Cracking the Boards:
USMLE STEP 2

Cracking the Boards:
USMLE STEP 2
Second Edition

by John J. Mariani, M.D.

RANDOM HOUSE, INC.
NEW YORK

www.randomhouse.com/princetonreview

Princeton Review Publishing, L.L.C.
2315 Broadway
New York, NY   10024
E-mail: comments@review.com

Copyright © 2000 by Princeton Review Publishing, L.L.C.

ISBN: 0-375-76164-0

Editor: Rachel Warren
Production Coordinator: Stephen White
Production Editor: Diahl Ballard
Illustrations by: The Production Department of The Princeton Review

Manufactured in the United States of America on partially recycled paper.

9 8 7 6 5 4 3 2 1

Second Edition

This book is dedicated to Daniella, for her love, support, and patience, without which it would not have been possible.

ACKNOWLEDGMENTS

The author would like to thank: Evan Schnittman, Jackie Jendras, and Laurie Barnett for their support and confidence; David Kelley, Paul Maniscalco, and Paul Edelblut for their teamwork; Kristen Azzara for her attention to detail; and the production department, Julieanna Lambert and Scott Harris, who put the whole thing together.

The author extends a very special thanks to Rachel Warren for her friendly criticism, subtle guidance, and flexible deadlines.

Contents

Internal Medicine 69

Ob/Gyn 134

Surgery   267

Practice Test   317

Preface

This book is designed to help medical students and physicians prepare for the computer-based administration of Step 2 of the United States Medical Licensing Examination (USMLE). My experience with Step 2, both as an examinee and as a Princeton Review instructor, is that a case-based review is the most effective way to prepare for the test. The general format of USMLE Step 2 is a clinical scenario followed by a question, or a series of questions, that focus on either the diagnosis, pathogenesis, epidemiology, treatment, or prognosis of the condition described. For any given clinical scenario, several such questions are possible. In fact, it is not uncommon for the same clinical scenario to appear more than once in one Step 2 administration and, each time, test a different aspect of the clinical encounter.

This book is designed to prepare students for the USMLE Step 2 with the format of the test in mind. Clinical vignettes written in the style and format of USMLE Step 2 scenarios are presented. Following each clinical vignette is a discussion of the diagnosis, pathogenesis, epidemiology, treatment, and prognosis of the case. This organization prepares the USMLE Step 2 candidate for any question that could be linked to each particular clinical scenario.

The selection of the clinical vignette topics was made based on The Princeton Review's USMLE Step 2 research; only topics that are commonly stressed on Step 2 are presented in this book. In general, topics tested on Step 2 mirror the practice of clinical medicine in the United States, which means that common conditions are stressed more than rare ones. The clinical vignettes are arranged into six chapters (family medicine, internal medicine, Ob/Gyn, pediatrics, psychiatry, and surgery) for the sake of organization, but Step 2 questions often test across several subject areas simultaneously.

USMLE Step 2 questions contain a description of a clinical encounter, but not in the format of a complete history and physical examination as you'd find in a patient's medical record. Only certain details are presented; not every piece of history, examination, or laboratory data is available. Part of the challenge of the examination is to arrive at the correct answer based on the artificial limits of the information in the question. In this way, too, the clinical vignettes in this book adhere to the format of actual USMLE Step 2 questions; there may be aspects of the history, physical exam, or laboratory data that are not provided that normally would be in a typical history and physical exam.

This book will maximize a USMLE Step 2 candidate's preparation effort. A review of the clinical vignettes and accompanying discussions will provide a firm foundation for facing the USMLE Step 2.

—John J. Mariani, M.D.
Medical Director,
The Princeton Review

Introduction

BASIC INFORMATION ABOUT THE USMLE

The USMLE is a three-step series of standardized tests that must be successfully completed before a student can apply for medical licensure. The USMLE is administered by the National Board of Medical Examiners (NBME) and the Educational Commission for Foreign Medical Graduates (ECFMG). In the United States, the license to practice medicine is governed by individual medical licensing authorities (state medical boards), which require successful completion of the USMLE as part of the licensing process.

The USMLE Step 2 focuses on clinical diagnosis and disease pathogenesis. The USMLE has been administered via computer at Sylvan Learning Centers worldwide since 1999. The new computer-based test (CBT) is administered throughout the year, and students may take the exam up to three times in a twelve-month period. The CBT consists of eight one-hour sections, each containing fifty items. Topic representation is randomly dispersed throughout the test; all CBT sections contain test items covering every subject area. Although each examinee has a different exam, all exam administrations are "content-equivalent." The total testing appointment is nine hours long, during which the examinee must complete a fifteen-minute orientation and the eight hours of testing. Students are allotted the remaining forty-five minutes for lunch and breaks to be taken at their own pace throughout the day. They can add to their break time by taking less than the time allowed for the tutorial or for any of the blocks of test questions. They cannot add to their actual testing time. The examination is designed so that breaks occur between blocks of questions.

The NBME has announced that while initially its computer-based exam will be linear (not adaptive), its goal is to introduce computer-adaptive sequential testing (CAST) in the future. In adaptive sequential testing, the examinee's performance on a given section influences the level of difficulty of questions on subsequent sections, and it is possible to go back to items and skip around within a section. Our research indicates that the exam will be adaptive with regards to subject matter; for example, if an examinee performs well in internal medicine but poorly in psychiatry, the computer will administer harder internal medicine questions and easier psychiatry questions on subsequent sections. The NBME has stated that it does not plan to announce when the exam will switch to section-adaptive testing, but that "students will know when they take the exam."

SCORING

The USMLE scoring process is complex. A raw score is converted into two equivalent scores, one on a three-digit scale and one on a two-digit scale. Currently, the minimum passing score for Step 2 corresponds to the seventh percentile among U.S. and Canadian medical students, as published in General Instructions, Content Descriptions and Sample Items, the booklet students receive after registering to take the exam.

A two-digit score of 75 always corresponds to the minimum passing score on the two-digit scale. Percentile information will no longer be provided with the scaled scores. The ECFMG does not furnish score distribution information from the data on graduates of overseas medical schools.

The NBME has announced that during the initial computer-based testing for each Step, approximately three months may be required for scores to become available. After this initial testing period, scores will be made available for mailing within approximately two weeks of the test date.

According to the NBME, an examinee must answer 55 to 65 percent of the total items on Step 2 correctly to attain a passing score. That is the most specific information either administering organization provides on raw-to-scale score conversion.

WHY THE USMLE IS DIFFERENT FROM OTHER STANDARDIZED TESTS

The NBME has gone out of its way to prepare an exam that assesses only a student's readiness for the next step in his or her medical education or career, not how well he or she takes a test. It is a very well-designed, content-based exam that requires comprehensive and detailed knowledge of the clinical sciences. For some students, this may be a relief. Many, many other standardized tests are intentionally written to trip test takers up, despite their command of the material. The NBME specifically steers its test writers away from defects in test writing, so students cannot employ strategies to get around the content-based objectives of the test. Because of this, the USMLE tests are more "technique-proof" than other standardized tests.

PURPOSE OF TECHNIQUES

Although the USMLE is not vulnerable to typical strategies for cracking standardized tests, all Step 2 examinees can use specific but limited techniques to maximize their performance. These techniques are not gimmicks that will magically give students a higher score, and at first they may seem awkward. With time and practice, however, these techniques will enable students to:

- Increase the pace of their reading
- Focus only on relevant details
- Eliminate more answer options when they are unsure of the correct answer

Because timing on this exam is so critical, we recommend that students first try the techniques explained in this guide on practice exams or during timed sections prior to taking the actual exam. Students should practice them until they can employ them smoothly. **Unless these pacing techniques become second nature, they not only won't work, but may actually slow students down.** We don't want test takers to concentrate on anything but how to choose the correct answer when they actually sit for the exam.

ANATOMY OF USMLE ITEMS

First, we'll quickly run through a little USMLE vocabulary.

1. **Items** or **Item Stems**: All the information following a number in the testing booklet. The items may present patient lab information or lab information needed to compute a result. The items may have associated gross or microscopic findings and radiographic images such as computed tomography (CT) scans or magnetic resonance imaging (MRI) studies. They may have complete or partial patient histories.

2. **Lead-in**: The specific sentence or question that asks test takers to find some connection between the stem and one of the options provided.

3. **Options**: Lettered words or phrases provided as possible answer choices. They follow the lead-in or precede a small set of items. For each numbered item, only one option will be considered the correct answer. There is no partial credit on this test.

4. **Answer**: The single option for each item that will be scored as correct.

5. **Distracters**: All of the options that will be scored as incorrect. They are always wrong, but are written so that if one or two pieces of information provided in the stem were just a bit different, each distracter could be correct. They're written not so much to confuse examinees (though they might), as they are to make sure they perceive the appreciable distinctions between each of them and the correct answer.

6. **Picture**: A gross or microscopic finding, chart, graph, radiograph, or any type of visual element.

TECHNIQUES

FAST FORWARD

An examinee looks at a new item and asks, "Is it long or short?" If the stem is longer than four lines, the very last sentence, phrase, or question should be read first so the examinee can determine what is being asked before reading the information provided. In NBME terms, the lead-in most often establishes the objective of the question. Armed with that knowledge, test takers can screen information in the stem that isn't relevant to the lead-in.

Similarly, as we will discuss later, when test takers hit a set of matching items, they should read the lead-in first to make sure they know what sort of relationship to look for between the numbered items and the lettered options.

TO SKIP OR NOT TO SKIP

The USMLE Step 2 is now administered via computer. What does this mean to students who have been bubbling in answers on paper-and-pencil multiple-choice tests their whole lives, or who are more comfortable with essay or oral exams? It actually isn't that big a change. Initially, the CBT will look very much like the old paper-and-pencil USMLE Step 2. The item formats are the same as the old paper-and-pencil exams, so the only differences will be the mechanics of answering the questions on the computer and the new, single-day format of the exam.

One advantage of not having to "bubble in" an answer sheet is that students don't have to worry about skipping around and accidentally marking the wrong question or skipping an item. Frame-shift errors (accidentally skipping or inserting an answer on the answer sheet and therefore making each subsequent answer choice out of sync) will be impossible. Examinees will have the ability to mark items for later review.

For paper-and-pencil exams, it has always been our advice to answer the questions in order so as to minimize the chance of making any sloppy answer sheet errors. With CBT, those errors are no longer a concern, so now we offer students a choice of techniques, **scanning and skipping** or **one-by-one**. We recommend that students try both techniques on practice exams and then decide which works best for them.

SCANNING AND SKIPPING

For some students, particularly those who have difficulty finishing all the items within a section, the option to skip around and decide which items they want to answer first will improve their efficiency. The items will be randomly distributed throughout the section with regard to topic representation and difficulty level. To maximize performance, some students may prefer to answer the questions they are more comfortable with first, and save the more difficult items for the end. The technique is to **scan** an item and decide if it should be answered now or **skipped** and answered later. The logic behind this strategy is that if students waste time on difficult items early in the section (items they are more likely to answer incorrectly), they may not have time to answer the easier items at the end of the section. Students should spend their time on items that they are likely to answer correctly. If they run out of time and the unanswered items were items they were likely to get wrong anyway, then they have used their time efficiently. The downside to this strategy is that it is necessary to invest time **scanning** items to decide whether they should be answered now or saved for later. If too much time is spent on **scanning**, the end result will be time wasted, not saved.

When a question is answered, students should **leave it alone**. It is a well-studied phenomenon that going back and changing answers is a bad strategy. Students are much more likely to change a correct answer to an incorrect one than the other way around.

ONE-BY-ONE

Other students will feel more comfortable attacking the items **one-by-one**, answering each question in the order it appears in a section. This technique will benefit those students who are confident that they are going to finish all the items in the section in the allotted time. The advantages to going **one-by-one** are: (1) no time is spent deciding whether an item should be skipped or not; (2) it is easier to calculate how many more items remain in the section for pacing purposes; (3) the overall flow of the exam is smoother when no time or energy is spent skipping around.

PROCESS OF ELIMINATION (POE)

A physician's skills as a diagnostician depend on his or her ability to rapidly reduce the number of disease entities, causative agents, or injured systems, etc., en route to prescribing efficacious treatment. This principle of reasoning also applies to sitting for the USMLE. A general concept in all standardized test taking is that distracters (or wrong answers) are easier to find than correct answers if examinees aren't already sure of the answer. With this in mind, students should immediately begin to strike down options they know to be false.

Students should examine each option and poke holes in it. If any part of the item stem falls apart while a student is considering a single option (lab values given in the stem don't match a lettered option, for example), they should move on—quickly. For example, if an item asks examinees to treat a patient with COPD, they should immediately eliminate an option that calls for 100 percent oxygen by facemask. Test takers should also be suspicious of any answer options that use extreme terms such as "always" or "never."

Process of Elimination is one of the most powerful tools that can be employed on this exam. It should be applied to every test item for which the examinee is not certain of the answer. Each time an answer option is eliminated, the probability of an examinee choosing the correct answer choice increases. For example, if a test taker randomly guesses on a question with five answer options, there is a 20 percent chance that he or she guessed correctly. If the examinee can eliminate one option that is definitely incorrect, that probability increases to 25 percent. If he or she can eliminate two options, the probability of getting the correct answer increases to 33 percent. On a 400-question test, test takers will not know the answer to every question cold. By using POE to increase the guessing percentage, their scores can be significantly increased over the course of the exam.

POE is not a "trick"; when students are able to discount answer choices, they are using hard-earned knowledge to do so. POE is a systematic approach that should be used throughout the exam. When they don't know the answer, students should never just guess randomly or choose the "letter of the day" (unless they are out of time). Using POE, they should always be able to eliminate at least one answer choice per question.

GUESSING

The only time it is acceptable to randomly guess the answer to a question is when an examinee is almost out of time (has only a few minutes left) and has not finished the section. **There is no guessing penalty on the USMLE.** It is always beneficial to fill in all of the answers. The most effective way to do this is for a student to select a single letter, such as "C," and mark all the remaining questions with it. Obviously, the more answer choices available, the less likely a student is to hit the bull's eye. Again, this type of guessing is only useful when there isn't enough time available for a student to employ POE.

PACING

This is a critical part of any standardized test performance. The USMLE Step 2 CBT sections require students to answer fifty items in one hour; that's an average of one minute and twelve seconds per question. In those seventy-two seconds, examinees must read the item and select an answer. Every time they spend more than seventy-two seconds on a question, that time must be made up somewhere else in the section.

NO CRUSADES

Examinees should not spend too much time on any one item. Often, Step 2 examinees reach a test item and say, "I knew this just yesterday—now I can't remember a thing about it, but I should sit here and answer this question if it's the last thing that I do." Launching a crusade against any one test item is a big mistake. There are 400 questions on the USMLE Step 2 exam, and no test taker is going to be sure of the answer to every single one. There will be questions to which the examinee will simply not know the answers. Before launching a crusade and losing precious time that could be used to answer easier questions, test takers should learn to cut their losses when up against a wall, be rational, use POE, and move on.

PICTURES

Some items are presented with additional information in the form of graphs, diagrams, slide and micrograph findings, photographs, or imaging studies. Examinees must be very open-minded when approaching these items to keep from getting trapped. They should avoid spending huge amounts of time (which on this test can be as little as two minutes) deciphering cryptic data representations at the expense of missing equally weighted, easier, nongraphical items. The visual information is not always necessary, but for some items examinees absolutely must read the image properly in order to choose the correct answer. The key here is to have a system: First, test takers should ignore the picture and try to answer the question without using the visual material. Then, after reading the item and the options, they should refer to the picture if necessary. Examinees should not look at the picture first and say, "I have no idea what this is and I will not be able to answer this question."

1. **Slides, Micrographs, Photographs, and Imaging Studies**—These pictures are imaging studies such as CT scans or MRIs, or microscopic preparations such as electron or light micrographs. As we have said, sometimes these items can be answered without looking at the picture. However, the picture can be useful or essential in choosing an answer.

2. **Graphs and Diagrams**—These tend to be more central to the item than the above. However, they invariably contain some superfluous information that can take too much time to decipher or eliminate. Therefore, when examinees come across one of these, they should go straight to the item to first determine *exactly* what they need to find in the graph. Test takers will definitely waste time if they look at the diagram or graph prior to reading the item and lead-in. Just because information is provided does not mean that it is relevant to answering the question. Test takers should consider it analogous to clinical medicine: Not every piece of history, physical exam, or lab data is relevant.

LAB VALUES

A table of standard laboratory values is available on the USMLE CBT as a "pop-up" screen. Test takers should have received their *Step 2 Computer-based Content and Sample Test Questions* booklet if they registered for the test. The lab values to be used on the actual test are provided in the "Sample Items" section of that booklet. Examinees should study them carefully. They are extremely helpful and should be consulted as students work through any practice items. Test takers should not assume that the normal lab values they used in lab research will be the same as the ones used on Step 2. Different hospital labs, different medical journals, and possibly even different faculty use different techniques and different units to present data. In order to avoid misinterpreting labs on the actual test, students must be clear on what Step 2 regards as "normal." So, if an item presents a lot of lab information, examinees should immediately check the normal values.

ITEM TYPES

SINGLE BEST MULTIPLE CHOICE

The majority of the 400 items on the USMLE Step 2 are multiple-choice items in this format. This item type has changed recently. The answer options may now range from A through J; in the past they only ranged from A through E. Most items using this format are still standard five-option multiple-choice questions, but some have more than five options. The principle is the same: A single option should be picked as an answer choice.

Here are examples of the standard "single best item type" with five answer choices:

1. A 19-year-old woman presents for evaluation of a three-week history of bleeding from her left breast nipple. She denies history of breast trauma. Prior medical and surgical histories are unremarkable. She does note that her aunt was recently diagnosed with breast cancer and is undergoing chemotherapy and radiation. Physical examination of the right breast reveals no evidence of masses, dimpling, skin retraction, or axillary adenopathy. The left breast is tender to palpation in the areola with no evidence of masses, dimpling, or skin retraction. The left axilla is free of adenopathy. The most likely diagnosis in this patient is which of the following?

    (A) Fibroadenoma
    (B) Fibrocystic change
    (C) Fibrosarcoma
    (D) Infiltrating ductal cell carcinoma
    (E) Intraductal papilloma

(E) is correct. A young female with pathologic nipple discharge requires further evaluation by the physician. The most common cause of bloody nipple discharge (90 percent of the time) is intraductal papilloma, a benign condition. The papilloma arises from an isolated mammary duct, which should be excised.

Choice A is incorrect. Fibroadenoma is a lobular, firm, well-circumscribed, solitary mass that is common in young females. Surgical excision is the treatment of choice in women over the age of 25. Younger patients may be treated with needle cytology and surveillance.

Choice B is incorrect. Fibrocystic change is associated with premenstrual breast tenderness and swelling. Patients with severe atypia or hyperplasia on biopsy are at risk for breast carcinoma.

Choice C is incorrect. Sarcoma of the breast represents a small percentage of breast cancers and is more common in females over the age of 40.

Choice D is incorrect. Infiltrating ductal cell carcinoma is the most common form of breast cancer. Lesions are typically hard, scirrhous, and infiltrating.

2. A 39-year-old man complains of a two-week history of vomiting. The last emesis was followed by approximately 500 cc of blood. He denies prior medical or surgical history. Social history is notable for drinking of 1 liter of liquor every other day and smoking one pack of cigarettes per day. Physical examination reveals a well developed male whose clothes smell of alcohol. Cardiac examination reveals a regular rate and rhythm. Pulmonary examination notes no evidence of wheezes, rhonchi, or rales. Gastrointestinal examination reveals mild mid-epigastric tenderness without evidence of peritoneal signs. Rectal examination reveals stool in the vault that is guaiac-positive. Laboratory values are as follows:

Hematocrit	35%
Hemoglobin	12.2 g/dL
White blood cell count	11,000/mm^3
Platelet count	340,000/mm^3

Serum

Sodium	139 mEq/L
Potassium	4.1 mEq/L
Chloride	100 mEq/L
Bicarbonate	26 mEq/L
Urea nitrogen	15 mg/dL
Creatinine	1.1 mg/dL

Urinalysis

Protein	trace
Heme	negative
Leukocyte esterase	negative
Nitrate	negative

The most likely diagnosis is
(A) esophageal varices
(B) gastritis
(C) Mallory-Weiss tear
(D) peptic ulcer disease
(E) syndrome of carcinoma

(C) is correct. Mallory-Weiss tears occur in the mucosa near the gastroesophageal junction. Patients are usually alcoholics and report a history of vomiting that precedes emesis of a large amount of blood. Physical examination is often unremarkable. Diagnosis is made by endoscopy and treatment strategies include H$_2$ receptor blockade.

Choice A is incorrect. Bleeding from esophageal varices is usually massive and often occurs without warning. Most cases are related to hepatic cirrhosis and resultant portal hypertension.

Choice B is incorrect. Gastritis that leads to bleeding may be erosive and associated with the ingestion of alcohol, aspirin, or ibuprofen. Erosions may also be noted after burns, systemic illness, or head injury.

Choice D is incorrect. Peptic ulcer of the duodenum, stomach, or surgical anastomosis may be associated with upper gastrointestinal bleeding.

Choice E is incorrect. Gastric or esophageal carcinoma patients complain of weight loss, progressive dysphagia, and minimal upper gastrointestinal bleeding.

3. A 25-year-old woman complains of vulvar itching, burning, and vaginal discharge with rancid odor for two weeks. She has a prior medical history of gestational diabetes mellitus and asthma for which she takes no medications. She is gravida 1 para 1 with a healthy 1-year-old male child at home. Currently, she lives alone and has had unprotected sexual intercourse with multiple male partners during the past several weeks. The vaginal discharge is yellow-green in color, frothy, and has a pH of 7.0. Vulvovaginal examination reveals vulvar edema and erythema and petechiae on the cervix. The vaginal vault has no evidence of mass lesions. Wet smear reveals large numbers of mature epithelial cells, white blood cells, and a fusiform protozoan organism. The most appropriate treatment includes

   (A) amoxicillin
   (B) ampicillin
   (C) metronidazole
   (D) miconazole
   (E) terconazole

(C) is correct. *Trichomonas vaginalis* is a protozoan organism that lives in the urethra and vagina. This organism can be freely transmitted during sexual intercourse. Symptoms of infection include vulvar itching, burning, copious discharge with rancid odor, dysuria, and dyspareunia. Examination may reveal edema and erythema of the vulva and petechiae of the upper vagina and cervix. The secretions are often yellow-green with a pH higher than 6.5. Wet smear will reveal the *Trichomonas* organism. Treatment is by oral metronidazole, and one-day therapy regimens result in a 90 percent cure rate.

Choice A is incorrect. Amoxicillin is not an appropriate treatment choice for *Trichomonas vaginalis*.

Choice B is incorrect. Ampicillin is not an appropriate treatment choice for *Trichomonas vaginalis*.

Choice D is incorrect. Miconazole is a topical synthetic imidazole for the treatment of *vaginal candidiasis*.

Choice E is incorrect. Terconazole is a topical synthetic imidazole for the treatment of *vaginal candidiasis*.

4. A 19-year-old female college student presents with a ten-day history of headache, malaise, sore throat, and dry cough that has become productive over the last four days. She states that several housemates have had similar symptoms during the last thirty days. She is still able to attend classes. Physical examination reveals a temperature of 38.2 C (100.8 F). Cardiac examination reveals no evidence of tachycardia, rubs, or murmurs. Pulmonary auscultation reveals scattered coarse rhonchi bilaterally without evidence of wheezes or rales. Gastrointestinal evaluation reveals no evidence of peritoneal signs. Laboratory studies obtained are as follows:

White blood cell count	16,700/mm^3
Hemoglobin	12.3 g/dL
Hematocrit	37%
Platelet count	320,000/mm^3

Serum

Sodium	139 mEq/L
Potassium	3.7 mEq/L
Chloride	99 mEq/L
Bicarbonate	24 mEq/L
Urea nitrogen	10 mg/dL
Creatinine	1.2 mg/dL
Alanine aminotransferase	30 U/L
Aspartate aminotransferase	25 U/L

Urinalysis

Heme	negative
Nitrate	negative
Leukocyte esterase	negative

The mainstay of diagnosis includes

(A) chest radiograph
(B) IgM cold agglutinins
(C) polymerase chain reaction
(D) rRNA hybridization
(E) white blood cell count

(B) is correct. The patient described is infected with *Mycoplasma pneumoniae*. This is a common cause of respiratory tract infections in college-aged students, especially among those who reside in close surroundings such as college dormitories. Symptoms include headache, fever, malaise, sore throat, and a cough that often becomes productive. Diagnosis may be made by evaluation of cold agglutinins of the IgM class directed at the I antigen of erythrocytes. This test is 80 percent positive at one week in patients with this condition.

Choice A is incorrect. Chest x-ray findings in this condition are nonspecific.

Choice C is incorrect. Polymerase chain reactions have shown promise in the detection of *Mycoplasma*, but are still currently in the experimental phase.

Choice D is incorrect. Ribosomal RNA hybridization has shown promise in the detection of *Mycoplasma*, but is still currently in the experimental phase.

Choice E is incorrect. While elevation of white blood cell counts may be noted in this condition, this is by no means diagnostic.

5. A 33-year-old woman who is HIV-positive reports progressive visual disturbance noted by a decrease in visual acuity. Funduscopic examination reveals large white areas proximal to the macula with perivascular exudates and hemorrhages. Otoscopy reveals movement of the tympanic membrane to pneumatic otoscopy without evidence of effusion. Shotty cervical adenopathy is noted bilaterally along the sternocleidomastoid muscle. Cardiac, pulmonary, and gastrointestinal examinations are unremarkable. Treatment of this condition involves which of the following agents?

(A) Oral erythromycin
(B) Oral ganciclovir
(C) Oral penicillin
(D) Oral prednisone
(E) Intravenous prednisone

(B) is correct. Treatment of CMV retinitis involves ganciclovir, foscarnet, and cidofovir. The drugs are given in an initial induction phase, and then a later life-long phase. Ganciclovir can also be given in an intraocular implantable form.

Choice A is incorrect. Oral erythromycin is not indicated in the treatment of CMV retinitis.

Choice C is incorrect. Oral penicillin is not useful in the management of CMV retinitis.

Choice D is incorrect. Oral corticosteroids are unproven in the treatment of CMV retinitis.

Choice E is incorrect. Intravenous prednisone is not of value in the treatment of CMV retinitis.

Examinees should go straight to the lead-in, found at the very end of the item stem, and read it before reading the rest of the stem. This will help test takers to know what to look for before the item stem leads them astray, as not all of the information in the item stem is directly relevant to answering the item correctly. In practice, patients often don't know what they are supposed to tell their physician, so in a history a physician may be confronted with many pieces of information, medical or otherwise, that are irrelevant to diagnosing and treating the problem at hand. On Step 2, this extraneous information causes examinees to waste time reading and trying to figure out where it fits in.

For the purposes of the USMLE, going straight to the lead-in will provide cues to help examinees find the discrete information needed to provide a diagnosis, determine the best means of prevention, or indicate what to expect to see in the patient's labs.

Here is an example of the extended single best item type, where the option range is greater than the standard A through E:

6.   A 25-year-old white man is referred to a psychiatrist. The patient has been unable to hold down a steady job, as he often misses work and has many arguments with his superiors. The patient reports having a history of intense, unstable relationships, usually broken off by him. The patient states that he feels uncomfortable in social situations. The patient denies any hallucinations or other psychotic symptoms. Sleep habits and appetite are normal. The most likely diagnosis is

   (A) agoraphobia
   (B) antisocial personality disorder
   (C) bipolar disorder
   (D) borderline personality disorder
   (E) cyclothymia
   (F) major depression
   (G) schizoid personality disorder
   (H) schizophrenia

(D) is correct. The key words here are "intense, unstable relationships," which, especially in the context of the USMLE, implies borderline personality disorder.

Choice A is incorrect. This disorder is characterized by the fear of being alone in public places, especially in situations from which a rapid exit would be difficult.

Choice B is incorrect. The patient would need to display signs of "lacking a conscience," committing acts against others without remorse, in order to be diagnosed with this disorder.

Choice C is incorrect. Bipolar disorder is characterized by alternating cycles of mania and depression. This patient has no history to support this diagnosis.

Choice E is incorrect. This is a less severe form of bipolar disorder. The symptoms can often be almost as severe as in bipolar disorder, but may not be of sufficient duration to meet the criteria for bipolar disorder.

Choice F is incorrect. The patient lacks any vegetative signs or symptoms.

Choice G is incorrect. This is characterized by a lifelong pattern of social withdrawal. Others often see sufferers as being eccentric, isolated, or lonely.

Choice H is incorrect. Markedly peculiar behavior, abnormal affect, unusual speech, bizarre ideas, and strange perceptual experiences characterize schizophrenia.

This is a more difficult type of item if the test taker does not know the answer straight away. After reading the item stem, examinees should try to answer the question without looking at the answer options. Once they have an answer in mind, they can scan the options for their answer. If they are unsure or draw a blank, they should use POE. It is harder to narrow down the choices when there are more answer options, but when an examinee is less than 100 percent sure, POE always improves the chances of arriving at the correct answer.

GROUPED SINGLE BEST ITEMS

The USMLE Step 2 also groups several single best items under a single case presentation. For these items, a case presentation is followed by a series of single best items. Usually, the questions following the case are related to each other and the answer to one item may influence the answer to the other items. For example, a question regarding a diagnosis will influence any questions about treatment.

Items 7–8

A 65-year-old man presents to the office for a routine examination. His past medical history is notable for hypertension and asthma. The patient was intubated for his asthma approximately fifteen years ago and was hospitalized for ten days. At the present visit, the patient reports that his wife died last week after battling a long illness. She was diagnosed with breast cancer five years ago and underwent modified radical mastectomy with chemotherapy and radiation. However, she succumbed to her disease with liver metastasis noted at autopsy. Upon further discussion with the patient, he reports a 2.3 kg (5 lb) weight loss, decreased appetite, and a lack of pleasure in his life at the present time. He seeks your guidance and advice. Laboratory studies obtained are as follows:

Hematocrit	42%
Serum	
Thyroxine (T_4)	8 µG/dL
Thyroid-stimulating hormone	2.5 µU/mL
Urea nitrogen	15 mg/dL

7. The most likely diagnosis is which of the following?
   (A) Adjustment disorder
   (B) Brief reactive psychosis
   (C) Depression–atypical
   (D) Depression–major
   (E) Schizoaffective disorder

(A) is correct. Adjustment disorder is such a common psychiatric condition that is often featured on the USMLE examination. This patient is suffering from normal grief secondary to the loss of a loved one. This is a traumatic event and the symptoms that this patient has are typical.

Choice B is incorrect. Brief reactive psychosis is unlikely given this patient's symptoms and their duration.

Choice C is incorrect. Atypical depression is more common in females with a history of psychiatric disorders.

Choice D is incorrect. Major depression is a possible sequela if adjustment disorder does not resolve in this patient.

Choice E is incorrect. Schizoaffective disorder is unlikely given this patient's symptoms and their duration.

8. The most effective treatment for this condition is which of the following?

    (A) Intensive psychotherapy
    (B) Levodopa
    (C) Sympathetic concern and reassurance
    (D) Tricyclic antidepressants

(C) is correct. The most appropriate initial treatment of adjustment disorder involves sympathetic concern and reassurance. Patients need to know that the symptoms they are experiencing are a part of the normal grieving process.

Choice A is incorrect. At this point, psychotherapy is not indicated for treatment of early adjustment disorder.

Choice B is incorrect. Levodopa, a treatment for Parkinson's disease, is not indicated in the management of adjustment disorder.

Choice D is incorrect. Tricyclic antidepressants are appropriate for a patient with complicated grief or depression and should not be prescribed unless the patient is quite symptomatic.

MATCHING ITEMS

Sometimes, the order of tasks is reversed. In matching items, the lettered options come first followed by a small set of numbered items. The items in this case do not pose questions or lead-ins. Instead, the numbered items are discrete statements, typically descriptions of patients. Examinees must correctly match each numbered description with a lettered option. Each lettered option may be the correct answer for one or more of the numbered items, or none of them. There are more lettered options than there are numbered items to answer, so they will not all be used.

Items 9–11

    (A) Adjustment disorder with depressed mood

    (B) Bipolar disorder

    (C) Cyclothymia

    (D) Dysthymia

    (E) Intoxication with pharmacologic-induced psychosis

    (F) Major depression

    (G) Schizophrenia

    (H) Uncomplicated bereavement

For each patient scenario below, select the best answer.

9. A 21-year-old woman with a family history of major depression in her father has a one-year history of job instability, occasional suicide attempts, and multiple short hospitalizations over the last two years. She experiences mild depression and hypomania. She is an intermittent drug and alcohol abuser.

(C) is correct. Cyclothymia has depressive and manic features either separately or intermingled. This disorder is more common in females and usually presents at about the age of 20. Affected individuals have job instability, occasional suicide attempts, and an increased risk of substance abuse.

10. A 59-year-old woman is anhedonic, sad, and tearful after the death of her husband due to a chronic illness. After intense mourning and resolution, her symptoms improve within two weeks.

(H) is correct. Uncomplicated bereavement usually follows severe loss or trauma and may produce symptoms of a full depressive syndrome. Affected individuals are able to work through their problems and see them to resolution through the process of grieving.

11. A 59-year-old woman is anhedonic, sad, and tearful after the death of her husband due to a chronic illness. She is now unable to work, forgets to eat three meals per day, and has lost 4.5 kg (10 lb) over the last month. She rarely goes outside to be with friends or relatives.

(A) is correct. This individual is experiencing features of adjustment disorder with depressed mood. This condition often occurs after a readily identifiable stress (death of a loved one) and results in impaired functioning and improves as the stress disappears. These patients are somewhere in between sadness and major depression.

The number of options in some of these questions can seem overwhelming, so examinees should not read the options first. They should make sure they know the type of relationship to look for by reading the set lead-in. Then they should go straight to the item and determine their answer. They should read one numbered item at a time and formulate their answer before looking at the list of options. The options are almost always listed alphabetically, which should help students locate their answer among the lettered options as quickly as possible.

POE only works for the options if each numbered item is considered separately. Even after an option is selected or eliminated as a correct answer for one item, it may end up being the correct answer for the next.

The very worst thing test takers can do is read the lettered options prior to reading the items. This will confuse their thinking and possibly induce a panic attack.

MATCHING ITEMS WITH MULTIPLE ANSWERS

For these items it is necessary to select more than one correct answer from the list per item. To answer the item correctly, examinees must pick the exact answer choices that the NBME has in mind. There is no partial credit given; test takers must pick the exact number and identity of answer options to get credit for the question. For example, if the item calls for three answer options, there are only three correct answers in the list and credit for the item will only be given if all of those three answer options are selected. Fortunately, there are not many of these items per exam.

Items 12–14

    (A) Increased pressure

    (B) Decreased pressure

    (C) Normal pressure

    (D) Increased polymorphonuclear leukocytes

    (E) Normal polymorphonuclear leukocytes

    (F) Increased protein

    (G) Decreased protein

    (H) Normal protein

    (I) Increased glucose

    (J) Decreased glucose

    (K) Normal glucose

    (L) Increased lymphocytes

For each patient with meningitis, select the appropriate cerebrospinal fluid indicator.

12. A 3-year-old boy with a fever of 39.4 C (103 F), headache, and nuchal rigidity is suspected of having bacterial meningitis.

(CHOOSE 4 ANSWERS)

(A, D, F, and J) are correct. The mot common causes of meningitis in a 3-year-old child include Gram-positive and Gram-negative bacteria. Typical cerebrospinal fluid analysis in such patients includes increased CFS pressure, increased polymorphonuclear leukocytes, increased protein, and decreased glucose levels.

13. A 28-year-old man with AIDS develops shaking chills and nuchal rigidity. He recently had a bout of CMV retinitis.

(CHOOSE 4 ANSWERS)

(C, L, H, and K) are correct. This patient with HIV disease and a recent bout of CMV retinitis might have viral meningitis. Typical cerebrospinal fluid findings in such patients include normal opening pressure, increased lymphocytes, and normal protein and glucose levels.

14. A 41-year-old man with a long history of untreated tuberculosis develops fevers, chills, and nuchal rigidity.

(CHOOSE 4 ANSWERS)

(A, L, F, and J) are correct. This patient with a prior history of tuberculosis and noncompliance with medications now has the new onset of neurological findings. This might suggest tuberculous meningitis. Typical CSF findings include increased opening pressure, increased lymphocytes, increased protein, and decreased glucose.

CALCULATIONS

Some items require simple calculations. In general, Step 2 is not a math test, but there are some basic skills that students will need to master prior to the exam. Calculators are not allowed into the test center, so all calculations must be worked out by hand. A "white board" and marker are provided for this purpose. For example:

15. A screening test for a newly discovered infectious agent is performed on the sera of 100 volunteers. It is known that ten of these volunteers are infected with the agent in question. The screening test results indicate that ten of the volunteers tested positive for the infectious agent in question. A confirmatory test is performed on the sera of the patients who had a positive screening test for the infectious agent. The confirmatory test, which has a specificity of 99.9%, is positive in 90% of the tested sera. What is the sensitivity of the screening test?

   (A) 0.1%
   (B) 1.0%
   (C) 10.0%
   (D) 90.0%
   (E) 100.0%

(D) is correct. Sensitivity = true (+)/true (+) + false (−). The true (+) = 10 × 90% confirmatory test = 9. It was know that ten of the original 100 were infected, so the screening test missed one of these cases, making the false negative # = 1. The equation is 9 / 9 + 1 = .9 = 90%. Specificity = True (−)/true (−) + false (+). Sensitivity is the ability to detect disease (low false (−)), specificity is the ability to exclude disease (low false (+)). Typically, good screening tests have a high sensitivity (low false (−)), and confirmatory tests have a high specificity (low false (+)).

In this case, examinees needed to know some basic formulas in order to plug in the given numbers. Examinees will need to be familiar with scientific notation and understand how the pH scale works. The math in general is relatively easy; what is being tested is the application of the appropriate formula.

INTERPRETING LABORATORY VALUES

Some items will offer the answer options as a group of lab values from which the test taker must select the most appropriate option based on the clinical description in the item stem. For example:

16. A 23-year-old woman presents to the emergency department with complaints of gradually worsening polyuria, polydipsia, and generalized weakness over the past week. She has a history of insulin-dependent diabetes and reports poor compliance

with her prescribed insulin regimen. Physical exam reveals tachypnea, hyperpnea, and a "sweet" breath odor. Which of the following blood gas values would most likely represent this patient's arterial blood gas?

	pH	PO_2	PCO_2	HCO_3
(A)	7.12	102	19	7
(B)	7.22	91	60	26
(C)	7.29	85	80	40
(D)	7.37	98	41	25
(E)	7.60	55	18	22

(A) is correct. This patient has diabetic ketoacidosis, which is characterized by a metabolic acidosis (low bicarb) secondary to ketone body formation and hypocapnia (compensatory respiratory alkalosis). Complete respiratory compensation for a metabolic acidosis does not occur.

Choice (B) is incorrect. This is an acute respiratory acidosis.

Choice (C) is incorrect. This is a chronic respiratory acidosis with a compensatory metabolic alkalosis (elevated bicarb).

Choice (D) is incorrect. This is a normal blood gas.

Choice (E) is incorrect. This is a respiratory alkalosis (hyperventilation) in response to hypoxia.

EXPERIMENTAL ITEMS

When the NBME introduces new items, it must first use them experimentally to gather performance data. This means that a number of items students encounter on the exam will not count toward their score. Test takers will not be able to tell which items are experimental.

Some items can ultimately end up unscored even if the NBME originally intended them as scored items. If a question tested well in another administration (probably as an experimental item) but everyone else who encountered it chose the same incorrect option, that particular item is assumed to be poorly written. The NBME usually throws such bad items out and recalibrates everyone's final scores before they are reported.

The most important thing for test takers to remember about experimental items is that it is impossible to identify them when taking the exam. **EXAMINEES SHOULD ASSUME THAT EVERY TEST ITEM COUNTS!**

REMEMBER...

- NO QUESTION SHOULD BE LEFT BLANK! There is no penalty for guessing. Examinees receive credit if they guess the correct answer, and there is no deduction for wrong answers.

- NO CRUSADES! If a test taker cannot answer a question, he or she should use POE and move on.

- TIMING IS EVERYTHING! Examinees should keep track of their pacing at regular intervals. The fear of not finishing will provide the motivation to keep going.

- FIRST GUESSES ARE MORE LIKELY TO BE CORRECT! Test takers who go back and change their answers are likely to change correct ones to incorrect ones. The only time an examinee should go back and change an answer choice is if an item stem provides an answer to a previous question.

KEEPING FAITH

Preparing for the USMLE Step 2 is a very difficult exercise in self-discipline. Preparing for this exam is analogous to an athlete preparing for the Olympics; test takers must condition themselves for the big event. The amount of studying required is tremendous. Anxiety over the eventual outcome and its implications can be disabling.

To be efficient and productive test takers, students must deal with these issues as they arise. Students should use their instructor and classmates as resources. Keeping a regular study schedule is essential, as this is not an exam that can be crammed for. Studying for this exam is definitely best done "one day at a time." Students must focus on what's in front of them and not worry about tomorrow, next week, or two years from now. If they stick to a schedule and work at it regularly, they will be able to move mountains (of books).

Anxiety is a normal state of mind during this process. If test takers aren't anxious, something is wrong. Anxiety should be used to motivate studies, not interfere with them. The key to success at this exam is an honest effort on a daily basis. The material needs to be chipped away at a little at a time, and if this is done regularly for a solid block of time prior to the exam, it can be manageable.

Test takers should sleep regular hours. In the weeks prior to the exam, students should get up at the same time they will need to be up for the exam. If a student is in a pattern of staying up late and sleeping late, it will be hard to change right before the exam. Rest is just as important as studying.

It is important to maintain mental health. Test takers should mix in some recreational activities with their studying. The key here is balance.

TEST DAY

Most of the rules test takers must adhere to when they arrive at the testing center will have been provided ahead of time in the Step 2 Computer-based Content and Sample Test Questions booklet, published by the NBME. Students should bring the registration card given to them by their school or the ECFMG and photo identification. Any calculators, beepers, cell phones, books, or watches (the computer will provide a clock timer) will not be allowed in the testing room.

1. Students must have a scheduling permit to take the examination.
2. Students must arrive at the test center at least thirty minutes early. If test takers arrive at the test location late, they may not be admitted to the examination.
3. Examinees will be offered a set of earplugs and will be given two double-sided, laminated erasable writing boards, a marker, and tissues to erase marks from the board.
4. A fifteen-minute tutorial will be presented first. If students are already familiar with the Step 2 tutorial and sample questions, they can exit from the tutorial immediately to start the first block of test questions. Any time saved from the fifteen-minute tutorial will be added to the overall break time.

5. Test takers should look at the timer regularly and adjust for pace. An average of seventy-two seconds should be spent per item.

6. Examinees are not penalized for wrong answers, so no questions should be left blank. When in doubt, students should use POE and move on. If time is running out, examinees should choose one letter and fill in all of the remaining items with that letter.

7. This is a very difficult test for everybody. It is supposed to be difficult and examinees are supposed to feel rushed, but should not let the test intimidate them.

Clinical Vignettes

ALCOHOLIC LIVER DISEASE

A 56-year-old man presents with complaints of nausea and vomiting, abdominal discomfort, and loss of appetite. The symptoms began approximately one month ago and have become progressively worse. He has lost 5 kg (11 lb) in the past month. The overt odor of alcohol is apparent on the patient's breath. The patient reports drinking "about a half-gallon of wine" every day for the past twenty years. Temperature is 38.2 C (100.8 F), pulse is 96/min, respirations are 16/min, and blood pressure is 110/55 mm Hg. The patient's sclera and skin appear jaundiced. "Spider" angiomas are noted on the patient's chest. Palmar erythema is present. Abdominal examination reveals an enlarged, tender liver, a palpable spleen, and moderate ascites. Laboratory studies show:

Hematocrit	33%	(Male: 41–53%)
Hemoglobin	11g/dL	(Male: 13.5–17.5 g/dL)
Leukocyte count	17,000/mm³	(4,500–11,000/mm³)
Platelet count	178,000/mm³	(150,000–400,000/mm³)
Prothrombin time	17 seconds	(11–15 seconds)
Serum		
Bilirubin, total	1.7 mg/dL	(0.1–1.0 mg/dL)
Alkaline phosphatase	139 U/L	(20–70 U/L)
Aspartate aminotransferase	178 U/L	(8–20 U/L)
Alanine aminotransferase	72 U/L	(8–20 U/L)
Amylase	56 U/L	(25–125 U/L)
Albumin	2.2 g/dL	(3.5–5.5 g/dL)

DIAGNOSIS

Alcoholic fatty liver should be suspected in alcoholic patients with hepatomegaly and normal or minimally deranged liver function tests. The clinical manifestations of alcoholic fatty liver are often minimal or entirely absent. Hepatomegaly, at times accompanied by tenderness, may be the only finding.

Alcoholic hepatitis should be considered in an alcoholic who has been drinking heavily and demonstrates jaundice; fever; an enlarged, tender liver; or ascites. The clinical severity of alcoholic hepatitis can vary enormously, ranging from asymptomatic or mild illness to fatal hepatic insufficiency. Typically, the clinical features of alcoholic hepatitis resemble those of viral or toxic liver injury. Patients often experience anorexia, nausea and vomiting, malaise, weight loss, abdominal distress, and jaundice. Fever, which can be as high as 39.4 C (103 F), is seen in about 50 percent of cases. On physical examination, tender hepatomegaly is common, and splenomegaly is found in about one-third of patients. Patients may have cutaneous "spider" angiomas and jaundice, and more severe cases may be complicated by ascites, edema, bleeding, and encephalopathy.

Alcoholic cirrhosis should be strongly suspected in patients with a history of prolonged or excessive alcohol intake and physical signs of chronic liver disease. Clinical features of cirrhosis derive from the morphologic alterations (and often reflect the severity of) hepatic damage, rather than the etiology of the underlying liver disease. Alcoholic cirrhosis may be clinically silent, and many cases are discovered incidentally at laparotomy or autopsy. In many cases, symptoms are insidious at onset. Anorexia and malnutrition lead to weight loss and a reduction in skeletal muscle mass. The patient may experience easy bruising, weakness, and fatigue. Eventually, the clinical manifestations of hepatocellular dysfunction and portal hypertension appear, including progressive jaundice, bleeding from gastroesophageal varices, splenomegaly, ascites, and encephalopathy. A firm, nodular liver may be an early sign of the disease; the liver may be either enlarged, normal, or decreased in size. Other frequent findings include palmar erythema, spider angiomas, parotid and lacrimal gland enlargement, clubbing of the fingers, splenomegaly, muscle wasting, and ascites with or without peripheral edema. Men may also have decreased body hair and/or gynecomastia and testicular atrophy. Dupuytren's contractures, which arise from fibrosis of the palmar fascia and the resulting flexion contracture of the digits, are associated with alcoholism, but are not specifically related to cirrhosis.

Routine hematologic and biochemical blood tests are usually normal in patients with alcoholic fatty liver, but there may be minimal elevations of the serum aspartate aminotransferase (AST); occasionally alkaline phosphatase and bilirubin levels are also elevated. In more advanced alcoholic liver disease, abnormalities of laboratory tests are more common. Anemia may result from acute and chronic gastrointestinal blood loss, coexistent nutritional deficiency (folic acid, vitamin B_{12}), hypersplenism, and a direct suppressive effect of alcohol on the bone marrow. Leukocytosis is often present in severe alcoholic hepatitis. Mild or pronounced hyperbilirubinemia may be found and is usually associated with elevations of serum alkaline phosphatase levels. The serum AST level is usually disproportionately elevated relative to alanine aminotransferase (ALT); i.e., the AST/ALT ratio is > 2. The serum prothrombin time is frequently prolonged, and reflects the reduced synthesis of clotting proteins; most notably the vitamin K-dependent factors. The serum albumin level is usually depressed.

Although a percutaneous needle biopsy is usually not necessary to confirm the typical findings of alcoholic hepatitis or cirrhosis, it may be helpful in distinguishing patients with less advanced liver disease from those with cirrhosis and in excluding other forms of liver injury, such as viral hepatitis.

PATHOGENESIS

The three principle alcohol-induced hepatic lesions are 1) alcoholic fatty liver (steatosis), 2) alcoholic hepatitis, and 3) alcoholic cirrhosis.

In alcoholic fatty liver, the liver is enlarged, yellow, greasy, and firm. Hepatocytes are distended by large, macrovesicular cytoplasmic fat vacuoles that push the hepatocyte nucleus up against the cell membrane. Accumulation of fat in the liver of an alcoholic results from the combination of impaired fatty acid oxidation, increased uptake and esterification of fatty acids to form triglycerides, and diminished lipoprotein biosynthesis and secretion.

Alcoholic hepatitis is characterized by hepatocyte degeneration and necrosis, often marked by ballooned cells and an infiltrate of polymorphonuclear leukocytes (PMN) and lymphocytes. The PMN may encircle damaged hepatocytes that contain Mallory bodies (alcoholic hyaline), which are clumps of perinuclear, deeply eosinophilic material. Mallory bodies are highly suggestive of, but not specific for, alcoholic hepatitis. Deposition of collagen around the central vein and perisinusoidal areas (central hyaline sclerosis) is associated with an increased likelihood of progression to cirrhosis. Alcoholic cirrhosis is characterized by diffuse fine scarring, fairly uniform loss of liver cells, and small regenerative nodules. It is only one of many consequences that results from chronic alcohol ingestion, and it often accompanies other forms of alcohol-induced liver injury.

With continued alcohol intake and destruction of hepatocytes, fibroblasts appear at the site of the injury and stimulate collagen formation. Weblike septa of connective tissue appear in periportal and pericentral zones and eventually connect portal triads and central veins. Although regeneration occurs within the small remnants of parenchyma, cell loss generally exceeds the rate of replacement. With continuing hepatocyte destruction and collagen deposition, the liver shrinks in size, acquires a nodular appearance, and becomes hard as "end-stage" cirrhosis develops. Disturbances in hormonal metabolism occur; for instance peripheral formation of estrogen is increased due to diminished hepatic clearance of the precursor **androstenedione** and the toxic effects of alcohol on the testes.

Although chronic alcoholism is the most common cause of cirrhosis, the quantity and duration of drinking necessary to cause cirrhosis remains unknown. The typical patient with cirrhosis has consumed a pint or more of whisky, several quarts of wine, or an alcoholic equivalent amount of beer daily for at least ten years. The amount and duration of ethanol consumption, rather than the type of alcoholic beverage or the pattern of ingestion, appear to be the determinants of liver injury.

EPIDEMIOLOGY

Alcoholic cirrhosis is the most common type of cirrhosis encountered in North America. Approximately 10 to 15 percent of alcoholics develop cirrhosis. Women, on average, tend to develop alcohol-induced liver injury after lower levels of consumption than men.

TREATMENT

Alcoholic hepatitis and cirrhosis are serious illnesses that require long-term medical supervision and careful management. An important component of the complete care of these patients is encouraging them to become involved in an appropriate alcohol counseling program. Therapy of the underlying liver disease is mainly supportive. Specific treatment is directed at particular complications, such as variceal bleeding and ascites.

In the absence of signs of impending hepatic coma, the patient should be placed on a diet that contains at least 1 g of protein per kilogram of body weight and 2,000 to 3,000 kcal per day. Daily multivitamin supplements should be prescribed, in addition to large amounts of thiamine in patients with Wernicke-Korsakoff syndrome.

All medicines must be administered with caution in the cirrhotic patient, especially those that are eliminated or modified through hepatic metabolism or biliary pathways. Patients may be sensitive to the affects of acetaminophen, particularly in conjunction with alcohol.

PROGNOSIS

Alcoholic fatty liver occurs in most heavy drinkers but is reversible on cessation of alcohol consumption and is not thought to be an inevitable precursor of alcoholic hepatitis or cirrhosis. In patients with severe alcoholic hepatitis associated with ascites and encephalopathy, the short-term prognosis is poor. The in-hospital mortality is approximately 50 percent. In milder cases, clinical recovery may be complete, but repeated bouts of alcoholic hepatitis usually lead to irreversible and progressive liver injury. Although alcoholic cirrhosis is usually a progressive disease, appropriate therapy and strict avoidance of alcohol may arrest the disease at most stages and permit functional improvement. Patients who have had a major complication of cirrhosis and continue to drink have a five-year survival rate of less than 50 percent. Ultimately, most patients with advanced cirrhosis die in hepatic coma, which is commonly precipitated by hemorrhage from ruptured esophageal varices or intercurrent infection.

ASTHMA

A 32-year-old woman presents to the emergency department with complaints of shortness of breath, cough, and wheezing for the past two hours. She has a history of asthma since the age of 10 and occasionally experiences severe attacks, usually in the spring. The patient has several inhaled therapies prescribed for her by her primary care physician and was instructed to use them on a regular schedule, but she admits that she rarely uses them. She was hospitalized and given intravenous corticosteroids once when she was 13, but has never been intubated. Temperature is 37 C (98.6 F), pulse is 110/min, and respirations are 24/min, with the patient demonstrating moderate respiratory distress. Auscultation of the chest demonstrates both inspiratory and expiratory wheezes, with a prolonged expiratory phase. A chest radiograph is obtained and shown below:

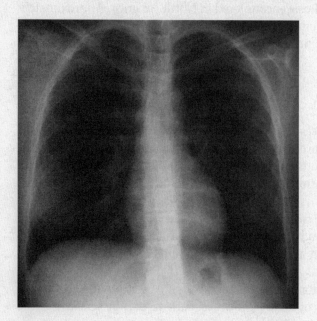 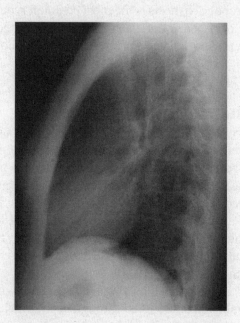

Chest radiograph PA and lateral view—normal study

DIAGNOSIS

The symptoms of asthma consist of a triad of coexisting dyspnea, cough, and wheezing. Typically, asthma is an episodic disease; acute exacerbations are interspersed with symptom-free periods.

At the onset of an attack, patients experience a sense of constriction in the chest, often with a nonproductive cough. Respiration becomes audibly harsh, wheezing in both phases of respiration becomes prominent, expiration becomes prolonged, and patients frequently have tachypnea, tachycardia, and mild systolic hypertension. The lungs become overinflated, and the anteroposterior diameter of the thorax increases. If the attack is severe or prolonged, the accessory muscles become visibly active, and a paradoxical pulse often develops. The end of an episode is frequently marked by a cough that produces thick, stringy mucus, that when examined microscopically often show eosinophils and Charcot-Leyden crystals. In extreme situations, wheezing may lessen markedly or even disappear, cough may become extremely ineffective, and the patient may begin a gasping type of respiratory pattern.

The diagnosis of asthma is established by demonstrating reversible airway obstruction. Reversibility is defined as a 15 percent or greater increase in the 1-second forced expiratory volume (FEV_1), following two puffs of a β–adrenergic agonist. When spirometry results are normal at presentation, the diagnosis can be made by showing heightened airway responsiveness to challenges with histamine, methacholine, or isocapnic hyperventilation of cold air. Once the diagnosis is confirmed, the effectiveness of therapy can be followed by measuring peak expiratory flow rates (PEFRs) and/or FEV_1.

The differentiation of asthma from other diseases associated with dyspnea and wheezing is usually not difficult, particularly if the patient is seen during an acute episode. An extremely common feature of asthma is nocturnal awakening with dyspnea and/or wheezing. Upper airway obstruction by tumor or laryngeal edema can occasionally be confused with asthma; patients will present with stridor and the harsh respiratory sounds will be localized to the trachea. Persistent wheezing localized to one area of the chest in association with paroxysms of coughing indicate endobronchial disease such as foreign-body aspiration, a neoplasm, or bronchial stenosis. The signs and symptoms of acute left ventricular failure occasionally mimic asthma, but the findings of moist basilar rales, gallop rhythms, blood-tinged sputum, and other signs of heart failure differentiate the diagnoses.

Recurrent episodes of bronchospasm can occur with carcinoid syndrome, recurrent pulmonary emboli, and chronic bronchitis. In chronic bronchitis, there are no true symptom-free periods, and one can usually obtain a history of chronic cough and sputum production as a background upon which acute attacks of wheezing are superimposed. Recurrent emboli can be very difficult to separate from asthma, and nuclear lung scans or pulmonary angiography may be required to establish the correct diagnosis. Eosinophilic pneumonias often produce asthmatic symptoms, as do various chemical pneumonias and exposure to some insecticides and cholinergic drugs.

PATHOGENESIS

Asthma is a disease of airways that is characterized by increased responsiveness of the tracheobronchial tree to multiple stimuli. It is manifested physiologically by a widespread narrowing of the air passages. The common denominator that underlies the asthmatic diathesis is a nonspecific hyperirritability of the tracheo-bronchial tree. Although the basic mechanism of the increased airway reactivity remains unknown, the most popular hypothesis at present is that of airway inflammation. Increased numbers of mast cells, epithelial cells, neutrophils, eosinophils, and lymphocytes are found in the bronchoalveolar lavage fluid of patients with asthma. The mediators released (which include histamine; bradykinin; the leukotrienes C, D, and E; platelet-activating factor; and prostaglandins [PGs] E_2, F_2a, and D_2) produce an intense, immediate inflammatory reaction that involves bronchoconstriction, vascular congestion, and edema formation.

Allergic asthma is often associated with a personal and/or family history of allergic diseases such as rhinitis, urticaria, and eczema. It is marked by positive wheal-and-flare skin reactions to intradermal injection of extracts of airborne antigens, with increased IgE in the serum, and/or with positive response to provocation tests involving the inhalation of specific antigen.

Patients with idiosyncratic asthma present with no personal or family history of allergy, with negative skin tests, and normal IgE levels. Many develop a typical symptom complex upon contracting an upper respiratory illness. The initial insult may be little more than a common cold, but after several days the patient begins to develop paroxysms of wheezing and dyspnea that can last for days to months.

The drugs most commonly associated with the induction of acute episodes of asthma are aspirin, coloring agents such as tartrazine, β–adrenergic antagonists, and sulfiting agents. There is a great deal of cross-reactivity between aspirin and other nonsteroidal compounds. β–adrenergic antagonists, including the selective β₁ agents, regularly obstruct the airway in asthmatics and should be avoided. Sulfiting agents, such as potassium metabisulfite, potassium and sodium bisulfite, sodium sulfite, and sulfur dioxide, which are widely used in the food and pharmaceutical industries as sanitizing and preserving agents, can also produce acute airway obstruction in sensitive individuals.

EPIDEMIOLOGY

Asthma is very common. It is estimated that 4 to 5 percent of the population of the U.S. is affected by it. Bronchial asthma occurs at all ages, but predominately in early life. About 50 percent of cases develop before age 10, and another third before age 40. In childhood, there is a 2:1 male/female ratio, but the sex ratio equalizes by age 30. The prevalence of aspirin sensitivity in asthmatics is approximately 10 percent and predominantly affects adults.

TREATMENT

Elimination of the causative agent(s) from the environment of an allergic asthmatic is the most successful means available for treating this condition. Desensitization or immunotherapy with extracts of the suspected allergens are widely used procedures, but they have not been proven to be highly effective. Patients with aspirin sensitivity can be desensitized by daily administration of the drug; this also induces cross-tolerance to other nonsteroidal anti-inflammatory agents.

The available agents for treating asthma are divided into two general categories: drugs that inhibit smooth muscle contraction (β–adrenergic agonists, methylxanthines, and anticholinergics) and agents that prevent and/or reverse inflammation (glucocorticoids, mast-cell stabilizing agents, inhibitors of mediator synthesis, and mediator-receptor antagonists.)

Agents Used for the Treatment of Asthma				
Category	Mechanism	Examples	Side effects	Comment
Adrenergic	Stimulate β-adrenergic receptors and activation of G proteins, which results in increased formation of cyclic AMP. Decrease the release of mediators and increase mucociliary transport.	Catecholamines (Epinephrine, Isoproterenol, Isoetharine)	Epinephrine and isoproterenol are not β_2-selective and have considerable chronotropic and inotropic cardiac effects. Epinephrine has substantial α-stimulating effects.	Short-acting (30 to 90 minutes.) Only effective when administered by inhalational or parenteral routes. Isoproterenol is devoid of α-activity and is the most potent agent of the group.
		Resorcinols (Metaproterenol, Terbutaline, Fenoterol) Saligenins (Albuterol, Salmeterol)	Main side effect is tremor. Devoid of cardiac side effects except at high doses.	Active by all routes of administration, but inhalation is preferred. Relatively long-lasting (4 to 6 h).
Methylxanthines	Undefined at present. Formerly thought to increase cyclic AMP by action on phosphodiesterase.	Theophylline, Aminophylline	Nervousness, nausea, vomiting, anorexia, and headache. At plasma levels greater than 30 mg/mL there is a risk of seizures and cardiac arrhythmias.	For maintenance therapy, long-acting compounds are given once or twice per day.
Anticholinergics	Produces bronchodilation by blocking muscarinic receptors in bronchial smooth muscle.	Atropine methylnitrate, Ipratropium bromide	Since these compounds are nonabsorbable, they are free of side effects.	May be of particular benefit in patients with coexistent heart disease, in whom use of adrenergics and methylxanthines may be dangerous. Major disadvantages are that they are slow-acting and of modest potency.

Glucocorticoids	Reduce airway inflammation.	Methylprednisolone (intravenous), Prednisone (oral), Beclomethasone (inhaled), Flunisolide (inhaled), Triamcinolone (inhaled)	Long-term oral or parenteral administration can suppress pituitary-adrenal axis and cause Cushing's syndrome. Thrush and dysphonia can be associated with inhaled agents.	Systemic administration is most beneficial in acute illness or progressively worsening chronic disease. Inhaled agents are useful during withdrawal from oral agents or maintenance therapy to reduce airway reactivity.
Mast cell-stabilizing agents	Inhibit the degranulation of mast cells, which prevents the release of inflammatory mediators.	Cromolyn, Nedocromil	None.	Used for prophylactic and chronic treatment. Most effective in atopic patients. Beneficial effects take 4 to 6 weeks to appear.
Antileukotrienes	Leukotriene receptor antagonists.	Zafirlukast, Montelukast	Headache, but is generally well tolerated.	Used for prophylaxis and chronic treatment.
Leukotriene pathway inhibitors	Inhibits 5-lipoxygenase, the enzyme that catalyzes the formation of leukotrienes from arachidonic acid.	Zileuton	Dyspepsia.	Used for prophylaxis and chronic treatment.

The most effective treatment for acute episodes of asthma is the administration of aerosolized β_2-agonists. Aminophylline can be added to the regimen to attempt to speed resolution. The effects of steroids in acute asthma are not immediate; they may not be seen for 6 hours or more after the initial administration. PEFR should be measured to monitor the response to treatment. If the PEFR does not improve with therapy, serial blood gas analysis is required. If the PCO_2 is within the normal range or elevated, an intensive care setting should be considered.

PROGNOSIS

The mortality rate from asthma is low; fewer than 5,000 annual deaths occur in the U.S. out of a population of approximately 10 million that have asthma. Typically, most attacks are short-lived, lasting minutes to hours. Unlike other airway diseases, such as chronic bronchitis, asthma is not progressive.

DENTAL CARIES

A 9-year-old boy is brought by his mother for a routine examination. The mother is concerned because the child refuses to see a dentist. He had a few routine dental evaluations several years earlier, but he complained that the examination was painful and now cries hysterically any time she suggests making an appointment. She requests that he be counseled regarding proper dental care and the potential consequences if he neglects his teeth.

DIAGNOSIS

Dental caries usually begins in the pits and fissures of the occlusal (biting) surfaces of the molar teeth. Incipient lesions first appear as opaque, white spots. With progressive loss of tooth tissue, cavitation occurs. Lesions of short duration cannot be diagnosed by inspection; they are usually detected by probing the affected pit or fissure. The second most frequent sites of caries are contact surfaces between the teeth. These areas are difficult to examine even for the dentist, who usually depends on intraoral radiographs. Caries lesions are least frequently detected in the necks (cervical areas) of the teeth near the gingiva.

The identification of high-risk patients is critical for preventing dental caries. Intact salivary gland function is the major host defense against dental caries. Without it, the patient will be susceptible to rampant dental caries. Patients at particular risk are those with Sjögren syndrome, Mikulicz disease, chronic graft-versus-host disease, and those receiving long-term therapy with drugs that cause xerostomia. Additional high-risk conditions for caries include gastroesophageal reflux, bulimia, rumination, Prader-Willi syndrome, mental retardation, and dystrophic epidermolysis bullosa. Hereditary fructose intolerance is associated with a reduced incidence of caries, because these patients must avoid fructose-containing foods.

Baby bottle tooth decay (BBTD) is an extensive form of tooth decay that occurs as a result of babies sleeping with a nursing bottle and typically occurs before 18 months of age. It is the only severe dental disease common in children younger than 3 years of age.

PATHOGENESIS

The development of dental caries is dependent on critical interrelationships between the tooth surface, dietary carbohydrates, and specific oral bacteria. The decay process is initiated by demineralization of the outer tooth surface due to the formation of organic acids during the bacterial fermentation of dietary carbohydrates. The frequency of carbohydrate consumption is a more important determinant of development of dental caries than is the actual quantity of carbohydrate consumed.

Dental caries have microbial specificity; cariogenic potential resides in a group of oral streptococci collectively designated *Streptococcus mutans*. These organisms initiate most dental caries of enamel surfaces. Once the enamel surface cavitates, other oral bacteria (in particular the lactobacilli) invade the underlying dentin and cause further destruction of tooth structure through a mixed bacterial infection.

EPIDEMIOLOGY

The prevalence of dental caries throughout the world has decreased markedly during the last two decades. This is believed to be due to advances in prevention—particularly the use of fluorides. Over half of the children in fluoridated areas are free of dental caries into their teens, but retention of teeth and aging of the population have both led to an increase in root caries. BBTD is relatively common, occurring in about 15 percent of medically underserved children in urban and rural areas, and in 50 percent or more children in some Native American groups.

TREATMENT

Contemporary dental therapies can salvage the majority of severely carious teeth. When an extraction is indicated, therapy must also address the problem that teeth surrounding the site of extraction will change their positions in the dental arch. This is particularly important in the primary and mixed dentitions of childhood and adolescence in order to prevent impaction or malposition of permanent successor teeth.

Clinical management of the pain and infection associated with untreated dental caries varies with the medical status of the patient. In general, dental infection localized to the dentoalveolar unit can be managed by local measures. Antibiotics are usually not indicated, except in those patients with compromised host defenses, impaired wound healing, or risk for endocarditis. In cases of dental infections that have spread beyond the dentoalveolar unit, antibiotics are indicated. Antibiotics can usually be given by the oral route in patients with unremarkable medical histories if the infection does not involve a vital area (submandibular space, facial triangle, or periorbital space). If the infection involves a vital area, or if oral antibiotics are ineffective, parenteral routes are indicated. Parenteral routes are also indicated for patients with compromised host defenses, impaired wound healing, or those at risk for endocarditis. Pain control with combinations of acetaminophen with codeine are usually adequate.

In otherwise healthy children, tooth decay is a preventable disease. The most effective preventive measure against dental caries is fluoridation of communal water supplies to approximately 1.0 ppm. In fluoride-deficient areas, similar caries prevention benefits are obtained from dietary fluoride supplements. The topical use of fluoride agents are beneficial to children at high risk for caries. Thorough daily brushing and flossing of the teeth also helps to prevent dental caries as well as periodontal disease. Decreasing the frequency of carbohydrate ingestion prevents dental caries.

PROGNOSIS

If left untreated, dental caries usually destroys most of the tooth and spreads into contiguous tissue, causing pain and infection. Microbial invasion of the dental pulp precipitates an inflammatory response (pulpitis) that can elicit significant pain (toothache). Pulpitis can progress to necrosis, with alveolar invasion of the alveolar bone (dental abscess, periapical abscess). This process may be very painful and is associated with the complications of sepsis and facial space infection.

DOMESTIC VIOLENCE

A 23-year-old gravid woman, with an estimated gestational age of 21 weeks, presents to the emergency department missing teeth, and with multiple ecchymotic areas on her face. The patient reports that she tripped and fell on the sidewalk. She reports sensing fetal movement and denies any uterine contractions, vaginal bleeding, or leaking fluid. Physical examination reveals some older-appearing ecchymotic areas on her back and thighs. A sonogram reveals a viable fetus with adequate amniotic fluid. Radiographic examination of the face and skull reveals no fractures.

DIAGNOSIS

Health care providers fail to diagnose most women suffering from abuse because of various barriers. Battered women feel great shame and fear for their safety if they confide in anyone. Some women have been abused for so long that they no longer see their spouse's behavior as abnormal and may even believe that they deserve the abuse. Domestic violence occurs in all socioeconomic, racial, religious, and educational backgrounds. Violence exists in both homosexual and heterosexual relationships, across all ages.

Routine assessment of all women is the key to improving diagnostic efforts. Certainly all women presenting to the emergency room for prenatal and postpartum care, as well as for routine doctor's visits, should be screened. It is clear that abuse increases in severity and frequency during a woman's pregnancy; one in six neonates will go home to a woman who was battered during her pregnancy. Patients should be assessed in private; not in the presence of a partner, other family members, or friends. It is appropriate to ask the patient if she is, or ever has been, in a relationship in which she was frightened or hurt.

PATHOGENESIS

Domestic violence is about the abuse of power and control. The batterer, typically a victim of abuse as well, has low self-esteem and desperately tries to control as many aspects of his wife or girlfriend's life as he can. This behavior often includes making all family and financial decisions, controlling her time and movements, dictating her career, and deciding when or whether she will be pregnant. He accomplishes this by threats, intimidation, and physical abuse. Couples involved in abusive relationships are typically caught in a cyclical pattern of behavior, described as a **cycle of violence**, which includes three phases. Phase one is the tension-building phase, in which the batterer is increasingly angry and irritable. Phase two is the actual battering incident, which may include anything from verbal and emotional abuse, a slap or push, to repeated beatings, rape, and even murder. Phase three has been called the Honeymoon Phase. During this time, the batterer is repentant, and tells his victim he loves her and will never hurt her again. This phase gives her hope and may therefore be the most dangerous phase of all. Studies have shown that, with time, the Honeymoon Phase gets shorter and shorter while the abusive incidents escalate in number.

EPIDEMIOLOGY

Domestic violence is the number-one cause of injury to women in the United States; 95 percent of domestic violence victims are women. One in five women has been or will be abused in an intimate relationship and 4,000 will die each year as a result. In over 50 percent of cases of domestic violence, the children are also injured.

TREATMENT

Suspected Domestic Violence

⇓

No injury noted/patient denies abuse⇐   ⇒Suspicious injury and/or patient reports abuse

⇓   ⇓

- Education regarding domestic violence   - Document using patient's own words

- Referrals to shelters/domestic violence services   - Document any injuries (photos, drawings)

- Frequent follow-up appointments   - Inquire about rape

- Educate regarding domestic violence

- Make safety assessment and plan

- Involve social work team

- Consider psychiatric referral

- Report as per individual state laws

PROGNOSIS

The number-one reason physicians fail to diagnose cases of domestic violence is that they do not ask the right questions. It is estimated that 22 to 35 percent of injured women presenting to the emergency room have been abused by their partners, but only 1 in 25 is correctly identified. Approximately 20 to 25 percent of women presenting to family practice clinics and 17 percent of obstetric patients are in violent relationships, but these numbers differ greatly from the numbers identified by physicians.

FAMILY PLANNING

A 38-year-old woman, gravida 3 para 3, presents to her primary care physician to discuss contraceptive methods. The patient is recently divorced and desires no further children. Presently, she is not sexually active, but wants "to be prepared" should she enter into a relationship. She has no history of coagulation disorders, breast cancer, or hypertension. She does not smoke. During her marriage, the patient and her husband used male condoms intermittently. For the future, she desires a method that she can control.

DIAGNOSIS

On average, a women's potential years of fertility extend from two years after her menarche to within several years of her menopause. The ability of a sexually active woman to control her fertility is an essential aspect of her overall well being. Each family planning decision, whether it involves contraception, sterilization, or pregnancy termination, must be individualized to the patient's and couple's needs and circumstances. If an undesired pregnancy occurs and the fetus has not reached a stage of viability, pregnancy termination or induced abortion may be an option.

PATHOGENESIS

It is estimated that one-third of sexually active women do not use contraception and that one-fourth of women did not use some form of birth control at the time of their first intercourse. It is also estimated that one-half of women who do use some form of contraception do so either inconsistently or incorrectly. As a result, more than one-half of the estimated 6 million conceptions in the U.S. each year are unintended. In women 40 years of age and older, the number is more than 75 percent; it exceeds 90 percent in women younger than 20 years of age.

EPIDEMIOLOGY

In the U.S., sterilization is the most common method used for contraception by couples; 11 percent of men and 28 percent of women are sterilized. Approximately 50 percent of women 40 to 44 years of age are sterilized. Oral contraceptives are used by 27 percent of women of reproductive age, hormone injections by 3 percent, and hormone implants and intrauterine devices each by 1 percent. Male condoms are used by 20 percent of couples.

TREATMENT

Many factors influence a woman's choice of birth control, including her attitude about delaying rather than preventing pregnancy, the need for prompt reversibility of the method, whether the method should be independent of coitus, and the appropriateness of the method relative to her religious and cultural beliefs. Other factors are the stability of the sexual relationship, the number of sexual partners, her partner's attitude toward contraception, the frequency of coitus, and the ability to predict and prepare for coitus.

	Available Methods of Contraception		
Method	Description	Advantages	Disadvantages
Periodic Abstinence	Includes calendar rhythm method, basal body temperature method, cervical mucus method, and symptothermal method.	Nonpharmacologic, nonmechanistic.	High failure rate, need to abstain from sexual intercourse for many days each menstrual cycle.
Condom, male	Covers entire length of erect penis.	Highly effective if used properly. Latex and polyurethane condoms reduce the rate of transmission of STDs.	Not very effective for contraception or disease prevention if used improperly or inconsistently.
Condom, female	Lubricated, 17 cm long sheath attached to two flexible rings.	Can be as effective as male condoms. Woman controls the method.	Can be awkward and uncomfortable for some users.
Diaphragm	Shallow latex cup with spring mechanism in its rim to hold it in place in the vagina.	Effective when used properly. Can be inserted up to four hours prior to intercourse.	Must be inserted with contraceptive cream or jelly prior to intercourse and must be left in place eight hours after the last ejaculation.
Cervical cap	Cup-shaped latex device that fits over the base of the cervix.	Can be inserted up to eight hours prior to intercourse and left in place for up to 48 hours.	Use of the cap requires more training than does the use of the diaphragm. Not as effective for parous women.
Spermicides	Foams, creams, suppositories, jellies, and films. Nonoxynol-9 is the most commonly used agent.	Nonoxynol-9 is also a microbicide, reducing the risk of STD transmission.	Must be inserted prior to each coital act.
Intrauterine device, copper	Copper-coated T-shaped device that is placed into the uterine cavity by a health care professional.	No systemic side effects, not associated with coitus, does not interfere with lactation, prompt return to fertility with removal. Effective for ten years.	Increased vaginal pain and bleeding at menses. Risk of uterine perforation at the time of insertion. No STD protection and may predispose to PID.
Intrauterine device, progesterone	T-shaped device that is placed into the uterine cavity by a health care professional. Progesterone is released from a reservoir.	No systemic side effects, not associated with coitus, does not interfere with lactation, prompt return to fertility with removal.	Must be replaced once a year. Increased vaginal pain and bleeding at menses. Risk of uterine perforation at the time of insertion. No STD protection and may predispose to PID.
Oral contraceptive, combination	Contain synthetic estrogen (ethinyl estradiol or mestranol) and progestin (norethindrone, norethindrone acetate, ethynodiol diacetate, norethynodrel, and norgestrel, levonorgestrel, desogestrel, or norgestimate). Ingested daily for 21 days followed by a 7-day steroid-free period during which withdrawal bleeding occurs.	Significant reductions in risk of endometrial and ovarian cancer. Lowered incidences of functional ovarian cysts, ovarian cancer, dysmenorrhea, and premenstrual syndrome.	Increased risk of thromboembolic disorder and hypertension. Contraindicated in women over the age of 35 who smoke. Slight increase in the risk of cervical, liver, and breast cancer.

Oral contraceptive, progestin alone	Contain only progestin	Absence of exogenous estrogen.	Progestin-only preparations do not consistently inhibit ovulation. Progestins can cause weight gain, acne, amenorrhea, and nervousness.
Levonorgestrel implants	Six silicone rubber rods are inserted subcutaneously. Provides contraception for five years.	Highly effective, its use is not related to coitus, absence of exogenous estrogen, no adverse effects on breast milk.	Irregular menstrual and intermenstrual bleeding.
Depot medroxyproges-terone acetate	Single intramuscular injection provides at least thirteen weeks of contraceptive efficacy.	Decreased risk of endometrial cancer. Useful for women who desire long interval birth spacing who cannot use estrogen-containing preparations.	Menstrual cycle dysfunction and weight gain. Overall slightly increased risk of breast, cervical, ovarian, or liver cancer.
Tubal sterilization	Mechanical occlusion or segmental destruction or suture ligation with partial salpingectomy.	Highly effective and permanent.	Intraperitoneal procedure requiring general or regional anesthesia. Surgical reversal is difficult. No STD protection.
Vasectomy	Transection and occlusion of both ends of the vas deferens.	Highly effective and permanent. Neither the volume nor the appearance of the ejaculate changes.	Surgical reversal is difficult. No STD protection.

Emergency contraception is offered to women who experience an act of unprotected sexual intercourse. Oral contraceptives in higher than normal doses can be used within 72 hours of unprotected sexual intercourse to reduce the chance of pregnancy by 75 percent. A copper IUD inserted within five days after sexual intercourse can also be used as an emergency contraceptive and has an efficacy of almost 100 percent.

The termination of pregnancy can be accomplished by either surgical or medical means. In the first trimester, the surgical approach entails dilation of the cervix and suction or sharp curettage of the decidua and products of conception. In the second trimester, dilation of the cervix with hydrophilic dilators (*Laminaria*) decreases trauma and injury to the cervix. The immediate complications of surgical evacuation of the uterus at any gestational age include hemorrhage, infection, retained products of conception, cervical laceration, perforation of the uterus with bowel injury, and risks associated with anesthesia. Medical methods for induced abortion up to 63 days' gestation include oral mifepristone (RU 486) or intramuscular methotrexate followed by the placement of intravaginal misoprostol.

PROGNOSIS

Contraceptive efficacy is calculated as the number of pregnancies that occur during a specific time interval of contraceptive use. The term "method effectiveness" refers to conception occurring with the correct use; it is defined as a method failure. The term "use effectiveness" refers to conception that occurs with both correct and incorrect use of the contraceptive method. The difference between use effectiveness and method effectiveness is small with contraceptive methods not related to coitus. Contraceptive methods that are coitally related and require consistent and proper use are less effective in actual use.

Contraceptive Effectiveness: Estimated Percentage of Unintended Pregnancies in the First Year of Contraceptive Use		
Method	Method Effectiveness	Use Effectiveness
No method	85%	85%
Periodic Abstinence	3.75%	20%
Withdrawal	4%	19%
Condom, male	3%	12%
Condom, female	5%	21%
Diaphragm	6%	18%
Cervical cap, nulliparous women	9%	18%
Cervical cap, parous women	26%	36%
Spermicides	6%	21%
Intrauterine device, copper	0.6%	0.8%
Intrauterine device, progesterone	1.5%	2%
Oral contraceptives, combination	0.1%	—
Oral contraceptives, progestin alone	0.5%	—
Levonorgestrel implants	0.1%	0.1%
Depot medroxyprogesterone acetate	0.3%	0.3%
Tubal sterilization	0.4%	0.4%
Vasectomy	0.1%	0.2%

HYPERCHOLESTEROLEMIA

A 41-year-old man presents for a routine evaluation. He says he is concerned about his health because his father and brother both died in their 40s of "heart attacks." The patient has an athletic build, is not overweight, and exercises regularly. He does not smoke or drink alcohol. His blood pressure is 115/75 mm Hg and pulse is 64/min. Physical examination demonstrates xanthomas over the Achilles tendons bilaterally and xanthelasmas on both sets of eyelids. Total serum cholesterol is 370 mg/dL.

DIAGNOSIS

Elevated levels of fasting plasma total cholesterol (hypercholesterolemia) in the presence of normal levels of triglycerides are almost always associated with increased concentrations of plasma low-density lipoproteins (LDL) cholesterol, since LDL carries approximately 70 percent of the total plasma cholesterol. Rarely, a patient with markedly elevated high-density lipoprotein (HDL) cholesterol may also have increased plasma total cholesterol levels.

Elevations of LDL cholesterol can result from single-gene defects, polygenic disorders, and secondary effects of other disease states. Some premature coronary heart disease (CHD) is due to mutations in major genes that are involved in lipoprotein metabolism, but elevated cholesterol levels in most patients with CHD reflect the adverse impact of a sedentary lifestyle, excess body weight, and a diet high in total and saturated fat on a susceptible genetic background. HDL cholesterol levels are an indicator of ability to protect against CHD. The role of very low density lipoproteins (VLDL) in atherogenesis is uncertain.

In untreated adults with heterogeneous familial hypercholesterolemia, total cholesterol levels are in the range of 275–500 mg/dL. Tendon xanthomas, which are due to both intracellular and extracellular deposits of cholesterol, are seen in about 75 percent of adults with heterogenous familial hypercholesterolemia. They most commonly involve the Achilles tendons and the extensor tendons of the knuckles. Tuberous xanthomas, which are softer, painless nodules on the elbows and buttocks, and xanthelasmas, which are barely elevated deposits of cholesterol on the eyelids, are also common in heterogenous familial hypercholesterolemia. In men with heterogenous familial hypercholesterolemia, CHD typically develops by the fourth decade of life. Homozygous familial hypercholesterolemia is characterized by plasma cholesterol levels > 500 mg/dL, large xanthelasmas, and prominent tendon and planar xanthomas. Individuals with homozygous familial hypercholesterolemia have an aggressive, premature CHD that can manifest in childhood.

Polygenic hypercholesterolemia accounts for most moderate hypercholesterolemia (240–350 mg/dL). In these cases, plasma triglyceride and HDL cholesterol levels are usually normal, and tendon xanthomas are not present.

PATHOGENESIS

Polygenic hypercholesterolemia is caused by the interaction of multiple genes with environmental factors that results in both the overproduction and reduced catabolism of LDL. Severity is probably affected by the consumption of saturated fat and cholesterol, age, and the amount and frequency of physical activity.

Familial hypercholesterolemia is due to a mutation in the gene for the LDL receptor, and is genetically heterogeneous. More than 200 different mutations in the gene have been identified. In this disorder, plasma levels of total and LDL cholesterol are elevated at birth and remain elevated throughout life. Plasma triglyceride levels are typically normal, and HDL cholesterol levels are normal or reduced. As would be expected with a decreased number of LDL receptors, the fractional clearance of LDL Apo B is decreased. LDL production is increase because more VLDL and intermediate-density lipoproteins (IDL) are secreted by the liver and more IDL particles are converted to LDL, rather than taken up by the hepatic LDL receptors. Familial defective Apo B100 is due to a missense mutation that reduces the affinity of LDL for the LDL receptor. Familial defective Apo B100 is a phenocopy of familial hypercholesterolemia.

Secondary causes of hypercholesterolemia include hypothyroidism, obstructive liver disease, nephrotic syndrome, anorexia nervosa, and acute intermittent porphyria. Drugs such as progestins, cyclosporines, and thiazides can also cause secondary hypercholesterolemia. Malnutrition, obesity, cigarette smoking, β-blockers, and anabolic steroids can cause low HDL levels.

EPIDEMIOLOGY

More than half of the CHD in the U.S. is attributable to abnormalities in the levels and metabolism of plasma lipids and lipoproteins. Familial hypercholesterolemia is a codominant disorder that occurs in the heterozygous form in approximately one in 500 individuals. The homozygous form of familial hypercholesterolemia occurs in one out of 1 million individuals. Familial defective Apo B100 is an autosomal dominant disorder: the prevalence and manifestations of both the heterozygous and homozygous forms of this disorder are similar to those produced by mutations of the LDL receptor.

TREATMENT

The treatment of elevated LDL cholesterol can be directed at either primary prevention of the complications of atherosclerosis, or secondary treatment after complications have occurred. The rationale for primary prevention is the link between elevated levels of LDL cholesterol and increased CHD risk.

For primary prevention, it is recommended that patients with multiple risk factors for CHD be treated aggressively. Risk factors include a family history of premature CHD (before the age of 55 years in a male parent or sibling, or below 65 in female relatives), hypertension, cigarette smoking, diabetes mellitus, and low HDL (< 35 mg/dL). CHD is more prevalent in older individuals (men > 45 years, women > 55 years); women with premature menopause who are not receiving estrogen replacement are also at risk. HDL cholesterol > 60 mg/dL is a negative risk factor.

The typical American diet derives about 35 percent of its calories from fat and contains 400–500 mg/day of cholesterol. Individuals with hypercholesterolemia should be encouraged to eat a diet that is lower in cholesterol and saturated fat, and less than 300 mg/day of cholesterol. In general, whole-milk dairy products, egg yolks, meats, palm oils, and coconut oil should be replaced with fresh fruits and vegetables, complex carbohydrates (especially whole-grain products), and low-fat dairy products. Shellfish are low in fat content and (except for shrimp) have low cholesterol levels. Nuts, bran, and olive oil are low in saturated fat and will have positive effects on LDL levels.

Three classes of lipid-lowering agents are recommended as first-line therapy against hypercholesterolemia: 1) bile acid-binding resins, 2) niacin, and 3) 3-hydroxy-3-methylglutaryl coenzyme A (HMG-CoA) reductase inhibitors. These agents may be used alone or in combination. Fibric acid derivatives such as gemfibrozil are second-line agents for hypercholesterolemia and are most effective in lowering triglyceride levels.

The bile acid-binding resins cholestyramine and colestipol interfere with reabsorption of bile acids in the intestine. This results in a compensatory increase in bile acid synthesis and up-regulation of LDL receptors in hepatocytes. They also cause a modest increase in HDL cholesterol, and are the primary agents used in the treatment of patients with elevated levels of LDL cholesterol and normal triglycerides. Gastrointestinal side effects include constipation, bloating, and gas.

Although the exact mechanism is not fully understood, niacin appears to inhibit the secretion of lipoproteins containing Apo B 100 from the liver. Niacin decreases total, VLDL, and LDL cholesterol, and raises HDL cholesterol levels. It is safe, but has unpleasant side effects, including uncomfortable cutaneous flushing with or without pruritus. Less common side effects include elevations of liver enzymes, gastrointestinal distress, impaired glucose tolerance, and elevated serum uric acid levels, with or without gouty arthritis.

HMG-CoA reductase inhibitors (lovastatin, simvastatin, pravastatin, fluvastatin, and atorvastatin) inhibit the rate-limiting step in hepatic cholesterol synthesis, which causes a rise in LDL receptor levels in hepatocytes and enhanced receptor-mediated clearance of LDL cholesterol from the circulation. HMG-CoA reductase inhibitors also reduce triglyceride levels and increase HDL levels, and are relatively free of side effects. Mild, transient elevations in liver enzymes occur with all of the agents at the highest doses. A rare but potentially serious adverse effect of HMG-CoA reductase inhibitors is myopathy.

The evidence that treatment to reduce plasma triglyceride levels leads to long-term health benefits is less compelling than that for the reduction of high LDL levels. However, efforts should be made to reduce triglycerides when they are at levels that may precipitate pancreatitis. Thus triglyceride levels > 500 mg/dL are generally treated, whereas lower levels (200–500 mg/dL) are not treated unless other CHD risk factors are present.

Prognosis

Reducing LDL cholesterol slows the progression and may actually induce the regression of CHD.

IMPOTENCE

A 44-year-old man with a 22-year history of diabetes mellitus presents with complaints of erectile dysfunction. He has not been able to achieve or sustain an erection for the past year. Previously he had no erectile or other sexual dysfunction. When questioned regarding nocturnal erections, the patient reports that he cannot recall the last time he awoke with an erection, which earlier in his life was a typical occurrence. Neurological examination reveals decreased peripheral sensory function, particularly in the lower extremities. The bulbocavernosus reflex is decreased in intensity.

DIAGNOSIS

Impotence is the failure to achieve erection, ejaculation, or both. Men with sexual dysfunction present with a variety of complaints, either singly or in combination: loss of desire (libido), inability to initiate or maintain an erection, ejaculatory failure, premature ejaculation, or inability to achieve orgasm. Sexual dysfunction may also be the presenting symptom of systemic disease.

The central issue in the evaluation of impotence is the separation of instances that are due to psychological factors from those due to organic causes. Often, the separation can be made on the basis of history. Anxiety and depressive states are common causes of impotence. Other psychological factors, such as disinterest in the sexual partner, fear of sexual incompetence, marital discord, guilt about deviant sexual attitudes, worry, fatigue, and ill health often operate in various combinations to reduce sexual impulse. With the exception of severe depression, men with psychogenic impotence usually have normal nocturnal and early morning erections. Nocturnal penile tumescence (NPT) normally occurs from early childhood through the eighth decade during rapid eye movement sleep, and the total time of NPT averages 100 minutes per night. Therefore, if the impotent man gives a history of rigid erections under any circumstances (but typically when awakening in the morning), the efferent neurologic and circulatory systems that mediate erection are intact and the dysfunction is probably due to a psychiatric disorder. If the history of nocturnal erections is questionable, measurement of NPT can be made with the use of a strain gauge. An alternative to NPT testing is the visual sexual stimulation test, which uses videotaped erotic material in a laboratory setting to measure erection by strain gauge.

If an organic etiology is likely, the history should be probed for indications of diabetes mellitus, manifestations of peripheral neuropathy or bladder dysfunction, symptoms referable to the vascular system such as intermittent claudication, and symptoms of penile disease, such as a history of priapism or penile curvature (Peyronie's disease). Men with vasculogenic impotence may present with total erectile impotence, decreased penile rigidity, or loss of erection during intercourse. A thorough drug history should be obtained. Although many drugs are associated with impotence, antihypertensives agents, cimetidine, and monoamine oxidase inhibitors are most likely to lead to erectile dysfunction. The patient should be questioned regarding any past surgery that may have produced neurologic damage. Smoking is not only a risk factor for atherosclerotic disease, but may also inhibit sinusoidal relaxation directly.

Physical examination should include a detailed genital examination to identify abnormalities of the penis; especially Peyroine's disease, which is usually felt as a fibrotic plaque on the dorsum of the penis. The testes should be palpated for size, symmetry, and abnormal masses; if their length is less than 3.5 cm, hypogonadism should be considered. Signs of feminization should be evaluated, such as gynecomastia and abnormal body hair distribution. All pulses should be palpated, and the presence of bruits evaluated. The neurological examination should measure anal sphincter tone, perineal sensation, and the bulbocavernosus reflex, which is elicited by squeezing the glans penis and noting the degree of anal sphincter constriction. An examination for peripheral neuropathy should include assessment of distal muscle function; the tendon reflexes in the legs; and vibratory, position, tactile, and pain sensation. Priapism can be distinguished from a normal erection by the absence of tumescence of the glans penis. The demonstration of sperm in a postcoital urine specimen establishes the diagnosis of retrograde ejaculation.

PATHOGENESIS

A variety of endocrine, vascular, neurologic, and psychiatric diseases can disrupt normal sexual and reproductive function in men. It is now believed that most impotent men have a component of underlying organic disease.

Erection is normally preceded by sexual desire, which is regulated in part by androgen-dependent psychological factors. Testicular androgens appear to be required for normal libido but not for the erectile mechanism itself. A loss of desire may be due to androgen deficiency (arising from either pituitary or testicular disease), psychological disturbance, or some types of prescribed or habitually abused drugs.

Penile erection is initiated by neuropsychologic stimuli that ultimately produce vasodilation of the sinusoidal spaces and arteries within the paired corpora cavernosa. The parasympathetic nervous system is the primary effector of erection. The physiologic mechanism of erection of the penis involves the release of nitric oxide (NO) in the corpus cavernosum during sexual stimulation. NO then activates the enzyme guanylate cyclase. This results in increased levels of cyclic guanosine monophosphate (cGMP), which produces smooth muscle relaxation in the corpus cavernosum and allows the inflow of blood.

The organic causes of erectile impotence can be grouped into endocrine, drug, local, neurologic, and vascular causes.

Organic Causes of Erectile Impotence in Men			
	Cause		Comment
Endocrine	Testicular failure		Uncommon, but easily recognized (measure plasma testosterone and gonadotropin levels) and treated.
	Hyperprolactinemia		Pituitary tumors can secrete prolactin, which suppresses the production of luteinizing hormone-releasing hormone.
Drugs	Antiandrogens	Histamine (H_2) blockers (e.g., cimetidine) Spironolactone Ketoconazole Finasteride	Can produce impotence, decreased libido, or impaired ejaculation.
	Antihypertensives	Central-acting sympatholytics (e.g., clonidine & methyldopa) Peripheral acting sympatholytics (e.g., guanadrel) β-blockers Thiazides	Angiotensin-converting enzyme, calcium channel-blockers, and peripheral vasodilators do not cause a significant incidence of sexual dysfunction.
	Psychiatric	Antidepressants (monoamine oxidase inhibitors, tricyclic antidepressants) Anticholinergics Antipsychotics	May impair sexual function via anticholinergic and sympatholytic actions.
	Central nervous system depressants	Sedatives (e.g., barbiturates) Antianxiety (e.g., diazepam)	
	Drugs of habituation or addiction	Alcohol Methadone Heroin Tobacco	
Penile diseases	Peyronie's disease		Not rare; patients present with painful plaque on the dorsum of the penis and may progress to development of penile curvature and decreased rigidity of erection. Can cause impotence due to fibrosis of the sinusoidal spaces of the corpora cavernosa, corporeal artery occlusion, or neurogenic mechanisms.
	Penile trauma		
	Previous priapism		

Neurologic	Anterior temporal lobe lesions		
	Disease of the spinal cord		If damage or lesion is above the sacral region, reflex erections may occur, whereas diffuse injury of the sacral spinal cord results in total impotence.
	Loss of sensory input	Tabes dorsalis Disease of dorsal root ganglia	
	Disease of nervi erigentes	Radical prostatectomy and cystectomy Rectosigmoid operations	The nerve supply to the penis runs on the posterolateral surface of the prostate, and if the nerves are spared during radical surgery, potency may be preserved. Transurethral prostatectomy does not cause organic impotence.
	Diabetic autonomic neuropathy		As much as 50 percent of men with diabetes mellitus develops impotence within six years of the onset of diabetes, and impotence may be the first sign of diabetic neuropathy. Vasculogenic dysfunction is a concomitant factor in most men with diabetic impotence.
	Polyneuropathies		Several factors contribute to neuropathic impotence, including abnormalities in afferent sensory pathways, motor neuropathy in the cavernosa nerves (needed for vasodilatation), and decreased level of neurotransmitters in the corpora cavernosa.
Vascular	Aortic occlusion (Leriche syndrome)		
	Atherosclerotic occlusion or stenosis		Impotence may result when disease process effects the pudendal and/or cavernosa arteries. Sinusoidal tissue itself may be adversely affected.
	Arterial damage from pelvic radiation		Commonly seen following pelvic radiation.
	Venous leak		
	Disease of the sinusoidal spaces		

Premature ejaculation seldom has an organic cause. It is usually related to anxiety in the sexual situation, unreasonable expectations about performance, or an emotional disorder. Absence of emission may be produced by 1) retrograde ejaculation, 2) sympathetic denervation, 3) androgen deficiency, or 4) drugs. Retrograde ejaculation may occur following surgery on the bladder neck, or it may develop spontaneously in diabetic men. Drugs such as guanethidine, phenoxybenzamine, phentolamine, and sertraline primarily impair ejaculation rather than erection or libido. If libido and erectile function are normal, the absence of orgasm is almost always due to a psychiatric disorder.

Priapism (failure of detumescence) is a persistent, painful erection that is often unrelated to sexual activity. It may be idiopathic but can be associated with sickle cell anemia, chronic granulocytic leukemia, spinal cord injury, or injection of vasodilator agents (such as alprostadil) into the penis. The disorder may be secondary to clotting of blood within the sinusoidal spaces of the penis or to abnormalities of the adrenergic-mediated mechanism for detumescence. Failure to treat priapism promptly can result in fibrosis and subsequent loss of erectile function.

EPIDEMIOLOGY

In the U.S., it is estimated that 2 million men are impotent because they suffer from diabetes mellitus; an additional 300,000 are impotent because of other endocrine diseases; 1.5 million are impotent because of the result of vascular disease; 180,000 because of multiple sclerosis; 400,000 because of traumas and fractures leading to pelvic fractures or spinal cord injuries; and another 650,000 as a result of radical surgery, including prostatectomies, colostomies, and cystectomies. The incidence of impotence in young men (< 35) is about 8 percent and that number may rise as high as 77 percent by age 80.

TREATMENT

Medical therapy with androgens offers little more than placebo benefit, except in hypogonadal men. If a prolactin-secreting tumor is present, either surgical removal or treatment with bromocriptine will usually result in the return of potency. Yohimbine, an α_2-adrenergic antagonist, is widely prescribed, but works only in psychogenic impotence, by placebo effect. Surgical therapy may be useful in the treatment of aortic obstruction, but potency will be lost rather than improved if the autonomic nerve supply to the penis is damaged. Penile revascularization is appropriate only in young men with traumatic arterial disease. Premature ejaculation is most successfully treated with behavioral therapy.

Sildenafil, a selective inhibitor of cyclic guanosine monophosphate (cGMP)-specific phosphodiesterase, is an orally administered medication that is available for the treatment of erectile dysfunction. Sildenafil enhances the effect of nitric oxide (NO) by inhibiting phosphodiesterase type 5 (PDE5), which is responsible for the degradation of cGMP in the corpus cavernosum. When sexual stimulation causes local release of NO, inhibition of PDE5 by sildenafil causes increased levels of cGMP in the corpus cavernosum; this results in smooth muscle relaxation and the inflow of blood to the corpus cavernosum. Sildenafil, at recommended doses, has no effect in the absence of sexual stimulation.

Self-injection with prostaglandin E$_2$ (alprostadil) produces erection in more than 90 percent of men with psychogenic, neurogenic, and mild-to-moderate vasculogenic impotence. Side effects include injection pain, priapism, and fibrosis. Commercially available mechanical devices that utilize a vacuum to produce an erection and a rubber band to restrict venous return at the base of the penis provide a successful nonsurgical alternative for many patients. Penile prostheses or implants are a therapeutic alternative in impotent patients refractory to other forms of therapy.

In the early stages of priapism, detumescence can sometimes be achieved by aspiration, irrigation of the corpora cavernosa, and injection of dilute vasoconstrictors. If this fails, surgical relief by shunting procedures may be necessary. In patients with sickle cell anemia, conservative measures such as transfusion, oxygenation, and irrigation are generally preferred to shunting procedures.

PROGNOSIS

The outcome of the treatment of impotence is variable and depends on the etiology, mode of treatment, and individual response to treatment.

LEAD POISONING

A 4-year-old boy is evaluated in the family medicine outpatient department for a scheduled visit. As part of a battery of routine screening questions, you ask the boy's mother about pica and possible environmental toxins. She reports that there has been a lot of construction in their home recently and that her son is constantly picking things up off of the floor and putting them in his mouth. Otherwise, the boy's history and physical examination are unremarkable. A serum lead level is ordered and is found to be 75 mg/dL.

DIAGNOSIS

Lead, a nonessential metal, is not a natural constituent of the human body; when present it represents a poisoning. Of critical importance in the diagnosis of lead poisoning is an accurate environmental history, particularly of exposure to lead-containing paint. A history of the presence of pica is strongly suggestive; however, pica is not a prerequisite for lead poisoning. Unless the symptoms of lead poisoning are obviously severe and evident, in most cases, the diagnosis needs to be established by blood lead testing. Lead poisoning is often diagnosed by screening asymptomatic children.

There is no direct correlation between blood lead levels and clinical manifestations. However, the probability of severe symptoms increases as the exposure to lead and blood lead levels rise. The most serious manifestation of lead poisoning is **acute encephalopathy**. This may appear without a prodrome or may be preceded by behavioral changes or **lead colic**, characterized by occasional vomiting, intermittent abdominal pain, and constipation. Encephalopathy includes persistent vomiting, ataxia, seizures, papilledema, impaired consciousness, and coma. Peripheral neuropathy, which is a common symptom in adults, is rarely seen in children, except for those with sickle cell disease. The symptoms of childhood lead poisoning (in the absence of clear signs of encephalopathy) are usually nonspecific and vague. Abdominal colic, behavioral abnormalities, attention disorders, hyperactivity, or severe unexplained retardation should raise the suspicion of lead poisoning.

Lead encephalopathy rarely occurs at blood lead levels below 100 mg/dL. However, children with blood lead levels even well below that level may present with a constellation of neurologic symptoms. These are usually more obvious at higher blood levels (hyperactivity, anorexia, decreased play activity), while at lower levels, the neurologic abnormalities become progressively less evident.

PATHOGENESIS

The high toxicity of lead results from its avidity for the **sulfhydryl (SH)** group of proteins. Lead binds irreversibly to the SH group of a protein and impairs its function. The enzyme **δ-aminolevulinic acid dehydratase**, which catalyzes the formation of the porphobilinogen ring (a key step in the heme synthetic pathway), is progressively inhibited by lead in an exponential manner, without any threshold. At high levels of exposure, the enzyme is nearly completely inactivated. This results in serious clinical consequences, such as the accumulation of **δ-aminolevulinic acid**, which is a neurotoxin.

Ferrochelatase is another enzyme in the heme synthesis pathway that is severely damaged by lead. This enzyme catalyzes the final step of heme synthesis—the insertion of iron into the protoporphyrin IX ring. This results in an accumulation of protoporphyrin in the erythrocytes, which permits a rapid and accurate measurement of the erythrocyte porphyrins. This measurement serves as a useful adjunct in detecting childhood lead poisoning because it reflects the biochemical effects of lead.

EPIDEMIOLOGY

The major source of lead ingested by children in the United States is the lead-containing paint present in most dwellings built before World War II. This is most dangerous as the paint deteriorates. Lead-containing dust is taken up by small children through respiration and their normal hand-to-mouth activities. Acidic fruit juices stored in poorly glazed ceramic vessels, lead dust carried home by lead industry workers, fumes from burning batteries, some Asian cosmetics, and some Mexican folk medicines have also resulted in sporadic cases of lead poisoning.

TREATMENT

The most important aspect of therapy is to remove the child from the source of exposure to lead. In most cases, this is the only necessary action. In symptomatic children, regardless of blood lead level, hospitalization is indicated. Children with lead levels of 70 mg/dL or more, even if asymptomatic, should always be considered a medical emergency. Treatment consists of chelation therapy; **dimercaprol (BAL)** followed by **edetate calcium-disodium (EDTA).** Repeated courses of treatment may be necessary until the blood lead level returns to a safe range (≤ 20 mg/dL). Treatment of children with lead encephalopathy consists of controlling convulsions, establishing an adequate urine flow, and administering chelation therapy. Careful control of fluids is necessary to avoid aggravating the increased intracranial pressure. Asymptomatic children with blood lead levels greater than 20 mg/dL should also be treated with chelation therapy.

PROGNOSIS

High levels of blood lead in children decreases their intelligence quotient an average of 1–2 points for each increase in blood lead from 10–20 mg/dL.

LYME BORRELIOSIS (LYME DISEASE)

A 27-year-old woman presents with complaints of headache, fever, chills, and joint pains. The symptoms began about two weeks ago and have gradually worsened. She also reports feeling more tired than usual. When questioned about any recent rashes, the patient responds that she had a circular red rash with a clear center on her leg approximately one month prior to the onset of the symptoms. Temperature is 38.1 C (100.5 F), pulse is 72/min, respirations are 14/min, and blood pressure is 120/80 mm Hg. Physical examination is unremarkable. No skin rashes are noted.

DIAGNOSIS

Lyme borreliosis (Lyme disease), a spirochetal illness caused by *Borrelia burgdorferi* and transmitted by tick bites, usually begins with a characteristic expanding skin lesion, erythema migrans (EM). Lyme disease is usually diagnosed by the recognition of a characteristic clinical picture with serologic confirmation. Although serologic testing may be negative for the first several weeks of infection, most patients will have a positive antibody response to *B. burgdorferi* after that time. A two-step approach is recommended in the serologic analysis of Lyme disease. Samples are first tested by ELISA and then equivocal or positive results are tested by Western blotting. The immune response in Lyme disease develops gradually. Titers of specific IgM antibody to *B. burgdorferi* peak between the third and sixth week after disease onset. The specific IgG response develops gradually over months. Culture of *B. burgdorferi* from clinical specimens is difficult.

The stages of the immune response are as follows:

Stage 1 (localized infection) is characterized by EM, which occurs at the site of the tick bite. It usually begins as a red macule or papule that expands slowly to form a large, annular lesion, most often with a bright red outer border and partial central clearing. The lesion is warm but often not painful. Perhaps as much as 25 percent of patients do not exhibit this characteristic skin manifestation.

Stage 2 (disseminated infection) may occur after several days or weeks, when the spirochete spreads hematogenously to many different sites. Patients frequently develop secondary annular skin lesions that are similar in appearance to the initial lesion. Skin involvement is frequently accompanied by severe headache, mild stiffness of the neck, fever, chills, migratory musculoskeletal pain, arthralgias, and profound malaise and fatigue. Other possible clinical manifestations of a disseminated infection include meningitis, cranial or peripheral neuritis, carditis, or atrioventricular nodal block. Except for fatigue and lethargy, the early signs and symptoms are typically intermittent and changing.

Stage 3 (persistent infection) occurs months to years later (usually after periods of latent infection), and is characterized by intermittent or chronic arthritis, chronic encephalopathy or polyneuropathy, or acrodermatitis. Within months after the onset of the infection, approximately 60 percent of the patients in the U.S. who receive no antibiotic treatment develop arthritis. The typical pattern is exemplified by intermittent attacks of oligoarticular arthritis in large joints, especially the knees.

It can be difficult to distinguish late Lyme disease from chronic fatigue syndrome or fibromyalgia. Compared with Lyme disease, chronic fatigue syndrome and fibromyalgia tend to produce more generalized and disabling symptoms, including marked fatigue, severe headache, diffuse musculoskeletal pain, multiple symmetric tender points in characteristic locations, pain and stiffness in many joints, diffuse dysesthesias, difficulty with concentration, and sleep disturbances. Patients with fibromyalgia or chronic fatigue syndrome lack evidence of joint inflammation, have normal neurologic testing results, and have a greater degree of anxiety and depression than do patients with chronic neuroborreliosis.

PATHOGENESIS

B. burgdorferi, the causative agent of the disease, is a fastidious, microaerophilic bacterium. After it is injected into the skin, *B. burgdorferi* may migrate outward, producing EM, and may spread hematogenously to other organs. The spirochete can adhere to many types of mammalian cells; it binds to certain ubiquitous host integrin receptors in the extracellular matrix, to vitronectin and fibronectin, and to matrix glycosaminoglycans. *B. burgdorferi* has a particular tropism for the tissues of the skin, nervous system, and joints. The spirochete is a potent inducer of proinflammatory cytokines, including tumor necrosis factor a and interleukin 1b. Histologic examination of all affected tissues reveals an infiltration of lymphocytes and plasma cells with some degree of vascular damage.

EPIDEMIOLOGY

Lyme disease is the most common vector-borne infection in the U.S. Persons of all ages and both sexes are affected in equal numbers. Most new cases have their onset during the summer months and occur in association with hiking, camping, hunting trips, and residence in wooded or rural areas.

The distribution of Lyme borreliosis correlates closely with the geographic ranges of certain ixodid ticks, which include *Ixodes dammini*, *I. pacificus*, *I. ricinus*, and *I. persulcatus*. *I. dammini* is the principal vector from Massachusetts to Maryland as well as in the midwestern states of Wisconsin and Minnesota. *I. pacificus* is the vector in California and Oregon. The *Ixodes* ticks have different animal hosts. For *I. dammini*, the white-footed mouse is the preferred host for immature larval and nymphal ticks. White-tailed deer, which are not involved in the life cycle of the spirochete, are the preferred host for *I. dammini*'s adult stage.

TREATMENT

Lyme disease can usually be treated successfully with orally administered antibiotics; the exceptions are cases that involve neurological abnormalities, which require intravenous therapy. For early Lyme disease, doxycycline is effective in men and nonpregnant women. Amoxicillin, cefuroxime, and erythromycin are second, third, and fourth-choice alternatives, respectively. In children, amoxicillin is effective. For objective neurological abnormalities, intravenous ceftriaxone is effective. Cefotaxime and penicillin are alternative choices for intravenous antibiotic therapy.

The risk of infection with *B. burgdorferi* after a tick bite is so low that antibiotic prophylaxis is not routinely indicated.

PROGNOSIS

The response to treatment is best early in the disease. The later stages of Lyme disease are treatable, but the convalescence may be longer. Eventually, most patients recover with minimal or no residual deficit.

MENTAL RETARDATION

A 9-year-old boy is brought by his parents for a routine evaluation. In reviewing his medical record, you note that one year earlier he had been referred to a child psychologist for evaluation and that he scored 70 on a standardized intelligence test. You inquire about his behavior and intellectual functioning. His parents report that he has always had difficulties with spoken and written language, but that his behavior is appropriate for his age, and he has a number of friends in the neighborhood. The parents, who are aware of the results of the intelligence testing, request advice and counseling regarding expectations for his adult performance, as well as any possible implications if they were to have additional children.

DIAGNOSIS

Mental retardation is defined as significantly subaverage general intellectual functioning that is accompanied by significant limitations in adaptive functioning. Onset must occur before 18 years. **General intellectual functioning** is defined by the intelligence quotient (IQ), obtained by one or more of the standardized, individually administered intelligence tests (e.g., Wechsler Intelligence Scales for Children, Stanford-Binet test, Kaufman Assessment Battery for Children). Impairments in *adaptive* functioning, rather than a low IQ, are usually the presenting symptoms in individuals with mental retardation.

Mental retardation is divided into four degrees of severity (mild, moderate, severe, and profound), which reflect the degree of intellectual impairment.

Classification of Mental Retardation		
Severity	**IQ range**	**Clinical features**
Mild	50–55 to 70	Understanding the use of language is often delayed to varying degrees, and speech difficulties may interfere with the development of independence into adult life. May acquire academic skills up to the sixth-grade level. During their adult years, mildly retarded persons usually achieve social and vocational abilities adequate for a minimum level of self-support. Makes up the largest percentage of those who are classified as mentally retarded, about 85 percent.
Moderate	35–40 to 50–55	Variable cognitive profiles of abilities are common for this group, and some persons may have higher visuospatial skills than language skills. Language development is variable, ranging from the ability to participate in simple conversation, to limited language, to the ability only to communicate basic needs. Others may show motor incoordination but are socially interactive and can engage in simple conversations. Completely independent living is rarely achieved in adulthood. This group makes up approximately 10 % of the mentally retarded population.
Severe	20–25 to 35–40	Similar to the moderately mentally retarded group with regard to the clinical picture and the presence of brain abnormality, as well as of associated handicaps. Significant number suffer marked motor impairment and associated deficits. In adulthood, supervision is needed for task performance. Makes up 3 to 4 % of the mentally retarded population.
Profound	Less than 20–25	Language comprehension and use are limited to understanding simple commands and making simple requests. A highly structured environment with continuous aid and supervision is needed. Constitutes 1 to 2 % of those diagnosed as mentally retarded.

Blood studies should include glucose, amino and organic acids, uric acid, ammonia, lactate, pyruvate, lead, copper, ceruloplasmin, very long chain fatty acids, and viral titers. Urine studies should include reducing substances, ketoacids, and mucopolysaccharides. Neuroimaging studies are helpful in identifying tumors, evidence of brain trauma, malformations, vascular abnormalities, intracranial calcification, and the state of myelination. Based on the findings from the history and physical, additional laboratory and diagnostic studies may be selected.

Distinguishing **dementia** from mental retardation is important, since mental retardation is defined as a developmental disability, while dementia is generally viewed as a chronic neurological disorder. The diagnosis of dementia requires that the memory impairment and other deficits in cognition represent a clear-cut decline from a prior, higher level of functioning. It should be determined whether cognitive development and adaptive development have always proceeded at a slow rate, or whether a regression from a state of average functioning occurred at some time in the person's life.

PATHOGENESIS

There are many confirmed and suspected causes of mental retardation. Currently, a specific cause for mental retardation can be identified in as many as two-thirds of cases. The etiology of mental retardation can be best conceptualized by the dynamic interaction of three main factors: 1) the person's genetic predisposition, 2) a wide range of environmental factors that impinge on the developing organism, and 3) the timing of exposures to endogenous and exogenous chemicals, microorganisms, radiation, and the status of the psychosocial milieu.

Important Etiologies of Mental Retardation	
Etiology	**Examples**
Acquired diseases	• CNS infections (e.g., encephalitis, meningitis) • Head trauma • Asphyxia • Intoxications (e.g., lead, other poisons) • Brain tumors
Environmental and pyschosocial factors	• Poverty • Neglect and abuse • Chronic parental illness • Nutritional deficiencies
Genetic	• Chromosomal disorders (e.g., Down's syndrome, fragile X) • Single-gene disorders (e.g., metabolic disorders, neurocutaneous disorders) • Polygenic inheritance
Gestational abnormalities	• Placental abnormalities • Placental-fetal circulatory abnormalities • Maternal malnutrition
Malformation syndromes	• Aicardi syndrome • Neural tube defects • Craniofacial anomalies
Perinatal trauma	• Prematurity • Hypoxia/asphyxia • Intracranial hemorrhage
Teratogens, intoxications, intrauterine infections	• Medications (e.g., anticonvulsants) • Drugs (e.g., cocaine) • Alcohol • Radiation exposure • Congenital infections (e.g., rubella, AIDS)

EPIDEMIOLOGY

Approximately 3 percent of the general population has an IQ less than two standard deviations below the mean. It is estimated that 80–90 percent of persons with mental retardation function within the mild range, whereas only 5 percent of the population with mental retardation is severely to profoundly impaired. The prevalence of mild retardation varies inversely with socioeconomic status, whereas moderate to severe disability occurs with equal frequency across all income groups.

TREATMENT

Although mental retardation is a chronic condition, a substantial degree of habilitation can be accomplished. Adaptive social growth and increased functional independence are most effectively accomplished through participation in normative community activities. Successful community integration depends on adequate skill in interpersonal communication, and persons with language impairments must be afforded the opportunity to learn alternate methods of communication. Mental retardation is not a disease or an illness in and of itself. Thought and perception are not characteristically disordered unless there is a concurrent major psychiatric disturbance.

PROGNOSIS

Persons with mild mental retardation are likely to live independent adult lives. Persons with moderate, severe, and profound mental retardation require different degrees of supervision as adults, depending on the degree of impairment in adaptive functioning.

OBESITY

A 54-year-old man presents for a routine health evaluation. He describes a sedentary lifestyle. He works for a publishing company and spends most of the day sitting at his desk. His only exercise is an occasional game of golf, during which he uses an electric golf cart. He does not smoke, drinks seven to ten alcoholic beverages per week, and eats "whatever is put in front of me." Family history is significant; his father suffered a fatal "heart attack" at the age of 59. Pulse is 92/min, respirations are 14/min, and blood pressure is 130/90 mm Hg. The patient is 1.8 m (71 in) tall and weighs 110kg (242 lb); his body mass index (BMI) is calculated to be 34 kg/m².

DIAGNOSIS

Obesity is a chronic disease that is increasing in prevalence and poses a serious risk for the development of diabetes mellitus, hypertension, heart disease, gallbladder disease, and certain forms of cancer. Obesity, a condition in which total body fat is higher than normal, is frequently used synonymously with the term "overweight" because the degree to which the patient is overweight can be measured more easily. Height and weight are easy and accurate measurements used for estimating or measuring total body fat. Body fat and fat distribution are affected by gender, age, degree of physical activity, and a number of drugs. In both men and women, body fat increases with age. In lean young men, body fat is less than 20 percent and may rise as they age to more than 25 percent. In young women, body fat stores may be below 30 percent and may increase gradually to more than 35 percent with age. At all ages after puberty, women have more body fat than men.

The most widely used formula for relating height and weight is the body mass index (BMI), which is weight/(height)², where weight is in kilograms and height is in meters. A BMI between 20 and 25 kg/m² is usually considered a good measurement for most individuals. Overweight is defined as measuring a BMI above 27 kg/m², and obesity is defined as a BMI > 30 kg/m². Determination of BMI, estimation of abdominal girth, and assessment of the presence of heart disease, diabetes mellitus, gallbladder disease, or hypertension in the family provide valuable information in the evaluation of an obese patient.

PATHOGENESIS

Obesity can be viewed as a consequence of the interaction between environmental forces and the individual genetic substrate, in particular with susceptibility genes. Genetic determinants can either play a major role in the pathogenesis of obesity or enhance susceptibility to its development. The dysmorphic forms of obesity in which genetics play a major role include the Prader-Willi syndrome, Ahlström's syndrome, the Laurence-Moon-Biedl syndrome, Cohen's syndrome, and Carpenter's syndrome.

Destruction of the ventromedial or the paraventricular nucleus of the hypothalamus can produce obesity by causing hyperphagia and a disturbance in the autonomic nervous system marked by increased parasympathetic and reduced sympathetic nervous system activity. Endocrine diseases, such as Cushing's disease and polycystic ovary syndrome, are associated with obesity. Drugs that can induce obesity include phenothiazines, antidepressants, antiepileptics (valproate, carbamazepine), steroids (glucocorticoids, megestrol acetate), and antihypertensives (terazosin).

Most forms of obesity are associated with enlarged fat cells and higher rates of basal lipolysis. In many forms of severe childhood-onset obesity, the total number of fat cells is increased. Fat cells serve as a reservoir for storage of fatty acids released during the clearance of chylomicrons, and can in turn release these stored fatty acids by the intracellular hormone-sensitive lipase. During conditions of dietary excess, fat cells synthesize long-chain fatty acids. Fat cells generate large quantities of lactate and metabolize glucose to provide glycerol-3-phosphate for triglyceride synthesis. The fat cell is also an important secretory organ; it produces the lipoprotein lipase, which is involved in hydrolyzing the triglycerides of very low density lipoproteins (VLDL) and chylomicrons, and components D (adipsin) and C3b. Adipocytes also produce cytokines such as tumor necrosis factor a, angiotensinogen, and leptin.

To maintain normal fat stores, dietary nutrients must be oxidized in the body in the proportion in which they occur in the diet. Since the dietary intake of carbohydrate nearly equals body stores of glucose, carbohydrate stores are more vulnerable to changes in dietary carbohydrate than either fat or proteins. There are three known predictors of weight gain: 1) a low metabolic rate; 2) a high respiratory quotient (the ratio of carbon dioxide produced to oxygen used); this indicates carbohydrate oxidation and the need to eat to replace carbohydrate; and 3) insulin resistance.

EPIDEMIOLOGY

The prevalence of obesity in the U.S. has increased relatively slowly in both genders over the past 40 years, but in the last decade it has increased by about 30 percent.

TREATMENT

The etiology of obesity is usually unknown; this makes a cure unlikely and palliation the therapeutic goal. Further complicating treatment is the fact that obesity is a stigmatized condition in which the overweight subject is frequently viewed as responsible for the condition.

Behavior modification is at the core of many current programs of weight reduction. The basic principles are those of operant conditioning and cognitive restructuring. Eating behavior is separated into its antecedents: the act of eating and the consequences of patterns that work toward solving the problem. Features of behavior modification of proven value in people who are successful in maintaining weight loss over an extended period of time include: 1) continued monitoring of food-related behaviors, 2) adoption of a low-fat diet, and 3) increased levels of physical activity.

For anyone considering a weight-reducing diet, the quantity of food intake and the avoidance of settings in which excess quantities of high-fat food are eaten are equally important. A diet with fewer than 25 percent fat calories is a reasonable goal. Exercise is not good as a primary strategy for weight reduction, but is crucial in maintaining weight loss.

The options for pharmacologic intervention in obesity include several appetite-suppressing agents. These drugs increase extraneuronal norepinephrine by enhancing its release (benzphetamine, phendimetrazine, phentermine, mazindol, and diethylpropion) or by blocking its uptake; by inhibiting α_1-adrenergic receptors (phenylpropanolamine); or by releasing serotonin and blocking its reuptake (fenfluramine). Appetite suppressing drugs should be reserved for patients with a BMI > 30 kg/m^2, or above 27 kg/m^2 if comorbid conditions are present. When appetite-suppressing drugs are discontinued, patients regain weight, in keeping with the concept that the drugs do not cure obesity, but only relieve its symptoms.

For individuals with a BMI > 35 kg/m^2 who have high risks for diabetes or family histories of early heart attacks, or individuals with BMI > 40 kg/m^2 without these problems, surgical manipulation of the gastrointestinal tract may be useful. The best long-term weight loss occurs with the gastric bypass operation, in which a small upper pouch is attached by a Roux-en-Y anastomosis to the jejunum. Vertical banded gastroplasty is also an effective option.

PROGNOSIS

The increased mortality associated with obesity results primarily from increased risks for cardiovascular disease, high blood pressure, diabetes mellitus, and possibly some types of cancer. Recidivism (weight regain) is common in obesity.

ROCKY MOUNTAIN SPOTTED FEVER

A 13-year-old boy is brought by his mother to his primary care physician's office with complaints of fever, nausea and vomiting, and a headache. He reports that the symptoms began five days ago and now has "aches and pains all over." He denies photophobia. Temperature is 39.2 C (102.6 F), respirations are 18/min, pulse is 120/min, and blood pressure is 90/50 mm Hg. Examination reveals a macular rash on his wrists and ankles. The patient is questioned regarding tick exposure, and he reports that he had discovered a tick on his leg after a hiking trip with his father ten days ago. Laboratory studies show:

Hematocrit	41%	(Male: 41–53%)
Leukocytes	8,500/mm³	(4.5–11,000/mm³)
Bands	8%	(3–5%)
Segmented neutrophils	58%	(54–62%)
Eosinophils	1%	(1–3%)
Basophils	0.5%	(0.0–0.75%)
Lymphocytes	28%	(25–33%)
Monocytes	4%	(3–7%)
Platelets	158,000/mm³	(150,000–400,000/mm³)
Erythrocyte sedimentation	50 mm/hr	(0–15mm/hr)

DIAGNOSIS

Rocky Mountain spotted fever (RMSF) is a severe rickettsial disease caused by *Rickettsia rickettsii*. Early in the illness when medical attention is usually sought, RMSF is difficult to distinguish from many self-limiting viral illnesses. During the first three days, fever, headache, malaise, myalgia, nausea, vomiting, and anorexia are the most frequent symptoms. The untreated illness progresses insidiously as vascular infection and injury advance.

Rash is evident in 14 percent of patients on the first day of illness and in 49 percent during the first three days. Vascular injury usually makes its appearance between the third and fifth febrile day; it is manifested by macules that are up to 5 mm in diameter on the wrists and ankles. Later, similar lesions develop on the remainder of the extremities and trunk. The pink foci of vasodilation become leaky, with local edema and conversion to maculopapules, which blanch on compression. Later, more severe vascular damage results in hemorrhage at the center of the maculopapules, creating petechiae that do not blanch upon compression. The manifestation of macules on the palms and soles, which is considered diagnostically important, usually occurs relatively late in the course of the disease, but does not occur at all in many cases.

Systemic and pulmonary microcirculations are the target of the vascular damage induced by intracellular rickettsial infection, and clinical manifestations represent this damage. Widespread increases in vascular permeability result in edema, decreased plasma volume, hypoalbuminemia, reduced serum oncotic pressure, and prerenal azotemia. Extensive involvement of the pulmonary microcirculation is associated with noncardiogenic pulmonary edema. Central nervous system involvement is an important clinical feature of RMSF. Encephalitis, which presents as confusion or lethargy, is due to vascular injury and is apparent in 25 percent of cases.

Clinical and epidemiologic considerations are more important than a laboratory diagnosis early in the illness. The most important epidemiologic factor is a history of exposure (within 12 days before onset) to a potentially tick-infested environment during a season of possible tick activity. However, only 60 percent of patients recall being bitten by a tick during the incubation period.

Serologic tests are usually negative at the time of presentation for medical care, but treatment should not be delayed. The indirect immunofluorescence assay can be used to confirm the diagnosis, and between 7 and 10 days after the onset of the illness, a diagnostic titer is usually detectable. Laboratory studies will show a normal white blood cell count, increased numbers of immature myeloid cells, and increased plasma concentrations of acute-phase response proteins. Hyponatremia due to the inappropriate secretion of antidiuretic hormone is common.

The differential diagnosis for early clinical manifestations of RMSF (fever, headache, and myalgia without a rash) includes influenza, enterovirus infection, infectious mononucleosis, viral hepatitis, leptospirosis, typhoid fever, Gram-negative or Gram-positive bacterial sepsis, and other rickettsial diseases. When a rash appears, the differential diagnosis should include rubeola, rubella, meningococcemia, disseminated gonococcal infection, secondary syphilis, toxic shock syndrome, drug hypersensitivity, idiopathic thrombocytopenic purpura, thrombotic thrombocytopenic purpura, Kawasaki syndrome, and immune complex vasculitis.

PATHOGENESIS

RMSF is caused by *R. rickettsii*, a Gram-negative bacillus. It is primarily transmitted by *Dermacentor variabilis* (the American dog tick) in the eastern two-thirds of the U.S. and California; by *Dermacentor andersoni* (the Rocky Mountain wood tick) in the western U.S.; by *Rhipicephalus sanguineus* in Mexico; and by *Amblyomma cajennense* in Mexico and Central and South America. Although it is maintained principally by transovarian transmission from one generation of ticks to the next, *R. rickettsii* can be acquired by uninfected ticks through the ingestion of a blood meal from rickettsemic small animals. The likelihood of an individual tick containing *R. rickettsii* is small.

R. rickettsii organisms are inoculated into the dermis along with secretions of the tick's salivary glands after roughly 6 hours of feeding. Rickettsiae spread throughout the body by the lymphatics and bloodstream. *R. rickettsii* has two major immunodominant surface-exposed proteins, OmpA and OmpB. OmpA functions as an adhesin for the host cell; OmpB, the most abundant outer-membrane protein, shares genetic sequences and limited antigens with typhus-group rickettsiae. The rickettsiae attach via OmpA to the endothelial cell membrane and induce their own engulfment. Once intracellularly located, they replicate in the cell by binary fission and spread from cell to cell, propelled by polar polymerization of the host cell's actin.

The pathological basis for tissue and organ injury in RMSF is increased vascular permeability with resulting edema, hypovolemia, and ischemia. After an incubation period of approximately one week, heavily infected endothelial cells begin to manifest as vascular injuries. It is the damage to these cells that results in increased vascular permeability, edema, the development of a host mononuclear-cell tissue response, and hemorrhage. Consumption of platelets may result in thrombocytopenia in up to half of those infected, but disseminated intravascular coagulation with hypofibrinogenemia is rare in RMSF. Serious potential complications of RMSF include hypoxemia, oliguria or anuric acute renal failure, seizures, hemorrhage and/or anemia, and severe thrombocytopenia.

EPIDEMIOLOGY

RMSF has been documented in 48 states and in Canada, Mexico, Panama, Colombia, and Brazil. Humans become infected during the active season of the vector tick species. In northern areas, cases occur mainly in the spring; in warmer southern states, most cases occur from May to September, although some are reported in the winter. The incidence of infection is highest among 5- to 9-year-old children.

TREATMENT

The drug of choice for the treatment of adults with RMSF is **doxycycline**, except for patients who are pregnant. Tetracyclines are known to stain the teeth of young children (< 9 years old). Although not as effective, chloramphenicol is recommended for use in pregnant women, and more cautiously, in young children. The most seriously ill patients are managed in intensive care units; careful fluid management is critical in these patients. Heparin is not a useful component of treatment and there is no evidence that glucocorticoids, although frequently administered, affect the outcome of RMSF.

The avoidance of tick bites is the only available preventive approach. Protective clothing and tick repellents can reduce the risk of tick bites. After possible exposure to ticks, it is wise to inspect the body and remove ticks as quickly as possible.

PROGNOSIS

The mortality rate of RMSF is approximately 5 percent. The case-fatality ratio is higher for males than females and increases with each decade of life above age 20. Pulmonary involvement with severe respiratory distress is a prominent factor in fatal cases. In untreated cases, death usually occurs within 2 weeks after the onset of illness.

SUBSTANCE ABUSE IN PREGNANCY

A 32-year-old woman with an estimated gestational age of 27 weeks presents to the family practice clinic for a scheduled prenatal visit. You review the patient's medical record and note that the pregnancy has been unremarkable to date; she has gained an acceptable amount of weight, a sonogram at 17 weeks demonstrated the fetus to have a weight in the 45th percentile, and to have a grossly normal anatomy. All laboratory results have been normal to date. Fundal height is appropriate for gestational age. Fetal heart rate is 145/min. During your examination, you note that she smells strongly of alcohol. You ask the patient if she thinks she has a problem with alcohol, and she replies, "Not at all, I just have a drink to relax now and then."

DIAGNOSIS

At the time of the initial prenatal visit, the patient should be questioned in a nonjudgmental way about legal and illicit drug use, including tobacco and alcohol. The use of a screening questionnaire can be both helpful and nonthreatening to the patient. However, since denial is an intrinsic component of addicted patients' behavior, any questionnaire is limited as a screening tool.

CAGE questionnaire
- C   Have you ever felt you ought to cut down on your drinking?
- A   Have people annoyed you by criticizing your drinking?
- G   Have you ever felt bad or guilty about your drinking?
- E   Have you ever had a drink first thing in the morning to steady your nerves or to get rid of a hangover (eye opener)?

PATHOGENESIS

Pregnancy-related problems due to substance abuse include increased rates of poor fetal growth, developmental delay, neonatal withdrawal, and increased exposure to sexually transmitted diseases, especially human immunodeficiency virus (HIV) and syphilis. Fetal risks are compounded by the propensity of addicted patients to obtain little or no prenatal care.

Pregnancy-related substance abuse consequences	
Substance	**Consequences**
Alcohol	There is no amount of alcohol consumption known to be safe in pregnancy, but fetal alcohol syndrome (FAS) is seen in women with heavy alcohol consumption (at least six 3-ounce drinks per day). FAS consists of: 1) growth retardation before or after birth, 2) a pattern of abnormal facial features or microcephaly, including shortening of the midfacial area (the nose and/or philtrum), and 3) central nervous system abnormalities–mental retardation, developmental delay, or abnormal neonatal developmental. Other alcohol-related birth defects include such structural abnormalities as ophthalmologic or otic anomalies, cardiac septal defects, hemangiomas, undescended testes, and hernias. There are also increased rates of spontaneous abortion, decreased immune function, hearing impairment, and developmental delay.
Cocaine	Causes adrenergic stimulation, resulting in vasoconstriction, tachycardia, and hypertension. Use of cocaine is associated with poor prenatal care and increased risks of placental abruption, prematurity, growth retardation, and, secondarily, fetal death and distress.
Nicotine	**Smoking is the single most common cause of impaired fetal growth.** Effects are dose-dependent and 15 to 25 percent of fetuses of smokers have intrauterine growth retardation. Nicotine use is also associated with premature rupture of the membranes, preterm labor, placental abruption, spontaneous abortion, and placenta previa. Post-delivery complications include persistent failure to thrive secondary to poor breast-feeding, increased risk of sudden infant death syndrome, asthma, frequent respiratory infections requiring hospitalization, and attention deficit disorder.
Opiates	Perinatal morbidities associated with opiate use include low birth weight, pregnancy-induced hypertension, and third-trimester bleeding. Neonatal complications include withdrawal syndrome, postnatal growth deficiency, microcephaly, neurobehavior problems, and an increased risk for sudden infant death syndrome. Withdrawal or detoxification is not recommended in pregnancy because of the risk of concomitant fetal withdrawal and possible fetal death.

EPIDEMIOLOGY

The true prevalence of substance abuse in pregnancy is difficult to assess because it varies with the population studied, but estimates range from 7.5 percent to 20 percent. Polypharmacy is the rule rather than the exception; the concomitant abuses of alcohol and nicotine are especially common. Most female smokers continue to smoke during pregnancy.

TREATMENT

Substance abuse affects all sectors of the population, and pregnant and parenting women comprise a special group with unique needs. Each woman requires an individualized treatment plan, but comprehensive services should include high-risk prenatal care with addiction treatment modalities such as individual, group, and family therapy. These women also need strong social service support, with encouragement toward education and job training. Residential treatment for women and their children should also be available to alleviate the social problems faced by these patients. Women with substance abuse problems have experienced higher rates of sexual and physical abuse as children and are also more likely to abuse their own children. In addition, they are likely to be the children of substance-abusing parents and to have been introduced to drugs by a male partner. These women are at high risk for involvement with the legal system; they may be under scrutiny by child protective services, or, in some states, even be subject to incarceration for delivering drugs to their fetuses. Since there is no treatment for FAS or other substance-related consequences, the goal for practitioners is prevention.

PROGNOSIS

Substance abuse/dependence is a chronic condition with a high rate of recidivism.

TUBERCULOSIS

A 42-year-old white woman presents to the emergency department with complaints of a cough productive of blood-tinged sputum, fever, night sweats, and general weakness. Her symptoms have gradually worsened over the past several weeks. The patient is HIV-positive and has been living in a homeless shelter for the past 6 months. She reports a weight loss of approximately 5 kg (11 lb) over the past 2 months. Temperature is 38.3 C (101 F), pulse is 100/min, blood pressure is 110/70 mm Hg, and respirations are 22/min. The patient is poorly groomed and appears malnourished. Auscultation of the chest demonstrates rales over the left upper lung field. A radiograph of the chest shows a left upper lobe infiltrate with cavitation.

DIAGNOSIS

Tuberculosis (TB) is caused by bacteria belonging to the *Mycobacterium tuberculosis* complex. It is usually classified as pulmonary or extrapulmonary, and predominantly affects the lungs, although in up to one-third of cases, other organs are involved. In order of frequency, the extrapulmonary sites most commonly involved in tuberculosis are the lymph nodes, pleura, genitourinary tract, bones and joints, meninges, and peritoneum, but all organ systems may be affected.

Early in the course of the disease, signs and symptoms of TB are often nonspecific and insidious, consisting mainly of fever and night sweats, weight loss, anorexia, general malaise, and weakness. However, in the majority of cases, a cough eventually develops, typically accompanied by the production of purulent sputum. Blood streaking of the sputum occurs frequently. Systemic features include fever and wasting.

Physical findings are of limited use in the diagnosis of pulmonary tuberculosis since many patients have no abnormalities detectable by chest examination, while others have detectable rales in the areas involved during inspiration, especially after coughing. The most common hematologic findings are mild anemia and leukocytosis.

The initial suspicion of pulmonary tuberculosis is often based on abnormal chest radiograph findings in a patient with respiratory symptoms. Primary pulmonary tuberculosis is typically localized to the middle and lower lung zones, and is usually accompanied by hilar or paratracheal lymphadenopathy. Secondary pulmonary tuberculosis results from endogenous reactivation of latent infection and is usually localized to the apical and posterior segments of the upper lobes, where high oxygen concentration favors mycobacterial growth. However, virtually any radiographic pattern, from a normal film or a solitary pulmonary nodule, to diffuse alveolar infiltrates in a patient with adult respiratory distress syndrome, may be seen. In the era of AIDS, no radiographic pattern can be considered pathognomonic.

Skin testing with the purified protein derivative (PPD) of tuberculin is the most widely used screening test for tuberculosis, but is of limited value in the diagnosis of active tuberculosis because of its low sensitivity and specificity. False-negative reactions are common in immunosuppressed patients and in those with overwhelming tuberculosis. Positive reactions are sometimes obtained when patients have been infected with *M. tuberculosis* but do not have active disease, and when persons have been sensitized by nontuberculous mycobacteria or bacillus Calmette-Guérin (BCG) vaccination.

Mycobacteria, including *M. tuberculosis*, do not stain readily and are often neutral on Gram's staining. However, once stained, the bacilli cannot be decolorized by acid alcohol, which is the reason for their classification as acid-fast bacilli (AFB). A presumptive diagnosis is given on the finding of AFB upon microscopic examination of a diagnostic specimen such as a smear of expectorated sputum or tissue. The definitive diagnosis of tuberculosis is dependent on the isolation and identification of *M. tuberculosis* from a diagnostic specimen. Because most species of mycobacteria, including *M. tuberculosis*, are slow growing, four to eight weeks may be required before their growth is detected.

PATHOGENESIS

Of the pathogenic species belonging to the *M. tuberculosis* complex, the most frequent and important agent of human disease is *M. tuberculosis* itself. *M. tuberculosis* is a rod-shaped, non-spore–forming, thin aerobic bacterium that measures about 0.5 μm by 3 μm. It is usually transmitted through the airborne spread of droplet nuclei produced by patients with infectious pulmonary tuberculosis. The probability of contact with a source case of *M. tuberculosis* infection, the intimacy and duration of that contact, the degree of infectiousness of the case, and the environment of the contact are all important determinants of transmission.

The risk of developing disease after being infected with *M. tuberculosis* depends largely on endogenous factors, such as the individual's innate susceptibility to disease and level of function of his or her cell-mediated immunity. Clinical illness directly following infection is classified as primary tuberculosis and is common among children up to 4 years of age. When infection occurs later in life, the chance is greater that the immune system will contain it, at least temporarily. The majority of individuals who will ultimately develop tuberculosis do so within the first year or two after infection. Dormant bacilli, however, may persist for years before being reactivated to produce secondary tuberculosis. Overall, it is estimated that about 10 percent of infected persons will eventually develop active tuberculosis.

A variety of diseases favor the development of active tuberculosis. The most potent risk factor for the development of active tuberculosis among individuals infected with *M. tuberculosis* is clearly HIV co-infection, which suppresses cellular immunity. The risk that latent *M. tuberculosis* will develop to cause active disease is directly related to the patient's degree of immunosuppression. Other conditions known to increase the risk of active tuberculosis among person infected with *M. tuberculosis* include silicosis; lymphoma, leukemia, and other malignant neoplasms; hemophilia; chronic renal failure and hemodialysis; insulin-dependent diabetes mellitus; immunosuppressive treatment; and conditions associated with malnutrition, such as gastrectomy and jejunoileal bypass surgery.

EPIDEMIOLOGY

In the mid-1980s in many industrialized countries, the number of tuberculosis cases, which had been falling steadily, stabilized and even began to increase. A number of factors—most notably infection due to human immunodeficiency virus (HIV); immigration from countries with high prevalences of tuberculosis; and social problems such as poverty, homelessness, and drug abuse—have been implicated in the increasing rate of tuberculosis infection. In the U.S., tuberculosis is a disease of young adult members of the HIV-infected, immigrant, and disadvantaged/marginalized populations.

Age is another important determinant of the risk of disease after infection. Among infected persons, the incidence of tuberculosis is highest during late adolescence and early adulthood. The risk may again increase in the elderly, possibly because of waning immunity.

$$R_x$$

TREATMENT

Five major drugs are considered first-line agents for the treatment of tuberculosis: isoniazid, rifampin, pyrazinamide, ethambutol, and streptomycin. The treatment regimen of choice for virtually all forms of tuberculosis in both adults and children consists of a two-month initial phase of isoniazid, rifampin, pyrazinamide, and ethambutol, followed by a four-month continuation phase of isoniazid and rifampin. Pyridoxine should be added to the regimen in persons at high risk of vitamin deficiency (e.g., alcoholics; malnourished persons; pregnant and lactating women; and patients with conditions that are also associated with neuropathy, such as chronic renal failure, diabetes, and HIV infection or AIDS). Bacteriologic evaluation is the preferred method of monitoring the response to treatment for tuberculosis. If a patient's sputum cultures remain positive at or beyond 3 months of therapy, treatment failure and drug resistance should be suspected. During treatment, patients should be monitored for drug toxicity. The most common significant adverse reaction is hepatitis.

By far the best way to prevent tuberculosis is the rapid diagnosis of infectious cases and the administration of appropriate treatment until cure. A major component of tuberculosis control in the U.S. involves the administration of isoniazid to persons with latent tuberculosis and at high risk for active disease. In most cases, candidates for prophylaxis are identified by PPD skin testing of high-risk groups of individuals. Some PPD-negative individuals are also candidates for prophylaxis; these include infants and children who have come in contact with infectious cases and HIV-infected persons who have been found to be anergic with other delayed-type hypersensitivity antigens, such as *Candida* and mumps. One contraindication to isoniazid prophylaxis is the presence of active liver disease. Since the most common risk of toxicity is hepatitis, persons at increased risk of toxicity (e.g., those aged 35 years or older, those consuming alcohol daily, and those with a history of liver disease) should undergo baseline and then monthly assessment of liver function during treatment.

PROGNOSIS

If properly treated, tuberculosis caused by drug-susceptible strains is curable in virtually all cases. However, the improper use of antituberculosis drugs, while reducing mortality, may result in large numbers of chronic infectious cases, often with drug-resistant bacilli. If untreated, the disease is fatal within five years in more than half of cases.

VAGINITIS

A 23-year-old woman presents to the family practice clinic with complaints of vaginal discharge and itching. The patient reports that for the past week she has had a foul-smelling vaginal discharge, as well as vaginal pruritus and dyspareunia. Her last menstrual period began two weeks earlier and lasted for three days. She has no history of sexually transmitted diseases and is sexually active with one male partner. On speculum examination, a profuse, yellow, foul-smelling discharge is noted. Vaginal pH is determined to be 7.0, and when a 10 percent solution of potassium hydroxide is added to the discharge, an amine odor is noted. Microscopic examination of a wet mount preparation demonstrates motile trichomonads.

DIAGNOSIS

Symptoms of **vaginitis** include increased vaginal discharge, vulvar irritation and pruritus, external dysuria, and a foul discharge odor. Although a small amount of vaginal discharge is normal, particularly at the midcycle, normal vaginal discharge should not have a foul odor or produce irritation or pruritus.

On inspection, the external genitalia may be normal or edematous, erythematous, excoriated, or fissured. On speculum examination, the vaginal mucosa may be erythematous. Discharge characteristics that are important to observe are viscosity, floccular appearance, color, and odor. Vaginal pH must be determined. A potassium hydroxide (KOH) odor test and a microscopic examination should be performed. Vaginal cultures are not particularly helpful except when used selectively to identify *Candida*.

Causes of Infectious Vaginitis			
Cause	**Clinical features**	**Diagnosis**	**Treatment**
Candidiasis	External irritation, dysuria, vulvar and vaginal pruritus are common. Classically, the vaginal walls are red and contain adherent, dry, white, curdy plaques.	KOH wet-mount examination. Vaginal discharge pH is normal (4.7 or less).	Local vaginal antifungal therapy (miconazole, clotrimazole, butoconazole, tioconazole, and terconazole). Oral fluconazole is also effective.
Trichomoniasis	Profuse, yellow, malodorous, often uncomfortable vaginal discharge and vulvar irritation.	Typically, vaginal pH is greater than 4.7 and forms an amine odor with 10 percent KOH solution. Motile trichomonads are demonstrated in the saline wet-mount smear.	Systemic therapy required. Metronidazole is the treatment of choice. Treat male partner simultaneously.
Bacterial vaginosis	Thin homogenous, fishy-smelling, gray vaginal discharge that adheres to the vaginal walls and often is present at the introitus.	Vaginal pH is greater than 4.7. Fishy amine odor produced by anaerobes is accentuated when 10% KOH solution is added. **Clue cells** (vaginal epithelial cells to which organisms are attached) are present.	Metronidazole and clindamycin are the most effective oral regimens. Topical metronidazole gel and clindamycin cream are as effective as oral therapy.

Other conditions that may cause excessive vaginal discharge include cervicitis, normal cervical mucus from cervical ectopy, vaginal foreign bodies (most commonly, retained tampons), and allergic reactions to douching or vaginal contraceptive agents. Atrophic vaginitis among postmenopausal women may produce burning and dyspareunia, but an infectious cause has not been established.

PATHOGENESIS

Women with infectious vaginitis have either abnormal organisms or a quantitative increase in normal flora. At least four types of infectious vaginitis are found: candidal, trichomonal, bacterial vaginosis, and in children, gonococcal. *Candida albicans* causes about 90 percent of vaginal yeast infections. *Trichomonas vaginalis* resides not only in the vagina, but also in the urethra, bladder, and Skene glands. Both anaerobes and *Gardnerella vaginalis* are normal inhabitants of the vagina, but overgrowth of the normal *Lactobacillus*-dominant flora by these bacteria causes bacterial vaginosis.

EPIDEMIOLOGY

Vaginitis is the most common gynecologic complaint. *Candida albicans* causes about 90 percent of vaginal yeast infections. About 15 percent of male sexual contacts of women with candidiasis have symptomatic balanitis. *Trichomonas vaginalis* is a common sexually transmitted organism, present in 3 to 15 percent of asymptomatic women. Most male contacts of women with trichomoniasis asymptomatically carry the organism in the urethra and prostate.

TREATMENT

The establishment of the correct diagnosis is mandatory because the selection of effective therapy depends on it; treatment of nonspecific vaginitis inevitably fails. Local vaginal therapy is typically used for candidiasis. Patients with frequently recurrent candidiasis should have a glucose tolerance test and human immunodeficiency virus testing, and should receive suppressive anticandidal therapy. In addition, some women with candidiasis have concurrent vaginal infections. Metronidazole is effective in treating trichomoniasis. Simultaneous treatment of the male sexual partner is recommended. Recurrent trichomoniasis is usually attributable to either a lack of compliance or reexposure to an untreated sexual partner. Bacterial vaginosis is treated with either oral or topical metronidazole or clindamycin.

PROGNOSIS

Typically, vaginitis is an easily treated condition. If therapy is unsuccessful, the diagnosis should be questioned.

ACQUIRED IMMUNODEFICIENCY SYNDROME

A 34-year-old woman known to be seropositive for human immunodeficiency virus (HIV) presents for a routine evaluation and is without complaints. The patient was diagnosed with HIV infection three years prior and has had no clinical symptoms or opportunistic infections. She takes no medications for her HIV disease. Her CD4+ T cell count one year ago was 534/mL. Temperature is 37 C (98.6 F), pulse is 72/min, respirations are 12/min, and blood pressure is 115/75 mm Hg. Physical exam is within normal limits. Pertinent negative findings include no adenopathy or oral thrush. A CD4+ T cell count is obtained and is 403/mL.

DIAGNOSIS

The clinical consequences of HIV infection encompass a spectrum that ranges from an acute syndrome associated with primary infection, to a prolonged asymptomatic state, to advanced disease. CD4+ T cell counts, along with HIV RNA serum levels, are used to determine prognosis and monitor response to therapy. HIV disease can be divided empirically (on the basis of the degree of immunodeficiency) into an early stage (CD4+ count > 500/mL), and intermediate stage (CD4+ count 200 to 500/mL), and an advanced stage (CD4+ count < 200/mL). The current definition of acquired immunodeficiency syndrome (AIDS) is complex. It is a system based on ranges of CD4+ counts and clinical categories. However, any individual with a CD4+ count lower than 200/mL has AIDS, regardless of the presentation of symptoms or opportunistic disease. Most AIDS-defining opportunistic infections and true malignancies occur in the advanced stage of the disease, but neurologic disease and Kaposi's sarcoma are not strictly related to the degree of immunodeficiency.

Approximately 50 to 70 percent of individuals with HIV infection experience an acute clinical syndrome approximately 3 to 6 weeks after primary infection. The syndrome is typical of an acute viral syndrome, and similar to that of acute infectious mononucleosis. Most patients recover spontaneously from this syndrome and have a mildly depressed CD4+ T cell count that remains stable for a variable period before beginning its progressive decline. In some patients, the CD4+ T cell count even returns to the normal range.

The median time from primary HIV infection to the development of clinical disease is approximately 10 years. HIV disease with active virus replication usually progresses during this asymptomatic period. The rate of disease progression is directly related to HIV RNA levels. With few exceptions, CD4+ T cell counts fall progressively during this asymptomatic period, at an average rate of approximately 50 cells/mL per year.

At some point, usually after the CD4+ T cell count has fallen below 500/mL, patients begin to develop signs and symptoms of clinical illness. Early symptomatic HIV disease is characterized by generalized lymphadenopathy, oral lesions (thrush, hairy leukoplakia, and aphthous ulcers), reactivation herpes zoster, and thrombocytopenia.

Opportunistic infections are late complications of HIV infection, and for the most part occur in patients with fewer than 200 CD4+ T cells per microliter. The causative agents characteristically include not only opportunistic infections such as *Pneumocystis carinii*, *Mycobacterium avium-intracellulare* complex, cytomegalovirus (CMV), and other organisms that normally do not cause disease in the absence of a compromised immune system, but common bacterial and mycobacterial pathogens as well.

Clinical disease of the nervous system accounts for a significant degree of morbidity in a high percentage of patients with HIV infection. Among the opportunistic infections and neoplasms that involve the central nervous system are toxoplasmosis, cryptococcosis, progressive multifocal leukoencephalopathy, CMV, HTLV-1, mycobacterial tuberculosis, syphilis, and primary CNS lymphoma. HIV encephalopathy, which is characterized by dementia and motor and behavioral abnormalities, generally occurs late in the course of HIV infection. Peripheral neuropathies are common in patients with HIV infection and occur at all stages of illness.

PATHOGENESIS

HIV is an RNA virus whose hallmark is the reverse transcription of its genomic RNA to DNA by the enzyme reverse transcriptase. The life cycle of HIV begins with the high-affinity binding of the gp120 protein via a portion of its V1 region (near the N terminus) to its receptor on the host cell surface, the CD4 molecule. CD4+ T lymphocytes and CD4+ cells of monocyte lineage are the principal targets of HIV. HIV disease eventually causes a profound immunodeficiency, which results from a progressive quantitative and qualitative deficiency of the subset of T lymphocytes referred to as helper or inducer T cells.

Active virus replication and progressive immunologic impairment occur throughout the course of HIV infection. Once the CD4+ T cell count falls below 200/mL, the patient becomes highly susceptible to opportunistic disease. Patients may experience constitutional signs and symptoms, or they may develop an opportunistic disease abruptly without any prior symptoms. The depletion of CD4+ T cells continues to be progressive and unrelenting throughout this phase. It is not uncommon for CD4+ T cell counts to drop as low as 10/mL, or even to zero.

Neurological problems that occur in HIV-infected individuals may be either primary to the pathogenic process of the HIV infection, or secondary to opportunistic infections and neoplasms.

EPIDEMIOLOGY

AIDS is the leading cause of death among Americans aged 25 to 44 years. HIV infection and AIDS have disproportionately affected minority populations in the U.S.; blacks and Hispanics constitute only 12 and 9 percent of the population, respectively, yet they account for 35 and 18 percent, respectively, of the adult/adolescent AIDS cases and for 58 and 23 percent, respectively, of AIDS cases in children.

TREATMENT

$$R_x$$

A variety of antiretroviral treatment strategies are currently being used. The timing of therapy initiation is somewhat controversial; some authorities recommend starting antiretroviral treatment from the time of diagnosis of HIV infection, while others recommend waiting until the CD4+ T cell count falls below 500/mL. Most current treatment strategies employ two nucleoside reverse transcriptase inhibitors and a protease inhibitor. HIV therapeutics is a rapidly evolving field and treatment recommendations are subject to frequent change.

Antiretroviral Agents		
Nucleoside analogues	**Non-nucleoside reverse transcriptase inhibitors**	**Protease inhibitors**
Zidovudine	Delavirdine	Ritonavir
Didanosine	Nevirapine	Nelfinavir mesylate
Zalcitabine		Saquinavir mesylate
Stavudine		Indinavir sulfate
Lamivudine		

Pneumocystis carinii pneumonia (PCP) rarely occurs before the CD4$^+$ T cell count drops below 200/mL or the CD4$^+$ percentage declines below 15 percent. At that point, PCP prophylaxis should be initiated. The preferred regimen is one double-strength tablet of trimethoprim/sulfamethoxazole daily. This also provides protection against toxoplasmosis, as well as certain bacterial infections. Alternative strategies include dapsone/pyrimethamine and clindamycin/primaquine, and aerosolized pentamidine for individuals unable to tolerate any systemic therapy. The gold standard of therapy for the patient with PCP or disseminated *Pneumocystis* is trimethoprim/sulfamethoxazole, and intravenous pentamidine can also be used to treat PCP.

Primary prophylaxis is indicated for *Mycobacterium avium-intracellulare* complex. This is rarely seen in patients with CD4$^+$ T cell counts above 100/mL. Clarithromycin, azithromycin, and rifabutin can delay the onset of *Mycobacterium avium-intracellulare* complex bacteremia. Treatment with clarithromycin and ethambutol is preferred for *Mycobacterium avium-intracellulare* complex infection in patients with HIV infection.

Toxoplasma gondii is the most common cause of secondary CNS infection in patients with AIDS; it is generally a late complication of HIV infection and usually occurs in patients with less than 100 CD4$^+$ T cells per microliter. The standard treatment for this is combination therapy with pyrimethamine and sulfadiazine.

Any HIV-infected person with at least a 5 mm induration upon Purified Protein Derivative (PPD) testing should receive a 1-year course of isoniazid. In addition, any patient with HIV infection who is anergic and at high risk of tuberculosis should be given one year of isoniazid therapy. Active tuberculosis often develops relatively early in the course of the HIV infection. Standard (four-drug) therapy for tuberculosis is generally as successful in the HIV-infected patient as it is in the HIV-negative patient.

Cryptococcus neoformans is the leading cause of meningitis in patients with AIDS, and generally occurs in patients with advanced disease. Standard therapy for meningitis in the HIV-infected patient is amphotericin B plus flucytosine. Histoplasmosis, a late complication of AIDS that typically presents as disseminated disease, is also treated with amphotericin. *Candida* sp. infections can be treated with either topical nystatin or clotrimazole troches, or in more severe cases, with ketoconazole or fluconazole.

CMV infection can be treated with ganciclovir, foscarnet, and cidofovir. Herpes simplex virus and varicella-zoster virus infections are treated with acyclovir.

Patients with HIV infection are at high risk for infection with encapsulated bacteria and should be given the pneumococcal polysaccharide vaccine as well as the *Haemophilus influenzae* type b vaccine.

PROGNOSIS

Ultimately, patients who progress to severe immunosuppression usually succumb to opportunistic infections or neoplasms. Opportunistic infections are the leading cause of morbidity and mortality in patients with HIV infection. Approximately 80 percent of AIDS patients die as a direct result of an infection other than HIV, most commonly bacterial infections. Patients with CD4$^+$ T cell counts below 200/mL are at high risk for infection with *Pneumocystis carinii*, while patients with CD4$^+$ counts below 100/mL are at high risk for infection with cytomegalovirus and the *Mycobacterium avium-intracellulare* complex.

ACUTE BACTERIAL MENINGITIS

A 19-year-old woman presents with complaints of headache, fever, nausea, vomiting, and a "stiff neck." Temperature is 38.9 C (102 F), pulse is 110/min, respirations are 20/min, and blood pressure is 100/60 mm Hg. Examination reveals photophobia and meningismus. Neurological exam is without focal deficits and funduscopic exam is normal. A computed tomography study of the head is obtained and shown below:

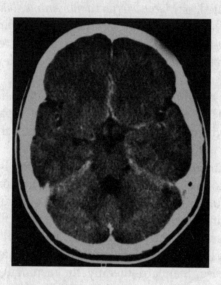

Axial computed tomography scan of the brain–normal study

A lumbar puncture is performed and the results of the cerebrospinal fluid (CSF) analysis are as follows:

CSF
Opening Pressure	300 mm H$_2$O	(l50–180 mm H$_2$O)
Total Leukocytes	2 × 10^6/mL	(< 5/mL)
Differential:		
Lymphocytes	8%	(60–70%)
Monocytes	3%	(30–50%)
Neutrophils	91%	(none)
Total Protein	230 mg/dL	(20–50 mg/dL)
Glucose	18 mg/dL	(40–70 mg/dL)
Gram Stain	Many Gram-negative cocci	
Culture	Pending	
Serum		
Glucose	110 mg/dL	(< 140 mg/dL)

DIAGNOSIS

In evaluating the patient with signs and symptoms of meningitis, examination of the CSF, usually by lumbar puncture (LP), is critical. This patient's CSF analysis is typical in that patients with bacterial meningitis usually present with an elevated opening pressure, neutrophilic pleocytosis, elevated protein concentration, and low glucose level. The presence of large numbers of red blood cells suggests a traumatic tap. The CSF glucose must be compared to a serum glucose level drawn at approximately the same time as the LP; normally, the CSF glucose concentration should be two-thirds of the serum glucose concentration. The CSF must be Gram-stained; identification of the organism is possible in 75 percent of cases and helps in determining the choice of antibiotic.

There are several infectious and noninfectious processes that can produce an acute meningitis syndrome and may be confused with acute bacterial meningitis. The major etiologies include parameningeal foci of infection (abscess), viral meningitis or encephalitis, CNS syphilis, Lyme disease, tuberculous meningitis, fungal meningitis, bacterial endocarditis, rickettsial infections, CNS neoplasms, cerebral vasculitis, granulomatous angiitis, and sarcoidosis.

PATHOGENESIS

Bacterial meningitis is the inflammatory response to bacterial infection of the pia-arachnoid and the cerebrospinal fluid of the subarachnoid space. The subarachnoid space is continuous over the brain, spinal cord, and optic nerves, and an infection in this space can extend throughout the cerebrospinal axis.

EPIDEMIOLOGY

Bacterial meningitis is a common disease in the United States. It accounts for more than 2,000 deaths annually. The bacterial etiologic agents of meningitis vary with age. Gram-negative bacilli (*Escherichia coli*), other enteric bacilli (*Pseudomonas* sp., *Listeria monocytogenes*), and group B streptococci are the major causative agents during the neonatal period. *Haemophilus influenzae* and *Neisseria meningitidis* are the main infectious causes of bacterial meningitis in children over one month of age. In adults, *N. meningitidis* and *Streptococcus pneumoniae* are the major causes, with aerobic Gram-negative bacilli playing a more frequent etiologic role, particularly in the elderly. *N. meningitidis* is the only cause of epidemics of meningitis.

TREATMENT

The treatment for bacterial meningitis is initially empiric, based on the age of the patient and probable infecting pathogens. The CSF Gram stain is usually helpful in determining the identity of the infectious agent. For neonates under one month of age, empirical therapy is usually ampicillin plus a third-generation cephalosporin, which will cover the most likely pathogens (*E. coli*, *S. agalactiae*, *L. monocytogenes*). In older infants (4–12 weeks*)*, *H. influenzae* or *S. pneumoniae* are also likely in addition to the typical neonatal causative agents, for which ampicillin plus a third-generation cephalosporin is sufficient. For older children and young adults, *N. meningitidis* or *S. pneumoniae* are the most likely cause of bacterial meningitis, and a third-generation cephalosporin (cefotaxime or ceftriaxone) is the drug of choice. For patients over the age of 50, aerobic bacilli and *L. monocytogenes* must be considered and the empirical regimen should include ampicillin, a third-generation cephalosporin, and possibly vancomycin. Patients are initially managed in an intensive care setting. CSF cultures may identify the infectious etiology and provide antibiotic sensitivity, permitting the narrowing of antibiotic coverage.

PROGNOSIS

The mortality rate of bacterial meningitis varies with the infectious agent; the case-fatality rate of *H. influenzae* is less than 5 percent, *N. meningitidis* is 13 percent, and *S. pneumoniae* is 19 percent. Permanent neurologic sequelae occur in one-third to one-half of survivors of bacterial meningitis. The major sequelae include hearing loss, mental retardation, cerebral palsy, seizures, and behavioral problems.

ACUTE LYMPHOBLASTIC LEUKEMIA

A 24-year-old man presents with complaints of fever, malaise, and fatigue. He notes that recently he has been bruising easily and when he brushes his teeth his gums bleed. These symptoms began three weeks ago. Temperature is 37 C (98.6 F), pulse is 96/min, blood pressure is 110/70 mm Hg, and respirations are 16/min. The patient appears pale. Examination is remarkable for sternal tenderness, a palpable spleen tip, and a number of small ecchymotic areas on the lower extremities. Laboratory studies show:

Hematocrit	8%	(Male: 41–53%)
Hemoglobin	6 g/dL	(Male: 13.5–17.5 g/dL)
Leukocytes	18,000/mm³	(4.5–11,000/mm³)
Bands	1%	(3–5%)
Segmented neutrophils	26%	(54–62%)
Eosinophils	0%	(1–3%)
Basophils	0.0%	(0.0–0.75%)
Lymphocytes	19%	(25–33%)
Monocytes	1%	(3–7%)
Lymphoblasts	53%	none
Platelets	18,000/mm³	(150,000–400,000/mm³)

DIAGNOSIS

Patients with acute lymphoblastic leukemia (ALL) present with signs and symptoms of marrow failure. Symptoms include pallor and fatigue, bleeding and bruising, and fever and infection—due to anemia, thrombocytopenia, and neutropenia, respectively. Patients with ALL can present with infiltration of the spleen, lymph nodes, liver, skin, or CNS. Bone pain, particularly sternal tenderness, is seen in many patients with lymphoblastic leukemia. Patients with leukemic meningitis generally present with headache, nausea, and cranial nerve palsies, but in order to make the diagnosis of acute leukemia, the marrow must be involved, with > 30 percent lymphoblasts, although a similar number of blasts in the peripheral blood also makes the diagnosis.

The risk of bleeding increases with platelet counts less than 20,000/mm³, and often involves skin and mucosal sites. An increased risk of infection occurs with an absolute neutrophil count of less than 500/mm³ and is the leading cause of death in patients with ALL.

PATHOGENESIS

There is no evidence that infectious agents are involved in the pathogenesis of pre-B or T cell ALL. There is an increased incidence of ALL in people with family members who have the disease. Individuals with Down's and Wiskott-Aldrich syndrome are at increased risk of developing ALL.

There is some relationship between immunophenotype and the subtype of ALL and clinical findings. Patients with Pre-B ALL, the classic childhood ALL, often have splenomegaly and usually have white blood cell counts less than 25,000/mm³. T cell ALL has a male predominance and is associated with CNS and mediastinal disease. B cell ALL often has extramedullary presentation with metabolic abnormalities.

The T cell phenotype is more common in adults than children. The t(9;22) is seen in about 20 percent of adults but is rare in childhood ALL.

Several metabolic abnormalities are seen in patients with ALL, such as uric acid nephropathy caused by the rapid turnover of acute leukemic cells. Both hypokalemia and hyperkalemia can also occur in patients with ALL. The cause of the hypokalemia in ALL is unknown, but hyperkalemia is often seen along with hypocalcemia and hyperphosphatemia as part of the tumor lysis syndrome that follows the initiation of therapy.

EPIDEMIOLOGY

The majority of patients with ALL are children and young adults. The incidence in adults is about 1/100,000 per year. ALL is more common in males than females, and in whites more than blacks.

TREATMENT

Optimal induction therapy for adults with ALL must include an anthracycline (daunorubicin or idarubicin), in addition to vincristine and prednisone. Children are treated with a combination of prednisone, vincristine, and asparaginase. Postremission therapy is critical to improve the duration of complete remission in patients with ALL. Cranial radiation with intrathecal methotrexate is an effective method of CNS prophylaxis. Febrile patients should be promptly treated with broad-spectrum antibiotics.

PROGNOSIS

Overall, more than 40 percent of patients with ALL are cured. Age is an independent prognostic variable in ALL; older adults (> 35 years) have a worse prognosis. Other adverse factors include delay in achieving complete remission, B cell phenotype, and high white cell count at presentation (> 50,000/mm³).

ACUTE MYELOID LEUKEMIA

A 71-year-old man presents with complaints of fatigue and weakness. The patient had been in his usual state of good health until approximately one month earlier, when he began feeling weak and tired. He also notes that his appetite has been poor and that he has lost at least 2.5 kg (5.5 lbs) in the last few weeks. When questioned about bleeding problems, the patient reports that recently, after cutting himself shaving, it took longer than normal for his blood to clot. Temperature is 37.5 C (99.5 F), pulse is 96/min, blood pressure is 120/75 mm Hg, and respirations are 16/min. Several ecchymotic areas are noted on the patient's lower extremities. His liver is enlarged and the spleen tip is palpable. Axillary, cervical, and inguinal lymphadenopathy is detected. Laboratory studies show:

Hematocrit	23%	(Male: 41–53%)
Hemoglobin	7.7 g/dL	(Male: 13.5–17.5 g/dL)
Leukocytes	18,000/mm^3	(4.5–11,000/mm^3)
Bands	2%	(3–5%)
Segmented neutrophils	28%	(54–62%)
Eosinophils	0%	(1–3%)
Basophils	0.0%	(0.0–0.75%)
Lymphocytes	12%	(25–33%)
Monocytes	2%	(3–7%)
Myeloblasts	56%	None
Mean corpuscular hemoglobin	29 pg/cell	(25.4–34.6 pg/cell)
Mean corpuscular volume	89 mm^3	(80–100 mm^3)
Platelets	61,000/mm^3	(150,000–400,000/mm^3)
Reticulocyte count	0.2%	(0.5–1.5% of red cells)

DIAGNOSIS

Patients with acute myeloid leukemia (AML) most often present with nonspecific symptoms that begin either gradually or abruptly and are the consequence of anemia, leukocytosis, leukopenia or leukocyte dysfunction, or thrombocytopenia. Most patients complain of fatigue or weakness at the time of diagnosis. Other nonspecific complaints, such as anorexia and weight loss, are common. Fever, with or without an identifiable infection, and/or signs of abnormal hemostasis (bleeding, easy bruising) may be present. Splenomegaly, hepatomegaly, lymphadenopathy, and sternal tenderness are often found at the time of diagnosis.

A normochromic normocytic anemia is usually present at the time of diagnosis and can be severe, and decreased erythropoiesis often results in a reduced reticulocyte count. The median presenting leukocyte count is about 15,000/mm^3, but 25 to 40 percent of patients will have counts less than 5,000/mm^3, and 20 percent will have counts greater than 100,000/mm^3. Platelet counts under 100,000/mm^3 are seen in 75 percent of patients, and about 25 percent of patients will have counts less than 25,000/mm^3.

Once the diagnosis of AML is suspected, a bone marrow aspirate and biopsy should be performed. The categorization of acute leukemia into biologically distinct groups is based on morphology, cytochemistry, and immunophenotype. The diagnosis of AML is established by the presence of at least 30 percent myeloblasts in blood and/or bone marrow. AML is organized into eight major subtypes, designated M0 to M7.

PATHOGENESIS

Heredity, radiation, chemical exposure, and drugs have all been implicated in the development of AML. There is no direct evidence of a viral etiology in AML.

Certain syndromes with associated somatic cell aneuploidy (trisomy 21, XXY, trisomy 13) have been tied to an increased incidence of AML. Inherited diseases with excessive chromatin fragility (Fanconi's anemia, Bloom syndrome, ataxia telangiectasia, Kostmann's syndrome) are also associated with an increased incidence of AML. Some other risk factors include exposure to benzene, smoking, and exposure to petroleum products, paint, embalming fluids, ethylene oxide, herbicides, pesticides, and electromagnetic fields.

Antineoplastic drugs, particularly alkylating agents and topoisomerase II inhibitors, are the leading cause of drug-related AML. Chloramphenicol, phenylbutazone, and less commonly chloroquine and methoxypsoralen have been reported to result in bone marrow failure that may evolve into AML. Therapeutic radiation alone contributes little to increased risk of acute leukemia, but can increase the risk in people also exposed to alkylating agents.

EPIDEMIOLOGY

The incidence of AML is approximately 2.3 per 100,000 people per year, and its incidence increases with age. Under 65 years, it is 1.3 per 100,000 people (per year), and above 65, the incidence is 12.2 per 100,000 people per year. The age-adjusted incidence is higher in men than women.

TREATMENT

$$R_x$$

Treatment of a newly diagnosed patient with AML is divided into two phases: induction and postremission management. The most commonly used regimens for inducing a complete remission consist of combination chemotherapy with cytarabine (cytosine arabinoside) and an anthracycline (daunorubicin or idarubicin). Cytarabine is a cell cycle S-phase–specific antimetabolite that becomes phosphorylated to an active triphosphate form that interferes with DNA synthesis. Anthracyclines are DNA intercalaters, their primary mode of action is to interact with topoisomerase II, leading to breakage of DNA. Postremission therapy is designed to eradicate any residual leukemic cells. Postremission therapy approaches in AML include intensive chemotherapy and allogeneic or autologous bone marrow transplant. Following chemotherapy, patients with AML require supportive care for the resulting granulocytopenia and thrombocytopenia. Infectious complications are the major cause of morbidity and mortality during induction and postremission chemotherapy for AML. Once relapse occurs, AML is generally curable only by bone marrow transplant.

PROGNOSIS

The single most important factor related to improved survival is attainment of a complete remission. Several factors have been identified that influence the likelihood of entering this, and chromosomal analysis of the leukemic cell provides the most important pretreatment prognostic information. Patients with t(8;21) and inv(16) have an extremely good prognosis. Patients with del(5q), −7 and abnormalities involving 12p have a very poor prognosis. Age at diagnosis is also an important pretreatment risk factor; advanced age (> 60 years) is associated with a poorer prognosis.

ACUTE MYOCARDIAL INFARCTION

A 67-year-old man presents with complaints of "crushing" chest pain for the past one hour. The patient was shoveling snow from his driveway and began to experience a heavy feeling in his chest. He sat and rested, but the discomfort became worse and became more of a "squeezing" type pain and at that time he began "sweating like a pig." When asked to describe the location of the pain, the patient makes a fist over his sternum and describes radiation to the left arm. The patient has no significant past medical history and reports that this is the first time he has ever experienced chest pain of this nature. When examined, the patient appears to be in acute distress, visibly sweating, and anxious. The patient is afebrile with a pulse of 92/min, respirations of 20/min, and a blood pressure of 120/80 mm Hg. Pulmonary exam is unremarkable. Cardiac examination demonstrates third (S_3) and fourth (S_4) heart sounds. Electrocardiogram is shown below. Serum analysis for cardiac markers is pending.

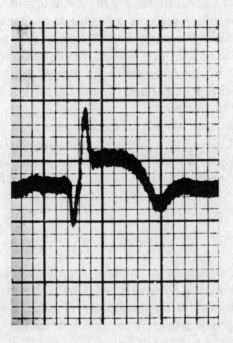

DIAGNOSIS

Pain is the most common presenting complaint of an acute myocardial infarction (MI), the character being of a deep and visceral nature. The combination of substernal chest pain that lasts longer than thirty minutes and associated diaphoresis is highly suggestive of an acute MI. Adjectives used to describe the pain are typically heavy, squeezing, crushing, stabbing, and burning. The pain usually involves the central chest area and epigastrium and may radiate to the arms. This is often accompanied by weakness, sweating, nausea, vomiting, anxiety, and a sense of impending doom.

The physical findings associated with an acute MI depend on both the severity of the infarct and the territory of myocardium supplied by the occluded vessel. Signs of ventricular dysfunction, in decreasing order of incidence, include: S_4 and S_3 heart sounds, decreased intensity of heart sounds, and paradoxical splitting of the second (S_2) heart sound. Left-sided heart failure secondary to an acute MI can lead to signs of pulmonary congestion on lung field examination. Jugular venous distention with clear lung fields can result from a right-sided infarct. Murmurs resulting from tricuspid or mitral insufficiency may be detected in cases of papillary muscle infarction. Arrhythmias may occur in the post-infarct period secondary to autonomic system imbalance, electrolyte disturbances, ischemia, and slowed conduction.

Electrocardiogram (ECG) analysis is very useful in the diagnosis of acute MI, but is far from perfect; a normal ECG in the setting of a high clinical suspicion does not rule out a diagnosis of an acute MI. Transmural infarction is likely if the ECG demonstrates Q waves or the loss of R waves. Nontransmural infarction is associated with transient ST-segment and T-wave changes. The ECG of the patient in the case above demonstrates the presence of a Q wave, ST-segment elevation, and T-wave inversion.

Necrotic myocardium releases certain proteins called serum cardiac markers into the blood in great quantities following an acute MI. The temporal pattern of the release of these proteins is valuable diagnostically, but is usually not helpful in making the initial urgent treatment decisions (reperfusion options). Typically, the initial treatment decisions are made on the clinical and ECG findings before the results of the blood tests are available. Creatine kinase (CK) level rises within 4 to 8 hours and generally returns to normal within 48 to 72 hours. CK is not specific for myocardium and may be elevated with skeletal muscle trauma. The MB isoenzyme of CK is not present in significant quantity in extracardiac tissue and is a more specific test than the CK alone. CK and CK-MB levels need to be evaluated over a 24-hour period to make the diagnosis of acute MI.

Abnormalities of wall motion are almost universally present in the setting of an acute MI, and echocardiography can be useful in helping to arrive at a diagnosis.

The pain of acute MI is similar to that of acute pericarditis, pulmonary embolism, acute aortic dissection, and costochondritis. These conditions must be considered in the differential diagnosis of chest pain.

PATHOGENESIS

MIs are usually due to an abrupt decrease in coronary blood flow following thrombotic occlusion of a coronary artery previously narrowed by atherosclerosis. Gradually developing coronary artery stenoses usually do not precipitate a MI because of the development of collateral vessels over time. Ultimately, the amount of myocardial damage is determined by the size of the territory supplied by the affected vessel.

EPIDEMIOLOGY

Approximately 1.5 million myocardial infarctions occur in the United States each year, making it one of the most common diagnoses in hospitalized patients. Approximately 50 percent of MIs can be linked to a precipitating factor, such as vigorous physical exercise, emotional stress, or a medical or surgical illness.

TREATMENT

Initial management of an acute MI includes control of cardiac pain, rapid identification of patients who are candidates for urgent reperfusion therapy, and triage of lower-risk patients. Aspirin is an essential component in the treatment of the patient with an acute MI. Typically, the first dose is chewed to facilitate the rapid inhibition of cyclooxygenase in platelets, thereby reducing thromboxane A_2 levels. Supplemental oxygen should be administered to patients who develop hypoxemia secondary to ventilation-perfusion abnormalities. Morphine is very effective at relieving the pain associated with MI, but can result in increased venous pooling and reduce cardiac output. Sublingual nitroglycerin can diminish or abolish chest discomfort. Intravenous β-blockers have been shown to reduce in-hospital mortality, presumably by decreasing cardiac oxygen demand.

Reperfusion therapy should be considered in patients who have ST-segment elevations of greater than 1 mm in at least two contiguous leads. The thrombolytic agents tissue plasminogen activator (t-PA), streptokinase, and anisoylated plasminogen streptokinase activator complex (APSAC) are approved for use in the setting of acute MI. These drugs all act by increasing the conversion of plasminogen to plasmin, which increases the lyses of fibrin thrombi. Thrombolytic therapy can reduce the relative risk of an in-hospital death by up to 50 percent if administered within the first hour of the onset of symptoms of myocardial infarction. Contraindications for thrombolytic therapy include a history of cerebrovascular hemorrhage or cerebrovascular event, severe hypertension, suspicion of aortic dissection, and active internal bleeding. The patient in this case would be an excellent candidate for thrombolytic therapy.

Primary percutaneous transluminal coronary angioplasty (PTCA) is also effective in restoring perfusion in acute MI. It is useful for patients who are not candidates for thrombolytic therapy, but are candidates for reperfusion. Coronary artery bypass surgery should be reserved for patients who are candidates for reperfusion, but whose anatomy is unsuited for angioplasty.

PROGNOSIS

The mortality rate for acute MI is approximately 30 percent, with more than half of these deaths occurring before the patient reaches the hospital. Approximately one of every 25 patients who survives the initial hospitalization dies in the first year after a MI.

ACUTE NEPHRITIC SYNDROME AND RAPIDLY PROGRESSIVE GLOMERULONEPHRITIS

A 29-year-old woman presents with complaints of a sore throat, headache, anorexia, nausea, vomiting, malaise, and decreased urine volume. Approximately ten days ago, the patient began to have symptoms of pharyngitis and did not seek medical attention. Temperature is 39.0 C (102.3 F), pulse is 84/min, blood pressure is 160/100 mm Hg, and respirations are 16/min. Physical examination demonstrates 3+ pitting of the lower extremities bilaterally. The pharynx is erythematous and injected; the tonsils are enlarged and covered with an exudate. Laboratory studies show:

Serum
Bicarbonate	18 mEq/L	(22–28 mEq/L)
Chloride	92 mEq/L	(95–105 mEq/L)
Creatinine	1.8 mg/dL	(0.6–1.2 mg/dL)
Potassium	5.3 mEq/L	(3.5–5.0 mEq/L)
Sodium	131 mEq/L	(136–145 mEq/L)
Urea nitrogen	32 mg/dL	(7–18 mg/dL)

Urinalysis
Microscopy	Dysmorphic red blood cells, red cell casts, and leukocytes seen
Dipstick	2+ proteinuria, 3+ heme

DIAGNOSIS

The acute nephritic syndrome and rapidly progressive glomerulonephritis (RPGN) are part of a spectrum of presentations of immunologically mediated, proliferative glomerulonephritis. The acute nephritic syndrome is characterized by the sudden onset of acute renal failure and oliguria (< 400 ml of urine per day). Extracellular volume expansion, edema, and hypertension develop because of impaired glomerular filtration rate (GFR) and an enhanced tubular reabsorption of salt and water. As a result of injury to the glomerular capillary wall, urinalysis typically reveals red blood cell casts, dysmorphic red blood cells, leukocytes, and subnephrotic proteinuria of < 3.5 g/day ("nephritic urinary sediment"). Hematuria is often macroscopic. In RPGN, patients develop renal failure over a period of weeks to months in association with a nephritic urinary sediment, subnephrotic proteinuria and variable oliguria, hypervolemia, edema, and hypertension.

Renal biopsy is the gold standard for diagnosis. Immunofluorescence microscopy is particularly helpful and identifies three major patterns in the deposition of immunoglobulin: 1) granular deposits of immunoglobulin, a sign of immune-complex glomerulonephritis; 2) linear deposition of immunoglobulin along the glomerular basement membrane, characteristic of anti-glomerular basement membrane disease; and 3) paucity or absence of immunoglobulin, typical of pauci-immune glomerulonephritis. Most patients (> 70 percent) with full-blown nephritic syndrome have immune-complex glomerulonephritis. Pauci-immune glomerulonephritis is less common (< 30 percent) in this setting, and anti-glomerular basement membrane disease is rare (< 1 percent). Among patients with RPGN, immune-complex glomerulonephritis and pauci-immune glomerulonephritis are equally prevalent (~ 45 percent each), and anti-glomerular basement disease is less common (< 10 percent).

Three serum markers often predict the immunofluorescence microscopy findings in nephritic syndrome and RPGN: 1) serum C3 level, 2) titers of anti-glomerular basement membrane antibody, and 3) the presence of antineutrophil cytoplasmic antibody (ANCA). Patients with immune-complex glomerulonephritis typically have low C3 levels (hypocomplementemia). Anti-glomerular basement antibodies are detectable in 90 to 95 percent of cases of anti-glomerular basement membrane disease. Most patients with pauci-immune glomerulonephritis have circulating ANCA.

PATHOGENESIS

The acute nephritic syndrome is the clinical correlate of acute glomerular inflammation, the classic pathologic correlate of the nephritic syndrome is proliferative glomerulonephritis. Renal blood flow and GFR fall as a result of obstruction of the glomerular capillary lumen by infiltrating inflammatory cells and proliferating resident glomerular cells. Renal blood flow and GFR are further compromised by intrarenal vasoconstriction and mesangial cell contractions that result from local imbalances of vasoconstrictor substances (such as leukotrienes, platelet-activating factor, thromboxanes, and endothelins) as well as vasodilator substances (nitric oxide and prostacyclin) within the renal microcirculation.

RPGN is the clinical correlate of more subacute glomerular inflammation; the classic pathologic correlate of RGPN is crescentic glomerulonephritis. The crescents are half–moon-shaped lesions in Bowman's space that are composed of proliferating parietal epithelial cells and infiltrating monocytes.

EPIDEMIOLOGY

The acute nephritic syndrome and RPGN can result from renal-limited primary glomerulopathy or secondary glomerulopathy complicating systemic disease. Anti-glomerular basement membrane disease is a rare disorder; it has an annual incidence of 0.5 per million. Immune complex glomerulonephritis may be idiopathic; it may represent a response to a known antigenic stimulus (viral, bacterial, fungal, and parasitic infection), or it may be part of a multisystem, immune-complex disorder (e.g., systemic lupus, erythematosus nephritis, Henoch-Schönlein purpura, cryoglobulinemia, or bacterial endocarditis). The major pauci-immune glomerulonephritides are idiopathic, renal-limited crescentic glomerulonephritis, microscopic polyarteritis nodosa, and Wegener's granulomatosis.

TREATMENT

Rapid diagnosis and prompt treatment are critical to avoid the development of irreversible renal failure. Treatment is dependent upon the etiology and the nature of the renal damage.

Poststreptococcal glomerulonephritis, a primary immune-complex glomerulonephritis, is the prototypical postinfectious glomerulonephritis and is a leading cause of acute nephritic syndrome. The treatment of poststreptococcal glomerulonephritis focuses on eliminating the streptococcal infection with antibiotics and providing supportive therapy until spontaneous resolution of the glomerular inflammation occurs. Diuretics and antihypertensive agents are used to control extracellular fluid volume and blood pressure.

Patients with anti-glomerular basement membrane disease are treated with immunosuppressive therapy, which includes emergency plasmapheresis, glucocorticoids, cyclophosphamide, and azathioprine. Pauci-immune glomerulonephritis is treated with glucocorticoids and cyclophosphamide. Dialysis and/or transplantation may be indicated in patients with end-stage renal disease.

PROGNOSIS

For anti-glomerular basement membrane disease, the speed of the initiation of therapy is a critical determinant of outcome; one-year renal survival approaches 90 percent if treatment is started before serum creatinine exceeds 5 mg/dL, but falls to about 10 percent if renal failure is more advanced. As many as 30 percent of patients with pauci-immune glomerulonephritis relapse following treatment-induced remission. Poststreptococcal glomerulonephritis carries an excellent prognosis and rarely causes end-stage renal disease.

ACUTE NEPHROTIC SYNDROME

A 48-year-old woman with a 20-year history of insulin-dependent diabetes mellitus presents for a routine evaluation. She complains of swelling around the ankles. Temperature is 37 C (98.6 F), pulse is 96/min, blood pressure is 120/80 mm Hg, and respirations are 16/min. Physical examination demonstrates 3+ pitting edema of the lower extremities bilaterally. Laboratory studies show:

Serum
    Albumin   1.9 g/dL   (3.5–5.5 g/dL)
    Cholesterol   340 mg/dL   (rec: < 200 mg/dL)
Urinalysis
    Dipstick   4+ proteinuria

DIAGNOSIS

The nephrotic syndrome is a clinical complex characterized by a number of renal and extrarenal features, the most prominent of which are proteinuria of > 3.5 g per 24 hours, hypoalbuminemia, edema, hyperlipidemia, lipiduria, and hypercoagulability.

In adults with nephrotic syndrome, renal biopsy is a valuable tool for establishing a definitive diagnosis, guiding therapy, and estimating prognosis. Renal biopsy is not required in the majority of children with nephrotic syndrome, because most of these cases are due to minimal change disease and respond to empiric treatment with glucocorticoids.

PATHOGENESIS

The key component of the nephrotic syndrome is proteinuria, which results from altered permeability of the glomerular filtration barrier (which consists of the glomerular basement membrane and podocytes with their slit diaphragms) to protein. The other components of the nephrotic syndrome are all secondary to urine protein loss.

In general, the greater the proteinuria, the lower the serum albumin level. The pathology of edema formation in nephrotic syndrome is poorly understood. The underfilling hypothesis postulates that hypoalbuminemia results in decreased intravascular oncotic pressure, which in turn leads to leakage of extracellular fluid from blood to the interstitium. Intravascular volume falls, stimulating the activation of the renin-angiotensin-aldosterone axis and the sympathetic nervous system, causing the subsequent release of vasopressin, and suppressing atrial natriuretic peptide release. These neural and hormonal responses promote renal salt and water retention, restoring intravascular volume and triggering further leakage of fluid to the interstitium.

Hyperlipidemia is believed to be a result of increased hepatic lipoprotein synthesis that is triggered by reduced oncotic pressure and can be compounded by increased urine loss of the proteins that regulate lipid homeostasis. Hypercoagulability is probably multifactorial in origin and is caused, at least in part, by increased urinary loss of antithrombin III, altered levels and/or activity of proteins C and S, hyperfibrinogenemia due to increased hepatic synthesis, impaired fibrinolysis, and increased platelet aggregability. Patients can develop spontaneous peripheral arterial or venous thrombosis, renal vein thrombosis, or pulmonary embolism. Other metabolic complications may include protein malnutrition and iron-resistant microcytic anemia due to transferrin loss. Hypocalcemia and secondary hyperparathyroidism can also occur as a result of vitamin D deficiency (due to enhanced urinary excretion of cholecalciferol-binding protein), and the urinary loss of thyroxine-binding globulin can result in depressed thyroxine levels.

EPIDEMIOLOGY

Nephrotic syndrome can complicate any disease that perturbs the negative electrostatic charge or architecture of the glomerular filtration barrier. Six conditions account for more than 90 percent of cases of nephrotic syndrome in adults: minimal change disease, focal and segmental glomerulosclerosis, membranous glomerulopathy, membranoproliferative glomerulonephritis, diabetic nephropathy, and amyloidosis.

TREATMENT

The treatment of nephrotic syndrome involves 1) specific treatment of the underlying morphologic entity and causative disease (if possible); 2) general measures to control proteinuria if remission is not achieved with immunosuppressive therapy and other measures; and 3) general measures to control nephrotic complications. Nonspecific measures that may reduce proteinuria include dietary protein restriction, angiotensin-converting enzyme inhibitors, and nonsteroidal anti-inflammatory drugs. Complications of nephrotic syndrome that may require treatment include edema, hyperlipidemia, thromboembolism, malnutrition, and vitamin D deficiency. Edema is managed with salt restriction and the use of loop diuretics.

Minimal change disease is usually successfully treated with glucocorticoids. Focal and segmental glomerulosclerosis is more difficult to treat, but glucocorticoids or cyclophosphamide and cyclosporine can be used. Membranous glomerulopathy may remit spontaneously, but immunosuppressive therapy is used in progressive cases. Membranoproliferative glomerulonephritis, which has a relatively benign course, has no effective treatment. For diabetic nephropathy, therapy is aimed at retarding the progression of disease through the control of blood sugar, systemic blood pressure, and glomerular capillary pressure. Treatment does little to slow the progression of the renal manifestations of amyloidosis; peritoneal dialysis or hemodialysis or kidney transplant may become necessary.

PROGNOSIS

The prognosis of nephrotic syndrome is dependent upon the underlying morphologic entity. Minimal change disease has an excellent prognosis, while the renal prognosis for focal and segmental glomerulosclerosis is relatively poor. Most patients with membranoproliferative glomerulonephritis survive without clinically significant impairment of GFR. Diabetic nephropathy is the leading cause of end-stage renal disease in the U.S. and accounts for 30 to 35 percent of patients on renal replacement therapy. Most patients with renal involvement of amyloidosis progress to end-stage renal disease.

ALZHEIMER'S DISEASE

An 85-year-old woman presents for an evaluation with her family after a recent episode of wandering from her home and becoming lost. The patient's granddaughter states, "My grandma has become so forgetful that she doesn't know how to use the phone or television. Sometimes she doesn't remember who I am and gets very angry, and she doesn't eat or clean herself." The patient's grandson notes that the patient, "welcomes me and asks me to come into her home very nicely, but doesn't know who I am and can't carry on a normal conversation." When questioned, the patient denies any difficulties, stating that, "I'm fine the way I am and don't need any help, but I don't know what these people want to do to me." The patient is oriented to person and place, but is unable provide the correct date or year. When asked to perform "serial 7's," she is unable to correctly subtract 7 from 100. When presented with a watch, she is unable to either name the object or read the time. Neurological exam reveals no focal deficits.

DIAGNOSIS

Initially, the memory loss associated with Alzheimer's disease (AD) may go unrecognized, but slowly the patients begin to have progressive difficulty with normal daily activities. Patients frequently get lost, have difficulty caring for themselves, and may be unable to do simple calculations or tell time. Language may be impaired, particularly naming objects or persons. Patients with AD often have motor apraxias and are unable to perform sequential motor tasks such as dressing or grooming. Hallucinations and delusions are common, but are usually simple and related to the patient's confusion. For example, the patient may mistake a visitor for a burglar because she does not recognize the individual. Loss of inhibitions or aggressive behavior can alternate with passivity and social isolation. Social graces, superficial conversation, and routine behavior may be retained despite significant impairment.

Treatable causes of dementia, including thyroid disease, vitamin deficiencies, brain tumor, intoxications, infection, and depression must be ruled out early in the disease course. Computed tomography and magnetic resonance imaging study changes are not specific for AD, but they can be useful in ruling out other disorders, including normal pressure hydrocephalus, multi-infarct dementia, and tumors.

PATHOGENESIS

Pathologically, there is diffuse atrophy of the cerebral cortex with secondary enlargement of the ventricular system. Microscopically, there are neuritic plaques containing Ab amyloid, silver-staining neurofibrillary tangles in neuronal cytoplasm, and Ab amyloid in the arterial walls of cerebral blood vessels.

EPIDEMIOLOGY

Alzheimer's disease is the most common cause of dementia in the United States, affecting approximately 3–4 million people. AD can occur in any decade of adulthood and is the most common cause of dementia in the elderly, affecting approximately 5 percent of all persons over the age of 70. The most important risk factors for AD are advanced age and a positive family history.

TREATMENT

There is no specific treatment for AD and the primary focus of care is supportive. Tetrahydroaminoacridine (tacrine), a cholinesterase inhibitor, is the only drug currently approved for the treatment of AD. Some patients appear to show an initial modest response to treatment, but the drug is not effective in the late stages of AD. Depression is common in the early stages of AD and should be treated. Behavioral symptoms, such as belligerence, hallucinations, insomnia, and agitation may be treated with a low dose of haloperidol.

PROGNOSIS

The progression of AD is variable. The typical duration is eight to ten years, but some patients may have prolonged plateaus without major deterioration. Death usually results from malnutrition, secondary infections, or heart disease.

AMYOTROPHIC LATERAL SCLEROSIS

A 47-year-old man presents with complaints of weakness in his right hand and difficulty chewing and swallowing. The patient reports that the symptoms began approximately 6 months ago and have become progressively worse. He is seeking medical treatment because the weakness in his dominate hand (right) is impairing his ability to write clearly. Upon further questioning, the patient also notes that he has diffuse "crampy" muscular discomfort upon arising in the morning. A review of symptoms is unremarkable, with pertinent negatives including an absence of sensory complaints and normal bladder and bowel function. Examination reveals an asymmetrical motor weakness affecting the distal right upper extremity, particularly the extensor functions of the hand. No sensory deficits are detected. An MRI is obtained.

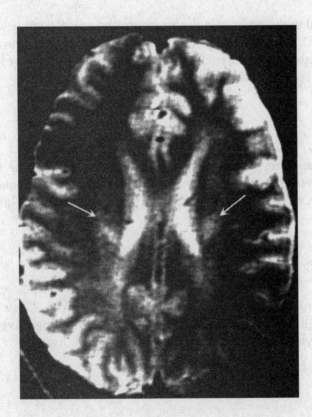

MRI demonstrating enlargement of the lateral ventricles

DIAGNOSIS

Amyotrophic lateral sclerosis (ALS) is a progressive neurodegenerative disorder that ultimately causes a loss of both upper and lower motor neurons. This patient's presentation is classic for the early stages of the disease. Early manifestations of ALS are variable; often the motor weakness is asymmetric and can affect bulbar and/or limb muscles. The initial presentation may involve either upper or lower motor neurons, but eventually both are affected. The hands usually show a predominance of extensor motor weakness. Sensory, bowel and bladder, and cognitive functions are not affected by ALS.

ALS is currently untreatable, and it is important to rule out treatable causes of motor neuron dysfunction. Cases that present atypically should be particularly suspect, including those in which only upper or lower motor neurons are affected, neurons other than motor neurons are affected, or there is evidence of a motor neuron conduction block.

PATHOGENESIS

The cause of sporadic ALS is not well defined. In ALS, the affected motor neurons undergo shrinkage, often with the accumulation of the pigmented lipid (lipofuscin) that normally develops in these cells with age. Proximal motor axons frequently display focal enlargements that are composed of accumulations of neurofilaments.

The loss of peripheral motor neurons in the brainstem and spinal cord denervates voluntary muscle fibers, which eventually atrophy (amyotrophy). The loss of cortical motor neurons results in thinning of the corticospinal tracts that travel in the lateral columns of the spinal cord. The loss of fibers in the lateral columns results in sclerosis of the affected tissue (lateral sclerosis).

EPIDEMIOLOGY

ALS is the most common form of progressive motor neuron disease; the incidence in the U.S. is approximately 1–3 per 100,000 and males are affected somewhat more frequently than females. ALS develops mainly as a sporadic disorder, but 5 to 10 percent of cases are inherited as an autosomal dominant trait.

TREATMENT

There is no treatment available to arrest the pathologic process of ALS. A new drug, riluzole, has been shown to moderately lengthen survival. The mainstay of treatment is supportive care. Some patients elect for respiratory support, which can be life-sustaining for end-stage disease.

PROGNOSIS

The disease is relentlessly progressive and eventually takes on a symmetric distribution, involving all motor groups. The median survival is 3 to 5 years, with death resulting from respiratory paralysis.

BREAST DISORDERS

A 43-year-old woman presents with complaints of a lump in her right breast. She examines her own breasts monthly and has not noticed this lump before. She denies any breast pain or nipple discharge. There is no history of breast cancer in her family. On examination, a 1 cm by 2 cm, mobile mass is detected in the upper-outer quadrant of the right breast. No dimpling or retractions of the skin are noted, and no other masses are detected in either breast. There is no nipple discharge bilaterally.

DIAGNOSIS

Women with breast symptoms should be evaluated. There is no lesion that is obviously benign; breast cancer must always be ruled out. Fine needle aspiration can serve as an intermediate step in cancer diagnosis, but the majority of patients will require histologic tissue confirmation with a breast biopsy. The most common benign condition of the breast is fibrocystic change. Pain is the most common symptom of fibrocystic change; it is often bilateral and particularly noticeable during the premenstrual phase. Unless proliferative changes with atypia are present, fibrocystic disease is not a risk factor for breast cancer. Fibroadenomas are benign breast masses. They are smooth, round, mobile lumps that can feel firm or rubbery, are usually painless, and tend to be discovered on breast examination. With fibroadenomas, mammography is not helpful in ruling out cancer; ultrasound and fine needle aspiration must be used to obtain cytologic material.

The most common benign causes of nipple discharge are mammary duct ectasia and nonpuerperal mastitis, both of which cause a multicolored discharge. Intraductal papillomas are the most common cause of bloody nipple discharge. Persistent bloody discharges should be investigated; the risk of cancer is increased when the 1) discharge is unilateral from a single duct, 2) discharge occurs in a postmenopausal patient, or 3) a mass is present.

Mastitis is an infection that can cause fever, pain, and swelling. It is the most common benign breast problem during pregnancy and lactation. Squamous metaplasia of the breast, a benign process that results from the transformation of glandular or mucosal epithelium into stratified squamous epithelium, is the most common form of nonpuerperal mastitis. It can mimic ductal ectasia or intraductal papillomas, and often occurs after trauma.

The optimal time for performing a breast examination is right after menstruation and prior to ovulation. Most commonly, the patient discovers the lump herself. Dermatologic disorders that could signal more serious conditions include edema, nevi, ulcers, or eczematoid reactions. A scaly, red eruption around the areola may be a sign of Paget disease. Half of breast cancers occur in the upper, outer quadrant of the breast, 18 percent beneath the nipple-areola, and 15 percent in the upper, inner quadrant.

Pertinent historical factors include the duration of the finding, the presence or absence of pain in relation to menses, and the presence or absence of dimpling of the skin. Pain is most common in cystic changes and less common in carcinoma. When the skin dimples, carcinoma is the likely underlying etiology. Nipple discharge must be evaluated; malignant discharges are usually unilateral, bloody, or spontaneous.

Once a lesion has been described as a mass, it must be analyzed to see whether it is benign or malignant. The diagnosis of breast cancer is made by surgical biopsy or radiologic core biopsy. Other indications for biopsy include marked erythema and edema suggestive of inflammatory carcinoma, unilateral discharge in a postmenopausal patient, serosanguineous or bloody nipple discharge, or persistent crusting of the nipple.

The American Cancer Society recommends annual mammography starting at age 40. Earlier screening should be performed in women who have had a prior breast cancer or who have first-degree relatives with breast cancer. Mammographic abnormalities are grouped into three categories: densities, microcalcifications, and parenchymal asymmetry. Mammography should be performed before any open biopsy. A mammogram may better delineate the palpable lesion and identify other lesions in the same or opposite breast that may need treatment.

EPIDEMIOLOGY

The incidence of breast cancer in the U.S. is approximately 180,000 new cases per year; there are 44,000 deaths per year due to this type of cancer. Breast cancer is the leading cause of death from cancer in women between the ages of 30 and 54 years, and represents 17 percent of the cancer incidence in women and 17 percent of the total cancer deaths. The female to male ratio is 150:1.

A family history of breast cancer can increase the risk by two to nine times in cases of bilateral premenopausal breast cancer that occurs in a first-degree relative. Nulliparous women, women whose menopause began after age 55, and women who had their first pregnancy after age 35 have a two to three times higher risk of breast cancer. Age is the most significant risk factor; breast cancer risk increases with age throughout a woman's life. In the U.S., breast cancer is more prevalent among women in the upper socioeconomic classes. There is an increased risk of breast cancer with moderate alcohol intake; the mechanism is unknown.

The incidence of fibrocystic change is greatest in women aged 20 to 50 years. Risk factors include nulliparity, late age of natural menopause, and high socioeconomic class. Fibroadenomas occur in all age groups but most commonly during the patient's second and third decade; their incidence decreases with advancing age.

PATHOGENESIS

Fibrocystic change is an enhanced or exaggerated reaction by breast tissue in response to fluctuating levels of ovarian hormones. The exact pathogenesis is not precisely known, but is thought to be related to an imbalance in estrogen and progesterone levels.

There are two categories of noninvasive breast cancer: ductal carcinoma *in situ* (DCIS) and lobular carcinoma *in situ* (LCIS); and two categories of invasive breast cancer: infiltrating ductal carcinoma and infiltrating lobular carcinoma. Infiltrating ductal carcinomas account for 72 percent of breast cancers, and infiltrating lobular carcinomas account for 10 to 15 percent. DCIS, LCIS, Paget disease, inflammatory carcinoma, and sarcomas account for the remaining cases.

Breast cancer is a hormone-dependent disease; women without functioning ovaries who never receive estrogen replacement do not develop breast cancer. Only about 10 percent of breast cancers can be linked directly to a germline mutation. A dominant oncogene plays a role in about 25 percent of breast cancer cases. The product of this gene is a member of the epidermal growth factor receptor superfamily called erbB2. Approximately 40 percent of breast cancer cases express a defected tumor suppression gene p53.

Breast cancer susceptibility genes, BRCA1 and BRCA2, have been identified and can be screened for. Families with high probability of a BRCA1 mutation are likely to have one of the following characteristics: 1) two or more breast cancer cases and one or more cases of ovarian cancer diagnosed at any age, 2) three or more breast cancer cases diagnosed before the age of 50 years, or 3) sister pairs with two breast cancers, two ovarian cancers, or a breast and ovarian cancer, all diagnosed before age 50. Women with BRCA1 have an 85 to 90 percent lifetime likelihood of developing breast cancer. The Li-Fraumeni syndrome is an inherited mutation in the tumor suppression gene p53, which leads to an increased incidence of breast cancer, osteogenic sarcomas, and other malignancies.

TREATMENT

Oral contraceptives can reduce the discomfort associated with fibrocystic change, and severe symptomatic fibrocystic change is treated with danazol. Other methods of relieving the discomfort associated with fibrocystic change include the use of a support bra, diuretics (especially premenstrually), and reducing caffeine and tobacco use.

The staging of breast cancer is critical for both prognosis and therapeutic decision-making, and is done using the tumor-node-metastasis system (TNM). The most common treatment options for invasive breast cancer include a modified radical mastectomy or breast conserving procedures that include lumpectomy and axillary lymph node dissection with irradiation. Breast conservation treatment is an appropriate method of primary therapy for the majority of women with Stage I and II breast cancer, and is preferable because it provides equivalent survival to total mastectomy and axillary node dissection while preserving the breast. The addition of radiation therapy to any form of mastectomy does not improve survival. However, radiation therapy can reduce the rate of local or regional recurrence, and for women with high-risk tumors, it may be considered following mastectomy.

Adjuvant therapy in high-risk groups has shown a definite and sustained reduction in both recurrence and mortality rates. Factors that influence disease prognosis and the decision for recommending adjuvant therapy include tumor size, nodal status, histology, menopausal status or age, grade, estrogen receptor status, speed of progression, prior treatment, and evidence of metastatic disease. The following drugs and combinations have been used for therapy: cyclophosphamide, methotrexate, and fluorouracil (CMF); cyclophosphamide, doxorubicin, and fluorouracil (CAF); or fluorouracil, doxorubicin, and cyclophosphamide (FAC). Paclitaxel is another drug that is effective in breast cancer, and tamoxifen reduces recurrence and mortality rates, but carries some increased risk of endometrial cancer.

Autologous bone marrow transplantation combined with high doses of chemotherapy can result in temporary improvements, but are unlikely to substantially alter the clinical course for most patients with advanced metastatic disease.

PROGNOSIS

Axillary lymph node status is the most important factor in the prognosis of patients with breast cancer. Tumor size is independently important in predicting recurrence; the primary prognostic factors used for metastatic disease are nodal status and tumor size. Tumor recurrences increase from 30 percent for patients with node-negative disease to 55 to 60 percent for patients with one to three lymph-positive nodes, and 85 to 90 percent for patients with four or more positive nodes.

Other prognostic factors include 1) estrogen receptor (ER) status, 2) vascular lymphatic invasion, 3) tumor proliferation activity, grade, and histologic subtype. ER-positive patients have an 8 to 10 percent better prognosis than ER-negative patients. Peritumor lymphatic and blood vessel invasion is an adverse prognostic factor, independent of menopausal status and tumor size. The risk of recurrence is 4.7 times greater for patients with vascular/lymphatic invasion compared to those without it. Favorable histologic subtypes include tubular, colloid (mucinous), and papillary tumors; intermediate histologic subtypes include invasive lobular and medullary lesions. Signet-ring carcinoma and sarcomatoid carcinoma carry an unfavorable prognosis.

Overall, the risk of recurrence is 2 to 5 percent per year from years two through six after initial occurrence and 1 percent a year thereafter.

5-Year Survival Rate for Breast Cancer by Stage	
Stage	5-year Survival (% of patients)
0	99
I	92
II	74
III	46
IV	14

CARDIOMYOPATHY

A 56-year-old man presents to the emergency department with complaints of shortness of breath. He has experienced gradual lessening of his exercise tolerance over the past several months. The patient also reports increasing frequency of awakening due shortness of breath at night, and needs to sleep with three pillows in order to feel comfortable. He gives a history of consuming approximately 10 alcoholic beverages per day for the past 40 years. Blood pressure is 100/60 mm Hg, pulse is 90/min, and respirations are 28/min. Auscultation of the chest demonstrates rales at the lung bases bilaterally. A third heart sound is noted and jugular venous distention is demonstrated. Pitting edema of the lower extremities is present. A chest radiograph is obtained and shown below:

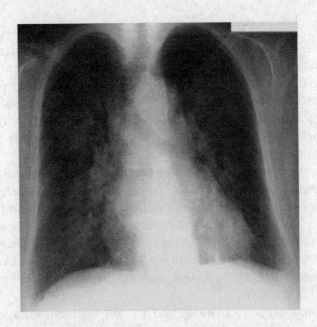

Chest radiograph–Congestive heart failure

DIAGNOSIS

Most patients with dilated cardiomyopathy gradually develop symptoms of left- and right-sided congestive failure manifested by dyspnea on exertion, fatigue, orthopnea, paroxysmal nocturnal dyspnea, peripheral edema, and palpitations. Variable degrees of cardiac enlargement and findings of congestive heart failure are noted. In patients with advanced disease, the pulse pressure is narrow and the jugular venous pressure is elevated. Third and fourth heart sounds are common, and mitral or tricuspid regurgitation may occur. Chest x-ray demonstrates enlargement of the cardiac silhouette due to left ventricular enlargement. Echocardiography shows left ventricular dilatation, with normal or minimally thickened or thinned walls, and systolic dysfunction.

Many patients with hypertrophic cardiomyopathy are asymptomatic and the first clinical manifestation of the disease may be sudden death. This occurs most frequently in children and young adults, often during or after physical exertion. In symptomatic patients, the most common complaint is dyspnea, but other symptoms include angina pectoris, fatigue, syncope, and near-syncope. The hallmark of obstructive hypertrophic cardiomyopathy is a systolic murmur, which is typically harsh, diamond-shaped, and begins well after the first heart sound. The electrocardiogram commonly shows left ventricular hypertrophy and widespread, deep, broad Q-waves that suggest an old myocardial infarction. Echocardiography, which is the mainstay of diagnosis for hypertrophic cardiomyopathy, typically demonstrates asymmetric left ventricular hypertrophy.

Restrictive cardiomyopathy results in an inability of the ventricle to fill, which limits cardiac output and raises filling pressure. Exercise intolerance and dyspnea are usually the most prominent symptoms of this type of cardiomyopathy. Persistently elevated venous pressure leads to dependent edema, ascites, and an enlarged, tender liver. The electrocardiogram typically shows low-voltage, nonspecific ST-T wave changes and various arrhythmias.

PATHOGENESIS

The cardiomyopathies are diseases that primarily involve the myocardium and are not the result of hypertension or congenital, valvular, coronary, arterial, or pericardial abnormalities. Cardiomyopathies can be classified into two fundamental types on an etiologic basis: 1) a primary type, consisting of heart muscle disease of unknown cause, and 2) a primary type, consisting of myocardial disease of known cause, or associated with a disease involving other organ systems. In many cases it is not possible to arrive at a specific etiologic diagnosis, and is therefore more useful to classify the cardiomyopathies on the basis of differences in their pathophysiology and clinical presentation.

In dilated cardiomyopathy, left and/or right ventricular systolic pump function is impaired, which leads to cardiac enlargement and often produces symptoms of congestive heart failure. Mural thrombi are often present, particularly in the left ventricular apex. Histological examination reveals extensive areas of interstitial and perivascular fibrosis. Although in many cases no cause is apparent, dilated cardiomyopathy is probably the end result of myocardial damage from a variety of toxic, metabolic, or infectious agents. A reversible form of dilated cardiomyopathy may be found in conjunction with alcohol abuse, pregnancy, selenium deficiency, hypophosphatemia, hypocalcemia, thyroid disease, cocaine use, and chronic uncontrolled tachycardia.

Hypertrophic cardiomyopathy is characterized by left ventricular hypertrophy, typically of a nondilated chamber, without obvious cause (such as hypertension or aortic stenosis). The two main features of the disease are: 1) heterogenous left ventricular hypertrophy, often with preferential hypertrophy of the interventricular septum, resulting in asymmetric septal hypertrophy, and 2) a dynamic left ventricular outflow tract pressure gradient related to a narrowing of the subaortic area resulting from the midsystolic apposition of the anterior mitral valve leaflet against the hypertrophied septum. The outflow tract gradient is manifested in about 25 percent of patients with hypertrophic cardiomyopathy. Diastolic dysfunction, characterized by increased stiffness of the hypertrophied muscle and resulting in elevated diastolic filling pressures, is present in all patients with hypertrophic cardiomyopathy.

Restrictive cardiomyopathies are characterized by abnormal diastolic function; the ventricular walls are excessively rigid and impede ventricular filling. Restrictive cardiomyopathy can be due to myocardial fibrosis, hypertrophy, or infiltration due to a variety of causes. Myocardial involvement with amyloid is a common cause of secondary restrictive cardiomyopathy. Other causes of restrictive cardiomyopathy include hemochromatosis, glycogen deposition, endomyocardial fibrosis, sarcoidosis, Fabry's disease, the eosinophilias, neoplastic infiltration, and myocardial fibrosis of diverse causes.

EPIDEMIOLOGY

Dilated cardiomyopathy is primarily a disease of middle-aged men and is more common in blacks. Approximately 20 percent of patients with dilated cardiomyopathy have familial forms of the disease. About half of all cases of hypertrophic cardiomyopathy have a positive family history compatible with autosomal-dominant transmission.

TREATMENT

Standard treatment of heart failure with salt restriction, diuretics, digitalis, and vasodilators may produce symptomatic improvement in patients with dilated cardiomyopathy. Mortality is reduced by angiotensin-converting enzyme inhibitors and a combination of hydralazine and isosorbide dinitrate. In patients with advanced disease who are refractory to medical therapy, cardiac transplantation should be considered.

For patients with hypertrophic cardiomyopathy, competitive sports and strenuous activity should be avoided. β-adrenergic blockers may alleviate angina pectoris and syncope in some patients. Calcium channel-blockers may reduce the stiffness of the ventricle and improve exercise tolerance. Dual chamber permanent pacing improves symptoms and reduces the outflow gradient in some patients. Surgical myotomy/myomectomy of the hypertrophied septum may result in lasting symptomatic improvement for those patients unresponsive to medical management.

Treatment for restrictive cardiomyopathy is usually directed at the underlying cause. Surgical treatment of endomyocardial fibrosis can result in symptomatic improvement.

PROGNOSIS

Most patients with dilated cardiomyopathy have an inexorable downhill course, and the majority, particularly those over 55 years of age, die within two years of the onset of symptoms. Death is due to either congestive heart failure or ventricular tachy- or bradyarrhythmia. The natural history of hypertrophic cardiomyopathy is variable. The major cause of mortality in hypertrophic cardiomyopathy is sudden death, which may occur in asymptomatic patients. Treatment for restrictive cardiomyopathy is usually disappointing, except for hemochromatosis.

CHRONIC LYMPHOCYTIC LEUKEMIA

A 64-year-old man presents for a routine physical examination. He has a ten-year history of hypertension that has been well controlled with nifedipine. He does not smoke cigarettes and drinks alcohol several times per week. Temperature is 37 C (98.6 F), pulse is 88/min, blood pressure is 120/80 mm Hg, and respirations are 12/min. Physical examination is unremarkable. A complete blood count shows:

Hematocrit	39%	(Male: 41–53%)
Hemoglobin	13 g/dL	(Male: 13.5–17.5 g/dL)
Leukocytes	22,000/mm³	(45–11,000/mm³)
Bands	1%	(3–5%)
Segmented neutrophils	8%	(54–62%)
Eosinophils	0%	(1–3%)
Basophils	0.0%	(0.0–0.75%)
Lymphocytes	90%	(25–33%)
Monocytes	1%	(3–7%)
Platelets	164,000/mm³	(150,000–400,000/mm³)

DIAGNOSIS

The most common chronic leukemia/lymphoma is B cell chronic lymphocytic leukemia (CLL). CLL presents as an asymptomatic lymphocytosis. Approximately 40 percent of patients with B cell CLL have only lymphocytosis with no anemia, thrombocytopenia, lymphadenopathy, or organomegaly. Constitutional symptoms are uncommon unless there is intercurrent infection, very extensive bulky disease, or histologic transformation to a more aggressive lymphoma. In Richter's syndrome, which occurs in about 5 percent of patients, rapidly growing nodal and extranodal masses are seen. With more extensive marrow compromise and/or splenic involvement, patients with B cell CLL can develop cytopenias or immunosuppression, which can cause symptoms.

The white cell count usually ranges between 10,000 and 200,000/mm³; 70 to 95 percent of this is small lymphocytes. The absolute neutrophil count is usually normal, and the red cell and platelet counts are mildly decreased. The marrow is universally involved, and the major diagnosis that must be excluded is a reactive lymphocytosis of normal T cells.

PATHOGENESIS

The malignant cells of CLL make up a minor subpopulation of B cells that express cell surface immunoglobulins IgM/D and the T cell-associated antigen CD5. There is no evidence that infectious agents are involved in the pathogenesis of CLL. There is, however, an increased incidence of CLL among persons with family members who have the disease.

EPIDEMIOLOGY

CLL is the most common type of adult leukemia in western countries. The incidence for CLL is 10/100,000 for persons over 70, but less than 1/100,000 for those under 50. CLL is more common in males than females, and in whites more than blacks, and the median presenting age is 60.

TREATMENT

Since most patients are asymptomatic at presentation with this disease, which can have a very long natural history without treatment, initial observation is generally recommended. The indications for treating patients include symptomatic lymphadenopathy or organ involvement, cytopenia due to progressive disease or autoimmune phenomena, or systemic symptoms. The treatment options for initial therapy are many, but generally involve alkylating agents with or without prednisone.

B Cell CLL Staging and Survival		
Stage	Clinical Features	Median Survival, in Years
0	Lymphocytosis	12
I	Lymphocytosis and adenopathy	9
II	Lymphocytosis and splenomegaly	7
III	Anemia	1–2
IV	Thrombocytopenia	1–2

PROGNOSIS

In B cell CLL, the clinical staging of patients is of prognostic importance. Other prognostic factors that predict a shorter survival time include a lymphocyte doubling time of less than 12 months, initial absolute leukocyte count > 50,000/mm^3, and an abnormal karyotype, most commonly trisomy 12. The extent of marrow involvement influences survival; a nodular infiltrate is more favorable than diffuse involvement.

CHRONIC MYELOID LEUKEMIA

A 61-year-old man presents with complaints of fatigue, lethargy, and decreased appetite. Symptoms have been present for at least several months, but the patient cannot say exactly when they started. He has lost approximately 7.5 kg (16.5 lb) in the past 6 months. Temperature is 37 C (98.6 F), pulse is 92/min, blood pressure is 115/75 mm Hg, and respirations are 14/min. Examination is remarkable for a palpable spleen tip. Laboratory studies show:

Hematocrit	32%	(Male: 41–53%)
Hemoglobin	10.7 g/dL	(Male: 13.5–17.5 g/dL)
Leukocytes	16,500/mm³	(4.5–11,000/mm³)
Bands	7%	(3–5%)
Segmented neutrophils	68%	(54–62%)
Eosinophils	6%	(1–3%)
Basophils	4%	(0.0–0.75%)
Lymphocytes	11%	(25–33%)
Monocytes	2%	(3–7%)
Myeloblasts	2%	None
Mean corpuscular hemoglobin	31 pg/cell	(25.4–34.6 pg/cell)
Mean corpuscular volume	92 mm³	(80–100 mm³)
Platelets	525,000/mm³	(150,000–400,000/mm³)

DIAGNOSIS

The clinical onset of the chronic phase of chronic myeloid leukemia (CML) is generally insidious. Some patients are diagnosed while still asymptomatic during health screening tests; others present with fatigue, malaise, and weight loss, or have symptoms resulting from splenic enlargement, such as early satiety and upper left quadrant pain or mass. Less common are features related to granulocyte or platelet dysfunction, such as infections, thrombosis, or bleeding. In most patients, the abnormal findings on physical examination are minimal to moderate splenomegaly, and mild hepatomegaly is occasionally found. Lymphadenopathy is unusual, except late in the course of the disease.

Elevated white blood cell counts with various degrees of immaturity of the granulocytic series are observed at diagnosis. Usually, there are fewer than 5 percent circulating blasts and fewer than 10 percent blasts and promyelocytes. Platelet counts are almost always elevated at diagnosis, and a mild degree of normochromic, normocytic anemia is present. Leukocyte alkaline phosphatase is characteristically low in CML cells.

The diagnosis of CML is established by identifying (cytogenically or molecularly) a clonal expansion of a hematopoietic stem cell that possesses a reciprocal translation between chromosome 9 and 22. Increased bone marrow cellularity, primarily of myeloid and megakaryocytic lineages, is found in almost all CML patients. The marrow blast percentage is generally normal or slightly elevated.

PATHOGENESIS

The product of the fusion gene resulting from the t(9;22) is believed to play a central role in the initial development of CML. No clear correlation with cytotoxic drugs, such as alkylating agents, has been found, and there is no evidence of a viral etiology. Cigarette smoking has been shown to accelerate the progression to blast crises and has an adverse effect on survival in CML.

The disease is characterized by the inevitable transition from a chronic phase to an accelerated phase and on to blast crisis. The events associated with the transition to the acute phase are poorly understood. Chromosomal instability of the malignant clone resulting, for example, in the acquisition of an additional t(9;22), trisomy 8, or 17p–, is a fundamental characteristic of CML. It is believed that the acquisition of resultant genetic and/or molecular abnormalities are critical to the phenotypic transformation.

Blast crisis is defined as an acute leukemia, with blood or marrow blasts > 30 percent. Based on morphologic, cytochemical, and immunologic features, blast cells can be classified as myeloid, lymphoid, erythroid, or undifferentiated. Approximately 50 percent of the total cases are classified as acute myeloid leukemia, 33 percent are classified as acute lymphoid leukemia, 10 percent are acute erythroleukemia, and the rest are undifferentiated.

EPIDEMIOLOGY

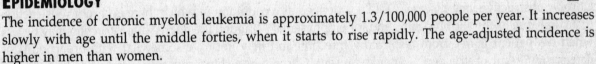

The incidence of chronic myeloid leukemia is approximately 1.3/100,000 people per year. It increases slowly with age until the middle forties, when it starts to rise rapidly. The age-adjusted incidence is higher in men than women.

TREATMENT

The goal of therapy in CML is to achieve prolonged, durable, nonneoplastic, nonclonal hematopoiesis. Allogenic bone marrow transplant is the only curative therapy for CML and, when feasible, is the treatment of choice. Marrow transplant is complicated by a high early mortality rate. In order to be qualified, patients should be relatively young (< 65) and have a healthy and histocompatible donor.

Interferon-α is the therapy of choice if bone marrow transplant is not feasible. The acute side effects of interferon-α are flulike symptoms. Chronic reactions include fatigue and lethargy, weight loss, myalgias, and arthralgias. The treatments for all forms of blast crises are generally ineffective.

PROGNOSIS

The clinical outcome of patients with CML is variable. The median survival is about four years. Negative prognostic factors include age > 60, spleen > 10 cm below the costal margin, blasts > 3 percent in blood, basophils > 7 percent in blood or > 3 percent in marrow, or platelets > 700,000/mm^3.

CHRONIC OBSTRUCTIVE LUNG DISEASE

A 58-year-old man presents with complaints of a chronic cough productive of thick sputum. The patient describes a several-year-history of a chronic cough that has progressively worsened over time. He has smoked one to two packs of cigarettes a day for the past 40 years. Temperature is 37 C (98.6 F), pulse is 92/min, respirations are 18/min, and blood pressure is 125/85 mm Hg. The patient is overweight and faintly cyanotic, but is not in any acute distress. Physical examination of the chest demonstrates a resonant note when percussed, and coarse rhonchi during inspiration and expiration. A pulse oximetry measurement shows 91 percent O_2 saturation. An arterial blood gas and hematocrit show:

pH	7.33	(7.35–7.45)
PCO_2	54 mm Hg	(33–45 mm Hg)
PO_2	57 mm Hg	(75–105 mm Hg)
Hematocrit	54%	(Male: 41–53%)

DIAGNOSIS

Chronic obstructive lung disease (COLD) is defined as a condition in which there is chronic obstruction to airflow due to chronic bronchitis and/or emphysema. Although the degree of obstruction may be less when the patient is free from respiratory infection and may improve somewhat with bronchodilator drugs, significant obstruction is always present. Chronic bronchitis and emphysema are two distinct processes; they most often present in combination in patients with chronic obstructive lung disease.

The diagnosis of chronic bronchitis is made by history, chronic airways obstruction is assessed physiologically, and emphysema can be diagnosed by high resolution computed tomography scan or histologic examination of sections of whole lung, fixed at inflation. Chronic bronchitis is a condition that is associated with excessive tracheobronchial mucus production sufficient to cause cough with expectoration for at least three months of the year for more than two consecutive years. Emphysema is defined as the permanent, abnormal distention of the air spaces distal to the terminal bronchiole with destruction of alveolar septa.

The clinical presentation of COLD varies in severity from simple chronic bronchitis without disability to a severely disabled state with chronic respiratory failure. Patients with this disease predominately due to emphysema tend to present with a long history of exertional dyspnea with minimal cough that is productive of small amounts of mucoid sputum, and tend to have an asthenic body build. These patients appear distressed, with obvious use of accessory muscles of respiration, and are tachypneic, with a prolonged expiration phase through pursed lips. Their lower intercostal spaces retract with inspiration, the chest percussion note is hyperresonant, and, on auscultation, the breath sounds are diminished, with high-pitched rhonchi heard toward the end of expiration. Arterial PO_2 is often in the mid-70s (mm Hg) and the PCO_2 is low to normal. On radiographic examination, the diaphragms are low and flattened, the bronchovascular shadows do not extend to the periphery of the lungs, and the cardiac silhouette is lengthened and narrowed.

Patients with predominant bronchitis usually have an impressive and long history of cough and sputum production, with an immodest history of cigarette smoking. Over the years, cough and sputum production progresses in frequency, duration, and severity. Patients with predominant bronchitis tend to be overweight and cyanotic. There is usually no apparent distress at rest, respiratory rate is normal or slightly increased, and there is no apparent usage of the accessory muscles of respiration. The chest percussion note is usually resonant, and on auscultation coarse rhonchi and wheezes that change in location and intensity can be heard after a deep and productive cough. Arterial PCO_2 values are chronically increased to the high 40s or low 50s (mm Hg); lowered PO_2 produces desaturation of hemoglobin, stimulates erythropoiesis, and results in hypoxic pulmonary vasoconstriction. With right ventricular failure, the cyanosis deepens and peripheral edema becomes prominent. There are no roentgenographic features that are definitive for chronic bronchitis. The two radiographic findings most commonly encountered are thickened bronchial walls (manifested by tubular shadows) and a generalized increase in bronchovascular markings.

PATHOGENESIS

Chronic bronchitis is associated with hypertrophy of the mucus-producing glands found in the submucosa of large, cartilaginous airways. However, the major site of obstruction is the small airways, where the characteristic findings are goblet cell hyperplasia, mucosal and submucosal inflammatory cells, edema, peribronchial fibrosis, intraluminal mucus plugs, and increased smooth muscle. The bronchitic inflammation seen here differs from the predominately eosinophilic inflammation of asthma because of the predominance of neutrophils and the peribronchiolar location of fibrotic changes. The protease inhibitor α-antitrypsin (α-1AT) is an acute-phase reactant. Either deficient or absent serum levels of α-1AT are found in some patients with the early onset of emphysema. The panacinar process predominates at the bases of the lung.

Emphysema is classified according to the pattern of involvement of the acini of the lung distal to the terminal bronchiole. In centriacinar emphysema, the distension and destruction are mainly limited to the respiratory bronchioles and there is relatively little change peripherally in the acinus. Panacinar emphysema involves both the central and peripheral portions of the acinus, which results, if the process is extensive, in a reduction of the alveolar-capillary gas exchange surface and the loss of elastic recoil properties.

Cigarette smoking is the most common single factor that leads to chronic airway obstruction, and it also adds to the effects of every other contributory factor. Chronic bronchitis is more prevalent in workers who engage in occupations that expose them to either inorganic or organic dusts, or to noxious gases. Exacerbations of bronchitis can be related to periods of exposure to heavy pollution containing sulfur dioxide and particulate matter.

Although chronic bronchitis and emphysema are usually combined, one process may predominate over the other. Both chronic bronchitis and emphysema result in airway narrowing; they both cause the residual lung volume (RV) and functional residual capacity (FRC) to be higher than normal. Elevations in total lung capacity (TLC) are frequent. Maldistribution of inspired gas and blood flow is always present to some extent. In chronic bronchitis and emphysema, there are increases in both wasted ventilation and wasted blood flow. Patients with emphysema have a decreased vital capacity (VC) and diminished maximal expiratory flow rates.

EPIDEMIOLOGY

The average age at the time of diagnosis is approximately 60 years for emphysema-predominant, and 50 years for bronchitis-predominant COLD.

TREATMENT

Cessation of smoking is the only certain means of influencing the progression of the chronic obstructive airway syndromes, and although such behavior modification is most effective at the early stages of the disease. It is also effective in slowing the rate of decline in lung function in the advanced stages. In patients in whom occupational or environmental exposures are thought to play a role, change of occupation or relocation of dwelling is advised.

The most common pathogenic bacteria found in respiratory infections in patients with chronic obstructive lung disease are *Haemophilus influenzae*, *Streptococcus pneumoniae*, and *Moraxella catarrhalis*. Therefore, antibiotics that are effective against β-lactamase–producing organisms are indicated when treating pulmonary infections in patients with COLD.

Bronchodilator drugs, including methylxanthines, sympathomimetics (strong β_2-adrenergic activity), and anticholinergics, are often quite helpful in alleviating symptoms of COLD. Theophylline, the most commonly used methylxanthine, can be given orally or parenterally. Selective β_2-stimulating drugs such as albuterol, terbutaline, and metaproterenol can be given both orally and by aerosol. Ipratropium bromide, an anticholinergic agent administered by metered-dose inhaler, is an effective bronchodilator in chronic bronchitic patients. Glucocorticoids are not proven to benefit patients with chronic obstructive lung disease.

For patients with severe arterial hypoxia (PO_2 of 55–60 mm Hg) in association with cor pulmonale, erythrocytosis, and signs of right heart failure, continuous O_2 therapy is indicated. If the PO_2 is persistently < 55 mm Hg, with or without cor pulmonale, continuous O_2 therapy is indicated.

PROGNOSIS

It is never too late to quit smoking cigarettes; although smoking cessation does not result in complete reversal of more pronounced obstruction, there is a significant slowing of the decline in lung function in all smokers who give up cigarettes. In general, in patients with chronic obstructive lung disease, there is a slow and relentless diminution in ventilatory function. Patients with predominant emphysema have a poorer prognosis after the onset of respiratory failure than do those with predominant bronchitis. Morbidity, mortality, and frequency of subsequent acute respiratory illnesses are higher in patients with chronic bronchitis.

COMMUNITY-ACQUIRED PNEUMONIA

A 76-year-old woman presents with complaints of a three-day history of right-sided chest pain, fever, chills, and a one-day history of cough productive of brown sputum. Temperature is 39.7 C (103.4 F), pulse is 100/min, blood pressure 115/70 mm Hg, and respirations are 22/min and shallow. Chest examination reveals decreased breath sounds, egophony, and dullness to percussion all localized to the right lung base. Laboratory studies are as follows:

Hematocrit	39%	(36–46%)
Leukocytes	18,500/mm³	(45–11,000/mm³)
Bands	9%	(3–5%)
Segmented neutrophils	76%	(54–62%)
Eosinophils	1%	(1–3%)
Basophils	0.0%	(0.0–0.75%)
Lymphocytes	13%	(25–33%)
Monocytes	1%	(3–7%)
Platelets	178,000/mm³	(150,000–400,000/mm³)

A chest radiograph is obtained and shown below:

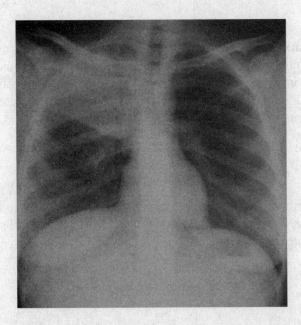

Chest radiograph PA view–right upper lobe infiltrate

DIAGNOSIS

Community-acquired pneumonia is typically characterized by sudden onset of fever, cough productive of purulent sputum, and pleuritic chest pain. Physical examination usually demonstrates signs of pulmonary consolidation (dullness, increased fremitus, egophony, bronchial breath sounds, and rales.)

The most common bacterial pathogen in community-acquired pneumonia is *Streptococcus pneumoniae*, but it may also be due to other bacterial pathogens such as *Heamophilus influenzae* or oral flora.

Community-acquired pneumonia may also have an atypical presentation characterized by a more gradual onset, a dry cough, and more extrapulmonary symptoms, such as headache, myalgias, fatigue, sore throat, nausea, vomiting, and diarrhea. Atypical pneumonia is classically produced by *Mycoplasma pneumoniae*, but can also be caused by *Legionella pneumophila*, *Chlamydia pneumoniae*, oral anaerobes, and *Pneumocystis carinii*.

Chest radiographs are useful for determining the presence and location of pulmonary infiltrates, assessing the extent of pulmonary infection, detecting pleural involvement, and gauging the response to antimicrobial therapy. Most primary pulmonary pathogens produce focal lesions, while hematogenous infections are usually multicentric in distribution. Oral anaerobes, *Mycobacterium tuberculosis*, and fungi can produce cavitary lesions. Anaerobic abscesses are located in dependent, poorly ventilated regions of the lung and characteristically have air-fluid levels. Empyema is the most common complication of pneumococcal pneumonia and occurs in about 2 percent of cases.

Sputum examination is the mainstay of the evaluation of a patient with acute bacterial pneumonia. Sputum cultures are used to determine antimicrobial sensitivity. In most patients with pneumococcal pneumonia, the white blood cell count is > 12,000/mm^3, but in 5 to 10 percent of hospitalized patients, the count is < 6,000/mm^3; this level is associated with a high risk of death.

PATHOGENESIS

The pneumonic process may primarily involve the interstitium (atypical presentation) or the alveoli (typical presentation.) Involvement of the entire lobe is called lobar pneumonia. The term bronchopneumonia refers to infections in which the pneumonic process affects only alveoli that are contiguous with the bronchi. Necrosis of lung tissue as a result of the infection and inflammatory processes can result in cavity and/or abscess formation.

EPIDEMIOLOGY

In patients who are hospitalized with community-acquired pneumonia, the most frequent pathogens are *S. pneumoniae*, *H. influenzae*, *C. pneumoniae*, and *L. pneumophila*. *M. pneumoniae* usually causes mild illness and is common among outpatients with community-acquired pneumonia.

TREATMENT

Most cases of community-acquired pneumonia (in otherwise healthy adults) do not require hospitalization. Oral antimicrobial therapy, usually administered on an empiric basis, should take care of *S. pneumoniae*. The β-lactams (penicillin G, amoxicillin-clavulanate, cefuroxime) have long been the standard therapy, but some locations have reported that as many as 10 to 20 percent of strains are resistant.

Patients who are ill enough to be hospitalized should have empiric parenteral antimicrobial therapy initiated until microbiologic evaluations are complete. Penicillin and ampicillin remain the drugs of choice for infection due to penicillin-susceptible pneumococci.

The pneumococcal vaccine contains capsular polysaccharide from the 23 most prevalent serotypes. This vaccine is recommended for immunosuppressed individuals who are at increased risk of pneumococcal infection, including patients with splenic dysfunction or asplenia, multiple myeloma, lymphoma, Hodgkin's disease, HIV infection, or organ transplantation. The pneumococcal vaccine is also recommended for adults who are immunocompetent, but are at an increased risk of pneumococcal infection and/or a serious complication of such infection, including patients with diabetes mellitus, alcoholism, cirrhosis, advanced cardiovascular disease, chronic renal insufficiency, and all persons older than 65 years of age.

PROGNOSIS

Successful host defense against the systemic spread of infection requires a functioning reticuloendothelial system, opsonins, and adequate numbers of neutrophils. Patients who develop overwhelming sepsis due to pneumonia generally lack one or more of these.

DIABETES MELLITUS

A 58-year-old man presents to his primary care physician with complaints of excessive thirst and frequent urination. Over the past several months he has noticed that he has become increasingly thirsty and drinks more fluids, but experiences no relief. He reports that he must awaken frequently during the night to urinate. He states that "I can't keep up. The more I drink, the more I need to urinate, but I still feel thirsty." His appetite has also increased during this period. The patient is significantly overweight. His height is 183 cm (72 in) and his weight is 125 kg (275 lb). Pulse is 92/min, blood pressure is 145/85 mm Hg, and respirations are 16/min. Capillary whole blood glucose level is 320 mg/dL.

DIAGNOSIS

Diabetes mellitus can be divided into two categories: autoimmune (type 1) and nonautoimmune (type 2). The term type 1 diabetes is often used as a synonym for insulin-dependent diabetes mellitus (IDDM), and type 2 diabetes is considered equivalent to noninsulin-dependent diabetes mellitus (NIDDM). This second linkage is not ideal, because a subset of patients with apparent NIDDM later become fully insulin-dependent and prone to ketoacidosis. When classifying diabetes, the term "insulin dependence" is not equivalent to the ongoing administration of insulin therapy; instead the term means that the patient is at risk for diabetic ketoacidosis in the absence of insulin. Many patients classified as noninsulin-dependent require insulin for control of hyperglycemia, but do not become ketoacidotic if insulin is withdrawn.

Diabetes mellitus is characterized by metabolic abnormalities and long-term complications involving the eyes, kidneys, nerves, and blood vessels. The manifestations of symptomatic diabetes mellitus vary from patient to patient. Most often, symptoms are due to hyperglycemia (polyuria, polydipsia, polyphagia), but the first event may be an acute metabolic decompensation that results in diabetic coma. Symptoms of NIDDM begin gradually, and this diagnosis is frequently made when an otherwise asymptomatic patient is found to have an elevated plasma glucose level on routine laboratory examination. The onset of external symptoms for IDDM may be abrupt, with thirst, excessive urination, increased appetite, and weight loss developing over several days.

The diagnosis of symptomatic diabetes is not difficult. Patients present with signs and symptoms attributable to an osmotic diuresis and have hyperglycemia. Asymptomatic patients with persistently elevated fasting plasma glucose concentrations are also easy to diagnose. Patients who are potentially diabetic but have normal fasting glucose concentrations are more problematic. These patients are usually given an oral glucose tolerance test and, if abnormal values are found, a diagnosis of impaired glucose tolerance or diabetes is given.

Criteria for the Diagnosis of Diabetes	
Fasting (overnight)	Venous plasma glucose concentration of > 7.8 mmol/L (140 mg/dL) on at least two separate occassions.
Following ingestion of 75 g of glucose	Venous plasma glucose concentration > 11.1 mmol/L (200 mg/dL) at 2 hours and on at least one other occasion during the 2-hour test (two values > 11.1 mmol/L (200 mg/dL) must be obtained for diagnosis).

If the 2-hour value is between 7.8 and 11.1 mmol/L (140 and 200 mg/dL) and one other value during the 2-hour test period is greater than or equal to 11.1 mmol/L (200 mg/dL), a diagnosis of impaired glucose tolerance is given. Persons in this category are at an increased risk for the development of fasting hyperglycemia or symptomatic diabetes, but progression is not predictable in individual patients.

Pathogenesis

The pathogenesis of IDDM begins with a genetic susceptibility to the disease, and an unknown environmental event initiates the disease process in such susceptible individuals. The pancreatic destructive process is almost certainly autoimmune in nature, although the details remain obscure. Viral infection is one triggering mechanism, but noninfectious agents may also be involved. By the time IDDM appears, most of the β-cells in the pancreas have been destroyed.

Patients with NIDDM have two physiological defects: abnormal insulin secretion and resistance to insulin action in target tissues. In contrast to IDDM, plasma insulin levels are normal to high in absolute terms, although they are lower than predicted for the level of plasma glucose seen. A relative insulin deficiency is present. For unknown reasons, patients with NIDDM do not develop ketoacidosis but are susceptible to development of hyperosmolar, nonketotic coma. Although insulin resistance in type 2 NIDDM is associated with decreased numbers of insulin receptors, most of the resistance is postreceptor in nature. The major environmental factor is obesity. It is highly likely that NIDDM is polygenic in origin.

Epidemiology

Diabetes mellitus is the most common endocrine disease. It is estimated that the prevalence of diabetes in the U.S. is about 2 percent, and that NIDDM is seven to eight times more common than IDDM. IDDM usually begins before age 40. In the U.S., peak incidence is around age 14. NIDDM usually begins in middle life or later, and the typical patient is overweight.

Treatment

The importance of diet in the management of diabetes varies with the type of disease. In insulin-dependent patients, particularly those on intensive insulin regimens, the composition of the diet is not of critical importance, since adjustment of the insulin can cover wide variations in food intake. In noninsulin-dependent patients who are not being treated with exogenous insulin, more rigorous adherence to diet is required, since the endogenous insulin reserve is limited. These patients cannot respond to the increased insulin demand produced by excess calories or increased intake of rapidly absorbed carbohydrates.

NIDDM that cannot be controlled by dietary management often responds to sulfonylureas, which are generally safe and easy to use. Sulfonylureas (chlorpropamide, tolazamide, tolbutamide, glyburide, and glipizide) act primarily by stimulating the release of insulin from the β-cells. Metformin, a biguanide useful in NIDDM patients who are not responsive to diet and exercise, may be prescribed as monotherapy in obese diabetics but is usually added as an adjunctive agent in patients whose disease is not controlled by maximal doses of sulfonylureas. The primary action of metformin is thought to be an inhibition of hepatic gluconeogenesis, and it may also enhance glucose disposal in muscle and adipose tissue.

Insulin is required for the treatment of all patients with IDDM and many patients with NIDDM. It is fairly easy to control the symptoms of diabetes with insulin, but it is difficult to maintain a normal blood sugar throughout a 24-hour period, even through multiple injections of regular insulin or infusion pumps. The multiple subcutaneous insulin injection technique involves the administration of intermediate- or long-acting insulin in the evening as a single dose together with regular insulin prior to each meal. Home glucose monitoring by the patient is necessary if the goal is the return to normal of the plasma glucose level. Continuous subcutaneous insulin infusion involves the use of a small, battery-driven pump that delivers insulin subcutaneously into the abdominal wall.

PROGNOSIS

Major Complications of Diabetes Mellitus	
Complication	Clinical Features
Diabetic ketoacidosis	Complication of IDDM. Requires insulin deficiency coupled with a relative or absolute increase in glucagon concentration. Often caused by cessation of insulin intake, but may result from physical (e.g., infection, surgery) or emotional stress. Characterized by 1) maximal gluconeogenesis and impaired peripheral utilization of glucose, which causes severe hyperglycemia, and 2) activation of the ketogenic process, which leads to a metabolic acidosis.
Hyperosmolar, nonketotic coma	Typically occurs in the setting of NIDDM. It is a syndrome of profound dehydration that results from a sustained hyperglycemic diuresis under circumstances in which the patient is unable to drink enough water to keep up with urinary fluid losses. Patients present with extreme hyperglycemia, hyperosmolarity, volume depletion, and central nervous system signs ranging from clouded sensorium to coma.
Circulatory abnormalities	Atherosclerosis is more extensive and occurs earlier than in the general population. Coronary artery disease and stroke are common. Peripheral vascular disease may cause intermittent claudication, gangrene, and, in men, organic impotence.
Retinopathy	Diabetic retinopathy is the leading cause of blindness in the U.S. However, most diabetic patients do not become blind. Approximately 85 percent of patients develop the complication. The fundamental characteristics of proliferative retinopathy are new vessel formation and scarring. This is treated with photocoagulation.
Diabetic nephropathy	Renal disease is the leading cause of death and disability in diabetics. Approximately one-half of the cases of end-stage renal disease in the U.S. are due to diabetic nephropathy. Approximately 35 percent of patients with IDDM, develop this condition. Prevalence in NIDDM varies from 15 to 60 percent depending on ethnic background. Diabetic nephropathy follows two distinct pathologic patterns: 1) a diffuse form, which is more common and is characterized by widening of the glomerular basement membrane together with generalized mesangial thickening, and 2) a nodular form, which is characterized by large accumulations of periodic acid-Schiff-positive material deposited at the periphery of the glomerular tufts (Kimmelstiel-Wilson nodule).
Diabetic neuropathy	Diabetic neuropathy can affect every part of the nervous system except the brain. The most common presentation is peripheral polyneuropathy, which is usually bilateral and characterized by numbness, paresthesias, severe hyperesthesias, and pain.
Diabetic foot ulcers	A special problem in diabetic patients, these ulcers appear to be due primarily to abnormal pressure distribution secondary to diabetic neuropathy. Vascular disease with diminished blood supply contributes to the development of ulcers, and infection is common.

HODGKIN'S DISEASE

A 32-year-old man presents with complaints of fatigue, malaise, weakness, and a weight loss of 5 kg (11 lb) over the past three months. He notes that recently he has woken up in the middle of the night drenched in sweat. Temperature is 37.8 C (100.1 F), pulse is 80/min, blood pressure is 120/75 mm Hg, and respirations are 12/min. Physical examination demonstrates multiple enlarged lymph nodes of the posterior cervical chain bilaterally. The nodes are firm, nontender, and freely mobile. A chest x-ray reveals mediastinal adenopathy. An open biopsy of one of the enlarged cervical nodes is performed and the histopathological specimen is shown below.

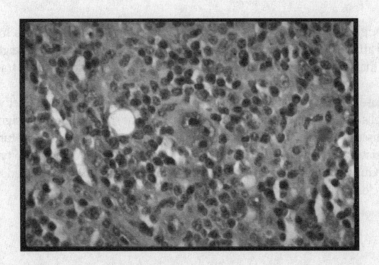

DIAGNOSIS

Hodgkin's disease usually presents as a localized disease and then spreads to contiguous lymphoid structures. Ultimately, it disseminates to nonlymphoid tissues where it can affect a potentially fatal outcome. Hodgkin's disease commonly presents with a newly detected mass or group of lymph nodes that are firm, freely mobile, and usually nontender. Approximately 60 percent of patients present with mediastinal adenopathy, sometimes first detected on routine chest x-ray. In 2 to 5 percent of patients, lymph nodes or other tissues involved with Hodgkin's disease can become painful after the ingestion of alcoholic beverages.

The majority of patients presenting with Hodgkin's disease have few or no symptoms related to the disease. However, 25 to 30 percent has some constitutional symptoms; the most common is low-grade fever, which can be associated with recurrent night sweats. Another important presenting symptom is unexplained weight loss of greater than 10 percent of the total body weight over 6 months or less. Other frequent symptoms include fatigue, malaise, and weakness. Pruritus occurs in approximately 10 percent of patients at initial diagnosis; it is usually generalized and may be associated with a skin rash.

Reed-Sternberg (RS) cells, in the appropriate cytoarchitectural milieu, are required for the diagnosis of Hodgkin's disease. RS cells typically have a pale-staining acidophilic cytoplasm and one or two large nuclei with deeply acidophilic nucleoli. Two antigens expressed on the RS cell, CD15 and CD30, are diagnostically useful. Needle aspirations or needle biopsies are not adequate for the primary histologic diagnosis of Hodgkin's disease. Biopsy specimens are usually taken from lymph nodes but may occasionally be taken from other tissues.

The differential diagnosis for Hodgkin's is similar to that of non-Hodgkin's lymphoma. In patients with cervical adenopathy, infections including bacterial or viral pharyngitis, infectious mononucleosis, and toxoplasmosis must all be excluded. Other malignancies, such as non-Hodgkin's lymphoma, nasopharyngeal cancers, and thyroid cancers can present with localized cervical adenopathy. RS cells and their variants may be immunologically distinguished from the neoplastic cells of most non-Hodgkin's lymphomas by their lack of a characteristic pattern of expression of T and B cell-associated antigens. Mediastinal adenopathy must be distinguished from infections, sarcoid, and other tumors. Reactive mediastinitis and hilar adenopathy from histoplasmosis can be confused with lymphoma since it occurs in otherwise asymptomatic people.

PATHOGENESIS

The etiology of Hodgkin's lymphoma is unknown. Hodgkin's disease is 99 times more common in an identical twin of an affected person than in the general population, which suggests a genetic contribution. There is evidence that the Epstein-Barr virus plays a role in the pathogenesis of a subset of cases of Hodgkin's disease.

Hodgkin's disease is a heterogenous disease derived from subpopulations of activated lymphohematopoietic cells. RS cells are definitely of hematopoietic lineage, but specific lineage assignment is difficult. In Hodgkin's disease tissues, the majority of the cells are small lymphocytes with a mature T cell phenotype, together with a variable number of B cells. Hodgkin's disease is divided into four types: 1) lymphocyte predominant, 2) nodular sclerosis, 3) mixed cellularity, and 4) lymphocyte depleted. RS cells may have monoclonal or polyclonal immunoglobulin gene arrangements.

EPIDEMIOLOGY

Approximately 7,500 new cases of Hodgkin's disease are diagnosed annually in the United States. In non-Hodgkin's lymphomas, there is a linear increase in incidence with age, but in Hodgkin's disease the age-specific incidence curve is bimodal, with an initial peak in young adults (15 to 35 years) and a second peak after age 50. Hodgkin's disease is more prevalent in males, particularly in young adult males.

TREATMENT

Following biopsy and histopathologic classification of Hodgkin's disease, the patient must be staged in order for the optimal therapy to be selected.

Ann Arbor Staging System for Hodgkin's Disease	
Stage I	Involvement of single lymph node region or single extralymphatic site
Stage II	Involvement of two or more lymph node regions on the same side of the diaphragm
Stage III	Involvement of lymph node regions on both sides of diaphragm; may include spleen
Stage IV	Disseminated involvement of one or more extralymphatic organs, with or without lymph node involvement

Pathologic staging is accomplished using invasive tests, including biopsy specimens obtained from different sites, usually during a staging laparotomy. The presence of extralymphatic disease is designated by the suffix "E." The presence of systemic symptoms (fever, night sweats, weight loss) is designated by the suffix "B" and their absence is noted with the suffix "A."

Patients with early-stage disease, such as IA or IIA, can be effectively treated with radiation; patients with more disseminated disease are most effectively treated with combination chemotherapy alone. The chemotherapeutic combination most successfully used to treat advanced stage disease is MOPP, which is composed of mechlorethamine (nitrogen mustard), vincristine, procarbazine, and prednisone.

PROGNOSIS

With appropriate treatment, about 85 percent of patients with Hodgkin's disease can be cured. Radiotherapy may cure more than 80 percent of people with localized Hodgkin's disease, and chemotherapy may cure more than 70 percent of those with disseminated disease. Nearly half of those not cured with primary treatment are cured with salvage therapy.

HUMAN IMMUNODEFICIENCY VIRUS INFECTION

A 24-year-old woman presents requesting counseling regarding the prevention of human immunodeficiency virus (HIV) infection. She is currently in a sexual relationship with a man who is an injecting drug user (IDU) whose HIV status is unknown. The patient does not use injecting drugs, has never received a blood transfusion, and has had four lifetime sexual partners. She uses condoms for birth control, but not consistently.

DIAGNOSIS

HIV is transmitted by both homosexual and heterosexual contact; by blood and blood products; and by infected mothers to infants either intrapartum, perinatally, or via breast milk. There is no evidence that HIV is transmitted by casual contact or that the virus can be spread by insects.

The diagnosis of HIV infection depends upon the demonstration of antibodies to HIV and/or the direct detection of HIV or one of its components. Antibodies to HIV generally appear in the circulation 4 to 8 weeks after infection. The standard screening test for HIV is the enzyme-linked immunosorbent assay (ELISA), which has a sensitivity of over 99.5 percent. The most commonly used confirmatory test is the Western blot. A Western blot that demonstrates antibodies to products of all three of the major genes of HIV (gag, pol, and env) is conclusive evidence of infection with HIV. The polymerase chain reaction (PCR) is the gold standard for the diagnosis of HIV infection. It is used in at-risk neonates or when standard serologic testing has failed to provide a definitive result.

PATHOGENESIS

HIV is predominantly sexually transmitted worldwide. Although one-half of the reported cases of AIDS in the U.S. are among homosexual men, the yearly incidence of new cases of AIDS contracted through heterosexual transmission is steadily increasing, mainly among minorities, and particularly female minorities. Heterosexual transmission is the most common mode of infection worldwide, particularly in developing countries. In the U.S., there is a 20-fold greater chance of transmission from man to woman than from woman to man through vaginal intercourse. There is also a close association between genital ulcerations and transmission, from the standpoints of both susceptibility to infection and infectivity. Infections with microorganisms such as *Treponema pallidum*, *Haemophilus ducreyi*, and herpes simplex virus are important causes of genital ulcerations, which are in turn linked to the transmission of HIV.

The virus is present in seminal fluid and in cervical and vaginal fluid. HIV can be transmitted by blood and blood products, both among individuals who share contaminated paraphernalia (needles and syringes) for injection drug use and in those who receive transfusions of blood and blood products. Transfusions of whole blood, packed red blood cells, platelets, leukocytes, plasma, fresh frozen plasma, and concentrates of clotting factors are all capable of transmitting HIV. Most cases of health care worker seroconversion occur as a result of needle-stick injuries.

HIV infection can be transmitted from an infected mother to her fetus during pregnancy as early as the first and second trimester or to her infant during delivery. However, maternal transmission to the fetus occurs most commonly in the perinatal period. Postnatal transmission from mother to infant can occur; colostrum and breast milk serve as vehicles of infection.

It is not known whether saliva can transmit HIV infection. Although the virus can be isolated from virtually any body fluid, there is no evidence that HIV infection can occur as a result of exposure to tears, sweat, or urine.

EPIDEMIOLOGY

HIV infection is a global pandemic; the current estimate of the number of cases of HIV infection among adults worldwide is approximately 22 million; among children it is approximately 1 million. The estimated prevalence of HIV infection in the U.S. is approximately 0.3 to 0.4 percent, and is highest among adults in their late twenties and thirties and among minorities.

The risk of being infected in the U.S. via transfused screened blood is approximately 1 in 500,000. The risk of HIV infection resulting from a skin puncture from a needle or a sharp object contaminated with blood from a person with a documented HIV infection is approximately 0.3 percent. In the U.S., approximately 1,600 newborns per year are infected with HIV by their mothers.

TREATMENT

Education, counseling, and behavior modification are the cornerstones of an HIV prevention strategy. Widespread voluntary testing of individuals who have practiced or are practicing high-risk behavior, together with counseling of infected individuals, is recommended. The practice of safe sex is the most effective way for sexually active, uninfected individuals to avoid contracting HIV infection and for infected individuals to avoid spreading infection.

Abstinence from sexual relations is the only absolute way to prevent sexual transmission of HIV. However, there are a number of relatively safe practices that can markedly decrease the chances of transmission of HIV infection. Partners engaged in monogamous relationships who wish to be assured of safety should both be tested for the HIV antibody. When the status of the partner is not known, or when one partner is positive, there are a number of options. Use of latex condoms, preferably together with the HIV-inhibiting spermicide nonoxynol-9, can markedly decrease the chance of HIV transmission. Receptive oral fellatio is not a safe sexual practice.

The most effective way to stop the transmission of HIV infection among IDUs is to stop their drug use. Unfortunately, oftentimes that is extremely difficult to accomplish unless the addict enters a treatment program. For those who will not or cannot participate in a drug treatment program and who continue to inject drugs, the avoidance of sharing needles and other paraphernalia is the next best way to avoid transmission of infection. Paraphernalia can be cleaned with undiluted household bleach.

Methods used to protect the blood supply include 1) screening of all blood for the HIV p24 antigen and for HIV antibody by ELISA, with a confirmatory Western blot; 2) the self-deferral of donors on the basis of risk behavior; 3) the screening out of HIV-negative individuals with surrogate laboratory parameters of infection, such as hepatitis B and C; 4) serologic testing for syphilis; and 5) the heat-treatment of clotting factor concentrates.

Health care workers can minimize their risk of occupational HIV infection by following adherence to universal precautions; refraining from direct patient care if the patient has exudative lesions or weeping dermatitis, and disinfecting and sterilizing reusable devices employed in invasive procedures. The premise of universal precautions is that every specimen should be handled as if it came from someone infected with a pathogen.

Zidovudine treatment of HIV-infected pregnant women from the beginning of the second trimester through delivery, and of the infant for six weeks following birth can dramatically reduce the rate of intrapartum and perinatal transmission of HIV infection, from 22.6 percent when untreated to 7.6 percent when treated with zidovudine. In developed countries, where bottled formula and milk are available, breast feeding is absolutely contraindicated when a mother is HIV-positive.

PROGNOSIS

Anyone who practices high-risk behavior is at risk for HIV infection. The risk of infection among IDUs increases with the duration of the injecting drug use, the frequency of the needle sharing, and the use of injection drugs in geographic locations with a high prevalence of HIV. There is a small but definite occupational risk of HIV transmission among health care workers.

HUNTINGTON'S DISEASE

A 45-year-old man presents with complaints of "feeling sad and not wanting to be around people," as well as being "fidgety." A review of systems reveals that the patient also has had a gait disturbance and dysarthria for several months. Past medical history is noncontributory. Family history is significant for the patient's father having a progressive "nervous disease" in his 50s that led to his "going senile" several years before his death. Examination notes that the patient displays involuntary grunting, grimacing, and choreiform movements. The MRI study is shown below.

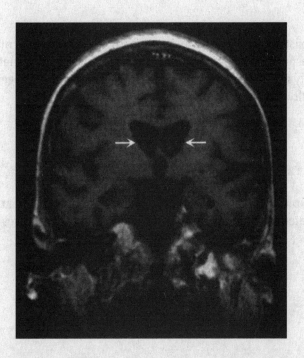

MRI demonstrating mylin tracts undergoing Wallerian degeneration

DIAGNOSIS

The clinical presentation of Huntington's disease (HD) is chorea and behavioral disturbances; in the early stages it is often confused with schizophrenia. Its onset is typically in the fourth or fifth decade of life and is usually subtle at first, often unrecognized by the patient and his or her family. The movement disorder is progressive and may eventually be disabling. The gait is poorly coordinated and is described as having a dance-like quality. Memory impairment occurs late in the course of the disease. Depression and social withdrawal are common.

Atrophy of the caudate nuclei can be demonstrated by the middle and late stages of the disease. Imaging studies will be significant for enlarged lateral ventricles (caudate forms the lateral margins of the lateral ventricles.)

PATHOGENESIS

HD is an autosomal, dominantly inherited genetic disorder and the HD genetic defect is located on chromosome 4p. The HD gene codes for a protein called huntingtin, which is found throughout the brain but whose normal function is unknown. In patients with HD, there is gliosis and neuronal loss, particularly of the medium-sized spiny neurons in the caudate and putamen. The basal ganglia show a marked decrease in γ-aminobutyric acid (GABA) production.

TREATMENT

No effective therapies exist for HD and care is supportive. The movement disorder and behavioral changes may partially respond to phenothiazines or benzodiazepines. Genetic counseling and testing should be offered to family members. A diagnostic blood test for the disease gene exists and persons who test positive will eventually develop symptoms if they live long enough.

PROGNOSIS

The disease duration is typically about fifteen years, but has a wide range. Early onset (before the age of 20; juvenile HD) is associated with a more rapid progression and in these cases the disease has a duration of approximately 8 years.

MULTIPLE SCLEROSIS

A 31-year-old woman presents with complaints of "having trouble walking and blurry vision for the last 6 months." The patient describes her gait difficulties as "tripping over my own feet." Upon further questioning, the patient describes a history of intermittent "pins and needles" in a variable distribution on her limbs and trunk. Testing of visual acuity demonstrates a moderate loss of acuity in the left eye only. Additionally, a scotoma of the left visual field is detected. Funduscopic exam is normal bilaterally. Neuromuscular examination reveals an asymmetric motor weakness of the right lower extremity. A sensory deficit of the dorsal aspect of the left forearm is discovered. Observation of the patient's gait reveals a subtle dragging of the right foot. A magnetic resonance imaging scan is obtained.

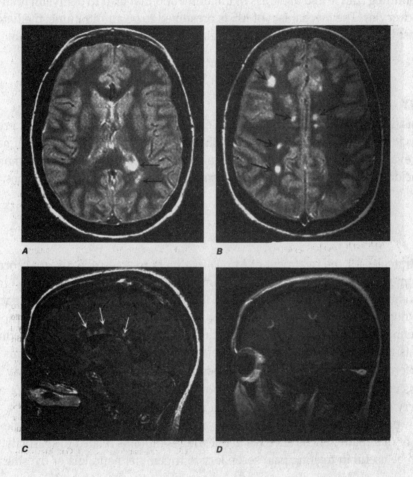

MRI demonstrating multiple sclerosis plaques

DIAGNOSIS

The onset of multiple sclerosis (MS) is variable. At first, symptoms may be dramatic or they may be so mild as not to motivate the patient to seek medical attention. The presenting symptoms of MS are diverse, the most common include muscle weakness, sensory loss, paresthesias, optic neuritis, diplopia, ataxia, and vertigo. The differential diagnosis of MS varies for each case, depending on the specific symptoms. No clinical sign or diagnostic test finding is unique to MS. Usually, the presence of relapsing and remitting symptoms attributable to different areas of white matter (especially in a young adult) is a strong indicator of MS. Typically, examination reveals more widespread signs of neurological disease than would be expected from the interview.

PATHOGENESIS

Pathologically, MS is characterized by multiple scarred areas contained within the white matter that are visible on macroscopic examination of the central nervous system. These lesions, termed plaques, have a relapsing and remitting course and are areas of inflammation that lead to demyelination and, eventually, loss of oligodendrocytes. The mechanism of MS is presumed to be autoimmune, mediated by T lymphocytes, and is most likely initiated by environmental exposure in genetically susceptible individuals.

EPIDEMIOLOGY

Multiple sclerosis (MS) is the second most frequent cause of neurologic disability that presents in early to middle adulthood (the most frequent is trauma). MS is more common in temperate climates and, in both hemispheres, prevalence increases with distance from the equator. MS is twice as common in females as males and its incidences rises steadily from the teens to mid-thirties and then declines.

TREATMENT

There are two strategies for the treatment of MS: 1) treatment to arrest the disease process and progression and 2) treatment to manage symptoms. It is important to score the longitudinal functional consequences of MS to help guide treatment decisions. For the patient who has an initial attack of demyelination disease in whom a diagnosis of MS is likely, but who lacks recurrent signs and symptoms (which are required for a definite diagnosis of MS), a combination of methylprednisolone and prednisone should be used. For patients with relapsing forms of MS, there are three prophylactic treatments available, interferon-β1b, interferon-β1a, and copolymer 1. Patients with chronic progression may be treated with immunosuppressive agents such as methotrexate or azathioprine, although they are only moderately effective and carry significant short- and long-term risks.

Patients with progressive disease may develop muscle spasticity with stiffness, flexor spasms, and clonus. Baclofen or diazepam may be effective in relieving symptoms related to spasticity. Carbamazepine or phenytoin can be useful in treating pain secondary to trigeminal neuralgia or dyesthesias.

PROGNOSIS

The clinical course of MS is highly variable. Favorable prognostic factors include early onset (excluding childhood), visual or sensory symptoms alone at presentation, a relapsing-remitting course, and minimal neurological impairment 5 years after onset. Poor prognostic factors include truncal ataxia, severe action tremor, and a primary progressive disease course.

NON-HODGKIN'S LYMPHOMA

A 72-year-old woman presents with complaints of newly discovered lumps in her axillae, neck, and groin. She first noticed the lumps 6 weeks ago, but did not think they were important since they were painless. She has been in her usual state of good health and denies any complaints of fever, chills, or night sweats. Her medical history is unremarkable. Temperature is 37 C (98.6 F), pulse is 76/min, blood pressure is 110/70 mm Hg, and respirations are 12/min. Physical examination reveals diffuse adenopathy of the axilla, inguinal area, and anterior and posterior cervical chain. The enlarged nodes are nontender and mobile.

DIAGNOSIS

More than two-thirds of patients with non-Hodgkin's lymphoma present with persistent, painless peripheral lymphadenopathy. Unlike patients with Hodgkin's disease who may present with weight loss, fever, or night sweats, fewer than 20 percent of patients with non-Hodgkin's lymphoma presents with systemic complaints. Non-Hodgkin's lymphomas can present with thoracic, abdominal, and/or extranodal symptoms. Although it is much less common than in Hodgkin's disease, approximately 20 percent of patients presents with mediastinal adenopathy. Involvement of retroperitoneal, mesenteric, and pelvic nodes is common in most histologic subtypes of non-Hodgkin's lymphoma. Patients who seek medical attention because of an abdominal mass, massive splenomegaly, or primary gastrointestinal lymphoma present with complaints similar to those caused by other space-occupying lesions. These complaints include chronic pain, abdominal fullness, early satiety, symptoms associated with visceral obstruction, or even acute perforation and gastrointestinal hemorrhage.

The differential diagnosis of generalized lymphadenopathy necessitates the exclusion of infectious etiologies including bacteria, viruses (e.g., infectious mononucleosis, cytomegalovirus, and HIV), and parasites. A firm lymph node larger than 1 cm that is not associated with a documentable infection and persists longer than four weeks should be considered for biopsy.

PATHOGENESIS

Non-Hodgkin's lymphomas can occur in the context of drug-induced immunosuppression and acquired or congenital immunodeficiency. There is some evidence that infectious agents are involved in the pathogenesis of some non-Hodgkin's lymphomas. Non-Hodgkin's lymphoma develops in up to 30 percent of HIV-infected individuals and 40 to 50 percent of those cases are associated with Epstein-Barr virus. Occupational exposures associated with an increased risk of non-Hodgkin's lymphoma include farming, welding, and work in the lumber industry. There is an increased incidence of non-Hodgkin's lymphoma in survivors of nuclear explosions or other radiation exposures. Non-Hodgkin's lymphoma can also occur as a late complication of prior chemotherapy and/or radiation therapy.

Non-Hodgkin's lymphomas can be grouped into two categories based on the patient's natural history: indolent lymphomas and aggressive lymphomas. About 90 percent of non-Hodgkin's lymphomas are of B cell origin. Histologic subtypes that are considered indolent lymphomas include follicular center lymphoma, marginal zone lymphoma, and mycosis fungoides. Histologic subtypes that are considered aggressive lymphomas include follicular center lymphoma (large cell), mantle cell lymphoma, diffuse large B cell lymphoma, aggressive T cell lymphomas, and AIDS-related lymphomas.

EPIDEMIOLOGY

About 45,000 new cases of non-Hodgkin's lymphoma occur each year in the U.S.; it ranks as the sixth-most common cause of cancer-related death.

TREATMENT

After the initial excisional biopsy and determination of the pathologic and immunologic subtype of the disease, a staging workup should be undertaken. Blood tests should be obtained, including complete blood counts, liver function tests, routine chemistries, serum protein electrophoresis, and serum β_2-microglobulin. Chest radiography and a computed tomography scan of the abdomen are essential for accurate staging, and a bone marrow biopsy must be performed. Staging laparotomy is not usually performed in non-Hodgkin's lymphoma.

Ann Arbor Staging System for Non-Hodgkin's Disease	
Stage I	Involvement of single lymph node region or single extralymphatic site
Stage II	Involvement of two or more lymph node regions on the same side of diaphragm
Stage III	Involvement of lymph node regions on both sides of diaphragm; may include spleen
Stage IV	Disseminated involvement of one or more extralymphatic organs, with or without lymph node involvement

The majority of patients with non-Hodgkin's lymphomas present with advanced disease; few are pathologic stages I and II. Early-stage disease can be treated very successfully with radiotherapy alone. More advanced disease is treated with combination chemotherapy, for which the C-MOPP (cyclophosphamide, mechlorethamine, vincristine, prednisone, and procarbazine) or CHOP (cyclophosphamide, doxorubicin, vincristine, and prednisone) regimens are used. Patients with the disease who are resistant to conventional or salvage therapeutic regimens can still be induced into a complete remission with very high-dose chemotherapy and radiotherapy combined with a bone marrow transplant.

PROGNOSIS

The response to treatment is the most important prognostic indicator. Early-stage patients treated with radiotherapy have a five-year, relapse-free survival of 60 to 80 percent, with overall five-year survival approaching 100 percent. The prognosis for patients with intermediate- and high-grade non-Hodgkin's lymphoma who fail to achieve a complete remission or who relapse following aggressive therapy is very poor. There is little difference in five-year survival between whites and blacks.

PARKINSON'S DISEASE

A 70-year-old Asian woman presents with complaints of "shaking" and "trouble walking." On examination, a resting tremor is observed, which is manifested by a slow rhythmic flexion-extension of the fingers and hands, as well as rhythmic pronation-supination of the forearms. The patient's facial expression is fixed; she is noted to blink infrequently and have widened palpebral fissures. There is moderate resistance of the extremities to passive movement, with the resting posture of the limbs at flexion. The patient is observed to have difficulty walking across the room, leans forward, and walks with small shuffling steps. Tendon reflexes are normal bilaterally and plantar responses are flexor bilaterally.

DIAGNOSIS

Parkinsonism is a syndrome that consists of tremor, rigidity, bradykinesia, and a characteristic gait and posture disturbance. It is a chronic progressive disorder in which idiopathic parkinsonism is present. A common clinical feature of Parkinson' disease is rigidity, which accounts for the flexed posture of many patients. Parkinson's disease gait is characterized by difficulty in initiating walking; small, shuffling steps; no arm swing; and unsteady sense of balance. Some patients walk with a festinating gait in an effort to prevent themselves from falling over due to an abnormal center of gravity. A depressed mood is common and advanced cases may progress to dementia.

Several disorders simulate Parkinson's disease. The changes in voice and decrease in spontaneous activity seen in depression, particularly in the elderly, can be confused with Parkinson's disease. Essential (benign, familial) tremor can be mistaken for Parkinson's disease, but essential tremor commonly affects the head, while Parkinson's affects the face and lips without involving head movements. The apraxic gait disturbance caused by normal-pressure hydrocephalus is similar to the Parkinson's disease gait disturbance, but normal-pressure hydrocephalus is also associated with urinary incontinence, dementia, and imaging studies that demonstrate dilation of the ventricular system without cortical atrophy. Several neurologic diseases can present with parkinsonism (see chart below) and it is important to distinguish these from Parkinson's disease for prognostic and therapeutic purposes.

Neurological Disorders That Present With Parkinsonism and Distinguishing Features	
Disease	Distinguishing Features
Wilson' s disease	Kayser-Fleischer rings Low serum copper and ceruloplasmin levels Family history Early age of onset
Huntington' s disease	Family history Dementia Genetic studies
Shy-Drager Syndrome	Impaired autonomic function Pyramidal, cerebellar, or lower motor signs

Creutzfeldt-Jakob disease	Rapidly progressive dementia Myoclonus Characteristic EEG findings
Striatonigral degeneration	Cerebellar deficits
Progressive supranuclear palsy	Abnormalities of voluntary eye movements Pseudobulbar palsy Axial dystonia
Cortical-basal ganglionic degeneration	Aphasia Apraxia Intellectual decline

PATHOGENESIS

The etiology of Parkinson's disease is unknown and it is not clear if there is a significant genetic component. Symptoms of Parkinson's disease are caused by the loss of nerve cells in the substantia nigra. Cell loss also occurs in the globus pallidus and putamen. The loss of dopaminergic cells in the substantia nigra results in reduced thalamic excitation of the motor cortex, which is clinically evident by the difficulty that parkinsonian patients have in initiating movements. Parkinsonism can be induced in primates (including humans) by exposure to 1-methyl-4-phenyl-1,2,3,6-tetrahydropyridine (MPTP).

EPIDEMIOLOGY

Parkinson's disease is a common condition, with a prevalence of 1 to 2 per 1,000 of the general population and 1 per 100 among people older than 65 years of age. Parkinson's disease generally affects adults in middle or late life, occurs in all ethnic groups, and has an equal sex distribution.

TREATMENT

There are several approaches to treatment for the patient with Parkinson's disease, but multidrug symptomatic pharmacologic treatment is standard. Anticholinergic drugs, including benztropine, procyclidine, and trihexyphenidyl, are helpful in relieving tremor. Amantadine, which potentiates the release of endogenous dopamine, is effective in improving the symptoms of mild parkinsonism. Levodopa, the metabolic precursor of dopamine, must be administered with an extracerebral dopadecarboxylase inhibitor (carbidopa) and provides symptomatic relief, especially for bradykinesia. Dopamine agonist drugs such as bromocriptine and pergolide directly stimulate dopamine receptors, providing symptomatic relief.

Neuroprotective therapy should be considered unless the patient has end-stage disease. Selegiline, a selective monoamine oxidase B inhibitor, may reduce oxidative damage and slow disease progression. The transplantation of fetal dopaminergic cells remains an experimental treatment and its long-term benefit remains uncertain.

PROGNOSIS

Treatment can improve symptoms and may slow progression, but Parkinson's disease remains a chronic disorder that leads to progressive disability over time.

PNEUMOCYSTIS CARINII PNEUMONIA

A 36-year-old white man who is HIV-positive presents with complaints of progressive shortness of breath, fever, and a nonproductive cough for the past week. His last known CD4+ count was 75 cells/mL. The patient is a homeless injecting drug user who is not currently being treated for his HIV infection. The patient reports a history of a "yeast infection of the throat" one year prior for which he was hospitalized. His temperature is 39 C (102.2 F), blood pressure is 100/60 mm Hg, pulse is 110/min, and respirations are 42/min. Arterial blood gas reveals a pH of 7.29, a PCO_2 of 20 mm Hg, and a PO_2 of 65 mm Hg. A chest radiograph is ordered and shown below:

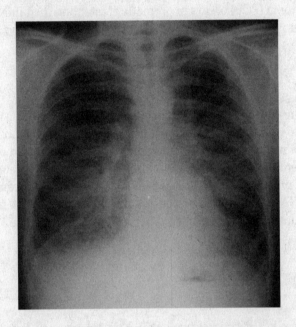

Chest radiograph PA view–interstitial infiltrate

DIAGNOSIS

Many infectious and noninfectious agents can produce the clinical picture of *Pneumocystis carinii* pneumonia (PCP). Patients generally present with a fever and a cough that is nonproductive or minimally productive of white sputum, and the course can be indolent in HIV-positive patients who meet the criteria for AIDS. PCP should always be considered in the evaluation of HIV-positive patients with CD4+ counts less than 200 cells/mL, fever, and pulmonary complaints.

Physical diagnosis is usually unremarkable. Radiographs of the chest may appear normal or show a faint bilateral interstitial infiltrate. Arterial blood gas usually demonstrates hypoxemia and an elevated arterial-alveolar gradient.

Histopathological staining makes a definitive diagnosis. Sputum induction is a simple, noninvasive technique. Fiber optic bronchoscopy is the gold standard of *P. carinii* diagnosis, but is expensive and invasive. The most invasive procedures, transbronchial biopsy and open lung biopsy, are used only in cases in which a diagnosis cannot be made by lavage.

PATHOGENESIS

Impaired cellular immunity is the major host factor that predisposes to pneumocystosis. Within the lung, *P. carinii* attaches to the alveolar type I pneumocytes. As the host's immune system fails, the *P. carinii* organisms multiply and gradually fill the alveolar space, leading to the characteristic foamy, vacuolated exudate. Severe disease may include interstitial edema, fibrosis, and hyaline membrane formation.

EPIDEMIOLOGY

Pneumocystis carinii pneumonia (PCP) occurs in premature, malnourished infants; children with primary immunodeficiency diseases; patients receiving immunosuppressive therapy; and people with AIDS.

TREATMENT

The drug of choice for pneumocystosis is trimethoprim-sulfamethoxazole (TMP), a folic acid synthesis inhibitor. The other major drug used to treat *P. carinii* is pentamidine, which has a method of action against *P. carinii* that is unknown. Alternative treatments include TMP plus dapsone and clindamycin plus primaquine.

For HIV positive patients with CD4+ cell counts of < 200/mL who are at high risk of developing pneumocystosis, primary prophylaxis is indicated. For all patients recovering from PCP, secondary prophylaxis is indicated. TMP is the prophylactic regimen of choice. Alternative treatments include dapsone, pyrimethamine-dapsone-leucovorin, and aerosolized pentamidine.

PROGNOSIS

In the typical case of untreated PCP, progressive respiratory compromise leads to death. Therapy is most effective when instituted early in the course of the infection, before extensive alveolar damage occurs. Despite the increased recognition of PCP and prophylaxis against it, *P. carinii* remains a leading cause of opportunistic infection and death among AIDS patients in industrialized countries.

SYSTEMIC LUPUS ERYTHEMATOSUS

A 32-year old woman presents with complaints of fatigue, malaise, intermittent fever, muscle and joint pains, and weight loss. She is a school teacher and over the past month has had to miss 10 days of work because of her symptoms. Her appetite has been poor and she has lost approximately 4 kg (8.8 lb) in the last month. Temperature is 37.9 C (100.3 F), pulse is 80/min, respirations are 14/min, and blood pressure is 135/85 mm Hg. An erythematous malar rash and patchy alopecia are noted. Physical examination demonstrates diffuse lymphadenopathy; the enlarged lymph nodes are nontender and mobile. Laboratory studies show:

Erythrocyte sedimentation rate	93 mm/hr	(Female 0–20 mm/hr)
Hematocrit	31%	(Female: 36–46%)
Hemoglobin	10.3 g/dL	(Female: 12.0–16.0 g/dL)
Leukocytes	4,000/mm³	(4.5–11,000/mm³)
Mean corpuscular volume	89/mm³	(80–100/mm³)
Platelets	110,000/mm³	(150,000–400,000/mm³)

DIAGNOSIS

Systemic lupus erythematosus (SLE) is a disease of unknown etiology in which tissues and cells are damaged by pathogenic autoantibodies and immune complexes. At onset, SLE may involve only one organ system, or it may be multisystemic. Severity varies from mild and intermittent to persistent and fulminant. Systemic symptoms are usually prominent and include fatigue, malaise, fever, anorexia, and weight loss.

Common Clinical Manifestations of SLE		Patients positive during course of disease
Systemic	Includes fatigue, malaise, fever, anorexia, nausea, and weight loss	95%
Musculoskeletal	Includes arthralgias, myalgias, nonerosive polyarthritis, myopathy, myositis, hand deformities, ischemic necrosis of bone	95%
Cutaneous	Includes malar rash, discoid rash, photosensitivity, oral ulcers, and other rashes (maculopapular, urticarial, bullous, subacute cutaneous lupus)	80%
Hematologic	Includes anemia (of chronic disease), hemolytic anemia, leukopenia, lymphopenia, thrombocytopenia, circulating anticoagulant, splenomegaly, lymphadenopathy	85%
Neurologic	Includes cognitive dysfunction, organic brain syndromes (psychosis, seizures), headache, peripheral neuropathy	60%

Cardiopulmonary	Includes pleurisy, pericarditis, myocarditis, endocarditis (Libman-Sacks), pleural effusions, lupus pneumonitis, interstitial fibrosis, pulmonary hypertension, adult respiratory distress syndrome/hemorrhage	60%
Renal	Includes proteinuria, cellular casts, nephrotic syndrome, renal failure	50%
Gastrointestinal	Includes nonspecific (anorexia, nausea, mild pain, diarrhea), vasculitis with bleeding or perforation, ascites, abnormal liver enzymes	45%
Thrombosis	Venous or arterial	15%
Fetal loss		30% (of pregnancies)
Ocular	Includes retinal vasculitis, conjunctivitis/episcleritis, sicca syndrome	15%

The presence of characteristic antibodies confirms the diagnosis of SLE. Autoantibodies are detectable at disease onset. A positive antinuclear antibody (ANA) test is not specific for SLE; a positive test supports the diagnosis of SLE, and a negative ANA test makes the diagnosis unlikely, but not impossible. Antibodies to double-stranded DNA (dsDNA) and to Smith are relatively specific for SLE.

Common SLE Autoantibodies		
Autoantibody	Incidence	Comment
Antinuclear antibodies	98%	Antibodies directed against multiple nuclear antigens. Repeatedly negative tests make SLE unlikely.
Anti-dsDNA	70%	Anti-dsDNA is relatively disease specific; anti-ssDNA is not. High titers are associated with nephritis.
Anti-Sm	30%	Specific for SLE
Anti-RNP	40%	High titer is seen in syndromes with features of polymyositis, lupus, scleroderma, and mixed connective tissue disease.
Anti-Ro (SS-A)	30%	Associated with Sjögren's syndrome, subacute cutaneous lupus, ANA-negative lupus, lupus in the elderly, neonatal lupus, congenital heart block, and can cause nephritis.
Anti-La (SS-B)	10%	Always associated with anti-Ro. Risk for nephritis is low if present. Associated with Sjögren's syndrome.
Antihistone	70%	More frequent in drug-induced LE (95%) than in spontaneous SLE.
Antiphospholipid	50%	Three types: lupus anticoagulant (LA), anticardiolipin (aCL), and false-positive test for syphilis. LA and aCL are associated with clotting, fetal loss, thrombocytopenia, and valvular heart disease.

SLE can be confused with rheumatoid arthritis; various forms of dermatitis; neurologic disorders such as epilepsy, multiple sclerosis, and psychiatric disorders; and hematologic disorders such as idiopathic thrombocytopenic purpura.

PATHOGENESIS

SLE results from tissue damage caused by pathogenic subsets of autoantibodies and immune complexes. The abnormal immune responses include polyclonal and antigen-specific T and B lymphocyte hyperactivity and inadequate regulation of that hyperactivity. These abnormal immune responses probably depend upon interactions between susceptibility genes and the environment. Ten to 15 percent of people with SLE have more than one affected family member, and there is an increased concordance for the disease in monozygotic, compared with dizygotic, twins. Certain genes, especially major histocompatibility complex class II and class III, are associated with the disease and with selected autoantibodies. C4AQO, a defective class III allele that fails to encode a functional C4A protein, is the most common genetic marker associated with SLE. Environmental factors that cause SLE to flare up are largely unknown, but ultraviolet-B light is one known factor.

Several drugs can cause a syndrome that resembles SLE, including procainamide, hydralazine, isoniazid, chlorpromazine, D-penicillamine, practolol, methyldopa, quinidine, interferon-α, and possibly hydantoin, ethosuximide, and oral contraceptives. The syndrome is rare, however, with all but procainamide and hydralazine. There is a genetic predisposition to drug-induced lupus, which is partly determined by drug acetylation rates.

EPIDEMIOLOGY

Women, usually of childbearing age, account for 90 percent of cases, but SLE can affect children, men, and the elderly. It is more common in blacks than in whites.

TREATMENT

There is no cure for SLE. Treatment is directed toward controlling acute, severe flares, and maintenance therapy. Arthralgias, arthritis, myalgias, fever, and mild serositis can be treated with nonsteroidal anti-inflammatory drugs (NSAIDs), including salicylates. NSAID toxicities such as elevated serum transaminases, aseptic meningitis, and renal impairment are especially frequent in SLE. The dermatitides of SLE, fatigue, and lupus arthritis may respond to antimalarials.

Life-threatening, severely disabling manifestations of SLE that are responsive to immunosuppression should be treated with high doses of glucocorticoids. Side effects of chronic glucocorticoid therapy include cushingoid habitus, weight gain, hypertension, infection, capillary fragility, acne, hirsutism, accelerated osteoporosis, ischemic necrosis of bone, cataracts, glaucoma, diabetes mellitus, myopathy, hypokalemia, irregular menses, irritability, insomnia, and psychosis. Cytotoxic agents (azathioprine, chlorambucil, and cyclophosphamide) can be used in patients with SLE to control active disease, reduce the rate of disease flares, and possibly reduce steroid requirements. Side effects of cytotoxic drugs include bone marrow suppression, increased infection with opportunistic organisms, irreversible ovarian failure, hepatotoxicity (azathioprine), bladder toxicity (cyclophosphamide), alopecia, and increased risk for malignancy.

Some manifestations of SLE do not respond to immunosuppression, including clotting disorders, some behavioral abnormalities, and end-stage glomerulonephritis. Anticoagulation with warfarin is the therapy of choice for preventing venous and arterial clotting in patients with SLE. Psychoactive drugs can be used when indicated, and renal transplant or dialysis may be indicated for patients with end-stage renal failure.

INTERNAL MEDICINE

PROGNOSIS

Survival in patients with SLE is 90 to 95 percent at two years, and slowly decreases over time to 63 to 75 percent at twenty years. Factors associated with poor prognosis include high serum creatinine levels, hypertension, nephrotic syndrome, anemia, hypoalbuminemia, and hypocomplementemia at the time of diagnosis, and low socioeconomic status. Most patients experience exacerbations interspersed with periods of relative quiescence. True remissions with no symptoms, which require no therapy, occur in up to 20 percent of patients.

VIRAL ENCEPHALITIS

A 38-year-old man is brought to the emergency department by ambulance. His wife found him at home "confused and sleepy" and when she tried to arouse him, he "started thrashing around, swinging his arms and legs." She further reports that he has had a fever, headache, and stiff neck for the past 2 days, and had become increasingly lethargic. She states that he has no significant past medical history, is taking no medications or illicit drugs, and has never suffered a seizure before. Examination reveals a lethargic, confused man who is not oriented to person, place, or time. Interview of the patient is difficult; his answers are unrelated to the questions and are at times incomprehensible. He appears to be speaking to people who are not present in the room. Temperature is 38.9 C (102 F), pulse is 110/min, respirations are 18/min, and blood pressure is 120/80 mm Hg. Neurological exam reveals no focal neurological deficits. Funduscopic examination reveals no evidence of papilledema. A lumbar puncture is performed and the results of the cerebrospinal fluid (CSF) analysis are below.

CSF

Opening Pressure	170 mm H_2O	(150–180 mm H_2O)
Total Leukocytes	3×10^3 /mL	(< 5/mL)
Differential		
Lymphocytes	98%	(60–70%)
Monocytes	2%	(30–50%)
Neutrophils	91%	(none)
Total Protein	93 mg/dL	(20–50 mg/dL)
Glucose	58 mg/dL	(40–70 mg/dL)
Gram Stain	No organisms seen	
Culture	Pending	

Serum

Glucose	104 mg/dL	(< 140 mg/dL)

DIAGNOSIS

The presentation of viral encephalitis is similar to that of viral meningitis, except that in encephalitis the brain parenchyma is involved in the infectious and inflammatory process in addition to the meninges. Viral encephalitis and meningitis both present with fever, headache, and meningismus. Additionally, patients with viral encephalitis commonly present with an altered level of consciousness, an abnormal mental state, and evidence of either focal or diffuse neurologic signs and symptoms. Focal or generalized seizures occur in more than 50 percent of patients with severe encephalitis. The range of presenting signs and symptoms for viral encephalitis is great; virtually every possible type of neurologic disturbance has been reported.

Examination of the CSF is essential in all patients suspected of having viral encephalitis unless contraindicated by the presence of severely increased intracranial pressure. The typical CSF fluid analysis for viral encephalitis is the same as viral meningitis and consists of a lymphocytic pleocytosis, a mildly elevated protein level, and a normal CSF fluid glucose level (compare to serum glucose—normal CSF fluid glucose is two-thirds that of the serum glucose level). A lymphocytic pleocytosis is critical for a diagnosis of viral encephalitis; 95 percent of patients with documented viral encephalitis have a CSF lymphocyte count greater than 5×10^3 per mL. The absence of this should prompt a careful search for other causes of encephalitis. A decreased CSF glucose level is atypical for viral encephalitis and should suggest the possibility of fungal, tuberculous, parasitic, leptospiral, syphilitic, sarcoid, or neoplastic meningitis. It is very difficult to culture viruses from the CSF in cases of encephalitis.

Patients with suspected encephalitis usually undergo imaging studies (computed tomography, magnetic resonance imaging) to help identify or exclude alternative diagnoses. These may demonstrate the existence of a focal or diffuse encephalitic process. The presence of focal findings is suggestive of herpes simplex virus (HSV) encephalitis.

The first step in the evaluation of a patient suspected of having viral encephalitis is to exclude nonviral (both infectious and noninfectious) causes. The most common illnesses that present in a similar way as viral encephalitis include vascular diseases; abscess and empyema; fungal, parasitic, rickettsial, and tuberculous infections; tumors; Reye's syndrome; toxic encephalopathy; subdural hematoma; and systemic lupus erythematosus. The next step is to distinguish HSV from any other possible viral causes of encephalitis, since a specific antiviral therapy for HSV is available (acyclovir). It is difficult to distinguish the specific viral etiology on clinical grounds alone, and HSV is identified or excluded by performing polymerase chain reaction on CSF fluid.

PATHOGENESIS

There is a multitude of viruses that has been reported to cause encephalitis; the most common include arboviruses, enteroviruses, HSV-1, and mumps; less common causes of encephalitis include cytomegalovirus, Epstein-Barr virus, human immunodeficiency virus, measles, and Varicella-Zoster virus.

EPIDEMIOLOGY

In the United States, there are approximately 20,000 cases of viral encephalitis per year. The season of the year, geographic location, travel history, age of the patient, and history of tick or animal bite are important clues that can help focus the diagnostic possibilities.

TREATMENT

Supportive care for viral encephalitis is indicated and is usually initially in an ICU setting. Patients require continuous monitoring of blood pressure and respiratory function. Seizures should be treated with standard anticonvulsant regimens and prophylactic therapy should also be considered, given the high frequency of seizures (> 50 percent) in patients with severe encephalitis.

Acyclovir, which is phosphorylated by viral thymidine kinase and inhibits viral DNA polymerase, is effective in the treatment of HSV encephalitis and may be useful in cases of viral encephalitis due to either EBV or VZV. Ganciclovir and foscarnet are effective in the treatment of CMV encephalitis. Ganciclovir is a deoxyguanosine analogue that is phosphorylated by viral kinases; it acts as a competitive inhibitor of CMV DNA polymerase. Foscarnet is a pyrophosphate analogue that inhibits viral DNA polymerases.

PROGNOSIS

There is a great deal of variation in the incidence and severity of sequelae in patients surviving viral encephalitis. In the case of Eastern equine encephalitis virus infection, approximately 80 percent of survivors have severe neurologic sequelae, but survivors of EBV, California encephalitis virus, and Venezuelan equine encephalitis infections rarely have serious sequelae. In cases of HSV encephalitis, even with treatment, neurologic sequelae are frequent, especially in those over 35 years of age.

ANTEPARTUM TESTING—BIOPHYSICAL PROFILE

A 36-year-old woman, gravida 4 para 3, with an estimated gestational age (EGA) of 37 weeks by menstrual dating and confirmed by ultrasound measurements at 17 weeks EGA, presents with complaints of decreased fetal movements for the past one day. She denies regular uterine contractions, vaginal bleeding, or leakage of fluid per vagina. This patient has had three prenatal visits over the course of her pregnancy. She is afebrile, with a pulse of 72/min, blood pressure of 95/55 mm Hg, and respirations of 18/min. Examination reveals a gravid abdomen at term. Pelvic examination shows the cervix to be long, closed, and posterior. Electronic fetal monitoring recorded over a 20-minute time period is shown below.

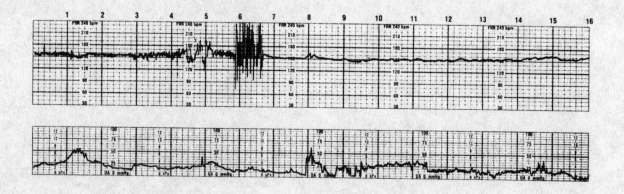

A biophysical profile is then performed.

Fetal Breathing Movements	2
Fetal Movements	2
Fetal Tone	2
Fetal Reactivity	0
Qualitative Amnionic Fluid Volume	2
Biophysical Profile Score	8/10

DIAGNOSIS

The biophysical profile measures five fetal variables over a period of 30 minutes and assigns a score for each (see chart below).

Biophysical Profile Components

Fetal Breathing Movements
Fetal Movements
Fetal Tone
Fetal Reactivity
Qualitative Amnionic Fluid Volume

Biophysical Profile Scoring and Interpretation

10	Normal Nonasphyxiated Fetus
8/10 (normal fluid)	Normal Nonasphyxiated Fetus
8/10 (decreased fluid)	Chronic Asyphyxia Suspected
6	Possible Fetal Asphyxia
4	Possible Fetal Asphyxia
0 to 2	Almost Certain Fetal Asphyxia

TREATMENT

The biophysical profile is thought to be a more sensitive assessment of fetal well-being than nonstress testing alone. For patients with a nonreactive NST and normal amniotic fluid volume who score above 8/10, fetal well being is reassured. If there is a decreased amount of fluid and the patient scores 8/10 or less, there is a suspicion of chronic fetal asphyxia and delivery must be considered. If it is a term pregnancy, delivery is indicated. If it is not a term pregnancy, the management must take into account fetal lung maturity as well as concerns of possible fetal asphyxia.

ANTEPARTUM TESTING—LATE DECELERATIONS

A 37-year-old woman, gravida 3 para 2, with an estimated gestational age (EGA) of 39 weeks by menstrual dating and confirmed by ultrasound measurements at 19 weeks EGA, presents with complaints of regular uterine contractions for the past 12 hours. She denies vaginal bleeding or leakage of fluid per vagina, and reports normal fetal movements. She has had an uncomplicated pregnancy, followed with regular prenatal visits since the first trimester. She is afebrile, with a pulse of 60/min, respirations of 18/min, and a blood pressure of 100/60 mm Hg. Pelvic examination shows the cervix to be partially effaced, 2–3 cm dilated, and anterior. A small amount of blood is noted on the examiner's gloved hand.

At the time of pelvic examination, an amniotomy is performed and a fetal scalp electrode is placed. Electronic fetal monitoring is shown below.

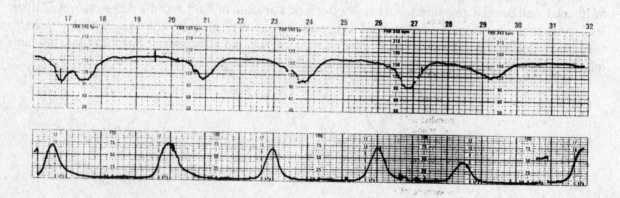

A fetal scalp blood sample is obtained and the pH is found to be 7.19

DIAGNOSIS

Fetal heart rate decelerations that follow uterine contractions (late decelerations) have been shown to be associated with uteroplacental insufficiency. This patient has demonstrated repetitive late decelerations secondary to spontaneous uterine contractions. After a finding of repetitive late decelerations, the next investigations would serve to assess fetal well-being. A fetal scalp electrode would be placed and a sample of fetal scalp would be obtained to get blood for pH analysis. The fetal scalp electrode, which measures fetal heart rate directly, is more accurate than the external fetal heart rate monitor, which uses Doppler ultrasound technology. The cervical exam in the setting of spontaneous regular uterine contractions indicates that the patient is in early labor. This patient is remote from delivery and is demonstrating signs of uteroplacental insufficiency and the suspicion of fetal compromise is high. The fetal scalp blood pH confirms this finding. A scalp pH of 7.19 is consistent with fetal acidosis secondary to asphyxia.

TREATMENT

Immediate delivery is indicated for this fetus (a scalp pH below 7.20 is an indication for immediate delivery) and an emergent cesarean section is required.

Fetal Scalp Blood Sampling

pH > 7.25	No Intervention
7.25 < pH > 7.20	Repeat fetal scalp blood sample within 30 minutes
pH < 7.20	Deliver

For patients who present with a fetal heart rate tracing such as the one shown above that demonstrates repetitive, late decelerations and for whom further investigations of fetal acid-base status are not possible (if the cervix is closed), emergent cesarean delivery is indicated.

ANTEPARTUM TESTING—NONSTRESS TEST

A 32-year-old female, gravida 1 para 0, with an estimated gestational age (EGA) of 38 weeks by menstrual dating and confirmed by ultrasound measurements at 18 weeks EGA, presents with complaints of decreased fetal movement for the past 6 hours. She denies regular uterine contractions, vaginal bleeding, or the loss of any fluid per vagina. Her pregnancy has been uncomplicated and she has had regular prenatal care since the first trimester. She is afebrile, pulse is 80/min, and respirations are 18/min. Examination reveals a gravid abdomen at term that is nontender. Pelvic exam shows the cervix to be long, closed, and posterior. Electronic fetal monitoring is as below:

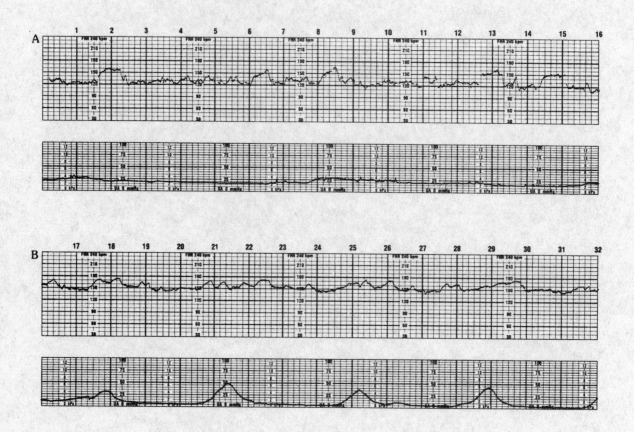

DIAGNOSIS

The evaluation of fetal well being is a critical process in the care of the pregnant patient. The nonstress test (NST) is the first screening measure used to evaluate fetal well-being. The patient is attached to an electronic fetal monitor that measures the fetal heart rate (Doppler) and uterine activity (tocodynamometer). The NST is interpreted as reactive or nonreactive. The criteria for a reactive NST is the occurrence of two accelerations of at least 15 beats per minute sustained for at least 15 seconds within a 20-minute period. Fetal heart rate accelerations are well correlated with fetal movements, even those that are maternally undetected. Lack of fetal heart rate accelerations can be a manifestation of fetal hypoxia.

TREATMENT

For this patient, whose NST was reactive, fetal well being has been assured. This patient should be given follow-up appointments and counseled to return if she detects decreased fetal movement in the future, but requires no further intervention.

PROGNOSIS

A reactive NST predicts good perinatal outcome in approximately 95 percent of cases. The predictive value of a nonreactive NST is low; the false positive rate exceeds 50 percent in most studies. A nonreactive NST must be followed by other methods of antepartum testing, such as the contraction stress test and the biophysical profile.

OB/GYN

ANTEPARTUM TESTING—FETAL HEART RATE PATTERNS (VARIABLE DECELERATIONS)

A 25-year-old woman, gravida 1 para 0, with an estimated gestational age of 39 weeks by menstrual dating presents with complaints of regular uterine contractions and a "gush" of clear fluid. Pelvic examination shows the cervix to be 100 effaced, 8 cm dilated, and anterior. The vertex is determined to be direct occiput anterior at 0 station. An intravenous line is placed and admission blood samples are obtained. Electronic fetal monitoring is shown below:

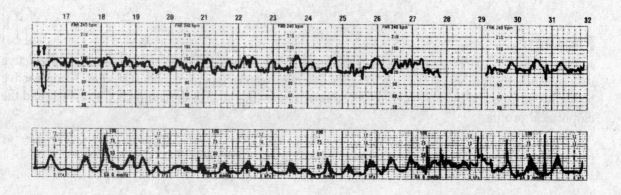

DIAGNOSIS

This patient is in active labor and demonstrating variable decelerations. Variable decelerations are variable in nearly all respects: duration, intensity, and timing relative to uterine contractions, and are usually the result of umbilical cord compression. Since cord compression most often occurs during uterine contractions, variable decelerations often coincide with uterine contractions, but may also occur during antepartum monitoring with fetal movement. There is an association of variable decelerations with oligohydramnios; cord compression events are more common when amniotic fluid volume is less than normal. The presence of variable decelerations is an indication for careful monitoring of the fetus, but does not necessarily present an indication for delivery. The variable decelerations need to be graded (mild, moderate, and severe) based on their size and duration and when they are present, other aspects of the heart rate tracing need to analyzed. A fetal scalp electrode should be placed to assess beat-to-beat variability, as the loss of variability is a concerning sign. The slow return of the variable deceleration to baseline is a sign of fetal intolerance to cord compression.

TREATMENT

The management of a laboring patient with variable decelerations requires the consideration of many factors. First, the quality of decelerations must be considered: their frequency, severity, and duration must be noted. Next, the overall variability of the fetal heart rate tracing needs to be assessed. An overall assessment of fetal well being needs to be made while considering the duration of the decelerations and the anticipated time of delivery. If the variable pattern has been occurring regularly for a significant period of time and delivery is not imminent, a more direct assessment of fetal well being must be obtained, such as fetal blood scalp sampling.

Since cord compression during uterine contraction is the cause of most variable decelerations, infusion of fluid into the uterine cavity can be attempted to reduce cord compression. Amnio-infusion is a technique in which a crystalloid solution (typically Ringer's lactate) is infused via an intrauterine catheter to relieve cord compression and the resultant transient interruption of umbilical blood flow.

CERVICAL CARCINOMA

A 48-year-old white woman, gravida 2 para 2, presents for a routine gynecologic examination. She has a history of genital herpes and has had four lifetime sexual partners. The patient has smoked one pack of cigarettes per day for the past 25 years. She has used oral contraceptives continuously for the past 15 years. Pulse is 72/min, blood pressure is 110/70 mm Hg, and respirations are 14/min. Speculum examination is performed. No active herpetic lesions are apparent, the cervix is without any gross lesions, and the vaginal mucosa is normal in appearance. A Papanicolaou (Pap) smear is performed. Bimanual pelvic examination demonstrates a nontender cervix, a mobile and normal sized uterus, and no adnexal masses.

DIAGNOSIS

The early diagnosis of cervical carcinoma is based on periodic cytologic screening of the cervix. The Pap smear is the standard method of screening for cervical carcinoma. In addition to detecting early cervical cancer, the Pap smear can also assess hormonal status and assist in identifying sexually transmitted pathogens such as herpes simplex, human papillomavirus (HPV), *Chlamydia trachomatis*, and *Trichomonas vaginalis*, as well as benign conditions.

It is recommended that a pelvic examination with a Pap smear be performed annually in women when they reach the age of 18 or become sexually active, whichever comes first. After a woman has had three or more consecutive normal examinations, the Pap smear may be performed less frequently in low-risk women. Pap smears should continue to be obtained yearly in women with one or more risk factors for cervical cancer (e.g., HIV or HPV infection, history of preinvasive cervical disease, or high-risk sexual behavior). A Pap smear should also be performed annually in women who have had a hysterectomy for pelvic cancer or *in situ* disease.

The Pap smear is easily obtained; with the cervix visualized, a plastic or wooden spatula is used to scrape the squamocolumnar junction and areas on the cervix or vagina that may look suspicious. In premenopausal women, the squamocolumnar junction is likely to be within the endocervical canal, and for this reason, a second specimen is taken from the endocervix with a cotton swab or cytobrush.

Colposcopy is most commonly used for evaluating the cervix in patients with an abnormal Pap smear. When the cervix is treated with 3 to 5 percent acetic acid, flat condyloma or dysplastic areas will turn white or develop a vascular pattern with a mosaic appearance or punctation. The squamocolumnar junction and transformation zone are thoroughly inspected, and a biopsy of the suspicious areas is performed. Nonpregnant patients with an abnormal Pap smear should also have an endocervical biopsy.

The most common symptom of cervical cancer is abnormal vaginal bleeding or discharge. Abnormal bleeding may take the form of postcoital spotting, metrorrhagia, menorrhagia, or postmenopausal spotting. Serosanguineous or yellowish vaginal discharge, frequently associated with a foul odor, may accompany an advanced or necrotic carcinoma. Pelvic pain may result from locally advanced disease or tumor necrosis. Extension of the tumor to the pelvic side wall may cause sciatic pain or back pain associated with hydronephrosis. Urinary or rectal symptoms can be associated with bladder or rectal invasion by advanced-stage carcinoma.

The physical findings associated with invasive carcinoma of the cervix are varied. Early lesions may be focally indurated or ulcerated, or present as elevated and granular areas that bleed readily on contact. More advanced tumors may be endophytic or exophytic. Endophytic tumors tend to develop within the cervical canal and produce an enlarged, hard, barrel-shaped cervix. Exophytic tumors have a polypoid or papillary appearance.

PATHOGENESIS

HPV is a likely etiologic agent of cervical squamous cell carcinoma, but while HPV is thought to be a component of neoplastic transformation, it is unlikely to be an entirely sufficient cause in and of itself. High oncogenic risk-type HPV viruses include types 16, 18, 31, 45, and 56. Cell-mediated immunity also appears to be a factor in the development of cervical cancer. Immunocompromised women may not only be at higher risk for the disease, but also demonstrate more rapid progression from preinvasive to invasive lesions, and an accelerated course once invasive disease has been diagnosed. Squamous cell carcinoma accounts for approximately 85 to 90 percent of cervical cancers, and adenocarcinoma of the cervix accounts for 10 to 15 percent.

Cervical intraepithelial neoplasia (CIN), also called dysplasia, refers to a lesion that may progress to invasive carcinoma. The significant features included in the criteria for the diagnosis of intraepithelial neoplasia are cellular immaturity, cellular disorganization, nuclear abnormalities, and increased mitotic activity. If mitosis and immature cells are present in the lower one-third of the epithelium, the lesion is designated as CIN 1. Dysplasia that involves the middle third is designated CIN 2. If it involves the upper third, it is designated CIN 3, and if it involves the full thickness it is diagnosed as carcinoma *in situ* (CIS). The natural history of CIN 1 lesions is that approximately 60 percent regress, 30 percent persist, 10 percent progress to CIN 3, and 1 percent progress to invasive carcinoma. The risk of CIN 3 lesions progressing to invasive carcinoma is at least 12 percent.

In invasive disease, the tumor cells commonly spread through parametrial lymphatic vessels, expanding and replacing parametrial lymph nodes and eventually replacing normal parametrial tissue. The lymph node groups most commonly involved are the obturator, external iliac, and hypogastric. When the primary tumor has extended beyond the confines of the cervix, the upper vagina is frequently involved and anterior extension through the vesicovaginal septum is very common. The most common areas for hematogenous spread are the lung, liver, and bone.

	Staging of Cervical Carcinoma	
Stage	Features
0	Carcinoma *in situ*, intraepithelial carcinoma
I	Carcinoma is strictly confined to the cervix
II	Carcinoma extends beyond the cervix, but not to the pelvic wall. Carcinoma involves the vagina, but not as far as the lower third.
III	Carcinoma has extended to the pelvic wall. On rectal examination, there is no cancer-free space between the tumor and the pelvic wall. The tumor involves the lower third of the vagina. All cases of hydronephrosis or nonfunctioning kidney are included, unless known to be due to another cause.
IV	Carcinoma has extended beyond the true pelvis or has clinically involved the mucosa of the bladder or rectum.

EPIDEMIOLOGY

In the United States, cancer of the uterine cervix is the sixth most common solid cancer in women after carcinoma of the breast, lung, colorectum, endometrium, and ovary. The mean age for diagnosis for cervical cancer is 52.2 years. Although the incidence of cervical cancer in the U.S. has declined significantly over the past 50 years, the rates among blacks, Hispanics, and Native Americans remain at least twice as high as those among whites. These differences are at least partially accounted for by the strong correlation between cervical cancer incidence and socioeconomic factors.

First intercourse before age 16 is associated with a two-fold increased risk of cervical cancer compared with that for women whose first intercourse occurred after age 20. The risk of cervical cancer is also directly proportional to the number of lifetime sexual partners. Cigarette smoking is an important etiologic factor in squamous cell carcinoma of the cervix; the increased risk for smokers is approximately two-fold. Long-term oral contraceptive users have about a two-fold increased risk of developing cervical carcinoma.

TREATMENT

Management of cervical squamous intraepithelial lesions depends on a combination of cytology, colposcopic findings, and results of directed biopsy. Cryosurgery, carbon dioxide laser, and loop electrosurgical excision are used in the treatment of cervical squamous intraepithelial lesions. Cervical conization can be both a diagnostic and therapeutic procedure.

Surgery and radiation therapy are the two therapeutic modalities that are commonly used to treat invasive cervical carcinoma. Primary surgical management is limited to disease that does not have obvious parametrial involvement. Radiation therapy can be used for all stages of the disease. Radical hysterectomy results in vaginal shortening and may be complicated by pulmonary embolism, ureterovaginal and vesicovaginal fistulae, and urinary dysfunction resulting from partial denervation of the detrusor muscle. Vaginal stenosis is the most common chronic complication of radiation therapy and is seen in up to 70 percent of cases. Radiation therapy may also be complicated by proctosigmoiditis, hemorrhagic cystitis, rectovaginal and vesicovaginal fistulae, or small bowel obstruction. Ovarian function is lost in virtually all patients who undergo radiation therapy. Chemotherapy is indicated for patients with extrapelvic metastases or those with recurrent disease who are not candidates for radiation therapy or exenterative surgery.

PROGNOSIS

Clinical stage at the time of presentation is the most important determination of subsequent survival, regardless of treatment modality. Overall survival is correlated with the degree of tumor differentiation. Large tumor volume is associated with decreased survival. Survival is inversely related to the number and location of lymph nodes metastases; survival decreases as more distant nodes are involved. With regard to histologic subtype, there is no difference in survival between squamous and adenocarcinomas, but adenosquamous histology is associated with decreased survival.

ENDOMETRIAL CANCER

A 67-year-old white woman, gravida 3 para 3, is 14 years postmenopausal and presents with complaints of several episodes of light vaginal spotting over the past month. She underwent an endometrial aspiration biopsy for a single episode of vaginal bleeding several months ago and the pathological report was "tissue insufficient for diagnosis." She has no significant past medical history and takes no medications. Examination shows a healthy-appearing thin woman with no abdominal or pelvic masses, atrophy of the lower genital tract, a mobile uterus, and no adnexal or cul-de-sac masses.

DIAGNOSIS

Postmenopausal bleeding should be thought of as endometrial adenocarcinoma until proven otherwise. Any bleeding in a postmenopausal patient should be promptly evaluated, although only about 20 percent of these patients are found to have a genital malignancy. Currently there is no reliable screening method for asymptomatic women, and postmenopausal uterine bleeding is the only common sign of endometrial carcinoma.

If bleeding is not present at the time of examination, it is not possible to prove that the bleeding is uterine in origin; vaginal atrophy combined with minor trauma can cause bleeding. However, postmenopausal bleeding requires a definitive histologic examination of the endometrium to rule out endometrial adenocarcinoma. If an endometrial aspiration biopsy is nondiagnostic, a more sensitive and specific procedure is required. Dilation and curettage, a blind procedure, is no more accurate than an aspiration biopsy. Diagnostic hysteroscopy and selected biopsy allows for visualization of the uterine cavity and a directed biopsy can be performed if necessary.

PATHOGENESIS

Endometrial hyperplasia occurs during periods of long-term, unopposed estrogen stimulation. The rate at which endometrial hyperplasia progresses to endometrial carcinoma has not been accurately determined, but the greater the degree of atypia, the higher the rate.

Approximately 80 percent of endometrial cancers are endometrioid, with 15 to 25 percent of these demonstrating squamous differentiation. Papillary serous and clear cell cancers each account for about 5 percent of endometrial cancers, but they have significantly worse prognoses than that of endometrioid adenocarcinoma. Approximately 5 percent of uterine malignancies are sarcomas.

EPIDEMIOLOGY

Endometrial carcinoma is the most common malignancy of the female genital tract; it accounts for approximately 7 percent of all cancers in women. In the United States, endometrial cancer will develop in about 1 in every 45 women during their lifetime. The vast majority of these malignancies occur after menopause, typically between the ages of 50 and 65.

There are many factors that increase the risk for developing endometrial carcinoma. Unopposed estrogen stimulation is a primary risk factor. The risk increases with higher doses of estrogen and prolonged use, but can be markedly reduced by the use of progestin and, in fact, the use of combination (progestin-containing) oral contraceptives decreases the risk of endometrial cancer. Conditions that lead to long-term estrogen stimulation, such as polycystic ovary syndrome and other feminizing ovarian tumors are associated with an increased risk of endometrial adenocarcinoma.

Endometrial Carcinoma Risk Factors	
Increase Risk	Decrease Risk
Unopposed estrogen stimulation	Ovulation
Unopposed menopausal replacement therapy	Progestin therapy
Menopause after age 52	Combination oral contraceptives
Obesity	Menopause before age 49
Nulliparity	Normal weight
Feminizing ovary tumors	Multiparity
Diabetes	
Polycystic ovary syndrome	
Tamoxifen therapy for breast cancer	

TREATMENT

The primary treatment for endometrial cancer is surgery consisting of the removal of the uterus, cervix, and adnexal structures. Surgical staging procedures, including careful exploration of the abdomen and pelvis and lymphadenectomy are often done at the same time.

Staging for Endometrial Cancer	
Stage	Description
IA	Tumor limited to the endometrium
IB	Invasion to less than one-half of the myometrium
IC	Invasion to more than one-half of the myometrium
IIA	Endocervical glandular involvement only
IIB	Cervical stroma involvement
IIIA	Tumor invades serosa and/or adnexa
IIIB	Vaginal metastases
IIIC	Metastases to pelvic and/or para-aortic lymph nodes
IVA	Tumor invasion of bladder and/or bowel mucosa
IVB	Distant metastases, including intra-abdominal and/or inguinal lymph nodes

Therapeutic options for patients with documented extrauterine disease (stages III and IV) include pelvic radiation, extended field radiation to cover the periaortic lymph nodes, whole-abdomen radiation, and systemic hormonal therapy (progestins) or chemotherapy. The most widely used chemotherapy agents include doxorubicin and cisplatin or carboplatin.

PROGNOSIS

Prognosis in endometrial carcinoma is related to tumor grade, tumor stage, and histologic type. Depth of myometrial invasion is an important prognostic factor that directly correlates with the likelihood of extrauterine disease. Advanced patient age at diagnosis is associated with a poorer outcome. Black women with endometrial cancer have a much poorer prognosis than do white women, even with correction for age and tumor stage.

ENDOMETRIOSIS

A 29-year-old woman, gravida 0 para 0, presents with complaints of painful menses and infertility. The patient, who is in a monogamous relationship, has been attempting to become pregnant for the past 2 years without success. In the past year she has experienced pain during intercourse. Her menses, which have become increasingly painful, occur regularly on a 28–day cycle, and usually last 5 days. Pelvic exam demonstrates tender nodules on the uterosacral ligaments bilaterally. The uterus is normal-sized and mobile. No adnexal masses are detected and the ovaries are freely mobile and nontender. A pelvic ultrasound is ordered and shown below:

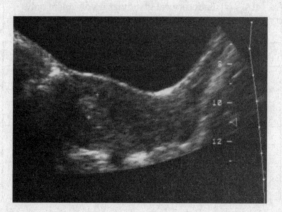

Ultrasound longitudinal view–normal female pelvis

DIAGNOSIS

Endometriosis is a common gynecologic problem in reproductive-age women, characterized by the presence of endometrial glands and stroma outside the endometrial cavity and uterine musculature. The common signs and symptoms of endometriosis are pelvic pain, dysmenorrhea, dyspareunia, abnormal uterine bleeding, and infertility. The type and severity of symptoms depend on the extent of disease, its location, and the organs involved, but even limited amounts of disease may cause significant symptomatology.

Although these symptoms are present in other gynecologic disorders, endometriosis should be suspected in any woman who has the classic symptoms of pelvic pain, dysmenorrhea, dyspareunia, abnormal menstrual bleeding, and infertility. No one constellation of signs or symptoms is pathognomonic of endometriosis. Many women with endometriosis are completely asymptomatic, and endometriosis should be considered in all reproductive-age women with infertility or an adnexal mass.

Clinical signs of endometriosis include localized tenderness in the cul-de-sac or uterosacral ligament; palpable tender nodules in the cul-de-sac, uterosacral ligament, or rectovaginal septum; pain with uterine movement; tender, enlarged adnexal masses; or fixation of the adnexa or uterus in a retroverted position. However, many patients with these clinical findings on pelvic exam later turn out not to have endometriosis. Direct visualization by laparoscopy is the optimal technique in diagnosing pelvic endometriosis.

The pelvis is the most common site of endometriosis, but endometriotic implants may occur nearly anywhere in the body. The most common sites of endometriosis, in decreasing order of frequency, are the ovaries, anterior and posterior cul-de-sac, posterior broad ligaments, uterosacral ligaments, uterus, fallopian tubes, sigmoid colon, appendix, and round ligaments. Other sites less commonly involved include the vagina, cervix, and rectovaginal septum. Uncommon locations include the inguinal canal, abdominal or perineal scars, ureters, urinary bladder, umbilicus, kidney, lung, liver, diaphragm, vertebrae, and extremities.

PATHOGENESIS

The histogenesis of endometriosis is poorly understood, but emerging evidence supports the causative role of retrograde menstruation and implantation of endometrial tissue. The incidence of retrograde menstruation is similar in women with and without endometriosis. Therefore, it is likely that other factors play a role. Factors might include the quantity of endometrial tissue reaching the peritoneal cavity, or the capacity of a woman's immune system to remove the refluxed menstrual debris. Direct transplantation is the probable explanation for endometriosis that develops in episiotomy, cesarean section, and other scars following surgery. Endometriosis in locations outside the pelvis likely develops from dissemination of endometrial cells or tissue through lymphatics or blood vessels. Another possible explanation for the histogenesis of endometriosis is that undifferentiated peritoneal cells undergo either spontaneous or induced differentiation into endometrial tissue, although there is no conclusive evidence that this takes place.

Anatomic alterations of the pelvis that increase tubal reflux of menstrual endometrium may increase a woman's risk of developing endometriosis. The incidence of endometriosis is higher in young women with genital tract obstructions that prevent expulsion of menses into the vagina, thereby increasing the likelihood of tubal reflux.

EPIDEMIOLOGY

The true prevalence of endometriosis in the general population is not known. The age at the time of diagnosis is commonly 25 to 35 years. Endometriosis is rarely diagnosed in postmenopausal women, and has not been found in prepubertal girls. If a patient has endometriosis, a first-degree female relative has a 7 percent likelihood of being similarly affected.

TREATMENT

The appropriate treatment of endometriosis depends on the severity of symptoms, the extent of disease, the location of disease, the patient's desire for future fertility, and the age of the patient. Minor pain due to endometriosis can be controlled with nonsteroidal anti-inflammatory drugs and/or analgesics.

Endometriotic implant growth is highly dependent on ovarian steroids. Medical therapies for endometriosis, which include oral contraceptives, progestins, danazol, and gonadotropin-releasing hormone (GnRH) analogues, are used to induce physiologic states mimicking either pregnancy or menopause in order to inhibit or delay progression of the disease. Progestins alone or in combination with estrogen induce a physiologic state that simulates pregnancy. Danazol and GnRH analogs induce a physiologic menopause-like state.

Surgery is indicated when the symptoms are severe, incapacitating, or acute, and when the disease is advanced. Surgery is preferred over medical therapy for advanced stages of disease with anatomic distortion of the pelvic organs, endometriotic cysts, or obstruction of the bowel or urinary tract. Women who are over 35 years of age, infertile, or symptomatic following expectant or medical management should be treated surgically.

For conservative surgery, which conserves the uterus and as much ovarian tissue as possible, laparoscopy is the preferred approach. Definitive surgery (which involves hysterectomy with or without removal of the fallopian tubes and ovaries) is indicated when significant disease is present and future pregnancy is not desired, or when incapacitating symptoms persist following medical therapy or conservative surgery. Perimenopausal women may be managed expectantly even when the disease is advanced, because endometriotic implants usually regress in the absence of ovarian hormone production after menopause.

Prognosis

Medical therapy with progestins, danazol, or GnRH analogues will ameliorate pelvic pain, but they do not enhance fertility. In most cases, surgical therapy at the time of initial diagnosis effectively relieves pain and may enhance fertility. If pregnancy occurs, regression or complete resolution of the disease is common. However, endometriosis is a recurrent disease, and definitive treatment, including the removal of pelvic organs, may ultimately be necessary.

HELLP SYNDROME

A 21-year-old white woman, gravida 1 para 0, with an estimated gestational age of 39 weeks is admitted to the labor and delivery suite with complaints of "leaking fluid" per vagina and "labor pains." Her admission blood pressure is 140/95 mm Hg and urine dipstick demonstrates 3+ proteinuria. Examination shows generalized edema and hyperreflexia. Pelvic exam demonstrates a positive nitrazine test; the cervix is dilated to 4 cm and fully effaced. Laboratory values show:

Hematocrit	28%	(37–48%)
Platelets	90,000/mL	(130,000–400,000/mL)
Prothrombin Time	12.1 seconds	(control—12.4 seconds)
Partial Prothrombin Time	27.2 seconds	(control—27.3 seconds)
Serum		
Bilirubin	1.4 mg/dL	(0.3–1.0 mg/dL)
Lactate dehydrogenase	700 IU/L	(100–190 IU/L)
Aspartate aminotransferase	90 IU/L	(0–35 IU/L)

DIAGNOSIS

HELLP syndrome is characterized by Hemolytic anemia, Elevated Liver enzymes, and Low Platelet count. It is important to recognize HELLP syndrome when it occurs and equally important to recognize that patients with it may be somewhat atypical in their presentation, occasionally not manifesting the hypertension or proteinuria until relatively late in the course of the disease. The most consistent laboratory finding in HELLP syndrome is thrombocytopenia (platelet count < 100,000/mL). It is sometimes difficult to distinguish between HELLP syndrome and other disorders associated with liver dysfunction or hemolytic anemias (e.g., idiopathic thrombocytopenic purpura, hemolytic uremic syndrome, gallbladder disease, and viral hepatitis).

EPIDEMIOLOGY

The reported incidence of HELLP syndrome in preeclampsia ranges from 2 to 12 percent and is present in 10 percent of patients with eclampsia. White women are more commonly affected by this syndrome than are black women.

TREATMENT

Patients with HELLP syndrome should be considered as having severe preeclampsia, regardless of their degree of hypertension or proteinuria, and the ultimate cure is delivery. Consideration of prompt delivery, regardless of fetal age, is warranted. Magnesium sulfate therapy is indicated. For patients remote from term and without evidence of disseminated intravascular coagulation, a more conservative approach can be considered. Patients must have their blood pressure, coagulation profiles, and platelets monitored routinely.

INFERTILITY AND ASSISTED REPRODUCTION

A 38-year-old woman, gravida 0 para 0, and her partner, a 40-year-old man, present for an infertility consultation. The couple has had regular intercourse without contraception for the last 18 months. The woman has never been pregnant and has used contraception regularly since she became sexually active. She reached menarche at 12 years of age and has had regular periods since the age of 15. She has no history of sexually transmitted diseases, no significant past medical history, and takes no medications. Review of systems is noncontributory. The man reports that he fathered a child in a previous relationship when he was 25 years old.

DIAGNOSIS

In general, if no contraception is used, a couple with relatively normal fertility will conceive within one year of regular coitus. No conception within one year of trying implies infertility, but if it is proven that conception is impossible, the proper term is sterility. Presently, the core infertility workup should include the following: semen analysis, documentation of ovulation, and testing of the anatomy and function of the female reproductive system. Therefore, infertility categories can be defined by three diagnostic test groups: 1) male gamete factor, 2) female gamete factor, and 3) female genital tract factors.

If the male partner produces no sperm, then azoospermia is the diagnosis, and the couple has sterility on the basis of male gamete factor. Compromises of spermatogenesis that result in decreased number, motility, or fertilizing capability of spermatozoa are much harder to define because of both the surprising fertility of some men with poor counts and the great variability in counts that is known to occur even in normal, fertile men.

The periodic shedding of an ovum is necessary for conception, and women who are physiologically anovulatory, such as prepubertal children, castrated women, and late postmenopausal women, are sterile. All available measures of ovulation in the clinical setting are indirect, including menstrual rhythm, basal body temperature, changes in cervical mucus, systemic symptomatology, ovulation test kits, endometrial biopsy, serum progesterone levels, and ultrasound monitoring of follicle growth and collapse. Therefore, since all tests of ovulation have some false-positive and some false-negative results, infertility caused by an ovulatory problem in reproductive-age women is difficult to define.

Female genital tract factors are easily evaluated. Cervical factor infertility, which is often suggested by poor sperm motility or poor sperm survival in cervical mucus after intercourse, can be assessed by a postcoital test (motile sperm present in cervical mucus). Assessment of the upper female genital tract, including the uterus, fallopian tubes, and peritoneal cavity, is most efficiently accomplished by performance of a single combined procedure of laparoscopy, hysteroscopy, and hydrotubation. Hysterosalpingography or saline infusion sonogram provides a useful adjunct in the assessment of the uterine cavity.

PATHOGENESIS

There is a large number of clinical conditions, both inherited and acquired, that can affect male gamete production, female gamete production, or the female genital tract. One measurable factor that clearly affects fertility is maternal age; marital age-specific fertility rates show a dramatic decline after 35 years of age and are essentially nil for a number of years before the median age of menopause. Much of this decline can be attributed to gradual alteration in ovulatory function; delay in childbearing also increases the risk of development of endometriosis and intercurrent injury, such as tubal occlusion and pelvic adhesions from pelvic inflammatory disease.

EPIDEMIOLOGY

Infertility is a common problem in the U.S.; about 2.5 million married couples (approximately 15 percent) are infertile. The number of infertile couples and the overall incidence of infertility in the U.S. have not changed significantly in the past several decades.

TREATMENT

Assisted reproductive technology (ART) is replete with many procedures, which are mainly variations on the standard theme of in vitro fertilization (IVF) and embryo transfer (ET). The steps of IVF-ET are 1) ovarian stimulation, 2) monitoring, 3) ultrasound-guided or laparoscopic oocyte retrieval, 4) IVF, and 5) uterine preembryo replacement. In addition to IVF, the various other technologies and their corresponding acronyms include gamete intrafallopian transfer (GIFT), zygote intrafallopian transfer (ZIFT), tubal embryo transfer (TET), intrauterine insemination (IUI), transuterine tubal insemination (TUTI), gamete manipulations, and intracytoplasmic sperm injection (ICSI).

The most common method of ovarian stimulation is pituitary down-regulation with gonadotropin-releasing hormone (Gn-RH) analogues, followed by high-dose gonadotropin stimulation. After appropriate ovarian stimulation has been achieved, Gn-RH and gonadal stimulation are discontinued and human chorionic gonadotropin is administered (as the luteinizing hormone substitute) to induce ovulation. Oocytes are retrieved by either laparoscopy or ultrasound-guided transvaginal aspiration. Gametes or embryos (after IVF) are then replaced by a variety of techniques.

Common Infertility Diagnoses and Treatments			
Diagnosis	Incidence	Diagnostic Tests	Therapies
Multifactorial	40%	Complete survey: Semen analysis, midluteal serum progesterone, laparoscopy or hysteroscopy with hydrotubation or hysterosalpingogram.	Treat one or more specific factors, IUI, GIFT, IVF-ET
Endometriosis	17%	Laparoscopy	Prospective observation, suppression with medication, or conservative resection
Male factor	12%	Semen analysis	Prospective observation or donor insemination, IUI, GIFT, IVF-ET, ICSI

Ovulatory dysfunction	11%	Midluteal serum progesterone, late-luteal endometrial biopsy	Directed therapies for endocrine diseases, clomiphene, human menopausal gonadotropin, or gonadotropin-releasing hormone
Tubal factor/pelvic adhesions	8%	Laparoscopy with hydrotubation or hysterosalpingogram	Laser laparoscopy or lysis of adhesions and tuboplasties at laparotomy
Cervical factor	1%	Postcoital test	Prospective observation, IUI, GIFT, IVF-ET
Uterine factor	1%	Hysteroscopy or hysterosalpingogram	Hysteroscopic resection, metroplasty at laparotomy
Idiopathic	10%	Complete survey: semen analysis, midluteal serum progesterone, laparoscopy or hysteroscopy with hydrotubation or hysterosalpingogram.	Prospective observation, empirical therapy with clomiphene or antibiotics, IUI, GIFT, IVF-ET

Prognosis

For the majority of infertile couples, infertility is correctable by either routine treatment or ART. Newer ART technologies, such as ICSI for males with severe oligospermia, cause dramatic improvement in couples diagnosed with several previously untreatable types of infertility.

MENSTRUAL DYSFUNCTION

A 34-year-old woman, gravida 1 para 1, presents with complaints of irregular menstrual bleeding. For the past 6 months she has experienced an increase in both the number of days of menstrual bleeding and menstrual flow. She says that her menses now last 8 to 10 days. The first 4 to 5 are productive of a very heavy menstrual flow and she needs to use in excess of 10 pads per day. She complains that she feels weak during the first few days of her menses and has had to miss several days of work each month. Her menses occur at regular 28-day intervals and there is no intermenstrual bleeding. She has no history of sexually transmitted diseases, is using condoms for birth control, and is sexually active with one partner, her husband. She has no medical problems and takes no medications. A review of systems is noncontributory. Breast exam reveals no masses. External genitalia are normal in appearance with a normal female hair distrubution pattern. Speculum examination demonstrates a parous cervix. Pelvic examination detects an enlarged, nodular, mobile uterus, with normal adnexa.

DIAGNOSIS

Menstrual dysfunction is a symptom of an underlying abnormality of the reproductive system. The abnormality may be developmental, endocrinologic, or the result of an acquired anatomic lesion. It may also be caused by ovarian failure, normally timed (menopause) or premature. The mean duration of menses is 5.2 days, with blood loss ranging from 35 to 43 mL per cycle. Uterine bleeding is considered abnormal if it occurs more often than every 21 days, lasts longer than 8 days, or is intermenstrual. Although excessive menstrual blood loss is defined as more than 80 mL per cycle, any menstrual pattern outside of a person's normal routine deserves investigation.

Abnormal Uterine Bleeding: Descriptive Terms	
Intermenstrual bleeding	Bleeding that occurs between regular menstrual periods
Menometrorrhagia	Bleeding that is excessive in amount, prolonged in duration, and may occur at regular or irregular intervals
Menorrhagia	Bleeding that is excessive in both amount and duration, at regular intervals
Metrorrhagia	Bleeding of usually normal amount but at irregular intervals
Oligomenorrhea	Bleeding at intervals of greater than 40 days that is usually irregular
Primary amenorrhea	The failure of menarche to occur before 16 years of age
Polymenorrhea	Bleeding at intervals of less than 22 days that may be regular or irregular
Secondary amenorrhea	The cessation of menses for at least 12 months in a postmenarchal woman

The evaluation of abnormal uterine bleeding should begin by excluding pregnancy as a cause. A complete history and careful pelvic examination must be performed early in the diagnostic evaluation of abnormal uterine bleeding. Abnormal uterine bleeding may be further evaluated by endometrial biopsy, transvaginal ultrasound, and/or hysteroscopy. Blind dilatation and curettage has an unacceptably high false-negative rate and fails to detect small but clinically significant lesions.

Amenorrhea, or the absence of menstruation, is not symptomatic of disease. The causes of amenorrhea can be categorized into four subgroups: 1) hypothalamic dysfunction, 2) pituitary dysfunction, 3) ovarian failure, and 4) anatomic abnormalities of the reproductive tract. Pregnancy must always be considered a possibility in women with secondary amenorrhea. As an initial screening test, a determination of serum prolactin should be obtained, because the level of this hormone is elevated in most women with amenorrhea caused by abnormal pituitary function. A detailed history and careful physical examination may uncover other signs or symptoms of pituitary disease that require the measurement of thyroid-stimulating hormone (TSH), growth hormone (GH), or adrenocorticotropic hormone (ADH) in the serum. In women with normal development of secondary sexual characteristics and primary amenorrhea, the pelvic exam becomes the most important element of the evaluation. If a normal vagina, cervix, and uterus are present, then hypothalamic, pituitary, and ovarian causes of the amenorrhea must be explored.

PATHOGENESIS

For successful reproduction, the human endometrium must receive and respond to appropriate hormonal signals that prepare it for embryo implantation. When conception does not occur, these hormonal messages initiate mechanisms that lead to the orderly shedding and controlled regeneration of this tissue. Menstruation is initiated by the precipitous fall in progesterone that occurs during the late luteal phase. About 70 percent of the total menstrual blood loss occurs in the first two days of menses. The establishment of hemostasis in the menstrual endometrium is achieved by the formation of hemostatic plugs by degranulated platelets and progressive vasoconstriction in the vasculature of the basal layer. At the time of menstruation, most of the functional layer of the endometrium sloughs and is replaced by a fibrinous eschar punctured by remnants of endometrial glands and the recently occluded spiral arterioles. The process of sloughing of the endometrium, clearing of the fibrinous mesh, and the total reepithelialization of the desquamated region is completed within 4 to 6 days of the initiation of menstruation.

The follicular phase of the menstrual cycle is a period of rapid endometrial growth induced by increasing ovarian estradiol production. The endometrium continues to increase in thickness throughout the follicular phase, with the superficial, or functional, layer as the primary site of mitotic activity. Endometrial depth is maximal in the late follicular phase, with further increase in thickness inhibited by postovulatory progesterone production by the corpus luteum. After proliferation of the stroma and glandular epithelium has halted, angiogenesis in the functional layer of the endometrium continues under the influence of progesterone. By the end of the luteal phase, a well-differentiated microvasculature has developed within the functional layer, consisting of spiral arterioles, capillaries, and venules.

Causes of Menstrual Dysfunction		
Dysfunction	Causes	Comment
Amenorrhea	Hypothalamic dysfunction	May be structural or functional. Includes congenital syndromes (Kallmann, Prader-Willi, Laurence-Moon-Biedl), systemic stresses (significant weight loss, excessive exercise, and severe emotional distress), and destructive processes or neoplastic lesions.
	Pituitary dysfunction	Amenorrhea may result from either a destructive process or a tumor creating pituitary dysfunction, or from pituitary tumors that secrete an excess of a particular trophic hormone. Amenorrhea secondary to abnormal pituitary function is frequently associated with elevated serum concentrations of prolactin. Psychomimetic and other drugs can induce mild hyperprolactinemia, resulting in amenorrhea. Hypothyroidism may also be associated with hyperprolactinemia. Hypopituitarism is associated with low prolactin levels and amenorrhea.
	Ovarian failure	Diagnosis of gonadal failure is made by serum FSH concentrations higher than 40 mIU/mL on two occasions. Hypergonadotropic hypogonadism is a heterogeneous disorder presenting with primary amenorrhea in about 15 percent of cases and secondary amenorrhea in the remaining 85 percent. Possible causes include, but are not limited to, Turner's syndrome, chemotherapy, galactosemia, and 17α-hydroxylase deficiency.
	Anatomic abnormalities	When the pelvic examination is abnormal, incomplete Müllerian development is the most likely cause. Other causes include imperforate hymen, transverse vaginal septum, atresia of the cervix, and Asherman's syndrome.
Abnormal uterine bleeding	Uterine leiomyomata	The finding of uterine leiomyomata in association with disorders of menstruation is exceedingly common. Pelvic ultrasound is useful for diagnosis and assessment of the number, size, and location.
	Anovulatory uterine bleeding	A symptom of an endocrine disturbance; the endometrium is chronically stimulated, inducing proliferation without secretory transformation and orderly shedding. In most cases it is associated with chronic oligoanovulation or polycystic ovary syndrome.
	Endometritis	Uterine tenderness and a history consistent with sexually transmitted diseases suggest the diagnosis. Endometrial biopsy is the most specific and sensitive test for determining the presence of this disorder.
Premenstrual syndrome	Precise cause unknown	Associated with alterations in mood, social behavior, and cognitive function. Occurs during the luteal phase of ovulatory menstrual cycles. Psychological disorders, including depression and anxiety, must be ruled out. The diagnosis can be made with the greatest accuracy by having patients keep a menstrual calendar and carefully recording daily symptoms.
Dysmenorrhea	Either of primary etiology or secondary to other conditions	Painful menstruation that may present as an isolated disorder or in association with other conditions. May be a symptom of endometriosis, cervical stenosis, endocervical polyps, and lesions of the uterine cavity. When it presents as an isolated disorder it usually occurs in nulliparous young women with a normal pelvic examination, in which cases the dysfunction is usually increased prostaglandin $F_{2\alpha}$ production by the endometrium. In cases associated with other disorders, therapy is directed toward the underlying cause.

EPIDEMIOLOGY

Menorrhagia occurs in 9 to 14 percent of healthy women, and most have normal duration of menses. The predominant cause of dysfunctional uterine bleeding in the postmenarchal and premenopausal years is anovulation secondary to alterations in neuroendocrinologic function. Ovulatory dysfunctional uterine bleeding occurs most commonly after the adolescent years and before the perimenopausal years. Secondary amenorrhea may occur at any time during the menstrual years. In about 10 percent of women, premenstrual symptoms are severe enough that medical attention is sought. Primary dysmenorrhea typically occurs before the age of 20.

TREATMENT

The successful treatment of abnormal uterine bleeding depends on an accurate diagnosis. In the case of bleeding associated with anovulation, a careful search may identify an underlying endocrinopathy. Treatment directed toward the underlying disorder usually results in the resumption of regular menses. When chronic anovulation is present, therapy must be preceded by an endometrial biopsy. In the absence of hyperplasia or neoplasia, cyclic oral contraceptives or progestins are uniformly successful. When abnormal uterine bleeding persists despite cyclic progestin treatment, a search for an anatomic cause must be initiated. Anovulatory bleeding occurring at the extremes of reproductive age requires specific treatment. The adolescent usually presents after many days of menstrual bleeding has failed to cease spontaneously. In this instance, the uterine bleeding arises from a denuded (rather than a hypertrophic and disordered) endometrium. Proliferation of the remaining endometrium with estrogen, not stabilization with progestin, is required.

Most cases of abnormal uterine bleeding due to anatomic causes can be treated either medically or by minimally invasive surgical techniques, avoiding hysterectomy. In the case of uterine leiomyomata, the therapeutic options depend on the number, size, and locations of the fibroid tumors. The hysteroscope is valuable in the diagnosis of anatomic lesions that affect the endometrial cavity, and is also a valuable therapeutic instrument.

Treatment of patients with amenorrhea associated with elevated gonadotropin levels involves estrogen replacement and therapy directed toward concurrent disorders. Women with secondary hypergonadotropic amenorrhea may be treated with estrogen-progestin replacement regimens.

The mainstay of treatment for premenstrual syndrome is the use of agents that suppress ovarian function, including oral contraceptive pills, GnRH agonist, and progestins. Simple interventions, such as exercise, alteration of diet, and the avoidance of salt, alcohol, and caffeine, may result in dramatic improvement.

The treatment of primary dysmenorrhea is either with nonsteroidal anti-inflammatory agents, which block prostaglandin synthesis through inhibition of the enzyme cyclooxygenase, or oral contraceptive pills, which inhibit endometrial prostaglandin synthesis by the action of progesterone and lessen and regulate menstrual flow. In cases of secondary dysmenorrhea, the underlying cause must be addressed.

PROGNOSIS

Excessive menstrual blood loss is the single most common indication for hysterectomy and accounts for significant lost productivity by the female population.

PLACENTAL ABRUPTION

A 27-year-old woman, gravida 3 para 2, at 32 weeks estimated gestational age, presents to the labor and delivery suite with complaints of painful uterine contractions and vaginal bleeding. Her pulse is 120/min, blood pressure is 80/40 mm Hg, and respirations are 22/min. Electronic fetal monitoring shows a fetal heart rate of 120/min. An external tocodynamometer demonstrates frequent uterine contractions. The uterine fundus is firm and tender. Transabdominal ultrasonography demonstrates a posteriorly implanted placenta with a large retroplacental clot seen; there is no evidence of placenta previa.

DIAGNOSIS

Abruptio placentae refers to premature separation of the normally implanted placenta before birth of the fetus. This most often takes place in the third trimester, but it can happen any time after 20 weeks of gestation. Frequently, the placental separation is an acute process that increases in severity over a few hours, but it can have a variable presentation. It may be self-limiting or may become quiescent and then recur. The placental separation may be complete or partial, or may involve only the placental margin. The latter is commonly referred to clinically as marginal sinus rupture.

The diagnosis of placental abruption is essentially a clinical one because no pathognomonic laboratory tests are available. The classic findings are vaginal bleeding, abdominal pain, uterine contractions, and uterine tenderness. Uterine contractions are characteristically of high frequency and low amplitude, with elevated baseline uterine tone. In 80 percent of patients, the abruption presents as vaginal bleeding, but in the remaining 20 percent, the blood remains trapped or concealed.

There are several serious complications associated with placental abruption. Placental abruption is the most common cause of consumptive coagulopathy during pregnancy. The major mechanisms are disseminated intravascular coagulation (DIC) and, to a lesser degree, retroplacental bleeding. Acute renal failure secondary to hypovolemia can occur in the setting of placental abruption. Pituitary necrosis (i.e., Sheehan syndrome) may also occur secondary to hypovolemia and resultant ischemia. Although the incidence of fetomaternal hemorrhage in patients with abruption is low, it is five times higher in women who have placental abruption secondary to trauma. Fetomaternal hemorrhage is associated with fetal and neonatal anemia, fetal cardiac arrhythmias, and fetal death.

The clinical manifestations vary greatly depending on the degree of detachment, and the diagnosis requires a high degree of suspicion. Ultrasonography is not very reliable for establishing the diagnosis of abruption; negative findings do not exclude life-threatening placental abruption.

PATHOGENESIS

Separation of the placenta is initiated by bleeding into the decidua basalis. The bleeding usually originates from the small vessels in the basal layer of the decidua, but it may be from fetoplacental vessels. The bleeding splits the decidua and spreads beneath the placenta, shearing it off. As a hematoma forms, it causes additional separation of the placenta from the uterine wall, with destruction and compression of adjacent placental tissue.

A number of etiological factors, such as maternal smoking, a short umbilical cord, uterine anomalies, advanced maternal age, daily physical work, and poor nutrition have been associated with some cases, but the cause is obscure in most patients. Maternal hypertension is the most consistently identified predisposing factor. Cocaine-induced transient hypertension is clearly associated with placental abruption. A direct blow to the uterus, forceful external version, placental site bleeding from a needle puncture at amniocentesis, and sudden decompression of the overdistended uterus are rare causes of placental abruption, but have all been implicated. Physical trauma, which complicates approximately one in twelve pregnancies, represents an important cause of abruption.

EPIDEMIOLOGY

Placental abruption complicates approximately 1 percent of pregnancies, is the most common cause of intrapartum fetal death, and accounts for nearly 15 percent of perinatal mortality. A history of placental abruption increases the risk of recurrence in a subsequent pregnancy by at least ten-fold.

TREATMENT

When abruption is suspected, management depends on the stage of gestation and the condition of the mother and infant. For less severe cases, especially ones in which the mother's condition is stable and the fetus is immature, expectant management is indicated. However, even with a mild abruption, the patient needs to be observed closely with external fetal heart rate monitoring. The severity of placental separation can progress, particularly after abdominal trauma. With any signs of maternal or fetal compromise, or if the patient is past 37 weeks of gestation, it is usually best to prepare for delivery. The immediate objectives of treatment are to restore blood loss, maintain constant surveillance of the fetus, and anticipate and treat clotting defects.

With greater degrees of abruption, a more aggressive approach and prompt delivery will be included in the treatment plan. Cesarean section is indicated in many cases, but vaginal delivery is possible in patients in whom there is no evidence of fetal distress and blood loss is not excessive.

PROGNOSIS

The effects of abruptio placentae on the fetus depend mainly on the degree of disruption at the uteroplacental interface. Permanent neurologic impairment occurs in up to 14 percent of surviving infants. Marginal separation may have no apparent effect, and intermediate degrees produce variable effects. In cases of complete or near-complete abruption, fetal death from anoxia is virtually certain.

PLACENTA PREVIA

A 19-year-old woman, gravida 2 para 1, at 33 weeks estimated gestational age, presents with complaints of painless vaginal bleeding. She states that the bleeding started approximately one hour ago and the volume is equivalent to normal menstrual flow. The patient reports normal fetal movement and denies feeling any uterine contractions. Maternal pulse is 104/min, blood pressure is 90/55 mm Hg, and respirations are 18/min. External electronic fetal heart rate monitoring shows the fetal heart rate baseline to be 130/min, with good variability. An external tocodynamometer does not detect any uterine contractions. Transabdominal ultrasound demonstrates a complete placenta previa.

DIAGNOSIS

Placenta previa is defined as implantation of the placenta in the lower uterine segment, with the placenta either overlying or reaching the cervix, usually in advance of the fetal presenting part. Placenta previa can be categorized into three types:

- Total previa: the internal os is entirely covered by the placenta

- Partial previa: the os is partially covered; expressed as the percentage covered at the time the diagnosis is made.

- Marginal previa: the placental edge reaches the internal os and may extend into the os as the cervix dilates. A low-lying placenta that is implanted in the uterine segment but doesn't reach the cervical os has similar clinical manifestations.

The mean gestational age at diagnosis is 32.5 weeks of gestation; about one-third of patients present before 30 weeks gestation and an additional one-third after 36 weeks of gestation, but it can occur as early as 20 weeks of gestation. Asymptomatic placenta previa may be incidentally diagnosed by routine sonography. Classically, placenta previa presents as painless vaginal bleeding in the third trimester. During late pregnancy, the lower uterine segment thins, and the softening cervix begins to efface and dilate. If the placenta is implanted in the lower pole, the size and margins of the implantation site become altered by these uterine changes. Bleeding can be precipitated by pelvic examination, intercourse, or labor. However, it often begins without any inciting cause; the patient may simply awaken in the middle of the night in a pool of blood.

Painless vaginal bleeding in the second half of pregnancy should be assumed to be placenta previa until proven otherwise, particularly if it is associated with multiparity, a soft uterus, an abnormal presentation, or a floating presenting part. Because more than one-half of patients who experience painless vaginal bleeding have placenta previa, it is of major importance to confirm it or rule it out.

Transabdominal ultrasound is the initial diagnostic technique of choice because of its safety and availability. Transvaginal ultrasound can be more instructive than transabdominal, but it must be used cautiously. Vaginal examination, although able to provide a definitive diagnosis of placenta previa, can provoke hemorrhage sufficient to endanger the lives of the mother and fetus. It should be performed only if absolutely necessary to make the diagnosis, and only after preparations for immediate cesarean delivery have been made.

Conditions occurring with placenta previa in up to 15 percent of cases include:

- Placenta accreta—abnormal adherence of the chorionic villi to the myometrium, associated with partial or complete absence of the decidua basalis and stratum spongiosum.

- Placenta increta—a form of placenta accreta where the chorionic villi invade the myometrium.

- Placenta percreta—condition in which chorionic villi have invaded the full thickness of myometrium up to or through the serosa of the uterus, causing incomplete or complete uterine rupture, respectively.

A ruptured vasa previa is a rare cause of bleeding in late pregnancy or during labor, and is often associated with placenta previa or multiple gestation. When there is velamentous insertion of the cord in the lower uterine segment, the umbilical vessels course through the membranes unsupported, in advance of the fetal presenting part, and extending across the cervical os. The vessels are commonly torn at the time of spontaneous or artificial rupture of the membranes. Fetal exsanguination can follow rapidly, and fetal mortality is at least 50 percent.

PATHOGENESIS

The specific cause of placenta previa is unknown, but a number of factors may affect the location of implantation in any pregnancy. These include abnormalities of endometrial vascularization, delayed ovulation, and prior trauma to the endometrium or myometrium. Multiple pregnancy predisposes women to placenta previa because of the increased surface area of placenta or placentas. In patients who have intrauterine synechiae or a scar from a uterine incision after such operations as cesarean section, hysterotomy, myomectomy, or metroplasty, it is quite common to find that subsequent placental sites include the area of the scar. There is a six-fold increase in the incidence of placenta previa in patients who have had a delivery by low cervical cesarean, regardless of whether the uterine incision was vertical or transverse. Placental migration occurs during the course of pregnancy and the earlier in pregnancy that sonography is performed, the more frequently the placenta appears to cover the cervix; many cases of placenta previa identified in the second trimester resolve spontaneously prior to term.

EPIDEMIOLOGY

The overall incidence of placenta previa in the U.S. is 1 in 200 births. It is more common in parous women, occurring in only 1 in 1,500 nulliparas and in up to 1 in 20 grand multiparas.

TREATMENT

All patients with significant bleeding should be admitted to the hospital, be placed at bed rest, and closely monitored. An intravenous catheter should be inserted, blood drawn for type and screen, intravenous fluids started, and serial vital signs and hematocrit levels checked. The status of the fetus should be evaluated with continuous electronic fetal heart rate monitoring.

The management of placenta previa is dependent upon the gestational age of the fetus, the amount of bleeding, and the condition of the mother and fetus. In the patient who is remote from term, expectant management is the treatment of choice. The goal is to extend the period of gestation long enough without compromising maternal health. Because nearly one-third of patients fail expectant management, the use of antenatal steroids to reduce the incidence of respiratory distress syndrome is indicated in patients presenting between 26 and 32 weeks of gestation.

Repetitive bleeding and transfusions may require emergency cesarean delivery at any time. In asymptomatic patients, a well-planned elective delivery at 36 to 37 weeks of gestation is indicated. Amniocentesis studies to determine fetal maturity can help inform the best time for delivery. Waiting longer than necessary invites possible episodes of hemorrhage that can endanger the mother and fetus.

Cesarean delivery has replaced vaginal delivery for all but a small number of patients with minor degrees of placenta previa. Unusual circumstances under which the vaginal approach might be considered include a dead fetus, major fetal abnormalities, a clearly previable fetus, active labor with engagement of the fetal head, and uncertainty about the degree of placenta previa.

PROGNOSIS

All types of placenta previa are associated with potential life-threatening hemorrhage during labor. The fetus is not usually adversely affected unless placental exchange is compromised by major placental detachment or maternal hypovolemia from blood loss. However, placental previa is associated with an increased incidence of congenital abnormalities and fetal growth retardation. Preterm delivery is the greatest threat to the infant, and the stage of pregnancy during which the first bleeding occurs is an important factor in perinatal outcome. The maternal mortality rate from placenta previa is less than 1 percent, and perinatal mortality is less than 5 percent.

PREECLAMPSIA—TERM PREGNANCY

A 19-year-old woman, gravida 1 para 0, presents to the prenatal clinic at 38 weeks estimated gestational age with complaints of a headache, "trouble seeing," and an inability to remove her rings from her fingers. Examination reveals nondependent edema of the face and hands, pitting edema of the lower extremities, and hyperreflexia. Her blood pressure is 150/100 mm Hg. The uterine fundal height is appropriate for the patient's estimated gestational age. Electronic fetal monitoring reveals a reassuring fetal heart rate pattern and no uterine contractions. Review of the patient's prenatal records demonstrates that the patient has gained 2.2 kg (5 lb) since her last examination two weeks ago. Urine dipstick shows 2+ proteinuria.

DIAGNOSIS

Preeclampsia is diagnosed as the developments of hypertension plus proteinuria or edema. Proteinuria almost always develops later than hypertension. Edema is a less predictive sign of preeclampsia since one-third of woman develop generalized edema by 38 weeks. Headache and visual disturbances are particularly ominous and a severe headache almost invariably precedes the first eclamptic convulsion. Blood pressure is the key diagnostic feature and the degree of hypertension is indicative of the severity of the disease. A sudden increase in weight is characteristic of preeclampsia and is due almost entirely to abnormal fluid retention. Hyperreflexia is characteristic of preeclampsia.

PATHOGENESIS

Vasospasm is the basic pathophysiologic mechanism implicated in preeclampsia and eclampsia. Vascular constriction causes resistance to blood flow and causes arterial hypertension. It is also thought that vasospasm exerts a damaging effect on the vessels, leading to the characteristic vascular changes in the liver, kidneys, and placenta seen in preeclampsia. Despite extensive investigation, the etiology of this disease is unknown.

EPIDEMIOLOGY

Preeclampsia is the most common hypertensive disorder of pregnancy. Preeclampsia is primarily a disease of nulliparous women and more commonly affects teenagers or women older than 35. It rarely develops earlier than 20 weeks of gestation, and when it does, is usually associated with a hydatidiform mole.

Risk Factors for Preeclampsia

Nulliparity
Multiple Gestation
Previous Preeclampsia-Eclampsia
Family History of Preeclampsia-Eclampsia
Preexisting Hypertension or Renal Disease
Diabetes
Molar Pregnancy
Nonimmune Hydrops Fetalis

TREATMENT

The cure for preeclampsia is delivery of the fetus. The age of the fetus is the critical factor in formulating a management plan. For women at or near term, induction of labor is usually indicated. This patient should be admitted to the hospital, have laboratory studies performed (complete blood count, liver function tests, serum creatinine), begin treatment immediately with magnesium sulfate, and labor should be induced (if vaginal delivery is indicated) or a surgical delivery should be performed (if cesarean section is indicated). Magnesium sulfate is necessary as an anticonvulsant prophylaxis during labor since clinical signs or symptoms cannot predict the progression to eclampsia.

PROGNOSIS

A number of organs and systems exhibit deterioration of function as a consequence of preeclampsia-eclampsia. The maternal hypertension leads to increased afterload and reduced cardiac output, and in extreme cases can lead to pulmonary edema. Women with preeclampsia tend to exhibit hemoconcentration, presumably secondary to generalized vasoconstriction. The extracellular fluid volume may be expanded beyond a level that is normal for uncomplicated pregnancies. Thrombocytopenia and reduction of plasma clotting factors may occur, and the function of the kidney, liver, brain, and retina may be affected.

Eclampsia may develop in neglected or fulminant cases of preeclampsia. It is most common in the last trimester and occurs more frequently as term approaches. The seizures are grand mal and may appear before, during, or after labor. Nearly all cases of postpartum preeclampsia occur within 24 hours of delivery. If the onset of convulsions occurs more than 48 hours postpartum, another diagnosis should be considered.

PRETERM LABOR

A 36-year-old woman, gravida 3 para 2, with an estimated gestational age of 28 weeks, presents with complaints of "cramps" every four minutes. Her prior obstetrical history is significant for a preterm delivery at 29 weeks estimated gestational age. The patient denies leakage of fluid per vagina or any vaginal bleeding. Her temperature is 37 C (98.6 F), blood pressure is 100/60 mm Hg, pulse is 80/min, and respirations are 20/min. Electronic fetal monitoring demonstrates regular uterine contractions and a reassuring fetal heart rate pattern. Examination reveals a negative nitrazine test. Cervix is dilated to 2 cm and partially effaced.

DIAGNOSIS

If the gestational age is between 20 and 37 weeks, the diagnosis of preterm labor may be made if there is evidence of cervical change or if the patient has regular uterine contractions occurring every ten minutes or less.

A critical factor in the diagnosis and management of preterm labor is determining if the membranes remain intact. Ruptured membranes may be caused by, or lead to, chorioamnionitis. A sonogram should be performed to determine gestational age and assess amniotic fluid levels.

PATHOGENESIS

In the majority of cases, the exact cause or causes of preterm labor is not known. The table below lists the main known causes of preterm labor.

Causes of Preterm Labor	
Spontaneous rupture of membranes	Spontaneous preterm labor is ccommonly preceded by spontaneous rupture of membranes. May be due to local infection.
Amniotic fluid infection	Up to one-third of the cases of preterm delivery are associated with chorioamnionic membrane infection.
Anomalies of conception	Malformations of the fetus or placenta increase the likelihood of preterm labor.
History of preterm delivery or late abortion	A woman who previously gave birth remote from term is more likely to do so again, even if no predisposing factor is identified.
Overdistended uterus	Polyhydramnios or multiple gestations increase the risk of preterm labor.
Fetal death	Death in utero remote from term is often followed by spontaneous preterm labor.

Cervical incompetency	An incompetent cervix can efface and dilate, not as a result of uterine activity, but because of an intrinsic cervical weakness.
Uterine anomalies	Uterine anomalies are uncommonly identified in cases of premature labor and delivery.
Abnormal placentation	Abruptio placentae and placenta previa are more likely to be associated with preterm labor.
Retained intrauterine device	There is an increased risk of preterm labor when an intrauterine device is present during pregnancy.
Maternal systemic disease	Severe systemic maternal disease may cause preterm labor and delivery.

TREATMENT

Prior to treating preterm labor, the physician must decide if a further intrauterine stay will be more likely to benefit or harm the fetus. Absolute contraindications to tocolytic therapy include fetal demise, lethal fetal anomaly, severe preeclampsia/eclampsia, severe hemorrhage, and chorioamnionitis.

Bed rest and intravenous hydration are always the first steps in treating preterm labor. Commonly used tocolytic agents include β-sympathomimetic agents (terbutaline and ritodrine), prostaglandin synthetase inhibitors (indomethacin), magnesium sulfate, and calcium channel blockers. β-2 agonists are also used frequently.

PRETERM RUPTURE OF MEMBRANES

A 22-year-old Asian woman, gravida 3 para 2, with an estimated gestational age of 28 weeks, presents with complaints of a "gush of leaking water" per vagina one hour earlier. The patient denies any vaginal bleeding or abdominal pain. Examination of the patient demonstrates a uterine fundal height consistant with the patient's estimated gestational age, temperature of 37 C (98.6 F), pulse of 86/min, respirations of 18/min, and blood pressure of 100/60 mm Hg. Sterile speculum examination reveals a pool of clear fluid in the posterior fornix. This fluid cause a blue change in color when applied to nitrazine paper and microscopic examination of the air-dried fluid shows "ferning" at low magnification. Ultrasound examination of the uterus demonstrates oligohydramnios. A digital examination of the cervix is not performed. Electronic fetal monitoring shows a baseline fetal heart rate of 135/min with spontaneous accelerations and no decelerations. No uterine contractions are detected by the tocodynamometer.

DIAGNOSIS

The diagnosis of membrane rupture must be considered in patients who complain of leakage of watery vaginal discharge. Preterm rupture of the membranes is defined as such prior to 38 weeks estimated gestational age. The fluid loss associated with membrane rupture may be sudden, producing a "gush," or may be gradual. The diagnosis must also be considered in patients admitted with preterm labor or ultrasound-demonstrated oligohydramnios. The patient must be questioned carefully regarding the timing of the loss of fluid, the color and consistency of the fluid, and if any odor was noted. Preterm rupture of the membranes can be confused with urine leakage (not uncommon in pregnancy), loss of the cervical mucous plug, or vaginal discharge associated with infection.

Nitrazine paper turns from yellow to blue when exposed to any alkaline fluid (pH > 7). Normal amniotic fluid pH is 7.0 to 7.5, while the normal vaginal pH is 4.5 to 5.5. False positives can result from alkaline urine, blood, semen, vaginal discharge caused by bacterial vaginosis, or *Trichomonas* sp. infection. Examination of dried amniotic fluid on a glass slide will demonstrate arborization ("ferning"). Ultrasound examination can help diagnose preterm rupture of the membranes, but a normal amount of amniotic fluid does not exclude this diagnosis.

In rare cases, usually in preterm pregnancies where the diagnosis remains uncertain, more invasive techniques can be employed, such as transabdominal injection of dye (indigo carmine, Evans blue, fluorescein) into the amniotic fluid. The use of methylene blue is contraindicated because of the risk of fetal methemoglobinemia. A tampon in the vagina can then detect any amniotic fluid leakage. Digital cervical exam is deferred in most cases because of the risk of ascending infection. Visualization of the cervix at the time of sterile speculum examination can usually provide sufficient information regarding the status of the cervix.

PATHOGENESIS

Most often, preterm rupture of the membranes is spontaneous and occurs for unknown reasons.

TREATMENT

The management of preterm rupture of the membranes is dictated by the gestational age of the fetus, the presence of documented fetal lung maturity, the presence of labor, and whether chorioamnionitis is present or suspected.

There are several issues that should be considered in the management of *preterm* rupture of the membranes but that play no role in the management of *premature* rupture of membrane. These are tocolysis, the administration of steroids (to enhance fetal lung maturity), and antibiotic prophylaxis. For preterm rupture of the membranes, the major concern is weighing the benefits of further intrauterine development against the risk of chorioamnionitis, which is the main risk of preterm rupture of the membranes for both the fetus and mother.

Amniotic fluid obtained from either the vaginal pool or amniocentesis should be sent for analysis of fetal lung maturity. The administration of steroids should be considered in cases of fetal lung immaturity. For this patient with no evidence of chorioamnionitis and a reassuring fetal heart rate patterns, conservative management, which would likely include prophylactic antibiotic therapy, is indicated.

PROGNOSIS

Preterm membrane rupture is associated with other obstetrical complications, including multifetal gestation, breech presentation, chorioamnionitis, and intrapartum fetal distress. As a consequence of these associations, patients with preterm rupture of membranes are more likely to be delivered by cesarean section. Patients with preterm rupture of membranes are very likely to develop spontaneous labor and deliver a preterm infant.

RAPE VICTIM

A 27-year-old woman presents to the emergency department with complaints of being sexually assaulted 4 hours earlier. She is sobbing in an uncontrolled manner and refusing to remove her clothing in preparation for physical examination. She is afebrile, pulse is 110/min, blood pressure is 110/65 mm Hg, and respirations are 22/min and shallow. Urine dipstick is unremarkable.

DIAGNOSIS

The evaluation of a rape victim requires compassionate care and the physician must carefully manage medical, emotional, and legal responsibilities. It is not the physician's responsibility to determine if a rape occurred and the documentation of the history and physical should be objective and nonjudgmental. A thorough history of the event, including specific acts performed, is required. A general medical-gynecologic history should be taken, including the last episode of consensual intercourse and if the patient has bathed since the attack. During the physical examination, swabs and smears of body fluids from any cavity penetrated should be collected for legal evidence. Gathering scrapings from the patient's fingernails and combing the victim's pubic hair are part of the routine evaluation of a rape victim. Specimens for *Chlamydia trachomatis* and *Neisseria gonorrhoeae* must be collected. Baseline serologic studies for herpes, hepatitis B, HIV, and syphilis should be considered and performed with the patient's consent. A urine pregnancy test should be performed to rule out an existing pregnancy prior to initiating any prophylactic treatments.

EPIDEMIOLOGY

Rape is a common act. Approximately 200,000 rapes are reported nationwide each year and this is likely to represent no more than 50 percent of the actual rapes committed. Victims are reluctant to report rapes because of embarrassment, fear of retribution, feelings of guilt, or a lack of knowledge of their rights. Sexual assault happens to people of all ages and races in all socioeconomic groups. Although the perpetrator may be a stranger, he or she is often an individual that is well known to the victim.

TREATMENT

The patient should be offered prophylactic antibiotics for coverage of common sexually transmitted diseases, typically a combination of ceftriaxone and doxycycline. Prophylaxis against pregnancy should be made available to the patient. Regimens of synthetic estrogens are effective if the attack has occurred in the past 72 hours. Acute crisis counselors are available in many emergency rooms and should be requested as soon as possible. The patient should be offered follow-up appointments for reviewing the results of the baseline testing and repeating the serologic studies.

In cases where the victim is a minor, most states require reporting of any possible or suspected child abuse. The responsibility for reporting rests with the physician.

RUPTURE OF THE MEMBRANES—TERM PREGNANCY

A 27-year-old woman, gravida 4 para 3, with an estimated gestational age (EGA) of 38 weeks by menstrual dating (confirmed by ultrasound measurements at 19 weeks EGA) presents with complaints of a continual leakage of clear fluid per vagina for the past 3 days. The patient denies any uterine contractions and reports vigorous fetal movement. The patient is afebrile, has a pulse of 80/min and respirations of 18/min. Sterile speculum examination reveals a pool of clear fluid in the posterior fornix and the cervix is long, closed, and posterior. This fluid causes a change in color to blue when applied to nitrazine paper and microscopic examination of the air-dried fluid shows "ferning" at low magnification. Ultrasound examination demonstrates a normal amniotic fluid volume. A 20-minute period of electronic fetal monitoring shows a baseline fetal heart rate of 140/min, with two spontaneous accelerations of 15 beats per minute over the baseline, each acceleration lasting more than 15 seconds. The tocodynamometer tracing is without evidence of uterine contractions.

DIAGNOSIS

The leakage of fluid from the vagina of a pregnant patient should be considered amniotic in origin until proven otherwise. After a careful history is obtained, a sterile speculum exam is critical to arriving at a diagnosis. Fluid obtained from the vaginal pool should be analyzed to determine its origin. Nitrazine paper turns from yellow to blue when exposed to any alkaline fluid (pH > 7). Normal amniotic fluid pH is 7.0 to 7.5, while normal vaginal pH is 4.5 to 5.5. Examination of dried amniotic fluid on a glass slide will demonstrate arborization ("ferning"). Ultrasound measurement of amniotic fluid volume is not always helpful in making the diagnosis of rupture of the membranes. It can be normal in cases (like this one) in which only a small amount of fluid has leaked out.

TREATMENT

The management of the term patient with rupture of the membranes (in the absence of labor) must take into consideration fetal well being. Once the diagnosis of rupture of the membranes is made, the next critical step is to evaluate the patient for any evidence of chorioamnionitis. Clinical signs of chorioamnionitis include elevated maternal temperature, fetal tachycardia, and uterine tenderness. Laboratory studies that are useful in assessing chorioamnionitis include maternal white blood cell count and differential, and analysis of fluid obtained via amniocentesis, which should include cell count and culture.

If there is no evidence of chorioamnionitis, other investigations to evaluate fetal well–being should be instituted, such as nonstress testing and biophysical profile. A plan of expectant management for term rupture of the membranes is reasonable when there is no evidence of chorioamnionitis and fetal well–being is reassured by antepartum testing. Induction of labor, if indicated, should be used in cases where the patient does not enter spontaneous labor, has evidence of chorioamnionitis, or if fetal well being is questioned. In cases where vaginal delivery is not indicated and the gestational age is certain, a cesarean section should performed after the diagnosis of rupture of the membranes is made.

Prognosis

Rupture of the membranes without spontaneous uterine contractions occurs in about 8 percent of term pregnancies. Patients with rupture of the membranes at term will begin labor spontaneously after 48 hours in 85 percent of cases. Prolonged rupture of membranes is associated with an increased risk of chorioamnionitis, puerperal endometritis, and neonatal sepsis.

SEXUALLY TRANSMITTED DISEASE SCREENING

A 23-year-old woman, gravida 0 para 0, presents with complaints of mild lower abdominal pain for the past five days, vaginal spotting, and a thick, yellow vaginal discharge. She reports taking oral contraceptives as her sole method of pregnancy prevention for the past 5 years and has had 7 sexual partners in that period of time. The patient's last menstrual period was normal and concluded one week ago. Temperature is 37.1 C (99.0 F). Examination reveals purulent vaginal discharge; tenderness on palpation and motion of the cervix; a small, nontender uterus; and normal adnexa. Microscopic examination of the vaginal discharge demonstrates many white blood cells, squamous epithelial cells, and many bacteria.

DIAGNOSIS

Patients with a history of multiple sex partners and no history of the use of barrier contraception are at risk for sexually transmitted diseases. Laboratory identification of the infectious agent is required prior to any treatment. A diagnosis of mucopurulent cervicitis can be made in the setting of gross visualization of mucopurulent material and the presence of 10 or more polymorphonuclear leukocytes per high-powered field. Cultures for gonorrhea and chlamydia, serological testing for syphilis, and HIV testing and counseling are indicated. Early pelvic inflammatory disease should be considered when acute cervicitis is present, but other signs and symptoms are needed to support this diagnosis such as fever, and uterine and adnexal tenderness.

PATHOGENESIS

Sexually Transmitted Infections			
Organism	Disease	Treatment	Comment
Bacteria			
Neisseria gonorrhoeae	Gonorrhea	Ceftriaxone or cefixime. Treatment for chlamydia given concurrently.	Can infect the urethra, Bartholin glands, and endocervix.
Chlamydia trachomatis	Chlamydiosis	Azithromycin and doxycycline are the most effective.	Obligate intracellular bacterium. Most often asymptomatic.
Treponema pallidum	Syphilis	Penicillin	Diagnosis confirmed with serology.
Haemophilus ducreyi	Chancroid	Azithromycin, ceftriaxone, erythromycin, amoxicillin/clavulanate, or ciprofloxacin	Gram-negative organism that forms a school-of-fish pattern when seen in the Gram-stain preparation. Painful ulcer with a ragged, undermined edge and raised border. Tender, unilateral adenopathy is common.
Calymmatobacterium granulomatis	Granuloma inguinale	Tetracycline, trimethoprim/ sulfamethoxazole, erythromycin, or the quinolones	Rare in temperate climates. Papular lesion ulcerates and develops a soft, red, painless granuloma.
Gardnerella vaginalis, G. anaerobes	Vaginosis	Metronidazole and clindamycin.	Overgrowth of normal inhabitants of the vagina results in a thin, homogeneous, fishy-smelling, gray vaginal discharge.
Mycoplasma hominis	Mycoplasmosis	Tetracyclines	Ubiquitous, but not highly virulent.
Ureaplasma urealyticum	Mycoplasmosis	Tetracyclines	Ubiquitous, but not highly virulent.
Viruses			
Herpesvirus hominis (herpes simplex virus)	Genital herpes	Oral acyclovir or valacyclovir	Latent HSV localizes in the sacral ganglion and most patients develop secondary (recurrent) infections.
Cytomegalovirus (CMV)	CMV infection	Treatment dependent upon severity of infection and sequelae.	Systemic illness

Hepatitis B virus	Hepatitis B	Treatment dependent upon severity of infection and sequelae.	Systemic illness
Human papillomavirus	Condyloma acuminatum	Cryotherapy, or topical application of podophyllin, podofilox, or trichloroacetic acid.	DNA virus, over seventy types identified. Recurrence occurs in about 50 percent of cases despite treatment.
Molluscum contagiosum virus	Molluscum contagiosum	Usually a self-limited disease, Liquid nitrogen or cantharidin can be applied directly to the lesion.	DNA poxvirus. Discrete, pearly, skin-colored, dome-shaped, smooth papules that have a central umbilication from which a plug of cheesy material can be expressed.
Human immunodeficiency virus	Acquired immunodeficiency syndrome	Treatment dependent upon severity of infection and sequelae.	Systemic illness
Protozoa			
Trichomonas vaginalis	Vaginitis	Metronidazole	Causes a profuse, yellow, malodorous, often uncomfortable vaginal discharge. Motile trichomonads are demonstrated on saline wet-mount smear.
Fungi			
Candida albicans	Vaginitis	Local vaginal therapy with miconazole, clotrimazole, butoconazole, tioconazole, or terconazole. Oral treatment with fluconazole or itraconazole.	Causes vulvar and vaginal pruritus with red vaginal walls that contain adherent, dry, white, curdy plaques. Risk factors include pregnancy, diabetes, and the use of immunosuppressive drugs and broad-spectrum antibiotics.
Acarids			
Sarcoptes scabiei	Scabies	5 percent permethrin cream	Human itch mite, one of the most common causes of itching dermatoses throughout the world.
Phthirus pubis	Pediculosis pubis	1 percent permethrin cream	Pubic lice, intensely pruritic.

The cervix may become infected by a wide variety of viral, protozoal, and fungal organisms. All of the sexually transmitted diseases may produce ulcerative lesions of the cervix. The most common infections of the cervix are caused by *Neisseria gonorrhoeae*, *Chlamydia trachomatis*, genital herpes, and human papillomavirus. *C. trachomatis* is the cause of a mucopurulent cervicitis in most women.

EPIDEMIOLOGY

The female reproductive tract is susceptible to a large number of infectious agents, and sexually transmitted infections are common.

TREATMENT

Treatment is not warranted before the results of the screening tests for the most common sexually transmitted diseases are available. Follow-up should be soon after the initial presentation and, if treatment is warranted, further timely reevaluations are indicated to monitor response because of the risk of a progressive, ascending infection. The treatment for gonorrhea is a single intramuscular injection of ceftriaxone. The treatment for chlamydia is oral doxycycline. The treatment of syphilis is benzathine penicillin. After identification of the infectious organism(s), treatment of sexual partners is indicated.

PROGNOSIS

The impact of sexually transmitted diseases on the physical condition of women ranges from minor annoyance to serious illness and, in some instances, even death.

ACUTE BRONCHIOLITIS

A 6-month-old female infant is brought to the emergency room by her parents, who are concerned about her difficulty breathing. The parents report that the infant had a "cold" with a "runny nose," fever, and slight cough for the past three days, but in the last 24 hours the cough has gotten worse and she has had difficulty breathing for the past few hours. The parents also note that she has not been interested in food for the past 24 hours. Temperature is 38.5 C (101.3 F), heart rate is 112/min, and respirations are 70/min. Examination reveals a tachypneic infant in extreme respiratory distress. A paroxysmal, wheezy cough accompanies almost every respiration. Auscultation of the chest demonstrates fine crackles bilaterally and a prolonged expiratory phase with wheezing and cough. A chest roentgenogram reveals hyperinflation of the lungs and an increased anteroposterior diameter on lateral view. Leukocyte count is normal.

DIAGNOSIS

The diagnosis of bronchiolitis is based on clinical findings, but the principal agent, respiratory syncytial virus (RSV), may be identified in nasopharyngeal secretions by culture or antigen assay. Asthma is the condition most commonly confused with acute bronchiolitis. Asthma typically has a recurrent pattern and is responsive to bronchodilators. Pneumonia is typically associated with an infiltrate on chest roentgenogram and if it is bacterial in origin, will present with an elevated white blood cell count. In acute bronchiolitis, the white blood cell count is usually normal. Children with bronchiolitis typically have decreased feeding secondary to the respiratory distress; the child cannot stop respiratory efforts long enough to feed adequately.

PATHOGENESIS

Acute bronchiolitis is characterized by bronchiolar obstruction due to edema and mucus accumulation. The obstruction increases air resistance in small air passages during inspiration and expiration, but because the radius of an airway is reduced during expiration, the result is air trapping and overinflation. The resulting ventilation/perfusion mismatch results in hypoxemia.

EPIDEMIOLOGY

Bronchiolitis is common among young children. Approximately 10 to 15 percent of children experience this illness in the first year of life. The majority of cases occur in the winter and spring when the associated viral agents are most prevalent in the community.

TREATMENT

The management of the child with bronchiolitis depends on the severity of the illness. Infants with respiratory distress should be hospitalized, but only supportive treatment is indicated. Approximately 5 percent of children require hospitalization. Supportive measures appropriate for acute bronchiolitis include administration of oral or intravenous fluids, antipyretic agents, and supplemental humidified oxygen if indicated.

Ribavirin aerosol, an antiviral agent, should be considered in high-risk patients, such as those with preexisting congenital heart disease or bronchopulmonary dysplasia. Antibiotic therapy is not indicated unless there is secondary bacterial pneumonia. Corticosteroids are not beneficial and may be harmful under certain conditions. Bronchodilators may be beneficial and a trial course of treatment should be attempted in seriously ill children.

PROGNOSIS

The most critical phase of the illness is within the first 72 hours after the onset of cough and dyspnea. After this critical period, recovery is complete within a few days. The case fatality rate is below 1 percent.

ACUTE EPIGLOTTIDITIS

A 3-year-old female child is brought to the emergency room by her parents, who report that she has had a fever and sore throat for the past 24 hours and, within the last thirty minutes, has developed difficulty breathing. Temperature is 39.4 C (103 F), pulse is 110/min, respirations are 20/min, and blood pressure is 100/60 mm Hg. Examination reveals inspiratory stridor, flaring of the alae nasi, and inspiratory retractions of the suprasternal notch, supraclavicular and intercostal spaces, and subcostal area. Oropharyngeal exam reveals an inflamed pharynx. A lateral roentgenogram of the upper airway is obtained and suggests a swollen epiglottis.

DIAGNOSIS

Acute epiglottiditis is a dramatic, potentially lethal syndrome of upper airway obstruction. Epiglottiditis is characterized by a fulminating course of high fever, sore throat, dyspnea, and rapidly progressive respiratory obstruction. Within a matter of hours, it may progress to complete obstruction of the airway and death unless adequate treatment is provided. The causative agent is almost always bacterial, and is typically due to *Haemophilus influenzae*, type b.

The differential diagnosis for patients with suspected upper airway obstruction include severe croup, bacterial tracheitis, foreign body aspiration, and retropharyngeal and peritonsillar abscess. Confirmation of the diagnosis requires direct observation of the inflamed and swollen supraglottic structures and a cherry-red, enlarged epiglottis. This examination should be performed in an operating room by physicians skilled in endotracheal intubation and tracheostomy, since an instrument-assisted examination of the pharynx in patients with epiglottiditis may induce a reflex laryngospasm. A roentgenogram of the upper airway can be helpful in demonstrating either the presence or absence of an enlarged epiglottis prior to direct examination under controlled conditions.

PATHOGENESIS

The bacterial infection causes intense inflammation of the epiglottis and sometimes the surrounding area as well, including the arytenoids and arytenoepiglottic folds, vocal cords, and subglottic area.

EPIDEMIOLOGY

Acute epiglottiditis usually occurs in children 2 to 7 years old. The peak incidence occurs at about 3.5 years of age. The incidence of acute epiglottiditis has been reduced dramatically due to the usage of the *Haemophilus influenzae* type b vaccine (Hib vaccine).

TREATMENT

All patients with the diagnosis of epiglottiditis must have an artificial airway established by either nasotracheal intubation, or less often by tracheostomy, regardless of the degree of apparent respiratory

PEDIATRICS

distress. As many as 6 percent of children with epiglottiditis who do not receive an artificial airway die, compared to less than 1 percent of those who do. Antibiotic therapy suitable for *Haemophilus influenzae*, including cefotaxime, ceftriaxone, or ampicillin with sulbactam, must be instituted immediately. Children with suspected epiglottiditis should not be placed in the supine position because of the risk of gravity-induced change in the position of the epiglottiditis. Patients with suspected epiglottis should be attended by a physician and have intubation equipment on hand at all times.

PROGNOSIS

With adequate treatment, the illness rarely lasts more than 2 to 3 days. No clinical features have been recognized that predict fatality.

ATTEMPTED SUICIDE

A 17-year-old female is brought to the emergency department by ambulance after a suicide attempt. The patient's mother called the ambulance after finding her daughter in the bathroom vomiting repeatedly. She described her daughter's appearance as "white as a ghost and sweating like a pig." In the bathroom, the mother found an empty bottle of acetaminophen and a "suicide note," in which the patient made mention of her parents' impending divorce as a motivating factor in her decision to "end the pain." The patient's mother reports that her daughter has been staying out late without permission lately and has come home visibly intoxicated on a number of occasions. The patient's school attendance and performance has worsened noticeably in the past six months.

A nasogastric tube is placed and gastric lavage is performed. Activated charcoal is administered. Acetylcysteine treatment is initiated. Serum bilirubin, transaminase activity, acetaminophen levels, and prothrombin time measurement are pending.

DIAGNOSIS

Threats or attempts of suicide should be taken seriously and seen as acts communicating desperation. It is difficult to assess the seriousness of the intent by the actual potency of the method. Other factors to be considered are the extent of premeditation and the likelihood of rescue. Leaving a suicide note is evidence of premeditation and a sign of seriousness of intent. The majority of suicide attempts are impulsive, with two-thirds of attempters reporting that they had thought about the act for less than one hour beforehand. Any attempt or gesture should be regarded as serious, regardless of the apparent seriousness of the intent, since most successful suicides occur among persons who have made earlier attempts or gestures. The most common method of attempting suicide by adolescents is the ingestion of medication. Firearms serve as the major method of death in adolescent suicide, with carbon monoxide and medication overdoses also being common. Males are more likely to use violent methods. Among preadolescents, jumping from heights is the most common method, followed by self-poisoning, hanging, stabbing, and running into traffic.

Among adolescents who commit suicide, three-quarters report difficulties with one or both parents. The families of adolescents who attempt suicide are more likely to have existing marital difficulties and child abuse. Alcohol intoxication is a prominent factor in adolescent suicide.

EPIDEMIOLOGY

Over the past two decades, the overall suicide rate has remained stable, but the rate for 15- to 24-year-olds has increased two- to three-fold. Females aged 15 to 19 have the highest rate of suicide attempts, up to 1 in 100 may attempt each year. Male adolescents outnumber females in completed suicides. In the U.S., suicide is the third leading cause of death for all adolescents, and among white adolescents it is second. Overall, suicide accounts for 10 percent of all deaths among adolescents. Native American teenagers have the highest risk, followed by white males. Black females have the lowest risk among adolescents. Suicide is rare under the age of 10 and only 1 percent of suicides occur in those younger than age 15.

TREATMENT

The management of patients who attempt suicide includes an assessment for any precipitating life events prior to the attempt, psychotherapeutic help to enable the patient to deal with crisis, and preventive measures to help the patient prevent or cope with subsequent crises. The physician assessing the suicidal behavior of an adolescent should carefully explore the 48 to 72 hours of the patient's life that preceded the suicide attempt. The degree of premeditation or impulsivity must be assessed. It is critical to understand whether the patient intended to be stopped or discovered before the attempt was completed. Consultation with a psychiatrist is essential in the evaluation of patients who attempt suicide.

Up to 10 percent of patients who attempt suicide require inpatient psychiatric care. Indications for inpatient psychiatric admission include patients with serious psychiatric disorders, those at risk of suicide or another attempt, and those who need to be removed from a stressful environment that is likely to precipitate another attempt.

PROGNOSIS

Approximately 40 percent of patients who attempt suicide have made a previous attempt, and between 13 and 35 percent of attempters will make another attempt in the next 2 years. There are factors that may be helpful in identifying people at risk for making another suicide attempt: problems with alcohol, the diagnosis of antisocial personality disorder, previous inpatient or outpatient psychiatric treatment, a previous suicide attempt that led to an admission, and living alone. Depression and general psychopathological factors are related to completed suicides.

ATTENTION DEFICIT/HYPERACTIVITY DISORDER

A 4-year-old boy is brought by his parents for an evaluation of his hyperactivity. The child's parents describe him as restless, easily distracted, and poorly behaved. He is often impulsive and refuses to follow instructions. His preschool teacher has had a great deal of trouble controlling him and has told his parents that if his behavior does not improve, he will not be able to stay in the class. The child has no significant medical history and takes no medications. He is sitting quietly next to his parents during the interview.

DIAGNOSIS

Attention deficit/hyperactivity disorder (ADHD) is characterized by poor ability to attend to a task, motor overactivity, and impulsivity. Children with this disorder are fidgety, have difficulty remaining in their seats in school, are easily distracted, find it hard to waiting their turn, impulsively blurt out answers to questions, have difficulty following instructions and sustaining attention, shift rapidly from one uncompleted activity to another, talk excessively, intrude on others, often seem not to listen to what is being said, lose items regularly, and often engage in physically dangerous activities without considering possible consequences. They often provoke others to anger and rarely learn from their mistakes.

Laboratory studies do not establish the diagnosis of ADHD. During examination of a child who is said to be hyperactive, it is not uncommon for signs and symptoms to be absent. Many hyperactive children are able to suppress characteristic behavior in a structured situation. Children in whom attention deficit problems are suspected should be evaluated for conduct disorder problems and learning disabilities. Sensory impairment, particularly auditory impairment, should be investigated in children who present with difficulty concentrating. Petit mal epilepsy should be ruled out, because it can mimic the concentration and attention problems seen in children with ADHD. Various medications (antipsychotics, anticonvulsants) may also cause overactivity and attention problems. Children with anxiety, dysthymic, and depressive disorders may show increased activity and social disturbances similar to those seen in ADHD. Gilles de la Tourette syndrome may coexist with ADHD.

PATHOGENESIS

The cause of ADHD is poorly understood. Children with ADHD differ from normal children in terms of cognitive style, levels and types of arousal, and response to rewards. ADHD, developmental disorders, alcohol abuse, conduct disorder, and antisocial personality disorder have all been shown to be more common in first-degree relatives of children with ADHD than in the general population.

EPIDEMIOLOGY

The prevalence of ADHD in the U.S. is approximately 1.5 to 4 percent. The syndrome is four to six times more likely to occur in males than females. In about half the cases, the age of onset occurs before 4 years of age.

TREATMENT

A comprehensive program is needed to lend structure to the child's environment and decrease the effects of the handicap by helping with academic and social learning. Formal operant conditioning techniques that reward the child with stars or tokens contingent on improved behavior are often helpful. Children should have a regular daily routine that they are expected to follow and for which they are rewarded with praise. Rules should be simple, clear, and as few in number as possible, and they should be coupled with firm limits that are enforced fairly and sympathetically through restrictions and deprivation for transgressions. Overstimulation and fatigue should be avoided. Behavior therapy is a more effective treatment than pharmacotherapy for the aggressive behaviors seen in children with ADHD.

Stimulant medications should be used only as a part of an ongoing treatment plan of behavioral and psychosocial therapy that involves the child, the parents, and the school. Methylphenidate, dextroamphetamine, pemoline, and various tricyclic antidepressants are efficacious in reducing overactivity, increasing attention span, and improving interaction between the child and other family members. But despite short-term improvements with stimulant medications, there is little evidence that stimulants improve retention, retrieval of information, or control of anger. Stimulant drugs can cause complications such as increased nervousness and jitteriness, and major short-term side effects include anorexia, upper abdominal pain, and difficulty sleeping. Long-term stimulant side effects may include increased heart rate and growth suppression. The growth of children receiving stimulants should be monitored, and drug-free holidays should be employed.

PROGNOSIS

Although hyperactivity may be short-lived, other symptoms of ADHD may persist into later life. The most predictive symptom of later psychopathologic conditions is the presence of aggression in childhood. Children with ADHD who are treated with multiple therapies (i.e., medications, psychotherapy, and parent counseling) are less likely to be delinquent in adolescence. Up to 25 percent of children with ADHD do not respond positively to stimulant medications.

AUTISTIC DISORDER

A 4-year-old boy with autistic disorder is brought by his parents for a routine evaluation. He does not respond to your verbal commands. He is holding a one-foot length of yellow plastic rope, which he is waving around in circles. His parents note that he has been playing with this same plastic rope for the past year and has no interest in any other toys. It is difficult to examine the boy because he will not stay in one place and is grabbing at things around him, attempting to put them in his mouth. He repeatedly spits saliva on his hands and rubs the saliva on any objects within his reach. His parents report that he has been very difficult to mange and want to know if this behavior is likely to get better on its own, or if there are any treatments available.

DIAGNOSIS

Autistic disorder develops before 30 months of age and is characterized by a qualitative impairment in verbal and nonverbal communication, in imaginative activity, and in reciprocal social interactions. Among the most notable symptoms and signs are nondeveloped or poorly developed verbal and nonverbal communication skills, abnormalities in speech patterns, impaired ability to sustain a conversation, abnormal social play, lack of empathy, and an inability to make friends. Stereotypical body movements, a marked need for sameness, very narrow interests, and a preoccupation with parts of the body are also frequent. The autistic child is withdrawn and often spends hours in solitary play. Ritualistic behavior prevails, reflecting the child's need to maintain a consistent, predictable environment. Tantrum-like rages may accompany disruptions of routine. Eye contact is minimal or absent. Visual scanning of hand and finger movements, mouthing of objects, and rubbing of surfaces may indicate a heightened awareness and sensitivity to some stimuli, whereas diminished responses to pain and lack of startle responses to sudden loud noises reflect lowered sensitivity to other stimuli. If speech is present, echolalia, pronomial reversal, nonsense rhyming, and other idiosyncratic language forms may predominate. Intelligence usually falls in the functionally retarded range; however, the deficits in language and socialization make it difficult to obtain an accurate estimate of the autistic child's intellectual potential.

Other pervasive developmental disorders and childhood psychosis are:

- **Asperger Disorder**—Characterized by a qualitative impairment in the development of reciprocal social interaction. Patients with Asperger disorder often demonstrate repetitive behaviors and restricted, obsessional, idiosyncratic interests. They do not, however, have the same language impairments that characterize autism.

- **Childhood Disintegrative Disorder**—Also known as Heller dementia, this is a rare condition of unknown etiology. Characterized by normal development up to 2–4 years of age, followed by severe deterioration of mental and social functioning, with regression to a very impaired "autistic" state. Language, social skills, and imagination are profoundly affected; bowel and bladder control may be lost; motor stereotypies are often present. Outcome is worse than for autistic disorder.

- **Rett Disorder**—This is an X-linked dominant disorder exclusively effecting girls (it is lethal to the male fetus). Development proceeds normally until approximately 1 year of age, at which time language and motor development regress and acquired microcephaly becomes apparent. These girls present with midline hand-wringing and unusual sighing. Autistic behaviors are typical.

PEDIATRICS

- **Childhood Schizophrenia**—Prominent symptoms include thought disorder, delusions, and hallucinations. The latter two symptoms, in addition to later onset, higher intelligence scores, and fewer perinatal complications, differentiate schizophrenia from autism. Schizophrenic children often appear to be chaotic. They may have paranoid delusions, aggressive behavior, hebephrenic silliness, social withdrawal, and alternating moods not apparently related to environmental stimuli. Auditory hallucinations are seen in 80 percent of schizophrenic children.

PATHOGENESIS

The cause of autistic disorder is unknown, but genetic factors have been implicated. There is an 80 percent concordance rate for monozygotic twins and a 20 percent concordance rate for dizygotic twins. Autism can be associated with other neurologic disorders, particularly tuberous sclerosis, seizure disorders, and, to a lesser extent, fragile X syndrome. Theories of causation include abnormal neurotransmitter functioning (dopamine, catecholamines, serotonin), brain injury, constitutional vulnerability, developmental aphasia, deficits in the reticular activating system, structural cerebellar lesions, forebrain hippocampal lesions, neuroradiologic abnormalities in the prefrontal and temporal lobe areas, and interplay between psychogenic and neurodevelopmental factors.

EPIDEMIOLOGY

The prevalence of autistic disorder is 3–4/10,000 children. The disorder is much more common in males than in females (3–4:1).

TREATMENT

Treatment is geared toward the individual's particular needs. Therapy with the very young focuses on speech and language, special education, parent education, training and support, and pharmacotherapy for certain target symptoms. Older children and adolescents with relatively higher intelligence but poor social skills and psychiatric symptoms (e.g., depression, anxiety, obsessive-compulsive symptoms) may require psychotherapy, behavioral or cognitive therapy, and pharmacotherapy. Working with families of autistic children is vital to the child's overall care.

Behavior modification is a major part of the overall treatment for autism. Pharmacotherapy is sometimes used to treat hyperactivity, tantrums, physical aggression, self-injurious behaviors, stereotypies, and anxiety symptoms. Haloperidol is effective in diminshing various generalized behaviors (anger, aggression, uncooperativeness, overactivity). Other medications used to treat psychiatric symptoms in autistic children include the stimulants, the serotonin-specific reuptake inhibitors, and clonidine.

PROGNOSIS

Prognosis is guarded. Some children, especially those with the ability to speak, may grow up to live marginal, self-sufficient, albeit isolated, lives in the community. However, for others, chronic placement in institutions is the ultimate outcome. Seizures and self-injurious behavior become more common with advancing age.

CEREBRAL PALSY

A 7-month-old girl is brought by her parents for an evaluation. Her parents report that she has difficulty crawling. She can pull herself along with her arms, but she tends to drag her legs behind her. The mother reports a normal pregnancy and an uncomplicated vaginal delivery. Examination of the child demonstrates bilateral spasticity in the legs, with brisk reflexes, ankle clonus, and a bilateral Babinski sign. When the child is suspended by the axillae, a scissoring posture of the lower extremities is maintained.

DIAGNOSIS

Cerebral palsy (CP) is a static encephalopathy that may be defined as a nonprogressive disorder of posture and movement, often associated with epilepsy and abnormalities of speech, vision, and intellect resulting from a defect or lesion of the developing brain. CP is classified by a description of the motor handicap in terms of physiologic (spastic, athetoid, rigid, ataxic, tremor, atonic, or mixed), topographic (monoplegia, paraplegia, hemiplegia, triplegia, quadriplegia, diplegia, or double hemiplegia), and etiologic (prenatal, perinatal, or postnatal) categories and functional capacity. The physiologic classification identifies the major motor abnormality, whereas the topographic taxonomy indicates the extremities involved. CP is also commonly associated with a spectrum of developmental disabilities, including mental retardation; epilepsy; and visual, aural, vocal, cognitive, and behavioral abnormalities. The motor handicap may be the least of the child's challenges.

Infants with spastic hemiplegia have decreased spontaneous movement on the affected side and show hand preference at a very early age. The arm is often more involved than the leg, and difficulty in hand manipulation is obvious by 1 year of age. About one-third of patients with spastic hemiplegia has a seizure disorder, and about 25 percent has cognitive abnormalities, including mental retardation. Spastic diplegia refers to bilateral spasticity of the legs. The first indication of spastic diplegia often occurs when the infant begins to crawl. The child uses the arms in a normal reciprocal fashion but tends to drag the legs. Most children with spastic diplegia have normal intellectual development. Spastic quadriplegia is the most severe form of CP, marked by motor impairment of all extremities and a high association with mental retardation and seizures. Associated developmental disabilities, including speech and visual abnormalities, are particularly prevalent in children with spastic quadriplegia. Athetoid CP, which is relatively rare, is characterized by hypotonia, poor head control, slurred speech, and impaired voice modulation, but intellect is preserved in most patients.

A thorough history and physical examination should rule out progressive disorders of the central nervous system, including degenerative diseases, spinal cord tumor, or muscular dystrophy. Depending on the severity and nature of the neurologic abnormalities, a baseline electroencephalogram and computed tomography (CT) scan may be indicated to determine the location and extent of structural lesions or associated congenital malformations. Additional studies may include tests of hearing and visual function.

PATHOGENESIS

For most cases of CP, a cause is not identified. However, a substantial number of children with CP has congenital anomalies external to the central nervous system, which may have placed them at increased risk for developing asphyxia during the perinatal period. Birth asphyxia is an uncommon cause of CP; most high-risk pregnancies result in neurologically normal children.

EPIDEMIOLOGY

CP is a common disorder, with an estimated prevalence of 2 per 1,000 in the population. Despite considerable advances in obstetric and neonatal care during the past 2 to 3 decades, there has been virtually no change in the incidence of CP.

TREATMENT

A multidisciplinary approach is most helpful in the management of CP. A team of physicians from various specialties, as well as occupational and physical therapists, speech pathologists, social workers, educators, and developmental psychologists are needed for the care of a child with CP. Parents should be taught how to handle their child in daily activities such as feeding, carrying, dressing, bathing, and playing in ways that will limit the effects of abnormal muscle tone. They also need to be instructed in the supervision of a series of exercises designed to prevent the development of contractures, especially a tight Achilles tendon. There is no proof that physical or occupational therapy prevents the development of CP in the infant at risk or that it will correct the neurologic deficit, but there is ample evidence that therapy optimizes the development of the affected child.

Children with spastic diplegia are treated initially with the assistance of adaptive equipment, such as walkers, poles, and standing frames. A rhizotomy procedure, in which the roots of the spinal nerves are divided, can produce considerable improvement in selected patients with severe spastic diplegia. Surgical soft-tissue procedures can reduce muscle spasm around the hip girdle. A tight heel cord in a child with spastic hemiplegia may be treated surgically by tenotomy of the Achilles tendon. The quadriplegic patient is managed with motorized wheelchairs, special feeding devices, modified typewriters, and customized seats.

PROGNOSIS

CP is a chronic, nonprogressive disorder for which lifetime care is required.

CHILD ABUSE AND NEGLECT

A 2-month-old girl is brought to the emergency department by her parents after suffering an accidental burn injury. The parents report that they were preparing to bathe the infant in the kitchen sink, when without warning she immersed her feet in the water, which had not yet reached a suitable temperature. The infant has an obvious scalding injury to her feet and lower legs bilaterally in a "stocking" pattern. Several small bruises of different colors are noted on the infant's buttocks and back.

DIAGNOSIS

Physical abuse is suspected when an injury is unexplained or explained implausibly. A tentative diagnosis of physical abuse or neglect is usually based on the history and physical findings. The existence of bruises, scars, and fractures of various stages of healing is highly suggestive of abuse. If an injury is incompatible with the history provided or the child's development, suspected abuse should be reported. With abused children, there is often delay in seeking medical help.

Bruises are the most common manifestation of child abuse and may be found on any body surface. Accidental bruises from impact trauma are most likely to be found on leading surfaces overlying superficial bone edges, such as the shins, forearms, hips, and brows. Bruises to the buttocks, genitalia, back, and backs of the hands are less likely to be due to an accident. The shape of the injury may suggest the object used. Paddles, belts, hands, and other instruments leave specific marks. Bilateral, symmetrical, and geometric injuries should raise suspicion of child abuse. Bruises change color over time; bruises of different colors are not compatible with a single event.

Most inflicted fractures are due to wrenching or pulling injuries that damage the metaphysis. A classic finding in child abuse is a chip fracture in which a corner of the metaphysis of a long bone is torn off, with damage to the epiphysis and periosteum. Inflicted fractures of the shaft are more likely to be spiral than transverse; spiral fractures of the femur before the age of walking are usually inflicted.

Approximately 10 percent of cases of physical abuse involve burns. The shape or pattern of a burn may be diagnostic when it reflects the geometric pattern of an object or method of injury. Immersion burns occur when a child is exposed to scalding water; these are most common in infants.

The most common cause of death from physical abuse is from head trauma. More than 95 percent of serious intracranial injuries that occur during the first year of life are the result of abuse. Injured infants may present with coma, convulsions, apnea, and increased intracranial pressure. Retinal hemorrhages are considered markers for acceleration/deceleration injuries, but they may also may occur in association with normal birth, coagulopathies, blood dyscrasias, and more rarely in meningitis, endocarditis, and severe hypertension.

Intraabdominal injuries are the second most common cause of death in physically abused children. Affected children may present with recurrent vomiting, abdominal distention, absent bowel sounds, localized tenderness, or shock. Because the abdominal wall is flexible, the force of the blow is usually absorbed by the internal organs and the overlying skin is free of bruises. The most common finding is a ruptured liver or spleen.

Sexual abuse includes any sexual activity with a child (before the age of legal consent) that is for the sexual gratification of an adult or a significantly older child. Sexual abuse includes oral-genital, genital-genital, genital-rectal, hand-genital, hand-rectal, or hand-breast contact; exposure of sexual anatomy; forced viewing of sexual anatomy; and showing pornography to a child or using a child in the production of pornography. Sex acts perpetrated by young children are learned behaviors and are associated with sexual abuse or exposure to adult sex or pornography. Symptoms associated with sexual abuse include 1) vaginal, penile, or rectal pain; erythema; discharge; or bleeding; 2) chronic dysuria, enuresis, constipation, or encopresis; and 3) premature puberty in a female. Specific behaviors associated with sexual abuse include sexualized activity with peers, animals, or objects; seductive behavior; and age-inappropriate sexual knowledge and curiosity.

Screening tests should be obtained in all cases of bruising in order to rule out a bleeding diathesis. These tests should include a prothrombin time, partial thromboplastin time, and a platelet count. When physical abuse is suspected in a child, a roentgenologic bone survey consisting of films of the skull, thorax, and long bones should be ordered; in addition, pelvis, finger, toe, and spine films may be indicated. Fractures considered highly specific to child abuse include metaphyseal, rib, scapular, outer end of the clavicle, vertebral, and finger in preambulating children; fractures of different ages; bilateral fractures; and complex skull fractures.

PATHOGENESIS

Child maltreatment encompasses a spectrum of abusive actions (acts of commission) and lack of actions (acts of omission) that result in morbidity or death. Physical abuse may be narrowly defined as intentional injuries to a child by a caretaker that result in bruises, burns, fractures, lacerations, punctures, and organ damage. Physical neglect and other acts of omission may result in failure to thrive, develop, and learn. Nutritional neglect is the most common cause of underweight infants and may account for more than one-half of the cases of failure to thrive. Emotional abuse includes intentional verbal or behavioral acts that result in adverse emotional consequences; emotional neglect occurs when a caretaker intentionally does not provide nurturing verbal and behavioral actions that are necessary for healthy development.

Immediate family members are the perpetrators in approximately 55 percent of abuse cases; the most common perpetrators are the father (21 percent), mother (21 percent), boyfriend of the mother (9 percent), babysitter (8 percent), and stepfather (5 percent). The average age of abusers is 25 years. The presence of spousal abuse increases the likelihood of child abuse. Substance abuse is a common finding in families with abused children. More than 90 percent of abusing parents have neither psychotic nor criminal personalities; they tend to be lonely, unhappy, angry, young, and single parents who did not plan their pregnancies, have little or no knowledge of child development, and have unrealistic expectations for child behavior. Ten to 40 percent of abusive parents has experienced physical abuse in childhood. Physical abuse is most likely to occur when a high-risk parent is responsible for the care of a high-risk child. High-risk children include premature infants, infants with chronic medical conditions, colicky babies, and children with behavioral problems. Mentally retarded children are more at risk for abuse and neglect.

Sexual abuse may be perpetrated by family members (incest), acquaintances, or, least often, by strangers. Sexual mistreatment of children by family members and non-relatives known to the child are the most common types of sexual abuse. The abuse of daughters by fathers and stepfathers is the most common form of reported incest, although brother-sister incest is considered to be the most common type.

EPIDEMIOLOGY

The actual incidence of child abuse and neglect is unknown. The number of reports to children's protective services and law enforcement agencies has steadily increased since mandated reporting began in the 1960s. In 1992, reports of all types of abuse were filed at an incidence of 45 per 1,000; a total of 2.9 million reports were filed, and 1,261 children died of maltreatment. Of reported children, 85 percent were younger than 5 years of age and 45 percent were younger than 1 year of age. The rate of reports decreases in older children. Neglect accounts for more deaths than does physical abuse. Approximately 10 percent of injuries to children younger than 5 years of age who are seen in emergency departments are due to abuse; 15 percent of children under 1 year of age who are admitted for burns, and 50 percent of children admitted with fractures, are abused.

TREATMENT

Appropriate medical, surgical, and psychiatric therapy for the injuries should be promptly initiated. The law requires that a child suspected of being abused or neglected be reported immediately to child protection services. A caseworker will confer with the physician to determine whether the child will be safe if released to a parent, or whether the child should be taken to an agency office. Hospital admission is indicated for children 1) whose medical or surgical condition requires inpatient management; 2) in whom diagnosis is unclear; and 3) when no alternative safe place for custody is available. Siblings should receive full examination within 24 hours of the recognition of child abuse in the family. Approximately 20 percent of them will be found to have signs of physical abuse. Children and siblings at risk for serious abuse can be placed in homes of appropriate relatives or emergency receiving homes.

A major role of the physician in primary abuse prevention is to identify parents at high risk for being unable to accept, love, and properly care for their offspring. Parental risks include a history of family violence, drug addiction, depression, or lack of support; socioeconomic problems; serious psychiatric illness; mental retardation; young parental age; closely spaced pregnancies; single parent status of the mother; negative parental comments about the newborn infant; lack of evidence of maternal attachment; infrequent visits to a new baby whose discharge is delayed because of prematurity or illness; anger toward or spanking of a young infant; and severe neglect of infant hygiene. Mentally or physically handicapped and chronically ill children should also be recognized as being at risk for abuse and neglect. Abuse and serious neglect may be prevented when at-risk families receive intensive training and support during pregnancy and after delivery. Prevention efforts include early and frequent contact between mother and baby in the delivery room, rooming-in, increased parental contact with premature infants, extra help calming the crying infant, more frequent office visits for at-risk infants, ongoing counseling regarding discipline and the use of nonphysical responses to annoying behaviors, public health nurse visits or trained home visitors, close follow-up of acute and chronic illnesses, telephone lifelines, arrangement for daycare or preschool, and assistance in family planning.

PROGNOSIS

Early studies of abused children returned to their parents after no intervention indicated that about 5 percent was killed and 25 percent was seriously reinjured. With comprehensive, intensive treatment of the entire family, 80 to 90 percent of families involved in child abuse or neglect can be rehabilitated to provide adequate care for their children. Approximately 10 to 15 percent of such families, especially those with a history of substance abuse, can only be stabilized and will require an indefinite continuation of supporting services (which may include drug monitoring) until their children are old enough to leave home. Termination of parental rights or continued foster placement is required in 2 to 3 percent of cases. As adults, victims of sexual abuse may have difficulties with close relationships; females may enter abusive relationships with men; have a variety of somatic complaints of the genitourinary and other systems; and need psychiatric help for depression, anxiety, substance abuse, disassociation, and eating disorders.

PEDIATRICS

CROUP

A 4-year-old male child is brought to his pediatrician's office by his parents who report that he has had fever and a worsening cough for the past three days. Temperature is 37.8 C (100 F), heart rate is 100/min, and respirations are 24/min and labored. Examination reveals a child in moderate respiratory distress; inspiratory stridor, a brassy cough, and marked suprasternal, intercostal, and subcostal retractions are evident. A roentgenographic examination of the nasopharynx and upper airway is obtained.

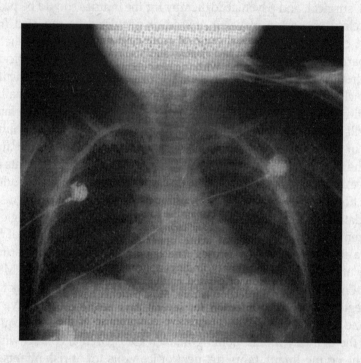

Radiograph of patient with croup, showing typical signs—subglottic narrowing ("steeple sign")

DIAGNOSIS

Croup (laryngotracheobronchitis) is the most common form of acute upper airway obstruction. It is almost always of viral etiology; parainfluenza 3 virus is the most common agent. The typical first episode occurs in children between 6 months and 6 years of age, with symptoms of an upper respiratory infection. The typical brassy cough (usually characterized as sounding like the barking of a seal), inspiratory stridor, and respiratory distress may develop slowly or acutely. Symptoms are characteristically worse at night. Signs of lower airway disease, such as wheezing and a productive cough, may be present. Although the majority of children with croup is not seriously ill, the airway obstruction may become severe enough to require placement of an artificial airway. As the obstruction increases, the stridor becomes continuous and is associated with worsening cough and increased respiratory distress.

The pattern of severe laryngotracheobronchitis may be difficult to distinguish from acute epiglottiditis. In croup, the subglottic space is the major site of obstruction. This is due to the viral inflammation and resulting edema. Roentgenographic examination of the nasopharynx and upper airway of a patient with croup may demonstrate the characteristic subglottic narrowing ("steeple sign") seen in the radiograph above.

PATHOGENESIS

The edema resulting from viral inflammation is the main pathological mechanism in croup. Parainfluenza virus infection accounts for approximately 75 percent of cases of croup. Inflammatory edema, destruction of ciliated epithelium, and exudate lead to an acute upper airway obstruction. The inflammation may extend to the bronchi and bronchioles.

EPIDEMIOLOGY

Most patients with viral croup are between the ages of 3 months and 5 years. The incidence of croup is higher in males. Croup occurs most commonly during the cold season of the year, and approximately 15 percent of patients have a strong family history of croup.

TREATMENT

Agitation and crying aggravate the respiratory symptoms, so children should be kept as calm as possible, preferably in an upright position. A cool mist may help prevent drying of the secretions around the larynx. Antibiotic treatment is not indicated, since croup has a viral etiology.

Children with severe croup require hospitalization and should be carefully monitored. The same precautions should be taken as are taken in cases of acute epiglottiditis. Aerosolized racemic epinephrine may temporarily reduce the edema, but the edema and obstruction will return and require repeated treatments. The use of corticosteroids is probably indicated for hospitalized children with croup, but is considered controversial by some sources.

PROGNOSIS

The duration of illness is typically fewer than 5 days. Most patients with croup progress only as far as the slight dyspnea and stridor before they start to recover.

PEDIATRICS

CYSTIC FIBROSIS

A 6-week-old white male infant is brought to his pediatrician by his parents, who are concerned about his chronic cough. The parents report that he is usually very hungry, eats a lot, and has large, greasy, foul-smelling stools. Additionally, the parents note that the infant's grandmother thinks he "tastes too salty." The infant has not gained any weight since his last visit two weeks ago. Vital signs are normal. The infant is observed to have a repetitive cough productive of a small amount of sputum. Expiratory wheezes are noted upon auscultation of the chest. A quantitative sweat test is positive (Cl⁻ ≥ 60 mEq/L).

DIAGNOSIS

Cystic fibrosis (CF) is the major cause of severe chronic lung disease and exocrine pancreatic insufficiency in children. The degree of mutational heterogeneity and environmental factors appear to be responsible for the highly variable clinical manifestations of CF. The diagnosis of CF is based on a positive sweat test (Cl⁻ ≥ 60 mEq/L) in conjunction with one or more of the following: chronic obstructive pulmonary disease, exocrine pancreas insufficiency, or a positive family history. The list of possible presenting signs and symptoms that are an indication for sweat testing is long.

Indications For Sweat Testing

Pulmonary
- Chronic or recurrent cough
- Chronic or recurrent pneumonia
- Recurrent bronchiolitis
- Atelectasis
- Hemoptysis
- Mucoid *Pseudomonas aeruginosa* infection
- Staphylococcal pneumonia

Gastrointestinal
- Meconium ileus, meconium plug syndrome
- Steatorrhea, malabsorption
- Pancreatitis
- Hepatic cirrhosis in childhood
- Rectal prolapse
- Deficiency of vitamin A, D, E, or K

Other
- Family history of CF
- Failure to thrive
- Salty tasting skin, salt crystals on skin
- Digital clubbing
- Hyponatremic hypochloremic alkalosis in infants
- Nasal polyps
- Pansinusitis
- Aspermia

PATHOGENESIS

CF is an autosomal recessive disorder. The more than 400 gene mutations that contribute to the CF syndrome occur at a single locus on the long arm of chromosome 7. The CF gene codes for a protein called CF transmembrane regulator (CFTR). CFTR is expressed largely in the epithelial cells of the airways, gastrointestinal tract, sweat glands, and the genitourinary system. Although a number of the most common mutations of the CF gene have been identified, DNA analysis cannot currently be used for general screening. However, DNA analysis is used extensively for carrier detection in CF families and spouses of know carriers.

There are four fundamental pathophysiologic derangements in cystic fibrosis: failure to clear mucous secretions, a paucity of water in mucous secretions, an elevated salt content in sweat and other serous secretions, and chronic infection limited to the respiratory tract. The respiratory epithelium of patients with CF exhibits marked impermeability to chloride and excessive reabsorption of sodium. This leads to a relative dehydration of the airway secretions, which results in impaired mucociliary transport and airway obstruction. Chronic bronchial infections with *Haemophilus influenzae*, *Staphylococcus aureus*, and/or *Pseudomonas aeruginosa* develop and lead to a chronic cough, sputum production, hyperinflation, bronchiectasis, and eventually pulmonary insufficiency and death. The rate of progression of lung disease is the chief determinant of morbidity and mortality. Approximately 90 percent of patients with CF develop exocrine pancreatic insufficiency early in life, sometimes at the time of birth, due to inspissation of mucus in the pancreatic ducts and consequent autodigestion of the pancreas. The exocrine pancreatic insufficiency results in maldigestion with secondary malabsorption, leading to steatorrhea, azotorrhea, and secondary vitamin deficiency states. Approximately 10 percent of patients with CF are born with a meconium ileus, an intestinal obstruction secondary to inspissated meconium. The inspissation of mucus in the reproductive tract leads to dysfunction. In females, the cervical mucus is abnormal and fertility is low, and males are almost universally azoospermic.

EPIDEMIOLOGY

CF occurs in approximately 1 of 3,000 white live births and 1 of 17,000 black live births in the United States, and is the most common lethal genetic disease affecting whites. The CF gene is more prevalent in Northern and Central Europeans. The high frequency of the CF gene has been hypothetically ascribed to resistance to the morbidity and mortality of cholera.

TREATMENT

The management of the complications of cystic fibrosis is complex. The objective of pulmonary therapy is to clear secretions from airways and control infection. Aerosol therapy is used to deliver medications and water to the lower respiratory tract. Chest physiotherapy and exercise are used to help remove mucus from the airways. Pharmacologic therapies help to clear mucus and improve airway performance. Pulmonary infections require antibiotic therapy. Administering exogenous pancreatic enzymes treats pancreatic insufficiency. Fat-soluble vitamins are given in twice-normal doses. Meconium ileus often requires surgical intervention.

PROGNOSIS

CF is a life-limiting disorder; the current median cumulative survival is 30 years, but patients vary greatly in the severity of their disease. Some infants with severe lung disease die in infancy, but most patients survive infancy and are relatively healthy into adolescence or early adulthood.

FAILURE TO THRIVE

A 15-month-old boy is brought to the pediatric outpatient department for a scheduled routine examination. The infant's mother reports that he has not been eating as much as usual and seems not to be hungry when offered food. She has not noticed any problems with his digestion or his ability to swallow. He has not had fever or diarrhea. Weight and height measurements demonstrate that the infant has dropped from the 75th percentile to the 25th percentile since his last visit three months ago. Physical examination is unremarkable.

DIAGNOSIS

Failure to thrive (FTT) is the diagnosis of infants or children whose physical growth is significantly less than that of their peers, and it often is associated with poor developmental and socioemotional functioning. FTT usually refers to growth below the 3rd or 5th percentile or a change in growth that has crossed two major growth percentiles (i.e., from above the 75th percentile to below the 25th) in a short time. The degree of FTT is usually measured by calculating each growth parameter (weight, height, and weight/height ratio) as a percentage of the median value for age.

The clinical presentation of FTT ranges from failure to meet expected age norms for height and weight, to alopecia, loss of subcutaneous fat, reduced muscle mass, dermatitis, recurrent infections, marasmus, and kwashiorkor. In developed countries, the most common presentation is poor growth detected in an ambulatory setting; in developing countries, recurrent infections, marasmus, and kwashiorkor are more common presentations.

PATHOGENESIS

The causes of insufficient growth include 1) failure of a parent to offer adequate calories, 2) failure of the child to take sufficient calories, and 3) failure of the child to retain sufficient calories.

Major Organic Causes of Failure to Thrive	
System	**Cause**
Cardiopulmonary	Congestive heart failure, asthma, bronchopulmonary dysplasia, cystic fibrosis, anatomic abnormalities of the upper airway, obstructive sleep apnea
Congenital	Chromosomal abnormalities, congenital syndromes (e.g., fetal alcohol syndrome), perinatal infections
Endocrine	Hypothyroidism, diabetes mellitus, adrenal insufficiency or excess, parathyroid disorders, pituitary disorders, growth hormone deficiency
Gastrointestinal	Gastroesophageal reflux, celiac disease, pyloric stenosis, cleft palate/cleft lip, lactose intolerance, Hirschsprung's disease, milk protein intolerance, hepatitis, cirrhosis, pancreatic insufficiency, biliary disease, inflammatory bowel disease, malabsorption
Infectious	Parasitic or bacterial infections of the gastrointestinal tract, tuberculosis, human immunodeficiency virus disease
Metabolic	Inborn errors of metabolism
Neurologic	Mental retardation, cerebral hemorrhages, degenerative disorders
Renal	Urinary tract infection, renal tubular acidosis, diabetes insipidus, chronic renal insufficiency
Other	Lead poisoning, malignancy, collagen vascular disease, recurrently infected adenoids and tonsils

In the United States, psychosocial FTT is more common than organic FTT. Psychosocial FTT is most often due to poverty or poor child-parent interaction. Organic and inorganic etiologic factors may occur together.

EPIDEMIOLOGY

The prevalence of FTT depends on the population studied. Approximately 5 to 10 percent of low-birthweight children and children living in poverty may have FTT. Family discord, neonatal problems (other than low birthweight), and maternal depression are also associated with FTT.

TREATMENT

The treatment of FTT requires consideration of all of the elements that contribute to a child's growth: health and nutrition, family issues, and the parent-child interaction. An appropriate feeding atmosphere at home is important; children should eat with other people and they should not be force-fed. For children with organic FTT, the underlying medical condition should be determined and treated. For older infants and young children with psychosocial FTT, high-calorie foods, such as peanut butter, whole milk, cheese, and dried fruits should be emphasized, and high-calorie supplementation may be necessary. Weight gain in response to adequate caloric feedings usually establishes the diagnosis of psychosocial FTT.

PROGNOSIS

FTT in the first year of life, regardless of cause, is particularly ominous. Maximal postnatal brain growth occurs during the first 6 months of life; the brain grows as much during the first year of life as during the rest of a child's life. Approximately one-third of children with FTT are developmentally delayed and have social and emotional problems.

PEDIATRICS

IMMUNIZATION

A 1-month-old male infant is brought to the doctor by his parents for a routine evaluation. The parents report that he has been breast-feeding successfully and is gaining weight. The infant received a hepatitis B vaccination soon after birth and is presently scheduled to receive a booster. The infant's parents are concerned about their child "receiving too many shots" and inquire if breast-feeding is sufficient to prevent disease.

DIAGNOSIS

Vaccination refers to the administration of any vaccine or toxoid. Immunization describes the process of artificially inducing immunity by administering an antigenic substance, such as an immunobiologic agent. Administration of an immunobiologic agent cannot be automatically equated with the development of adequate immunity.

A constant task of physicians is maintaining individual immunity and, along with public health workers, herd immunity. Even after the entire population is fully vaccinated, the task is not complete because it will be imperative to immunize subsequent generations as long as the threat of disease persists. The target population for common and highly contagious childhood diseases, such as measles, is the whole universe of susceptibles, and the time to immunize is as early in life as is feasible.

All 50 states require immunization for school entry, and as a result, up to 90 percent of all children are immunized against nine vaccine-preventable diseases at the time they enter school (excluding newer vaccines such as HBV and HIB). Current practice dictates that all children in the U.S. receive diphtheria, tetanus, and pertussis (DTP); polio; measles; mumps; rubella; *Haemophilus influenzae* (Hib); hepatitis B; and varicella; unless contraindicated. In some diseases, such as rubella, infection is primarily a threat to the fetus (young infants and children are not at risk), so that although it is not clinically necessary to immunize early in life, the goal is to ensure immunity before females enter the reproductive group.

Most infants in the U.S. begin a course of immunization, but a substantial number fails to complete the series on schedule. There are four major barriers to successful infant and childhood immunization within the health care system: low public awareness and lack of public demand for immunization; inadequate access to immunization services; missed opportunities to administer vaccines; and inadequate resources for public health and preventive programs.

Modern vaccines, although relatively safe and effective, are associated with some mild to life-threatening adverse effects. All patients or their parents or guardians should be informed of both the benefits and the risks associated with vaccination. The use of mandated vaccines benefits society by reducing morbidity, the cost of care for preventable diseases, and childhood mortality, but vaccines are often associated with severe adverse reactions or sequelae in some children. These reactions may be local or systemic, and may include serious anaphylaxis and urticaria. No vaccine can be expected to be 100 percent effective; therefore, some immunized persons may develop disease after exposure.

Limited studies of HIV-infected infants and children show no increased risk of adverse events from live or inactivated vaccines. It is unnecessary to test for HIV before making immunization decisions for asymptomatic children. Live, attenuated vaccines are normally contraindicated in other immuno-compromised patients, such as those with the congenital immunodeficiency syndromes and those receiving immunosuppressive therapy.

PATHOGENESIS

Active immunization consists of inducing the body to develop defenses against disease by the administration of vaccines or toxoids that stimulate the immune system to produce antibodies and cellular immune responses to protect against the infectious agent. The principle approaches involve the use of live, usually attenuated, infectious agents, and the use of inactivated or detoxified agents or their extracts, or specific products of recombination (e.g., hepatitis B). Live, attenuated vaccines are thought to induce an immunologic response more like the one elicited by natural infection than killed vaccines. Inactivated, or killed, vaccines consist of inactivated whole organisms (e.g., pertussis vaccine), detoxified exotoxins alone (e.g., tetanus toxoid), endotoxins linked to carrier proteins, soluble capsular material (e.g., pneumococcal polysaccharide), conjugated capsular material (e.g., Hib conjugate vaccine), extracts of some component (e.g., hepatitis B), or components of the organism (e.g., subunit influenza).

When active immunization is unavailable or has not been given before exposure, passive immunization provides temporary immunity to an unimmunized person exposed to an infectious disease. This type of immunization consists of providing temporary protection through the administration of exogenously produced antibody. Three types of preparations are used in passive immunization: standard human immune serum globulin, special immune serum globulins with a known antibody content for specific agents, and animal serums and antitoxins. Passive immunization occurs through the transplacental transmission of antibodies to the fetus, which provides protection against several diseases for the first three to six months of life, and the injection of immune globulin for specific preventive purposes.

EPIDEMIOLOGY

Because infectious diseases know no geographic or political boundaries, uncontrolled disease anywhere in the world poses a threat to the health of children in the U.S. Worldwide, measles continues to kill an estimated 1.5 million children each year, and it is estimated that 20 to 35 percent of all deaths in children younger than 5 years of age are associated with vaccine-preventable diseases.

TREATMENT

More than 50 biologic products are available in the U.S., and 11 antigens are used for routine immunization of infants and children, including diphtheria and tetanus toxoids and pertussis vaccine; trivalent polio, measles, mumps, and rubella vaccines; Hib; and hepatitis B vaccines. Immunizing agents include vaccines, toxoids, and antibodies containing preparations from human or animal donors.

Multiple simultaneous vaccines can be given safely and effectively. Intervals between doses longer than those recommended delay, but do not diminish, the ultimate protective response, but giving vaccines at shorter than recommended intervals may impair responses.

Recommended Schedule for Routine Active Vaccination of Infants and Children									
Vaccine	At Birth	1–2 Mo	2 Mo	4 Mo	6 Mo	6–18 Mo	12–15 Mo	15 Mo	4–6 yrs
Diphtheria, tetanus, pertussis (DTP)			DTP	DTP	DTP			DTP	DTP
Polio, live oral (OPV)			OPV	OPV	OPV				OPV
Measles, mumps, rubella (MMR)							MMR		MMR
Haemophilus influenzae type B conjugate (Hib)			Hib	Hib			Hib		
Hepatitis B (Hep B)	Hep B	Hep B				Hep B			

Annual immunization against influenza is inappropriate for normal children but should be given to children at high risk of infections of the lower respiratory tract, including those with congenital or acquired heart disease; disorders that compromise pulmonary function, including cystic fibrosis, severe asthma, neuromuscular and orthopedic conditions that distort or weaken the thoracic cage, and pulmonary dysplasia; chronic azotemic renal disease or the nephrotic syndrome; diabetes mellitus; and chronic, severe anemia, such as thalassemia or sickle cell anemia. Immunodeficient and immunocompromised children may also benefit from annual immunization against influenza.

The 23-valent pneumococcal vaccine is not recommended for routine use in children. As with other polysaccharide vaccines, its efficacy is minimal in children under 2 years of age. It is recommended for children older than 2 years of age who are at risk of severe, life-threatening pneumococcal infection, such as those with sickle cell disease, asplenia syndrome, cerebrospinal fluid leak, and HIV infection or other immunosuppressive disease states.

For certain infections, active or passive immunization soon after exposure prevents or attenuates the disease. Measles immune globulin given within 6 days of exposure may prevent or modify infection, and administration of the measles vaccine within the first few days after exposure may prevent symptomatic infection. Although the clinical manifestations of rubella are minimized by postexposure passive immunization, viremia, fetal infections, and congenital rubella syndrome may not be prevented by immunization. The administration of immune globulin is recommended only for women developing rubella during pregnancy who will not consider abortion. Tetanus immune globulin is used in patients with tetanus along with toxoid vaccine for those who have not been immunized. Administration of rabies immune globulin and rabies vaccine in the immediate postexposure period is highly effective. The use of immune globulin within two weeks of exposure to hepatitis A is likely to prevent clinical illness. HBV immune globulin also prevents disease after exposure.

Response to vaccines is usually gauged by measuring specific antibody concentrations in the serum. Antibody titers serve as a dependable indicator of immunity, but seroconversion measures only one parameter of the host response. The absence of measurable antibody may not mean that the individual is unprotected.

PROGNOSIS

Immunization represents one of the most cost-effective means of preventing serious infectious disease. The widespread use of vaccines led to the global eradication of smallpox and the elimination of poliomyelitis from the U.S. Immunization has nearly eliminated congenital rubella syndrome, tetanus, and diphtheria, and has dramatically reduced the incidence of pertussis, rubella, measles, mumps, and *H. influenzae* type b meningitis in the U.S.

NEONATAL NECROTIZING ENTEROCOLITIS

A 1-week-old premature infant, delivered at 27 weeks estimated gestational age secondary to severe maternal preeclampsia, develops abdominal distention and gastric retention while being cared for in the neonatal intensive care unit. The infant did well after delivery and was started on enteral feedings on the third day of life. Stool guaiac is positive. Plain abdominal roentgenogram demonstrates abdominal distention, hepatic portal venous gas, and bubbly appearance of pneumatosis intestinalis.

DIAGNOSIS

Neonatal necrotizing enterocolitis (NEC) is a serious disease of newborns characterized by varying degrees of mucosal or transmural necrosis of the intestine. Onset usually occurs in the first 2 weeks of life, but can appear as late as 2 months of age in very low birth weight infants. Meconium is passed normally, and the first signs of NEC are abdominal distention with gastric retention, which usually develops after the onset of enteric feedings. Bloody stools are seen in 25 percent of patients. The onset is often insidious, and sepsis may be suspected before an intestinal lesion is noted. Progression may be rapid, but it is unusual for the disease to progress from mild to severe in 72 hours.

Plain abdominal films may demonstrate pneumatosis intestinalis, a finding that is diagnostic of NEC in the newborn infant; 50 to 75 percent of patients have pneumatosis when treatment is started. Portal vein gas is a sign of severe disease, and pneumoperitoneum indicates an intestinal perforation.

The differential diagnosis of NEC includes systemic or intestinal infections, obstruction, and volvulus. Indomethacin may produce focal intestinal perforation and pneumoperitoneum, but patients taking indomethacin usually appear to be less ill than those with NEC.

PATHOGENESIS

The etiology of NEC is unknown. Many factors may contribute to the development of NEC, which is characterized by a necrotic segment of intestine, gas accumulation in the submucosa of the bowel wall (pneumatosis intestinalis), and progression of intenstinal necrosis leading to perforation, sepsis, and death. The distal ileum and proximal colon are involved most frequently.

EPIDEMIOLOGY

No particular race or sex is markedly more susceptible to the disease. Incidence of NEC ranges from 1 to 5 percent of admissions to neonatal intensive care units. Very small, ill, preterm infants are particularly susceptible to NEC, but the disease does also occur occasionally in term infants.

TREATMENT

Prevention of NEC may be possible with judicious feeding protocols and the use of breast milk. Intensive therapy is indicated for suspected and diagnosed cases. Cessation of feeding, nasogastric decompression, and intravenous fluids is indicated. Cultures of blood, stool, and cerebrospinal fluid should be taken. Broad-spectrum antibiotics that cover nosocomial infections should be started.

The course of NEC should be monitored by frequent abdominal imaging studies to examine for intestinal perforation. Pneumoperitoneum and brown paracentesis fluid suggest perforation. Hematocrit, platelet, electrolyte, and acid-base determinations should be followed serially. Failure to respond to medical management, a single fixed bowel loop, erythema of the abdominal wall, evidence of perforation, or a mass are indications for exploratory laparotomy, resection of necrotic bowel, and external ostomy diversion.

Prognosis

Medical management fails in about 20 percent of patients in whom there is pneumatosis intestinalis at diagnosis; of these cases, the mortality rate is greater than 25 percent. Strictures develop at the site of the necrotizing lesion in about 10 percent of patients.

Complications of NEC, following massive intestinal resection, include short bowel syndrome (malabsorption, growth failure, and malnutrition), complications of total parenteral alimentation due to central venous catheters (sepsis, thrombosis), and cholestatic jaundice that may progress to cirrhosis.

PARVOVIRUS B19 INFECTION

A 6-year-old boy is brought in for an evaluation by his mother who complains of his nonproductive cough, fever, and rash. The child's mother states that the rash started 4 days ago on the boy's face, saying it looked like he had been "slapped in the face." Over the next few days the rash spread to his trunk and he developed a mild, nonproductive cough and slight fever. The boy complains of a headache, but denies photophobia, nausea, or vomiting. He has no significant medical history and takes no medications. Review of his immunization record demonstrates completion of all indicated vaccination series. The child's temperature is 38.2 C (100.8 F). He has a diffuse, erythematous, macular rash over his face, trunk, and proximal extremities. The rash is prominent on the extensor surfaces of the proximal extremities, but the palms and soles are not affected.

DIAGNOSIS

The most common manifestation of parvovirus B19 is erythema infectiosum, also known as fifth disease, which is a benign, self-limited exanthematous illness occurring in childhood. Affected children are afebrile and not ill-appearing. The hallmark of fifth disease is a characteristic rash, which occurs in three stages: 1) an erythematous facial flushing that gives the appearance of slapped cheeks, 2) the rash spreads rapidly to the trunk and proximal extremities as a diffuse macular erythema, and 3) central clearing occurs, giving the rash a lacy, reticulated appearance. The palm and soles are spared; the rash tends to be more prominent on extensor surfaces. The prodromal phase is mild and consists of low-grade fever, headache, and mild URI (upper respiratory infection) symptoms. Arthritis and arthralgia can occur as a complication of fifth disease or as the only clinical manifestation of B19 infection.

Individuals with chronic hemolytic conditions, such as sickle cell disease, thalassemia, hereditary spherocytosis, and pyruvate kinase deficiency, may experience transient red cell aplasia after contact with B19. The transient arrest of erythropoiesis and absolute reticulocytopenia induced by B19 infection leads to a sudden fall in serum hemoglobin. Patients have fever, malaise, and lethargy, as well as signs and symptoms of profound anemia, such as pallor, tachycardia, and tachypnea. Rash is rarely present. Children with sickle hemoglobinopathies may also have a concurrent vaso-occlusive pain crisis.

Patients with impaired humoral immunity are at risk for chronic infections with parvovirus B19. Chronic anemia is the most common manifestation of parvovirus infection in immunosuppressed patients; it is sometimes accompanied by other cytopenias or complete marrow suppression. Chronic infections are seen in children with cancer receiving cytotoxic chemotherapy, children with congenital acquired immunodeficiency syndrome (AIDS), and patients with defects in IgG class-switching who are unable to generate neutralizing antibodies.

The rash of erythema infectiosum must be differentiated from rubella, measles, enteroviral infections, and drug reactions. In older children with rash and arthritis associated with B19, the differential diagnosis includes juvenile rheumatoid arthritis, systemic lupus erythematosus, and other connective tissue disorders.

Determination of anti-B19 IgM is the best marker of recent or acute infection; however, laboratory tests for the diagnosis of B19 infection are not generally available. The diagnosis of erythema infectiosum is usually based on clinical observation of the typical rash and the exclusion of other conditions. The virus cannot be isolated by culture.

PATHOGENESIS

Parvovirus B19, a small, DNA-containing virus, is a member of the genus Parvovirus in the family Parvoviridae. Parvovirus B19 does not infect animals, and animal parvoviruses do not infect humans. B19 is composed of an icosahedral protein capsid without an envelope that contains single-stranded DNA that is approximately 5.5 kb in length.

Parvoviruses replicate in dividing cells, and because of their limited genome, they require host cell factors in late S phase to replicate. B19 can only be propagated in erythropoietin-stimulated cells derived from human bone marrow or primary fetal liver culture. The primary target of B19 infection is the erythroid cell line, specifically the erythroid precursors near the pronormoblast stage. The virus lyses these cells, which leads to a progressive depletion and a transient arrest of erythropoiesis, and reticulocyte count falls to near zero. The tropism for erythroid cells is related to the erythrocyte P blood group antigen. The virus has no apparent effect on the myeloid cell line. Humoral immunity is crucial in controlling infection.

Individuals with conditions of chronic hemolysis and increased red cell turnover are very susceptible to the perturbations in erythropoiesis caused by B19 infection. Persons with impaired ability to produce specific antibodies are likely to be at risk for more serious or persistent infection with B19, which usually manifests as chronic red cell aplasia (but neutropenia, thrombocytopenia, and marrow failure are also described).

Transmission of B19 is by the respiratory route, presumably via large droplet spread. However, B19 is also transmissible by blood and blood products. This is exemplified by hemophiliac children receiving pooled donor clotting factor. The incubation period for erythema infectiosum ranges from 4 to 28 days (the average is 16 to 17 days). The incubation period for other clinical manifestations, such as aplastic crises, is shorter because viremia precedes the rash. The transmission rates in households range from 15 to 30 percent in susceptible contacts.

Primary maternal infection is associated with nonimmune fetal hydrops and intrauterine fetal demise. The second trimester seems to be the most sensitive time, but fetal losses are reported at every stage of gestation.

EPIDEMIOLOGY

Infections with parvovirus B19 are common and worldwide. Clinically apparent infections (rash, illness, and aplastic crisis) are most prevalent in school-age children, and 70 percent of cases occurs among children 5 to 15 years old. Although community outbreaks show seasonal peaks in the late winter and spring, sporadic infections can occur year-round.

TREATMENT

There is no specific antiviral therapy for B19 infection, and no vaccine is available. Intravenous immunoglobulin (IVIG) may be helpful in cases of anemia and bone marrow failure in immunocompromised children. In patients whose immune status is not likely to improve, such as in AIDS, administration of IVIG may produce only a temporary remission, and periodic reinfusions may be required.

Preventive strategies are based on the understanding of the particular clinical syndrome. Children with erythema infectiosum are not likely to be infectious at presentation because rash and arthropathy represent immune-mediated, postinfectious phenomena. Isolation is unnecessary and ineffective after diagnosis. Children with B19-induced red cell aplasia (aplastic crisis) are infectious when they present and have a more intense viremia. These children typically require transfusion and supportive care until their hematologic status is stable. They should be isolated in the hospital to prevent spread to susceptible patients and staff.

PROGNOSIS

For patients with erythema infectiosum, the rash resolves spontaneously without desquamation but tends to wax and wane over a one- to three-week period. It can recur with exposure to sunlight, heat, exercise, and stress. Children with leukemia undergoing chemotherapy, those with congenital immunodeficiency states, and patients with AIDS are at risk for chronic B19 infections.

SCOLIOSIS

A 10-year-old girl without complaints presents for a routine examination. The patient is examined from behind while in a standing position, and her right shoulder is noted to be lower than her left. The pelvis is determined to be level, ruling out a leg-length discrepancy. The patient is then instructed to place her palms together and bend forward with her hands directed between her feet. A "hump" is noted in the right posterior thorax, while a corresponding depression is found on the opposite side of the spine.

DIAGNOSIS

Scoliosis represents a rotational malalignment of one vertebra on another, which results in rib rotation when the curve is in the thoracic area, and paravertebral muscle rotation when it is in the lumbar region. On the convex portion of the curve, the ribs are rotated posteriorly, creating a "hump," and in the concave portion of the curvature, they are rotated anteriorly, creating a "valley."

To evaluate a patient for scoliosis, the back should be examined with the patient in the standing position and viewed from behind. The shoulders and waist should be evaluated for symmetry. The levelness of the pelvis is assessed first. Leg-length discrepancies result in pelvic obliquity that can produce the clinical appearance of scoliosis. When the pelvis is level or has been leveled with blocks, the spine is examined for asymmetry, deformity, and areas of tenderness. The symmetry of the back is then determined. The presence of a hump or asymmetry is the hallmark of a scoliotic deformity. The corresponding area opposite the hump is typically depressed due to spinal rotation.

A complete physical examination is required for any child or adolescent with scoliosis because the deformity may be indicative of an underlying disease process. Idiopathic scoliosis is usually a painless disorder. Any child with scoliosis and back pain requires a careful neurological examination for neuromuscular or intraspinal disorders.

Posteroanterior (PA) and lateral standing radiographs of the entire spine must be obtained for assessment of scoliosis, kyphosis, lordosis, congenital malformations and, if the iliac crests are visible, the skeletal maturity of the patient. The degree of curvature is measured from the most tilted or end vertebra of the curve superiorly and inferiorly. Other radiographic procedures that may occasionally be necessary in the evaluation of spinal deformities include computed tomography, magnetic resonance imaging (MRI), myelography, and tomography. MRI is the procedure of choice for evaluating for coexistent spinal cord defects in children with congenital scoliosis.

PATHOGENESIS

Scoliosis refers to alterations in normal spinal alignment that occur in the anteroposterior or frontal plane. The majority of scoliotic deformities are idiopathic. Others, however, can be congenital, associated with a neuromuscular disorder or syndrome (cerebral palsy, Duchenne muscular dystrophy, spinal muscular atrophy, myelodysplasia, and arthrogryposis), or compensatory from a leg-length discrepancy or intraspinal abnormality.

Idiopathic scoliosis is the most common form of scoliosis. It occurs in healthy, neurologically normal children, but its exact cause is unknown. Children with idiopathic scoliosis tend to show subtle changes in proprioception and vibratory sensation, which suggests abnormalities of spinal cord posterior-column function. Idiopathic scoliosis can be divided into three groups on the basis of age at onset: 1) infantile; birth to 3 years of age; 2) juvenile; 4 to 10 years of age; and 3) adolescent; 11 years of age and older. Adolescent scoliosis is the most common form and accounts for approximately 80 percent of cases of idiopathic scoliosis. Infantile scoliosis is very rare in the U.S. Juvenile scoliosis is not common, but in many children with the diagnosis of adolescent scoliosis, onset actually occurred when they were juveniles, but was not diagnosed at that time.

Abnormalities of vertebral development during the first trimester of pregnancy often result in structural deformities of the spine that are evident at birth or become obvious in early childhood. Congenital scoliosis can be classified as 1) partial or complete failure of vertebral formation (wedge vertebrae or hemivertebrae); 2) partial or complete failure of segmentation (unsegmented bars); or 3) mixed. These deformities may be isolated or in combination with other organ system malformations. Congenital genitourinary malformations occur in 20 percent of children with congenital scoliosis, with unilateral renal agenesis being the most common abnormality. Spinal dysraphism is a general term for coexistent vertebral and spinal cord defects; it occurs in about 20 percent of children with congenital scoliosis. Spina bifida occulta is the most common and benign defect, and myelomeningocele is the most severe.

EPIDEMIOLOGY

The incidence of idiopathic scoliosis is only slightly greater in girls than in boys, but scoliosis is more likely to progress and require treatment in girls than in boys. Hereditary tendencies also occur—approximately 20 percent of children with scoliosis have family members with the same condition. Although the daughters of affected mothers are more likely than other children to experience scoliosis, the magnitude of curvature in an affected individual is not related to the magnitude of curvature in relatives.

TREATMENT

Treatment of idiopathic scoliosis is based on curve progression and the age of the patient. No treatment is necessary for nonprogressive deformities. The risk for curve progression varies according to sex, age, menarchal status, curve location, and curve magnitude. Although the female:male ratio of occurrence of idiopathic adolescent scoliosis is approximately 1:1, the risk for curve progression is much higher for females. Premenarchal girls with curves of more than 20 degrees have a significantly higher risk for progression than girls one to two years after menarche with similar curves. Curves of less than 25 degrees are observed and reevaluated radiographically at 4- to 6-month intervals.

The treatment of progressive idiopathic adolescent scoliosis is orthotic or surgical. Exercises alone are ineffective. Progressive curves between 25 and 45 degrees in skeletally immature patients are managed by orthoses, while curves greater than 45 degrees require surgery. When surgery is necessary, a variety of techniques may be used, but most generally involve a posterior spinal fusion and some type of segmental spinal instrumentation.

The risk for progression of spinal deformity in children with congenital scoliosis varies depending on the growth potential of the malformed vertebra. Overall, 25 percent of patients with congenital scoliosis will not demonstrate curve progression and do not require treatment, but 75 percent of patients will demonstrate curve progression, and 50 percent will require treatment. Orthotic treatment is of limited value because these curves tend to be rigid.

Prognosis

Orthoses are 60 to 75 percent effective in controlling curve progression. They do not provide permanent correction of the deformity.

ALCOHOLISM

A 48-year-old man is brought to the emergency room after being found unresponsive on a park bench. The patient is poorly groomed, wears tattered clothing, and smells strongly of alcohol. After fluid hydration and intravenous multivitamins, the patient becomes alert and is questioned regarding his history of alcohol use. He reports having his first drink at age 14 and, by late high school, he claims to have been a daily drinker. He describes his father and brother as "drunks." The patient successfully completed college and was employed as an accountant while using alcohol on a daily basis. After ten years of employment at the same company, he was fired due to his alcohol-related absenteeism and poor work performance. The patient reports that, at the time he was fired, he was drinking every morning and would develop "the shakes" if he did not drink alcohol throughout the day. Since that time he has held occasional odd jobs but has been homeless for the past 3 years.

DIAGNOSIS

Alcoholism is a chronic and progressive disease characterized by a loss of control over the use of alcohol, with subsequent social, legal, psychological, and physical consequences. For most people, the pattern of severe difficulties with alcohol becomes apparent in the mid-20s to mid-30s. Alcohol dependence is characterized by a history of alcohol-related problems, including compulsive intake of alcohol, alcohol taking an increasingly important place in a person's life, and evidence of physical withdrawal symptoms. The physical dependence upon alcohol appears to be related to tolerance. The phenomenon of tolerance is described as the ability to tolerate higher and higher doses of a substance (in this case, alcohol). As the body adapts in order to resist the effects of alcohol, it may reach a condition in which it cannot function optimally unless alcohol is present. Other possible signs of alcoholism include a persistent desire and unsuccessful efforts to cut down on drinking despite recurrent consequences, and drinking larger amounts or over longer time periods than intended. The diagnosis of alcohol dependence is fairly obvious once the pattern of alcohol-related life problems has been observed.

Alcohol withdrawal is characterized by a coarse tremor of the hands, insomnia, anxiety, and increased blood pressure, heart rate, body temperature, and respiratory rate. The distinction between the terms "alcohol abuse" and "alcohol dependence" is that the criteria for alcohol abuse do not include tolerance, withdrawal symptoms, or a pattern of compulsive use; they include only the harmful consequences of repeated use.

CAGE QUESTIONNAIRE

- C   Have you ever felt that you ought to cut down on your drinking?
- A   Have people annoyed you by criticizing your drinking?
- G   Have you ever felt bad or guilty about your drinking?
- E   Have you ever had a drink first thing in the morning to steady your nerves or to get rid of a hangover (eye opener)?

PATHOGENESIS

At some time during life, 90 percent of the population of the U.S. drinks alcohol. Initial alcohol intake is usually related to social, religious, or psychological factors. Alcohol ingestion produces changes in feeling states and subsequently increases the likelihood that a person will have a psychological drive to continue to drink the substance despite potentially severe adverse consequences. However, the factors that influence the decision to drink, or those that contribute to temporary problems, are probably different from those that contribute to the development of alcohol dependence. There is a three- to four-fold increase in risk of severe alcohol problems in close relatives of people with alcohol problems, which supports a genetic basis for alcoholism.

There are three ways in which the body develops tolerance to alcohol. Behavioral tolerance is the process of learning how to perform tasks effectively despite the effects of alcohol. Pharmacokinetic tolerance is the adaptation of the metabolizing system to clear alcohol from the body more rapidly. Cellular tolerance is the adaptation of the nervous system that allows it to function despite high blood alcohol levels. The adaptation of the body to prolonged exposure to and high doses of alcohol is likely to produce physical dependence, which is the basis of the alcohol withdrawal syndrome.

EPIDEMIOLOGY

Alcoholism is probably the most common serious, diagnosable behavioral or psychiatric disorder. The lifetime risk for alcohol dependence is approximately 10 percent for men and 3 to 5 percent for women. The rate of alcohol abuse may be as high as 20 percent for men and 10 percent for women.

TREATMENT

Once alcoholism is diagnosed, the general steps involved in treatment are confrontation, detoxification, and rehabilitation. The goal of confrontation is to break through patients' denial and help them to recognize the existing and potential adverse consequences if the disorder is not treated. The first step in detoxification is a thorough physical examination. Severe alcohol withdrawal is characterized by delirium tremens, a state of confusion, and is sometimes accompanied by visual, tactile, or auditory hallucinations. A small percentage of alcoholics also demonstrates one or two generalized seizures, usually within 48 hours of stopping drinking. Severe alcohol withdrawal is unlikely in the absence of a severe medical disorder or combined drug abuse. The second step of detoxification is to offer rest, adequate nutrition, and multivitamins (especially thiamine). Rehabilitation efforts are directed at increasing and maintaining high levels of motivation for abstinence and helping patients readjust to a lifestyle free of alcohol.

Counseling or therapy may be carried out in an individual or group setting. Counseling efforts are directed at helping patients build a lifestyle free of alcohol, which includes a sober peer group, social and recreational events that do not involve drinking, and a way of recognizing situations in which the risk for relapse is high. Self-help groups such as Alcoholics Anonymous that provide help twenty-four hours a day enable patients to associate with a sober peer group and provide role models for recovering alcoholics in the form of the sober members of the group.

Unless the patient is one of the 10 to 15 percent of alcoholics who have an independent mood disorder, schizophrenia, or anxiety disorder, psychotropic medications are not indicated. One possible exception to this rule is the alcohol sensitizing agent disulfiram, which may be used to place the patient in a condition in which drinking alcohol precipitates an uncomfortable reaction.

PROGNOSIS

It is impossible to predict whether any specific person will maintain abstinence. The following are favorable prognostic indicators: the absence of a diagnosis of antisocial personality disorder or drug dependence; evidence of a supportive general life, and whether or not the patient stays for the full course of the initial rehabilitation. Cirrhosis of the liver is found in 15 percent of alcoholic persons.

ANTISOCIAL PERSONALITY DISORDER

A 23-year-old man is referred by the court for a psychiatric evaluation after his ninth shoplifting arrest in the past year. The information provided by the criminal justice system indicates that he has a long history of arrests dating back to early adolescence for a variety of crimes against persons and property. When asked about the events leading to the arrest and the subsequent referral for evaluation, the patient replies, " I don't know what that judge's problem is, I was just walking through that store! The security guards set me up; made it look like I was stealing something." When questioned about his long criminal history, he dismisses it as, "some nonsense, I never took anything from anybody who didn't have it coming to them." The patient has never been able to maintain regular employment for longer than six months at a time and, when questioned about his irregular work history, replies, "Why should I work for somebody else while they get rich? I need to take care of myself." The patient reports having a wife and young child whom he deserted two years ago. When asked about how he felt about abandoning his family, the patient replied, "She was a nag, always bugging me about my drinking and getting a job. She'll be all right, the system will take care of her." When questioned about alcohol and drug use, the patient reports daily alcohol use and the occasional use of heroin and cocaine.

DIAGNOSIS

Antisocial personality disorder is characterized by a pervasive pattern of disregard for and violation of the rights of others, and presents by early adulthood. Impulsivity is a central feature of the disorder and is often manifested by a failure to exercise normal caution. Persons with antisocial personality disorder believe that coercion or personal profit motivates all people, including themselves. They value others for what they can provide and believe that in order to survive, they need to extort and manipulate wherever they can. This perspective manifests itself in a variety of unlawful behaviors such as theft, evasion of debts and taxes, and physical intimidation. Persons with antisocial personality disorder may appear to derive pleasure from the problems they cause others, often acting in a manner that could be described as cruel or sadistic. However, their acts may be motivated only by self-serving purposes, and they may show a simple disregard for the effects of their actions on others.

Persons with antisocial personality disorder lack fidelity, loyalty, and honesty, which prevents them from forming mutually satisfactory relationships. Their infidelity, evasion of responsibility, and betrayal of promises prevents them from functioning well as a spouse or a parent. The inner experiences of persons with antisocial personality disorder are flat and barren; they view all other people as cold and self-serving.

PATHOGENESIS

Genetic factors appear to play a role in antisocial personality disorder but do not fully account for the disorder's development. Frequent exposure to substance abuse and criminal behavior during childhood are risk factors for the development of antisocial personality disorder. Other risk factors include childhoods notable for erratic, neglectful, harsh, and abusive parenting; attention deficit/hyperactivity disorder in childhood; and sociological variables including poverty in an urban setting, illegitimate or adoptive status, membership in a large family, frequent divorce, and poorly structured schooling.

EPIDEMIOLOGY

The prevalence of antisocial personality disorder in the general population is 2 to 3 percent. It is three to four times more common in men than women and is most prevalent in lower socioeconomic urban populations. An increased frequency of occurrence of depression, substance abuse, somatization disorder, and antisocial personality disorder are found in the family histories of persons with antisocial personality disorder.

TREATMENT

Psychosocial modalities have only selective value in the treatment of antisocial personality disorder, and biological therapies are not effective at all. Traditional treatment settings are not typically useful; more effective, treatment can occur in specialized therapeutic community programs. The antisocial behaviors need to be intensely and directly confronted on a daily and immediate basis.

PROGNOSIS

Antisocial behaviors tend to peak in early adulthood and gradually diminish with age. The reduction in antisocial behaviors may be due to the negative social, economic, legal, and interpersonal consequences that develop over time. For a significant number of persons with antisocial personality disorder, the cessation of antisocial behavior may be marked by the introduction of chronic substance abuse or other psychiatric symptoms, and as many as one-third may eventually develop alcoholism.

BIPOLAR DISORDERS

A 28-year-old-man is brought to the emergency room by ambulance and is accompanied by the police. The police report that the patient was involved in an altercation in a bar after acting very inappropriately with several other customers and the staff. The police report that, according to the bartender, the patient insisted on buying drinks for everyone in the bar even if they did not want them and then went up to people who refused and proclaimed that he had "hit it big and wanted to celebrate." The police go on to report that he sexually harassed the waitress, touching her inappropriately and insisting that she sit on his lap. When the bartender intervened, the patient proceeded to shove him and yell, "Who do you think you are, telling me what to do! Don't you know who I am? I could buy and sell you in a minute!" When questioned about his behavior, the patient responds, "I have every right in the world to be buying drinks in that bar, don't they know who I am? And on a similar note, do you know how the market closed today? I have a great deal of money riding on an important trade. And why are the police harassing me?" The patient's speech is very rapid and pressured. When asked about the speed of his speech, the patient responds, "I've got a million ideas racing through my head, that's why my firm had to fire me today, they knew that with my expertise and speed I was going to take over the place soon." When asked about his sleep habits, the patient exclaims, "Sleep! Who needs it? I get a few hours every night or two. I am too busy to waste time sleeping."

DIAGNOSIS

Bipolar disorders are characterized by the presence of at least one excited (manic or hypomanic) episode. Manic episodes consist of disturbances of mood, psychomotor activity, circadian function, and cognitive function. The clinical features of mania are generally the opposite of depression. Some patients with bipolar disorder may have only manic episodes, but most eventually have at least one or more depressive episode. The symptoms of a manic episode are listed below.

Manic Episode—Characteristic Symptoms

1. Inflated self-esteem or grandiosity
2. Decreased need for sleep
3. More talkative than usual or pressure to keep talking
4. Flight of ideas or subjective experience that thoughts are racing
5. Distractibility
6. Increase in goal-directed activity or psychomotor agitation
7. Excessive involvement in pleasurable activities that have a high potential for painful consequences

The Diagnostic and Statistical Manual of Mental Disorders, 4th Edition (DSM-IV) criteria for a manic episode requires that three or more of these symptoms be present during a period of at least one week. There are three major types of bipolar disorders. The diagnosis of **bipolar I disorder** requires only the presence of a manic episode, but most patients will experience a depressive episode during their lifetime. **Bipolar II disorder** is characterized by the presence or history of one or more major depressive episodes, and the presence or history of at least one hypomanic episode. **Cyclothymic disorder** is characterized by hypomanic symptoms combined with depressive symptoms that do not meet the criteria for major depressive disorder.

PATHOGENESIS

Genetic vulnerability and biochemical abnormalities are clearly involved in the development of the bipolar disorders, but psychological factors play a role in the precipitation of manic episodes. Genetic transmission is more firmly established for bipolar I disorder than for major depressive disorder. In family members of bipolar patients, both bipolar I disorder and major depressive disorder are more common.

EPIDEMIOLOGY

The lifetime prevalence of bipolar disorder I is approximately 0.4 to 1.6 percent. The lifetime prevalence of bipolar II disorder is approximately 0.5 percent. The lifetime prevalence of cyclothymic disorder is approximately 0.4 to 1.0 percent. Manic episodes are about equally prevalent in men and women and the prevalence of bipolar disorders does not vary by race. The average age of onset of the bipolar disorders is between 20 and 40 years, but they may present at any time during adulthood. A family history of depression is the most important risk factor for the development of bipolar disorders.

TREATMENT

For acute mania, lithium remains the treatment of choice. The antimanic action of lithium may take several weeks to manifest and can be augmented with other agents, particularly in the early phases of treatment. Traditionally, lithium has been augmented with antipsychotics, but more recently carbamazepine, valproic acid, and high-potency benzodiazepines (clonazepam and lorazepam) have been used. Lithium is used for the maintenance treatment of patients with bipolar disorders. Monitoring of trough levels (performed in the early morning before the first dose is given) at one- to two-month intervals is recommended. Long-term maintenance treatment with antipsychotics should be avoided, if possible, because bipolar patients have an increased risk of developing tardive dyskinesia.

Side effects of lithium include gastrointestinal disturbances (particularly diarrhea), impaired thyroid function, and neuropsychiatric syndromes (tremor, confusion, and myoclonic twitches). Lithium impairs antidiuretic hormone function at the level of adenylate cyclase and often produces a syndrome of diabetes insipidus.

Pregnant patients should not be treated with lithium because of the increased risk for Ebstein's anomaly, a teratogenic malformation of the cardiac and great vessels. There is a substantial risk of spina bifida associated with the use of valproate. Carbamazepine is associated with an increased risk of minor congenital malformations, developmental delay, and spina bifida.

The treatment of depressive episodes in a patient with bipolar disorder is very different from the treatment of a patient with major depressive disorder. Agents used for the treatment of major depressive disorder (selective serotonin reuptake inhibitors, cyclic antidepressants, monoamine oxidase inhibitors) may induce a switch into hypomania or mania, or speed up the rate of cycling in rapid-cycling patients. These antidepressant agents need to be used with caution and other options, such as the addition of a mood stabilizer (lithium, carbamazepine, or valproate), should be considered.

Adjunctive psychotherapy can be useful in the treatment of bipolar disorder. Approximately one third of patients do not respond or respond only partially to lithium, and even for those who do respond, adjunctive psychotherapy can be helpful in addressing the psychological and behavioral problems associated with bipolar disorder. Adjunctive psychotherapy can also improve compliance with medication.

PROGNOSIS

The bipolar disorders are medical illnesses that are disabling in the short term and potentially recurrent and disabling in the long term. Long-term prophylaxis is generally indicated for the patient with bipolar disorder, particularly if the patient has a family history of bipolar illness. On average, manic episodes predominate in youth, and depressive episodes predominate later in life.

BORDERLINE PERSONALITY DISORDER

A 27-year-old woman is referred to the psychiatric outpatient clinic after hospitalization for a suicide attempt. When questioned about the circumstances surrounding the suicide attempt, the patient angrily responds, "I was furious with my boyfriend. I thought he loved me, I thought he was the greatest thing in the whole world, but now I know different. He is a completely worthless human being!" A series of healed linear scars is noted on her forearm. When questioned regarding the origin of the scars, the patient responds, "that happened because of my mother, when I was in college I told her not to go on vacation for two weeks and she did, so I cut myself." The patient reports having 8 different jobs in the past 5 years. She attended college for three semesters, but dropped out because she "hated everyone there."

DIAGNOSIS

The borderline personality disorder is characterized by a pervasive pattern of instability in interpersonal relationships, self-image, and affect. Patients with borderline personality disorder have marked impulsivity (beginning by early adulthood) and are severely dysfunctional. Their relationships are unstable, intense, and stormy. They have sudden and dramatic shifts in their views of others, typically alternating between extremes of idealization and devaluation. An important defense mechanism used by persons with borderline personality disorder is splitting, in which widely divergent views of themselves or others are present simultaneously, and people are divided into groups of the idealized (all good) and the devalued (all bad). The impulsive actions of persons with borderline personality disorder are distinctive for their potential or actual self-damaging effects. Repetitive suicide threats, gestures, and attempts, including overdoses and self-mutilation, are common. These self-destructive acts are usually precipitated by threats of separation from others, rejection, or the demands of intimacy. Patients are chronically dysphoric, displaying a mixture of depression, anger, loneliness, and emptiness.

PATHOGENESIS

The available evidence suggests that borderline personality disorder is of multifactorial origins. It appears to be the result of a variety of nonspecific, predisposing neurobiological, early developmental, and socializing factors.

EPIDEMIOLOGY

Borderline personality disorder occurs in 2 to 3 percent of the general population and is the most common personality disorder seen in clinical settings. It occurs three times more often in women than it does in men. Borderline personality disorder is five times more common among first-degree relatives of those who have the disorder than it is in the general population.

R_x

TREATMENT

Long-term individual psychotherapy can be helpful to persons with borderline personality disorder, but they often discontinue treatment impulsively and angrily. The response to pharmacological treatment is inconsistent; some patients benefit from low doses of antipsychotics or monoamine oxidase inhibitors. Serotonin-specific reuptake inhibitors can diminish both impulsive and mood-related symptoms, and are usually tried first because of their safety.

PROGNOSIS

The course of borderline personality disorder is variable. Persons with borderline personality disorder may attain some stability in their interpersonal relationships and vocational functioning, but others often experience profound dysfunction in those same important aspects of life. Persons with borderline personality disorder have an increased risk of suicide, and 8 to 10 percent eventually die this way.

COCAINE DEPENDENCE

A 27-year-old man presents to the emergency room with complaints that "my heart feels like it is going to explode out of my chest." The patient appears diaphoretic, anxious, agitated, and hypervigilant. The patient is very talkative and his speech is pressured. Initially, he is very suspicious of the hospital staff and is unwilling to give his name or other identifying information. Blood pressure is 190/120 mm Hg, pulse is 130/min, and temperature is 38.2 C (100.8 F). The patient admits to using cocaine intravenously within the past hour. When questioned further regarding his cocaine use, the patient reports that he started using cocaine intranasally several years ago on an intermittent basis, but over the past year he has progressed to using cocaine, either intravenously or by smoking crack-cocaine, on a daily basis. He lost his job as a consequence of his cocaine use approximately a year ago and is currently homeless. The patient reports several arrests for drug possession and petty crimes within the past year.

DIAGNOSIS

Cocaine dependence is defined as a cluster of physiological, behavioral, and cognitive symptoms that, taken together, drive the patient to continue to use cocaine despite significant problems related to such use. Cocaine abuse is a term used to categorize a pattern of maladaptive use of cocaine that leads to clinically significant impairment or distress within a 12-month period, but in which the symptoms have never met the criteria for cocaine dependence.

Cocaine can be taken orally, by injection, by absorption through nasal and buccal membranes, or by inhalation and absorption through the pulmonary alveoli. The half-life of a single dose of cocaine in the blood is about 30 to 90 minutes. Intravenous injection or freebase inhalation produces an intensely pleasurable sensation, which only lasts a few minutes. The other psychological and physiological effects decline more slowly. Cocaine intoxication is characterized by euphoria, suspiciousness, hypervigilance, anxiety, hyperactivity, talkativeness, and grandiosity. Signs and symptoms of central nervous system stimulation include tachycardia, cardiac arrhythmias, elevated or lowered blood pressure, pupillary dilation, perspiration, or chills. Common symptoms of cocaine withdrawal include dysphoria, fatigue, insomnia or hypersomnia, increased appetite, psychomotor retardation or agitation, and anhedonia.

As cocaine use progresses, some persons place greater priority on obtaining and using cocaine than on meeting other social obligations or avoiding such threats as toxicity or arrest. They may engage in illegal activities to raise money or trade sex for the drug. Major medical complications of cocaine use are listed in the table below.

Major Medical Complications of Cocaine Use

Cardiovascular
    Intracranial hemorrhage
    Aortic dissection, rupture
    Arrhythmias
    Myocardial ischemia and infarction
    Renal infarction
    Intestinal infarction
    Myocarditis
    Shock
    Sudden death

Central Nervous System
   Seizures
   Transient focal neurological deficits
   Subarachnoid hemorrhage
   Intracranial hemorrhage
   Cerebral infarction
   Toxic encephalopathy
Respiratory
   Pulmonary edema
   Pneumothorax
   Respiratory arrest
Metabolic
   Hyperthermia
   Rhabdomyolysis
Reproductive
   Spontaneous abortion
   Placental abruption
   Premature rupture of the membranes
   Intrauterine growth retardation
   Congenital malformations
   Neonatal delayed neurobehavioral development

Cocaine use can induce paranoia, suspiciousness, and overt psychosis, which can be difficult to distinguish from acute paranoid schizophrenia. Users of cocaine may exhibit behavior similar to that seen in hypomanic or manic patients.

PATHOGENESIS

Substance dependence is the result of a process in which social, psychological, cultural, and biological factors influence substance-using behavior. Social and cultural factors largely influence the initial use and continued availability of cocaine. The pharmacological properties of cocaine are believed to play a very important role in the perpetuation of use and subsequent progression to dependence; cocaine has potent mood-elevating and euphorigenic actions, particularly when injected or inhaled. Although some physical dependence does develop, an aversive withdrawal syndrome like the one experienced by those addicted to opioids or sedatives probably does not play as important of a role in perpetuating the use of cocaine. The odds of cocaine dependence are increased among persons with alcohol dependence, schizophrenia, bipolar disorder, or antisocial personality disorder, but it is unclear how this comorbidity is etiologically linked to cocaine. Learning and conditioning are believed to be important factors in the perpetuation of cocaine use.

EPIDEMIOLOGY

The lifetime prevalence rate for cocaine dependence or abuse is 0.2 percent. Although cocaine use has fluctuated dramatically over the past 20 years, epidemiological evidence does not reveal notable and consistent changes in the incidence and prevalence of cocaine-related disorders.

TREATMENT

The general principles of treatment for cocaine dependence are similar to those for other drugs of abuse. It is generally believed that discontinuance of the use of cocaine must be the goal of treatment and that any use of cocaine will lead to a return to dependence. Psychological treatment approaches include cognitive-behavioral, psychodynamic, and general supportive techniques. In addition, patients may be encouraged to participate in Cocaine Anonymous, Narcotics Anonymous, or Alcoholics Anonymous for additional support. There are currently no pharmacological treatments that produce decreases in cocaine use.

PROGNOSIS

The treatment of cocaine dependence may have various outcomes ranging from complete relapse resulting in continued cocaine dependence to total abstinence from cocaine and other drugs.

EATING DISORDERS
(ANOREXIA NERVOSA AND BULIMIA NERVOSA)

A 15-year-old female adolescent is brought to her family physician by her parents who report that she is "starving herself to death." The patient appears very thin and has a pale skin tone. Her parents describe her eating "rituals"; she cuts her food into small pieces, moves it around her plate, and eats very slowly, avoiding foods with high fat and carbohydrate contents. The patient's parents report that they suspect that their daughter is abusing laxatives and "making herself vomit." They estimate that their daughter has had a 9 kg (20 lb) weight loss over the preceding year. The patient becomes angry at this point, crying out, "I have to eat like that, look how fat I am!" The patient reports that she is 157 cm (62 in) tall and weighs 38.5 kg (85 lb), which she emphasizes is "too heavy for someone my size, look how fat my legs are!" According to the patient's chart, menarche occurred at age 12 years 8 months, but the patient reports amenorrhea for the past year.

DIAGNOSIS

The differential diagnosis for eating disorders must include an evaluation for any medical illnesses (such as cancer) that could account for the weight loss. Weight loss can also occur in certain mental disorders, particularly depression. However, depressed patients have decreased appetites, whereas anorexia nervosa patients have normal appetites. The patient with anorexia nervosa typically is preoccupied with the caloric content and serving size of food, which is not seen in depressed patients.

The diagnostic criteria for anorexia nervosa include: refusal to maintain body weight at or above a minimally normal weight for age and height, intense fear of gaining weight or becoming fat despite being underweight, disturbances in self-evaluation of one's own body weight or shape, and amenorrhea in postmenarchal females. The DSM-IV recognizes two types of anorexia nervosa: a *restricting type*, in which the patient does not regularly engage in binge eating or purging behavior (i.e., self-induced vomiting or the misuse of laxatives, diuretics, or enemas) and a *binge eating/purging type* in which the patient regularly engages in binge eating or purging behavior during the current episode of anorexia nervosa.

It is critical to distinguish anorexia nervosa from bulimia nervosa. The diagnosis of bulimia nervosa cannot be made if binge eating and purging occur exclusively during episodes of anorexia nervosa. Patients with bulimia nervosa suffer from powerful and intractable urges to overeat; have disturbances in self-evaluation of body weight or shape; seek to avoid the fattening effects of food by inducing vomiting, abusing purgatives, or both; and have a morbid fear of becoming fat, but they do not meet the criteria for anorexia nervosa (in that they maintain a near-normal body weight). The patient described above would meet the criteria for anorexia nervosa, binge eating/purging type.

PATHOGENESIS

Anorexia and bulimia nervosa are illnesses that have a variety of predispositions; many persons in a population may have the predisposition, but only some actually develop it. Culturally, there is a strong prejudice against obesity and great value is placed on thinness. A family history of depressive disorders, alcoholism, obesity, or an eating disorder increases the risk for the development of an eating disorder.

There is a 50 percent rate of concordance for anorexia nervosa among monozygotic twins versus a 10 percent concordance rate among dizygotic twins. At the individual level, predisposing factors for eating disorders include a sense of personal helplessness, fears of losing control, and self-esteem that is highly dependent upon the opinions of others.

EPIDEMIOLOGY

The eating disorders anorexia nervosa and bulimia nervosa have become more common in the past 25 years and affect primarily women, who account for 90 to 95 percent of all cases. Prevalence studies have found that anorexia nervosa is found in about 0.5 percent of young girls and bulimia nervosa in about 1.5 percent. Eating disorders often develop in adolescence; most patients develop the disorder between the ages of 12 and 25. Recent studies have not found an increased incidence in the upper social classes as was once a widely held belief.

TREATMENT

The complicated psychological and medical nature of anorexia nervosa requires a comprehensive treatment plan. Most patients can be treated as outpatients through a program that includes monitoring eating and weight, monitoring appropriate biochemical indices (nutritional and electrolytes), and psychotherapy. Individual and family therapy, based on a variety of behavioral, psychodynamic, and cognitive approaches, is indicated. However, patients who have lost a substantial amount of weight and who have not been able to gain weight during outpatient treatment require inpatient treatment. Emergency admissions may also be required for metabolic or suicidal crises. Pharmacotherapy has been shown to be of limited value in the treatment of anorexia nervosa. Anxiety, which may be a prominent feature of anorexia nervosa, can be treated with benzodiazepines or antipsychotics. The treatment for bulimia nervosa is similar to that for anorexia nervosa, except that pharmacotherapy is of greater value. A variety of antidepressant medications, including desipramine, imipramine, trazodone, and fluoxetine, have been shown to reduce binge eating and vomiting.

PROGNOSIS

Eating disorders display an extremely varied course, ranging from mild illnesses to lifelong disorders. Recent studies have documented an 18 percent mortality rate from either complications of anorexia nervosa or suicide in chronic patients.

EXTRAPYRAMIDAL SIDE EFFECTS
OF ANTIPSYCHOTIC DRUG THERAPY

A 23-year-old man hospitalized for a psychotic episode complains to the staff of a stiff neck and back, and states that it "feels like someone is pulling on my muscles." The patient was started on antipsychotic medication two days prior. Temperature is 37 C (98.6 F), blood pressure is 110/70 mm Hg, and pulse is 80/min. On physical exam, the patient's head is firmly turned to the left and his back is arched rigidly. It is not possible to change the position of patient's head.

DIAGNOSIS

The extrapyramidal symptoms of antipsychotic drug therapy include acute dystonias, parkinsonian syndrome, tardive dyskinesia, and neuroleptic malignant syndrome. One or more extrapyramidal symptoms may occur simultaneously. Acute dystonias, which consist of intermittent and sustained spasms of the muscles of the head and neck, are one of the most frightening extrapyramidal side effects experienced by patients. The dystonias lead to involuntary movements including opisthotonos (tetanic spasms in which the spine and extremities are bent forward convexly), retrocollis (drawing back) and torticollis (drawing sideways) of the neck, oculogyric crises, grimacing, dysarthria, and dysphagia.

The parkinsonian syndrome typically consists of rigidity, cogwheeling, and tremors. The neuroleptic malignant syndrome, which is comprised of hyperthermia, severe muscular rigidity, autonomic instability, and changing levels of consciousness, can be fatal. Tardive dyskinesia is a movement disorder that may occur after long-term antipsychotic medication treatment. Patients with tardive dyskinesia have characteristic abnormal movements, including those of the mouth and tongue (lip smacking, sucking, puckering), facial grimacing, choreoathetoid movements of the fingers and toes, and slow writhing movements of the trunk.

PATHOGENESIS

Extrapyramidal symptoms are believed to be caused by altered dopamine dynamics in the dopamine receptor blockade in the substantia nigra and caudate nucleus. The biological risk factors for the development of neuroleptic malignant syndrome are unknown. The exact mechanism of tardive dyskinesia is also unknown, but it is theorized that it results from an increased sensitivity of dopamine receptors in the basal ganglia.

EPIDEMIOLOGY

Acute dystonias occur in 10 percent of patients during the first hours and days of initiating antipsychotic therapy. Parkinsonism syndrome may take days or weeks to appear fully. The neuroleptic malignant syndrome is rare, and tardive dyskinesia takes months or years to develop. At least 10 to 20 percent of patients treated with antipsychotics for more than a year experience tardive dyskinesia.

PSYCHIATRY

TREATMENT

Anticholinergic agents (diphenhydramine, benztropine) are the most effective treatments for extrapyramidal side effects. Neuroleptic malignant syndrome is treated with dantrolene and supportive care (antiparkinsonian medications, fluid and electrolyte replacement, and blood pressure management). Once tardive dyskinesia is diagnosed, the need for antipsychotic therapy should be evaluated since many patients will have a remission if therapy is discontinued. Most patients with tardive dyskinesia require continuation of antipsychotic therapy for chronic schizophrenia, but the lowest effective antipsychotic dosage should be given in order to decrease the risk of progression. Antiparkinsonian medications worsen tardive dyskinesia, while antipsychotics typically suppress it.

PROGNOSIS

Acute dystonias usually last for only a few hours and almost always disappear within 24 to 48 hours after the discontinuation of antipsychotic therapy. Parkinsonian symptoms improve in response to a reduction in the dose of the antipsychotic agent and the addition of anticholinergic agents. Neuroleptic malignant syndrome is potentially fatal, but can resolve within a week with treatment and supportive care. Tardive dyskinesia does not appear to be a progressive disorder for most patients; it typically develops rapidly and then stabilizes, often abating even if antipsychotic therapy is continued.

FACTITIOUS DISORDER

A 34-year-old woman presents to the emergency department with complaints of fever, right lower quadrant abdominal pain, and nausea and vomiting. Attempts at obtaining a medical history are futile; the patient is only willing to discuss her current condition, stating, "I'm in too much pain to answer a lot of useless questions." The patient's temperature is 37.5 C (99.5 F), pulse is 90/min, respirations are 18/min. Abdominal examination reveals exquisite right lower quadrant tenderness, with the patient exhibiting guarding and rebound tenderness. The patient's abdominal exam is also notable for multiple surgical scars. As the nurse is attempting a venipuncture to obtain blood for a complete blood count and electrolyte analysis, the patient becomes very argumentative, telling the nurse that "he doesn't know what he is doing" and "obviously that isn't the best place to draw blood." Further efforts to obtain the details of the patient's prior medical and surgical history are without success. The patient refuses to answer any questions and screams out, "Can't you see that I have appendicitis and need emergency surgery!" A review of the patient's hospital medical records reveals that one year prior, she underwent an emergency laparotomy for presumed appendicitis. At the time of surgery, evidence of a prior appendectomy was noted and no organic basis for her symptoms could be identified. The surgeon's preoperative note documented that the patient clearly denied ever having a prior appendectomy.

DIAGNOSIS

A diagnosis of factitious disorder is made in a patient who intentionally causes his or herself to be ill for the sole purpose of becoming a patient. The patient may go to great extremes to convincingly mimic the signs and symptoms of various medical and psychiatric disorders. Some examples of this phenomenon include: urinalysis contaminated with blood or feces, surreptitious self-administration of epinephrine, surreptitious injection of insulin, self-inoculation of bacteria, self-insertion of gas, needles, or metallic fragments in joint areas to mimic arthritic symptoms. These actions are deliberate and thought out; the patient is often well educated about the nature of the illness he or she is feigning, but the symptoms appear to be beyond the patient's ability to control. When the patient is presented with painful or life-threatening procedures, he or she displays an inappropriate lack of overt anxiety, and many patients will demand specific treatments. When confronted with evidence or suspicions of the deception, the patient usually becomes angry and leaves the hospital, typically accusing the physician of incompetence or malpractice.

The first step in the evaluation of a patient for factitious disorder is to evaluate for medical or psychiatric disorders that may be causing or contributing to the signs and symptoms that the patient displays. Patients with factitious disorder often suffer from associated true medical complications (e.g., may have abdominal adhesions from multiple surgeries.) The criteria for making a diagnosis of factitious disorder are that the patient intentionally feigns physical or psychological signs and symptoms, is motivated by the desire to assume the sick role, and external incentives (economic, legal, physical well being) are absent. In factitious disorder, the behavior is planned and intentional, but the motivation is largely unconscious. Somatoform disorder is exemplified by patients who demonstrate symptoms for which there is no demonstrable organic basis. The production of symptoms in somatoform disorder is unconscious; the patient believes that the illness is real. In malingering, symptoms are intentionally feigned to achieve an overt and tangible goal such as obtaining monetary compensation, obtaining shelter, or avoiding police.

PATHOGENESIS

Clearly there are complex forces at work that produce the bizarre presentation of a person motivated to compulsively deceive hospital staff and self-inflict harm. Patients know they are acting, but cannot stop themselves. Over time, they become increasingly more medically knowledgeable, which allows them to carefully craft their factitious signs and symptoms.

EPIDEMIOLOGY

The factitious disorders encompass a wide variety of patients and by nature are difficult to diagnose, which makes obtaining systematic epidemiologic data difficult. Factitious disorders typically begin in early adulthood and the episodes may follow a real illness, loss, or abandonment. No genetic or familial pattern has been established. Most studies of factitious disorder report that the diagnosis is more common in persons employed in or familiar with medically related occupations.

TREATMENT

The treatment of factitious disorder is very difficult and full resolution of symptoms is rare. The standard approach is confrontation in a supportive, nonaccusatory manner with assurances that care and treatment will continue. Psychiatric hospitalization is usually indicated where appropriate psychodynamic and behavioral therapies can be initiated. At this time, other possible concomitant psychiatric disorders, typically depressive disorders, borderline personality disorder, or substance-related disorder should be investigated.

PROGNOSIS

Factitious disorder has a varied course and prognosis ranging from a few brief episodes to a chronic, lifelong disorder.

GENERALIZED ANXIETY DISORDER

A 23-year-old woman presents with complaints of "being worried all the time." The patient reports, "I have always been nervous and high-strung, but over the past year I seem to have been worried about *everything* and it is starting to get hard for me to make it through the day." The patient is very nervous when driving to work, afraid that she will get into an accident. While at her job as an editor, she finds herself worrying that she is making errors, despite rechecking her work frequently. She finds the anxiety and worry uncontrollable; nothing that she can do, say, or think seems to alleviate it. Recently, she has had to take several days off from work because she has been very fatigued and has had difficulty concentrating on her tasks. For the past year she has suffered from neck and back pain, which she attributes to muscle tension. During the day, she feels very restless and on edge, but at night she has difficulty falling asleep and does not feel well rested in the morning.

DIAGNOSIS

Generalized anxiety disorder (GAD) is defined as excessive anxiety and worry for 6 months or longer, and is accompanied by at least three of six somatic symptoms.

Generalized Anxiety Disorder Symptoms

- Restlessness or feeling "keyed up" or on edge
- Difficulty concentrating or mind going blank
- Irritability
- Easy fatigability
- Muscle tension
- Sleep disturbance (difficulty falling or staying asleep, or restless, unsatisfying sleep

The anxiety is difficult to control and causes significant impairment in social or occupational functioning and/or marked distress in the patient. A diagnosis of GAD is not made if the anxiety is a feature of another Axis I disorder or is due to substance intake or a general medical condition. Patients may suffer from tension headaches and back and neck pain. Patients may complain of shortness of breath, palpitations, sweating, dizziness, hot and cold flashes, and frequent urination. They may also experience disturbances in gastrointestinal function. Patients with GAD are irritable and easily startled. Other conditions that should be considered in the differential diagnosis of GAD include panic disorders, depressive disorders, hypochondriasis, and substance-related disorders.

PATHOGENESIS

The etiology of GAD is currently unknown, but anxiety involves both psychological and physiological processes.

EPIDEMIOLOGY

Anxiety disorders are among the most common psychiatric disorders, and GAD is probably the most common anxiety disorder. The age of onset is usually in the late teens or early 20s. Woman are twice as likely to be affected by GAD as men.

TREATMENT

The treatment for GAD includes both psychological and pharmacological approaches; psychotherapy appears to augment the efficacy and shorten the duration of pharmacotherapy. Cognitive behavior techniques (cognitive restructuring, relaxation, breathing, psychoeducation, and exposure) can be used to reduce the severity of symptoms of GAD, but they do not induce a complete remission. Benzodiazepines are generally used to pharmacologically treat GAD. Tolerance to the sedative and psychomotor side effects of benzodiazepines develop within a few weeks, but tolerance to their antianxiety effects is rare. Prolonged use of benzodiazepines produces a physiological dependence, which induces a resultant withdrawal syndrome upon discontinuation of therapy; benzodiazepines must be tapered slowly when discontinued. Buspirone, a partial 5-hydroxytryptamine$_{1A}$(5-HT$_{1A}$) agonist, is effective in the treatment of GAD. Cyclic antidepressants, which are effective in treating panic disorder, can also be effective in treating GAD. β-blockers, which are typically not effective in treating GAD when used alone, can be used to treat the palpitation, tremor, and perspiration associated with anxiety.

PROGNOSIS

GAD tends to run a chronic and fluctuating course, with periodic exacerbations and remissions. Without treatment of the anxiety, extended periods of remission are unlikely.

HISTRIONIC PERSONALITY DISORDER

A 34-year-old white man presents to the psychiatric outpatient clinic with complaints of "things not going right." He is meticulously dressed, deeply tanned, and well groomed. The patient collapses into a chair, lets out a deep sigh, and states in an exasperated tone, "Everything is closing in on me, I am being abandoned by those I care about most." When asked to go into further detail, the patient describes how his wife of ten years is threatening to leave him because of his flirtatious behavior. He goes on to say, "She just doesn't understand, this is the way I am. I need to get close with people when I meet them to better understand them." When asked to describe his wife, he states, "She is a truly wonderful, wonderful person—we are extraordinarily close." When asked to elaborate on the nature of their relationship, he is unable to provide any specific details about their interactions, other than to say, "I love her with all my being, without her my heart would be a dark, unfathomable void."

DIAGNOSIS

Histrionic personality disorder is characterized by a pervasive pattern of excessive emotionality and attention seeking, typically beginning by early adulthood. Persons with histrionic personality disorder tend to be expressive, gregarious, dramatic, and flamboyant. Typically, they express emotion with inappropriate exaggeration. Their colorful displays of emotion can be engaging, but may appear insincere; their emotions may seem shallow or rapidly shifting. Their style of speech is dramatic and lacking in detail. Persons with histrionic personality disorder tend to exaggerate the intimacy of their relationships and are often uncomfortable when they are not the focus of attention. They may attempt to draw attention to themselves by being very lively, dramatic, charming, or flirtatious. They may also be inappropriately sexually seductive in appearance or behavior, and may express their seductiveness indiscriminately. They are often overly concerned with their physical attractiveness and spend excessive time and effort on their appearances.

PATHOGENESIS

Increasing evidence indicates that typical histrionic traits are part of a person's constitutional makeup and are necessary predispositions for the development of histrionic personality disorder.

EPIDEMIOLOGY

The prevalence of histrionic personality disorder in the general population is estimated to be approximately 2 to 3 percent. Clinicians tend to diagnose the disorder in women more frequently than in men, but studies using rigorous diagnostic criteria report that is equally prevalent in men and women. Studies suggest that histrionic personality disorder runs in families.

TREATMENT

The primary treatment of histrionic personality disorder is individual psychotherapy. Patients with histrionic personality disorder often present for treatment of depression, vague physical problems, or relationship difficulties.

PROGNOSIS

The personality traits of self-centeredness, tendency to exaggerate, and lack of attention to detail cause difficulties in forming mutually satisfactory intimate relationships, determining appropriate behavior in social situations, and maintaining employment in certain occupations.

MAJOR DEPRESSIVE DISORDER

A 36-year-old female presents with complaints of "feeling sad all the time." The patient reports that for the past 3 months she has felt increasingly depressed. She goes on to report that she has been having increasing difficulty performing her routine tasks at home and work and feels very "sluggish." She is an executive and reports that it has become increasingly difficult to concentrate at work and that her productivity has decreased notably, so much so that her immediate supervisor has remarked upon it. The patient goes on to relate that she feels, "tremendously guilty over not being able to perform at work, I feel absolutely worthless. I don't know how my coworkers can stand me." During this time, she has felt very tired and unable to exercise, which she typically does on a daily basis. She reports feeling no interest in pursuing other normally pleasurable activities, such as reading or going to the movies. When questioned about her sleep patterns, the patient responds, "It has been terrible. I have trouble falling asleep and staying asleep every night." The patient denies having a specific plan for suicide, but remarks that "I wouldn't mind if a bus ran me over." The patient denies any history of manic episodes or symptoms.

DIAGNOSIS

Major depressive disorder is the most common mood disorder. Characteristically, patients with major depressive disorder display disturbances in mood, psychomotor activity, cognitive function, and vegetative function. The symptoms of a major depressive episode are described below.

Major Depressive Episode Characteristic Symptoms

1. A depressed mood most of the day nearly every day
2. Markedly diminished interest or pleasure in all (or almost all) activities most of the day nearly every day
3. Significant weight loss when not dieting, or weight gain; or a decrease or increase in appetite nearly every day
4. Insomnia or hypersomnia nearly every day
5. Psychomotor agitation or retardation nearly every day
6. Fatigue or loss of energy nearly every day
7. Feelings of worthlessness or excessive or inappropriate guilt nearly every day
8. Diminished ability to think or concentrate or indecisiveness nearly every day
9. Recurrent thoughts of death, recurrent suicidal ideation without a specific plan, or a suicide attempt or specific plan for committing suicide

The DSM-IV criteria for a major depressive episode requires that five or more of these symptoms be present during the same 2-week period and that at least one of the symptoms is either a depressed mood or the loss of interest or pleasure. The DSM-IV diagnostic criteria for major depressive disorder requires the presence of a major depressive episode without any history of a manic or hypomanic episode. Depressive symptoms that do not meet the criteria for major depressive episode characterize dysthymic disorder.

PATHOGENESIS

Depressive disorders should be conceptualized as complex neuroendocrinometabolic disorders that involve many different organ systems throughout the body. Their pathophysiology is not restricted to brain function. Abnormalities in the physiology of the biogenic amines (norepinephrine, epinephrine, dopamine, and serotonin) are thought to be associated with the pathophysiology of major depressive disorder. Biogenic amines, which are released into the synaptic space and act at pre- and postsynaptic receptors, have diverse effects on brain function. Alterations in the sensitivity of the postsynaptic receptors may be related to both the action of antidepressants and the pathophysiology of the depressive disorders. Various endocrine changes are associated with the depressive disorders, including alterations in the hypothalamic-pituitary-adrenal, the hypothalamic-pituitary-thyroid, and the hypothalamic-pituitary-growth hormone axes.

Stressful negative life events and chronic stress appear to predispose a person to episodes of major depressive disorder. Certain personality attributes, which develop early in life as a result of biological tendencies, coupled with social environment, are closely related to the risk of mood disorders later in life. Persons predisposed to develop a depressive disorder have been shown to lack energy, be more introverted, worry, be more dependent, and be hypersensitive. Major depressive disorder is frequently comorbid with the Axis II disorders.

EPIDEMIOLOGY

The lifetime prevalence of major depressive disorder is 10 to 25 percent for women and 5 to 12 percent for men. Dysthymic disorder has a lifetime prevalence of 6 percent. The prevalence of mood disorders does not vary by race. The average age of onset of major depressive disorder falls between the ages of 20 and 40 years. A family history of depression is the most important risk factor for the development of major depressive disorder. The rates for major depressive disorder are highest among separated and divorced persons, and lowest among single and married persons. Unemployment is also a risk factor for major depressive disorder.

TREATMENT

Depression is a serious, potentially life-threatening medical illness. Current models of treatment recognize the importance of combining both psychosocial and pharmacological approaches in most patients. Common antidepressant medications and their side effects are listed in the table on the next page.

Common Antidepressant Medication Side Effects		
Class	Examples	Side Effects
Selective serotonin reuptake inhibitors	fluoxetine, sertraline, paroxetine	Nausea, weight loss, sweating, sedation, dry mouth, and sexual dysfunction
Serotonin nonselective reuptake inhibitors	venlafaxine	Agitation with insomnia, internal sense of being driven, headache, tremor, gastrointestinal upset, and sexual dysfunction
Heterocyclics	nortriptyline, imipramine	Sedation, weight gain, hypotension, anticholinergic properties, lethal in overdose
Monoamine oxidase inhibitors	tranylcypromine, phenelzine	Dietary restrictions necessary, sedation, weight gain, hypotension, many drug incompatibilities
Other	Trazodone	Sedation, weight gain, priapism
	Buspirone	Minimal sedation and weight gain

Selective serotonin reuptake inhibitors (SSRI) are one of the leading types of antidepressants sold in the U.S., mainly because of their relatively benign side effects. Antidepressants must be administered for several days to weeks before their response can be evaluated. Once an antidepressant treatment is found to help alleviate an acute episode of major depressive disorder, treatment should be continued for 6 to 9 months to reduce the risk of relapse.

Many types of psychotherapeutic approaches based on a variety of concepts are now in use, including psychoanalysis, interpersonal therapy, behavioral therapy, and cognitive-behavioral therapy. The choice of treatment, the duration of treatment, and whether or not to use more than one treatment modality at a time is based on the phase of the illness, patient characteristics, the presence of chronicity and dysthymia, or the presence of bipolar disorder.

PROGNOSIS

The prognosis for recovery from an acute episode is good for most patients with major depressive disorder. However, two-thirds of patients will experience recurrences throughout life and have varying degrees of residual symptoms between episodes. Major depressive disorder is treatable, despite its chronicity. Suicide is a complication that occurs in approximately 15 percent of depressive patients.

NARCISSISTIC PERSONALITY DISORDER

A 34-year-old man presents to the psychiatric clinic with complaints of "marriage trouble." The patient begins the interview by describing his wife's complaints. He states, "She says that I don't listen to her; that I don't care what goes on with her. I don't know what her problem is; I make a ton of money. I'm the best at what I do, and she has everything she could ever want." When asked how it made him feel to hear his wife state that she is not satisfied with him, he replies, "I think she just complains a lot. She is lucky to have me." He describes his coworkers as "a bunch of incompetent morons that I am burdened with." It is suggested to the patient that he may need to make some changes in his behavior if his marriage is to succeed, to which he replies, "Changes? The only change I'm going to make is to change doctors. I knew I shouldn't have come here, you people don't know what you're doing. I need someone better trained to help me."

DIAGNOSIS

Narcissistic personality disorder is characterized by a pervasive pattern of grandiosity, a need for admiration, and a lack of empathy, all of which begin in early adulthood. Persons with narcissistic personality disorder typically have an aggrandized sense of self-importance, overestimate their abilities, and inflate their accomplishments. They expect to be recognized as superior, special, or unique. Patients are often preoccupied with fantasies that confirm and support their grandiosity; these fantasies often involve admiration and special privileges they believe should be forthcoming. Their sense of entitlement may be exhibited by behaviors that demonstrate their expectation of special treatment, such as assuming they should not have to wait in line while others should. They generally lack the ability to empathize with the desires, experiences, and feelings of others, and have an unemotional style of interpersonal involvement.

Patients with narcissistic personality disorder typically have vulnerable self-esteem, which makes them particularly sensitive to injury from criticism, defeat, and rejection. Their interpersonal relationships are inevitably impaired because of problems derived from their feelings of entitlement, need for admiration, and disregard for the sensitivities of others.

PATHOGENESIS

Temperaments characterized by high energy, tension, and conscientiousness may nonspecifically predispose persons to the disorder. Some theories suggest that pathological narcissism develops from ongoing childhood experiences of having fears, failures, dependence, or other signs of vulnerability responded to with criticism, disdain, or neglect.

EPIDEMIOLOGY

It is estimated that the prevalence of narcissistic personality disorder in the general population is less than 1 percent. The disorder is diagnosed in men more frequently than in women.

TREATMENT

Individual psychotherapy is the basic treatment for patients with narcissistic personality disorder.

PROGNOSIS

There is considerable variability in the course of narcissistic personality disorder. Most patients show improvement in their occupational adjustments and interpersonal relationships over time.

OBSESSIVE-COMPULSIVE DISORDER

A 29-year-old man is referred to the psychiatric clinic by his dermatologist, who notes his "excessive" hand washing. When questioned about his hand-washing habits, the patient states that he washes his hands 40 to 50 times a day. His rationale is that; "I just can't leave the house before I get them really clean. I know it sounds crazy, but if I touch anything on the way out of the house I have to wash them again." When questioned further about ritualistic behaviors, the patient volunteers that he needs to check to make sure the stove is turned off fifteen to twenty times before he leaves the house and often has to go around to all the appliances to make sure they are unplugged several times before leaving. These behaviors often cause him to be late for appointments, and he was recently fired from a job because of his tardiness. The patient also reports intrusive recurring thoughts, usually of a sexual nature. He has stopped attending church because of the recurring sexual thoughts; he was frightened of his impulse to shout obscenities at the priest.

DIAGNOSIS

Obsessive-compulsive disorder (OCD) is characterized by either obsessions or compulsions that are a significant source of distress, are time consuming, or interfere significantly with a person's normal routine, occupational functioning, or social activities or relationships. Obsessions are defined as recurrent and persistent thoughts that are intrusive and inappropriate and cause the patient anxiety and distress. Compulsions are repetitive behaviors that the patient feels driven to perform in response to an obsession. Compulsions are aimed at preventing or reducing distress or preventing some dreaded event or situation, but are unconnected realistically with what they are designed to neutralize or prevent. Obsessions are usually anxiety-provoking, while compulsions are usually anxiety-relieving. A typical obsession would be exaggerated cleanliness, and a typical related compulsion would be hand washing. Mental compulsions include praying, counting, and repeating words silently.

Patients who reveal the nature of their obsessions may appear bizarre or irrational, but they almost always retain full insight and recognize that their thoughts and impulses are unreasonable. Symptoms can usually be placed into one of the following categories: checking rituals, cleaning rituals, obsessive thoughts, obsessive slowness, or mixed rituals. Checking or cleaning rituals are the most common and virtually all patients have multiple symptoms.

OCD is frequently confused with obsessive-compulsive personality disorder (see page 242). OCD is an Axis I disorder, while obsessive-compulsive personality disorder is an Axis II disorder.

PATHOGENESIS

Imaging studies and neurochemical evidence suggest a neurological etiology for OCD.

EPIDEMIOLOGY

A lifetime prevalence of OCD in the U.S. is estimated to affect between 2 and 3 percent of the general population. OCD typically begins in early adulthood, and over 80 percent of those affected develop symptoms before age 35.

TREATMENT

Pharmacotherapy is the treatment of choice for OCD; antidepressants, particularly clomipramine, are the most effective. Patients with OCD generally receive medication in combination with other styles of treatment, particularly behavioral therapy. Psychoanalysis and psychodynamic-oriented psychotherapy are not effective in the treatment of OCD, but supportive psychotherapy in combination with pharmacotherapy can be helpful. Behavior therapy produces the most significant changes in rituals.

PROGNOSIS

Generally, OCD is a chronic illness with a waxing and waning course, even with treatment. Complete cures are unusual, but approximately 90 percent of patients can expect moderate to marked improvement with treatment.

OBSESSIVE-COMPULSIVE PERSONALITY DISORDER

A 38-year-old man presents to the psychiatric clinic with complaints of "difficulties at work." The patient is a well-groomed, impeccably dressed man who appears serious and stiff at the interview. He is an attorney at a large firm and has always been praised for his thoroughness, devotion, and attention to detail. He was recently promoted and is now in charge of a large project; there are several other attorneys working under his leadership. The patient relates that he is having a great deal of difficulty supervising the team members because "they don't do anything right. I have laid out exactly how everyone should proceed, but they insist on doing it their own way and I have had to redo most of their work myself. We are falling very far behind schedule." When questioned further about his planning, he states that he made daily schedules for each of the members of the team, delineating what he or she should spend their time doing in 10-minute intervals. He is unmarried and without any close friends. When asked about his social life, he states, "My work is my life; I spend my weekends at the office. I don't leave a stone unturned when I am working on a case."

DIAGNOSIS

Obsessive-compulsive personality disorder typically begins in early childhood and is characterized by a pervasive pattern of preoccupation with orderliness, perfectionism, and mental and interpersonal control at the expense of flexibility, openness, and efficiency. Persons with this disorder have high standards and strive for perfection, to the point that they delay or do not complete tasks because they have not met their own overly strict standards. A common associated feature is indecisiveness; they so are painstakingly preoccupied with details, rules, lists, order, organization, and schedules that they lose sight of the main point of the activity. They may also allocate their time poorly, at times leaving the most important tasks to the last minute. They are controlling; for example they might give others highly detailed instructions about how a task should be done and may be annoyed if alternative methods are suggested. Patients with obsessive-compulsive personality disorder are excessively devoted to their work, typically to the exclusion of social activities.

Persons with obsessive-compulsive personality disorder are capable of intimacy and loyalty, but tend to express emotions in a formal, controlled manner. They may have a miserly spending style toward themselves or others, typically hoarding money for some future catastrophe. They also are unable to discard worn-out or worthless objects, even when they have no sentimental value. The net effect of these traits makes it difficult for persons with obsessive-compulsive personality disorder to engage in meaningful relationships.

The use of a similar name for Axis I obsessive compulsive disorder can lead to confusion, but the two disorders are distinct and, with the exception of hoarding, have different criteria. Obsessive-compulsive disorder is characterized by repetitive, unwanted thoughts (obsessions) and ritualistic behaviors, rather than broad personality traits.

Pathogenesis

Erikson's view of the anal stage of development as a time of expression of autonomy versus shame may identify the disorder's origins. The child's expression of drives, emotions, and willful autonomy may be met by excessive parental disapproval, which may cause the child to stifle emotional expression and focus on the details of childhood tasks. Obsessive-compulsive personality traits are probably reinforced by cultures that place a great value on hard work and the subordination of individual expression to outside demands.

Epidemiology

The prevalence of obsessive-compulsive personality disorder is estimated to be 1 percent in the general population. The disorder appears to be twice as prevalent among men as it is among women.

Treatment

Individual psychotherapy is the treatment of choice for obsessive-compulsive personality disorder. Persons with obsessive-compulsive personality disorder may seek treatment because they feel that their lives are pleasureless and unfulfilling or because they are encountering difficulties with work or relationships.

Prognosis

Persons with obsessive-compulsive personality disorder have problems in relationships because of their stubbornness and inflexibility, and as a result may live barren lives with few friends and little intimacy. Their perfectionism, perseverance, and attention to detail may be useful in certain occupations, but to meet the criteria for the personality disorder, those traits must be so extreme as to be maladaptive.

OPIOID DEPENDENCE

A 28-year-old woman presents to the emergency room with complaints of "feeling sick." The patient reports that she has been using heroin intravenously for the past 5 years, but has not used any for the past 12 hours. The patient is homeless and supports her drug use through prostitution. The patient complains that, "I am sweating a lot, my nose is running, I have diarrhea, my skin feels prickly, and I feel very nervous."

DIAGNOSIS

Opioid dependence is characterized by a maladaptive pattern of opioid use that leads to clinically significant impairment or distress, manifested by a number of signs and symptoms including tolerance; withdrawal; using opioids in larger amounts or over longer time periods; unsuccessful efforts to cut down or control use; a great deal of time spent in activities necessary to obtain opioids; giving up important social, occupational, or recreational activities because of opioid use; and continued opioid use despite adverse consequences. The diagnosis of opioid dependence can be relatively straightforward if the patient is willing to be honest, but can be troublesome if the patient is motivated to conceal past patterns of opioid use. Because of the tolerance to many of the actions of opioid drugs that is developed after chronic use, even the careful observer may not detect opioid effects in a patient.

Opioid withdrawal is rarely life threatening in healthy adults, but its effects can vary greatly in intensity depending on the patient's typical dose, the rate at which the opioid is removed from the receptors, and the duration of the patient's use. Typical symptoms include craving, anxiety, dysphoria, yawning, perspiration, lacrimation, rhinorrhea, restless and broken sleep, dilated pupils, aches, piloerection, and hot and cold flashes. In more severe cases, additional symptoms include nausea, vomiting, diarrhea, weight loss, low-grade fever, and increased blood pressure, pulse, and respiratory rate.

PATHOGENESIS

Substance dependence is the result of a process in which multiple interacting factors (social, psychological, cultural, and biological) influence substance-using behavior. This biopsychosocial perspective sees the actions of the substance as critical, but claims that not all persons exposed to the substance will experience its effects in the same way. Only a fraction of people who experiment with opioids develop serious problems. Opioids have potent mood-elevating and euphorigenic effects, particularly when they are injected or inhaled. Repeated opioid use typically induces a physical dependence that results in an aversive withdrawal syndrome when brain opioid levels decline. This appears to play a key role in perpetuating use. Tolerance does not develop uniformly to all of the actions of opioid drugs. Very high tolerance can develop to the analgesic, respiratory depression, and sedative actions of opioids, but markedly less tolerance is developed to their miotic effects and the inducement of bowel constipation.

There are several opioid receptors that have been identified. The μ receptor, primarily found in the central nervous system, is where classic opioids such as morphine bind and produce their effects. The κ receptor is where drugs such as butorphanol and nalbuphine exert their effects. The δ receptor is the preferential binding site for endogenous met-enkephalin.

EPIDEMIOLOGY

In the U.S., the lifetime prevalence of heroin use is estimated to be 1.5 percent and the lifetime prevalence of heroin dependence is estimated to be 0.4 percent. Rates of alcohol and drug abuse, mental illness, and antisocial personality disorder are higher in the families of heroin users.

TREATMENT

The first step of opioid treatment is withdrawal. Patients who have not been dependent on opioids for more than a year or who have not previously made any attempts at withdrawal are not appropriate candidates for prolonged opioid therapy. Oral methadone is often used to ameliorate the severity of opioid withdrawal. Clonidine, an α_2-agonist, can also be used to suppress some aspects of the opioid withdrawal syndrome. Opioid antagonists such as naltrexone may be used as part of treatment.

The treatment of opioid dependence may involve outpatient, inpatient, residential, or day-care settings. Treatment may involve group, individual, or family therapy. Many opioid users benefit from participation in self-help groups such as Narcotics Anonymous (NA).

In the U.S., more than 100,000 patients are receiving methadone maintenance treatment at any given time. Methadone is an μ-receptor agonist that produces euphoria, analgesia, and other typical morphine-like effects. However, when given chronically by the oral route, patients develop tolerance to these effects. Methadone has a long half-life (approximately 24 hours) and when given orally has a reliable but slow absorption and consistent bioavailability. This combination of tolerance, a long half-life, and slow onset of action buffers the patient against any sharp peak of subjective effect.

PROGNOSIS

Most patients, whether treated with either a drug-free or methadone maintenance model, do not achieve long-term opioid abstinence. For a substantial number of opioid-dependent persons, it is prolonged incarceration that ends the opioid use. The majority of patients treated in methadone programs shows significantly decreased opioid and nonopioid drug use, criminal behavior, and symptoms of depression; and increased gainful employment. Patients who discontinue methadone maintenance treatment against medical advice are very unlikely to have sustained abstinence from opioids.

PANIC DISORDER/AGORAPHOBIA

A 34-year-old woman presents to a psychiatrist with complaints of being "too scared to leave my house." The patient reports that she is overwhelmed with fear when in crowds, that she begins to sweat, feels her heart pounding, feels that it is difficult to breath, and thinks, "I am going to die." These attacks began approximately 2 years ago and have become progressively worse, increasing in both frequency and intensity. For the past 6 months she has been refusing to take public transportation, avoiding driving alone over bridges, and avoiding standing in line at the supermarket. Over the past 2 months, she has been unable to leave the house unaccompanied because of an overwhelming fear that a panic attack will occur in public and that she will "go crazy and not be able to control myself." The patient reports that she has had numerous medical evaluations, all of which have been normal.

DIAGNOSIS

Panic attacks are sudden rushes of fear that are accompanied by several somatic symptoms such as difficulty breathing, palpitations, and dizziness. Panic disorder is a common, chronic illness characterized by recurrent, unexpected panic attacks and the associated avoidance and worry related to their possible occurrence. Panic attacks are different from generalized or free-floating anxiety; they are discrete periods that reach peak intensity within seconds or minutes and subside soon afterward. Panic attacks are different from phobic anxiety in that they are not always predictable.

Typical Panic Attack Symptoms

1. Abdominal distress or nausea
2. Chest discomfort or pain
3. Chills or hot flashes
4. Derealization or depersonalization
5. Diaphoresis
6. Fear of losing control or "going crazy"
7. Fear of dying
8. Feeling dizzy, unsteady, light-headed, or faint
9. Feeling of choking
10. Palpitations, pounding heart rate, or tachycardia
11. Paresthesias
12. Sensation of shortness of breath or smothering
13. Shaking or trembling

The somatic symptoms of panic often mimic those of common catastrophic medical events such as myocardial infarction. Panic attacks are a common symptom of many psychiatric and medical conditions. However, in panic disorder, the panic attacks are not due to another medical or psychiatric condition and are not the result of the effects of a substance or medication. In panic disorder, the panic attacks recur unexpectedly, causing the patient persistent concern about experiencing attacks and the implications of the next attack or its consequences. Patients with panic disorder demonstrate a significant change in behavior that is related to the attacks. Patients with panic disorder may or may not have associated agoraphobia.

Several nonpsychiatric medical conditions and organic factors can mimic the symptoms of panic disorder.

Medical Conditions Mimicking Panic Disorder	
Condition	Symptoms
Thyroid Dysfunction	Patients with hyper- and hypothyroidism commonly experience symptoms of anxiety
Parathyroid Dysfunction	Hyperparathyroidism may present as panic disorder
Adrenal Dysfunction	Pheochromocytomas can cause symptoms of anxiety, headaches, tachycardia, sweating, flushes, trembling, and hypertension
Vestibular Dysfunction	Can cause vertigo with accompanying nausea, vomiting, ataxia, and anxiety
Cardiac conditions	Arrhythmias, supraventricular tachycardia, and mitral valve prolapse may produce symptoms similar to panic attacks
Hypoglycemia	Somatic symptoms may be similar to certain symptoms of a panic attack
Seizure disorders	Particularly temporal lobe epilepsy. May manifest with symptoms of panic anxiety
Intoxication syndromes	Intoxication with CNS stimulants (amphetamines, caffeine, cocaine) can cause panic attacks
Withdrawal syndromes	CNS depressant withdrawal (alcohol, barbiturates) can cause panic attacks

Agoraphobia is characterized by anxiety about being in places or situations from which escape might be difficult or in which help may not be available in the event of an unexpected or situationally predisposed panic attack. Persons with agoraphobia typically fear situations that include being outside the home alone; being in a crowd or on a bridge; or traveling by bus, train, or automobile. Agoraphobic persons avoid these situations, or else endure them with marked distress or anxiety or only in the presence of a companion. Agoraphobia typically occurs in the setting of panic disorder, but can rarely occur without panic disorder. In these cases, fear and avoidance are associated with the possibility of suddenly developing a paniclike symptom (dizziness, sudden diarrhea, loss of bladder control).

PSYCHIATRY

PATHOGENESIS

The etiology of panic disorder is addressed by both psychological and biological theories. Psychological theories of panic disorder are based on conditioning, personality, and cognitive hypotheses. Biological theories of panic disorder are based on the observations that panic attacks can be both blocked and induced by the administration of various pharmacologic agents.

EPIDEMIOLOGY

The lifetime prevalence rate of panic disorder is estimated to be between 1.5 to 2 percent. Approximately 3 to 4 percent of the population report panic attacks but do not meet the full criteria for panic disorder. Women are two to three times more likely than men to develop panic disorder or experience panic attacks. Family history is a significant risk factor for being affected by panic attacks or developing panic disorder. Panic disorder typically begins in late adolescence or early adulthood. The onset of panic disorder after age 45 is rare.

The prevalence of agoraphobia is not well defined. In clinical populations, agoraphobia is almost never seen without an accompanying history of panic disorder or attacks. Women are two to three times more likely than men to develop agoraphobia. There is also a heritable contribution to agoraphobia.

TREATMENT

Treatments of panic disorder include pharmacotherapy, cognitive-behavioral therapy, and a combination of the two. Several different agents have been demonstrated to be effective in the acute treatment of panic disorder. These include tricyclic antidepressants, monoamine oxidase inhibitors, and high-potency benzodiazepines. Serotonergic agents may also be useful, but this is less well documented. Certain specific drugs are *not* useful in treating panic disorder: bupropion, maprotiline, L-deprenyl, buspirone, and ritanserin. β-adrenergic receptor antagonists such as propranolol may block palpitations and other cardiovascular symptoms, but do not block actual panic attacks.

Cognitive-behavioral treatments are administered in four parts: 1) cognitive therapy and psychoeducation, 2) applied relaxation, 3) respiratory control techniques, and 4) in vivo exposure. Cognitive therapy and psychoeducation are directed toward addressing beliefs and misinterpretations that may contribute to the induction and continuation of panic attacks. Relaxation training is directed toward reducing arousal levels and may help give the patient a sense of control over panic attacks. Respiratory control techniques are designed to help control the hyperventilation that typically accompanies panic attacks. Exposure therapy, in which the patient is confronted with the feared stimulus, is used for avoidance symptoms.

PROGNOSIS

The lifetime course of panic disorder is chronic but fluctuating. Persons with panic disorder are more likely to suffer from major depressive disorder. Substance abuse is also a frequent sequela of panic disorder. This is typically brought on in an effort to self-medicate. Overall, despite its chronicity, the long-term prognosis of patients with panic disorder is good, with most patients eventually able to lead relatively normal lives.

PARANOID PERSONALITY DISORDER

A 28-year-old man presents to the psychiatry outpatient clinic for a follow-up visit. During the previous clinic visit, the patient stated that his reason for seeking counseling was because of anxiety concerning an impending career decision, but he did not want to go into detail about it because he was unsure if the psychiatrists at the clinic "were on his side." Now the patient has returned to discuss his issues, but still appears guarded and serious. When asked about the nature of his concerns, he responds that he is considering leaving his current employer because "they have been using me for years, taking my ideas and making millions off of them." He has a job interview scheduled at another company, but is uncertain whether he should show up for it. He feels that "these companies are all in this together. They share the information they steal from me and if I change jobs, this company will probably work with my old employers to continue to profit from my work." The patient divorced his wife two years prior because "she was always sneaking around behind my back." Asked if he had any direct evidence of her infidelity, he states, "I knew what was going on. She was tricky, but I knew what she was up to."

DIAGNOSIS

Paranoid personality disorder is characterized by a pervasive distrust and suspicion of others, such that their motives are interpreted as malevolent. Patients with paranoid personality disorder often suspect without cause that others will exploit, harm, or take advantage of them. They doubt the loyalty of their friends, associates, and spouses or sexual partners. They are reluctant to confide in others because of the fear that the information will somehow be used against them. They constantly scrutinize the behavior of others in search of evidence of deception, and often misinterpret benign remarks or events. Their attitudes are intense and strongly defended. Persons with this disorder typically appear argumentative, sarcastic, guarded or aloof, and have difficulty relaxing. They may function stably in the work place, particularly if their work does not require cooperation with others. When under extreme stress they may have overtly paranoid thinking, but it does not usually reach the level of psychosis.

The diagnosis of paranoid personality disorder does not imply the presence of overt psychosis. Paranoid schizophrenia, unlike paranoid personality disorder, is characterized by persistent psychotic symptoms such as hallucinations and bizarre delusions. Paranoid personality disorder and schizotypal personality disorder have the traits of suspiciousness and paranoia in common, but paranoid personality disorder lacks the cognitive and perceptual disturbances that are characteristic of schizotypal personality disorder.

PATHOGENESIS

The cause of paranoid personality disorder remains largely unknown.

EPIDEMIOLOGY

The prevalence of paranoid personality disorder is estimated to be in the range of 0.5 to 2.5 percent of the population. Paranoid personality disorder appears to be somewhat more common in men than in women.

TREATMENT

People with paranoid personality disorder are difficult psychotherapy patients because of their distrust and suspicion of others. Nevertheless, the main focus of treatment is for the therapist to build a trusting relationship with the patient.

PROGNOSIS

Clinical experience suggests that paranoid personality disorder is characterized by a chronic course, particularly in the absence of treatment. Paranoid personality disorder may be associated with major depression, agoraphobia, obsessive-compulsive disorder, and suicide attempts.

PARAPHILIAS

A 36-year-old man is referred for an evaluation by the criminal justice system. The patient was arrested for exposing his genitals to a neighbor. He explains that he experiences an overwhelming desire to expose his genitals and that he finds the shock and fear of his unsuspecting female victims very exciting. Typically, he feels compelled to masturbate immediately after the event. The patient reports feeling guilty and ashamed for engaging in this behavior and has vowed repeatedly never to do it again, but the desire often overwhelms him and he has performed this act in excess of fifty times. The patient has been married for seven years and describes sexual relations with his wife as "dull."

DIAGNOSIS

Paraphiliacs experience intense sexual urges and sexual fantasies that involve nonhuman subjects, children, or nonconsenting persons; or the suffering or humiliation of one's self or partner. Paraphilias are characterized by specialized sexual fantasies, masturbatory practices, sexual props, and requirements of or for the sexual partner. The table below lists some paraphilias and their distinguishing features.

Paraphilias	
Pedophilia	Recurrent, intense, sexually arousing fantasies, sexual urges, or behaviors involving sexual activity with a prepubescent child or children
Exhibitionism	Recurrent, intense, sexually arousing fantasies, sexual urges, or behaviors involving the exposure of one's genitals to an unsuspecting stranger
Voyeurism	Recurrent, intense, sexually arousing fantasies, sexual urges, or behaviors involving the act of observing an unsuspecting person who is naked, in the process of disrobing, or engaging in sexual activity
Frotteurism	Recurrent, intense, sexually arousing fantasies, sexual urges, or behaviors involving touching and rubbing oneself against a nonconsenting person
Sexual masochism	Recurrent, intense, sexually arousing fantasies, sexual urges, or behaviors involving the act of being humiliated, beaten, bound, or otherwise made to suffer
Transvestic fetishism	Heterosexual male with recurrent, intense, sexually arousing fantasies, sexual urges, or behaviors involving cross-dressing
Sexual sadism	Recurrent, intense, sexually arousing fantasies, sexual urges, or behaviors involving acts in which the psychological or physical suffering of a victim is sexually exciting
Fetishism	Recurrent, intense, sexually arousing fantasies, sexual urges, or behaviors involving the use of nonliving objects

Paraphilias not specified in the chart include sexual excitement derived from telephone scatologia (obscene telephone calls), necrophilia (corpses), partialism (exclusive focus on a part of the body), hypoxyphilia (partial suffocation or strangulation), zoophilia (animals), coprophilia (feces), klismaphilia (enemas), and urophilia (urine). The DSM-IV requires that, for the diagnosis of a paraphilia, the behavior in question be present for at least six months and cause clinically significant distress or impairment in social, occupational, or other important areas of functioning.

PATHOGENESIS

Sexual psychopathology is a subset of personality development. This means that the three major factors that influence personality development—biology, environment, and the synthetic-integrative functions of the mind—must be important in the development of paraphilias. The efficacy of antiandrogen medication in the control of driven or violent sexual behavior suggests that the behavior is centrally mediated and androgen-sensitive.

EPIDEMIOLOGY

Paraphilic behavior appears to peak between the ages of 15 and 25 and then gradually declines. Paraphilias appear to occur predominately in men. As many as 10 to 20 percent of paraphiliacs may have been molested as children (before age 18). As many as 20 percent of women with paraphilias may have been the targets of exhibitionism and voyeurism.

TREATMENT

Cognitive-behavioral techniques, psychoanalysis, and psychotropic agents are used in the treatment of paraphilias. Medroxyprogesterone can be used in male patients whose driven hypersexuality is out of control.

PROGNOSIS

The prognosis in the treatment of paraphilias is generally guarded. The degree of compulsion in the paraphilias appears to decrease as the patient ages.

SCHIZOAFFECTIVE DISORDER

A 27-year-old man is brought to the emergency room by the police after they received a concerned call from the patient's family. The patient's family reports that the patient is "mentally ill" and has been taking antipsychotic medications intermittently since 20 years of age, and in the last year he has been "depressed on and off." The family members go on to note that for over 2 months, he has been profoundly depressed, not eating or sleeping well, not leaving the apartment, and not engaging in activities that he normally finds pleasurable. During this time of depression, the family believes that he has been hearing voices. The family members believe that, in between the bouts of depression, the patient continued to experience psychosis (hearing voices and paranoid delusions). The patient is dressed in soiled, mismatched clothes and is poorly groomed. When questioned about how he is feeling, the patient responds, "Tell them all I feel sad, the microwaves are melting my brain. That's all."

DIAGNOSIS

Patients with schizoaffective disorder have significant and enduring mood symptoms that overlap with prominent psychotic symptoms. The psychotic symptoms continue to be present even during substantial intervals of the illness in which the patient lacks prominent mood symptoms. There is considerable variation in the possible presenting symptoms of schizoaffective disorder. All or any of the psychotic symptoms may be present during an acute episode, including delusions, hallucinations, and evidence of a thought disorder. Prominent mood disorder symptoms are also present in schizoaffective disorder. These may be of either the manic or depressive variety. The psychotic and mood disorder symptoms impair social, occupational, and self-care functioning. Schizoaffective disorder is characterized by an episodic nature. Intervals of intense illness interrupt quiescent periods during which psychosocial functioning is adequate.

PATHOGENESIS

The etiology of schizoaffective disorder is unknown. There are several different theories regarding its cause, including that it is a variant of schizophrenia; a variant of a mood disorder; that it is related to both schizophrenia and affective disorder; or that it is a third psychosis, distinct from both schizophrenia and affective disorder.

EPIDEMIOLOGY

The prevalence of schizoaffective disorder is estimated to be between 0.5 to 0.8 percent of the general population. The age of onset of schizoaffective disorder is typically late adolescence or early adulthood.

TREATMENT

Psychiatric hospitalization is often required during acute psychotic episodes. Antipsychotics, lithium, and antidepressants are used in the treatment of schizoaffective disorder; their combination should be dictated by the nature of the patient's symptoms. These agents are used both for acute and maintenance treatment.

PROGNOSIS

The course and outcome of schizoaffective disorder tend to be more favorable than those of schizophrenia, but less favorable than a pure mood disorder.

SCHIZOID PERSONALITY DISORDER

A 39-year-old man is accompanied to the outpatient psychiatry clinic by his sister. During the assessment interview, the sister says that she made the appointment for her brother because she is "worried about him." She goes on to relate that her brother, who is 5 years her junior, has lived with her since high school, has never dated, and has no close friends. She complains that although he is able to financially support himself, he "has no life." The sister is planning to get married and is worried about what will become of her brother if she leaves him and he is forced to live by himself. The patient sits passively while his sister discusses her concerns with abundant emotion. When questioned about his thoughts and feelings on these matters, the patient replies in a flat, even-toned voice, "I am fine by myself." The sister yells, "All he does is sit at home and fiddle with his computer. He never goes out, he has no friends! What's going to happen to him when I leave?" The sister begins crying. The patient continues to remain expressionless and indifferent while his sister speaks, and when he is asked to further express how he feels about his sister's concerns, he responds, "I'll be all right."

DIAGNOSIS

Schizoid personality disorder is characterized by a pervasive pattern of detachment from social relationships and a restricted range of emotional expression in interpersonal relationships. Patients with schizoid personality disorder are typically described as "loners." They usually have no close friends or confidants, with the possible exception of a spouse or first-degree relative. They rarely marry and are uninterested in sexual experiences with others. They generally find few activities pleasurable. Persons with schizoid personality disorder have difficulty experiencing and expressing emotions; in particular anger and aggression. Their bland, colorless, and constricted affect is notable. Schizoid personality disorder shares certain features in common with other odd cluster personality disorders (social isolation and restricted affectivity), but it lacks the cognitive and perceptual distortions of schizotypal personality disorder and the suspiciousness and paranoid ideation of paranoid personality disorder.

PATHOGENESIS

Schizoid personality disorder may be related to schizophrenia, particularly in its negative symptoms. The social isolation typical of schizoid personality disorder is thought to be due to a lack of desire for intimacy or involvement with others. There is also evidence that patients with schizoid personality disorder often have histories of grossly cold or neglectful parenting. Psychodynamic theories suggest that these early traumatic life experiences may create an expectation that relationships will not be gratifying and result in a defensive withdrawal from others.

PSYCHIATRY

EPIDEMIOLOGY

The prevalence of schizoid personality disorder in the general population is estimated to be in the range of 0.5 to 0.7 percent. This disorder appears to be more common in men than in women.

TREATMENT

Patients with schizoid personality disorder rarely seek treatment and usually avoid therapy when it is recommended. When they do seek treatment, it is usually precipitated by an acute stressor or the encouragement of a family member. Some patients respond well to psychodynamic psychotherapy. The role of drug therapy in this disorder has not been investigated.

PROGNOSIS

The course and prognosis of schizoid personality disorder are not well studied.

SCHIZOPHRENIA

A 19-year-old man is brought to the emergency room by ambulance and is accompanied by the police. The ambulance crew and police were called to the patient's college dormitory to investigate complaints that he was throwing things out the window and yelling obscenities. Fellow students report that the patient has been "acting strange lately. He has not been himself." They go on to report that he has not been grooming himself, stays in his room alone, and has not attended class or social functions for the past several months. The patient's roommate states that when the patient was a freshman he achieved high grades, but for the past six months he has done very poorly academically. The patient is in four-point restraints, screaming, "You can tie me down, but I won't let you control my mind." Attempts at questioning the patient are unsuccessful. He refuses to answer questions and instead yells, "I am the chosen one, decreed by the French high command, your gamma rays cannot make me balance the knives at large!"

DIAGNOSIS

No laboratory tests or biological markers are available for the diagnosis of schizophrenia. All diagnostic criteria entail observing and interviewing patients and obtaining clinical histories from persons who are significant in their lives. DSM-IV requires the presence of at least two characteristic symptoms that endure for a significant portion of time, during at least a one-month period. The list of characteristic symptoms includes delusions, hallucinations, disorganized speech, grossly disorganized or catatonic behavior, and negative symptoms. The DSM-IV also requires the presence of social and occupational dysfunction for a duration of at least 6 months. Additionally, the DSM-IV requires the exclusion of schizoaffective disorder as well as mood disorders with psychotic features, and that the schizophrenic illness not be a consequence of substance abuse or of a general medical condition.

Schizophrenia typically presents during adolescence or early adulthood. The usual presentation is a psychotic episode that is preceded by a period of progressive behavioral symptoms, but a psychotic state can appear suddenly in a person who has no prior history of behavioral symptoms. Persons with schizophrenia often appear odd. For instance, their grooming and personal hygiene may be neglected. Social withdrawal is also a common symptom in schizophrenia, but some patients may be bizarrely intrusive, displaying no understanding of the usual social and interpersonal boundaries. Schizophrenic patients display disorders of thought and speech, including a loosening of associations, clang associations (rhyming and punning), verbigeration (repetition of meaningless words or phrases), echolalia (involuntary parrot-like repetition of a word or sentence just spoken by another person), neologisms (made up words or phrases), and thought blocking. Classically, a flat or blunted affect is common in schizophrenia. There are a number of bizarre behaviors associated with schizophrenia, including catatonic stupor, echopraxia (involuntary imitation of movements made by another), stereotyped behavior, and negativism (tendency to do the opposite of or to stubbornly resist what one is requested to do). Delusions, hallucinations, and illusions are common in schizophrenia, and auditory hallucinations are the most common clinically observed hallucination.

PATHOGENESIS

The exact cause or causes of schizophrenia are not well understood. The syndrome probably represents more than one etiological and disease process. Genetic factors are important in some cases, but the exact genes and their contribution to the pathophysiology of the illness is not clear. Although it is not clear if schizophrenia is a neurodevelopmental or a neuropathological disorder, the preponderance of evidence supports the neurodevelopmental theory.

Studies of brain structure show that schizophrenic patients have relatively less brain tissue than do healthy control subjects, either as a result of its failure to develop or its subsequent loss over time. The dopamine hypothesis of schizophrenia is based on two important observations: 1) drugs that increase activity in the dopaminergic system (amphetamine, levodopa, methylphenidate) can induce a paranoid psychosis similar to schizophrenia in normal subjects, and worsen symptoms in schizophrenic patients; and 2) drugs that block postsynaptic dopamine receptors reduce the symptoms of schizophrenia.

EPIDEMIOLOGY

Schizophrenia affects approximately 1 percent of the world's population. First-degree relatives of a schizophrenic person have approximately a five- to ten-fold greater chance of developing schizophrenia. Children in whom both parents have schizophrenia have a 35 percent chance of developing schizophrenia, as compared to a 1 percent chance if neither parent has schizophrenia. Overall, men and women are affected equally by schizophrenia, but men are more likely to experience an onset of symptoms between the ages of 15 and 25, while women generally experience an onset of symptoms between the ages of 25 and 35. A disproportionate number of schizophrenic persons are born during the winter months. Schizophrenia is more prevalent among members of lower social classes (defined by income, occupation, education, and place of residence.) One explanation for this finding could be that socioenvironmental factors found at lower socioeconomic levels are a cause of schizophrenia (social causation theory). Another explanation, which is currently favored, is that lower socioeconomic status is a consequence of schizophrenia (social drift theory).

TREATMENT

Antipsychotic medications used to treat schizophrenia target the postsynaptic dopamine receptors in the brain (see the table on the next page). These drugs diminish symptom expression and reduce relapse rates. Clozapine, an atypical antipsychotic, is effective in ameliorating psychotic symptoms in patients refractory to typical antipsychotics. There is a 1 to 2 percent risk of agranulocytosis associated with the use of clozapine, and careful monitoring is necessary. Risperidone, a first-line atypical antipsychotic medication, does not have an association with agranulocytosis. Other agents may be used to augment antipsychotic treatment, including lithium, carbamazepine, antidepressants, and benzodiazepines. The side effects of antipsychotics range from mild discomfort to permanent movement disorders.

Commonly Used Antipsychotic Agents		
Class	Generic Name	Chlorpromazine Equivalence
Phenothiazines	Chlorpromazine	100
	Thioridazine	100
	Fluphenazine	2
	Perphenazine	8
Thioxanthenes	Thiothixene	4
	Chlorprothixene	100
Butyrophenones	Haloperidol	2
Dibenzodiazepines	Clozapine	100
Benzisoxazole	Risperidone	0.6

Intensive psychotherapy alone is less effective than drug treatment and is not considered an alternative to the use of antipsychotic medications, but supportive psychotherapy can increase the effectiveness of drug treatment. Psychological treatments for schizophrenia include both individual and group therapies.

PROGNOSIS

Deterioration is not inevitable, but schizophrenia is usually a chronic and disabling disease. The short-term outcome for first-admission patients is that, after two years of illness, approximately 60 percent will have relapsed. The long-term outcome is more complicated; the course of schizophrenia is extremely variable and characterized by remissions and relapses. The suicide risk of persons with schizophrenia is twenty times that of the general population. At least 10 percent of schizophrenic persons commits suicide, most during the first ten years of illness.

SCHIZOTYPAL PERSONALITY DISORDER

A 37-year-old man is brought to the psychiatric emergency room by his mother, who is concerned about his persistent social isolation. The patient's mother describes how the patient lives alone, has no friends or social contacts, and recently lost his job as a stock person at the local grocery store. The patient is dressed in a bizarre manner. He is wearing a shirt that is too small, socks of two different colors, and a stained and tattered raincoat. The patient replies to questions in a flat, detached manner, without looking directly at the examiner. When asked about why he lost his job, the patient replies, "They were not on my side, they didn't appreciate or value my power." When asked to elaborate, the patient mutters softly, "I already told you." The patient is questioned about friendships and social activities, to which he responds, "I don't really like being around people that much, it makes me nervous. I don't need friends." The patient denies any auditory or visual hallucinations.

DIAGNOSIS

Schizotypal personality disorder is characterized by a pervasive pattern of social and interpersonal deficits. This pattern includes an acute discomfort with and reduced capacity for close relationships, along with cognitive or perceptual distortions and eccentricities of behavior that typically begin by early adulthood. The cognitive and perceptual distortions may include ideas (not delusions) of reference, odd beliefs or magical thinking, unusual perceptual experiences, and suspiciousness or paranoid ideation. These patients are not psychotic; they are able to test reality and determine that such distortions are internally rather than externally generated. Patients with schizotypal personality disorder may have odd speech. It may be vague, circumstantial, metaphoric, elaborate, stereotyped, concrete, include idiosyncratic phrasing, or use words unusually. Patients may have odd, eccentric, or peculiar mannerisms or dress.

Persons with schizotypal personality disorder have significant difficulties with personal relationships. They typically have excessive social anxiety, often due to paranoid fears about the motivations of others. Persons with schizotypal personality disorder have difficulty expressing a full range of affects and often relate to others in an inappropriate, stiff, or constricted manner. Schizotypal personality disorder is associated with anxiety, depression, and dysthymic disorder. Up to 50 percent of patients has a history of major depressive disorder.

Schizotypal personality disorder can be distinguished from schizophrenia by the absence of psychosis. It can be distinguished from paranoid and schizoid personality disorders by the presence of cognitive and perceptual distortions, eccentricity or oddness, and profound social discomfort. Although persons with schizotypal personality disorder experience profound social discomfort, they differ from avoidant personality disorder in that they lack the desire to form social attachments.

PATHOGENESIS

There is evidence for a common genetic predisposition for schizophrenia and schizotypal personality disorder. This evidence includes familial risks as well as shared biological abnormalities associated with chronic attention and cognitive dysfunctions, which appear to reflect structural alterations of the central nervous system.

EPIDEMIOLOGY

Schizotypal personality disorder is estimated to have a prevalence of 3 to 5 percent in the general population, and it may be slightly more common in men than in women. Schizotypal personality disorder is more common among the first-degree relatives of schizophrenic patients, and the risk of schizophrenia is higher in relatives of persons with schizotypal personality disorder.

TREATMENT

Most persons with schizotypal personality disorder do not seek treatment, and when they do it is usually for associated symptoms, such as depression or anxiety. Patients with schizotypal personality disorder may respond to antipsychotic medications. Social rehabilitative treatments using supportive and educational methods are useful as well.

PROGNOSIS

The course of schizotypal personality disorder is relatively stable with continued severe impairment. Approximately 10 to 20 percent of patients with schizotypal personality disorder go on to develop schizophrenia.

SLEEP DISORDERS

A 31-year-old woman presents with complaints of "trouble sleeping." The patient reports that she has had great difficulty falling asleep for the past 3 months. Even when she falls asleep, she has difficulty staying asleep, and she wakes up frequently throughout the night. She goes on to complain that, "Every little sound in the house bothers me; I wake up over the slightest noise or movement." The patient states that, even after a full night of sleep, she does not feel rested. The patient, who is an architect, believes the symptoms began while she was working on a challenging project. She decided to seek evaluation now because she is having trouble focusing on her work during the day due to her constant sleepiness. She has had to stop participating in evening social activities because she doesn't want to get "too wound up." At bedtime, she has a great deal of anxiety over whether she will be able to fall asleep or not, which she feels is contributing to her sleeping problems.

DIAGNOSIS

Sleep disorders can be divided into three main classifications: 1) primary sleep disorders, 2) parasomnias, and 3) sleep disorders associated with medical or psychiatric disorders.

Primary sleep disorders are not due to another mental disorder, a general medical condition, or a substance. Parasomnias are abnormal behavioral or physiological events that occur in association with sleep, sleep stages, or the sleep-wake transition. Numerous medical and psychiatric conditions, including substance use, have the potential to affect sleep. The classification of common sleep disorders is noted in the table on the next page.

Sleep Disorders		
Primary Sleep Disorders	Dyssomnia	Abnormalities in amount, quality, or timing of sleep (more common in females).
	Primary Insomnia	Difficulty initiating or maintaining sleep, or nonrestorative sleep.
	Primary Hypersomnia	Excessive daytime sleepiness or prolonged sleep almost daily for at least a month.
	Narcolepsy	Repeated irresistible attacks of refreshing sleep, cataplexy, and recurrent intrusions of elements of REM sleep into the transition between sleep and wakefulness (hypnopompic or hypnagogic hallucinations).
	Breathing-Related Sleep Disorders	Sleep disruption due to abnormal ventilation that leads to excessive sleepiness or insomnia.
	Circadian Rhythm Sleep Disorder	Sleep disruption resulting from a mismatch between endogenous circadian sleep-wake cycle and exogenous demands of timing and duration of sleep.
Parasomnias	Nightmare Disorder	Repeated occurrence of frightening dreams that lead to awakenings with full alertness.
	Sleep Terror Disorder	Repeated occurrence of abrupt awakenings, usually beginning with panicky scream or cry. Episodes are accompanied by autonomic arousal and behavioral manifestations of intense fear. The person is difficult to awaken or comfort. No detailed dreams recalled.
	Sleepwalking Disorder	Repeated episodes of complex motor behavior initiated during sleep, including getting up from the bed and walking. Marked by reduced alertness and responsiveness, blank stare. Limited recall of the events of the episode.
Sleep Disorders Related to a Medical or Psychiatric Disorder	Sleep Disorders Related to Another Mental Disorder	Sleep disturbance is temporally and causally related to another mental disorder, including mood disorders, psychoses, anxiety disorder, panic disorder, and alcoholism.
	Substance-induced Sleep Disorder	Disturbance occurs due to intoxication or withdrawal from alcohol, amphetamines, cocaine, caffeine, opioids, sedative-hypnotics, and anxiolytics.
	Sleep Disorder Due to a General Medical Condition	Disturbance in sleep is due to a general medical condition, but is severe enough to warrant independent clinical attention.

PATHOGENESIS

Sleep disorders comprise a diverse group of conditions with a variety of etiologies. Psychological, physiological, and environmental factors play varying roles across the spectrum of sleep disorders.

EPIDEMIOLOGY

Sleep disorders are common disorders that affect one-third of people at some time in their lives. Dyssomnia is more common in females than it is in males. Narcolepsy occurs in equal rates in men and women. There is a familial tendency to develop sleep apnea syndrome and it is the most prevalent dyssomnia that is encountered in sleep disorder centers.

TREATMENT

Benzodiazepines and imidazopyridines are the most commonly prescribed sedative-hypnotic medications used to treat insomnia. Nonprescription formulas include sedating antihistamines and protein precursors. The chronic use of sleeping pills is not recommended. Stimulants are used in sleep disorders that produce hypersomnolence; pemoline or methylphenidate are used for the extreme sleepiness of narcolepsy, and anxiolytics are used when anxiety represents a critical component of the sleep disorder. Since mood disorders are one of the most common etiologies of insomnia, a sedating antidepressant taken at bedtime can be helpful in treating both the depression and the insomnia. Behavioral treatments include sleep hygiene education (rules for good sleep rituals), stimulus control therapy (cues for sleeping), sleep restriction therapy and feedback (restricting the amount of time spent in the bed), relaxation therapy (self-hypnosis and breathing exercises), and chronotherapy (resetting the biological clock).

Continuous positive airway pressure is effective in alleviating sleep apnea. Sleep apnea is the only primary dyssomnia for which surgery is common, and uvuolopalatopharyngoplasty is helpful for patients with oropharnygeal obstruction. Bright light therapy is used for patients with sleep-wake cycle irregularities.

PROGNOSIS

Outcomes to treatments for sleep disorders vary widely; follow-up and refinement of therapy are essential. Relief from unrelenting sleeplessness or debilitating daytime hypersomnolence can provide incalculable benefit to the patient's well being, quality of life, safety, and overall health.

SUICIDE

A 55-year-old man is brought to the emergency department by ambulance after a suicide attempt. The patient was found in the garage by his wife. He had shot himself with a rifle. The patient's wife reports that her husband has been unemployed for a period of time and was being treated by a psychiatrist for depression. She also describes the patient as having a "drinking problem." Despite resuscitation efforts, the patient expires.

DIAGNOSIS

Many suicides among psychiatric patients are preventable. The psychiatric and social risk factors for suicide in psychiatric patients include: a past suicide attempt, a chronic psychiatric disorder, recent hospital discharge, living alone, unemployment, being unmarried, and a predisposition to depressive symptoms. Mood disorder is the diagnosis most commonly associated with suicide. Approximately 30 to 65 percent of suicide victims has primary depression. More depressed men commit suicide than depressed females. The chances that a depressed person will commit suicide are increased if the person is single, separated, divorced, widowed, or recently bereaved.

PATHOGENESIS

The circumstances surrounding a suicide attempt typically involve a recent life change, particularly interpersonal stress, such as serious arguments with a spouse, having a new person in the home, the serious illness of a family member, serious personal physical illness, and legal problems. Approximately 70 percent of suicide victims are found to have one of two psychiatric disorders: depression or alcoholism. Physical illness is estimated to be a contributing factor in many suicides. Certain diseases of the nervous system in which an associated mood disorder is known to exist are associated with an increased risk of suicide and include epilepsy, multiple sclerosis, head injury, cardiovascular disease, Huntington's disease, dementia, and AIDS. Endocrine conditions that cause mood disorders are associated with increased suicide risk and include Cushing's disease, anorexia nervosa, Klinefelter's syndrome, and porphyria.

EPIDEMIOLOGY

Suicide accounts for 0.4 to 0.9 percent of all deaths in the U.S., making it the eighth leading cause of death. Psychiatric patients have a three- to twelve-fold greater risk of suicide, and the lifetime risk of suicide for alcoholics is approximately 3 percent, which is at least twice the risk of the general population and 60 to 120 times greater than the nonpsychiatrically ill in the general population. The suicide rate of heroin addicts is 20 times that of the general population. Almost 10 percent of schizophrenics die by committing suicide. Suicide rates increase with age; the elderly make up 10 percent of the entire population, but account for 25 percent of suicides.

A review of world literature demonstrates that there is a preponderance of female suicide *attempters* in all countries. Men in all age ranges commit suicide more often than do women, mainly because men tend to use more violent methods than women do. The suicide rate among whites is nearly twice that of non-whites; two out of every three suicides are white males. Married persons have the lowest suicide rates, and the higher the social class, the greater the risk of suicide. Unemployed persons have a greater rate of suicide than employed persons do, and persons in certain occupations are traditionally considered to be at an increased risk for suicide: musicians, dentists, law enforcement officers, lawyers, and insurance agents.

TREATMENT

Since nearly all suicide victims have a treatable psychiatric disorder and typically communicate their self-destructive plans to those around them, suicide should be considered a preventable cause of death. The evaluation for suicide includes a complete psychiatric history and mental status exam, with particular inquiry into depressive symptoms and suicidal thoughts, intents, plans, and attempts. Lack of future plans, making a will, and giving away personal property may indicate an increased risk for suicide. Patients may be treated as either inpatients or outpatients, depending on a variety of clinical parameters and the judgment of the clinician.

PROGNOSIS

Patients who attempt suicide and patients who commit suicide represent different populations, with some overlap. Approximately 1 percent of patients who attempt suicide will commit suicide in the following year. The lifetime risk of suicide among suicide attempters ranges from 1 in 8 to 1 in 50, depending on sex and age. Risk factors for eventual suicide in persons who attempt suicide include: age over 45; male sex; unemployment or retirement; separation, divorce, or having been widowed; living alone; poor physical health; having received medical treatment in the last 6 months; having a psychiatric disorder; having made previous suicide attempts by violent means; and writing a suicide note.

ABDOMINAL AORTIC ANEURYSM

A 74-year-old man presents for a routine examination. He is without complaints. Abdominal examination reveals a large, nontender, pulsatile mass that is palpated at the umbilicus and inferiorly. Respirations are 16/min, blood pressure is 140/90 mm Hg, and pulse is 80/min. Abdominal ultrasound demonstrates an abdominal aortic aneurysm that is 7 cm in diameter. Laboratory studies show:

Leukocyte count	7,300/mm^3	(4,500–11,000/mm^3)
Hematocrit	43%	(Male: 41–53%)
Hemoglobin, blood	14.3 g/dL	(Male: 13.5–17.5 g/dL)
Platelet count	258,000/mm^3	(150,000–400,000/mm^3)
Prothrombin time	12 seconds	(11–15 seconds)
Partial thromboplastin time	29 seconds	(25–40 seconds)

DIAGNOSIS

Aortic aneurysms do not usually produce symptoms, but as they expand they may become painful. Symptoms may be caused by compression or rupture of adjacent tissue by aneurysms. Mural thrombi within the aneurysm may embolize peripherally.

Most aneurysms (75 percent) are discovered while they are still asymptomatic, either as pulsatile masses or unexpectedly during the course of an evaluation for an unrelated condition. Physical examination is accurate in a vast majority of cases. The infrarenal aorta lies at the level of the umbilicus, and the pulsatile mass should be detected in that region. The proven accuracy, safety, and low cost of ultrasonography make it the procedure of choice for the diagnosis and follow-up of aneurysms. Computed tomography (CT) has the advantage of providing an accurate characterization of the entire aorta. CT can provide information about the character and thickness of the aortic wall, and is particularly helpful in evaluating patients with symptoms; it can detect as little as 10 mL of blood outside the lumen of the aorta. Magnetic resonance imaging (MRI) can provide a much more detailed image than either CT or ultrasonography, but is very costly, and there are difficulties in scanning obese patients and patients with pacemakers. Arteriography is not accurate in determining the size or presence of an aneurysm, but can be helpful in defining associated vascular anatomy, particularly the renal arteries. Absolute indications for arteriography include symptoms of mesenteric ischemia, hypertension or renal dysfunction, horseshoe kidney, or claudication or other signs and symptoms of coexistent lower extremity occlusive disease.

Occasionally, an aneurysm may leak, causing pain and tenderness; this constitutes a medical emergency. More often, acute rupture occurs without any prior warning.

PATHOGENESIS

An aneurysm is defined as the pathological dilation of a segment of a blood vessel, and a true aneurysm involves all three layers of the vessel wall. Pseudoaneurysm refers to conditions in which the intimal and medial layers are disrupted and the dilatation is lined by adventitia only (and sometimes by perivascular clot). The infrarenal aorta is the most common site for the development of an abdominal aortic aneurysm. Aortic aneurysms are typically fusiform in shape and usually arise below the origins of the renal arteries, extending a variable distance beyond the aortic bifurcation. Aneurysms tend to grow an average of 0.4 cm per year, but growth occurs at an uneven rate. Abdominal aortic aneurysms are almost always associated with atherosclerosis.

EPIDEMIOLOGY

The most common type of aneurysm presented for treatment is the abdominal aortic aneurysm (AAA). These aneurysms are found in 2 percent of the elderly population. They exist predominantly in males, in which they are nine times more common. There is a familial tendency for the development of aneurysms in 20 percent of patients with AAA, which is either sex-linked or autosomally inherited. The relative risk for first-degree relatives of affected individuals is 11.6.

TREATMENT

Indications for operative resection with graft replacement include prevention of rupture, atheroembolization, associated occlusive disease, and pressure or erosion into contiguous structures. The decision to recommend surgery must weigh the immediate risk of operation against the risk of rupture, which is directly related to the size of the aneurysm. Aneurysms greater than 6 cm in diameter have a significant risk of rupturing and should be operated on unless severe comorbid conditions exist. The five-year risk of rupture for aneurysms that are less than 5 cm in diameter is 1 to 2 percent, but it is 20 to 40 percent for aneurysms greater than 5 cm in diameter. Diastolic hypertension and chronic obstructive pulmonary disease are other risk factors for the rupture of an AAA.

Patients with coronary artery disease (CAD) undergoing aneurysm resection have an increased risk of myocardial infarction, ischemia-related pulmonary edema, and cardiac death. Preoperative cardiac revascularization reduces the operative risk of those patients with CAD who undergo AAA repair.

PROGNOSIS

Prognosis is related to both the size of the aneurysm and the severity of coexistent coronary artery and cerebral vascular diseases. The operative mortality rate for AAA repair is approximately 2 to 5 percent. Renal failure, ischemic colitis, and spinal cord ischemia are potential complications of AAA repair. The mortality rate following the rupture of an AAA is approximately 90 percent; of patients who reach the hospital alive, the mortality rate averages 50 percent.

ACUTE APPENDICITIS

A 32-year-old man presents to the emergency department with complaints of abdominal pain. The pain began approximately 12 hours earlier and was initially focused in the umbilical area. Approximately 6 hours later, the pain worsened and shifted to the right lower quadrant. The pain is constant and worsens with any movement. He has had mild nausea and had one episode of vomiting several hours earlier. The patient has not been hungry nor has he eaten since the pain began. Temperature is 38.1 C (100.5 F), pulse is 100/min, and blood pressure is 120/80 mm Hg. The patient is lying very still on a stretcher with his right hip flexed. He exhibits voluntary guarding to abdominal examination. Tenderness is maximal in the right lower quadrant. Rebound tenderness is present in the right lower quadrant. White blood cell count is 14,000/mm^3. A computed tomography study of the abdomen is obtained and shown below:

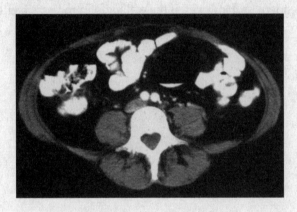

CT abdomen–normal study

DIAGNOSIS

Abdominal pain is the prime symptom of acute appendicitis. In the classical presentation, the pain is initially diffusely centered in the lower epigastrium or umbilical area, is moderately severe, and is steady, sometimes with intermittent cramping superimposed. Typically, within 4 to 6 hours, the pain localizes in the right lower quadrant, but although this classic pain sequence is usual, it is not invariable. Variations in the anatomic location of the appendix can account for the variations in the presentation of the somatic phase of the pain. Anorexia nearly always accompanies appendicitis, and if the patient is not anorexic, the diagnosis should be questioned. Vomiting occurs in approximately 75 percent of patients, but is not prominent or prolonged. Most patients give a history of obstipation from before the onset of abdominal pain, but diarrhea occurs in some patients, particularly small children.

The physical findings associated with appendicitis are determined principally by the anatomic position of the inflamed appendix, as well as by whether the organ has already ruptured. Uncomplicated appendicitis is associated with minimal elevations of temperature, rarely more than 1 C. Patients with appendicitis typically prefer to lie supine, with the thighs, particularly the right thigh, drawn up. When asked to move, patients with appendicitis do so slowly and gingerly because any motion increases the pain. The classic right lower quadrant signs are present when the inflamed appendix lies in the anterior position. Direct rebound tenderness is usually maximally present in the right lower quadrant. Rovsing's sign, which is pain in the right lower quadrant when palpatory pressure is exerted on the left lower quadrant, also indicates peritoneal irritation. A patient's muscular resistance to palpation of the abdominal wall roughly parallels the severity of the inflammatory process. If the appendix is located retrocecally, the anterior abdominal findings may be less striking and tenderness may be greatest in the flank. If the inflamed appendix hangs into the pelvis, abdominal findings may be absent and tenderness detected only on rectal exam.

A mild leukocytosis (10,000–18,000/mm^3) with a moderate polymorphonuclear predominance is usually present in patients with uncomplicated acute appendicitis. Plain films of the abdomen are rarely helpful in diagnosing acute appendicitis, although they can be useful in ruling out additional pathology. Sonography can be useful in the evaluation of suspected appendicitis. Sonography can identify a normal-appearing appendix; an inflamed, noncompressible appendix; fecaliths; inflammatory pericecal fluid; and in females can be used to survey other pelvic organs for pathology. Computed tomography (CT) is at least as accurate as sonography, but is more expensive and involves radiation exposure.

Rupture should be suspected when the temperature is higher than 39 C (102 F) and white blood cell count is greater than 18,000/mm^3. In most cases of rupture, the inflammatory process is contained and the patients display localized rebound tenderness. However, if the walling-off process is ineffective, generalized peritonitis will be present.

The differential diagnosis of acute appendicitis is outlined in the table below.

Differential Diagnosis of Acute Appendicitis	
Disease	Key Features
Acute Mesenteric Adenitis	Most often confused with acute appendicitis in children. Almost invariably an upper respiratory infection is present or recently resolved. Tenderness not as sharply localized as in appendicitis.
Acute Gastroenteritis	Very common in children. Acute, self-limited infection characterized by watery diarrhea, nausea, vomiting. No localizing signs. Laboratory values normal.
Disease of the Male	Torsion of the testis, acute epididymitis, and seminal vesiculitis can present with epigastric pain.
Meckel's Diverticulitis	Clinical picture very similar to acute appendicitis, but preoperative differentiation is unnecessary since the complications and treatment are the same.
Perforated Peptic Ulcer	Closely simulates appendicitis if spilled gastroduodenal contents gravitate down the right gutter to the cecal area and if the perforation seals fairly soon, minimizing upper abdominal findings.
Regional Enteritis	Can simulate appendicitis by presenting with fever, right lower quadrant pain and tenderness, and leukocytosis.
Urinary Tract Infection	Acute pyelonephritis, particularly on the right side, may mimic a retroileal acute appendicitis. Chills, right costovertebral angle tenderness, pus cells, and particularly bacteria in the urine can be used to differentiate between the two.
Intussusception	Typically occurs in children under the age of 2 (appendicitis is very uncommon under the age of 2). Typically occurs in a well-nourished infant who is suddenly struck by colicky pain. Preferred treatment of intussusception is reduction by barium enema; however, treatment of acute appendicitis by barium enema may be catastrophic.
Ureteral Stone	If lodged near the appendix, may simulate a retrocecal appendicitis. Pain referred to the labia, scrotum, or penis; hematuria; and/or the absence of fever or leukocytosis suggests a stone rather than appendicitis. Pyelography is used to confirm diagnosis.
Gynecologic Disorders	The rate of erroneous diagnosis of acute appendicitis is highest in young adult females. Pelvic inflammatory disease, ruptured ovarian follicle, twisted ovarian cyst or tumor, endometriosis, and ruptured ectopic pregnancy can be erroneously diagnosed as appendicitis. Laparoscopy plays a significant role in diagnosis.
Henoch-Schönlein Purpura	Occurs two to three weeks after a streptococcal infection. Abdominal pain may be prominent, but joint pains, purpura, and nephritis are typically present as well.
Other Lesions	Diverticulitis or perforating carcinoma of the cecum or sigmoid may be impossible to distinguish from appendicitis.

PATHOGENESIS

Acute appendicitis is primarily caused by obstruction of the lumen, which is typically caused by fecaliths. Less common causes of appendiceal obstruction include hypertrophy of lymphoid tissue; inspissated barium from previous x-ray studies; vegetable and fruit seeds; and intestinal worms, particularly ascarids. The severity of the inflammatory process is related to the degree of obstruction. Fecaliths are found in approximately 40 percent of cases of simple acute appendicitis, 65 percent of cases of gangrenous appendicitis, and 90 percent of cases of gangrenous appendicitis with rupture.

The probable sequence of events following the occlusion of the lumen is that: 1) a closed-loop obstruction is produced by the proximal block. The continued normal secretion of the appendiceal mucosa rapidly produces distention; 2) distention stimulates nerve endings of visceral, afferent pain fibers, which produce vague, dull, diffuse pain in the mid-abdomen or lower epigastrium; 3) increased intraluminal pressure causes venous congestion and vascular compromise of the appendiceal mucosa; 4) the resident bacteria of the appendix rapidly multiply and invade the compromised appendiceal mucosa; 5) the inflammatory process involves the serosa of the appendix and, in turn, the parietal peritoneum in the region; this produces the characteristic shift in pain to the right lower quadrant. A variety of anaerobes, aerobes, or facultative bacteria have been cultured from peritoneal fluid, abscess contents, and appendiceal tissue in patients with gangrenous or perforated appendicitis. The most commonly identified are *Bacteroides fragilis*, *Escherichia coli*, and *Peptostreptococcus* sp.

EPIDEMIOLOGY

Appendicitis is one of the most common acute surgical diseases. The incidence of appendicitis is approximately 52 cases per 100,000 population. Appendicitis occurs more frequently in males, with a ratio of approximately 1.3:1, especially at the time of puberty. Currently, 84 percent of all appendectomies are performed for acute pathology. The rate of normal appendectomy is approximately 16 percent, with females comprising 68 percent of patients found to have a normal appendix at exploration.

TREATMENT

Immediate appendectomy is the recommended treatment of acute appendicitis because of the progression to rupture. The accuracy of the preoperative diagnosis should be approximately 85 percent; if it is consistently less, unnecessary operations will be performed. If it is more, too few operations will be performed and patients with atypical appendicitis will be managed expectantly when they should have prompt surgical intervention.

Preoperative antibiotics are effective in reducing the risk of infectious complications. Open appendectomy and laparoscopic appendectomy are both acceptable methods: Laparoscopy may be preferable in women of childbearing age, in patients in whom the diagnosis remains in question, in patients concerned about cosmesis, and in obese patients who would require a large incision for the open approach.

PROGNOSIS

The mortality from appendicitis in the U.S. is 0.2 percent per 100,000 population. The principle factors in mortality are whether rupture occurs before surgical treatment and the age of the patient. The overall mortality rate in unruptured acute appendicitis is 0.06 percent, which is a little higher than that of the administration of a general anesthetic. The overall mortality rate in ruptured acute appendicitis is 3 percent, and the mortality rate of ruptured appendicitis in the elderly is approximately 15 percent. Death is usually attributable to uncontrolled sepsis.

The morbidity rates of acute appendicitis parallel mortality rates, with higher rates of morbidity in cases of rupture and in the elderly. Most of the serious, early complications are septic and include abscess and wound infection. Intraabdominal abscesses are less common.

BURNS

A 34-year-old man is brought to the emergency department by ambulance after sustaining a burn injury. The man works as a cook and was accidentally scalded by boiling water and steam. The patient's entire right upper extremity and anterior trunk have a mottled, pink and white appearance. The areas of skin that were covered by clothing appear to be more seriously affected. Pulse is 110/min, blood pressure is 90/60 mm Hg, and respirations are 22/min.

DIAGNOSIS

The severity of injury caused by burns is proportionate to the total surface area of the total burn, the depth of the burn, the age of the patient, and his or her associated medical problems or injuries. A general idea of burn size can be made by using the *Rule of Nines* (see table below).

Body Part	Percentage of Total Body Surface Area (TBSA)	Total
Each upper extremity	9% × 2	18%
Each lower extremity	18% × 2	36%
Anterior trunk	18%	18%
Posterior trunk	18%	18%
Head and neck	9%	9%
Perineum	1%	1%

Rule of Nines

For smaller burns, an accurate assessment of burn size can be made using the patient's hand, which amounts to 2.5 percent of TBSA. Children under the age of four have much larger heads and smaller thighs in proportion to body size than do adults; in infants, the head accounts for nearly 20 percent of TBSA.

Burn depth is the primary determinant of damage to the patient's long-term appearance and function. First-degree burns involve only the epidermis. They do not blister, become erythematous due to dermal vasodilation, and are quite painful. Second-degree burns extend into the dermis. Initially they have a pink or mottled white and pink appearance (white areas have no blood flow), and blisters are seen. Third-degree (full-thickness) burns involve all layers of the dermis and appear white, cherry red, or black, and may or may not have deep blisters associated with them. Fourth-degree burns involve all layers of the skin, subcutaneous fat, and deeper structures, and have a charred appearance.

PATHOGENESIS

Cutaneous burns are caused by the application of heat, cold, or caustic chemicals to the skin. When heat is applied to the skin, the depth of injury is proportionate to the temperature applied, the duration of contact, and the thickness of the skin. Common causes of burns are discussed in the table on the next page.

Common Causes of Burns		
Burn Type	Cause	Comment
Scald Burns	H_2O at 60 C (140 F) creates a full-thickness burn in 3 s. Freshly brewed coffee = 82 C (180 F). Cooking oil = 204 C (400 F). Roofing tar or asphalt = 204–260 C (400–500 F).	In civilian practice, scalds, usually from hot water, are the most common cause of burns. Deliberate scalds are the most common form of reported child abuse. Exposed areas tend to be burned less deeply than areas covered with clothing as clothing retains heat.
Flame Burns	House fires, flammable liquids, automobile accidents, and ignition of clothing from stoves or space heaters.	Second-most common. Patients whose bedding or clothes have been on fire rarely escape without some full-thickness burns.
Flash Burns	Explosions of natural gas, propane, gasoline, and other flammable liquids cause intense heat for a very brief period of time.	Third-most common. Generally distributed over all exposed skin; clothing is protective. Mostly dermal, depth depends on the amount and type of fuel.
Contact Burns	Contact with hot metals, plastic, glass, or hot coals.	Usually limited in extent, but invariably very deep. It is common for patients involved in industrial accidents to have associated crush injuries. Contact burns are often fourth-degree burns.

Direct thermal injury results in an increase in total body capillary permeability. Burn shock is characterized by decreased cardiac output, extracellular fluid, and plasma volume; and oliguria. Thermal injury causes severe immunosuppression, both cellular and humoral, that is directly related to the size of the burn wound.

EPIDEMIOLOGY

Thermal burns and related injuries are a major cause of death and disability in the U.S.; approximately 2 million individuals annually are burned seriously enough to seek health care; 70,000 of these require hospitalization, and about 5,000 die. More than 90 percent of burns is completely preventable; nearly half are smoking- or alcohol-related.

TREATMENT

Burn patients often require years of supervised rehabilitation, reconstruction, and psychosocial support. The ultimate goal of burn wound management is closure and healing of the wound. Early surgical excision of burned tissue with extensive debridement of necrotic tissue and grafting of skin or skin substitutes greatly decreases the mortality of severe burns. For deeper burns, the eschar is surgically removed and the wound is closed; grafting techniques and procedures are employed for immediate placement of flaps. Scarring, a virtual certainty with deep burns, can be minimized by appropriate early surgical intervention and long-term scar management.

Proper fluid management is critical for survival in major thermal injury. Crystalloid and colloid solutions are administered to restore and preserve tissue perfusion. Broad-spectrum antimicrobial agents, which include silver nitrate, mafenide acetate, and silver sulfadiazine, are applied directly to the burn wounds. In general, prophylactic systemic antibiotics have no role in the management of burn wounds and in fact can lead to colonization with resistant organisms. Nutritional support is directed primarily toward the provision of calories to match energy expenditures and the provision of nitrogen to replace or support body protein stores.

Prognosis

Ninety-six percent of patients admitted to burn centers survive, and 80 percent of them returns to the preburn physical and social situation within a year of injury. The likelihood of scar formation is related to the depth of dermis involvement. The longer the burn takes to heal, the less dermis remains, the greater the inflammatory response, and the more severe the scarring. Infectious complications are the major cause of morbidity and mortality in serious burn injury patients.

CHOLECYSTITIS

A 63-year-old woman presents with complaints of fever, nausea, vomiting, and abdominal pain. She typically experiences right upper quadrant pain after a fatty or fried meal. Temperature is 38.3 C (101 F), pulse is 92/min, blood pressure is 96/60 mm Hg, and respirations are 16/min. Abdominal exam reveals right upper quadrant tenderness, particularly along the right costal margin. The right upper quadrant demonstrates rebound tenderness, and palpation during inspiration increases the intensity of the pain to such a degree that the patient halts breathing. Laboratory studies are as follows:

Leukocyte count	17,000/mm^3	(4,500–11,000/mm^3)
Segmented neutrophils	74%	(54–62%)
Bands	9%	(3–5%)
Eosinophils	1%	(1–3%)
Basophils	0	(0–0.75%)
Lymphocytes	14%	(25–33%)
Monocytes	2%	(3–7%)
Hematocrit	39%	(Female: 36–46%)
Serum		
Bilirubin		
Total	2.0 mg/dL	(0.1–1.0 mg/dL)
Direct	1.0 mg/dL	(0.0–0.3 mg/dL)
Alkaline phosphatase	50 U/L	(20–70 U/L)
Aspartate aminotransferase	15 U/L	(8–20 U/L)
Alanine aminotransferase	16 U/L	(8–20 U/L)
Amylase	56 U/L	(25–125 U/L)

An ultrasound study of the right upper quadrant is ordered.

DIAGNOSIS

The diagnosis of acute cholecystitis is usually made on the basis of a characteristic history and physical examination. The sudden onset of right upper quadrant (RUQ) tenderness, fever, and leukocytosis are highly suggestive. Most patients with acute cholecystitis give a history that is compatible with chronic cholecystitis and cholelithiasis. The onset of symptoms is frequently related to eating a heavy, fatty, or fried meal. The pain is usually moderate to severe and experienced in the RUQ and epigastrium, but may radiate to the back. Vomiting may be severe, and patients with acute cholecystitis characteristically have a low-grade fever. Tenderness along the right costal margin is characteristic and is often associated with rebound tenderness and spasm. The gallbladder may be palpable. Deep inspiration or cough during subcostal palpation of the RUQ usually produces increased pain and inspiratory arrest (Murphy's sign) in cholecystitis. Mild to marked jaundice may be present, depending upon the presence or degree of common duct obstruction. A serum bilirubin level greater than 6 mg/dL suggests the presence of associated choledocholithiasis. Patients with acute cholecystitis usually have a leukocytosis with a shift to the left. Ultrasound can be used to identify calculi and/or a thickening in the wall of the gallbladder and is the diagnostic procedure of choice. Radionucleotide biliary studies are valuable diagnostic tools in cases of suspected acute cholecystitis as well.

Patients with chronic cholecystitis typically present with moderate, intermittent abdominal pain in the RUQ and epigastrium, although chronic cholecystitis may be asymptomatic for years. A history of intolerance of fatty or fried foods is common.

The differential diagnosis of acute cholecystitis includes perforation or penetration of a peptic ulcer, appendicitis, pancreatitis, hepatitis, myocardial ischemia or infarction, pneumonia, pleurisy, and herpes zoster involving an intercostal nerve.

PATHOGENESIS

Acute cholecystitis is usually associated with an obstruction of the neck of the gallbladder or cystic duct caused by stones impacted in Hartmann's pouch. The calculus exerts direct pressure on the mucosa, which results in ischemia, necrosis, and ulceration with swelling, edema, and impairment of venous return. Necrosis can lead to perforation with pericholecystic abscess formation, fistulization, or bile peritonitis. Positive bile cultures are noted in 60 percent of patients; *Escherichia coli*, *Klebsiella* sp., *Streptococcus* sp., *Enterobacter aerogenes*, *Salmonella* sp., and *Clostridium* sp. have all been identified. Acute cholecystitis may also be caused by generalized sepsis, the vascular effects of collagen disease, terminal states of hypertensive vascular disease, and thrombosis of the main cystic artery. Less than 1 percent of acutely inflamed gallbladders contains a malignant tumor. Emphysematous cholecystitis begins with acute cholecystitis, followed by ischemia or gangrene of the gallbladder and infection by gas-producing organisms (*Clostridium* sp.). Emphysematous cholecystitis occurs most frequently in elderly men and in diabetic patients.

Chronic cholecystitis is almost always associated with the presence of gallstones, and results from repeated episodes of subacute or acute cholecystitis, or from repeated, mechanical irritation of the gallbladder wall. Chronic cholecystitis may progress to symptomatic gallbladder disease or acute cholecystitis. The following table lists complications of cholecystitis.

Complications of Cholecystitis			
Complication	Signs and Symptoms	Pathogenesis	Comment
Empyema	High fever, severe RUQ pain, marked leukocytosis, prostration.	Progression from acute cholecystitis with persistent cystic duct obstruction.	High risk of Gram-negative sepsis and/or perforation.
Hydrops	Frequently asymptomatic, but chronic RUQ pain can occur.	Prolonged obstruction of the cystic duct.	Cholecystectomy indicated since empyema, perforation, or gangrene may complicate the condition.
Gangrene	Associated withG perforation.	Ischemia of the wall and patchy or complete tissue necrosis.	Associated with vasculitis, diabetes mellitus, empyema, or torsion.

Perforation	Patients with free perforation may experience a sudden transient relief of RUQ pain.	Gangrene usually predisposes for perforation, but may also occur in chronic cholecystitis without warning.	Cholecystectomy indicated, possibly with drainage. Localized perforations are usually contained. Free perforation is less common, but mortality rate is 30%.
Fistula	Associated with development of gallstone ileus.	Results from inflammation and adhesion formation. Fistulae into the duodenum are most common.	Can be diagnosed by the finding of gas in the biliary tree on plain abdominal x-ray.
Gallstone ileus	The majority of patients do not give a history of either prior biliary tract symptoms or complaints of acute cholecystitis.	Mechanical obstruction resulting from the passage of a large gallstone into the bowel lumen. Site of obstruction is usually the ileocecal valve.	Laparotomy with stone extraction is the procedure of choice.
Limey (milk of calcium) bile	Clinically innocuous.	Secretion of calcium salts into lumen of gallbladder produces calcium precipitation and diffuse, hazy, opacified bile.	Cholecystectomy recommended because limey bile most often occurs in a hydropic gallbladder.
Porcelain gallbladder	Associated with limey bile.	Calcium salt deposition within the wall of chronically inflamed gallbladder.	Cholecystectomy is indicated because porcelain gallbladder is associated with the development of carcinoma of the gallbladder.

EPIDEMIOLOGY

Acute cholecystitis can occur at any age, but the greatest incidence occurs between the ages of 40 and 80. Whites are affected more often than are blacks, and women more often than men. Gallstones are found in 90 to 95 percent of cases of acute cholecystitis, and less than 1 percent of acutely inflamed gallbladders contains a malignant tumor. The incidence of common duct calculi is about 7–15 percent in both acute and chronic cholecystitis.

TREATMENT

Acute cholecystitis is best treated by early surgery. Most surgeons prefer to operate within 24 to 48 hours after the onset of symptoms (early cholecystectomy). In the majority of cases, a laparoscopic cholecystectomy is successful. However, the incidence of conversion to open cholecystectomy is greater in patients with acute cholecystitis as compared to patients without inflammation. Emergent cholecystectomy is indicated in patients in whom a complication of acute cholecystitis such as empyema, emphysematous cholecystitis, or perforation is confirmed or suspected.

Although surgical intervention is the mainstay of therapy for acute cholecystitis and its complications, a period of in-hospital stabilization may be required before cholecystectomy. Oral intake is eliminated, nasogastric suction is initiated, and extracellular volume depletion and electrolyte abnormalities are repaired. Intravenous antibiotic therapy is indicated for patients with severe acute cholecystitis.

PROGNOSIS

The mortality for early elective or early cholecystectomy in patients under the age of 60 is 0.5 percent. The mortality rate for emergent cholecystectomy is approximately 3 percent.

CHOLELITHIASIS AND CHOLEDOCHOLITHIASIS

A 45-year-old woman presents with complaints of intermittent right upper quadrant pain that radiates to the right shoulder. The patient has been experiencing intermittent right upper quadrant pain for the past year, but the intensity and frequency have increased in the past few weeks. She notes that the pain worsens after she eats a fatty or fried meal, and she typically experiences nausea and vomiting along with the pain. During the past week, her urine has been very dark, while her stools have been very light-colored. Temperature is 37 C (98.6 F), pulse is 100/min, and blood pressure is 110/70 mm Hg. The patient's skin and sclera appear jaundiced. Examination of the abdomen is unremarkable. Laboratory studies are as follows:

Leukocyte count	8,000/mm^3	(4,500–11,000/mm^3)
Hematocrit	40 percent	(Female: 36–46 percent)
Prothrombin time	17 seconds	(11–15 seconds)
Serum		
Bilirubin		
Total	9.0 mg/dL	(0.1–1.0 mg/dL)
Direct	6.0 mg/dL	(0.0–0.3 mg/dL)
Alkaline phosphatase	140 U/L	(20–70 U/L)
Aspartate aminotransferase	70 U/L	(8–20 U/L)
Alanine aminotransferase	85 U/L	(8–20 U/L)
Amylase	48 U/L	(25–125 U/L)

An ultrasound study of the right upper quadrant is ordered.

DIAGNOSIS

Biliary colic, the most common manifestation of gallstones, is caused by temporary obstruction of the outflow of bile from the gallbladder. This results in intermittent spasmodic pain in the right upper quadrant, which often radiates to the shoulder or scapula and is often precipitated by a fatty or fried meal. The attacks are self-limiting but tend to recur in an unpredictable manner. Temperature and leukocyte count are typically normal. The bilirubin and alkaline phosphatase levels are normal or slightly elevated, and hyperamylasemia may be present.

The manifestations of choledocholithiasis are variable. Biliary obstruction is typically chronic and incomplete, but may be acute or complete. Patients characteristically complain of colicky pain in the right upper quadrant that radiates to the right shoulder, with intermittent jaundice, pale stools, and dark urine. Liver function tests demonstrate evidence of obstructive jaundice, with elevated alkaline phosphatase, elevated serum bilirubin, and a prolonged prothrombin time (decreased vitamin K absorption).

Potentially useful procedures in the diagnosis of cholelithiasis are discussed in the table below.

Diagnostic Evaluation of the Gallbladder			
Diagnostic Procedure	Advantages	Limitations	Other
Plain abdominal x-ray	Low cost. Readily available.	Low yield.	Has pathognomic findings in calcified gallstones, limey (milk of calcium) bile, porcelain GB, emphysematous cholecystitis, gallstone ileus.
Gallbladder ultrasound	Rapid, accurate identification of gallstones (> 95%), simultaneous scanning of GB, liver, bile ducts, pancreas; safe in pregnancy.	Not useful when in the setting of bowel gas, massive obesity, ascites, or a recent barium study.	Procedure of choice for detection of stones.
Oral cholecystogram	Low cost. Readily available. Accurate identification of gallstones (90–95%). Identification of GB anomalies.	Relative contraindication in pregnancy, very small stones may be undetected, more time-consuming than GB ultrasound.	Useful in identification of gallstones if diagnostic limitations prevent GB ultrasound.
Radioisotope scans (HIDA, dimethyl iminodiacetic acid, etc.)	Accurate identification of cystic duct obstruction. Simultaneous assessment of bile ducts.	Relative contraindication in pregnancy. Low-resolution cholecystogram.	Indicated for confirmation of suspected acute cholecystitis, less sensitive and less specific in chronic cholecystitis.

PATHOGENESIS

Gallstones form as a result of the solids cholesterol, bile pigment, and calcium settling out of solution. Other constituents include iron, phosphorus, carbonates, proteins, carbohydrates, mucus, and cellular debris. In the U.S., most stones are made up of cholesterol, bile pigment, and calcium, and have a particularly high content of cholesterol. The solubility of cholesterol depends on the concentration of bile salts, phospholipids, and cholesterol in bile. However, pure cholesterol stones are uncommon; they are usually large, have smooth surfaces, and are solitary. Bilirubin pigment stones are usually associated with hemolytic jaundice or situations in which the bile is abnormally concentrated, and have a character-istic smooth, glistening, green or black surface. Bile stasis, which includes temporary cessation of bile flow into the intestine and stagnation in the gallbladder, also plays a major role in the formation of gallstones.

Most commonly, duct calculi are formed within the gallbladder and then migrate down the cystic duct into the common bile duct; these are classified as secondary stones. The formation of primary stones in the ducts is less common. In patients infected with *Clonorchis sinensis*, stones may form within the hepatic ducts or the common bile duct itself. Small stones may then pass through the common duct into the duodenum, but the narrow lumen (2 to 3 mm) of the distal duct frequently obstructs their passage. The presence of calculi in the distal duct leads to edema, spasm, or fibrosis of the distal duct, which further worsens the biliary obstruction. Chronic biliary obstruction may cause secondary biliary cirrhosis or ascending cholangitis. Gallstone pancreatitis is associated with the presence or passage of common bile duct stones.

EPIDEMIOLOGY

Gallstones are quite prevalent in most western countries. In the U.S., autopsy series have demonstrated gallstones in at least 20 percent of women and 8 percent of men over the age of 40. It is estimated that approximately 16 to 20 million people in the U.S. have gallstones, and approximately 1 million new cases of cholelithiasis develop each year. In cases of asymptomatic gallstones, the risk of developing symptoms or complications that require surgery is very small; approximately 1 to 2 percent per year. Common duct stones may be single or multiple and are found in 10–15 percent of patients with cholelithiasis.

TREATMENT

The treatment of symptomatic cholelithiasis is cholecystectomy, preferably by the laparoscopic approach. Lithotripsy is not regarded as an appropriate therapy because a diseased organ will likely form new stones and the flushing effect of bile is not equivalent to that of urine. In general, patients with asymptomatic gallstones should not be treated. Cholecystectomy for asymptomatic stones may be appropriate for elderly patients with diabetes and for individuals who will be isolated from medical care for an extended period of time.

The indications for the treatment of choledocholithiasis include the presence of common duct stones in a symptomatic patient; a dilated extrahepatic duct; jaundice; recurrent chills and fevers consistent with cholangitis; and gallstone pancreatitis. Common duct stones can be removed by endoscopic retrograde cholangiopancreatography (ERCP). Destruction of the sphincter of Oddi (sphincterotomy) at the time of ERCP will permit stones that were not extracted (or ones that form at a later date) to pass into the duodenum. At the time of cholecystectomy, the common duct can be opened, the stones removed, and a T tube inserted. In cases in which a dilated common duct and multiple stones are present, a choledochoduodenostomy can provide definitive treatment.

The administration of agents that increase the solubility of cholesterol and promote gallstone dissolution has limited utility. Chenodeoxycholic acid and ursodeoxycholic acid decrease HMG-CoA reductase activity, which replenishes the bile acid pool and reduces cholesterol synthesis and secretion. Medical therapy is reserved for those patients who are not candidates for, or refuse, elective cholecystectomy and patients with recurrent calculus disease after cholecystectomy.

PROGNOSIS

The mortality rate is less than 1 percent for patients undergoing laparoscopic cholecystectomy. In 4 to 5 percent of the cases of laparoscopic cholecystectomy, surgeons must convert to an open cholecystectomy. Bile duct injuries occur in approximately 4 percent of patients undergoing laparoscopic cholecystectomy. Cholecystectomy causes a greater fraction of the bile salt pool to cycle around the enterohepatic circulation, which increases the bile salt and phospholipid secretion. This results in greater solubility of cholesterol and decreases the likelihood of the formation of additional calculi.

DIVERTICULAR DISEASE

A 77-year-old woman presents with complaints of lower left quadrant abdominal pain. The pain began 3 days ago and has gradually worsened. She has been constipated for the past 3 days, and denies any complaints of dysuria. Temperature is 38.3 C (101 F), pulse is 96/min, and blood pressure is 110/60 mm Hg. The left lower quadrant is tender to palpation. A tender mass is noted on rectal and vaginal examination. Laboratory studies show:

Serum		
Leukocyte count	16,500/mm³	(4,500–11,000)/mm³
Segmented neutrophils	73%	(54–62%)
Eosinophils	1%	(1–3%)
Lymphocytes	12%	(25–33%)
Monocytes	4%	(3–7%)
Hemoglobin	12 g/dL	(12–16 g/dL)
Urinalysis		
White blood cells	none	
Red blood cells	none	
Protein	negative	
Leukocyte esterase	negative	

DIAGNOSIS

Diverticulosis refers to the presence of colonic diverticula. When infection is associated with these diverticula, the term diverticulitis is used. Patients with acute diverticulitis typically complain of left lower abdominal pain. The pain may radiate to the suprapubic area, left groin, or back. They may also note a change in bowel habits, usually constipation but occasionally diarrhea. Fever and chills may be present. They may also complain of urgency or frequency of urination if the inflammation is adjacent to the bladder. Rectal bleeding is uncommon in the setting of diverticulitis.

The physical findings associated with diverticulitis depend upon the severity and location of the infection. The most common finding is tenderness over the left lower abdomen. A tender mass in the left lower quadrant suggests a phlegmon or abscess. Abdominal distention may be present as a result of an ileus or the partial obstruction of small bowel due to the inflammatory process. Rectal examination may demonstrate pelvic tenderness.

The diagnosis of diverticulitis can usually be made on the basis of history and physical examination; computed tomography (CT) is the test of choice to confirm its diagnosis. CT can detect the location of the inflammation and determine the presence of an abscess, ureteral obstruction, or fistula. Ultrasound or, less frequently, contrast enema, can also be used when the diagnosis is uncertain.

PATHOGENESIS

A diverticulum is an abnormal sac or pouch protruding from the wall of a hollow organ. A true diverticulum, which is a rare finding, is composed of all of the layers of the intestinal wall, while a false diverticulum lacks a portion of the normal bowel wall. The commonly observed diverticula of the colon consist of protrusions of mucosa through the muscular layers of the wall; they lack a muscular coat and are therefore false diverticula. Diverticulitis refers to an infection associated with diverticula; although the infectious process commonly associated with diverticular disease is pericolic in nature and affects the surrounding soft tissue (mesentery or adjacent organs) in addition to the serosal surface of the colon.

The exact cause of diverticulosis is unknown. The diverticula are actually herniations of mucosa through the colon at sites at which arterioles penetrate the muscular wall. These locations are primarily on the mesenteric side of the antimesenteric teniae. Diverticulosis is also characterized by a marked thickening of the affected colonic wall. This muscular abnormality precedes the appearance of the diverticula and occurs mainly in the sigmoid colon. A low-fiber diet appears to be associated with a narrow sigmoid colon, and a narrow lumen allows small regions of the sigmoid colon to be isolated into compartments that are then subjected to high pressures. It is thought that high-pressure contractions produce the herniations of mucosa. Diverticula occur most often in the sigmoid; in more than 50 percent of patients, the diverticular disease is confined to the sigmoid. Less frequently (40 percent of patients) it involves the descending colon as well, and the entire colon is affected in a small number of patients (5 to 10 percent).

Diverticulitis is the result of a perforation of a diverticulum that leads to extravasation of feces from the lumen to the serosal surface of the colon. Typically, the amount of fecal contamination is very small and the body's natural defenses contain the infection. If the contamination is significant, or if the patient is immunocompromised, abscess formation or even generalized peritonitis can occur.

EPIDEMIOLOGY

Diverticulosis is rare before age 30 and becomes more common with increasing age. It is present in approximately 75 percent of the U.S. population over the age of 80, and men and women appear to be affected equally. Diverticular disease has become more common as the amount of fiber consumed by individuals in the U.S. has declined.

TREATMENT

The treatment of diverticulitis depends upon the severity of the disease. For patients with minimal signs of infection, outpatient therapy with a clear liquid diet and broad-spectrum antibiotics is appropriate. Patients with significant evidence of infection should be hospitalized for bowel rest, intravenous fluids, and intravenous broad-spectrum antibiotics. Nasogastric suction is not indicated unless an ileus or obstruction is present. For patients who recover from simple, uncomplicated diverticulitis, a high-fiber diet is recommended. In cases of recurrent diverticulitis, resection of the diseased colon is considered.

Diverticular abscesses may be treated with percutaneous, transrectal, or transvaginal drainage. These approaches are preferable to a celiotomy because they minimize the potential of contaminating other areas of the peritoneal cavity. The spreading of generalized peritonitis is a rare complication of diverticulitis, but it may occur if the fecal contamination is significant or if the patient is immunocompromised. In these cases, diversion of the fecal stream, intravenous broad-spectrum antibiotics, and nutritional support should permit resolution of the peritonitis. Fistula formation between the sigmoid colon and other organs (bladder, vagina, small intestine, and skin) is a relatively frequent complication of diverticulitis (and is the most common cause of a sigmoid-vesicular fistula). Fistulas require definitive surgical treatment.

PROGNOSIS

Seventy percent of patients who recover from a simple, uncomplicated episode of diverticulitis will have no recurrence. However, in patients who suffer a second attack of diverticulitis, the risk of subsequent attacks is greater than 50 percent.

FRACTURES

A 12-year-old boy is brought to the emergency department by ambulance after falling from a tree. Pulse is 96/min, blood pressure is 110/60 mm Hg, respirations are 22/min, and temperature is 37 C (98.6 F). The child is alert and oriented, responding appropriately to questions. A cervical spine survey demonstrates no fractures. He complains of pain in his right leg. The right leg appears grossly normal and the skin is intact. The right leg just below the knee joint is tender and the child will not allow flexion at the knee joint. A radiograph of his right knee joint is shown below.

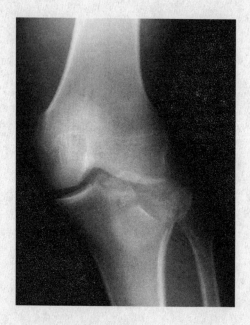

Tibial plateau fracture

DIAGNOSIS

HISTORY AND PHYSICAL EXAMINATION

A **fracture** is defined as a linear deformation or discontinuity of bone produced by forces that exceed the ultimate strength of the material. The clinical manifestations of a fracture include pain, swelling, deformity, ecchymosis, instability, and crepitus. Fractures are described anatomically according to their location in the bone (intraarticular, epiphyseal, metaphyseal, diaphyseal), the plane of the fracture (transverse, oblique, spiral), the number and type of fragments, and whether the fracture is open (compound) or closed. In an **undisplaced fracture**, a plane of cleavage exists between the fracture fragments without separation. In **displaced fractures**, the convention is to describe the direction of displacement of the distal fragment with reference to the proximal fragment (medial, lateral, posterior, etc.). **Comminution** refers to presence of multiple fracture fragments. **Angulation** refers to angular deformity between the long axes of the fracture fragments. The diagnosis of a fracture is usually confirmed radiographically with two radiographs taken at right angles to each other. Joints above and below the fracture site should be included in the radiograph in order to rule out associated injuries.

PATHOGENESIS

Classification of Common Types of Fractures	
Type	**Description**
Pathological fractures	Occur when the strength of the bone is below normal, as is seen in infections, tumors, or metabolic bone disease, or after the creation of surgical defects in bone.
Spiral fractures	Produced by torsional force, the fracture line is helical.
Stress fractures	Occur when a bone is subjected to repetitive stresses that are individually insufficient to cause fracture but cumulatively lead to fatigue failure; results from force on a bony structure during use, as opposed to resulting from exogenous trauma.
Greenstick fractures	Result from axial loading of bone with compaction of bony trabeculae, and generally occur in vertebral bodies.
Compression fractures	Incomplete fracture resulting from failure of a portion of the cortex under tension, with part of the opposing cortex still intact, but plastically deformed. These are typically seen in children.
Torus fractures	Retain partial cortical continuity, but with buckling or failure in compression of the opposing cortex. Seen in children, commonly occurs in the radius, ulna, or both.
Plastic deformation	Occur as deformation without fracture, can occur with loads that exceed the elastic limit of the bone, but not its ultimate strength, and is more common in children.
Fat embolism	Fat embolism is an extremely common pathologic finding after trauma. However, the fat embolism syndrome of pulmonary dysfunction, coagulopathy, and neurologic disturbances associated with increased circulating fat globules is uncommon.

EPIDEMIOLOGY

The direction and magnitude of force applied to a bone and the rate of loading all are important in determining the fracture pattern that will result. Open fractures are generally higher-energy injuries, resulting in more comminution and soft-tissue injury and, consequently, greater impairment of bone blood supply.

TREATMENT

Immediate threat to a patient's life from an injured extremity is unusual, but can be a consequence of subsequent hemorrhage and shock. Use of pneumatic trousers (medical anti-shock trousers, or MAST) during transport may help to maintain blood pressure and decrease blood loss from lower-extremity injuries. Multiple fractures, even when closed, can induce shock from internal hemorrhage, particularly if major pelvic injuries are present. Assessment of possible spinal injury is imperative, and transport using a backboard and sandbags or other head supports helps to minimize the chances of causing additional injury. One of the most important determinations is whether a fracture is open or closed. Open fractures constitute an orthopedic surgical emergency because of the risk of deep infection; in particular, osteomyelitis.

The injured extremity should be evaluated as quickly as possible for neurovascular compromise, soft tissue and bony injuries, and joint instability. Peripheral pulses and capillary refill must be evaluated, and motor and sensory examinations performed. After the neurovascular examination has been performed and soft-tissue trauma or wounds are evaluated, fractured extremities are splinted to minimize further injury. Plaster splints, pillow splints, or air splints can be used to stabilize the extremity. Fractures involving the humerus or shoulder can be splinted with a sling. Fractures of the femur are best temporarily stabilized in a traction splint. Occasionally, a completely nondisplaced fracture is not apparent on initial films; in this event immobilization with follow-up films in 1 to 2 weeks is indicated.

The major aim in the treatment of open fractures is the prevention of infection. This is best accomplished by aggressive and immediate debridement of the wound and fracture site in a sterile operative environment, and initiation of empiric intravenous prophylactic antibiotic therapy. Infection in a fracture, once established, can be extremely difficult to eradicate and markedly increases the risk of nonunion. Primary closure of open fractures is rarely, if ever, indicated.

PROGNOSIS

Early aggressive treatment of hypovolemic shock greatly reduces the likelihood of morbidity and mortality.

INTESTINAL OBSTRUCTION

A 49-year-old man presents with complaints of crampy abdominal pain, nausea, vomiting, and abdominal distention that began 3 days ago and has become progressively worse. His last bowel movement was 3 days ago. Medical history is significant for an emergent laparotomy and splenectomy after a car accident 3 years ago. Temperature is 37 C (98.6 F), respirations are 14/min, pulse is 112/min, and blood pressure is 100/60 mm Hg. Examination shows a distended abdomen that is nontender. Auscultation reveals loud, high-pitched borborygmi. Laboratory studies show:

Leukocyte count	13,000/mm³	(4,500–11,000/mm³)
Hematocrit	59%	(Male: 41–53%)
Serum		
Urea nitrogen	50 mg/dL	(7–18 mg/dL)
Creatinine	1.8 mg/dL	(0.6–1.2 mg/dL)

A plain film of the abdomen is obtained and shown below:

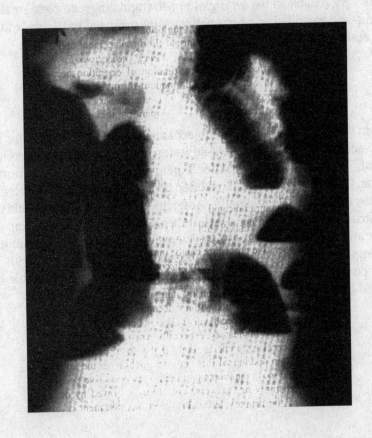

Acute mechanical obstruction of the small intestine

DIAGNOSIS

Acute intestinal obstruction, when it is due to a volvulus around a mechanical adhesion, usually begins with a sudden onset of abdominal pain. The four cardinal symptoms and signs of intestinal obstruction are crampy abdominal pain, nausea and vomiting, obstipation, and abdominal distention. The more distal the obstruction, the more feculent the nature of the vomitus. If the obstruction is not total, chronic nausea and vomiting can occur.

Localized tenderness progressing to rebound tenderness accompanied by fever, tachycardia, and leukocytosis suggest that bowel viability is compromised. Physical diagnosis cannot absolutely distinguish between strangulated and nonstrangulated obstructions.

Intestinal obstruction typically results in losses of 4 to 8 L of intravascular and extracellular fluid into the small bowel. The most common early laboratory signs of obstructions are elevation of blood urea nitrogen and creatinine levels, hemoconcentration, hyponatremia, and hypokalemia. Simple mechanical obstructions are accompanied by a modest increase in leukocyte count; strangulated obstructions are associated with leukocyte counts in the 15,000 to 25,000/mm^3 range, seen with a polymorphonuclear predominance with many immature forms; very high white blood cell counts (40,000–60,000/mm^3) suggest primary mesenteric vascular occlusion.

Radiographs are very reliable in the setting of nonstrangulating, complete small bowel obstruction; the distention of fluid- and gas-filled loops of small intestine arranged in a "step ladder" pattern with air-fluid levels and an absence or paucity of colonic gas are both pathognomonic.

PATHOGENESIS

Intestinal obstruction may be mechanical or nonmechanical (adynamic or dynamic ileus). Obstructions of the small bowel secondary to postoperative adhesions make up 60 to 80 percent of admissions for intestinal obstruction; hernias account for 15 to 20 percent; and malignant tumors make up 10 to 15 percent of admission. Colonic obstruction most often arises from cancer (60 percent), diverticulitis (15 percent), or volvulus, especially in the elderly. Adynamic ileus, which is probably the most common overall cause of obstruction, is mediated via the hormonal component of the sympathoadrenal system, and may occur after any peritoneal insult. Dynamic (spastic) ileus is very uncommon and results from extreme and prolonged contraction of the intestine. Dynamic ileus can result from heavy metal poisoning, uremia, porphyria, and extensive intestinal ulcerations. The possible causes of intestinal obstruction are listed in the table on the next page.

Causes of Intestinal Obstruction

I. Mechanical obstruction of the lumen
   A. Blockage of the lumen
      1. Meconium
      2. Intussusception
      3. Gallstones
      4. Impactions (feces, barium, bezoar, worms)
   B. Lesions intrinsic to the bowel
      1. Congenital
         a) Atresia and stenosis
         b) Imperforate anus
         c) Duplications
         d) Meckel's diverticulum
      2. Traumatic
      3. Neoplastic
      4. Inflammatory
         a) Regional enteritis
         b) Diverticulitis
         c) Chronic ulcerative colitis
      5. Other
         a) K^+-induced stricture
         b) Radiation stricture
         c) Endometriosis
   C. Lesions extrinsic to the bowel
      1. Adhesive band constriction
      2. Hernia and wound dehiscence
      3. Extrinsic masses
         a) Neoplasms
         b) Abscesses and hematomas
         c) Annular pancreas
         d) Anomalous vessels
II. Inadequate motility
   A. Neuromuscular defects
      1. Megacolon
      2. Paralytic ileus
         a) Intestinal distention
         b) Peritonitis
         c) Retroperitoneal lesions
         d) Electrolyte imbalance
         e) Toxemias
      3. Spastic ileus
   B. Vascular occlusion
      1. Arterial
      2. Venous

Interference with the mesenteric blood supply (strangulated obstruction) is the most serious complication of intestinal obstruction. Strangulated obstruction frequently occurs secondary to adhesive band obstruction, hernia, and volvulus. When both the afferent and efferent limbs of a loop of bowel are obstructed, it is referred to as a closed-loop obstruction. Closed-loop obstructions are dangerous because they have the propensity for rapid progression to strangulation. Colon obstruction, with the exception of volvulus, usually does not strangulate.

EPIDEMIOLOGY

Intestinal obstruction accounts for at least 20 percent of all admissions to a surgical service. More than 9,000 deaths result from intestinal obstruction and operation annually. Patients with previous intraabdominal procedures have a 5 percent incidence of intestinal obstruction.

TREATMENT

The initial management of a patient with intestinal obstruction is a comprehensive laboratory and radiographic evaluation (chest and abdominal plain films). Nasogastric suction and fluid resuscitation should be initiated. The placement of a long tube (Miller-Abbott) is useful in the setting of a postoperative obstruction. A barium enema is performed to determine if the obstruction is in the colon, except in cases of suspected acute diverticulitis, in which a contrast examination of the colon is contraindicated. Nasogastric suction decompression is usually effective in the setting of a partial small bowel obstruction. The treatment of ileus is supportive and nonoperative; continuous decompression is performed.

Surgery soon after admission is indicated in the following types of obstruction: strangulation, closed-loop obstruction, colon obstruction, and early, simple mechanical obstruction. If surgery is required, the timing is critical. The surgery should be carried out before a closed-loop obstruction develops and/or the bowel becomes compromised. Surgical procedures for the relief of intestinal obstruction include procedures that do not require the opening of bowel (such as lysis of adhesion, reduction of intussusception, reduction of incarcerated hernia), enterotomy for the removal of obturation obstruction (gallstone, bezoars), resection of the obstructing lesion or strangulated bowel with primary anastomosis, short-circuiting anastomosis around an obstruction, or the formation of a cutaneous stoma proximal to the obstruction.

PROGNOSIS

The overall mortality rate for small bowel obstruction is approximately 10 percent. The prognosis of adynamic ileus is usually good. The mortality rate for colonic obstruction is about 20 percent, and the mortality rate in strangulated obstruction is 25 percent.

INTRACRANIAL TUMORS

A 56-year-old woman presents to the walk-in clinic with complaints of a headache, nausea, and vomiting. She appears drowsy and is not oriented to the date or day of the week. A right hemiparesis is noted on physical exam. While waiting to have a magnetic resonance imaging (MRI) study of the brain, she has a generalized tonic-clonic seizure that resolves with intravenous diazepam treatment. She is given a loading dose of phenytoin and the MRI obtained is shown below:

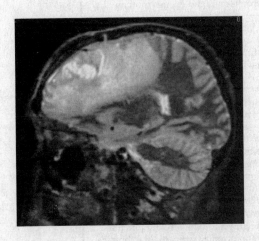
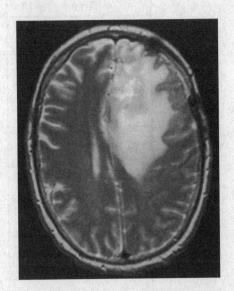

Left cerebral mass

DIAGNOSIS

Intracranial tumors, arising either from within or on the surface of the brain, exert both local and generalized effects because of their presence within a closed, bony structure. Local effects of the tumor are either irritative or destructive. Focal seizures occur because of irritation of an adjacent cortex, while a focal neurologic deficit develops because of compressive forces on nearby brain tissue. More generalized effects come from raised intracranial pressure due to the presence of the mass, including obstructive hydrocephalus, hemorrhage, cerebral edema, or mass effect from the bulk of the tumor within the closed skull. The symptoms from the generalized effects may be headache, occasional nausea and vomiting, decreased level of consciousness, and/or slowed cognitive function.

SURGERY

PATHOGENESIS

Common Brain Tumors		
Type	**Percent**	**Comment**
Gliomas	40–50	Includes astrocytomas, medulloblastomas, oligodendrogliomas, and ependymomas.
Meningiomas	12–20	Relatively benign tumors that arise from the arachnoid layer of the meninges, usually occurring in the fourth through sixth decades of life. They affect women more often (65%) than men.
Pituitary tumors	5–15	May be functional on nonfunctional. Mass effect may alter pituitary function.
Neurilemomas	3–10	Mainly eighth nerve. Schwannomas constitute 8% of all intracranial tumors and are almost twice as common in females as in males.
Metastatic tumors	5–10	25% of all intracranial tumors are metastatic. Malignant cells invade the central nervous system hematogenously and tend to lodge at the gray and white matter junction. Most common primary sites are lung, breast, kidney, testis, colon, and skin.
Blood vessel	< 1	Hemangionblastomas usually occur in the cerebellum. Associated with Hippel-Lindau disease (autosomal disorder consisting of central nervous system hemagioblastomas, retinal angiomatosis, renal and pancreatic cysts, and renal carcinoma).
Tumors of developmental defects	2–3	Includes dermoids, epidermoids, teratomas, chordomas, paraphyseal cysts, craniopharyngiomas
Pinealomas	0.5–0.8	Are actually germinomas, more common in males, and tend to occur in the second and third decades.
Miscellaneous	1–3	Sarcomas, papillomas of the choroid plexus, lipomas, lymphomas

EPIDEMIOLOGY

Nervous system tumors represent almost 10 percent of all neoplasia. Of these, 15 to 20 percent occur in children. Nearly 70 percent of adult tumors are found above the tentorium (supratentorial), whereas 70 percent of childhood tumors are found below (infratentorial). Central nervous system tumors are the most common solid tumors in children.

TREATMENT

Astrocytomas are generally treated with surgery for diagnosis and debulking, followed by radiation therapy. Malignant gliomas are treated with surgery, radiation, and chemotherapy. Meningiomas are treated with surgery. Medulloblastomas are treated with aggressive surgical removal of the tumor, followed by irradiation of the brain, and possibly chemotherapy. Schwannomas are treated with surgery. Pinealomas (germinomas) are extremely radiosensitive and do not require surgery.

PROGNOSIS

The five-year survival rate for astrocytomas with surgery and subsequent radiation is 35 to 50 percent. Malignant gliomas are uniformly fatal, despite aggressive therapy. The recurrence rate of meningiomas is approximately 10 percent. The 5-year recurrence rate of medulloblastomas is at least 25 percent.

LOWER GASTROINTESTINAL HEMORRHAGE

A 73-year-old man is brought to the emergency department by ambulance with rectal bleeding. The bleeding began 1 hour ago and has been constant since then. His temperature is 37 C (98.6 F), pulse is 120/min, and blood pressure is 80/40 mm Hg. Physical exam demonstrates active rectal bleeding. A nasogastric tube is passed into the stomach and reveals no evidence of gastroduodenal bleeding. Laboratory studies show:

Leukocyte count	8,000/mm³	(4,500–11,000/mm³)
Hematocrit	24%	(Male: 41–53
Hemoglobin, blood	8 g/dL	(Male: 13.5–17.5 g/dL)
Platelet count	173,000/mm³	(150,000–400,000/mm³)
Prothrombin time	14 seconds	(11–15 seconds)
Partial thromboplastin time	37 seconds	(25–40 seconds)

DIAGNOSIS

The definition of massive lower gastrointestinal bleeding is the loss of more than 3 units of blood over a 24-hour period. Diverticulosis and angiodysplasia are the most common causes of life-threatening colonic hemorrhage. Other possible causes of lower gastrointestinal hemorrhage include inflammatory bowel disease, ischemic colitis, tumors, and anticoagulant therapy, but although these other conditions are associated with blood loss, life-threatening hemorrhage is rare. In the management of a patient with lower gastrointestinal hemorrhage, it is more important to identify the exact location of the bleeding point immediately than it is to identify the cause of the bleeding.

PATHOGENESIS

Colonic diverticula, which are located primarily in the sigmoid colon, are formed at the location where the colonic arterioles penetrate the muscular wall of the bowel. The presence of diverticula may weaken the blood vessels over time, predisposing them to rupture. Massive lower gastrointestinal hemorrhage can result from diverticulosis, but it is rare for diverticulosis to be the cause of significant chronic bleeding. Most often, the vascular disruption occurs on the mucosal side of the artery, and the bleeding is virtually always into the colonic lumen.

The exact cause of angiodysplasia is unknown, but it is thought to result from chronic obstruction of the submucosal veins secondary to repeated muscular contractions of the colon. Over time, the venules become dilated, and this eventually leads to the formation of small arterial-venous communications. When the disease becomes more advanced, dilation of a submucosal vein, appearing as a vascular tuft, may be seen on angiography. These arterial-venous communications are most common in the cecum, but can be found throughout the large bowel.

EPIDEMIOLOGY

Acute lower gastrointestinal hemorrhage most commonly affects older patients. The two most common causes of hemorrhage from the colon are diverticulosis and angiodysplasia, which both appear to be acquired conditions. These disorders are rare in the young, but appear with increasing frequency after age 50, and may occur simultaneously.

R_x

TREATMENT

The management of lower gastrointestinal bleeding consists of simultaneously replacing the lost intravascular volume and identifying the site of hemorrhage so appropriate treatment can be given.

Evaluation and Treatment of Lower Gastrointestinal Hemorrhage

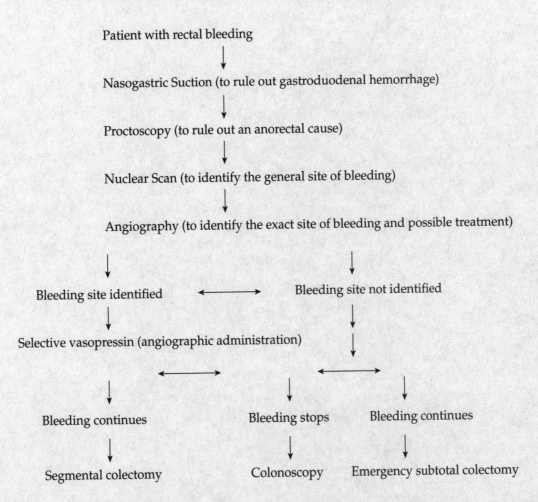

Gastroduodenal hemorrhage is a frequent cause of rectal bleeding and should be excluded immediately by placement of a nasogastric tube. Colonic bleeding will stop spontaneously in 85 percent of patients with gastroduodenal hemorrhage, and the site of bleeding may be impossible to identify once the hemorrhage has stopped. In patients in which the bleeding site is identified by selective angiography, treatment with vasopressin will stop the bleeding in 85 percent of patients. Emergent colonoscopy, after administration of oral electrolyte lavage, may be considered as both a diagnostic and treatment option. Celiotomy is the last-resort treatment; every reasonable effort should be made to identify and control the bleeding with nonoperative techniques.

PROGNOSIS

The prognosis of a patient with lower gastrointestinal hemorrhage is highly variable and is mainly dependent upon the patient's general medical condition and the amount of blood loss. Although most episodes of lower gastrointestinal bleeding stop spontaneously, between 10 and 25 percent of patients eventually require surgery to control bleeding.

MALIGNANT HYPERTHERMIA

A 34-year-old man who underwent a laparoscopic cholecystectomy several hours earlier develops a fever of 40.3 C (104.5 F) while in the post-anesthesia care unit. The surgery was uncomplicated and there was no evidence of infection. Pulse is 120/min, respirations are 24/min, and blood pressure is 90/50 mm Hg. His skin is diaphoretic and mottled in appearance. Physical examination is notable for marked skeletal muscle hypertonicity. Laboratory studies are as follows:

Hematocrit	46%	(Male: 41–53%)
Hemoglobin	15 g/dL	(Male: 13.5–17.5 g/dL)
Leukocyte count	17,000/mm³	(4,500–11,000/mm³)
Platelet count	78,000/mm³	(150,000–400,000/mm³)
Prothrombin time	17 seconds	(11–15 seconds)
Serum		
Bicarbonate	14 mEq/L	(22–28 mEq/L)
Calcium	12.7 mEq/L	(8.4–10.2 mEq/L)
Chloride	98 mEq/L	(95–105 mEq/L)
Creatine kinase	789 U/L	(Male: 25–90 U/L)
Lactate dehydrogenase	267 U/L	(45–90 U/L)
Magnesium	1.3 mEq/L	(1.5–2.0 mEq/L)
Potassium	5.8 mEq/L	(3.5–5.0 mEq/L)
Sodium	138 mEq/L	(136–145 mEq/L)

DIAGNOSIS

Malignant hyperthermia is a rare anesthetic complication that is characterized by a rapid rise in body temperature, usually during the initiation of a general anesthetic after administration of succinylcholine or potent inhalation agents, particularly halothane. Metabolic acidosis and electrolyte imbalances quickly develop, with associated hypercalcemia. The final stages of the event are marked by temperatures approaching 42 C (107.6 F), oxygen desaturation, hypercapnia, and cardiac dysrhythmia.

A patient with a high core temperature, along with appropriate clinical findings (dry skin, hallucinations, delirium, pupil dilation, muscle rigidity, and/or elevated levels of creatine phosphokinase) is likely to have malignant hyperthermia.

Signs and symptoms of malignant hyperthermia

- muscle rigidity (e.g., masseter spasm and rigidity)
- tachypnea and tachycardia
- cardiac dysrhythmias
- myoglobinuria
- skin mottling and cyanosis
- unstable blood pressure
- increased end-tidal carbon dioxide (ETCO$_2$)
- rapidly rising core body temperature.

PATHOGENESIS

Malignant hyperthermia is an inherited abnormality of skeletal muscle sarcoplasmic reticulum that causes a rapid increase in intracellular calcium levels in response to halothane and other inhalational anesthetics, or to succinylcholine. The mode of inheritance of malignant hyperthermia is autosomal dominant, with reduced penetrance and variable expressivity, but sporadic cases and patterns of recessive autosomal hereditary have occasionally been seen.

Agents associated with malignant hyperthermia

- ethyl chloride
- ethylene
- diethyl ether
- gallamine
- halothane
- lidocaine
- mepivacaine
- methoxylflurane
- trichloroethylene
- succinylcholine

EPIDEMIOLOGY

The incidence of malignant hyperthermia reaction during anesthesia is estimated to be from 1:15,000 in children, to 1:50,000 in adults. The acute malignant hyperthermia syndrome is more prevalent in young individuals, and more than 50 percent of cases occur before the age of 15. The MHS patient normally appears to be in good health, but suffers from subclinical myopathy, which can be dramatically exposed when triggering agents are used during anaesthesia.

Population at risk for developing malignant hyperthermia during anesthesia:

- survivors of a malignant hyperthermia reaction, or patients with a positive caffeine-halothane contracture test

- first-degree relatives of such patients or members of known malignant hyperthermia-susceptible families with neuromuscular disorders, with increased levels of creatine kinase (CPK) in serum

- patients who suffer from Duchenne muscular dystrophy, King-Denborough syndrome or central core myopathy

- patients who have exhibited masseter muscle spasm during anaesthesia with halothane and succinylcholine

- patients with a history of neuroleptic malignant syndrome or heat stroke

TREATMENT

A family history of complications associated with anesthetics is a warning of this possibly lethal complication, and prevention is the safest method of limiting the risk to susceptible patients. Cessation of anesthesia and the administration of intravenous dantrolene sodium are the immediately indicated therapies. Procainamide should also be administered to patients with malignant hyperthermia because of the likelihood of the occurrence of ventricular arrhythmias. Support measures must be initiated promptly, including positive pressure ventilation on 100 percent oxygen, correction of the acidosis and electrolyte imbalance, cooling blankets, monitoring of urine output, and treatment of possible myoglobinuria. After the acute episode, oral administration of dantrolene (up to 1 to 2 mg/kg four times a day) may be necessary for 1 to 3 days to prevent recurrences.

Attempting to lower the already normal hypothalamic set point with antipyretics is ineffective. Physical cooling with sponging, fans, cooling blankets, and even ice baths should be initiated immediately in conjunction with the administration of intravenous fluids and dantrolene. If insufficient cooling is achieved by external means, internal cooling can be achieved by gastric or peritoneal lavage with iced saline. In extreme circumstances, hemodialysis or even cardiopulmonary bypass with cooling of blood may be performed.

PROGNOSIS

Mortality from acute fulminant malignant hyperthermia episodes is approximately 10 percent. Delay in the early recognition and prompt treatment of a malignant hyperthermia episode can result in the sudden, unexpected death of a surgical patient from cardiac arrest, brain damage, body system failure, or disseminated intravascular coagulation.

MALIGNANT MELANOMA

A 52-year-old man presents with complaints of a "mole" on his face. He reports that the lesion has become darker in color and grown in size over the past six months. Examination of the face demonstrates a flat, irregularly pigmented lesion with irregularly shaped borders, which measures approximately 1.5 cm by 1.75 cm. A thorough examination of the skin fails to detect any other pigmented lesions. The remainder of the physical examination is unremarkable.

DIAGNOSIS

The important clinical features of melanoma include a pigmented lesion with an irregular, raised surface, and irregular borders. About 5 to 10 percent of melanomas are not pigmented. Lesions that change in color and size and ulcerate over a period of a few months are suspicious and should be biopsied.

There are four common distinct types of melanoma. These are, in order of decreasing frequency, superficial spreading, nodular, lentigo maligna, and acral lentiginous. The superficial spreading type, which represents 70 percent of melanomas, can occur anywhere on the skin except the hands and feet. They are flat, commonly contain areas of regression, and measure 1–2 cm in diameter at the time of diagnosis. The nodular type accounts for 15 to 20 percent of melanomas. These lesions are darker and raised. The histologic criterion for a nodular melanoma is a lack of radial growth peripheral to the area of vertical growth. The lentigo maligna type, which accounts for 5 to 10 percent of melanomas, occur mostly on the neck, the face, and the back of the hands of elderly people. These lesions are always surrounded by dermis with heavy solar degeneration. The rarer acral lentiginous type is distinctly different. It occurs on the palms and soles and in the subungual regions. Although melanoma among dark-skinned people is relatively rare, the acral lentiginous type accounts for a higher percentage of melanoma in dark-skinned people than in people with less pigmented skin.

PATHOGENESIS

Melanoma arises from transformed melanocytes and can appear anywhere that melanocytes have migrated during embryogenesis. The eye, central nervous system, gastrointestinal tract, and even the gallbladder have been reported as primary sites of the disease. Over 90 percent are found on the skin; but 4 percent of melanomas are discovered as metastases without an identifiable primary site.

Nevi are benign melanocytic neoplasms found on the skin of most people. Dysplastic nevi are rare and contain a histologically identifiable focus of atypical melanocytes. This type of nevus may represent an intermediate between a benign nevus and a true malignant melanoma. The relative risk of developing melanoma increases with the number of dysplastic nevi a patient develops.

Once the melanocyte has transformed into the malignant phenotype, the growth of the lesion is radial in the plane of the epidermis. Even though microinvasion of the dermis can be observed during this radial growth phase, metastases do not occur. Only when the melanoma cells form nests in the dermis are metastases observed. The transformed cells in the vertical growth phase are morphologically different and express different cell-surface antigens than those in the radial phase or of the dysplastic nevus.

EPIDEMIOLOGY

The rise in the rate of melanoma is the highest of any cancer in the U.S. The incidence of melanoma is approximately 13 per 100,000; there were 32,000 new cases of melanoma reported in the U.S. in 1991.

TREATMENT

The treatment for melanoma is primarily surgical; it is the only hope for cure and the best treatment for regional control and palliation. All suspicious lesions should undergo excisional biopsy. A 1 mm margin of normal skin should be taken if the wound can be closed primarily. Once a diagnosis of melanoma is made, the biopsy scar and any remains of the lesion need to be removed to eradicate any remaining tumor. All clinically positive lymph nodes should be removed by regional nodal dissection. When patients develop distant metastases, surgical therapy may be indicated. Solitary lesions in the brain, gut, or skin that are symptomatic should be excised when possible.

The most promising area of melanoma treatment is in the use of immunologic manipulation. The only adjuvant therapy known to influence survival so far is the use of intravenous interferon α-2b in patients with lesions of 4 mm of invasion or more or nodal metastasis. Radiation therapy is the treatment of choice for patients with symptomatic multiple brain metastases. Hyperthermic regional perfusion of the limb with a chemotherapeutic agent (e.g., melphalan) is the treatment of choice for patients with local recurrence or in-transit lesions (local disease in lymphatics) that are on an extremity and not amenable to excision.

PROGNOSIS

A tumor/nodal involvement/distant metastasis (TNM) system is used for staging melanoma. The critical measurement for the "T" component (tumor) is the depth of tumor invasion; the greater the depth of invasion, the poorer the prognosis. Evidence of tumor in regional lymph nodes is a poor prognostic sign; the ten-year survival rate drops precipitously with the presence of lymph node metastasis. The presence of distant metastasis is a grave prognostic sign; the median survival ranges from 2 to 7 months, depending on the number and site of metastases. Other independent prognostic factors include:

- Anatomic location—People with lesions on the extremities do better than people with melanomas of the trunk or face.

- Ulceration—Presence of ulceration in a lesion carries a worse prognosis; these melanomas act more aggressively than nonulcerated ones.

- Sex—Women have melanomas in more favorable anatomic sites, and these lesions are less likely to contain ulcerations. However, even with correction for these factors, women have a higher survival rate than men.

- Histologic type—Nodular melanomas have the same prognosis as superficial spreading types when lesions are matched for depth of invasion. Lentigo maligna types, however, have a better prognosis even after correcting for thickness, and acral lentiginous lesions have a worse prognosis.

SURGERY

PANCREATITIS

A 48-year-old woman presents with complaints of epigastric pain that radiates to the back, nausea, and vomiting. The symptoms began following a large, fatty meal 2 days ago and have become progressively worse. Her temperature is 37 C (98.6 F), pulse is 120/min, and blood pressure is 90/55 mm Hg. Examination demonstrates diffuse abdominal tenderness, particularly in the epigastrium. Bowel sounds are absent. No masses are detected. Laboratory studies show:

Leukocyte count	11,000/mm^3	(4,500–11,000/mm^3)
Hematocrit	50%	(Female: 36–46%)
Serum		
Bilirubin		
Total	3.0 mg/dL	(0.1–1.0 mg/dL)
Aspartate aminotransferase	15 U/L	(8–20 U/L)
Alanine aminotransferase	20 U/L	(8–20 U/L)
Amylase	310 U/L	(25–125 U/L)

DIAGNOSIS

Pancreatitis is clinically characterized by acute abdominal pain, elevated concentrations of pancreatic enzymes in the blood, and an increase in the amount of pancreatic enzymes excreted in the urine. Pancreatitis may occur as a single episode or may recur. A typical attack begins with severe and persistent epigastric or upper abdominal pain that often radiates to the back. Frequently, the attack follows the ingestion of a large meal and is associated with nausea and persistent vomiting.

Examination of the abdomen reveals tenderness most marked in the epigastrium, and bowel sounds are decreased or absent. There are usually no palpable masses, but when one is present, it most often represents a swollen pancreas (phlegmon), pseudocyst, or abscess. Severe dehydration, tachycardia, and hypotension may be present. In about 1 percent of patients, a bluish color is evident around the umbilicus (Cullen's sign) or in the flanks (Grey Turner's sign). This is an indication of necrotizing pancreatitis, in which blood has dissected to those areas from the retroperitoneum near the pancreas.

Serum amylase concentration rises to more than 2.5 times the normal concentration within 6 hours of an acute episode and usually remains elevated for several days. The level of serum amylase does not correlate with the severity of the episode of pancreatitis. Serum lipase levels are more reliable than amylase in diagnosing acute pancreatitis. Electrolyte derangements may be present when vomiting has been significant and dehydration is severe. A hypokalemic, hypochloremic, metabolic alkalosis is most common. Hypocalcemia and hypomagnesemia can also occur. The hematocrit may be elevated due to dehydration, or low secondary to pancreatic or retroperitoneal blood loss in necrotizing pancreatitis. White blood cell count is usually normal unless suppurative complications are present. Liver function tests are usually normal, but mild elevations of serum bilirubin concentration (< 2 mg/dL) may be seen due to partial common bile duct obstruction.

The best way to confirm the presence of gallstones when biliary pancreatitis is suspected is with ultrasound examination. Ultrasound may also reveal an edematous, swollen pancreas, peripancreatic fluid collection, or pseudocysts. A computed tomography (CT) scan of the pancreas should be obtained in all patients with acute pancreatitis whose illness has not begun to resolve within 2 or 3 days, or whenever complications are suspected. Possible findings include a normal-appearing pancreas, pancreatic edema, a mass of inflamed peripancreatic tissue and pancreas (phlegmon), pancreatic and/or peripancreatic fluid collections (acute pseudocysts), or abscess. The adequacy of pancreatic perfusion can be estimated if intravenous contrast is used.

Chronic pancreatitis is clinically characterized by recurring, acute episodes of abdominal pain that are indistinguishable from those of acute pancreatitis. As the disease progresses, pancreatic function becomes impaired. The exocrine insufficiency is manifested as steatorrhea and malabsorption, and the endocrine insufficiency causes diabetes, which often requires insulin for its management.

PATHOGENESIS

Acute pancreatitis is a nonbacterial inflammation of the pancreas caused by the activation, interstitial liberation, and digestion of the gland by its own enzymes. In the U.S., the most common cause of acute pancreatitis is cholelithiasis. The table on the next page lists the possible causes of acute pancreatitis.

Common Causes of Acute Pancreatitis		
Etiology	Mechanism	Comment
Gallstone	Transient obstruction of the pancreatic duct by a gallstone at the ampulla of Vater.	Usual age of onset is mid to late 40s, women more commonly affected than men. Gallstones recovered in feces of 90 percent of patients suggesting that the obstruction is brief.
Alcohol	Induces spasm of the sphincter of Oddi. Causes precipitation of enzyme protein and calcium in ducts, which leads to obstruction. Can also increase permeability of pancreatic ducts.	Usual age of onset is mid-30s, men more commonly affected than women. Approximately 10 to 15 percent of persons who consume large amounts of alcohol develop pancreatitis.
Hypercalcemia	Can cause intraductal precipitation of calcium stones. Can also increase permeability of pancreatic ducts.	Most commonly due to hyperparathyroidism. Can cause acute and chronic pancreatitis.
Hyperlipidemia	May involve the release of large amounts of toxic fatty acids into the pancreatic capillary circulation by pancreatic lipase.	More common in the setting of elevated chylomicrons and very low density lipoproteins. Dietary or pharmacological control of the hyperlipidemia minimizes the chances of recurrent episodes.
Heredity	Mendelian dominant trait. One form due to mutation in the gene for trypsin.	Symptoms of acute pancreatitis appear in most patients between the ages of 12 and 14. Many patients progress to chronic pancreatitis.
Drugs	Various mechanisms.	Uncommon but important causes. Most common include: steroids, azathioprine, 6-mercaptopurine, thiazide diuretics, furosemide, sulfonamides, tetracycline, and estrogens.
Pancreas divisum	Embryologic ventral and dorsal pancreatic anlagen fail to fuse, resulting in most drainage through the accessory papilla, which may not be large enough.	Most common congenital anatomic variant. Associated with recurrent pancreatitis in young adulthood. Can progress to chronic pancreatitis.
Idiopathic	Unknown	Accounts for 15 to 20 percent of all cases, however, one-third of all patients with no obvious cause will eventually be found to have cholelithiasis.

During a mild attack (edematous pancreatitis), the morphologic changes are characterized by pancreatic and peripancreatic edema and fat necrosis, but pancreatic necrosis is absent. In its severe form (necrotizing pancreatitis), extensive pancreatic and peripancreatic fat necrosis, pancreatic parenchymal necrosis, and hemorrhage into and around the pancreas are evident. During these episodes of acute inflammation, both the exocrine and endocrine functions of the gland are impaired for weeks or even months. If the cause and any complications of pancreatitis are eliminated, the pancreas usually returns to normal.

Severe episodes of acute pancreatitis may be associated with both systemic and local complications. Possible systemic complications include respiratory insufficiency with adult respiratory distress syndrome, renal failure, and depressed myocardial function. Local complications might include the development of pancreatic or peripancreatic infection and pseudocyst formation.

Chronic pancreatitis is characterized by a permanent and usually progressive destruction of pancreatic tissue. The acinar cells are destroyed first and replaced by dense, fibrous scar tissue. Eventually, the islet cells are also damaged by this sclerotic process, and cysts and pseudocysts occur frequently. In the U.S., the most common cause of chronic pancreatitis is alcoholism. In contrast to acute pancreatitis, the morphological changes in chronic pancreatitis are irreversible and often progressive, even if the cause is removed. The only exception is obstructive chronic pancreatitis, which can improve somewhat after the obstruction is removed.

EPIDEMIOLOGY

In the U.S., the incidence of acute pancreatitis is approximately 5,000 cases per year. Gallstone pancreatitis accounts for about 40 percent of all cases of pancreatitis and about 90 percent of cases of acute pancreatitis in the U.S. Alcoholic pancreatitis accounts for 40 percent of all cases of pancreatitis, and about 75 percent of cases of chronic pancreatitis.

TREATMENT

The treatment of uncomplicated acute pancreatitis is medical and primarily directed at the restoration of fluid and electrolyte balance and the avoidance of secretory stimulation of the pancreas. Nasogastric suction is indicated in all but the mildest cases. Oral intake should be withheld until the ileus has resolved and pain is absent. Fluid resuscitation is critical; large volumes of fluid can be sequestered in the retroperitoneum, adjacent to the pancreas. About 30 percent of patients with acute pancreatitis develop arterial hypoxemia and require O_2 supplementation.

Peritoneal lavage can be used in patients with severe acute pancreatitis and intraperitoneal fluid in order to remove toxins and various metabolites and minimize their systemic absorption. In most cases of biliary pancreatitis, the gallstone dislodges spontaneously, but if it does not, the stone can be removed by either endoscopic retrograde cholangiopancreatography or surgery.

Surgery is contraindicated in uncomplicated acute pancreatitis. In most cases of biliary pancreatitis, the pancreatitis resolves within two or three days and cholecystectomy can then be performed. For severe pancreatitis, the biliary tree should be drained through cholecystotomy, but this procedure should be delayed. Infected pancreatic necrosis should be treated with surgical debridement. Pancreatic abscess can be treated surgically or, if possible, by percutaneous drainage.

Noninterventional, expectant management of a pancreatic pseudocyst is the best course in patients with minimal symptoms. A pseudocyst that does not resolve spontaneously may lead to serious complications. If the pseudocyst is expanding and is complicated by rupture, hemorrhage, or abscess, surgery is indicated.

PROGNOSIS

The mortality rate for all patients with acute pancreatitis is approximately 10 percent. Necrotizing pancreatitis associated with infection shows a mortality rate of about 35 percent.

Ranson's criteria are widely used for prognosticating patients with acute pancreatitis (see table below).

Ranson's Prognostic Criteria for Acute Pancreatitis	
Present on Admission	Developing within the first 48 hrs
Age > 55	Hematocrit fall > 10%
White blood cell count > 16,000/mm^3	Blood urea nitrogen increase > 8 mg/dL
Blood glucose > 200 mg/dL	Serum Ca_2^+ < 8 mg/dL
Serum lactate dehydrogenase > 350 U/L	Arterial PO_2 < 60 mm Hg
AST > 250 U/L	Base deficit < 4 mEq/L
	Estimated fluid sequestration > 600 mL

Morbidity and mortality rates correlate with the number of criteria present: 0–2 = 2 percent mortality; 3–4 = 15 percent mortality; 5–6 = 40 percent mortality; 7–8 = 100 percent mortality.

PNEUMOTHORAX

A 31-year-old man presents to the emergency department with complaints of left-sided chest pain and shortness of breath. The patient reports that the pain and shortness of breath began suddenly about 1 hour earlier. Temperature is 37 C (98.6 F), pulse is 100/min, respirations are 28/min, and blood pressure is 125/80 mm Hg. The patient is tall and thin. Although the patient demonstrates tachypnea and increased respiratory effort, he does not appear to be in acute distress. He is able to answer questions without any difficulty. Examination of the chest reveals distant breath sounds and hyperresonance to percussion on the left side. The trachea is in the midline. Neck veins are not dilated. A room air arterial blood gas shows:

pH	7.46	(7.35–7.45)
PCO_2	30 mm Hg	(33–45 mm Hg)
PO_2	77 mm Hg	(75–105 mm Hg)

A chest x-ray is obtained.

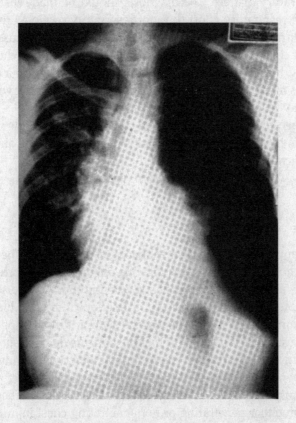

Chest radiograph demonstrating pneumothorax

DIAGNOSIS

The most common presenting symptom of a spontaneous pneumothorax is chest pain, followed by dyspnea. If the lung is more than 25 percent collapsed, a decrease in breath sounds is evident on auscultation and the affected side is hyperresonant to percussion. Young patients without underlying lung disease can be relatively asymptomatic at rest, with the nearly complete collapse of one lung and arterial blood gases that are nearly normal. A more dramatic presentation that includes tachypnea, cyanosis, and hypoxia is seen in patients with underlying lung disease and limited ventilatory reserve.

The characteristic radiographic finding of a pneumothorax is the absence of lung markings and a faintly visible line that defines the edge of the lung. When the lung collapses almost completely, it is visible as an irregular density attached to the hilum. When the lung surface is separated from the chest wall by 3 cm or more, the patient may have 50 percent lung collapse (by volume). Pneumothorax can vary from being so slight as to be missed on the initial radiographic examination, to being a massive, continuing air leak that displaces the mediastinum, depresses the diaphragm, and compresses the opposite lung, such as the tension pneumothorax. With any chest injury, it is wisest to presume that a pneumothorax is present until proven otherwise.

A developing tension pneumothorax may not be obvious at first; pain may be the primary complaint, with no evidence of respiratory distress. The diagnosis should be made instantly upon observation of dilated neck veins making respiratory effort (but not respiratory motions) that are unable to move air. The diagnosis can be confirmed by observation of a hyperresonant percussion note over the injured hemithorax, and absent or distant breath sounds. Difficulty in ventilation during resuscitation or high-peak inspiration pressures during mechanical ventilation strongly suggest a diagnosis of tension pneumothorax. The diagnosis is made by the finding of an enlarged hemithorax with no breath sounds and a shift of the mediastinum to the contralateral side.

The diagnosis of an open pneumothorax (sucking chest wound) is made if the patient has normal or collapsed neck veins and is making respiratory motions but is not moving air. Confirmation is made by inspection of the patient's chest and observation of the wound.

PATHOGENESIS

Pneumothorax is the presence of gas in the pleural space. A spontaneous pneumothorax occurs without antecedent trauma to the thorax. A primary spontaneous pneumothorax occurs in the absence of underlying lung disease, while a secondary spontaneous pneumothorax occurs in its presence. Primary spontaneous pneumothoraces are usually due to rupture of apical pleural blebs, which are small cystic spaces that lie within or immediately under the visceral pleura. Primary spontaneous pneumothoraces occur almost exclusively in smokers, and suggest that the patients do have subclinical lung disease. Most secondary spontaneous pneumothoraces are due to chronic obstructive pulmonary disease, but pneumothoraces have been reported with virtually every pulmonary disease.

Pneumothorax is usually the result of injury to the lung or the tracheobronchial tree; traumatic pneumothorax results from either penetrating or nonpenetrating chest injuries. Esophageal perforation may be followed by a pneumomediastinum that ruptures into the pleural cavity. The amount of bleeding into the peritoneal cavity depends on whether the pneumothorax is associated with blunt injury and fractured ribs, or is the result of a penetrating wound. Iatrogenic pneumothorax is a type of traumatic pneumothorax that is becoming more common. The leading causes of this type of pneumothorax are transthoracic needle aspiration, thoracentesis, and the insertion of central, intravenous catheters.

A tension pneumothorax is a pneumothorax in which the pressure in the pleural space is positive throughout the respiratory cycle. A tension pneumothorax typically occurs during mechanical ventilation or resuscitative efforts. When an injury to the lung parenchyma has occurred, air can enter the pleural space with each respiratory effort and the flap-valve effect of the injury prevents that air from reentering the bronchial tree to be expired. Tension develops within the pleural space until equilibration with the negative pressures is reached. At that time, effective ventilation ceases and venous blood can no longer enter the chest. A shift of the mediastinum and compression of the large veins result in a decreased cardiac output that may lead to sudden death.

An open pneumothorax occurs when a full thickness segment of the chest wall has been destroyed and the negative intrapleural pressure sucks air directly through the chest wall defect rather than through the trachea into the alveoli. It occurs most commonly after shotgun blasts, explosions with flying debris, or other impalement injuries. It may or may not be associated with underlying parenchymal damage.

EPIDEMIOLOGY

Up to 80 percent of patients with spontaneous pneumothorax are young adults; usually male without clinically significant pulmonary disease. A tall, asthenic habitus is common. In patients over age 40, significant pulmonary disease is usually present, most frequently emphysema in tobacco addicts.

TREATMENT

Treatment of the more common pneumothoraces depends on symptoms of respiratory insufficiency, the extent of the pneumothorax, and the presence of significant hemothorax. A decision not to remove the pleural air implies that the patient has had a minor injury and conditions for observation are ideal.

The initial recommendation for primary spontaneous pneumothorax is simple aspiration. If the lung does not expand or if the patient has a recurrent pneumothorax, tube thoracostomy with instillation of a sclerosing agent such as doxycycline is indicated. Nearly all patients with secondary spontaneous pneumothorax should be treated with tube thoracostomy, with instillation of a sclerosing agent. Patients with either primary or secondary spontaneous pneumothoraces who have a persistent air leak or an unexpanded lung after five days of tube thoracostomy should have a thoracoscopy with bleb resection and pleural abrasion.

Aspiration of the air with a needle and insertion of an intercostal catheter is a reasonable method of treatment for patients who have up to a 50 percent collapse. In patients who exhibit collapse greater than 50 percent, those with hemopneumothorax, and those whose pneumothorax is the result of penetrating trauma, an intercostal catheter should be inserted and attached to a water seal, with 10–25 cm H_2O of negative pressure. In the majority of patients, lung reexpansion and cessation of the air leak occur within a few hours or days. If not, a major bronchial injury may be present, and a thoracotomy may be required after appropriate diagnostic procedures. Traumatic pneumothoraces should be treated with tube thoracostomy. The treatment of iatrogenic pneumothoraces differs according to the degree of respiratory distress and can primarily involve observation, the administration of supplemental oxygen, aspiration, or tube thoracostomy.

Tension pneumothorax must be treated as an emergency. The immediate release of tension is accomplished by the placement of a large-bore needle into the pleural space through the second anterior intercostal space. The diagnosis is confirmed if large amounts of gas escape from the needle after insertion. This should be followed immediately by the insertion of a thoracostomy tube.

PROGNOSIS

Approximately one-half of patients with an initial primary spontaneous pneumothorax will have a recurrence, but thoracoscopy or thoracotomy with pleural abrasion is almost 100 percent successful in preventing recurrences. Pneumothorax in patients with lung disease is more life threatening than in normal individuals because of their lack of pulmonary reserve.

TRAUMA

A 24-year-old man is brought to the emergency department by ambulance after being injured in a motorcycle accident. The ambulance crew reports finding the patient unresponsive approximately 7 meters (25 feet) from his motorcycle. Initial evaluation demonstrates an unresponsive, intubated patient making spontaneous respiratory efforts, with a rapid, weak pulse. Auscultation of the chest demonstrates bilateral and equal breath sounds. Pulse is 136/min and blood pressure is 80/40 mm Hg. After intravenous solution of 3 L of lactated Ringer's solution, his blood pressure is 110/70 mm Hg, pulse is 110/min, and he has spontaneous respirations of 20/min.

DIAGNOSIS

The initial treatment of seriously injured patients consists of a primary survey, resuscitation, secondary survey, diagnostic evaluation, and definitive care. Very often these processes can be administered simultaneously. The evaluation and treatment of trauma patients often begins in the field by emergency medical services personnel.

Many trauma patients cannot provide specific information about the mechanism of their injury. For this reason, emergency medical personnel and police are trained to evaluate an injury scene and should be questioned. In cases of trauma caused by automobile accident, the speed of the accident, the angle of impact (if any), the use of restraints, airbag deployment, the condition of the steering wheel and windshield, whether the patient was ejected from the vehicle, and whether anyone was dead at the scene should all be ascertained. Vital signs and mental status in the emergency department should be compared with those at the scene; improvement or deterioration provides critical prognostic information.

PATHOGENESIS

Trauma or injury is defined as damage to the body caused by an exchange with environmental energy that is beyond the body's resilience. More energy is transferred over a wider area during blunt trauma than during trauma from a gunshot or stab wound. As a result, blunt trauma is associated with multiple, widely distributed injuries, while penetrating injuries result in damage that is localized to the path of the bullet or knife.

Patients who have sustained blunt trauma are separated into two categories: high energy transfer and low energy transfer, according to their risk for multiple injuries. Injuries that involve high energy transfer include auto-pedestrian accidents; motor vehicle accidents in which the car's change of speed exceeds 20 mph, or in which the patient has been ejected; motorcycle accidents; and falls from heights greater than 20 feet. For motor vehicle accidents, the greatest risk factors that reflect the magnitude of injury from the field are the death of another occupant in the vehicle and an extrication time longer than 20 minutes. Low-energy trauma, such as being struck with a club or falling from a bicycle, usually does not result in widely distributed injuries, but potentially lethal laceration of internal organs can still occur because of a potentially substantial net energy transfer to that location.

Penetrating injuries are classified according to the wounding agent, i.e., stab wounds, gunshot wounds, or shotgun wounds. Gunshot wounds are further subdivided into high- and low-velocity injuries, because the speed of the bullet is much more important than its weight when determining kinetic energy. High-velocity gunshot wounds are rare in the civilian setting, but close-range shotgun wounds (which are more common) are comparable to high-velocity gunshot wounds because the total energy of the load is delivered to a small area (often with devastating results). Long-range shotgun wounds usually result in a diffuse pellet pattern of comparatively low energy.

EPIDEMIOLOGY

Trauma is a major public health issue; it remains the most common cause of death for individuals between the ages of 1 and 44 years, and is the third most common cause of death for all ages. There are approximately 100,000 deaths due to trauma in the U.S. per year, of which motor vehicle accidents account for nearly 50 percent of these, while homicides, suicides, and other causes comprise the other half. The magnitude of the incidence of trauma is much larger than these death rates indicate, however, since most injured patients survive.

TREATMENT

The primary survey, which is the identification and treatment of conditions that constitute an immediate threat to life, is referred to as the ABCs—a check on Airway, with cervical spine protection; Breathing; and Circulation. Ensuring the presence of an adequate airway is the first priority in the primary survey. All blunt trauma patients require cervical spine immobilization until injury is ruled out. Patients who are conscious and have a normal voice do not require further attention to their airway. Exceptions to this rule include patients with penetrating injuries to the neck and an expanding hematoma; evidence of chemical or thermal injury to the mouth, nares, or hypopharynx; extensive subcutaneous air in the neck; complex maxillofacial trauma; or airway bleeding. Patients who have an abnormal voice or altered mental status require further airway evaluation. Altered mental status is the most common indication for intubation because of the patient's inability to protect their airway. Options for airway access include nasotracheal, orotracheal, or operative intervention. Nasotracheal intubation can be accomplished only in patients who are breathing spontaneously and is contraindicated in the apneic patient.

Once a secure airway is obtained, adequate oxygenation and ventilation must be administered. All injured patients should receive supplemental oxygen therapy and be monitored by pulse oximetry. Conditions that may constitute an immediate threat to life because of inadequate ventilation include: tension pneumothorax, open pneumothorax, or flail chest/pulmonary contusion. These diagnoses can be made with a combination of physical examination and chest x-ray.

After a secure airway and adequate ventilation are established, circulatory status is determined. A rough first approximation of the patient's cardiovascular status can be obtained by palpating peripheral pulses. At this point in the patient's treatment, hypotension should be assumed to be caused by hemorrhage. Blood pressure and pulse should be measured every fifteen minutes. Hemorrhaging should be controlled externally before restoring circulating volume. Intravenous access for fluid resuscitation is begun with two large-bore peripheral catheters. Blood should be drawn and immediately sent for typing and hematocrit measurement. For patients requiring vigorous fluid resuscitation, saphenous vein cutdowns at the ankle or percutaneous femoral vein catheter introducers is preferred. In hypovolemic pediatric patients (younger than 6 years of age) in whom peripheral access cannot be obtained, intraosseus cannulation of the proximal tibia is indicated.

Initial fluid resuscitation is with a 1 L intravenous bolus of normal saline, lactated Ringer's solution, or other isotonic crystalloid in an adult, or 20 mL/kg of body weight lactated Ringer's solution in a child.

The goal of fluid resuscitation is to reestablish tissue perfusion. Urine output is a quantitative and relatively reliable indicator of organ perfusion. Adequate urine output is 0.5 mL/kg/hr in adults, 1 mL/kg/hr in children, and 2 mL/kg/hr in infants younger than 1 year of age. Classic signs and symptoms of shock are tachycardia, hypotension, tachypnea, mental status changes, diaphoresis, and pallor.

An abnormal mental status should prompt an immediate reevaluation of the ABC's and consideration of an evolving central nervous system injury. Acute changes in mental status can be caused by hypoxia, hypercarbia, or hypovolemia, or they may be an early sign of increasing intracranial pressure.

When the conditions that constitute an immediate threat to life have been attended to, the secondary survey is performed. The patient is examined in a systematic fashion to identify occult injuries. Special attention should be given to the patient's back, axillae, and perineum (because injuries in these areas are easily overlooked). A Foley catheter should be inserted to decompress the bladder, obtain a urine specimen, and monitor urine output. In cases of persistent hypovolemic shock in which an attempt to place a Foley catheter is unsuccessful, a percutaneous suprapubic cystostomy tube should be placed. A nasogastric tube should be inserted to decrease the risk of gastric aspiration and allow inspection for blood that would be suggestive of occult gastroduodenal injury. Patients should undergo a digital rectal examination for an evaluation of sphincter tone and to look for blood, perforation, or a high-riding prostate.

Selective radiographs are obtained early in the emergency room evaluation. For patients with severe blunt trauma, anteroposterior chest and pelvic radiographs should be obtained as soon as possible. Additional diagnostic studies are often indicated on the basis of mechanism of injury, location of injuries, screening x-rays, and the patient's overall condition.

Regional Assessment		
Region	**Evaluation**	**Comment**
Head	Presence of lateralizing findings are important. Otorrhea, rhinorrhea, "raccoon eyes," and Battle's sign (ecchymosis behind the ear) can be seen in basilar skull fractures. Patients with significant closed head injury should have a CT scan performed. For penetrating injuries, plain skull films should be obtained as well, since they provide information that CT does not.	Examination of the head should focus on potentially treatable neurologic injuries. Significant penetrating injuries are usually produced by bullets from handguns, but other weapons or instruments can injure the cerebrum via the orbit or through the thinner temporal region of the skull.
Neck	Cervical spine series includes a lateral view with visualization of C7–T1, an anteroposterior view, and a transoral odontoid view. If pain or tenderness persists in spite of normal appearance on plain x-ray films, a CT scan should be done. Penetrating injuries of the anterior neck are significant because of the density of critical structures in this region.	Attention should be focused on signs and symptoms of an occult cervical spine injury. All patients should be assumed to have cervical spine injuries until proven otherwise.
Chest	Widening of the mediastinum on anteroposterior chest x-ray strongly suggests a tear of the descending thoracic aorta. Penetrating thoracic trauma can be evaluated by physical examination, plain posteroanterior and lateral chest x-rays with metallic markings of entrance and exit wounds, and central venous pressure measurement.	Blunt trauma to the chest may involve the chest wall, thoracic spine, heart, lungs, thoracic aorta and great vessels, and the esophagus.

SURGERY

Abdomen	The presence of abdominal rigidity or gross abdominal distention in a patient with truncal trauma is an indication for prompt surgical exploration. Laparotomy is mandatory in cases of gunshot wounds that penetrate the peritoneal cavity. Stab wounds must be explored to determine if the peritoneum has been violated. Diagnostic peritoneal lavage is the most sensitive test available for determining the presence of intraabdominal injury. Blunt abdominal trauma is evaluated by ultrasound imaging.	In general, it is not necessary to determine which intraabdominal organs are injured, only whether an exploratory laparotomy is necessary.
Pelvis	Plain x-rays reveal gross abnormalities, but CT scanning may be necessary. Urethrograms should be done in stable patients before placing the Foley catheter to avoid false passage and subsequent stricture.	Blunt injury to the pelvis frequently produces complex fractures.
Extremities	Injury of the extremities from any cause requires plain x-ray films to evaluate fractures. Ligamentous injuries, particularly those of the knee and shoulder that are related to sports activities, can be imaged with MRI. Arteriography is helpful in locating vascular injuries.	

PROGNOSIS

Predicting the outcome of a trauma patient is difficult due to the large number of variables involved. The number of injured organs, major fractures, blood loss, and the presence of shock are crude predictors of outcome. The most common causes of death for trauma patients are head injury, exsanguination from cardiovascular injuries, and sepsis with multiple organ failure.

Practice
Test

SIMULATED FULL-LENGTH PRACTICE USMLE STEP 2

The next section includes a simulated full-length USMLE Step 2. This examination is not an actual USMLE Step 2, and in fact, the NBME has never released a full-length USMLE Step 2. Although the actual USMLE Step 2 is now administered on computer, the questions look very much the same as they did when the exam was administered as a paper and pencil exam. the USMLE Step 2 CBT consists of the same types of multiple-choice questions that appeared on the paper and pencil exam. This simulated full-length USMLE Step 2 was developed to provide students an opportunity to practice with a simulated exam of the same length and structure as the actual USMLE Step 2. Detailed explanations are included. Students may choose to go through the exam adhering to actual USMLE Step 2 time limits or may review questions one by one at their own pace.

Keep in mind the actual testing conditions. The testing day for Step 2 lasts 9 hours. Each exam is composed of groups of questions called "blocks." The Step 2 examination consists of 8 blocks of approximately 50 questions. You will have 60 minutes to complete each block of questions. Once you start working on a block, you cannot stop the exam clock. The computer will keep track of how much time you have left in each block and for the entire exam. The questions in a block will appear on the computer screen one at a time. You will read the material available and select an answer to the question. You can select an answer by pointing to the answer and "clicking" with the computer's mouse or by typing the letter (A, B, C, etc.) on the computer's keyboard that corresponds to the answer. When you are finished with a question, you choose to move on to the next question. Once you complete the block or the time allotted for the block runs out, you cannot go back to the questions in that block.

You can take breaks, including a lunch break, between blocks of questions. You will have at least 45 minutes of break time for the entire testing day. You can take this break time at your own pace throughout the testing day. If you finish one or more blocks early, you can take this extra time as break time. The brief tutorial at the beginning of the exam is included on the USMLE CD-ROM provided by the NBME or ECFMG. If you are already familiar with the tutorial and choose to skip it on the exam date, you can use this extra time for breaks. Your testing day is over when you have completed all blocks of questions or when you run out of time, whichever happens first. You should be careful not to use all of your break time too early in the testing day.

Please Note: Although current at the time of publication, the format of Step 2 is subject to change. These changes may affect the length of the testing day for these exams and the ability of examinees to review and change their answers to questions within a block. Notice of any changes will be posted on the USMLE web site at http://www.usmle.org.

SECTION 1 BEGINS HERE

Directions (Items 1–50): Each of the numbered items is followed or preceded by a set of options. For each item, select the BEST lettered option to answer the question or complete the statement. Locate the corresponding item number in the appropriate section of your answer sheet and completely fill in the circle containing the lettered option you have selected.

1. A 52-year-old black male presents to his primary care physician with complaints of overwhelming sadness for the last several months. He admits to a 4.5 kg (10 lb) weight loss, difficulty sleeping with early morning awakenings, and constipation. His physician diagnoses major depression and writes a prescription for trazodone. When counseling the patient about this medicine, which of the following potentially dangerous side effects should the physician emphasize?

   (A) Malignant hypertension
   (B) Pancytopenia
   (C) Priapism
   (D) Seizures
   (E) Urinary retention

(C) is correct. While many of the antidepressant mediations may cause impotence, trazodone is well-recognized as cause of priapism. Choice A is incorrect. Monoamine oxidase inhibitors may precipitate hypertension when taken with food or other drugs that contain certain amine compounds; trazodone does not. Choice B is incorrect. Newer antipsychotic medications, such as clozaril, are noted for their propensity to cause idiosyncratic pancytopenia. Choice D is incorrect. Seizures are a recognized complication of combining bupropion with other tricyclic antidepressants, particularly in patients with eating disorders. Trazodone is not known to have this effect. Choice E is incorrect. Tricyclic antidepressants may result in urinary retention because of their anticholinergic activity. Trazodone is not a tricyclic antidepressant.

2. A 63-year-old white male presents with a six-week history of fevers as high as 38.2 C (102 F), sweats, and fatigue. He has a new diastolic heart murmur, II/VI in intensity, heard loudest at the base and without radiation. Blood cultures are drawn and grow gram-positive cocci in chains. Which of the following is the most likely pathogen?

   (A) *Pseudomonas aeruginosa*
   (B) *Staphylococcus aureus*
   (C) *Staphylococcus epidermidis*
   (D) *Streptococcus pneumoniae*
   (E) *Streptococcus viridans* group

(E) is correct. This patient has subacute endocarditis with a new murmur of aortic insufficiency. The pathogen most often isolated from patients with subacute bacterial endocarditis is streptococci from the *viridans* group, which are common oral flora. The blood culture findings support this diagnosis, being typical for the appearance of *Streptococcus* on gram stain (gram-positive cocci in chains). Choice A is incorrect. *Pseudomonas aeruginosa* is an uncommon cause of endocarditis in patients who do not abuse intravenous drugs. It commonly attacks the tricuspid valve, causing the soft systolic murmur of tricuspid regurgitation. Choice B is incorrect. *Staphylococcus aureus* is a common cause of acute bacterial endocarditis, which is rapidly fatal without treatment (within 6 weeks). Staphylococci appear as gram-positive cocci in clusters on gram stain. Choice C is incorrect. *Staphylococcus epidermidis* is a cause of acute endocarditis. It is also a common pathogen in endocarditis after heart valve replacement surgery. Staphylococci appear as gram-positive cocci in clusters on gram stain. Choice D is incorrect. *Streptococcus pneumoniae*, although a common cause of pneumonia and meningitis, is an uncommon cause of endocarditis.

3. A 24-year-old woman complains of growths on her vagina for the last month. These growths have persisted and enlarged, but are not painful. She states that she had a similar occurrance of such lesions at age 18, which responded to medical therapy. She is sexually active with multiple partners of both sexes and uses a vaginal sponge and creme as contraceptive methods. Physical examination reveals small, raised, shaggy lesions on her vagina ranging in size from 1 to 7 mm. They are noted on both the labia majora and the perineum. Rectal examination reveals evidence of a prior thrombosed external hemorrhoid that was treated surgically. Which of the following is the most likely diagnosis?

(A) Chancroid
(B) Condyloma acuminatum
(C) Condyloma latum
(D) Genital herpes
(E) Molluscum contagiosum

(B) is correct. Condyloma acuminata (venereal warts) causes soft, fleshy growths on the vulva, cervix, perineum, and anus. Diagnosis is made on physical examination and confirmed with biopsy of the lesions. Treatment of uncomplicated warts can be accomplished with topical podophyllin. Treatment with 5-fluorouracil, cryosurgery, or surgical excision is required for more extensive lesions. Choice A is incorrect. Chancroid is associated with papules or pustules that are red and irregularly shaped on a yellow or grey base. The regional lymph nodes are often tender. Choice C is incorrect. Condyloma lata are found in syphilis and are flat lesions that are red and firm. They have a broad base and are nontender. Choice D is incorrect. Genital herpes is associated with a variable number of papules with raised margins and irregular borders. There is no associated lymphadenopathy or induration. Choice E is incorrect. Molluscum contagiosum is associated with lesions that have central umbilication and are more common over the lower abdomen. The appearance of these lesions is described as yellow and cheesy.

4. A 44-year-old sexually active woman complains of 4 hours of severe generalized abdominal pain and intermittent vaginal bleeding that has increased over the last 2 days. Her prior medical history is notable for irritable bowel syndrome and hyperthyroidism. Her medications include a synthetic antithyroid preparation. Her prior obstetrical history is notable for abruptio placentae with her only pregnancy at age 33, which resulted in a stillborn product. Presently, she complains of dizzinness, nausea, and constipation. Her last menstrual period was 40 days ago, and her menstrual periods typically occur every 26 days. Physical examination reveals a blood pressure of 96/70 mm Hg, a pulse of 110/min, respirations of 18/min, and lower abdominal tenderness to deep palpation. Pelvic examination reveals a slightly open cervix with no evidence of blood in the vaginal vault. Which of the following is the most appropriate next step in the workup and management of this patient?

(A) Complete blood count
(B) Culdocentesis
(C) Transabdominal sonography
(D) Transvaginal sonography
(E) Urine pregnancy test

(E) is correct. Any sexually active female in the reproductive age group who presents with pain, menstrual bleeding, and/or amenorrhea should have ectopic pregnancy as a part of the differential diagnosis. The initial step in the management of this patient should include a urine pregnancy test, which can detect human chorionic gonadotropin as early as 14 days after conception, and is positive in greater than 90 percent of cases of ectopic pregnancy. Choice A is incorrect. A complete blood count can identify anemia secondary to intraabdominal bleeding in the setting of an ectopic pregnancy, but in this hemodynamically stable patient, it is not the first test that should be ordered. Choice B is incorrect. Culdocentesis can aid in the identification of hemoperitoneum, which might indicate the presence of ectopic pregnancy. While aspiration of blood suggests a ruptured ectopic pregnancy, a negative culdocentesis does not rule out this condition. Choice C is incorrect. Transabdominal sonography is a useful adjunct to quantification of hCG levels and cannot rule out a pregnancy outside the uterine cavity. It can, however, confirm the intrauterine presence of a gestational sac. Choice D is incorrect. Transvaginal sonography is more sensitive than transabdominal sonography and can detect pregnancy when the hCG level is 1,500 mIU/mL or greater.

5. A 27-year-old white male presents to the emergency department with complaints of urethral discharge for several days. Subsequent urine culture and urethral swab cultures for *Neisseria gonorrhoeae* and *Chlamydia trachomatis* is negative. The patient also notes several weeks of joint aches in his right knee, left hip, and right shoulder. He denies fever, chills, or sweats. His exam confirms his joint complaints as well as small joint effusions. Which of the following is the most likely diagnosis?

   (A) Disseminated *Neisseria gonorrhoeae*
   (B) Psoriatic arthritis
   (C) Reiter's syndrome (reactive arthritis)
   (D) Rheumatoid arthritis
   (E) Systemic lupus erythematosus

(C) is correct. Reiter's syndrome or reactive arthritis causes a nonpurulent, asymmetric, and additive arthritis of the large joints and may cause dactylitis. Individuals usually are HLA-B27 positive. Urogenital lesions, such as urethritis and prostatitis, are common, as is anterior uveitis. Choice A is incorrect. Disseminated *Neiserria gonorrhoeae* is a severe acute illness that causes high fever. Involved joints are septic and thus grossly erythematous and exquisitely painful. Choice B is incorrect. Psoriatic arthritis is a chronic inflammatory arthritis found in 5–42 percent of patients with psoriasis. Dactylitis is the common finding, along with nail changes. Choice D is incorrect. Rheumatoid arthritis is a chronic inflammatory arthritis. It is symmetric, with common involvement of the wrists, knees, and metacarpal joints. Choice E is incorrect. Systemic lupus erythematosus is a chronic multisystem autoimmune disease. Arthritis may be prominent, but is generally symmetric.

6. A 34-year-old primigravid woman who is pregnant by home pregnancy test presents for evaluation. She has a history of systemic lupus erythematosus and takes prednisone daily. Doppler ultrasound reveals evidence of fetal heart tones. Abdominal examination reveals normoactive bowel sounds with a fundal height at 5 cm below the umbilicus. Her serum electrolytes are normal. Which of the following is a possible fetal cardiac defect in this pregnancy?

   (A) Coarctation of the aorta
   (B) Complete heart block
   (C) Transposition of the great vessels
   (D) Tricuspid atresia
   (E) Ventricular septal defect

(B) is correct. Maternal systemic lupus erythematosus increases the rate of abortion and may result in a perinate with cardiac arrhythmia, most notably complete heart block. Choice A is incorrect. Coarctation of the aorta can result from embryonic exposure to hyperglycemia, as seen in maternal diabetes mellitus. Choice C is incorrect. Transposition of the great vessels can result from embryonic exposure to hyperglycemia, as seen in maternal diabetes mellitus. Choice D is incorrect. Tricuspid atresia can result from embryonic exposure to teratogens. Choice E is incorrect. Ventricular septal defect can result from embryonic exposure to hyperglycemia, as seen in maternal diabetes mellitus.

7. A 35-year-old woman misses her period. Shortly thereafter, she complains of a heavy sensation in her breasts with tingling and soreness. She also has nausea and vomiting throughout the day that is worse in the morning. After a few weeks of these symptoms, the patient feels a "fluttering" sensation in her abdomen. Convinced that she is pregnant, the patient goes to the doctor's office. On physical examination, the abdomen appears enlarged, and no masses are palpable. The uterus is a normal size, smooth, and mobile. Adnexa are not palpable. The cervix is long and closed. The vulvovaginal mucosa is a pink hue. Urine pregnancy test is negative. The most likely diagnosis in this patient is

    (A) hydatidiform mole
    (B) normal pregnancy
    (C) ovarian cyst
    (D) pseuodocyesis
    (E) uterine leiomyoma

(D) is correct. Pseudocyesis occurs in young females with a strong unfulfilled desire for pregnancy. It is associated with all of the subjective symptoms of true pregnancy, e.g., nausea, vomiting, breast soreness, and fetal movement. Patients may cease menses. The abdomen may appear enlarged. However, there are no pelvic signs of pregnancy, and urinary pregnancy test is negative. If the patient is still convinced of pregnancy, then psychiatric consultation is in order. Choice A is incorrect. Urine pregnancy test is negative. Molar pregnancy presents with hyperemesis gravidarum and a uterus larger than expected for dates. Choice B is incorrect. Urine pregnancy test is negative. Choice C is incorrect. Ovarian cysts may simulate pregnancy, but this patient's adnexa are not palpable. Choice E is incorrect. Uterine leiomyoma may simulate abdominal and uterine enlargement of pregnancy, but this patient's uterus is normal in size and smooth.

8. A couple has four children, two boys and two girls. Both of the boys suffer from a rare metabolic disease. Both the mother and father are unaffected. Unfortunately, the history of the boys' grandparents is unavailable. What is the most likely mode of inheritance?

    (A) Autosomal dominant
    (B) Autosomal recessive
    (C) Mitochondrial inheritance
    (D) Sex-linked dominant
    (E) Sex-linked recessive
    (F) Too little information

(F) is correct. Without additional information, it is impossible to differentiate the mode of inheritance, other than to exclude autosomal dominant (one of the parents would be afflicted) or sex-linked dominant (the carrier expresses the trait, therefore, the mother would be affected). Choice A is incorrect. If the mode of inheritance was autosomal dominant, one of the boys' parents would be afflicted. Choice B is incorrect. This is a possible mode of inheritance (both parents are silent carriers and each child would have a one-fourth chance of being afflicted, i.e., inherit both recessive genes). However, several other modes are also possible. Choice C is incorrect. This is a possible mode of inheritance. Typically, the mother (often a silent carrier) transmits the trait to most or all of her offspring with phenotypic heterogenicity. An example of this mode of inheritance is Kearns-Sayre syndrome. Choice D is incorrect. In sex-linked dominant inheritance, the carrier expresses the trait; in this question, the mother is unaffected. Choice E is incorrect. This is a possible mode of inheritance. In sex-linked recessive inheritance, the mother is a silent carrier. Each male offspring has a 50 percent chance of being afflicted (that is, inheriting his mother's affected X chromosome). However, several other modes are also possible.

9. A 25-year-old white man who is seropositive for HIV has a red mass at the angle of his jaw. It is painful and oozes yellow-green pus slightly. The patient denies fever, chills, headache, malaise, cough, abdominal pain, or weight loss. He was first tested for HIV and found to be seropositive last year during a routine exam. He has not received any therapy and his last CD4$^+$ count was 1,000/mm^3. He takes ibuprofen for occasional tension headaches. He has no known drug allergies. He denies any recent colds or illnesses. He is currently sexually active and uses condoms. He does not smoke, drink alcohol, or use any intravenous drugs. He occasionally smokes marijuana. On physical examination, he is afebrile with stable vital signs. The neck is supple. There is a red, indurated, subcutaneous mass with draining sinuses on the right submandibular region. Oral dentition is poor. Lungs are clear. Cardiovascular examination is within normal limits. The abdomen is soft and nontender. Extremities are without abnormalities. The skin is otherwise intact. Complete blood count is within normal limits. Chest x-ray is negative. Gram stain of pus drained from the jaw lesion reveals gram-positive filaments in a smear of tightly knit clusters. Acid-fast staining is negative. The most likely diagnosis is

(A) actinomycosis
(B) erysipelas
(C) impetigo
(D) nocardiosis
(E) osteomyelitis

(A) is correct. This patient has a cervicofacial infection with *Actinomyces israelii* with a classic presentation. Systemic signs and symptoms are rare. Poor oral dentition is a predisposing factor. Diagnosis is via visualization of gram-positive hyphae in grains representing clumps of organisms. This species is anaerobic. Treatment is penicillin. Choice B is incorrect. Erysipelas is a brawny cellulitis caused by *Streptococcus pyogenes*. Choice C is incorrect. Impetigo is a superficial infection of skin that results in honey-colored, crusted lesions caused by *Staphylococcus* species or group A β-hemolytic *Streptococcus*. Choice D is incorrect. Nocardiosis is weakly acid-fast and aerobic. Choice E is incorrect. Osteomyelitis is not likely because there are no systemic signs.

10. A 17-year-old boy presents to the emergency room after falling on his outstretched hand while attempting to catch a pass thrown during a football game. He has a prior medical history of a solitary right kidney, but still engaged in contact sports despite recommendations from physicians not to do so. He complains of right wrist pain. Physical examination reveals exquisite tenderness in the right anatomic snuff-box and a decrease in right wrist range of motion, especially with flexion and extension. Examination of the left wrist reveals good range of motion in flexion, extension, and internal and external rotation. Radiographs reveal no evidence of a fracture. Which of the following is the most likely diagnosis?

(A) Ligamentous injury of the wrist
(B) Lunate dislocation
(C) Perilunate dislocation
(D) Scaphoid fracture
(E) Smith's fracture

(D) is correct. Scaphoid fracture is usually seen in young adults who fall on an outstretched hand. Physical examination may reveal tenderness in the anatomic snuff-box. Radiographs may not reveal evidence of fracture. However, if fracture is suspected, plaster casting and repeat x-ray studies should be undertaken. Choice A is incorrect. Radiographic findings in ligamentous injury to the wrist often reveal an increased gap between the scaphoid and the lunate, and a decreased scaphoid height on the AP view. Choice B is incorrect. Lunate dislocations occur with wrist hyperextension, and radiographs may show disruption of the axial alignment of the lunate, radius, and capitate bones. Choice C is incorrect. Perilunate dislocations occur with wrist hyperextension. Radiographs may show disruption of the axial alignment of the lunate, radius, and capitate bones. Choice E is incorrect. Smith's fracture occurs with a fall on the dorsum of the wrist. This type of injury results from a radius fracture with volar angulation. Treatment strategies include closed reduction.

11. A 35-year-old white female presents to her primary care physician very distraught. Her boyfriend of 4 years has recently been diagnosed with HIV. The patient has had unprotected sex with her boyfriend on numerous occasions. She denies any complaints, including recent weight loss, fevers, or adenopathy. Her HIV ELISA test is negative. Which of the following is the most appropriate next step?

(A) Assure the patient she does not have HIV
(B) Begin triple-drug therapy for HIV
(C) Begin zidovudine therapy
(D) Obtain a CD4+ count
(E) Repeat HIV ELISA test in six months

(E) is correct. Although it is encouraging that her HIV test is negative, it is possible that she is in the window period of infection prior to antibody response, and thus prior to a positive HIV ELISA test. Rechecking the HIV test in six months is appropriate. If it is again negative, she should be assured, barring reexposure, that she is HIV-negative. Choice A is incorrect. Although it is encouraging that her HIV test is negative, it is possible that she is in the window period of infection prior to antibody response, and thus prior to a positive HIV ELISA test. She must have a repeat HIV test in six months. Barring reexposure, she may then be assured that she does not have HIV. Choice B is incorrect. Prophylaxis against HIV infection is only absolutely indicated for those with needle-stick exposure and consists of a triple-drug regimen; it is not indicated in this situation. Choice C is incorrect. Prophylaxis against HIV infection is only absolutely indicated for those with needle-stick exposure and consists of a triple-drug regimen, not zidovudine alone. Prophylaxis is not indicated in this situation. Choice D is incorrect. CD4+ counts are useful in monitoring the course of HIV disease and, in particular, risk of certain opportunistic infections, but not in diagnosis.

12. A 31-year-old primigravid woman who is pregnant by home pregnancy test presents for evaluation. She has a history of deep venous thrombosis and takes warfarin daily. Doppler ultrasound reveals evidence of fetal heart tones. Abdominal examination reveals normoactive bowel sounds with a nonpalpable fundal height. Urine β-HCG testing in the office is positive. Which of the following is a possible fetal defect in this pregnancy?

(A) Clear cell carcinoma of the vagina
(B) Congenital heart disease
(C) Nasal hypoplasia
(D) Neonatal jaundice
(E) Stained teeth

(C) is correct. Warfarin is a medication used as an anticoagulant for patients with deep venous thrombosis. This agent is a potential teratogen and is associated with nasal hypoplasia, stippled epiphyses, growth retardation, and mental retardation. Fetal bleeding is also possible. Choice A is incorrect. Clear cell carcinoma of the vagina is associated with maternal use of diethylstilbestrol. Choice B is incorrect. Congenital heart disease can be associated with maternal use of anticonvulsants during pregnancy. Choice D is incorrect. Neonatal jaundice is associated with maternal use of sulfonamides during pregnancy. Choice E is incorrect. Staining of the newborn's teeth is associated with maternal use of tetracycline during pregnancy.

Items 13–14

A 42-year-old white female with a long history of depression is brought to the emergency department after being found to be unresponsive by her husband. She is stuporous, but without focal neurologic deficits.

Laboratory studies show:

pH	7.10
PCO_2	22 mm Hg
PO_2	96 mm Hg
Serum	
Sodium	144 mEq/L
Potassium	4.1 mEq/L
Chloride	105 mEq/L
Bicarbonate	10 mEq/L
BUN	9 mg/dL
Creatinine	1.0 mg/dL
Glucose	80 mg/dL

13. Which of the following is a likely etiology of her profound acidosis?

(A) Ethylene glycol ingestion
(B) Hyperventilation
(C) Respiratory failure
(D) Salicylate overdose
(E) Sertraline overdose

(A) is correct. This patient has an increased anion gap [sodium – (chloride + bicarbonate) = 29] metabolic acidosis with a compensatory respiratory alkalosis. In the absence of renal failure, common causes of an anion gap metabolic acidosis are ingestion of toxic substances, such as ethylene glycol, isopropyl alcohol, large amount of ethanol, and methanol. A normal anion gap is 12 or less. Anion gap acidosis can cause diarrhea, early renal failure, and renal tubular acidosis. Choice B is incorrect. Hyperventilation alone, without underlying metabolic acidosis, results in alkalemia and a $PCO_2 < 40$. Choice C is incorrect. Respiratory failure can result from a profound acidemia secondary to the retention of carbon dioxide, hence a low pH with an elevated PCO_2 would be expected. Choice D is incorrect. Salicylate overdose/toxicity causes a mixed metabolic acidosis and respiratory alkalosis. Choice E is incorrect. Overdose of the serotonin-selective release inhibitors result in tachycardia and mild hypotension without profound acid/base disturbances.

14. What is the most appropriate first step in the management of this patient?

(A) Administration of activated charcoal
(B) Administration of bicarbonate
(C) Computed tomography of the head
(D) Electrocardiogram
(E) Endotracheal intubation

(E) is correct. This patient is profoundly acidotic and requires immediate intubation of her airway prior to any other intervention. Choice A is incorrect. Activated charcoal is indicated in many suspected overdoses. However, intubation of the airway is paramount. Choice B is incorrect. Administration of bicarbonate is a reasonable intervention, especially if tricyclic overdose is suspected. However, intubation of the airway is paramount. Choice C is incorrect. Computed tomography must be reserved until the patient is stabilized, especially in light of the lack of focal neurologic findings. Choice D is incorrect. Electrocardiogram is another reasonable intervention that might provide clues to the etiology of her acidosis, but should be reserved until intubation of the airway is obtained.

15. A 39-year-old man with a prior psychiatric history is noted by family members to be incoherent with disorganized behavior. His affect is grossly inappropriate but he does not exhibit muscular rigidity. He demonstrates looseness of associations during the mental status exam. He has a prior medical history of hyperthyroidism that is treated with oral antithyroid preparations. Physical examination is notable for a palpable thyroid gland without masses. Cardiac examination reveals a regular rate and rhythm. Pulmonary evaluation reveals no evidence of rales, rhonchi, or wheezes. Abdominal examination reveals normoactive bowel sounds. Which of the following is the most likely classification of this individual's illness?

(A) Catatonic
(B) Disorganized
(C) Paranoid
(D) Residual
(E) Undifferentiated

(B) is correct. This individual exhibits features of schizophrenia. The disorganized type of schizophrenia is notable for incoherence, marked loosening of associations, or grossly disorganized behavior. Individuals have a flat or grossly inappropriate affect. These subjects show no evidence of mutism, negativism, or rigidity. Choice A is incorrect. Catatonic schizophrenia is associated with stupor, mutism, negativity, and purposeless excitement. Choice C is incorrect. Paranoid schizophrenia is characterized by a preoccupation with systematized delusions or with frequent auditory hallucinations, without evidence of looseness of associations or disorganized behavior. Choice D is incorrect. Residual schizophrenia is noted for the absence of prominent delusions, hallucinations, incoherence, or grossly disorganized behavior. Choice E is incorrect. Undifferentiated schizophrenia has features of prominent delusions, hallucinations, incoherence, and grossly disorganized behavior.

16. A 24-year-old woman complains of vaginal growths on her labia for the past 4 months. These growths have persisted and are not painful. She had a similar occurrence of such lesions at age 18, which responded to medical therapy. She is sexually active with multiple male partners, with intermittent use of condoms as contraception. Pelvic examination reveals several papules with raised margins and irregular borders. The lesions involve the labia bilaterally. Rectal examination reveals no evidence of hemorrhoids. Which of the following is the most likely diagnosis?

(A) Chancroid
(B) Condyloma acuminatum
(C) Condyloma latum
(D) Genital herpes
(E) Molluscum contagiosum

(D) is correct. Genital herpes is associated with a variable number of papules with raised margins and irregular borders. There is no associated lymphadenopathy or induration. Treatment involves topical and/or oral antiviral agents. Choice A is incorrect. Chancroid is associated with papules or pustules that are red and irregularly shaped on a yellow or grey base. The regional lymph nodes are often tender. Choice B is incorrect. Condyloma acuminata (venereal warts) are soft, fleshy growths on the vulva, cervix, perineum, and anus. The lesions can be single or multiple. Diagnosis is made on physical examination and confirmed with biopsy of the lesions. Treatment of uncomplicated warts can be accomplished with topical podophyllin. Treatment with 5-fluorouracil, cryosurgery, or surgical excision is required for more extensive lesions. Choice C is incorrect. Condyloma lata are found in syphilis and are flat lesions that are red and firm. They have broad bases and are nontender. Choice E is incorrect. Molluscum contagiosum is associated with lesions that have central umbilication and are more common over the lower abdomen. The appearance of these lesions is described as yellow and cheesy.

17. A 51-year-old man who has worked in fur and glass factories for 20 years complains of a 4-month history of progressive anorexia, headache, and dizziness. His wife notes that his personality has changed during the past 6 months. Examination of his head reveals excessive lacrimation and conjunctivitis. Cardiac examination reveals a regular rate and rhythm. Pulmonary auscultation reveals no evidence of rales, rhonchi, or wheezing. Abdominal evaluation reveals normoactive bowel sounds without peritoneal signs. Skin examination reveals areas of patchy dermatitis. Which of the following is the most likely etiologic agent?

(A) Arsenic
(B) Lead
(C) Manganese
(D) Mercury
(E) Thallium

(A) is correct. Arsenic is a heavy metal that can cause various symptoms following chronic exposure. Typical industries that use arsenic include the fur and glass industries. Symptoms include lacrimation, conjunctivitis, anorexia, headache, and vertigo. Physical examination may reveal evidence of dermatitis. Intellectual impairment and drowsiness may also be noted. Choice B is incorrect. Lead poisoning is associated with abdominal colic, neuropathy, and encephalopathy. Patients may present with acute delerium and seizures. Treatment involves calcium lactate and chelating agents. Choice C is incorrect. Manganese poisoning is associated with headache, hypersomnia, and impotence, as well as uncontrollable laughing and crying spells. Choice D is incorrect. Mercury poisoning is associated with gastritis, bleeding gums, excessive salivation, and coarse tremor with jerky movements. Choice E is incorrect. Thallium poisoning is associated with abdominal pain, vomiting, alopecia, ataxia, retrobulbar neuritis, and impaired consciousness.

18. A 62-year-old white female presents to the emergency department one week after having a right total hip replacement. She complains of a painful, swollen, warm-to-the-touch right calf. Which of the following is the most appropriate initial intervention?

(A) Order computed tomography of her right leg, hip, and pelvis
(B) Order a duplex Doppler study of the patient's right lower extremity
(C) Order magnetic resonance imaging of her right hip
(D) Prescribe antibiotics for the patient's cellulitis
(E) Reassure her that this is normal postoperative swelling

(B) is correct. Deep venous thrombosis (DVT) is always a concern in the post-operative patient. Hip replacement surgery places patients at particularly high risk of DVT. The best initial evaluation of suspected DVT is a duplex Doppler study of the affected extremity. Choice A is incorrect. Computed tomography, although an excellent study to visualize bony structures, is not appropriate of the suspected etiology of the pain is a deep venous thrombosis. Choice C is incorrect. Magnetic resonance imaging is an excellent tool to visualize soft tissue detail, however, it is not appropriate if the suspected etiology of the pain is a deep venous thrombosis of the lower extremity. Choice D is incorrect. Although cellulitis may certainly present as a warm, swollen extremity, the patient's history is suspicious for DVT and this must be eliminated as a concern prior to treatment of the lesion as a cellulitis. Untreated DVT places the patient at risk of pulmonary embolism and death. Choice E is incorrect. This is not a normal postoperative finding and reassurance is not appropriate. Untreated DVT places the patient at risk of pulmonary embolism and death.

19. A 31-year-old healthy female is pregnant. As part of her routine prenatal screening, labs are sent and she is found to be anemic:

Hemoglobin	10 g/dL
Hematocrit	30%
Mean corpuscular volume	68 fL

Which of the following is her hemoglobin electrophoresis most likely to demonstrate?

(A) Increased hemoglobin A_2
(B) Normal
(C) Presence of Bart's hemoglobin
(D) Presence of hemoglobin H
(E) Presence of hemoglobin S
(F) Presence of hemoglobin SC

(A) is correct. This patient has β-thalassemia trait characterized by her asymptomatic, moderately severe anemia with a very low mean corpuscular volume. It is important to differentiate this anemia from that of iron deficiency, as β-thalessemia does not correct with iron supplementation. Long-term use of iron in these patients can cause iron overload. Hemoglobin electrophoresis demonstrates increased (from 2.5 percent to 5 percent) hemoglobin A_2. Choice B is incorrect. The patient has β-thalassemia and would have an abnormal hemoglobin electrophoresis as outlined above. Choice C is incorrect. Bart's hemoglobin is found in the most severe form of α-thalassemia, where no α-globin chains are produced and all hemoglobin molecules are tetramers of γ-chains. Death occurs in utero. Choice D is incorrect. Hemoglobin H is produced in α-thalessemia with deletion of three α-genes. Hemoglobin H is a tetramer of β-chains; it deposits to form Heinz bodies. Choice E is incorrect. Hemoglobin S is the abnormal hemoglobin of sickle cell disease, secondary to a substitution of a valine for a glutamate at the sixth position of the β-chain. Patients are symptomatic from a young age. Choice F is incorrect. Hemoglobin SC is abnormal hemoglobin of patients who have both hemoglobin S and hemoglobin C (substitution of a lysine for a glutamate and position six on the β-globin chain). Afflicted individuals have anemia with splenomegaly and occasional painful crises similar to those seen in sickle cell disease.

20. A 25-year-old man with mental retardation and manic depression has been institutionalized since the age of 12. Both of his parents were killed in an automobile accident when he was 7 years old. He is currently treated with lithium, and recent blood level testing indicates that his dose is therapeutic. Recent laboratory values are provided below:

Hematocrit	47%
Leukocyte count	7,900/mm^3
Platelet count	370,000/mm^3
Serum	
Sodium	133 mEq/L
Chloride	98 mEq/L
Potassium	3.4 mEq/L
Bicarbonate	24 mEq/L
Magnesium	1.9 mEq/L
Creatinine	1.2 mg/dL
Urea nitrogen	19 mg/dL

Multiaxial evaluation of this individual with regard to the severity of psychosocial stressors are included on which of the following?

(A) Axis I
(B) Axis II
(C) Axis III
(D) Axis IV
(E) Axis V

(D) is correct. Axis IV is used to code the psychosocial and environmental problems that can contribute to an individual's current psychosocial disorder. Stressors can affect the individual in a positive or negative fashion and such information may be important in formulating a therapeutic plan for an individual that will maximize removal of the psychosocial stressor. In this case, the death of both parents is considered to be a catastrophic event. Choice A is incorrect. Axis I consists of the clinical disorders that may be a focus of clinical attention. In this category, medical conditions such as diabetes mellitus, hypertension, thyroid disorders, and parathyroid disorders should be included. The multiaxial evaluation allows for categorization of physical, social, and psychological disorders to allow for maximization of patient diagnosis and subsequent care. Choice B is incorrect. Axis II consists of personality disorders and mental retardation. This individual, with his history of mental retardation, would have this condition noted as an axis II diagnosis. The multiaxial evaluation allows for classification of pathologic and psychologic conditions into different categories, which in turn allows greater ease of treatment. Choice C is incorrect. Axis III represents any physical disorder or general medical condition that is present in addition to the mental disorder. Choice E is incorrect. Axis IV represents the global assessment of functioning (GAF) scale. This scale judges the psychological and social continuum of mental health and mental illness.

21. A 23-year-old woman complains of small growths along her lower abdomen and around her vaginal orifice for the past 6 months. These growths have persisted and are not painful. She states that she had a similar occurrence of such lesions at age 18, which responded to medical therapy. She is sexually active with multiple male partners with intermittent use of condoms as a contraceptive method. Physical examination reveals multiple papules along the lower abdominal wall and circumferentially around the vaginal orifice. The core of each papule appears waxy. Microscopy reveals the presence of inclusion bodies. Rectal examination reveals no evidence of hemorrhoids. However, there is evidence of a healed anal fissure in the posterior midline. Which of the following is the most likely diagnosis?

(A) Chancroid
(B) Condyloma acuminatum
(C) Condyloma latum
(D) Genital herpes
(E) Molluscum contagiosum

(E) is correct. Molluscum contagiosum is associated with lesions that have central umbilication and are more common over the lower abdomen. The appearance of these lesions is described as yellow and cheesy. The diagnosis is made clinically. However, the presence of inclusion bodies can be noted on microscopic examination. Treatment involves dessication, cryotherapy, or curettage of the lesions. Choice A is incorrect. Chancroid is associated with papules or pustules that are red and irregularly shaped on a yellow or grey base. The regional lymph nodes are often tender. Choice B is incorrect. Condyloma acuminata (venereal warts) are soft, fleshy growths on the vulva, cervix, perineum, and anus. The lesions can be single or multiple. Diagnosis is made on physical examination and confirmed by biopsy of the lesions. Treatment of uncomplicated warts can be accomplished with topical podophyllin. Treatment with 5-fluorouracil, cryosurgery, or surgical excision is required for more extensive lesions. Choice C is incorrect. Condyloma lata are found in syphilis and are flat lesions that are red and firm. They have broad bases and are nontender. Choice D is incorrect. Genital herpes is associated with a variable number of papules with raised margins and irregular borders. There is no associated lymphadenopathy or induration. Treatment involves topical and/or oral antiviral agents.

22. A 67-year-old white male presents to his primary care physician complaining of early satiety worsening over the last three months, along with a 4 kg (10 lb) weight loss. What is the most appropriate first step?

(A) Barium enema
(B) Barium swallow
(C) Computed tomography of the abdomen
(D) Endoscopic retrograde cholangiopancreatography
(E) Esophagogastroduodenoscopy
(F) Magnetic resonance imaging of the abdomen
(G) Ultrasound of the abdomen

(E) is correct. This history is very troublesome and suspicious for gastric cancer. Esophagogastroduodenoscopy provides an opportunity both for evaluation and tissue sampling for a pathologic diagnosis. Other imaging modalities would provide valuable information, but do not provide tissue confirmation. Choice A is incorrect. The patient's symptoms of early satiety is referable to his upper gastrointestinal tract, in particular, his stomach. Choice B is incorrect. Barium swallow may visualize the suspected tumor, but does not provide for tissue confirmation (that is, gastric adenocarcinoma versus lymphoma or another lesion). Choice C is incorrect. Computed tomography is useful for staging tumor involvement prior to surgical intervention, but should be the first diagnostic step. Choice D is incorrect. Endoscopic retrograde cholangio-pancreatoscopy (ERCP) is useful in the evaluation of patients with suspected pancreatic and biliary lesions, not stomach cancer. Choice F is incorrect. Magnetic resonance imaging has limited utility in imaging suspected gastrointestinal malignancy. Computed tomography is able to provide much the same information at less cost. There are exceptions, such as further evaluation of suspected carcinoid and other tumors. Choice G is incorrect. Ultrasound is the first diagnostic test in the evaluation of jaundice, but is not the first step in the evaluation of suspected stomach pathology.

Items 23–24

You are reviewing an article that discusses the effect of finasteride on prostate size in patients with benign prostatic hyperplasia. One hundred male patients with benign prostatic hyperplasia without evidence of carcinoma were enrolled. Each patient underwent a prestudy ultrasound to document prostate size. The mean prostate size was 40 g with a range of 20 to 75 g and a standard deviation of 10 g. After 6 months of finasteride in increasing doses from 1–5 mg at night, each patient underwent a repeat ultrasound. The results are as follows: the mean prostate size was 30 g with a range of 20 to 75 g and a standard deviation of 8 g. The most frequent pretreatment ultrasound prostate size was 35 g. The most frequent post-treatment ultrasound prostate size was 30 g.

23. In interpreting the data provided, which of the following statements are true?

    (A) The pretreatment mode is 40 g
    (B) The post-treatment mode is 35 g
    (C) 68% of the pretreatment prostate sizes
        were between 35 and 45 g
    (D) 95% of the pretreatment prostate sizes
        were between 10 and 70 g

(C) is correct. When interpreting statistical data, it is important to keep several statistical terms on your mind. The mode is the most frequently observed score in a distribution of data. For the pretreatment group, the mean prostate size is 40 g with a standard deviation of 10. This means that 68 percent of the patients will have prostate sizes between 35 and 45 g. Choice A is incorrect. The pretreatment mode (prostate size) was 35 g. Choice B is incorrect. The post-treatment mode (prostate size) was 30 g. Choice D is incorrect. 99 percent of the values in a normal distribution will fall within three standard deviations from the mean.

24. A patient in the study was found to have a prostate size of 46 g on the postfinasteride ultrasound. In terms of percentile rank, how many patients have larger prostate sizes than his?

    (A) 5
    (B) 10
    (C) 20
    (D) 50
    (E) 75

(A) is correct. This patient's prostate size is 46 g. Since the mean prostate size in the post-treatment group was 30 g with a standard deviation of 8 g, a prostate size of 46 g is two standard deviations from the mean prostate size. In a normal distribution, 95 percent of scores will fall within two standard deviations from the mean. Therefore, this patient will fall in the 95% percentile and have 5 patients with larger prostates that he has in this study of 100 patients.

25. A 50-year-old woman presents for evaluation of new-onset bloody vaginal discharge as well as urinary frequency and dysuria. She notes that sexual intercourse has become painful. Vaginal speculum examination reveals a mass lesion in the upper portion of the vaginal vault. Laboratory values are as follows

Hematocrit	29%
Hemoglobin	9.5 g/dL
Mean corpuscular volume	69/mm³
White blood cell count	6,000/mm³
Platelet count	240,000/mm³

Serum

Sodium	133 mEq/L
Potassium	4.2 mEq/L
Chloride	101 mEq/L
Bicarbonate	25 mEq/L
Urea nitrogen	12 mg/dL
Creatinine	0.9 mg/dL

Urinalysis

Protein	negative
Heme	positive
Leukocyte esterase	negative
Nitrate	negative

The primary treatment option should include which of the following?

(A) Chemotherapy
(B) Intravesicular chemotherapy
(C) Radiotherapy
(D) Surgical excision
(E) Watchful waiting

(C) is correct. The primary treatment for vaginal carcinoma is radiotherapy, which will shrink large tumors rather well. Following radiotherapy, it is possible that chemotherapy or surgical excision will be viable options. This cancer typically occurs in females over the age of 40 with classic symptoms of vaginal bleeding and urinary symptoms from compression of the bladder. Choice A is incorrect. Chemotherapy provides poor results for patients with vaginal carcinoma. Choice B is incorrect. Intravesicular chemotherapy is appropriate for carcinoma in situ of the bladder. Choice D is incorrect. Surgical excision, while an appropriate additional therapy for this condition, should be attempted after radiotherapy. Choice E is incorrect. Watchful waiting is not an appropriate strategy for the management of vaginal carcinoma.

26. A newborn male is examined by the pediatrician after delivery and is found to have an extra digit on his left hand and foot. The mother was noted to have a history of alcohol and cold medicine abuse during her pregnancy. She states that she had routine prenatal care, and antenatal sonography revealed no evidence of anatomic abnormalities. The baby was born at 39 weeks gestation and had a birth weight of 3,300 g (7 lb 4 oz). Maternal serologies reveal rubella nonimmune status and a reactive rapid plasma reagin (RPR) test. The most likely explanation of the limb abnormalities is

(A) amelia
(B) meromelia
(C) micromelia
(D) polydactyly
(E) syndactyly

(D) is correct. Polydactyly describes the presence of extra fingers and toes. The extra digit often lacks proper muscular connections. This finding can be unilateral or bilateral. Choice A is incorrect. Amelia describes the absence of one or more extremities. Choice B is incorrect. Meromelia describes a situation in which the hands and feet are attached to the trunk by a small, irregularly shaped bone. Choice C is incorrect. Micromelia describes a condition in which all extremities are present, but are abnormally short. Choice E is incorrect. Syndactyly is an abnormal fusion of bones and commonly affects the fingers and toes.

27. A 22-year-old white female presents to her primary care physician with complaints of shortness of breath and wheezing worsening over the last month. She has a long history of asthma for which she uses an albuterol metered-dose inhaler as needed. She has been awakened each of the last 4 nights with wheezing and is having to use her albuterol inhaler several times a day. Her peak flow prior to an albuterol nebulizer treatment is 200 mL, and is 450 mL afterwards. Her diffuse expiratory wheezes clear and she feels remarkably better. Which of the following is the most appropriate first step in the management of this patient's asthma?

   (A) Begin home albuterol nebulizer treatments

   (B) Continue albuterol as needed and add an inhaled corticosteriod

   (C) Continue albuterol as needed as monotherapy

   (D) Continue albuterol as needed and add an oral corticosteriod

   (E) Continue albuterol as needed and add an oral leukotriene inhibitor

(B) is correct. This patient has failed as-needed bronchodilator therapy. The cornerstone to management of adult asthma is inhaled corticosteriods. The goal is to minimize the requirement of as-needed use of metered-dose inhaled bronchodilators such as albuterol. Choice A is incorrect. The cornerstone to management of adult asthma is inhaled corticosteriods. The goal is to minimize the requirement of as-needed use of metered-dose inhaled bronchodilators such as albuterol and obviate the need for nebulizer treatments. Choice C is incorrect. As-needed bronchodilator therapy is adequate for the asthmatic with only occasional symptoms. However, when patients begin to use as-needed bronchodilator therapy several times a day or have nighttime awakenings, initiation of an inhaled corticosteriod is indicated. Choice D is incorrect. The cornerstone to management of adult asthma is inhaled corticosteriods. The goal is to minimize the requirement of as-needed use of metered-dose inhaled bronchodilators such as albuterol and obviate the need for oral steroids, with their devastating side effects. Choice E is incorrect. Leukotriene inhibitors are an important recent addition to the armamentarium of asthma control, but should be reserved for use in the refractory asthmatic as a steroid-sparing agent.

A 5-year-old girl complains of mucus and blood-tinged vaginal discharge for the last 4 days. She also notes perianal pruritus. The mother is the only caretaker of this child and is always with her. She has no prior medical history. She currently takes no medications. Physical examination of the heart, lungs, and abdomen is unremarkable. Pelvic examination reveals perineal erythema. Vaginoscopy reveals a small piece of toilet paper in the lower vaginal vault.

28. The susceptibility of this child to this condition may be related to

   (A) estrogen hyperstimulation
   (B) contamination by feces
   (C) contamination by urinary stream
   (D) thickness of vaginal secretions
   (E) vaginal immunocompetence

(B) is correct. This child has vulvovaginitis. The susceptibility of young girls to such an infection is high because of the thin, atrophic vaginal mucosa that results from the body's lack of estrogen secretion. Contamination by feces due to poor hygiene is also a plausible mechanism of pathogenesis for this condition. Foreign bodies can often be found on vaginoscopy. Choice A is incorrect. Estrogen stimulation is lacking, and this is supported by the atrophic vaginal mucosa. Choice C is incorrect. Urinary contamination is not linked to the pathogenesis of this condition. Choice D is incorrect. The lack of estrogen makes vaginal secretions thin, which can predispose young girls to infection. Choice E is incorrect. The vaginal mucosa of the child has impaired immune mechanisms.

29. Which of the following is the most reliable radiographic study to be obtained in this patient?

   (A) Computed tomograph of the pelvis
   (B) Magnetic resonance images of the pelvis
   (C) Plain-film of the abdomen
   (D) Transabdominal ultrasonography
   (E) No radiographic study is reliable

(E) is correct. While the most common foreign body found in the vagina in vulvovaginitis is toilet paper, other objects such as beads and toys can also be found. Radiographs are not reliable for diagnosis since most objects are not radiopaque. Therefore, no radiographic study should be performed in this child. Choice A is incorrect. Computed tomograph of the pelvis will not provide reliable information in children with vulvovaginitis. Choice B is incorrect. Magnetic resonance images of the pelvis will not provide reliable information in children with vulvovaginitis. Choice C is incorrect. Plain films of the abdomen will not provide reliable information in children with vulvovaginitis. Choice D is incorrect. Transabdominal ultrasonography of the pelvis will not provide reliable information in children with vulvovaginitis.

30. A 24-year-old white female presents to the emergency department with three days of nausea, vomiting, and myalgias. Over the last twelve hours, she has developed a rash, dizziness, and fever. Her temperature is 39.0 C (104 F), blood pressure is 85/60 mm Hg, and heart rate is 120 beats/min. She has an erythematous rash sparing her palms and soles. Laboratory studies are as follows:

AST	100 U/dL
ALT	110 U/dL
Creatinine	2.3 mg/dL
BUN	65 mg/dL

Which of the following is the most likely diagnosis?

(A) Endocarditis
(B) Mononucleosis
(C) Rocky Mountain spotted fever
(D) Scarlet fever
(E) Toxic shock syndrome
(F) Urosepsis

(E) is correct. This young female patient has the classic findings of toxic shock syndrome: fever, hypotension, and rash that follow a few-day history of nausea and myalgias in a menstruating woman. The syndrome is mediated by a staphylococcal toxin (TSST-1). Mild hepatocellular damage and reversible renal insufficiency are common. Treatment is antibiotics directed against *Staphylococcus* and supportive care. In time, the rash will desquamate. Choice A is incorrect. The rapid time course argues against (even acute) endocarditis, as does the patient's young age and lack of systemic findings such as splinter hemorrhages, Roth's spots, and Janeway's lesions. Choice B is incorrect. Mononucleosis is a viral syndrome caused by infection with the Epstein-Barr virus. Most people are infected by late childhood. Symptoms range from fatigue and malaise to easy bruising. Early in the course of infection, bulky cervical lymphadenopathy and sore throat are common. Patients are generally not acutely ill (with hypotension). Choice C is incorrect. Rocky Mountain spotted fever is a tick-borne illness caused by the bacteria *Rickettsia rickettsii*. Untreated patients may have a rapidly fulminant course with profound thrombocytopenia. The rash begins on the hands and soles. Choice D is incorrect. Scarlet fever is a complication of Group A streptococcal pharyngitis. Some streptococcal organisms produce exotoxins, which causes fever and rash. The rash is maculopapular, "sandpaper" in texture, and accentuates in the skin folds. Choice F is incorrect. Urosepsis may cause profound hypotension, especially when caused by a gram-negative organism (which has endotoxin). However, premonitory symptoms in a young woman would include urinary symptoms such as dysuria, frequency, and urgency.

31. A 38-year-old man has a 2-year history of dysphagia and regurgitation of nonacidic material. He achieves minimal relief of his symptoms with oral over-the-counter antacid therapy. Physical examination reveals a palpable thyroid gland without masses. Cardiac examination reveals no evidence of rubs, murmurs, or gallops. Pulmonary auscultation reveals no evidence of wheezes or rhonchi. Gastrointestinal examination reveals mild tenderness in the mid-epigastric region without focal peritoneal signs. Rectal examination reveals a normal-sized prostate and guaiac-negative stool in the vault. Radiologic studies reveal a fluid-filled, dilated esophagus with a distal stricture. The most likely diagnosis is

(A) achalasia
(B) diffuse esophageal spasm
(C) esophageal carcinoma
(D) proximal web
(E) scleroderma

(A) is correct. Achalasia is characterized by dysphagia and regurgitation of nonacidic material. X-ray appearance of this condition includes a dilated, fluid-filled esophagus and a distal "bird-beaked" stricture. Typical manometric findings include high resting esophageal pressures with abnormal relaxation during swallowing. The esophageal body has continuous low-amplitude contractions after swallowing. Choice B is incorrect. Diffuse esophageal spasm is associated with substernal chest pain and dysphagia, and x-ray studies will reveal simultaneous, noncoordinated contractions. Choice C is incorrect. Esophageal carcinoma usually occurs in the middle third of the esophagus and is associated with progressive dysphagia and weight loss. Choice D is incorrect. Most webs are asymptomatic and their etiology is uncertain. The Plummer-Vinson syndrome consists of dysphagia, webs, and iron-deficiency anemia and occurs in middle-aged women. Choice E is incorrect. Scleroderma is associated with gastroesophageal reflux and dysphagia. X-ray studies often reveal aperistalsis of the esophagus and peptic stricture.

32. A 67-year-old white female presents to her primary care physician with complaints of vaginal bleeding for one week. She has been postmenopausal for the last 20 years. She does not use hormone replacement therapy. Her last pelvic exam and Pap smear four months ago were normal. Which of the following is the most appropriate first step?

  (A) Computed tomography of the pelvis
  (B) Dilatation and curettage
  (C) Endometrial biopsy
  (D) Hysteroscopy
  (E) Magnetic resonance imaging of the pelvis
  (F) Pelvic examination
  (G) Ultrasound of the pelvis

(F) is correct. Pelvic examination is the mandatory first step in the evaluation of postmenopausal bleeding in all cases prior to proceeding with further evaluation. The most concerning etiology is endometrial cancer, but pelvic exam may provide another obvious diagnosis such as cervical polyp or infection. Choice A is incorrect. Computed tomography is valuable for staging endometrial cancer prior to resection, but is not the appropriate initial evaluation of postmenopausal vaginal bleeding. Choice B is incorrect. Dilatation and curettage to obtain samples for pathologic examination is one accepted method of obtaining tissue for the diagnosis of endometrial cancer, but is not the first step in the evaluation of postmenopausal bleeding. Choice C is incorrect. Endometrial biopsy (which can be done in the office) with samples for pathologic examination is one accepted method of obtaining tissue for the diagnosis of endometrial cancer, but is not the first step in the evaluation of postmenopausal bleeding. Choice D is incorrect. Hysteroscopy is most valuable in the evaluation of infertility to elucidate structural lesions of the uterus. It has no role in the initial evaluation of postmenopausal bleeding. Choice E is incorrect. Magnetic resonance imaging has a role in the staging of endometrial cancer prior to resection, but is not the appropriate initial evaluation of postmenopausal vaginal bleeding. Choice G is incorrect. Ultrasound is useful in the evaluation of suspected endometrial cancer, being particularly useful in quantifying uterine thickness, but it is not the appropriate initial evaluation of postmenopausal vaginal bleeding.

33. A 37-year-old black female presents to the emergency room with blurry vision in her left eye for the last several days. She also notes an accompanying retro-orbital pain, present for about the same length of time. Her past medical history is only remarkable for a cesarean section three years ago upon the birth of the last of her three children. She does not smoke and only occasionally drinks a glass of wine with dinner. She has never suffered these symptoms before. Her ocular exam demonstrates 20/20 vision in her right eye and 20/80 vision in her left eye. Her left pupil is enlarged. Field testing shows a left paracentral scotoma with normal right eye visual fields. Which of the following is the most likely location of the patient's lesion?

  (A) Left lens
  (B) Left optic nerve
  (C) Left retina
  (D) Optic chiasm
  (E) Right occipital lobe

(B) is correct. The woman in question is suffering optic neuritis, a diagnosis supported by her left pupillary dysfunction, left visual acuity deficit, and left scotoma. None of the other answer choices are consistent with her symptoms. Choice A is incorrect. Lens lesions would result in symptoms similar to those of a cataract and would be painless. Choice C is incorrect. Damage to the retina would be expected following trauma and not result in a pupillary defect. Choice D is incorrect. Optic chiasm lesions cause a bitemporal hemianopia. Choice E is incorrect. An occipital lesion would cause a field cut, not a central scotoma.

34. A 42-year-old man presents to the emergency department with complaints of a headache that awakened him from sleep. The pain is sharp and stabbing in nature, like an "icepick" in his eye. It is associated with unilateral tearing, but no visual changes. He had a similar headache the previous night, and got no relief from aspirin or acetaminophen. Which of the following is the best initial treatment of this patient's headache?

(A) Intramuscular sumatriptan
(B) Intravenous metoclopramide
(C) Intravenous meperidine
(D) Intravenous morphine
(E) Nasal cannula oxygen

(E) is correct. This patient is suffering from a cluster headache. An effective abortive measure for a cluster headache is oxygen. Choice A is incorrect. Sumatriptan is an effective abortive medication used the treatment of migraine headache. Choice B is incorrect. Metoclopramide is being used increasingly as an abortive agent in the treatment of migraine headache. Choice C is incorrect. Meperdine is a frequently utilized narcotic analgesic used in the treatment of headache in the emergency department, but narcotics should be avoided if this cluster headache can be aborted with oxygen therapy. Choice D is incorrect. Morphine is a potent narcotic analgesic. The need for narcotics may be avoided if this cluster headache can be aborted with oxygen therapy.

35. A 57-year-old white male presents to his primary care physician with complaints of a nonproductive cough that has worsened over the last several months, as well as drenching night sweats on several occasions. He had a renal transplant 7 years ago. His current medications include cyclosporine, azathioprine, and prednisone. His chest roentgenograph demonstrates bulky, hilar adenopathy. Biopsy confirms lymphoma. Which of the following is the most appropriate next step?

(A) Begin external beam radiation to the chest
(B) Begin six cycles of chemotherapy
(C) Discontinue azathioprine and/or cyclosporine
(D) Remove renal allograft
(E) Search for a compatible bone marrow donor

(C) is correct. Iatrogenic immunosuppression is a risk factor for development of malignant lymphoma. A certain percent of these lymphomas will regress spontaneously with no further treatment if immunosuppression is discontinued. Choice A, Choice B, and Choice E are incorrect. A certain percent of these lymphomas will regress spontaneously with no further treatment if immunosuppression is discontinued. Choice D is incorrect. The risk for lymphoma stems from immunosuppression, not the allograft. Removal of the allograft is not indicated.

Items 36–39

    (A) Atenolol
    (B) Captopril
    (C) Furosemide
    (D) Hydrochlorothiazide
    (E) Sodium nitroprusside
    (F) Terazosin
    (G) Verapamil

For each patient with hypertension, select the most appropriate therapeutic agent.

36. A 41-year-old man with diabetes mellitus and asthma has hypertension. He has been treated medically for several years, with good blood pressure control. Physical examination reveals clear breath sounds bilaterally, with no evidence of rhonchi or rales. At his last visit to the physician, serum potassium was 3.1 mEq/L and serum triglycerides were 375 mg/dL.

(C) is correct. Patients who are taking diuretics should be aware of several metabolic effects of such agents. Loop diuretics such as furosemide are associated with the development of hyperglycemia, hypercholesterolemia, and hypertriglyceridemia. Hypokalemia and hyperuricemia are also possible metabolic derrangements.

37. A 69-year-old man with a history of hypertension has a recent history of urinary frequency, nocturia, and decreased force of stream. Cardiovascular examination reveals a systolic ejection murmur grade II/IV heard best at the apex, with no evidence of gallops. Transabdominal sonography reveals no evidence of hydronephrosis or hydroureter. The prostate gland was estimated to be 70 grams and the post-void residual was 150 cc. The patient's blood pressure on three successive occasions was 160/90 mm Hg.

(F) is correct. Terazosin is an α-adrenergic-blocker and is equivalent to that of the thiazide class of diuretics. This medication has minimal metabolic effects except for a mild reduction of serum triglycerides. This medication has the added benefit of decreasing urinary outflow obstruction in patients with benign prostatic hyperplasia. Thus, in this patient with hypertension and prostatism, terazosin is a reasonable treatment modality.

HT.

38. A 64-year-old man with a history of asthma and chronic bronchitis is hospitalized for an exacerbation of his asthma. Pulmonary auscultation reveals bilateral scattered wheezes with decreased breath sounds at the lung bases. Arterial blood gasses reveal a pH of 7.33, PCO_2 of 50 mm Hg, and a PO_2 of 67 mm Hg. His blood pressure is persistently at 150–160/90–95 mm Hg.

(G) is correct. Patients with hypertension and a history of asthma and chronic lung disease should not receive blockers (atenolol) because of the increased risk of bronchospasm. Angiotensin-converting enzyme inhibitors (captopril) should also be avoided in this individual, because they can increase respiratory secretions and can worsen coughing. Therefore, the most appropriate agent for this individual would be a calcium channel-blocker such as verapamil, which will cause bronchodilation as well as a decrease in blood pressure. Thus, this agent is appropriate in the patient with chronic lung disease who is also hypertensive.

39. A 42-year-old woman has a history of migraine headaches. She also has a history of subacute thyroiditis, which is treated with acetaminophen. On three successive visits to her primary care physician, her blood pressure has been approximately 160/90 mm Hg. Physical examination reveals tenderness over the right and left thyroid lobes without palpable mass lesions. Cardiovascular examinaton reveals a regular rate and rhythm, and pulmonary auscultation reveals good air exchange bilaterally.

(A) is correct. This patient has a history of migraine headaches and hypertension and requires treatment for her hypertension-blocking agents such as atenolol are helpful in such patients because they not only decrease blood pressure but have been shown to decrease the frequency of migraine attacks. Medications that are direct vasodilators (hydralazine) should be avoided in these patients, because the direct vasodilation effects might precipitate asthma attacks.

Items 40–44

   (A) Aortic insufficiency
   (B) Aortic stenosis
   (C) Atrial septal defect
   (D) Mitral regurgitation
   (E) Mitral stenosis
   (F) Mitral valve prolapse
   (G) Papillary muscle dysfunction
   (H) Pulmonic stenosis
   (I) Tricuspid regurgitation
   (J) Ventricular septal defect

Match the most likely cardiac lesion with each of the following clinical scenarios.

40. A 65-year-old male presents to the emergency department complaining of a fainting spell. He had no prodromal symptoms prior to this episode and was unconscious for a brief period of time before his wife found him on the floor. He has a harsh crescendo-decrescendo systolic murmur loudest over the left sternal border in the third and fourth intercostal spaces, with radiation to the neck.

(B) is correct. This patient has presented with syncope, which is one of the three sequelae of critical aortic stenosis (angina and congestive heart failure being the other two). The murmur is classic, with radiation to the neck. Additionally, pulsus parvus et tardus might be expected.

41. A 23-year-old male presents to the emergency department with fever. He is cachectic and has several pinpoint lesions in his left antecubital fossa. He has a faint, harsh, high-pitched systolic murmur over the left sternal border around the fifth intercostal space without radiation.

(I) is correct. This patient, who from his presentation would seem to abuse intravenous drugs, presents with a fever and a murmur characteristic of tricuspid regurgitation. TR is a common valvular lesion in intravenous drug abusers with endocarditis.

42. A 27-year-old white female with a history of generalized anxiety disorder presents to the emergency department with complaints of 6/10 substernal chest pain, unrelieved with one sublingual nitroglycerin administered by EMS. She has a mid-systolic click over the left mid-clavicular fifth intercostal space.

(F) is correct. Mitral valve prolapse is associated with generalized anxiety disorder. It is not uncommon for these patients to present with chest pain. The exam finding of a mid-systolic click is classic.

43. A 55-year-old black male with a long-standing history of insulin-dependent diabetes mellitus and hypertension presents to the emergency department complaining of crushing substernal chest pain and severe shortness of breath. His electrocardiogram has a large ST segment elevation in the anterior leads (V1–V6) consistent with an acute anterior wall myocardial infarction. He is very dyspneic at rest and has rales throughout both lung fields. He also has a harsh holosystolic murmur radiating to his axilla.

(G) is correct. Papillary muscle rupture is a known complication of large anterior wall myocardial infarction. A new harsh holosystolic murmur confirms the diagnosis of rupture and subsequent incompetence of the mitral valve.

44. A 66-year-old white female with a history of rheumatic heart disease presents to her primary care physician for her annual physical exam. Her cardiac exam is significant for low-pitched, rumbling diastolic murmur, best heard over the left mid-clavicular fifth intercostal space.

(E) is correct. The classic lesion of rheumatic heart disease is mitral stenosis typified by a rumbling diastolic murmur.

Items 45–50

(A) Ampicillin
(B) Ceftriaxone
(C) Ciprofloxacin
(D) Clindamycin
(E) Doxycycline
(F) Gentamicin
(G) Metronidazole
(H) Penicillin
(I) Rifampin
(J) Trimethoprim/Sulfamethoxazole
(K) Vancomycin

Choose the most appropriate antibiotic choice for each clinical scenario.

45. A 37-year-old white male presents to his primary care doctor complaining of severe abdominal pain and bloody diarrhea, which began after eating a chicken sandwich purchased from a street vendor. Stool culture isolates *Shigella* sp.

(C) is correct. Ciprofloxacin is the preferred treatment for infectious diarrhea (*Shigella*, *Salmonella*, and *Campylobacter*), reducing the symptomatic period by 42%. Trimethoprim/sulfamethoxazole was previously an acceptable alternative, but now many strains are resistant.

46. A 22-year-old white male army recruit presents to the infirmary complaining of a severe headache and photophobia. Exam is notable for meningismus.

(B) is correct. Meningitis is common among close-quartered individuals, such as college students and army recruits. The usual pathogen is *Neisseria meningitidis*, although *Streptococcus pneumoniae* is also a consideration. High doses of ceftriaxone is appropriate therapy.

47. A 35-year-old white female presents to her primary care doctor with complaints of dysuria, frequency, and urgency for the last day. She has no fever, nausea, vomiting, or costovertebral angle tenderness. She is allergic to penicillin.

(J) is correct. Uncomplicated cystitis is best treated with trimethoprim/sulfamethoxazole. The overwhelming majority of uncomplicated cystitis is due to Enterobacteriaceae sensitive to this antibiotic. Floroquinolone therapy is an acceptable alternative, though considerably more expensive and thus not first-line treatment.

48. An 18-year-old white male presents to the emergency department with a high fever, confusion, and a rash on his palms and soles. His laboratory studies are remarkable for thrombocytopenia. He has just returned from a camping trip in the North Carolina mountains.

(E) is correct. Doxycycline is the appropriate therapy for Rocky Mountain spotted fever (RMSF), which is characterized by fever and rash beginning on the palms and soles that spreads to the trunk. RMSF is most prevalent in the mid-Atlantic region and North Carolina.

49. A 32-year-old white female presents her primary care physician with complaints of malodorous vaginal discharge. Examination of the vaginal discharge shows "clue cells."

(G) is correct. *Gardnerella vaginalis* is a cause of vaginosis. Diagnosis is confirmed by visualizing clue cells. It is best treated with metronidazole.

50. A 27-year-old white female presents to the emergency department with complaints of vaginal discharge. She has large amounts of foul-smelling, foamy cervical discharge. Wet prep visualizes motile trichomonads.

(G) is correct. Metronidazole is first-line therapy for *Trichomonas vaginalis*. Diagnosis is confirmed by visualizing motile trichomonads on the wet prep.

SECTION 2 BEGINS HERE

Directions (Items 51–100): Each of the numbered items is followed or preceded by a set of options. For each item, select the BEST lettered option to answer the question or complete the statement. Locate the corresponding item number in the appropriate section of your answer sheet and completely fill in the circle containing the lettered option you have selected.

51. A 9-year-old boy has a one-year history of recurrent eye blinking, head jerking, and facial grimacing. Recently, he has progressed to multiple coughing attacks as well as grunting and sniffling. During the past week, he has begun to repeat his own words and the words of his family members. Teachers in school have noted that the child has difficulty concentrating and occassionally hits himself and jumps up and down. Which of the following is the most appropriate treatment for this individual?

   (A) Clonidine
   (B) Haloperidol
   (C) Pimozide
   (D) Propanolol
   (E) Thorazine

(B) is correct. This patient exhibits signs and symptoms of Tourette's syndrome. Multiple motor and vocal tics occur several times daily. Simple motor tics can include eye blinking and facial grimacing. Simple vocal tics include coughing and grunting. Complex motor tics include hitting oneself and jumping, while complex vocal tics include repeating one's own words and repeating other's words. Excessive swearing can also be noted. 85 percent of patients improve with haloperidol and its associated sedative properties. Choice A is incorrect. Clonidine is not as effective as haloperidol in the treatment of Tourette's syndrome. Choice C is incorrect. Pimozide is an antidopaminergic medication that is a second-line agent in the treatment of Tourette's syndrome. Choice D is incorrect. Propanalol is not recommended in the treatment of Tourette's syndrome. Choice E is incorrect. Thorazine is not recommended in the treatment of Tourette's syndrome.

52. A 33-year-old woman who is HIV-positive notes progressive visual disturbance manifesting as a decrease in visual acuity. Funduscopic examination reveals large, white areas proximal to the macula with perivascular exudates and hemorrhages. Otoscopy reveals movement of the tympanic membrane to pneumatic otoscopy without evidence of effusion. Cervical adenopathy is noted bilaterally along the sternocleidomastoid muscle. Cardiac, pulmonary, and gastrointestinal examinations are unremarkable. Treatment of this condition involves which of the following agents?

   (A) Oral erythromycin
   (B) Oral ganciclovir
   (C) Oral penicillin
   (D) Oral prednisone
   (E) Intravenous prednisone

(B) is correct. Treatment of cytomegalovirus retinitis involves ganciclovir, foscarnet, and cidofovir. The drugs are given in an initial induction phase, and then in a later life-long phase. Ganciclovir can also be given in an intraocular implantable form. Choice A is incorrect. Oral erythromycin is not indicated in the treatment of CMV retinitis. Choice C is incorrect. Oral penicillin is not useful in the management of CMV retinitis. Choice D is incorrect. Oral corticosteroids are unproven in the treatment of CMV retinitis. Choice E is incorrect. Intravenous prednisone is not of value in the treatment of CMV retinitis.

53. A 72-year-old black male presents to the emergency department with complaints of a severe left-sided headache for the last several days. It is exacerbated by combing his hair and chewing food. He has point tenderness over his anterior scalp. Which of the following is the most appropriate initial intervention?

(A) Carotid duplex Dopplers
(B) Computed tomography of the head
(C) Echocardiogram
(D) Electroencephalogram
(E) Magnetic resonance imaging of the head
(F) Temporal artery biopsy
(G) Trial of narcotic analgesics

(F) is correct. Severe headache and scalp tenderness raise the diagnosis of temporal arteritis. This diagnosis must be confirmed quickly, as untreated temporal arteritis, a large vessel vasculitis, can result in irreversible blindness. Choice A is incorrect. The history provides no evidence for an embolic phenomenon. Carotid duplex Dopplers are a useful tool for assessing carotid stenosis, a common source of atheroemboli. Choice B is incorrect. A focal headache may herald intracranial pathology, making CT scan an appropriate first step. However, in this case, the additional history of scalp tenderness, jaw claudication, and point tenderness make temporal artery biopsy the best first step. Choice C is incorrect. The history provides no evidence for an embolic phenomenon. Echocardiogram is a useful tool for assessing left atrial and left ventricular clots, a common source of atheroemboli, especially in patients with atrial fibrillation. Choice D is incorrect. No part of the history suggests a seizure disorder; an electroencephalogram is not warranted. Choice E is incorrect. A focal headache may herald intracranial pathology. MRI is an excellent study for assessing fine intracranial anatomy. However, in this case, the additional history of scalp tenderness, jaw claudication, and point tenderness make temporal artery biopsy the best first step. (And, prior to MRI, a CT scan would be appropriate) Choice G is incorrect. Temporal arteritis is a potentially vision-threatening emergency. Until serious pathology is excluded, a trial of narcotic analgesics is inappropriate and likely to be dangerous.

54. A 42-year-old white female with a history of fibromyalgia presents to her primary care physician with complaints of worsening diffuse muscular pain and fatigue. She takes no medications. What is the best initial treatment?

(A) Alprazolam
(B) Fluoxetine
(C) Glucocorticoids
(D) Ibuprofen
(E) Intramuscular gold
(F) Intramuscular methotrexate
(G) Narcotic analgesic
(H) Oral gold

(D) is correct. Fibromylagia is a syndrome of widespread musculoskeletal pain, stiffness, easy fatigability, multiple tender points, and nonrestorative sleep. Treatment is difficult, but should center around the use of regular exercise and nonsteroidal anti-inflammatory drugs. Treatment for concomitant depression or anxiety is advised, if present. Choice A is incorrect. Treatment of anxiety in patients with fibromyalgia is indicated only if they are having symptoms of anxiety. Choice B is incorrect. Treatment of concomitant depression in patients with fibromyalgia is indicated, and fluoxetine would be appropriate. However, this clinical scenario only provides symptoms of fibromyalgia, not depression. Choice C is incorrect. There is no role for the use of glucocorticoids in the treatment of fibromyalgia. Choice E is incorrect. Intramuscular gold is a remittive agent used primarily for the treatment of rheumatoid arthritis. It has no role in the treatment of fibromyalgia. Choice F is incorrect. Methotrexate is chemotherapeutic agent used in the treatment of resistant rheumatoid arthritis, among other applications. It has no role in the treatment of fibromyalgia. Choice G is incorrect. Narcotic analgesics should be avoided in the treatment of fibromyalgia. Choice H is incorrect. Oral gold is a remittive agent used primarily for the treatment of rheumatoid arthritis. It has no role in the treatment of fibromyalgia.

55. A 76-year-old man is confused 2 nights after his right total hip replacement. Previously, he had been living alone in the community and doing his own shopping and other activities of daily living. The patient is agitated, pointing out the snakes at his bedside (his IV fluid lines) and the bugs on the ceiling (ceiling tiles). He is disoriented to person, place, and time. His vital signs are stable. There is no evidence of hypoxia, fever, or focal neurologic deficits. Which of the following is the most appropriate next step?

(A) Administration of diphenhydramine
(B) Administration of diazepam
(C) Computed tomography of the head
(D) Psychiatric consultation
(E) Review of medications

(E) is correct. The patient is delirious. This is evidenced by his delusions (IV lines look likes snakes), agitation, and disorientation. The most frequent cause of delirium in the elderly is medication. Choice A is incorrect. Diphenhydramine is notorious for making the elderly more confused, presumably on the basis of its anticholinergic effects. Choice B is incorrect. Benzodiazepines should not be used as first-line therapy for delirium, especially in the elderly. Choice C is incorrect. In the absence of focal neurologic deficits, computed tomography is not immediately indicated in the delirious patient. Choice D is incorrect. The diagnosis and treatment of delirium, in this case, is straightforward and does not require psychiatric involvement.

56. A 65-year-old man is brought to the emergency department by his family for increasing confusion. They note several months of unremitting cough, weight loss of 6.8 kg (15 lb), and now worsening confusion. He is a cachectic white male. A chest roentgenograph demonstrates a right upper lobe mass. Serum electrolytes are as follows:

Sodium	115 mEq/dL
Potassium	4.0 mEq/dL
Chloride	90 mEq/dL
Bicarbonate	22 mEq/dL

Which of the following is the most likely pathology of this patient's lung tumor?

(A) Adenocarcinoma
(B) Carcinoid tumor
(C) Large cell carcinoma
(D) Small cell carcinoma
(E) Squamous cell carcinoma

(D) is correct. Small cell carcinoma is associated with a number of paraneoplastic syndromes due to the release of neuroendocrine products by the tumor. One of these syndromes is syndrome of inappropriate secretion of antidiuretic hormone (SIADH). Non-small cell lung tumors rarely cause SIADH in the absence of brain metastases. Choice A, Choice C, and Choice E are incorrect. These tumors comprise the "non-small cell" lung cancers and rarely possess neuroendocrine function with the exception of producing parathyroid-like hormone induced hypercalcemia. Choice B is incorrect. Carcinoid tumor is rarely primary to the lung, but rather primary to the gastrointestinal tract. Lung lesions are rare except in widely metastatic disease, and symptoms of flushing and diarrhea are prominent.

57. A 33-year-old man has a 3-week history of catatonic behavior, delusions, and auditory hallucinations after being fired from his job as an assistant vice president of a local business. At the present time, he appears to be in emotional turmoil and seems confused. Conversations with this individual are characterized by rapid shifts from one intense affect to another. Laboratory values are obtained:

Serum

Thyroid-stimulating hormone	4.1 µU/mL
Thyroxine	7 mg/dL
Triiodothyronine (RIA)	145 ng/dL

Which of the following is the most likely etiology of this condition?

(A) Presence of a preexisting personality disorder
(B) Prior history of cerebral tumor
(C) Prior history of schizophrenia
(D) Prior history of seizure disorder
(E) Prior history of substance abuse

(A) is correct. This individual has brief reactive psychosis. This condition is defined by a symptom constellation of less that one month's duration and follows an obvious stress on the patient's life. Patients exhibit an increase in volatility and lability, confusion, disorientation, and affective symptoms. This condition is highly associated with persons with a preexisting personality disorder and those who have experienced a major life stressor such as a natural disaster. Choice B is incorrect. A prior history of a cerebral tumor is not associated with the development of brief reactive psychosis. Choice C is incorrect. Schizophrenia is a part of the differential diagnosis of brief reactive psychosis. However, schizophrenia is considered when the duration of symptoms is at least 3 months. Choice D is incorrect. A prior history of seizures can cause symptoms similar to those of brief reactive psychosis. Therefore, this organic etiology must be considered as a part of the differential diagnosis of this condition. Choice E is incorrect. A prior history of substance abuse is part of the differential diagnosis of mood disorders, especially those of short duration such as in this case. However, this entity is less likely than the correct answer.

58. A 20-year-old white male college student majoring in chemical engineering presents to the student health center in the midst of final exams. He is concerned because late last night while studying, his roommate noted that he looked distinctly "yellow." He was able to eat several slices of pizza before finally going to bed without difficulty. Upon awakening this morning, the skin discoloration had resolved.

The patient's liver function tests are as follows:

ALT	15 U/L
AST	18 U/L
Bilirubin (total)	4.0 mg/dL
Bilirubin (direct)	0.4 mg/dL

Which of the following is the most appropriate next step?

(A) Computed tomography of the abdomen
(B) Dimethyl iminodiacetic acid (HIDA) scan
(C) Liver biopsy
(D) Reassure the patient
(E) Right upper quadrant ultrasonography

(D) is correct. This patient is suffering from Gilbert's disease, a partial deficiency of glucuronosyl-transferase. This is the most common cause of an unconjugated hyperbilirubinemia in the absence of hemolytic anemia. This patient should be reassured that his condition is benign and will likely recur in times of stress. Choice A is incorrect. Computed tomography is very useful for evaluation of hepatic masses that are not a concern in light of the history and lab data. Choice B is incorrect. The history provides no evidence for acute cholecystitis. Additionally, the hyperbilirubinemia is unconjugated, rather than conjugated, as would be expected in cholelithiasis. Therefore, a HIDA scan (a test useful for confirming obstruction of the cystic duct) in not indicated. Choice C is incorrect. Gilbert's syndrome is a benign condition. The risks inherent in liver biopsy (an invasive procedure) cannot be justified. Choice E is incorrect. Ultrasonography is an very useful initial evaluation of the gallbladder and biliary tree. However, this patient has no history or lab evidence for gallbladder or biliary tree pathology. Rather, he has an unconjugated hyperbilirubinemia.

59. A study is conducted to determine whether eating a low-fat diet during adolescence is protective against developing breast cancer later in life. The study tool is a self-administered questionnaire that asks subjects to elaborate on their eating habits during their adolescence. The subjects include 1,000 women with known breast cancer and 1,000 women who do not have breast cancer. All subjects were between the ages of 50 and 80 years old. Based on the study, women with breast cancer report consuming a diet higher in fat during their adolescence than women without breast cancer ($p < 0.05$). What is the most important defect in this study?

(A) Berkson's bias
(B) Detection bias
(C) Investigator bias
(D) Procedure bias
(E) Recall bias

(E) is correct. Recall bias occurs when subjects are asked to recall past events and one group is more likely than the other to remember certain events. In this example, subjects must recall eating habits from their adolescent years. Patients with breast cancer are more likely to be aware of research examining the relationship between diet and cancer than patients without breast cancer. Thus, breast cancer patients are more likely to recall the high fat foods they consumed during adolescence than women without breast cancer. Choice A is incorrect. Berkson's bias refers to differential study admission rates. The classic example is a study that uses hospitalized patients in which both cases and controls are more likely than the general population to have a certain risk factor present. Choice B is incorrect. Detection bias occurs when a new technique is developed that can diagnose a disease earlier in its development than was previously possible. In such cases, it appears that patients survive longer because their disease is detected earlier. Choice C is incorrect. Investigator bias would not play a role in this study because the questionnaires are self-administered. Choice D is incorrect. Procedure bias occurs when two groups are treated differently. If, for example, patients in a study get more medical attention that affects their progress, it affects the study outcome.

60. A 20-year-old white female presents with dysuria, urgency, and frequency. The patient has no past medical history and takes no medication. Physical examination is within normal limits except for the cervix, which has a purulent discharge. Otherwise, there are no vulvar lesions, lymphadenopathy, or adnexal tenderness. Gram stain of this exudate reveals gram-negative intracellular diplococci. Tissue culture is also likely to recover

(A) *Candida albicans*
(B) *Chlamydia trachomatis*
(C) *Mycoplasma hominis*
(D) *Staphylococcus aureus*
(E) *Treponema pallidum*

(B) is correct. This patient with evidence of gonorrheal infection, is also 40–50 percent likely to have a concomitant chlamydial infection. Treatment for both organisms should be initiated. One suitable regimen is ceftriaxone (125 mg IM) for gonorrhea, followed by doxycycline (100 mg BID × 7 days) to treat chlamydial infection. Choice A, Choice C, Choice D, Choice E are not necessarily associated with gonorrheal infection.

61. A 25-year-old woman, gravida 1 para 0, at 16 weeks gestation has painful swelling and warmth of her left knee. She has a recent history of multiple joint pain with swelling at her right wrist, left elbow, and left ankle that occurred over the past week. Now her left knee is similarly affected. She also has a rash on her palms and soles. The patient has no other past medical history. She takes a daily multivitamin with iron. She does not smoke or drink alcohol. The patient denies any intravenous drug use. Review of systems is otherwise entirely negative. Physical examination reveals a temperature of 37 C (98.6 F), a pulse of 100 beats/min., and a blood pressure of 90/60 mm Hg. The neck is supple and lungs are clear. Cardiovascular examination is within normal limits. The abdomen is soft and without tenderness. Extremities show about 10 small, necrotic pustules distributed over the palms and soles. The left knee is 4 cm greater in diameter than the right, swollen, erythematous, and tender, with decreased range of motion. Neurological examination reveals no focal deficits. White blood cell count is 10,000/mm^3. Rapid plasma reagin is nonreactive. Left knee x-ray reveals soft tissue swelling. Synovial fluid white blood cell count is 80,000/U/L. The test most likely to confirm this patient's diagnosis is

(A) blood culture
(B) erythrocyte sedimentation rate
(C) rheumatoid factor
(D) synovial fluid culture
(E) synovial fluid gram stain
(F) throat culture

(F) is correct. This patient has a purulent arthritis most likely due to infection with *N. gonorrhoeae*. It is seen most commonly in pregnant or menstruating females, with migratory polyarthralgias, purulent monoarthritis, and a skin rash. There is no fever. Patients often have no symptoms of urethritis. There are over 50,000 cells/U/L on synovial fluid white blood cell count. Choice A is incorrect. Blood culture is almost never positive. Choice B is incorrect. Erythrocyte sedimentation rate is not indicated at this time. It is also a highly nonspecific test for inflammation and is not used for diagnosis. Choice C is incorrect. A rheumatoid factor test is not indicated in this patient, as she is not likely to have rheumatoid arthritis. Choice D is incorrect. Synovial fluid culture is positive in less than 50 percent of patients. Choice E is incorrect. Synovial fluid gram stain is positive in less than 25 percent of patients.

62. A 45-year-old white presents to the emergency department with complaints of severe left-sided flank pain. Further evaluation reveals a kidney stone. He also has trouble with constipation and diffuse bone pain. Laboratory studies are as follows:

Calcium	12.8 mg/dL ↑
Phosphorus	2.5 mg/dL ↓

Which of the following is the most appropriate first step?

(A) Assay for parathyroid-like hormone
(B) Chest roentgenograph
(C) Computed tomography of the chest
(D) Cytoscopy
(E) Magnetic resonance imaging of the chest
(F) Repeat laboratory studies

(F) is correct. Prior to proceeding with a lengthy and expensive evaluation, the possibility of erroneous lab testing must be excluded. The assay for calcium, in particular, requires special technologist attention. Without a known underlying malignancy, most cases of hypercalcemia are secondary to a hyperfunctioning parathyroid adenoma. Choice A is incorrect. Parathyroid-like hormone is produced by nonsmall cell cancers of the lung. Without evidence of malignancy, there is no indication for this test. Choice B is incorrect. Chest roentgenograph would be a useful screening tool if there was suspicion of an underlying nonsmall cell lung cancer producing parathyroid-like hormone. Prior to rechecking the calcium value, the study is not indicated. Choice C is incorrect. Computed tomography is very useful in staging lung cancer. However, it has no role in the initial evaluation of hypercalcemia. Choice D is incorrect. The patient's current complaint is a kidney stone. Hydration and pain control are the hallmarks of treatment. Cystoscopy is not indicated. Choice E is incorrect. Magnetic resonance imaging is not indicated in the evaluation of hypercalcemia.

63. A 57-year-old white female with a history of rheumatoid arthritis presents to her primary care doctor complaining of fatigue, which has been worsening over the last few months. Her conjunctiva are pale. She has signs of active arthritis in several metacarpal joints and prominent ulnar deviation of her wrists. Laboratory studies are as follows:

Hemoglobin	9.8 g/dL
Hematocrit	28.9%
Mean corpuscular volume	90 fL
Serum	
Ferritin	Increased
Total iron binding capacity	Increased
Iron	Decreased

Which of the following most appropriate classification of her anemia?

(A) β-thalassemia trait
(B) Chronic disease anemia
(C) Folate deficiency
(D) Iron deficiency
(E) Vitamin B$_{12}$ deficiency

(B) is correct. Chronic disease anemia is characterized by a normocytic anemia (normal MCV) with low serum iron and high total iron binding capacity. The problem is the inability of iron to be incorporated into red blood cells, rather than deficiency of iron. In this case, chronic active rheumatoid arthritis is to blame. Choice A is incorrect. β-thalassemia is characterized by a microcytic anemia. The MCV is often very low, and almost always less than 70 fL. Choice C is incorrect. Folate deficiency is characterized by a megaloblastic anemia with an increased MCV. Choice D is incorrect. Iron deficiency results in a microcytic, hypochromic anemia with both low serum iron and total iron binding capacity. Choice E is incorrect. Deficiency of vitamin B$_{12}$ is characterized by a megaloblastic anemia with an increased MCV.

64. A 25-year-old white woman with asthma works at an accounting firm as a secretary. Her coworkers noticed a change in her behavior that occurred 2 weeks ago, which is quite dramatic. Whereas she had been quiet, conservative, and hardworking in a meek way before, she now enters the office with a grand flourish and announces how great the world is, and how she feels "on top of things." She invited everyone in the firm, including the head accountant, to a huge party at an expensive club she rented for the occasion. She increasingly neglects her work duties and has of late skipped whole days without explanation. Finally, she is brought to the emergency room with an acute asthma exacerbation because she has not been using her inhaler and has been smoking heavily. On physical examination, she is anxious and has red eyes. She has difficulty moving air through her lungs and talks very rapidly in a hoarse voice. Urine toxicology screen is negative. Blood alcohol level is 200 mg/dL. Upon further questioning, she wishes she could die. The most likely diagnosis is

(A) bipolar I disorder
(B) bipolar II disorder
(C) cyclothymic disorder
(D) mixed episode
(E) substance-induced mood disorder

(A) is correct. This patient has had a manic episode. This, plus or minus a history of major depressive episode, makes for the diagnosis of bipolar I disorder. Three of the following must be present for at least 1 week: inflated self-esteem; decreased need for sleep; pressured speech; flight of ideas; distractibility; increase in goal-directed activity; excessive involvement in pleasurable activities that have a high potential for painful consequences. Symptoms must not be due to the direct effects of a substance. Choice B is incorrect. Bipolar II disorder features at least one episode of major depression (depressed mood, anhedonia, weight changes, sleep disturbances, fatigue, psychomotor changes, indecisiveness, recurrent thoughts of death, feelings of worthlessness) with 1 hypomanic episode. Choice C is incorrect. Cyclothymic disorder features, over the past 2 years, repeated episodes of hypomania and depression (but not severe enough for major depressive episode)— leading to the diagnosis of cyclothymic disorder. The age of onset is in the teens or early adulthood. A hypomanic episode lasts about 4 days and is less severe than a manic episode. There is no history of hospitalization, psychotic features, or severe social or occupational impairment. Choice D is incorrect. Mixed episode features aspects of both a manic episode and a major depressive episode over a 1-week period. Choice E is incorrect. Substance-induced mood disorder features a mood disturbance caused by substance abuse. This patient has evidence of mood disturbance leading to substance abuse, not the other way around.

65. A 30-year-old white man with a history of alcohol abuse is seen for a psychiatric evaluation. He has a police record that began at age 17 and includes repeated arrests for theft, assault, and damage to property. He has no other medical or psychiatric conditions and takes no medications. The patient smokes 1 to 2 packs of cigarettes per day and uses alcohol in binges. He has used heroin, cocaine, and marijuana in the past, but denies current use. The patient lives alone, recently separated from his girlfriend. He has no contact with his mother, and he does not know who his father is. On mental status examination, he is pleasant and smiling, and cooperative to all questioning. Mood is euthymic and affect is pleasant. He has no hallucinations, suicidal ideation, or homicidal ideation. Reality testing is intact. When asked about past crimes, the patient dismisses them as mindless occurrences and does not appear apologetic. He states that he has been a troublemaker for as long as he can remember. Urine toxicology screen returns positive for cocaine. The patient is informed of this result and becomes visibly agitated. He vehemently denies ever having told a lie about his drug usage. The most likely diagnosis in this patient is

(A) borderline personality disorder
(B) narcissistic personality disorder
(C) obsessive-compulsive personality disorder
(D) antisocial personality disorder
(E) paranoid personality disorder

(D) is correct. This patient displays a pervasive pattern of disregard for and violation of the rights of others. He has repeatedly performed acts that are grounds for arrest, shown deceitfulness, irritability, aggressiveness, and lack of remorse. He also is at least 18 years old with a history of conduct disorder before 15 years of age. Choice A is incorrect. Borderline personality disorder features instability of self-image, interpersonal relationships, and mood. Patients have a marked reactivity of mood and chronic feelings of emptiness. Choice B is incorrect. Narcissistic personality disorder features a grandiose sense of self with extreme sensitivity to criticism. There is little ability to empathize with others and a need for excessive admiration. Choice C is incorrect. Obsessive-compulsive personality disorder has symptoms of preoccupation with details, rules, lists, order, organization, or schedules with over-conscientiousness, scrupulousness, and inflexibility about matters of morality. Choice E is incorrect. Paranoid personality disorder is characterized by preoccupation with recurrent suspicions, grudges, and reading hidden meanings in benign remarks.

66. A 28-year-old black man with sickle cell anemia has fever, chills, and a painful back. Pressing on his lower spine elicits pain. He has no history of trauma or recent surgery. He has had several sickle cell crises in the past and was last hospitalized 6 months ago. He takes folic acid daily. Otherwise, he takes no other medications, does not smoke, and does not drink alcohol. He denies any current illicit drug use. Physical examination reveals a temperature of 38.3 C (101 F) and stable vital signs. The neck is supple. Lungs are clear and cardiovascular examination is within normal limits. The abdomen is soft and nontender with normal bowel sounds. Lumbar spine is tender to palpation and slightly warm. MRI scan reveals extensive soft tissue swelling that crosses the L4, L5 disk space. The most likely organism that would cause this presentation in this patient is

(A) *Escherichia coli*
(B) *Neisseria gonorrhoeae*
(C) *Salmonella* sp.
(D) *Staphylococcus aureus*
(E) *Staphylococcus epidermidis*

(C) is correct. This patient has vertebral osteomyelitis—fever, chills, and painful spine with MRI confirmation of the disease. 95 percent of cases are due to a strain of pyogenic bacteria. In patients with sickle cell anemia, the most common organism is *Salmonella*—10 times more common than any other species. Choice A is incorrect. *Escherichia coli* is seen in intravenous drug users. Choice B is incorrect. *Neisseria gonorrhoeae* is not seen as a cause of vertebral osteomyelitis. Choice D and Choice E are incorrect. They constitute the cause in 75 percent of standard acute pyogenic bone infections.

67. A cohort study is designed to examine the association between elevated cholesterol levels and myocardial infarction. Study subjects were recruited from a weight-reduction program and included men and women ages 50 through 75 years old. Cholesterol levels were taken biannually using standardized protocols for serum analysis. Subjects were followed for 20 years and the number of myocardial infarctions was recorded based on hospital records. Analysis of the data showed a rate ratio of 3.5 ($p < 0.05$) indicating that people with elevated cholesterol levels were at 3.5 times the risk of having a myocardial infarction than those without elevated cholesterol levels. Which of the following describes the major flaw in the study?

(A) Confounding
(B) Differential misclassification
(C) Inappropriate analysis of the data
(D) Inappropriate use of a cohort study design
(E) Nondifferential misclassification

(A) is correct. Confounding occurs when a variable is associated with both the exposure and the disease/outcome. In this case, subjects were chosen from a weight reduction program, and therefore it is reasonable to assume that many, if not all, of the subjects are overweight. Obesity is known to be associated with elevated cholesterol levels (the exposure in this case) and myocardial infarction (the disease or outcome in this case). Thus the relationship between elevated cholesterol and myocardial infarctions in this study is influenced by the confounding variable, obesity. Choice B is incorrect. Differential misclassification is also a type of information bias. Differential misclassification occurs when an error in measurement of a particular variable is related to another variable. Such errors bias away from the null. The use of serum analysis to determine cholesterol levels and hospital records to determine if a subject has had a myocardial infarction are likely to be accurate measurements of the exposure and disease/outcome variable in this example. Choice C is incorrect. Inappropriate analysis of the data is incorrect because in a prospective cohort study (such as the one presented here), the rate ratio is an appropriate measurement of the relationship between the exposure and the disease. Choice D is incorrect. This is an entirely appropriate and effective use of the cohort study design. Choice E is incorrect. Nondifferential misclassification is a type of information bias. Information bias occurs when the measurement of a particular variable is inaccurate. In nondifferential misclassification, the error in measurement of a particular variable is not related to any other variables. Such errors bias toward the null.

68. A 24-year-old white man presents to his psychiatrist's office because he is depressed and lonely. He secretly likes a woman at his job as a clerk in an advertising firm. However, he is afraid she will reject him, humiliate him, and ultimately disapprove of him. He has never had a close relationship with anyone except for his sister, who now lives in another state. He believes he is a "complete loser." The patient appears nervous and speaks in a tense, low voice. He has no other medical conditions and takes no medications. He does not smoke, drink, or use illicit drugs. Family history is significant for breast cancer that caused the death of his mother at age 60. He denies any hallucinations, or suicidal or homicidal ideation. Reality testing and judgment are intact. The doctor asks him to speak up and the patient becomes visibly upset. The most likely diagnosis is

(A) dependent personality disorder
(B) schizoid personality disorder
(C) schizotypal personality disorder
(D) borderline personality disorder
(E) avoidant personality disorder

(E) is correct. The patient avoids interpersonal contact secondary to fear of criticism, disapproval, and rejection; is preoccupied with being criticized or rejected in social situations; views self as socially inept, personally unappealing, or inferior to others; is unusually reluctant to take personal risks because they may prove embarrassing; is unwilling to get involved with people unless certain of being liked; and takes rejection/criticism poorly. These attributes qualify this patient for avoidant personality disorder. Choice A is incorrect. Dependent personality disorder features pateints who are unable to make everyday decisions and need others to assume responsibility for most major areas of their lives. Patients have difficulty initiating projects and go to excessive lengths to obtain nurturance and support. Choice B is incorrect. Schizoid personality disorder presents as a pattern of detachment from social relationships and a restricted range of expressed emotions. Patients almost always choose solitary activities, have little interest in sexual experiences, a lack of close friends, appear indifferent, and have emotional coldness, detachment, or flattened affect. Choice C is incorrect. Schizotypal personality disorder has symptoms of ideas of reference, odd beliefs, magical thinking, unusual perceptual experiences, odd thinking and speech, and suspiciousness or paranoid ideation. Choice D is incorrect. Borderline personality disorder features frantic efforts to avoid real or imagined abandonment; a pattern of unstable and intense interpersonal relationships; recurrent suicidal behavior, gestures, or threats; affective instability due to a marked reactivity of mood; chronic feelings of emptiness; difficulty controlling anger; and transient, stress-related paranoid ideation.

69. A 42-year-old white woman develops fatigue, weakness, and a general feeling of lethargy. She also has nausea and vomiting, and has lost 4.5 kg (10 lb) in the past month. She reports a loss of appetite with increased thirst and urination. She has no other medical history, takes no medications, and has an allergy to sulfa. She works as a secretary in a law firm. She does not smoke cigarettes and drinks a glass of red wine every other day. The patient is married with 4 healthy children. Physical examination reveals a thin woman with dry mucous membranes. Lungs are clear. Cardio-vascular examination reveals tachycardia with a thready pulse. Percussion of the spine elicits pain. Neurologic examination reveals no focal abnormalities. X-ray films of the spine are within normal limits. Chest x-ray is also normal. Serum calcium is 13 mg/dL. Albumin is 3.4 g/dL. The most likely cause of this patient's clinical condition is

(A) cancer with bony metastases
(B) sarcoidosis
(C) hyperparathyroidism
(D) multiple myeloma
(E) psychogenic

(C) is correct. This patient has hypercalcemia caused by hyperparathyroidism. Signs and symptoms include easy fatigue, weakness, nausea, vomiting, anorexia, kidney stones, headache, pains in the back, thirst, polydipsia, and polyuria. Serum calcium over 15 mg/dL can lead to death. Treatment is volume repletion and inorganic phosphates. Choice A is incorrect. Cancer with bony metastases is also a common cause of hypercalcemia seen in patients with metastatic breast cancer. Choice B is incorrect. Sarcoidosis is not the most common cause of hypercalcemia. The patient's chest x-ray was normal. Choice D is incorrect. Multiple myeloma is not the most common cause. Spine films were within normal limits, and there is no history of fractures. Choice E is incorrect. This is not a reason here, because this patient has documented hypercalcemia.

A 24-year-old white male presents to the emergency room complaining of a painful right knee for the last 2 days and fever for the past 24 hours. He denies any antecedent trauma or past medical history. His temperature is 38.2 C (102 F). His right knee is exquisitely painful and erythematous with a prominent effusion. No other joints are involved.

70. Which of the following is the most appropriate step after joint aspiration?

    (A) Elevation and frequent ice treatments
    (B) Intravenous cefazolin
    (C) Intravenous ceftriaxone
    (D) Intravenous penicillin
    (E) Oral cephalexin

(C) is correct. In a young patient with a monoarticular acute arthritis, especially of the knee or wrist, *Neisseria gonorrhoeae* should be suspected foremost. Resistance of *Neisseria gonorrhoeae* to penicillin is increasing, requiring the use of ceftriaxone as first-line therapy. In the pediatric and elderly populations, streptococcal and staphylococcal septic arthritis requires different antibiotic choices. Choice A is incorrect. Septic arthritis is a joint-threatening condition that mandates rapid initiation of intravenous antibiotics, in this case, an antibiotic with good coverage for suspected gonococcal septic arthritis. Choice B is incorrect. Intravenous cefazolin provides good coverage for methicillin-sensitive staphylococci, but in this patient, an antibiotic with *Neisseria gonorrhoeae* coverage is needed. Choice D is incorrect. Resistance of *Neisseria gonorrhoeae* to penicillin is increasing, requiring the use of ceftriaxone as first-line therapy for suspected gonococcal septic arthritis. Choice E is incorrect. Septic arthritis is a joint-threatening condition that mandates rapid initiation of intravenous antibiotics, in this case, an antibiotic with good coverage for suspected gonococcal septic arthritis.

71. Which of the following is the most likely culture result from joint aspiration of the knee of this patient?

    (A) Gram-negative diplococci
    (B) Gram-negative rods
    (C) Gram-positive cocci in chains
    (D) Gram-positive cocci in clusters
    (E) Sterile culture

(E) is correct. *Neisseria gonorrhoeae* is a fastidious organism that is difficult to culture. Therefore, only 30 percent of joints infected with *Neisseria gonorrhoeae* have a positive culture. However, gram-negative diplococci may be seen on Gram stain or by immunofluorescent staining. Choice A is incorrect. *Neisseria gonorrhoeae* is a fastidious organism that is difficult to culture. Therefore, only 30 percent of joints infected with *Neisseria gonorrhoeae* have a positive culture. Choice B is incorrect. Gram-negative septic arthritis is rare and usually only occurs in the profoundly debilitated or immunocompromised. Choice C is incorrect. Although streptococcal septic arthritis is common in children and the elderly, *Neisseria gonorrhoeae* is the most common pathogen in young, otherwise healthy adults. Choice D is incorrect. Although staphylococcal septic arthritis is common in children and the elderly, *Neisseria gonorrhoeae* is the most common pathogen in young, otherwise healthy adults.

72. The normal hematocrit in a population of male high school students is found to be 45 percent with a standard deviation of 5 percent. What is the range of hematocrit levels that would encompass approximately 95 percent of this population?

(A) 30–50%
(B) 35–55%
(C) 40–50%
(D) 35–45%
(E) 35–65%

(B) is correct. Questions on biostatistics appear on every licensure examination. A 95 percent confidence interval would encompass two standard deviations from the average in both directions. With a standard deviation of 5, two standard deviations (10) above and below the mean would place the confidence interval between 35 and 55.

73. A 23-year-old Asian American woman, gravida 1 para 0, is at 32 weeks gestation when she develops nausea, vomiting, and dull right upper quadrant abdominal pain. She also has a slight fever. In the emergency room, she is found to have a temperature of 38 C (100.4 F). Her sclera are anicteric. Mucous membranes are dry. The abdomen is gravid with right upper quadrant tenderness to deep palpation. There is no rebound tenderness, but there is guarding. The cervix is long and closed with cervical motion tenderness elicited when the uterus is manipulated on pelvic examination. Fetal heart rate monitoring is begun and is reassuring for now. Ultrasound of the abdomen reveals a purulent mass in the right upper quadrant. The most common diagnosis in a pregnant patient presenting in this manner is

(A) acute cholecystitis
(B) acute pancreatitis
(C) appendicitis
(D) ruptured peptic ulcer
(E) small bowel obstruction

(C) is correct. Appendicitis is the most common acute surgical complication of pregnancy, occurring in 1:1,500 to 1:2,000 pregnancies. This patient has the usual visceral symptoms such as nausea, vomiting, and right upper quadrant pain because of the gravid uterus. These patients can also have pain with manipulation of the uterus. There may be complete absence of peritoneal signs even if there is a coexisting peritonitis. A WBC count is not helpful in pregnancy, and neither are x-rays. Diagnosis is by surgery, which has a 20 percent false negative laparotomy rate. Choice A is incorrect. Cholecystitis occurs with nausea, vomiting, jaundice, and evidence of increased total bilirubin and stones on ultrasound of the RUQ. Choice B is incorrect. Pancreatitis is secondary to cholelithiasis in pregnancy. There is usually no fever with this diagnosis. Choice D is incorrect. Ruptured peptic ulcer occurs with the sudden onset of violent pain. It is rare in pregnancy, and x-ray of the chest reveals air under the diaphragm. Choice E is incorrect. Small bowel obstruction occurs in 1–3:10,000 pregnancies. It is seen as colicky abdominal pain, nausea, vomiting, increased bowel sounds, and obstipation. Abdominal x-rays are helpful.

74. A 21-year-old female college student presents for psychiatric counseling to control her erratic eating patterns. Since she entered college, she has felt an overwhelming desire to achieve a thin, "glamorous" image. However, at parties, she feels a strong compunction to eat enormous amounts of fatty foods. She has since established a pattern in which she eats 2 to 3 large pizzas, 2 bags of potato chips, and a dozen donuts, and then proceeds to purge herself with laxatives. She also exercises 3 hours a day at the school gym. She is seeking help because this habit has become quite expensive, as she has these eating episodes almost every day now. She feels she has lost control of her life. She denies suicidal ideation at this time. Physical examination is significant for dental caries and erosion. Weight is 68.1 kg (150 lb) and height is 173 cm (5´8´´). Serum electrolytes are within normal limits. She agrees to outpatient psychotherapy. The most likely short-term prognosis of this patient is

(A) spontaneous remission in 1 to 2 years
(B) steady improvement with a waxing and waning course
(C) poor outcome with increasing severity of symptoms
(D) poor outcome with a 30 percent risk of mortality
(E) poor outcome because the patient is not taking antidepressants

(B) is correct. This patient has bulimia nervosa—recurrent episodes of binge eating with self image unduly influenced by body shape and weight. The diagnosis is better than anorexia. In the short run, patients in outpatient psychotherapy have greater than 50 percent improvement. It is a chronic disorder with lapses. If hospitalized, one-third have a poor outcome with chronic symptoms. Rarely, untreated patients have spontaneous remission in 1 to 2 years. Choice A is rare. Choice C is not true. Choice D is not true. Choice E is not true because antidepressants are only added if psychotherapy fails.

75. A 25-year-old man from Barbados develops a vesicular lesion in his groin area. There is a single, painless growth on his perineum that resolves in 1 week. One month later, the patient develops painful inguinal lymphadenopathy, fever, muscle aches, and joint pain. On examination, the patient has a groove sign over the inguinal lymph nodes, which are enlarged and painful. There is no urethral discharge or skin lesions. Otherwise, the rest of the physical examination is unremarkable. The patient is empirically treated with oral erythromycin while genital and lymph node aspirate cultures and complement fixation titers are pending. He shows signs of improvement. Which of the following organisms is the most likely cause of this patient's presentation?

(A) *Chlamydia trachomatis*
(B) *Haemophilus ducreyi*
(C) Herpes simplex virus
(D) *Neisseria gonorrhoeae*
(E) *Trichomonas vaginalis*

(A) is correct. This patient has signs and symptoms of lymphogranuloma venereum (LGV). This is an STD usually found in the tropics, caused by *C. trachomatis* types L1,2,3. The patient has a typical clinical presentation and course. There is first a vesicular lesion and then inguinal lymphadenopathy, fever, myalgia, and arthralgias. He has the typical groove sign on the skin overlying the enlarged, painful inguinal lymph nodes. Diagnosis is with complement fixation titers greater than 1:64. Treatment is oral erythromycin for 3–6 weeks. Choice B is incorrect. *H. ducreyi* results in chancroid—a soft sore with a necrotic ulcer base. Choice C is incorrect. Herpes infection would not show improvement with erythromycin. In this entity, multiple vesicular lesions are very painful. Choice D is incorrect. *N. gonorrhoeae* is a cause of urethritis or is asymptomatic in men. Choice E is incorrect. *T. vaginalis* is often asymptomatic in men or causes urethritis.

76. In the small town of Babyville (population 20,000), there are 6,500 women between the ages of 15 and 44. In 1997, 2,000 of those women became pregnant. Three hundred women decided to have an abortion before the 20th week of gestation. Intrauterine fetal deaths occurred in 200 women before the 20th week of gestation and in 100 women after the 20th week of gestation. Two hundred fifty babies died within the first year of life, 50 of those babies died in the first 28 days of life. There were no twins born in Babyville in 1997. What was the fertility rate Babyville in 1997?

(A) $(2,000/6,500) \times 1,000$
(B) $(1,500/6,500) \times 1,000$
(C) $(1,400/6,500) \times 1,000$
(D) $(2,000/20,000) \times 1,000$
(E) $(1,500/20,000) \times 1,000$
(F) $(1,400/20,000) \times 1,000$

(C) is correct. Fertility rate is defined as the number of live birth per 1,000 females in the population between the ages of 15 and 44 years. In this case, 2,000 women became pregnant, but 600 of those pregnancies did not progress to term. Thus there were 2,000 – 600 = 1,400 live births in 1997. The denominator is the number of women in the population between the ages of 14 and 44 years old, 6,500. In order to express the rate in births per 1,000 females it is necessary to multiply by 1,000. The answer is therefore $(1,400/6,500) \times 1,000$. Choice A and Choice B are incorrect because they include intrauterine deaths in the numerator. Choice D, Choice E, and Choice F are incorrect because they include the entire population of Babyville in the denominator. Choice D and Choice E are also incorrect because they include intrauterine deaths in the numerator. Be careful not to confuse fertility rate with birth rate. Birth rate is defined as the number of live births per 1,000 population. In this case, option Choice F is a calculation of the birth rate in Babyville for the year 1997.

77. A 22-year-old white female presents to the student health center at her university complaining of fatigue and a yellow appearance to her sclera. She was recently treated for an atypical pneumonia, presumed to be caused by *Mycoplasma pneumoniae*, with a course of azithromycin. Her lab work is as follows:

Hemoglobin	6.5 g/dL
Hematocrit	18.9%
Platelets	200,000/mm^3
White blood cell count	6,100/mm^3
Serum	
ALT	20 U/dL
Bilirubin (total)	4.5 mg/dL
Bilirubin (indirect)	4.1 mg/dL
Cold agglutinins	Positive

Which of the following classes of antibody is the most likely etiology of her anemia?

(A) IgA
(B) IgD
(C) IgE
(D) IgG
(E) IgM

(E) is correct. This patient is suffering a hemolytic anemia (evidenced by her anemia and unconjugated hyperbilirubinemia) mediated by "cold agglutinins," which are IgM antibodies. A well-recognized sequela of *Mycoplasma pneumoniae* is such an anemia, with IgM antibodies that react with the I antigen of the red blood cell membranes in 80 percent of patients (only a small percentage of which develop hemolytic anemia). Choice A is incorrect. IgA is a secretory antibody most often associated with the gastrointestinal tract. It is associated with a nephropathy (Berger's disease). Choice B is incorrect. IgD's function has remained elusive, but it is not implicated in hemolytic anemias. Choice C is incorrect. IgE is associated with allergic and anaphylactic phenomena, not with hemolytic anemia. Choice D is incorrect. IgG is implicated in "warm" hemolytic anemias, not "cold."

78. A 14-year-old girl who is on the junior high school track team has had a 9.1 kg (20 lb) weight loss over the past 2 months. She is trying to control her body weight to enhance her running ability. Currently, she is in the 10th percentile for height and weight. She has an intense fear of gaining weight and becoming fat. Her last menstrual period was 4 months ago and she denies ever being sexually active. Physical examination reveals a young, cachectic female in no apparent distress. Cardiovascular examination reveals bradycardia without rubs or murmurs. Pulmonary auscultation reveals no evidence of wheeze or rhonchi. Abdominal examination reveals normoactive bowel sounds. Which of the following is the most appropriate pharmacologic treatment for this individual?

(A) Cyproheptadine
(B) Diazepam
(C) Fluorazepam
(D) Temazepam
(E) Triazolam

(A) is correct. This individual has signs and symptoms of anorexia nervosa. This condition is associated with a refusal to maintain body weight over a normal weight for age and height, a weight of 15 percent below that expected for age. Patients may exhibit an intense fear of gaining weight or becoming fat even though they are underweight. Amenorrhea is also noted. Anorexics often resist medication. However, cyproheptadine is a promising treatment strategy. Choice B is incorrect. Diazepam is not indicated in the treatment of anorexia nervosa. Choice C is incorrect. Fluorazepam is indicated in the treatment of anxiety disorders. Choice D is incorrect. Temazepam is indicated in the treatment of anxiety disorders. Choice E is incorrect. Triazolam is not indicated in the treatment of anorexia nervosa.

79. A 37-year-old woman, gravida 2 para 1, goes to her obstetrician for a check-up at 15 weeks of estimated gestational age by ultrasound dating. She is found to have a blood pressure of 140/90 mm Hg and 2+ protein on urine dipstick without evidence of urinary tract infection. Her uterus is larger than expected for gestational age. There is evidence of bleeding at the closed cervical os. Ultrasound of the pelvis is undertaken and shows a "snowstorm appearance"; that is, multiple echoes without a normal sac or fetus. The most likely diagnosis in this patient is

(A) hydatidiform mole
(B) inevitable abortion
(C) normal intrauterine gestation
(D) severe preeclampsia
(E) twin gestation

(A) is correct. Hydatidiform mole is a proliferative trophoblastic abnormality associated with pregnancy. Symptoms include bleeding in the second trimester, uterus larger than expected for dates, nausea and vomiting (in one-third of patients). Preeclampsia in the second trimester is almost pathognomonic. Diagnosis is by passage of vesicular tissue and/or ultrasound of the pelvis showing multiple echoes without evidence of a normal gestational sac or fetus. Treatment by dilatation and curettage is effective in 80–85 percent of patients. Choice B is incorrect. Ultrasound would show a fetus and the cervical os would be open. Choice C is incorrect. Ultrasound does not show normal intrauterine gestation. Choice D is incorrect. A blood pressure of 140/90 mm Hg and 2+ protein does not qualify for severe preeclampsia. This diagnosis is suggested when one of the following is present: SBP > 160 mm Hg; DBP > 110 mm Hg; oliguria; proteinuria of 5 g or more in 24 hours; cerebral or visual disturbances; epigastric pain; pulmonary edema or cyanosis; thrombocytopenia; or intrauterine growth retardation. Choice E is incorrect. Ultrasound does not show twin gestation.

A 27-year-old black woman who works as a para-medic is involved in a head-on automobile collision with her ambulance and another car. The woman is uninjured and rushes to the car to extricate a little boy. However, the car bursts into flames, knocking her to the ground. She is unable to save the boy. After this event, the woman continues to have recurrent nightmares of the event. She cannot erase the eyes of the little boy from her mind. In her dreams, she cannot hear the boy, but she can see him screaming and his mouth moving, and he always dies. The woman quits her job and loses social contact with family and friends. Over the next year, she begins to drink alcohol in excess and finds herself unable to sleep, feeling intense self-directed hatred and hopelessness.

80. The most likely diagnosis is

    (A) acute stress disorder
    (B) adjustment disorder with anxiety
    (C) major depressive disorder
    (D) post-traumatic stress disorder
    (E) substance-induced anxiety disorder

(D) is correct. This patient has symptoms of re-experiencing the initial trauma and avoidance of stimuli associated with the trauma. These happen in response to exposure to events that involve actual death or injury or a threat to physical integrity of oneself or others and that evoke intense fear, helplessness, or horror. The symptoms may appear immediately after the trauma or may be delayed 6 months or more. The patient also has signs of social and occupational dysfunction with alcohol abuse to help her deal with her disorder. Choice A is incorrect. Acute stress disorder features anxiety or arousal, avoidance, reexperiencing, and acute or delayed dissociative symptoms that begin within 1 month of the event and last 2 days to 4 weeks in response to a traumatic event. Choice B is incorrect. Adjustment disorder features anxiety or impairment in excess of those that would normally be expected within 3 months of exposure to an obvious stress. Symptoms are expected to resolve within 6 months of the stress. Choice C is incorrect. This patient has some signs of depression such as hopelessness, sleep disturbances, and self-hate, but the etiology is related to the initial traumatic event, making the diagnosis of post-traumatic stress disorder more appropriate for this case. Choice E is incorrect. Substance-induced anxiety disorder features anxiety that occurs as a result of substance abuse.

81. The most appropriate therapy for this condition is

    (A) alcohol detoxification
    (B) biofeedback
    (C) electroconvulsive therapy
    (D) group therapy
    (E) short-acting benzodiazepines

(D) is correct. Treatment of this disorder consists of group therapy with discussion of the trauma. Other adjunctive therapies such as biofeedback and carbamazepine or selective serotonin reuptake inhibitors may be helpful as well. Choice A is incorrect. Alcohol detoxification is not the primary purpose of therapy. This patient may, however, have a substance abuse disorder secondary to her post-traumatic stress disorder. Choice B is incorrect. Biofeedback is an adjunctive therapy in this disorder. Choice C is incorrect. Electroconvulsive therapy is used to treat major depressive disorder after a failed trial of medications. Choice E is incorrect. Short-acting benzodiazepines are not indicated in this patient, for whom short-acting drugs may exacerbate symptoms and cause addiction.

82. A 64-year-old, right-handed Asian male is brought to the emergency department by his family after they found him unresponsive in his armchair. His blood pressure is 200/120 mm Hg and his heart rate is 100 beats/min. He is unable to move his right arm or leg and will not look to the right. He has intelligible speech and is unable to follow commands. He takes no medication and smokes a pack of cigarettes a day. What is the anatomical location of this patient's stroke?

(A) Basilar artery
(B) Left anterior cerebral artery
(C) Left middle cerebral artery
(D) Right anterior cerebral artery
(E) Right middle cerebral artery

(C) is correct. Complete middle cerebral artery strokes result in contralateral hemiplegia and hemianesthesia. When the dominant hemisphere is affected, aphasia is also present as well as hemineglect. Choice A is incorrect. Basilar artery stroke results in a variety of brainstem syndromes, depending on the area of ischemia. With complete occlusion, symptoms are **bilateral**. Choice B is incorrect. Anterior cerebral strokes are much less common than strokes involving the middle cerebral artery because of collateral circulation through the anterior communicating artery. When stroke does involve this artery, there is contralateral hemiparesis of the leg/foot with relative sparing of the upper extremity. Speech is slow and lacking in spontaneity (abulia). Choice D is incorrect. When stroke involves the anterior cerebral artery, there is **contralateral** hemiparesis of the leg/foot, with relative sparing of the upper extremity. Speech is slow and lacking in spontaneity (abulia). Choice E is incorrect. Complete middle cerebral artery strokes result in **contralateral** hemiplegia and hemianesthesia.

83. A 26-year-old man presents with a five-hour history of progressive low back pain. He denies history of recent trauma. His pain is unrelieved by rest and minimally relieved with oral anti-inflammatory agents. Physical examination reveals no evidence of scoliosis. Skin overlying the lumbar spine is erythematous and tender. Magnetic resonance imaging of the spine is remarkable for destruction of the L3 vertebral body and disc space. Laboratory studies obtained are presented below:

Erythrocyte sedimentation rate	40 mm/hr
Hematocrit	39%
Hemoglobin	13 g/dL
White blood cell count	14,500/mm^3
Serum	
Alanine aminotransferase	30 units/L
Creatinine	1.1 mg/dL

Which of the following is the most likely diagnosis?

(A) Ankylosing spondylitis
(B) Lumbar arachnoiditis
(C) Metastasis to the spine
(D) Osteoporosis
(E) Vertebral osteomyelitis

(E) is correct. This patient has signs and symptoms of vertebral osteomyelitis. This condition is associated with low back pain that is unrelieved by rest, focal spine tenderness, and an elevated erythrocyte sedimentation rate. The primary source of infection is often the lung, urinary tract, or skin, and destruction of the vertebral bodies and disc space is common. Choice A is incorrect. Ankylosing spondylitis typically occurs in males under the age of 40 with nocturnal back pain unrelieved by rest. Choice B is incorrect. Lumbar arachnoiditis may follow an inflammatory response to local tissue injury in the subarachnoid space. Choice C is incorrect. Back pain is the most common neurologic symptom in patients with systemic cancer. Metastatic carcinoma, multiple myeloma, and lymphoma can involve the spine. Choice D is incorrect. Osteoporosis is loss of bone substance resulting from medical disorders such as hyperparathyroidism and steroid use.

84. A 65-year-old man has a one-year history of ceaseless pacing and a shuffling gait. His wife notes that he has had some noticeable changes in his personality and social skills. He has decreased emotion and desire to partake in his usual activities, although he states that he feels fine. Immediate and recent memory loss have also occurred. During the last 2 months, he has become progressively withdrawn. He has no prior medical or surgical history. He currently takes no medications. He is a non-smoker and nondrinker. Recent laboratory studies are presented below:

Erythrocyte sedimentation rate   12 mm/hr

Serum

    Thyroid-stimulating hormone   3.7 µU/mL

    Thyroxine   8 mg/dL

    Creatinine   1.1 mg/dL

    Iron   185 mg/dL

Which of the following findings are most likely to be noted on an electroencephalogram of this patient?

(A) Diffuse slowing
(B) Global rapid activity
(C) Intermittent rapid and slow activity
(D) Partial slowing
(E) Normal activity

(E) is correct. The electroencephalogram (EEG) helps to rule in or out a diversity of conditions and can differentiate between organic and functional conditions. Patients with degenerative dementia of the Alzheimer type will have a normal EEG more than 50 percent of the time. However, reversible forms of dementia often produce abnormal EEG findings. Choice A is incorrect. Diffuse EEG slowing can be seen in patients with delirium. Choice B is incorrect. Drugs can alter the EEG tracing. For example, sedative-hypnotics increase fast activity. Choice C is incorrect. Intermittent rapid and slow activity on the EEG are not typical of primary degenerative dementia. Choice D is incorrect. Partial slowing of activity on the EEG is not typical of Alzheimer's disease.

85. A 66-year-old man is brought in for evaluation by his wife because she states that her husband is not acting like himself. According to his wife, he is unable to remember important personal information and other facts he knew in the past. However, he denies that he has memory loss. He cannot remember simple things such as what he had for breakfast that day. He is very distractible and is unable to focus his attention to participate in a conversation. He has experienced some misperceptions such as believing that someone is climbing into his bedroom window. These described deficits vary in severity over hours and days. The patient exhibits no evidence of anhedonia or flattening of affect. He states that he sleeps poorly at night and that his symptoms are worse in the dark. He is usually drowsy during the day. The patient and his wife deny any marital problems or recent evidence of psycho-social stress. Recent laboratory studies are shown below:

Erythrocyte sedimentation rate	8 mm/hr

Serum

Thyroid-stimulating hormone	4.0 µU/mL
Thyroxine	8 mg/dL
Creatinine	0.9 mg/dL
Iron	175 mg/dL

Which of the following is the most likely diagnosis?

(A) Delirium
(B) Dementia
(C) Depression
(D) Normal aging
(E) Normal grief reaction

(A) is correct. Delirium is a rapidly developing disorder of disturbed attention that fluctuates with time. Individuals often have clouding of consciousness, attention deficits, perceptual disturbances, and sleep-wake alteration. Disorientation, memory impairment, incoherence, and altered psychomotor activity may also be noted. It is often difficult to distinguish delirium from an acute functional psychosis. Electroencephalograms in this condition often reveal diffuse slowing. Treatment is usually supportive with an active search for the underlying cause of the delirium. Choice B is incorrect. Dementia is a loss of cognitive and intellectual functions sufficiently severe to interfere with social or occupational functioning. The most common cause of dementia is Alzheimer's disease. Choice C is incorrect. Depression in the elderly may coexist with dementia. Many patients with dementia become depressed as they understand the severity of their dementia. However, this patient does not exhibit classic signs of depression. Choice D is incorrect. Normal aging is associated with a decreased ability to learn new material and a slowing of thought processes. Occupational and social functioning are normal in these individuals. Choice E is incorrect. The history in this question gives no indication that the patient has suffered any recent loss of a loved one. His behavior is not typical of a grief reaction.

Items 86–90

    (A) Choreiform movement
    (B) Cog-wheeling rigidity
    (C) Dystonia
    (D) Essential tremor
    (E) Myoclonus
    (F) Pill-rolling tremor
    (G) Tardive dyskinesia

Match each clinical history with the most likely abnormal movement finding.

86. A 45-year-old woman with a family history of early death from mental illness is brought to her primary care physician by her family, who is concerned about her jerking movements and increasingly bizarre behavior, both of which have worsened over the last year. The patient has involuntary jerking movements of her upper extremities and trunk. Mental status exam reveals paranoia.

(A) is correct. Huntington's disease is an autosomal dominant degenerative brain disorder. Hallmarks of the disease are chorea (frequent, sudden jerks of any of the limbs or trunk with a dancing quality) and behavioral disturbance. Onset is usually in the fourth or fifth decade of life.

87. A 32-year-old executive presents to his primary care physician with complaints of a tremor. The tremor is precipitated by stressful situations such as important business meetings. The tremor is very fine and associated with no other neurological deficits.

(D) is correct. Essential tremor can develop at any age, but typically develops in middle or later life. It often involves one or both hands and spares the legs. It generally causes no disability. Treatment is propanolol.

88. A 36-year-old white male with a long history of schizophrenia treated with haloperidol is brought to the emergency room by a friend who noticed strange movement of the patient's face and lips with frequent lip-smacking. Neurologic exam is otherwise normal.

(G) is correct. Tardive dyskinesia is associated with the long-term use of high-potency neuroleptics, such as haloperidol. There is repetitive, involuntary movements of the tongue and lips. Unfortunately, the disorder is often not reversible with discontinuation of the drug.

89. A 32-year-old white female complains to her primary care physician of difficulty sleeping. She is awakened several times a night by an involuntary jerking of her legs, which stops spontaneously. She has tried drinking tonic water before bed without relief.

(E) is correct. Myoclonus is a common movement disorder and is a common cause of insomnia. Symptoms are usually nocturnal and involve the lower extremities. First-line treatment is clonazepam.

90. A 54-year-old white male presents to his primary care doctor with complaints of frequent falls. His wife has noted that he has a new resting tremor. Exam is remarkable for upper extremity rigidity as well as difficulty initiating and ceasing walking.

(B) is correct. Parkinson's disease is a common movement disorder usually presenting during middle age. There is a variable combination of tremor, rigidity, bradykinesia, and difficulty initiating and terminating gait leading to falls. Cog-wheeling rigidity is another classic finding.

    (A) Appendicitis
    (B) Hepatitis
    (C) Hyperemesis gravidarum
    (D) Gastroesophageal reflux
    (E) Inflammatory bowel disease
    (F) Pancreatitis
    (G) Peptic ulcer disease
    (H) Pica
    (I) Ptyalism

For each patient described below, select the most appropriate diagnosis.

91. A 29-year-old woman, gravida 5 para 2, is 20 weeks pregnant. She has a long history of intermittent bloody and watery diarrhea. Her symptoms have remained stable during the current pregnancy. Cardiac examination reveals a regular rate and rhythm. Pulmonary evaluation reveals clear lungs bilaterally without rales or rhonchi. Abdominal examination reveals normoactive bowel sounds with a fundal height 22 cm from the pubis. Anorectal evaluation reveals evidence of a healed left and right lateral anal fissure.

(E) is correct. This patient has symptoms of ulcerative colitis. Typical symptoms include bloody and watery diarrhea. Pregnancy does not exacerbate this disease. Severe disease is associated with an increased risk of spontaneous abortion and premature labor. Treatment consists of a low-residue diet, antidiarrheals, and sulfasalazine.

92. A 24-year-old woman, gravida 2 para 1, is 20 weeks pregnant. She complains of a 10-hour history of anorexia, nausea, vomiting, and right lower quadrant pain. Physical examination reveals a woman in acute distress. Temperature is 38.6 C (101.5 F). Cardiac examination reveals a regular rate and rhythm. Pulmonary auscultation reveals no evidence of rhonchi or rales. Gastrointestinal examination reveals tenderness to soft palpation in the right lower quadrant with localized guarding and rebound tenderness. Rectal examination reveals the presence of external hemorrhoids. Tenderness is noted during bimanual examination of the right lower quadrant. White blood cell count is 16,500 cells/mm³.

(A) is correct. This patient has signs and symptoms of acute appendicitis. The diagnosis is suspected when nausea and vomiting is preceded by anorexia and periumbilical or right lower quadrant pain. The gravid uterus may mask the diagnosis by altering the position of the appendix and inflammatory exudate. Appendectomy with or without antibiotic therapy is necessary.

93. A 29-year-old woman, gravida 4 para 3, is 24 weeks pregnant. She complains of a daily craving for ice, and lately she desires to eat laundry starch. Her symptoms have remained stable during the current pregnancy. Cardiac examination reveals a regular rate and rhythm. Pulmonary evaluation reveals clear lungs bilaterally without rales or rhonchi. Abdominal examination reveals normoactive bowel sounds with a fundal height 24.5 cm from the pubis. Anorectal evaluation reveals evidence of external hemorrhoids.

(H) is correct. This patient has symptoms of pica. Pica is a craving for non-foodstuffs such as laundry starch, ice, dirt, or clay, and is common in pregnancy. Its true incidence is underestimated due to denial. This condition can be quite serious when ingestion of materials interferes with needed food and mineral intake. Poor nutrition can result. Treatment consists of detection, counseling, and encouragement to control pica.

94. A 26-year-old woman, gravida 2 para 1, is 25 weeks pregnant. She complains of annoying, excessive salivation during her pregnancy. She feels as if she produces gallons of saliva each day. Her symptoms have remained stable during the last 2 weeks. Cardiac examination reveals a regular rate and rhythm. Pulmonary evaluation reveals clear lungs bilaterally without rales or rhonchi. Abdominal examination reveals normoactive bowel sounds with a fundal height 24.5 cm from the pubis. Anorectal evaluation reveals no evidence of external hemorrhoids.

(I) is correct. This patient has symptoms of ptyalism. Ptyalism, or excess salivation, can be quite bothersome to patients. Affected individuals can produce up to 1 liter of saliva per day. Treatment strategies include atropine, which produces a small decrease in secretions. Patients should be reassured that this condition will remit as the pregnancy progresses and is not dangerous.

95. A 26-year-old woman, gravida 2 para 2, is 23 weeks pregnant. She complains of a 4-day history of nausea and vomiting 4 to 8 times per day. She is unable to tolerate a diet except for ice chips. She notes a 2.3 kg (5 lb) weight loss during this time period. She appears ill with dry skin and parched oral mucus membranes. Cardiac examination reveals tachycardia and a weak pulse with a regular rate and rhythm. Pulmonary evaluation reveals clear lungs bilaterally without rales or rhonchi. Abdominal examination reveals normoactive bowel sounds with a fundal height 22 cm from the pubis. Palpation of the right and left lower quadrant reveals mild pain without peritoneal signs. Anorectal evaluation reveals no evidence of external hemorrhoids.

(C) is correct. Hyperemesis gravidarum is intractable emesis during pregnancy. It occurs in 4 out of every 1,000 pregnancies and is associated with severe gastrointestinal symptoms, weight loss, dehydration, ketosis, and electrolyte abnormalities. Hospitalization for fluid and electrolyte repletion is required. Diet can be reinstituted slowly and progressively.

Items 96–97

(A) Alprazolam
(B) Amitriptyline
(C) Benztropine
(D) Clonazepam
(E) Diphenhydramine
(F) Fluoxetine
(G) Lithium
(H) Phenelzine
(I) Secobarbital
(J) Trazodone

For the following descriptions of drugs, select the drug listed above that most aptly fits the description.

96. This drug is a specific inhibitor of serotonin reuptake by presynaptic neurons. It takes about 4 weeks to reach steady-state concentrations.

(F) is correct. This selective serotonin reuptake inhibitor (SSRI) is effective in major depression, eating disorders, panic disorder, obsessive compulsive disorder, and borderline personality disorder.

97. This drug is a nonspecific inhibitor of monoamine oxidase. Tyramine-containing foods should be avoided during ingestion and at least 2 weeks following the last dose to avoid a hypertensive crisis.

(H) is correct. This drug is used in depressive disorders. It is equal in efficacy to tricyclic antidepressants and SSRIs. However, it is used less frequently because of dietary precautions.

  (A) Cluster headache
  (B) Dental disease
  (C) Glaucoma
  (D) Hypertensive encephalopathy
  (E) Meningitis
  (F) Migraine
  (G) Postherpetic neuralgia
  (H) Pseudotumor cerebri
  (I) Sinusitis
  (J) Subarachnoid hemorrhage
  (K) Subdural hematoma
  (L) Temporal arteritis
  (M) Tension headache
  (N) Trigeminal neuralgia

For each patient with a headache, select the best diagnosis from the list above.

98. A 30-year-old man with a history of mild hypertension who is currently being treated with enalapril presents with a 2-week history of recurrent headaches. The patient describes the headache as a constant, nonthrobbing pain behind his right eye that generally occurs at night and often awakens him from sleep. The pain usually subsides after about 1 hour. He reports having similar headaches about a year ago, but says they went away without any treatment. On physical exam, the patient's blood pressure is 145/85 mm Hg, pulse is 90/minute, respirations are 16/minute, and temperature is 36.0 C (98.6 F). There is no focal tenderness upon palpation of his head. His lungs are clear to auscultation, heart beat is regular, and there is no organomegaly or palpable abdominal masses.

(A) is correct. This patient presents with the classical signs of a cluster headache. Often unilateral and nonthrobbing in character, cluster headaches usually occur in middle-aged men. They typically occur at night and last from 10 minutes to a few hours. Many patient report night time symptoms that occur daily, but resolve after a period of weeks to months.

99. A 55-year-old woman presents with a 2-week history of a boring pain on the left side of her head, above and just forward of her ear. When the headache began she thought it was just a cold because she had been feeling weak and somewhat feverish. Upon further questioning, the patient also reports that her scalp has been especially sensitive when she brushes her hair and that her jaw gets stiff at the end of meals. Her physical exam is notable for a blood pressure of 130/85 mm Hg, a pulse of 80/minute, respirations of 18/minute, and a temperature of 37.4 C (99.3 F). Her head is tender to palpation in the same distribution as the headache, but otherwise there are no abnormalities noted.

(L) is correct. This woman has the classic symptoms of temporal arteritis. Other associated findings include myalgia, arthralgia, and in 50 percent of untreated cases visual loss. Patients may also have an elevated Westergren erythrocyte sedimentation rate (usually between 29–144 mm/hr). Diagnosis is made by biopsy of affected temporal arteries. Treatment is steroids. In cases where visual loss is present, steroid treatment should be initiated stat.

100. A 23-year-old male presents to the emergency department with a one-day history of headache. He reports that he developed a sore throat over the last couple of days and yesterday began vomiting. This morning, he noticed that his neck was unusually stiff. His physical exam reveals a blood pressure of 135/80 mm Hg, pulse of 110/minute, respiration of 20/minute, and temperature of 40.0 C (104.0 F). He has a generalized petechial rash that, according to the patient, appeared earlier that day. Neck flexion in the supine position elicits involuntary flexion of his hips. Babinski's sign is present bilaterally.

(E) is correct. Meningitis is caused by infectious agents, a granulomatous process, neoplasms, or chemical irritants. It produces a headache that is throbbing in character, bilateral, and occipital or nuchal in location. Patients with bacterial meningitis typically have a constellation of signs and symptoms that include fever, headache, stiff neck, and vomiting. Meningeal signs such as Brudzinski's sign, flexion at the hips upon passive neck flexion, or Kernig's sign, pain upon extension of the leg when the thigh is flexed, are often present. Meningococcal meningitis may also present with a petechial or purpuric rash. Anyone with meningeal signs and a petechial or purpuric rash should be assumed to have meningococcal meningitis until proven otherwise. Choice B is incorrect. Headaches can be associated with temporomandibular joint (TMJ) dysfunction or an infected tooth. In TMJ dysfunction, the patient complains of preauricular facial pain, limited jaw movements, and tenderness of the muscles of mastication. An infected tooth causes a constant unilateral aching pain. Choice C is incorrect. Acute angle glaucoma produces pain around the eye that radiates to the forehead. Choice D is incorrect. Patients with hypertensive encephalapathy describe severe, throbbing pain. These patients will have blood pressures of 250/150 mm Hg or higher and may also demonstrate lethargy, hemiparesis, or focal seizures. Choice F is incorrect. The classic migraine headache is preceded by transient neurological symptoms such as visual changes. This is followed by a throbbing unilateral headache often associated with nausea, vomiting, and photophobia. Migraines can occur without the prodromal aura and can be bilateral. Choice G is incorrect. Postherpetic neuralgia is a sequella of herpes zoster, caused by varicella-zoster virus. The pain of postherpetic neuralgia is typically characterized as severe stabbing or burning. In the head, V_1 nerve is most commonly affected. Thus pain occurs in the distribution of V_1. Choice H is incorrect. Pseudotumor cerebri, also called benign intracranial hypertension, causes a diffuse headache with papilledema and decreased visual acuity. Choice I is incorrect. Sinusitis produces pain and localized tenderness in the frontal or maxillary sinus areas. Choice J is incorrect. Usually the result of a ruptured cerebral arterial aneurysm or an arteriovenous malformation, a subarachnoid hemorrhage is characterized by sudden unset, severe, generalized headache. Loss of consciousness, vomiting, and neck stiffness are common. (K) is incorrect. Subdural hematomas generally result from trauma. Patients may complain of a headache and usually have neurological findings. (M) is incorrect. A tension headache is a chronic headache usually described as a tight band around the head. (N) is incorrect. Thought to be caused by microvascular compression of trigeminal nerve roots, trigeminal neuralgia occurs mainly in middle to late life and produces pain to areas supplied by V_2 and V_3.

Directions (Items 101–150): Each of the numbered items is followed or preceded by a set of options. For each item, select the BEST lettered option to answer the question or complete the statement. Locate the corresponding item number in the appropriate section of your answer sheet and completely fill in the circle containing the lettered option you have selected.

101. A 39-year-old woman has a two-week history of catatonic behavior, delusions, and auditory hallucinations after being fired from her job as an executive of a corporation. She appears to be in emotional turmoil and is confused. Conversations with her are notable for rapid shifts from one intense affect to another. She is emotionally labile with confused and incoherent speech. She appears to be transiently disoriented and cannot remember events from her recent past. Laboratory values are reported below:

White blood cell count	6,500/mm³
Hematocrit	37%
Platelet count	320,000/mm³
Serum	
Sodium	139 mEq/L
Potassium	3.9 mEq/L
Chloride	106 mEq/L
Bicarbonate	28 mEq/L
Urea nitrogen	10 mg/dL
Creatinine	1.0 mg/dL
Thyroid-stimulating hormone	4.0 μU/mL
Thyroxine	9 mg/dL
Triiodothyronine (RIA)	145 ng/dL
Urinalysis	
Hemoglobin	negative
Nitrate	negative
Leukocyte esterase	negative

Which of the following is the most likely diagnosis?

(A) Brief reactive psychosis
(B) Post-traumatic stress disorder
(C) Psychotic disorder not otherwise specified
(D) Schizoaffective disorder
(E) Schizophrenia

(A) is correct. This individual has brief reactive psychosis. This condition is defined by a symptom constellation of less that one month's duration and follows an obvious stress on the patient's life. Patients exhibit an increase in volatility and lability, confusion, disorientation, and affective symptoms. This condition is highly associated with individuals who have a preexisting personality disorder and those who have experienced a major life stressor such as a natural disaster. Choice B is incorrect. Post-traumatic stress disorder occurs following a severe loss or stress such as rape, car accident, or natural disaster and is notable for marked anxiety, personality change, insomnia, and nightmares. Choice C is incorrect. This patient has symptoms that are clearly identifiable with a psychiatric disorder. Choice D is incorrect. Schizoaffective disorder is a vague and poorly defined disorder meant for people with evidence of both schizophrenia and major depression. Choice E is incorrect. Schizophrenia is the most common psychotic disorder, with varying degrees of severity. Affected individuals have an impaired sense of reality and may be confused and disoriented.

102. A 25-year-old primigravid woman who is pregnant by home pregnancy test presents for evaluation. She denies prior medical or surgical history. Doppler ultrasound reveals evidence of fetal heart tones. Abdominal examination reveals normoactive bowel sounds with a nonpalpable fundal height. Urine β-HCG testing in the office is positive. Which of the following nutrients requires the highest percent increase in supplementation during pregnancy?

(A) Calcium
(B) Niacin
(C) Vitamin A
(D) Vitamin D
(E) Vitamin E

(A) is correct. Calcium must be supplemented during pregnancy to meet fetal needs and preserve maternal calcium stores. Milk is the recommended substance to maintain calcium stores, because it is inexpensive and provides 1 gram of calcium and 33 grams of protein per quart. The pregnant patient requires an additional 400 mg of calcium above the 800 mg required by nonpregnant individuals. Choice B is incorrect. Fourteen mg of niacin are required daily by the non-pregnant patient, while 16 mg are required in the pregnant state. Choice C is incorrect. 800 mg of vitamin A are required daily in the nonpregnant state, while 1 gram is required in the pregnant state. Choice D is incorrect. 200 mg of vitamin D are required daily in the non-pregnant state, while 400 mg are required in the pregnant state. Choice E is incorrect. Eight mg of vitamin E are required daily in the nonpregnant state, while 10 mg are required in the pregnant state.

103. A 41-year-old woman with multiple myeloma treated with chemotherapy complains of a three-month history of progressive low back pain. She denies history of recent trauma. Her pain is unrelieved by rest and minimally relieved by oral anti-inflammatory agents. Physical examination of the heart, lungs, and abdomen is unremarkable. Examination of the spine reveals no evidence of scoliosis. Her skin is intact without obvious abnormalities. Laboratory studies obtained are presented below:

Erythrocyte sedimentation rate	20 mm/hr
Hematocrit	38%
Hemoglobin	12 g/dL
White blood cell count	7,500/mm³
Serum	
Alanine aminotransferase	30 U/L
Creatinine	1.0 mg/dL

Magnetic resonance imaging is remarkable for sparing of the disk space. Which of the following is the most likely diagnosis?

(A) Low back strain
(B) Lumbar arachnoiditis
(C) Metastasis to the spine
(D) Spondylolisthesis
(E) Vertebral osteomyelitis

(C) is correct. Back pain is the most common neurologic symptom in patients with systemic cancer. Metastatic carcinoma, multiple myeloma, and lymphoma can involve the spine. Pain is often unrelieved with rest. Magnetic resonance imaging reveals metastasis with sparing of the disc space. Choice A is incorrect. Without a history of trauma, low back strain is not a likely diagnosis. Choice B is incorrect. Lumbar arachnoiditis may follow an inflammatory response to local tissue injury in the subarachnoid space. Choice D is incorrect. Spondylolisthesis is slippage of the anterior spine, leaving the posterior elements behind. Lumbar radiculopathy can result. Choice E is incorrect. Vertebral osteomyelitis is associated with low back pain that is unrelieved by rest, focal spine tenderness, and an elevated erythrocyte sedimentation rate.

104. A 34-year-old man has a one-year history of emotional lability and looseness of associations. He is brought in for evaluation by his wife who has noted a change in his behavior and personality. He is given a self-administered personality test that produces a general description of his personality characteristics. Which of the following is the most likely examination that was administered to this individual?

    (A) Bender-Gestalt test
    (B) Draw-a-person test
    (C) Minnesota multiphasic personality inventory
    (D) Rorschach test
    (E) Thematic apperception test

(C) is correct. The Minnesota multiphasic personality inventory is a self-administered personality test that produces a general description of the patient's personality characteristics. Although this test is useful for a global description of the patient, its uses diagnostically are somewhat limited. Choice A is incorrect. The Bender-Gestalt test involves having the patient draw nine specific geometric figures on a blank sheet of paper to detect visiomotor impairment and organic defects. Choice B is incorrect. The draw-a-person test asks the patient to draw pictures of people of both sexes. Choice D is incorrect. The Rorschach test is an unstructured projective test that asks a patient to describe what he sees in a series of ten standardized ink blots. It can be used diagnostically to help identify psychoses and personality disorders. Choice E is incorrect. The thematic apperception test is a projective test similar to the Rorschach, which draws conclusions from the patient's responses to a series of suggestive and ambiguous drawings.

105. A 28-year-old primigravid woman who is pregnant by home pregnancy test presents for evaluation. She denies prior medical or surgical history. Doppler ultrasound reveals evidence of fetal heart tones. Abdominal examination reveals normoactive bowel sounds with a nonpalpable fundal height. Urine β-HCG testing in the office is positive. Which of the following pelvic types is most favorable for a vaginal delivery of her newborn?

    (A) Android
    (B) Anthropoid
    (C) Gynecoid
    (D) Platypelloid
    (E) Tetroid

(C) is correct. The gynecoid pelvis is the most favorable pelvis for vaginal delivery. This pelvis type is seen in 50 percent of women and is characterized by an oval inlet, straight sidewalls, nonprominent ischial spines, a wide subpubic arch, and a concave sacrum. Choice A is incorrect. The android pelvis is wedge-shaped, with convergent pelvic sidewalls and prominent ischial spines. Choice B is incorrect. The anthropoid pelvis is very common in African American women and is marked by an oval inlet with divergent pelvic sidewalls. Choice D is incorrect. The platypelloid pelvis is rare and characterized by a wide transverse diameter of the inlet. Choice E is incorrect. Tetroid is not a description of the female pelvis.

Items 106–107

A 28-year-old primigravida is 35 weeks pregnant. She tells you that she does not want to become pregnant again upon completion of the present delivery. Her prenatal care has been up-to-date. She has a history of hypertension in pregnancy, but takes no medications. She is currently in labor and has been contracting regularly at 10-minute intervals during the last 3 hours. She complains of sudden onset of suprapubic pain and vaginal discharge. Electronic fetal monitoring reveals the absence of uterine contractions. Her blood pressure is 70/40 mm Hg and her pulse is 140 beats/min. Cardiac examination reveals faint heart tones. Pulmonary examination reveals good breath sounds bilaterally. Abdominal examination reveals tenderness to palpation in the right and left lower quadrants. Bloody vaginal discharge is noted. Ultrasonography reveals extension of fetal extremities and an abnormal fetal position.

106. Which of the following is the most appropriate treatment for this individual?

(A) Embolization of the hypogastric artery
(B) Embolization of the uterine artery
(C) Hysterectomy
(D) Vaginal packing
(E) No further treatment is necessary

(C) is correct. This patient has signs and symptoms of uterine rupture. Rupture may be spontaneous or traumatic. Symptoms include bleeding during labor, suprapubic pain, and cessation of uterine contractions. Hemoperitoneum and hypovolemic shock can result. Treatment involves abdominal exploration and may require hysterectomy. Choice A is incorrect. Embolization of the hypogastric artery is an inappropriate treatment for rupture of the uterus. Choice B is incorrect. Embolization of the uterine artery is an inappropriate treatment for rupture of the uterus. Choice D is incorrect. Vaginal packing is inappropriate for a patient with hypovolemic shock and uterine rupture. Choice E is incorrect. Observation is inappropriate for a patient with hypovolemic shock and uterine rupture.

107. Which of the following strategies might prevent this condition from occurring?

(A) Classical cesarean section
(B) Encourage vaginal delivery
(C) Monitored oxytocin induction and labor stimulation
(D) Ureteral ligation
(E) Uterine artery ligation

(C) is correct. Since rupture of the uterus imposes a 10–40 percent maternal mortality and a 50 percent fetal mortality, this condition should be prevented. Strategies for prevention include careful monitoring of oxytocin induction and stimulation of labor. Choice A is incorrect. Low cervical cesarean sections have a lower risk of uterine rupture than classic procedures. Choice B is incorrect. While encouraging vaginal delivery, this mode should be avoided in situations such as cephalopelvic disproportion. Choice D is incorrect. There is no reason to ligate the ureters in this patient. Choice E is incorrect. Uterine artery ligation may stabilize an uncontrollable hemorrhage, but some bleeding may persist and require further treatment.

108. A 52-year-old black male presents to the emergency department with complaints of fever and chills for the last 24 hours, as well as photophobia for the last 12 hours. He had a renal transplant 5 years ago and his current medications include azathioprine, cyclosporine, and prednisone. His temperature is 38.7 C (103 F), blood pressure is 120/60 mm Hg, and heart rate is 110 beats/min. Exam confirms photophobia and there is prominent meningismus. A lumbar puncture is performed. What is the most appropriate initial treatment?

(A) Amphotericin
(B) Ampicillin
(C) Ampicillin/Gentamicin
(D) Ceftriaxone
(E) Ceftriaxone/Ampicillin
(F) Chloramphenicol

(E) is correct. *Listeria monocytogenes* meningitis is more common in the immunocompromised and may have an acute presentation that requires prompt attention to avoid a fatal outcome. Until the diagnosis is confirmed by culture of an organism, broad-spectrum antibiotics including coverage for *Listeria monocytogenes* (ampicillin) is indicated. Choice A is incorrect. Fungal meningitis is a concern in the immunocompromised, but is rare. Presentation is usually subacute. Choice B is incorrect. Ampicillin alone does not provide adequate coverage for the common causative organisms of meningitis, *Streptococcus pneumoniae* and *Neiserria meningitidis,* which remain the most common causes of meningitis, even in the immunocompromised. Choice C is incorrect. Gram-negative meningitis is rare, even in the immunocompromised. The combination of ampicillin/gentamicin does not provide adequate coverage for the common causative organisms of meningitis, *Streptococcus pneumoniae* and *Neiserria meningitidis,* which remain the most common causes of meningitis, even in the immunocompromised. Choice D is incorrect. Ceftriaxone alone does not provide coverage against *Listeria monocytogenes.* Choice F is incorrect. Prior to the advent of third-generation cephalosporins, chloramphenicol played an important role in the treatment of meningitis. However, third-generation cephalosporins are preferred secondary to their more favorable side effect profile.

109. A 54-year-old white male presents to his primary care physician for a follow-up visit regarding his blood pressure, which has remained persistently elevated over the last 3 months. He suffered an inferior wall myocardial infarction 6 months ago. He takes no medications. His blood pressure is 160/100 mm Hg and heart rate is 88 beats/min. Which of the following is the most appropriate treatment for this patient's hypertension?

(A) Follow-up in the 3 months
(B) Nitroglycerin patch
(C) Oral atenolol
(D) Oral captopril
(E) Oral clonidine
(F) Oral diltiazem

(C) is correct. The chronic use of oral β-blockers following myocardial infarction has been demonstrated to decrease total mortality. β-blockers are indicated for the routine secondary prevention of myocardial infarction and are the most logical choice for a patient with hypertension following myocardial infarction. Choice A is incorrect. This patient has demonstrated persistent hypertension with elevated blood pressure measurements on several occasions are requires treatment. Choice B is incorrect. Nitroglycerin should be reserved for the treatment of angina and myocardial ischemia, not hypertension. Choice D is incorrect. Angiotensin-converting enzyme inhibitors are indicated for patients with depressed cardiac function following myocardial infarction as secondary prevention. There is no mention of this patient's cardiac function. Choice E is incorrect. α-adrenergic blockers like clonidine should be reserved for refractory hypertension secondary to its side effect profile and risk of rebound hypertension when stopped. Choice F is incorrect. Calcium-channel blockers like diltiazem have not been shown to improve mortality following myocardial infarction.

110. A 21-year-old woman presents for evaluation of painful breasts. She complains of bilateral, multiple breast masses that fluctuate in size and discomfort in relation to her menstrual cycle. Her pain is most intense just prior to menses. Physical examination of both breasts reveals no evidence of masses, dimpling, skin retraction, or nipple inversion. Both axillae are without palpable adenopathy. Cardiovascular examination reveals a regular rate and rhythm with no evidence of rubs, murmurs, or gallops. Pulmonary auscultation reveals good breath sounds bilaterally and abdominal examination reveals no evidence of peritoneal signs. Which of the following is the most likely diagnosis?

    (A) Fat necrosis
    (B) Fibrocystic change
    (C) Galactocele
    (D) Infiltrating ductal cell carcinoma
    (E) Macromastia

(B) is correct. Fibrocystic change is associated with breast tenderness and premenstrual swelling. Fluctuation in mass size and discomfort is related to the menstrual cycle. Patients with severe atypia or hyperplasia on biopsy are at risk for breast carcinoma. Treatment is largely symptomatic. Patients should be advised to perform monthly breast self-examinations. Choice A is incorrect. Fat necrosis is associated with ecchymosis, skin retraction, and local tenderness, and may be related to breast trauma. Choice C is incorrect. Galactocele is a cystic dilation of a duct with a thick, inspissated, milky fluid that occurs near the time of lactation. Choice D is incorrect. Typically, scirrhous adenocarcinoma of the breast begins in the upper outer quadrant of the breast. It takes approximately 5 to 8 years for the typical breast cancer to become palpable (greater than 1 cm in size). Choice E is incorrect. Macromastia, usually unilateral, is a disorder of unknown etiology that may develop after pregnancy, and often regresses with antiestrogen therapy.

111. A 70-year-old right-handed white female presents to the emergency department with right-sided hemiplegia and aphasia of sudden onset that began an hour ago. Her husband relates her only medical history to be hypothyroidism. She smokes a pack of cigarettes per day. Exam confirms a left-middle cerebral artery stroke. Which of the following is a modifiable risk factor for stroke?

    (A) Age
    (B) Cigarette smoking
    (C) Family history
    (D) Gender
    (E) Left ventricular hypertrophy
    (F) Race
    (G) Stress avoidance

(B) is correct. The modifiable risk factors for stroke include: hypertension, cigarette smoking, cardiac disease (atrial fibrillation, infective endocarditis, mitral valve stenosis, and recent large myocardial infarction), sickle cell disease, history of transient ischemic attacks, and carotid artery stenosis. Choice A is incorrect. Age is not a modifiable risk factor. The risk of stroke increases exponentially with each decade of age. Choice C is incorrect. There is a genetic tendency toward stroke, or the risk factors for stroke, but family history is not a modifiable, risk factor. Choice D is incorrect. Men have a higher incidence of stroke, but gender is not a modifiable risk factor. Choice E is incorrect. Left ventricular hypertrophy is a risk factor for stroke, perhaps a surrogate marker for long-standing uncontrolled hypertension, but is not reversible or modifiable. Choice F is incorrect. Balcks have a higher incidence of stroke, but race is not a modifiable risk factor. Choice G is incorrect. Stress has not been shown to be a risk factor for stroke.

112. An 80-year-old white female trips in her kitchen and fractures her distal radius. Radiographs demonstrate severe osteopenia. Which of the following is the best first-line treatment for osteoporosis?

    (A) Bisphosphonates
    (B) Calcitonin
    (C) Calcium supplements
    (D) Estrogen replacement therapy
    (E) Weight-bearing exercise

(D) is correct. Each of the answer choices is a potentially useful measure in the treatment of osteoporosis. However, estrogen replacement therapy is the most useful, and, in the absence of contraindications like previous breast cancer, one of the safest and best tolerated. Choice A is incorrect. Oral bisphosphonates are the best alternative for patients with osteoporosis who are unable to take estrogen. Choice B is incorrect. Calcitonin is associated with many side effects, particularly allergic, but has a role for those intolerant of estrogen and bisphosphonates. Choice C is incorrect. Calcium supplements are a necessary adjuvant to any program to combat osteoporosis, but have not been proven effective as a single agent. Choice E is incorrect. Weight-bearing exercise is a useful adjuvant to any program to combat osteoporosis, but is not proven effective at preventing bone loss alone.

113. A 67-year-old white male presents to his primary care physician with complaints of left hip and leg pain. The pain is localized along the left wing of the ischium and in the distal femur. The skin over the affected bones is warm and mildly erythematous. Laboratory studies are as follows:

Serum

Calcium	9.6 mg/dL
Phosphorus	3.6 mg/dL
Alkaline phosphatase	460 U/L

Which of the following is the most likely diagnosis?

    (A) Compression fractures
    (B) Metastatic lesions
    (C) Multiple myeloma
    (D) Osteoarthritis
    (E) Osteosarcoma
    (F) Paget's disease
    (G) Rheumatoid arthritis

(F) is correct. Paget's disease is the second most common primary disease of bone (after osteoporosis). The inciting event is increased osteoclastic activity (reflected by high alkaline phosphatase levels). Eventually, abnormal structurally weak bone replaces the destroyed bone. Choice A is incorrect. Compression fractures are most common in the thoracic spine of patients with osteoporosis, or at the sight of bony metastatic lesions. Choice B is incorrect. Metastatic lesions often cause pain, but not skin warmth and erythema. Usually, there is a history of an underlying malignancy and hypercalcemia. Choice C is incorrect. Multiple myeloma often presents with bony pain, most typically in the ribs and spine. Choice D is incorrect. Osteoarthritis most commonly affects weight-bearing joints (such as the knees) and the small joints of the hands, not the ischium. Choice E is incorrect. Osteosarcoma arises in a small percentage of patients with long-standing Paget's disease. It is a primary bone tumor that usually affects younger persons. Choice G is incorrect. Rheumatoid arthritis is a systemic autoimmune disease with prominent destruction of the metacarpal joints and wrists, as well as the knees.

114. A 25-year-old woman complains of vulvar itching and vaginal discharge for 2 weeks. The discharge has a cottage cheese-like appearance and is without odor. Anorectal examination reveals small, internal hemorrhoids that prolapse with Valsalva's maneuver. Vaginal speculum examination reveals vulvar edema and erythema with white, curd-like concentrations of exudate on saline mount. Which of the following is the most appropriate treatment?

(A) Acyclovir
(B) Erythromycin
(C) Metronidazole
(D) Miconazole
(E) Tetracycline

(D) is correct. Candidiasis is associated with variable amounts of white discharge, a vaginal pH of 4–5, and the presence of mycelia on potassium hydroxide microscopic preparations. Treatment is topical 2 percent miconazole nitrate suppositories for 3 to 7 days. Choice A is incorrect. Acyclovir treats viral infections. Choice B is incorrect. Erythromycin is ineffective in the treatment of candidiasis. Choice C is incorrect. Metronidazole is the treatment of choice for bacterial vaginosis. Choice E is incorrect. Tetracycline is the treatment of choice for *Chlamydia* infections of the vagina.

115. A 54-year-old black male is brought to the emergency department by his family for confusion worsening over the last several weeks. He also has had a cough productive of scant blood-tinged sputum for the last several months, with an 8 kg (20 lb) weight loss. He has a localized right upper lobe wheeze and his deep tendon reflexes are absent. Which of the following in his most likely electrolyte abnormality?

(A) Hypercalcemia
(B) Hyperkalemia
(C) Hypernatremia
(D) Hypocalcemia
(E) Hypokalemia
(F) Hyponatremia

(A) is correct. The combination of weight loss, hemoptysis, and a localized wheeze are very suspicious for lung cancer. The absence of deep tendon reflexes makes hypercalcemia the most likely electrolyte disorder. Some squamous cell carcinomas of the lung secrete a parathyroid-like hormone, which causes hypercalcemia. Choice B is incorrect. Hyperkalemia does not cause hyporeflexia. Choice C is incorrect. Hypernatremia does not cause hyporeflexia. Choice D is incorrect. Hypocalcemia causes hyperreflexia and tetany in extreme cases. Choice E is incorrect. Hypokalemia may provoke cardiac arrhythmias, but does not cause hyporeflexia. Choice F is incorrect. Hyponatremia may cause confusion and seizures in severe cases. Lung tumors, especially small cell carcinoma, may cause the syndrome of inappropriate antidiuretic hormone release, causing profound hyponatremia.

116. A 28-year-old white female presents to her primary care physician with complaints of palpitations for the last several months. The palpitations occur several times a week. She is never dizzy, diaphoretic, or nauseous during these episodes. She has never lost consciousness. She has a prominent mid-systolic click, but no audible heart murmur. Which of the following is the most appropriate initial step in this patient's care?

(A) 24-hour Holter monitoring
(B) Cardiac catheterization
(C) Cardiology referral
(D) Cardiothoracic surgery referral
(E) Echocardiogram
(F) Loop event recorder monitoring
(G) Reassurance that her condition is benign

(E) is correct. This patient has a history and physical exam findings consistent with mitral valve prolapse. Palpitations are a common presentation. The lesion is benign, but may require dental and surgical prophylaxis if there is accompanying mitral valve regurgitation. Therefore, an echocardiogram is needed to evaluate her valvular lesion. Choice A is incorrect. The patient's palpitations are in all likelihood a symptom of her mitral valve prolapse, not an underlying arrhythmia. Therefore, further search for a cause of her palpitations is not warranted. Choice B is incorrect. There is no indication for cardiac catheterization. Catheterization is indicated prior to some valvular replacement operations. Choice C is incorrect. Management of mitral valve prolapse does not usually require a subspecialist. Choice D is incorrect. Unless there is symptomatic mitral regurgitation with mitral valve prolapse, a rare finding, there is no indication for cardiothoracic surgery referral. Choice F is incorrect. The patient's palpitations are in all likelihood a symptom of her mitral valve prolapse, not an underlying arrhythmia. Therefore, further search for a cause of her palpitations is not warranted. Choice G is incorrect. The patient's condition is likely benign, but may require dental prophylaxis. Therefore, echocardiography is indicated prior to simple reassurance.

117. A 28-year-old man who is on a camping trip and sleeping outdoors awakens suddenly, complaining of abdominal pain. He thinks he was bitten by a spider with a red hourglass mark on the abdomen. During the next 24 hours, he complains of generalized muscle pain, nausea, vomiting, and headache. He is brought to the emergency department for evaluation. Physical examination reveals an area of erythema and edema on the left lateral thigh. Which of the following is the most appropriate treatment for this individual?

(A) Antibiotics
(B) Glucocorticoids
(C) Muscle relaxants
(D) Plasmapheresis
(E) Systemic antivenin

(C) is correct. The black widow spider is the most common biting spider in the United States. The venom is neurotoxic and centers around the spinal cord. Symptoms include muscular pain, nausea, vomiting, and headache. Treatment consists of narcotics for pain relief and a muscle relaxant. Antivenin therapy is rarely required. Choice A is incorrect. While antibiotics are part of the treatment plan, they are secondary to pain control and relief of muscle spasm. Choice B is incorrect. Glucocorticoids are not required in the treatment of black widow spider bites. Choice D is incorrect. Plasmapheresis is not required in the treatment of black widow spider bites. Choice E is incorrect. Although an antivenin is available, it is rarely required for the treatment of black widow spider bites.

118. A 34-year-old white male with a 15-year history of Crohn's disease complains to his primary care physician about back pain and stiffness. He has morning stiffness and dull pain in his back that improves dramatically with exercise. The pain does not radiate and has never awoken him from sleep. Which of the following is most appropriate first step in diagnosing this patient?

(A) Computed tomography of the lumbar spine
(B) Computed tomography of the sacroiliac joints
(C) Magnetic resonance imaging of the lumbar spine
(D) Magnetic resonance imaging of the sacroiliac joints
(E) Nuclear medicine bone scan (total body)
(F) Plain roentgenographs of the lumbar spine
(G) Plain roentgenographs of the sacroiliac joints

(G) is correct. Spondylitis occurs in up to 25 percent of patients with inflammatory bowel disease. Patients typically complain of pain in the back or buttocks in the morning that is relieved with exercise. Treatment is centered around control of the underlying bowel disease. The best first step in evaluation is plain radiographs of the sacroiliac joints, which show the typical findings of ankylosing spondylitis and bilateral sacroiliitis. Choice A is incorrect. The patient's symptoms are typical for sacroiliitis, not low back pathology. A study of his lumbar spine would likely be unfruitful. Choice B is incorrect. Plain radiographs generally demonstrate the changes of sacroiliitis without the need for more expensive computed tomography. Choice C is incorrect. The patient's symptoms are typical for sacroiliitis, not low back pathology. A study of his lumbar spine would likely be unfruitful. Choice D is incorrect. Magnetic resonance imaging is not necessary, as far less expensive plain radiographs usually demonstrate the sacroiliitis. Choice E is incorrect. A nuclear medicine bone scan is abnormal in up to 50 percent of patients with inflammatory bowel disease, with increased uptake in the sacroiliac joints, many of them asymptomatic. This makes bone scan an inappropriate first test. Choice F is incorrect. The patient's symptoms are typical for sacroiliitis, not low back pathology. A study of his lumbar spine would likely be unfruitful.

119. A 35-year-old marathon runner is concerned about his cholesterol, which he recently had checked at a community health fair. He maintains a near-vegetarian diet and runs at least 5 miles a day. He does not smoke cigarettes. His lipid profile is as follows:

Total cholesterol	160 mg/dL
LDL cholesterol	90 mg/dL
HDL cholesterol	15 mg/dL

Which of the following is most likely to improve the patient's lipid profile?

(A) Increased exercise
(B) Intramuscular vitamin B_{12}
(C) One alcoholic beverage daily
(D) Oral cholestyramine
(E) Oral probucol
(F) Oral simvastatin

(C) is correct. Low levels of HDL cholesterol are an independent risk factor for the development of coronary artery disease. Increasing HDL levels in postmenopausal women is best done by introducing estrogen replacement therapy. In men, exercise (to which this patient is already committed) and moderate (a glass a day) consumption of alcohol has been demonstrated to boost levels of HDL. Choice A is incorrect. It is unlikely that any additional benefit in HDL levels would be gained from additional exercise. Choice B is incorrect. There is no role for the use of vitamin B_{12} in the treatment of cholesterol abnormalities. Choice D is incorrect. Cholestyramine, though difficult to take, has been shown to lower LDL cholesterol, but not raise HDL levels. Choice E is incorrect. Probuchol has been shown to lower LDL cholesterol, but also lowers HDL levels. Choice F is incorrect. Simvastatin, an HMG Co-A reductase inhibitor, reduces levels of LDL cholesterol, but does not raise HDL levels.

120. A 27-year-old white female presents to her primary care physician complaining of a right facial droop for the last two days. Her husband noticed an uneven smile yesterday, and now the patient is concerned about a droop of her right eyelid. Exam confirms a bilateral facial droop with loss of the right nasolabial fold and right ptosis and paralysis of the right orbicularis oculi muscle. Sensation is intact and cranial nerve examination is otherwise normal. Which of the following is the most likely diagnosis?

(A) Acoustic neuroma
(B) Bell's palsy
(C) Brainstem tumor
(D) Carotid body tumor
(E) Cholesteatoma
(F) Herpes zoster
(G) Trigeminal neuralgia

(B) is correct. Bell's palsy is the most common cause of facial nerve paralysis. Onset is abrupt with maximal deficits at 48 hours after onset. Treatment is corticosteriods. It is important to distinguish central from peripheral facial nerve palsy. Because of bilateral cortical innervation of the upper facial muscles, central lesions often spare the muscles of the upper face (frontalis and orbicularis oculi), while peripheral lesions result in complete unilateral facial paralysis. Choice A is incorrect. Acoustic neuromas are slow-growing tumors most frequently affecting the eighth cranial nerve. When the seventh cranial nerve is affected, the onset is insidious, not acute. Choice C is incorrect. A brainstem tumor would result in a "central seven," with sparing of the upper facial muscles. Choice D is incorrect. Carotid body tumors may cause a facial nerve palsy, but of insidious onset. Choice E is incorrect. Cholesteatomas may cause a facial nerve palsy, but of insidious onset. Choice F is incorrect. Herpes zoster may invade the geniculate ganglion and cause a facial nerve palsy. However, in such cases, a vesicular eruption is prominent. Choice G is incorrect. Trigeminal neuralgia (or tic douloureux) is a pain disorder characterized by paroxysms of excruciating facial pain, especially of the lips, gums, and cheeks.

121. A 45-year-old woman presents to the emergency department with complaints of excruciating right upper quadrant pain. She has suffered similar episodes in the past, but with less intense pain. The sharp pain occurs 30 minutes after a meal and lasts up to an hour. It is unrelieved with antacids. Exam confirms right upper quadrant tenderness without rebound or guarding. Which of the following is the most appropriate next step?

(A) Computed tomography of the abdomen
(B) Endoscopic retrograde cholangiopancreatography
(C) Exploratory laparotomy
(D) Magnetic resonance imaging of the abdomen
(E) Nuclear medicine biliary scan
(F) Ultrasound of the abdomen

(F) is correct. This woman is presenting with classic symptoms of biliary colic. Ultrasound is the imaging modality of choice in the initial evaluation of suspected biliary pathology. It is relatively inexpensive and noninvasive. Choice A is incorrect. Computed tomography is not an appropriate modality for the initial investigation of suspected biliary pathology. Choice B is incorrect. Endoscopic retrograde cholangiopancreatography is a diagnostic and possibly therapeutic modality for investigating suspected common bile duct stones (which can be removed with sphincterotomy) as well as other bile duct and pancreatic pathology. It is not an appropriate initial step in patients with suspected biliary pathology. Choice C is incorrect. Exploratory laparotomy is not warranted in this stable patient. Choice D is incorrect. Magnetic resonance imaging is not an appropriate modality for the initial investigation of suspected biliary pathology. Choice E is incorrect. Nuclear medicine biliary scans are helpful in confirming biliary pathology or for further investigation after a nondiagnostic ultrasound, especially in the patient with suspected acute cholecystitis. But, ultrasound is the best first step.

122. A 34-year-old woman presents to her primary care physician with complaints of headaches and spots before her eyes. The spots are in her peripheral vision and resemble small bolts of lightening. The spots may proceed or accompany a headache. Neurologic examination is normal. Which of the following is the most likely explanation for these findings?

(A) Angle closure glaucoma
(B) Cluster headache
(C) Migraine headache
(D) Multiple sclerosis
(E) Tension headache
(F) Transient ischemic attacks

(C) is correct. This patient has migraine headaches with scintillating scotomas, a common finding in patients with migraine. Choice A is incorrect. Angle closure glaucoma causes severe eye pain, nausea and vomiting, and loss of visual acuity; not scotoma. Conjunctival injection and corneal edema are common signs. Choice B is incorrect. Cluster headaches are severe unilateral headaches often associated with tearing of the eye, but not scotoma. Choice D is incorrect. The diagnosis of multiple sclerosis requires neurologic deficits separated by space and time. Persons with multiple sclerosis may have central scotomas as a result of optic nerve involvement. Scotomas are not generally associated with headache. Choice E is incorrect. Tension headaches commonly begin the back of the head and spread in a band-like manner to the frontal area. Tension headaches are not associated with visual phenomena. Choice F is incorrect. Transient ischemic attacks are associated with amaurosis fugax (a closing of a blind visual change) secondary to transient retinal ischemia with embolism of the retinal artery.

123. A 3-year-old girl is brought to the emergency department by police after neighbors heard a child crying in the apartment next door. The child was found sitting in the bathtub in excessively hot water. There was an electrical outlet within hands' reach of the bathtub. Her parents were not home at the time. Physical examination reveals erythema and edema of the anterior and posterior trunk with intact skin. There is no evidence of necrosis. Which of the following is the most likely diagnosis?

(A) Cigarette burn
(B) Electrical injury
(C) Epidermal necrolysis
(D) Scalding
(E) Stevens-Johnson syndrome

(D) is correct. Over 80 percent of burns to children under the age of 5 are scald burns. Scalding occurs when inadequately supervised children are put in bathtubs in which the water is excessively hot, and from which they cannot remove themselves. Child abuse may present as a thermal injury. Choice A is incorrect. Cigarette burn produces punctate areas of erythema, edema, and skin necrosis. Choice B is incorrect. Electrical injury is not likely in this individual. Choice C is incorrect. This child does not have evidence of skin loss. Therefore, epidermal necrolysis is not likely. Choice E is incorrect. Acute massive skin loss is not noted in this child. Therefore, Stevens-Johnson syndrome is unlikely.

124. A 45-year-old black male with diabetes mellitus presents to the emergency department with complaints of nausea and vomiting as well as right eye pain and headache for the last 12 hours. All symptoms were of acute onset. Exam reveals a profoundly injected right eye with severe photophobia and tearing. Laboratory studies are as follows:

Serum

Sodium	145 mEq/dL
Potassium	4.0 mEq/dL
Chloride	110 mEq/dL
Bicarbonate	25 mEq/dL
Creatinine	1.0 mg/dL
BUN	20 mg/dL
Glucose	240 mg/dL

Which of the following is the most appropriate initial step?

(A) Computed tomography of the head
(B) Endocrinology consultation
(C) Follow-up with primary care physician
(D) Intravenous hydration
(E) Intravenous insulin drip
(F) Ophthalmologic consultation

(F) is correct. Angleclosure glaucoma occurs when the iris blocks the drainage of aqueous humor from the anterior chamber of the eye. The result is an acute rise in intraocular pressure with severe eye pain, nausea and vomiting, and loss of visual acuity. Conjunctival injection and corneal edema are common signs. Treatment is urgent reduction in intraocular pressure first with hyperosmotic agents, then surgical iridectomy by an opthalmologist. Choice A is incorrect. The patient has no symptoms that cannot be easily accounted for by a acute angle closure glaucoma. Choice B is incorrect. The patient's moderately elevated blood glucose is likely a stress reaction to his glaucoma. Treatment is straightforward, insulin and control of the underlying eye disease, and does not require endocrinology input. Choice C is incorrect. This patient has presented with angle closure glaucoma, a vision-threatening ocular emergency, and needs the immediate services of an ophthalmologist. Choice D is incorrect. The best treatment for his moderately elevated blood glucose is insulin. Should the patient be unable to eat or drink, intravenous fluids should be instituted. Choice E is incorrect. The patient's moderately elevated blood glucose without an acidosis (normal bicarbonate) does not require an insulin drip. Subcutaneous therapy will suffice.

125. A 44-year-old white male presents to his primary care physician for a follow-up visit about his diabetes mellitus. He has had difficulty with management of his diabetes in the past, but following the recent death of his brother due to a heart attack, he has "turned over a new leaf." He brings in his glucose log with all values falling between 110 mg/dL and 175 mg/dL. His current medical regimen includes metformin and glipizide. His laboratory studies are as follows:

Hemoglobin A_{1C}	14%

Serum

Fasting blood glucose	320 mg/dL
Triglycerides	500 mg/dL

Which of the following is the most appropriate next step?

(A) Accuse the patient of forging his glucose log results
(B) Add insulin to the patient's medical regimen
(C) Add triglitazone the patient's medical regimen
(D) Commend the patient for his excellent glucose control
(E) Confront the patient regarding his diet and exercise regimen
(F) Increase the patient's dose of metformin

(E) is correct. The patient's glucose log and his laboratory studies are clearly contrary. The appropriate course of action is a nonaccusatory discussion with the patient about his disease and overall disease management. Choice A is incorrect. Finger-pointing and accusations only act to distance the patient, making any meaningful discussion of his diabetes impossible. Choice B is incorrect. The patient is failing oral therapy. Prior to the institution of new medication, there are important issues to discuss, i.e., the disparity between several pieces of lab data and the patient's own log. Choice C is incorrect. The patient is failing his current oral therapy. Prior to the institution of new medication, there are important issues to discuss, i.e., the disparity between several pieces of lab data and the patient's own log. Choice D is incorrect. The patient's self-reported glucose values do reflect excellent control. However, these values are contradictory to several pieces of lab data. Choice F is incorrect. The patient is failing oral therapy. Prior to the institution of new medication, there are important issues to discuss, i.e., the disparity between several pieces of lab data and the patient's own log.

126. A 62-year-old woman with a history of perineal condyloma infections, chronic hemorrhoids, and proctitis presents with anorectal bleeding and pain. She has a prior medical history of perineal fistulas that were treated with surgical excision 3 and 5 years ago. Physical examination reveals a 2.5 cm cauliflower-like mass approximately 4 cm from the anal verge. Which of the following is the most appropriate treatment for this individual?

   (A) Chemotherapy
   (B) Radiotherapy
   (C) Radiotherapy and chemotherapy
   (D) Subtotal proctocolectomy
   (E) Surgical resection of the polyp

(C) is correct. This patient has signs and symptoms of anal carcinoma. This condition is associated with chronic rectal irritation from hemorrhoids, perineal fistulae, leukoplakia, and trauma from anal intercourse. Women are more commonly affected then men, and typical presenting features include bleeding, pain, and perineal mass. Radiotherapy and chemotherapy together lead to a complete response in 80 percent of patients when the lesion is less than 3 cm. Choice A is incorrect. Chemotherapy alone is less effective than combination therapy for anal carcinoma. Choice B is incorrect. Radiotherapy alone is less effective than combination therapy for anal carcinoma. Choice D is incorrect. Subtotal proctocolectomy may be indicated for patients with large or recurrent lesions. Choice E is incorrect. Surgical resection of the polyp is less effective than combination therapy for anal carcinoma.

127. A 63-year-old man who has a 60-pack year history of smoking complains of gross hematuria. Physical examination of the heart, lungs, and abdomen is within normal limits. The prostate is approximately 40 grams and is symmetric. Intravenous pyelography reveals normal kidneys and ureters bilaterally. A small filling defect is noted within the floor of the urinary bladder. Cystoscopy is performed and reveals a sessile, papillary growth that is approximately 2 cm by 4 cm, proximal to the left ureteral orifice. Biopsies of the lesion are taken and are most likely to reveal

   (A) adenocarcinoma
   (B) carcinoid tumor
   (C) sarcoma
   (D) squamous cell carcinoma
   (E) transitional cell carcinoma

(E) is correct. The incidence of bladder cancer in the United States is approximately 60,000 cases per year with a median age of 65 years. Smoking accounts for 50 percent of the risk. More than 90 percent of tumors are derived from transitional epithelium. Hematuria is the initial sign in approximately 90 percent of patients. Superficial tumors can be removed at cystoscopy. Choice A is incorrect. Adenocarcinoma represents 2 percent of all bladder carcinomas. Choice B is incorrect. Carcinoid tumors represent less than 1 percent of all bladder carcinomas. Choice C is incorrect. Sarcoma represents less than 1 percent of all bladder carcinomas. Choice D is incorrect. Squamous cell carcinoma represents approximately 3 percent of all bladder cancers.

128. A 38-year old woman complains of intermittent chest pain while at rest for the past 3 years. She has a medical history of hyperthyroidism. Her current medications include synthetic thyroid supplements. Physical examination reveals a late systolic click with systolic ejection murmur. Echocardiogram reveals posterior displacement of the mitral leaflet late in systole. Which of the following is the most appropriate treatment for this individual?

(A) Calcium-channel blockers
(B) β-blockers
(C) Digoxin
(D) Furosemide
(E) Reassurance

(E) is correct. This patient has symptoms of mitral valve prolapse. This condition occurs because redundant mitral valve tissue is present, along with elongated chordae tendineae cordis. Asymptomatic patients should be reassured, but if systolic ejection murmur occurs, prophylaxis for endocarditis should be instituted. Choice A is incorrect. Calcium-channel blockers are not indicated in the treatment of mitral valve prolapse. Choice B is incorrect. β-blockers are not indicated in the treatment of mitral valve prolapse. Choice C is incorrect. Digoxin is indicated in conditions associated with left ventricular failure such as aortic regurgitation. Choice D is incorrect. Furosemide may be helpful in patients with severe cardiac symptoms to reduce preload.

129. A 14-year-old boy complains of progressive right leg pain that is typically severe at night and is relieved with aspirin. He is otherwise healthy with no other medical problems. Physical examination reveals no evidence of erythema or edema overlying the right femur. Right lower extremity x-ray reveals a sharply demarcated radiolucent nidus of osteoid tissue surrounded by sclerotic femoral bone. The most likely diagnosis is

(A) aneurysmal bone cyst
(B) chordoma
(C) histiocytic lymphoma
(D) osteoid osteoma
(E) unicameral bone cyst

(D) is correct. Osteoid osteoma affects children and adolescents age 10–20 years and has a male predominance. It usually arises in the femur and tibia. The cardinal feature is pain, which is more severe at night. Signs of inflammation are unusual. X-ray reveals a sharply demarcated radiolucent nidus of osteoid tissue surrounded by sclerotic bone. Choice A is incorrect. Aneurysmal bone cyst is a vascular lesion in the metaphyses of young children and may respond to radiation therapy. Magnetic resonance imaging may reveal blood-filled cystic spaces in affected areas. Treatment can also involve curettage or resection, except when the lesion is inaccessible. Choice B is incorrect. Chordoma is a tumor of notochord origin that is slow-growing and occurs in middle-aged adults. Choice C is incorrect. Histiocytic lymphoma occurs in the diaphyses of long bones in patients over the age of 20. Choice E is incorrect. Unicameral bone cyst is an expansile, benign bone lesion of childhood. Usually affecting the femur or humerus, this fluid-filled cavity can be associated with pathologic fractures. The lesion often resolves spontaneously after bone maturity.

130. A 37-year-old white female presents to her primary care physician with complaints of numbness in her left hand and arm and weakness in her right leg. Her symptoms began several days ago. She also recalls an episode of blurry vision in the past that persisted for several days, but resolved completely. Her exam is remarkable for diminished sensation to pinprick and light touch in her left arm (C6 nerve root distribution) and decreased motor strength in her right quadriceps. Which of the following is the most appropriate initial step in the evaluation of this patient?

(A) Cerebral angiogram
(B) Computed tomography of the brain
(C) Electroencephalogram
(D) Magnetic resonance imaging of the brain
(E) Nerve conduction studies

(D) is correct. This young female patient presents with neurologic deficits separated by time and space. The suspicion of multiple sclerosis should be very high. The best initial evaluation of a such a patient is magnetic resonance imaging, which demonstrates white matter plaques of demyelination. Choice A is incorrect. Angiography is a procedure with significant risks and should be reserved for those with clear indications such as suspected aneurysms, not the evaluation of suspected multiple sclerosis. Choice B is incorrect. Although less expensive and better tolerated than magnetic resonance imaging, the white matter plaques of multiple sclerosis are not easily visualized by computed tomography. Choice C is incorrect. There is no suspicion of a seizure disorder to warrant electroencephalography as a first step. Choice E is incorrect. Nerve conduction tests are useful in the investigations of peripheral neuropathy. However, the patient's symptoms point to a more diffuse disease like multiple sclerosis, not an isolated arm or leg lesion.

131. A 45-year-old white male presents to his primary care physician with complaints of increasing abdominal girth over the last several months. He has consumed at least a six-pack of beer a day for the last 25 years, and more than that on the weekends. Exam reveals a distended abdomen with shifting dullness and a fluid wave, as well as gynecomastia and testicular atrophy. Which of the following is the most appropriate first step?

(A) Computed tomography of the abdomen
(B) Gastroenterology consultation
(C) Exploratory laparotomy
(D) Magnetic resonance imaging of the abdomen
(E) Paracentesis
(F) Ultrasound of the abdomen

(E) is correct. Paracentesis with laboratory evaluation of the ascitic fluid is the first step in the evaluation of new ascites in a patient with accessible fluid. Study of the fluid will allow for the determination of exudate or transudate and generation of a differential diagnosis to guide further testing. Choice A is incorrect. Computed tomography of the abdomen has a role in the evaluation of new ascites after paracentesis in patients with accessible fluid. Computed tomography is very useful in visualizing mass lesions as well as many liver diseases. Choice B is incorrect. Initial evaluation of the patient with ascites does not require gastroenterology consultation. Choice C is incorrect. The initial investigation of new ascites does not involve laparotomy. Choice D is incorrect. The initial investigation of new ascites, after paracentesis, may involve computed tomography, but not the more expensive magnetic resonance imaging. Choice F is incorrect. Ultrasound is an excellent tool for initial investigation of biliary pathology, but is not the initial step in the evaluation of new ascites.

132. A 30-year-old man complains of a lump on the dorsal side of his wrist that extends into the joint. He has no prior surgical or medical history. Physical examination reveals a cystic lesion on the dorsal side of the wrist that extends into the joint space. Range of motion in flexion, extension, internal, and external rotation appear to be uninhibited. The lesion is 1 cm in diameter and is well circumscribed. There is no evidence of edema or fluctuance. The most appropriate treatment is which of the following?

(A) Chemotherapy
(B) Corticosteroids
(C) Radiotherapy
(D) Splinting
(E) Surgical excision

(E) is correct. This patient has a ganglion tumor. These tumors occur in four locations on the hand. One typical location is on the dorsal side of the wrist extending into the joint. The treatment of choice is surgical excision to include the entire cyst and its origin. Choice A is incorrect. Chemotherapy is an ineffective treatment for ganglion tumor. Choice B is incorrect. Corticosteroids are an ineffective treatment for ganglion tumor. Choice C is incorrect. Radiotherapy is an ineffective treatment for ganglion tumor. Choice D is incorrect. Splinting might relieve the pain associated with ganglion tumor because of immobilization, but surgical excision is the treatment of choice.

133. A new serologic test for antibody to the HIV virus is developed and compared with the standard immunoassay diagnostic test. The following data are obtained:

Immunoassay Testing

New test	Antibody	No antibody
Positive	80	40
Negative	20	960

The sensitivity of the new test is

(A) 10%
(B) 20%
(C) 67%
(D) 80%
(E) 96%

(D) is correct. Sensitivity is defined as positivity in disease diagnosis and can be determined from a collection of data by the following ratio: Sensitivity = the number of true positives/the number of true positives + false negatives. For the present example, sensitivity = 80/80 + 20 = 80%. Thus, sensitivity measures the true positive rate. Specificity, on the other hand, measures the true negative rate.

134. A 33-year-old man presents to the emergency department complaining of nausea and vomiting for 1 week. He admits to numerous abdominal surgeries. He states that his symptoms are the result of major life stresses, although he-will not elaborate on the specific details. Physical examination is within normal limits except for the abdominal portion, which is significant for mild tenderness to deep palpation in the left lower quadrant. There are also numerous scars. Bowel sounds are normoactive. The patient is admitted to the hospital for intravenous hydration and observation. While in the inpatient ward, a nurse observes the patient sticking himself with a needle and smearing the blood into his rectum. Later that day, a second nurse observes a similar incident. Which of the following is the most likely diagnosis?

(A) Body dysmorphic disorder
(B) Factitious disorder
(C) Hypochondriasis
(D) Malingering
(E) Somatoform pain disorder

(B) is correct. This individual has symptoms of factitious disorder. The symptoms are deliberately and consciously produced by the patient. Typical symptoms include nausea and vomiting, and patients may intentionally put blood into feces or artifically raise their temperatures to produce a physical illness. Patients may describe their complaints as follows: "my abdomen feels like a railroad yard," and "my heart feels like a race car." Physical examination may reveal multiple scars from prior surgical procedures. Treatment involves confrontation of the patient. Psychotherapy is rarely effective. In contrast, the malingerer should be handled formally (and often legally). Choice A is incorrect. Body dysmorphic disorder is a disorder of young adults in which patients become preoccupied with an imagined physical defect that they feel negatively affects their appearance. Treatment is often successful with antidepressants. Choice C is incorrect. Hypochondriasis involves an individual who is hyperalert to symptoms and presents them in great detail during the history. Many patients display anxiety or depression. Treatment is unpromising. Choice D is incorrect. The malingerer knowingly fakes symptoms for some obvious gain, such as getting drugs, avoiding the law, etc. Individuals are often evasive and uncooperative during the examination and therapy, and they tend to avoid medical procedures and sign out of the hospital against medical advice. Antisocial personality disorder and drug abuse are common associated conditions. The malingerer should be handled formally (and often legally). Choice E is incorrect. Somatoform pain disorder often occurs in women who experience pain for which no cause can be found. Often exacerbated by stress, this condition can disappear quickly or persist for years. This condition is felt to be similar to a conversion disorder.

135. A 42-year-old man presents to the emergency room complaining of nausea and vomiting for 1 week. He denies prior medical or surgical history. He has a history of drug abuse. Review of his medical records indicates numerous visits to the hospital during the past year for such complaints as severe headaches, bleeding from the rectum, chest pain, and tinnitus. During the last two documented emergency visits, you note that the patient had signed out of the hospital, refusing medical work-up, including computed tomography of the head and rigid sigmoidoscopy. He states that his symptoms are the result of major life stresses, although he will not elaborate on the specific details. An abbreviated physical examination is undertaken as the patient is extremely uncooperative. Cardiac examination reveals a regular rate and rhythm. Pulmonary auscultation reveals no evidence of rhonchi or wheezing. Gastrointestinal examination reveals mild tenderness to deep palpation in the left lower quadrant. Bowel sounds are normoactive. The patient is then given antiemetics and oral analgesics. You return in one hour and find that the patient has signed out of the hospital. Which of the following is the most likely diagnosis?

(A) Body dysmorphic disorder
(B) Factitious disorder
(C) Hypochondriasis
(D) Malingering
(E) Psychosomatic disorder

(D) is correct. The malingerer knowingly fakes symptoms for some obvious gain such as getting drugs, avoiding the law, etc. Individuals are often evasive and uncooperative during the examination and therapy, and they tend to avoid medical procedures and sign out of the hospital against medical advice. Antisocial personality disorder and drug abuse are common associated conditions. The malingerer should be handled formally (and often legally). Choice A is incorrect. Body dysmorphic disorder is a disorder of young adults in which patients become preoccupied with an imagined physical defect that they feel negatively affects their appearance. Treatment is often successful with antidepressants. Choice B is incorrect. In factitious disorder, the symptoms are deliberately and consciously produced by the patient. Typical symptoms include nausea and vomiting, and patients may intentionally put blood into feces or artifically raise their temperature to produce a physical illness. Patients may describe their complaints as follows: "my abdomen feels like a railroad yard," and "my heart feels like a race car." Physical examination may reveal multiple scars from prior surgical procedures. Treatment involves confrontation of the patient that they are factitious. Psychotherapy is rarely effective. Choice C is incorrect. Hypochondriasis involves an individual who is hyperalert to symptoms and presents them in great detail during the history. Many patients display anxiety or depression. Treatment is unpromising. Choice E is incorrect. A psychosomatic disorder is a physical disease partially caused or exacerbated by psychological factors.

Items 136–138

    (A) Acute postinfectious
        glomerulonephritis
    (B) Crescentic glomerulonephritis
    (C) Focal and segmental glomerulonephritis
    (D) Membranoproliferative
        glomerulonephritis
    (E) Membranous nephropathy
    (F) Mesangial proliferative
        glomerulonephritis
    (G) Minimal change disease

Match each renal disease with the most likely clinical scenario.

136. A 42-year-old white female with a long history of rheumatoid arthritis who receives gold injections weekly to control her joint inflammation is found to have new renal insufficiency on routine laboratory studies. Urinalysis is positive for 3+/4 proteinuria, but there are no other abnormalities.

(E) is correct. The use of gold is a well-recognized cause of membranous nephropathy as is penicillamine, hepatitis, and malignancy. Urine sediment is bland, but there is often significant proteinuria, even in the nephrotic range.

137. A 32-year-old white male with AIDS presents to his primary care doctor after he found his blood pressure to be 170/95 mm Hg at the grocery store. Blood pressure in the office is 179/100 mm Hg. Exam reveals new periorbital edema. Urinalysis is positive for 4+/4 proteinuria, but there are no other abnormalities.

(C) is correct. AIDS and heroin use are both associated with the development of focal and segmental glomerulonephritis. Nephrotic range proteinuria is common and sediment is bland.

138. A 40-year-old white male presents to his primary care physician with complaints of hemoptysis. A chest roentgenograph demonstrates nonspecific infiltrates. Renal insufficiency is noted on laboratory studies. Antibasement membrane antibodies are positive. Urinalysis is positive for 3+/4 protein and 3+/4 blood. Sediment demonstrates red blood cell casts.

(B) is correct. Goodpasture's syndrome, in which antibodies are generated against the glomerular basement membrane, often presents with hemoptysis. The renal lesion is a crescentic glomerulonephritis with hematuria and red blood cell casts, which behaves clinically as a rapidly progressive glomerulonephritis.

    (A) Amoxicillin
    (B) Aztreonam
    (C) Ceftriaxone
    (D) Clindamycin
    (E) Doxycycline
    (F) Erythromycin
    (G) Penicillin
    (H) Piperacillin
    (I) Trimethoprim-sulfamethoxazole

For each of the patients described below, select the most appropriate antibiotic for the etiologic organism.

139. An 18-year-old primigravida with a history of crack-cocaine abuse presents for her first prenatal examination. She has no known drug allergies and takes no medications. She smokes crack-cocaine daily. On examination, she is found to have an indurated, painless vulvar lesion on a gray base. Inguinal lymph nodes are palpable and nontender bilaterally. Darkfield microscopy of a sample scraped from the lesion reveals treponemes.

(G) is correct. This patient has the classic chancre of primary syphilis. The incidence of this sexually transmitted disease is greatly increased in prostitutes and crack cocaine users (who often become prostitutes to support their habits). Rapid plasma reagin and venereal disease research laboratory tests may still be negative in early primary syphilis. Treponemes are visible on darkfield microscopy of a fluid sample scraped from the base of the chancre. The treatment of choice is penicillin. Even if the pregnant woman is allergic to penicillin, this situation warrants desensitization.

140. A 25-year-old woman, gravida 2 para 1, develops dysuria. She is at 25 weeks gestation and has had an uncomplicated course of regular antenatal care. She takes no medication and has an allergy to penicillin that presents as a skin rash. Physical examination is within normal limits. Her cervix is long and closed, and there is no evidence of inflammation. Microscopic examination of a clean-catch urine sample reveals many white blood cells and no bacteria. Urine culture is negative. Thayer-Martin culture does not yield growth of any organisms. Repeat urine culture three days later is still negative. The patient continues to have dysuria.

(F) is correct. Patients with dysuria, pyuria, and negative urine cultures are likely to have chlamydial urethritis. Treatment is erythromycin or amoxicillin (if they can't tolerate erythromycin). Doxycycline is the drug of choice for chlamydial infections in non-pregnant patients, but is contraindicated in pregnancy because it stains the developing teeth of the fetus.

141. A 30-year-old patient is pregnant for the first time. During her first antenatal examination, she reveals that she has recently been treated for a sexually transmitted disease. She has no current symptoms or complaints. She is otherwise in good health and takes no medications at the present time. She is not allergic to any medications that she knows of. A Gram stain of endocervical secretions reveals Gram-negative intracellular diplococci. Modified Thayer-Martin media grows more of the same organisms.

(C) is correct. This patient has an infection with gonorrhea, which is quite often asymptomatic. The CDC-recommended treatment is ceftriaxone (250 mg IM). Gram stain shows the Gram-negative intracellular diplococci, but is not a very sensitive test. Culture is higher yield.

Items 142–146

(A) Behçet's syndrome
(B) Bowenoid papulosis
(C) Bullous pemphigoid
(D) Contact dermatitis
(E) Crohn's disease
(F) Herpes simplex
(G) Lichen sclerosus
(H) Perineal pseudoverrucous papules
(I) Pinworms
(J) Psoriasis

For each child with an anogenital skin lesion, select the most likely diagnosis.

142. A 5-year-old boy is brought to his pediatrician for evaluation of an anogenital rash and intermittent genital pain. He has no prior medical or surgical history. Physical examination of the heart, lungs, and abdomen is within normal limits. The anogenital area has bilateral edema and erythema. Groups of vesicles and blisters are noted. He has similar lesions on his face, neck, palms, and soles. Skin biopsy reveals dermal inflammation.

(C) is correct. This child has symptoms of genital pemphigoid. This condition can occur in early childhood and presents with edema, erythema, erosion, and genital pain. Classic skin lesions are vesicular with blistering. Confirmation requires skin biopsy. The diagnosis requires a high index of suspicion.

143. A 9-year-old boy with a long history of intermittent right lower quadrant pain and diarrhea presents to his pediatrician complaining of rectal pain with defecation. Cardiac examination reveals a regular rate and rhythm. Pulmonary auscultation reveals good breath sounds bilaterally. Anogenital examination reveals marked anal dilation. A small perirectal fistula is noted in the left lateral quadrant. A small skin tag is noted in the right inferior quadrant. There is no evidence of internal or external hemorrhoids.

(E) is correct. Crohn's disease is a familial inflammatory disorder of the gastrointestinal tract and can affect any site from the mouth to the anus. Perirectal involvement is common with this disease and can take many forms. Typical lesions include skin tags, fissures, fistulae, ulcerations, and abscesses. Anal dilation is also a common feature of this condition.

144. A 12-year-old girl with a history of uveitis and recurrent oral ulcers presents to her pediatrician for evaluation of vulvar pain and a skin rash. Physical examination reveals multiple small, oral, aphthous ulcers. Physical examination of the heart, lung, and abdomen is within normal limits. The vulva has several discrete areas of ulceration with the largest measuring 0.5 cm by 0.5 cm. The ulcers appear to be deep, but are painless to palpation.

(A) is correct. This patient has evidence of Behçet's syndrome. This condition is characterized by recurrent oral and genital ulcers and relapsing uveitis. Most patients have oral ulcers. Genital ulcers may be deep and heal with scarring, but are relatively painless. The diagnosis is made clinically.

145. A 2-month-old male infant presents to his physician for evaluation of diaper rash. He has no prior medical or surgical history. Physical examination of the heart, lungs, and abdomen is within normal limits. The anogenital area has beefy-red erythema with sharp borders. There are several other areas with a fine, silvery scale in the groin and under the arms.

(J) is correct. This patient has evidence of psoriasis. This chronic condition can begin in childhood. Typical features include sharply demarcated plaques with a fine, silvery scale. In infants and toddlers, psoriasis typically involves the anogenital area and skin folds. Skin biopsy is confirmatory.

146. A 13-year-old girl presents to her pediatrician for evaluation of an anogenital skin rash. She is sexually active with several male partners. She denies history of sexually transmitted diseases. Physical examination of the heart, lungs, and abdomen is within normal limits. The right side of the vulvovaginal area has numerous small, flat-topped papules with a velvety-brown appearance. The left side of the vulvovaginal area contains the same lesions in a mirror image of the contralateral side.

(B) is correct. This patient has evidence of Bowenoid papulosis. This condition is a human papillomavirus-associated condition. Classic lesions present in a mirror distribution and appear as flat-topped papules, often with a velvety-brown appearance. This condition typically occurs in young, sexually active adults.

Items 147–150

(A) Acute cholecystitis
(B) Acute large bowel obstruction
(C) Acute pancreatitis
(D) Appendicitis
(E) Chronic pancreatitis
(F) Crohn's disease
(G) Diverticulitis
(H) Esophageal carcinoma
(I) Gastric cancer
(J) Gastroenteritis
(K) Nephrolithiasis
(L) Reflux esophagitis
(M) Ruptured ectopic pregnancy
(N) Ruptured peptic ulcer
(O) Small bowel obstruction
(P) Strangulated inguinal hernia
(Q) Tubo-ovarian abscess
(R) Ulcerative colitis

For each of the following patients with abdominal pain, select the most likely cause.

147. A 48-year-old black man with a history of alcohol abuse presents to the emergency room with the abrupt onset of abdominal pain located in the mid-epigastric region. The pain radiates to the back and is worse with movement. The patient is nauseous and vomits several times. Past medical history is significant for alcohol abuse with a history of a drunk driving arrest in the past. His last binge occurred 12 hours ago and consisted of a fifth of vodka, a bottle of whiskey, and a case of beer. He takes no medications or illicit drugs and does not smoke. Physical examination is significant for mid-epigastric tenderness without rebound tenderness or guarding. Bowel sounds are absent. There is abdominal distention but no masses are felt. The patient also has a temperature of 39 C (102.2 F), a pulse of 120 beats per minute, and a blood pressure of 80/60 mm Hg while supine. Lungs have decreased breath sounds at the bases and the heart is without murmurs, rubs, or gallops. White blood cell count is 18,000/mm³. Serum glucose is 150 mg/dL, lactate dehydrogenase is 400 U/L, aspartate aminotransferase (SGOT) is 300 U/L, and amylase is 500 U/L. Chest x-ray reveals bilateral lower lobe atelectasis. Abdominal plain film reveals a dilated loop of small bowel in the left upper quadrant.

(C) is correct. This patient has acute pancreatitis with classic signs and symptoms of epigastric abdominal pain radiating to the back, nausea, vomiting, fever, sentinel loop on abdominal film, and linear focal atelectasis of the lower lung lobes. Acute pancreatitis is most commonly due to gallstones and alcohol use. This patient has a severe case as determined by Ranson's criteria on admission—WBC > 16,000/mm³, LDH > 350 U/L, AST > 250 U/L. Amylase is often elevated, but is not part of Ranson's criteria.

148. A 24-year-old white woman, gravida 0 para 0, complains of right lower quadrant abdominal pain for the past week. She has pain of moderate severity that is worse with intercourse. She also complains of low grade fever, nausea, and vomiting. Her last bowel movement was 4 days ago and was unremarkable. The patient has no significant past medical history. On physical examination, temperature is 38 C (100.4 F), pulse is 100 beats per minute, and blood pressure is 100/80 mm Hg. Lung and cardiovascular examinations are within normal limits. The abdomen has right lower quadrant tenderness to deep palpation, without rebound or guarding. A mass is felt on deep palpation of the right lower quadrant that is confirmed on pelvic exam. The patient also has cervical motion tenderness. Urine pregnancy test is negative. White blood cell count is 11,000/mm³. Abdominal plain film is suggestive of ileus. Ultrasound of the pelvis reveals fluid around the right salpinx and ovary.

(Q) is correct. This patient has a tubo-ovarian abscess, seen with recurrent infection on damaged adnexal tissue. Patients may have a tender adnexal mass, fever, tachycardia, and adynamic ileus. Complications include rupture with sepsis, infertility, and ectopic pregnancy. Treatment for this patient is long-term antibiotics and close follow-up to ensure shrinkage of the mass. Surgery is indicated if pharmacologic therapy fails.

149. An 80-year-old while man develops abdominal pain, cramping, and distention over 12 hours. He has not passed gas during this period of time. His last bowel movement was 2 days ago and was without gross evidence of blood. The patient also complains of nausea with complete lack of appetite during the same period of time. The patient has a history of prostate cancer and hypertension. He takes an angiotensin-converting enzyme inhibitor and a baby aspirin every day. The patient's prostate cancer was judged to be inoperable and placed on a watchful waiting protocol. Physical examination reveals a temperature of 39 C (102.2 F), a pulse of 110 beats per minute, and a blood pressure of 120/70 mm Hg. Lungs are clear. Cardiovascular exam is significant for tachycardia. The abdomen is distended with no bowel sounds present. There is rebound tenderness and guarding of the left lower quadrant. Stool is guaiac-positive. White blood cell count is 13,000/mm³. Abdominal plain film reveals an inflated U-shaped loop in the region of the sigmoid.

(B) is correct. This patient has an acute large bowel obstruction secondary to sigmoid volvulus. 90 percent of all volvuli in the United States occur at the sigmoid. Patients have an elevated white blood cell count, fever, abdominal pain, distention, and obstipation. The sigmoid twists around a narrow-based mesocolon and becomes air-filled, as seen on abdominal plain film. Treatment is with barium enema reduction or surgery if gangrene is suspected.

150. A 30-year-old white woman, gravida 0 para 0, with a history of infertility, develops bilateral lower quadrant abdominal pain and vaginal bleeding. At the emergency department she is found to be tachycardic and faints before a full history is elicited. The patient is afebrile with a pulse of 120 beats per minute, blood pressure of 60/palp mm Hg. The abdomen is diffusely tender to light palpation with guarding present. A tender right adnexal mass is palpable. Urinary human chorionic gonadotropin testing is positive. White blood cell count is 8,000/mm³. Hemoglobin is 8 g/dL.

(M) is correct. This patient has signs and symptoms of ruptured ectopic pregnancy—syncope, abdominal pain, uterine bleeding, and a positive pregnancy test. This patient probably has had low-grade chronic pelvic inflammatory disease with resultant infertility secondary to tubal factor. Therefore, she is at increased risk for ectopic pregnancy, which occurs most commonly at the ampulla. This patient needs stat laparoscopy/laparotomy.

SECTION 4 BEGINS HERE

Directions (Items 151–200): Each of the numbered items is followed or preceded by a set of options. For each item, select the BEST lettered option to answer the question or complete the statement. Locate the corresponding item number in the appropriate section of your answer sheet and completely fill in the circle containing the lettered option you have selected.

151. A 22-year-old white male presents to his college infirmary with complaints of headache and photophobia for the last 24 hours. His temperature is 38.5 C (102 F). He has prominent meningismus. Lumbar puncture is obtained with the following results:

Nucleated cells   100/mL

Cell count differential   Lymphocyte predominant

Protein   Mildly elevated

Glucose   Normal

Which of the following is the most appropriate first step?

    (A) Intravenous ampicillin
    (B) Intravenous ceftriaxone
    (C) Intravenous vancomycin
    (D) Observation
    (E) Oral cephalexin

(D) is correct. Aseptic (or viral) meningitis is common in the young age group. Fever, headache, and meningeal irritation with a lymphocytic pleocytosis of the cerebrospinal fluid with normal glucose and mildly elevated protein is the usual picture. The usual etiologic agent is an enterovirus. Treatment is supportive. Choice A is incorrect. Ampicillin has an important role in the treatment of *Listeria monocytogenes* meningitis; a bacterial meningitis of the very old and very young and the immunocompromised. Choice B is incorrect. Ceftriaxone has an important role in the treatment of suspected bacterial meningitis with excellent activity against the common pathogens, *S. pneumoniae* and *N. meninigitidis* as well *as H. influenzae*. In this case, the cerebrospinal findings are not consistent with a suspected bacterial meningitis. Choice C is incorrect. Vancomycin has a role in the treatment of suspected staphylococcal meningitis, a rare infection. Choice E is incorrect. There is no role for the use of oral antibiotics in any patient with suspected meningitis.

152. A 45-year-old white female presents to her primary care doctor complaining of itching and fatigue worsening over the last several months. She is markedly icteric. Laboratory tests are obtained and are as follows:

Serum

Sodium	140 mEq/dL
Potassium	4.0 mEq/dL
Chloride	110 mEq/dL
Bicarbonate	25 mEq/dL
BUN	12 mg/dL
Creatinine	1.0 mg/dL
Total bilirubin	7.8 mg/dL
Direct bilirubin	6.9 mg/dL
AST	25 U/dL
ALT	30 U/dL
Alkaline phosphatase	450 mg/dL
Antimitochondrial antibody titer	1:1,280

Which of the following is the most likely diagnosis?

    (A) Crigler-Najjar syndrome
    (B) Gilbert disease
    (C) Hepatitis A infection
    (D) Primary biliary cirrhosis
    (E) Rotor's syndrome
    (F) Sclerosing cholangitis

(D) is correct. Primary biliary cirrhosis often presents with pruritus or is asymptomatic with elevated alkaline phosphatase levels. It is most common in women between 35–60 (90 percent of cases). Antimitochondrial antibody test is a sensitive and specific test when positive (titer > 1:40). Choice A is incorrect. Crigler-Najjar is a hereditary unconjugated hyperbilirubinemia with severe deficiency or absence of glucuronosyltransferase. The syndrome is almost always symptomatic in infancy. Choice B is incorrect. Gilbert's disease is a mild deficiency of glucuronosyltransferase characterized by an increase in serum bilirubin with fasting or physiologic stress. The hyperbilirubinemia is unconjugated. Choice C is incorrect. Hepatitis A infection causes an acute, dramatic rise in transaminases, often in the thousands. Choice E is incorrect. Rotor's syndrome is a rare autosomal recessive condition associated with impaired hepatic storage of bilirubin and a conjugated hyperbilirubinemia. Choice F is incorrect. Sclerosing cholangitis is characterized by the progressive obliteration of the extrahepatic and occasionally intrahepatic ducts. It often presents with symptoms of biliary obstruction, including jaundice and pruritus as well as right upper quadrant pain. It is associated with inflammatory bowel disease.

153. A 72-year-old white female is brought to the emergency department by her husband because of her difficulty walking. This has been progressing over the last several months, along with increasing forgetfulness. He also notes that she has recently developed urinary incontinence. Testing of memory is abnormal, showing very poor short-term memory. Which of the following is the most appropriate first test?

(A) Computed tomography of the head
(B) Computed tomography of the spine
(C) Electroencephalogram
(D) Lumbar spine roentgenographs
(E) Magnetic resonance imaging of the head
(F) Psychiatric consultation
(G) Urine culture

(A) is correct. Normal pressure hydrocephalus is composed of a classic triad of urinary incontinence, dementia, and abnormal gait. There is hydrocephalus without cerebral atrophy on brain imaging. Unlike Alzheimer's disease, the gait disturbance is early and cortical atrophy is minimal. Treatment is a ventricular shunting. Choice B is incorrect. The patient's ambulatory dysfunction, based on her history, is best explained by normal pressure hydrocephalus. Exploration of other causes of ambulatory dysfunction is not warranted. Choice C is incorrect. Electroencephalogram is not indicated in this patient without a history consistent with seizure disorder or focal brain abnormality. Choice D is incorrect. The patient's ambulatory dysfunction, based on her history, is best explained by normal pressure hydrocephalus. Exploration of other causes of ambulatory dysfunction is not warranted. Choice E is incorrect. Computed tomography is less expensive and as likely to confirm the clinical diagnosis of normal pressure hydrocephalus as the more expensive magnetic resonance imaging. Choice F is incorrect. This patient's history is most consistent with normal pressure hydrocephalus, rather than a dementing or other psychiatric illness. Therefore, psychiatric consultation is not indicated. Choice G is incorrect. Urine culture is an important tool in the work-up of new incontinence, but in this case, the patient's underlying disease, normal pressure hydrocephalus, explains her incontinence.

154. A 67-year-old white female presents to her primary care physician with complaints of numbness in her right upper extremity, generalized weakness, and fatigue. Laboratory studies are obtained:

Hemoglobin	8.0 mg/dL
Hematocrit	25%
WBC	4.5/mL
Platelets	550×10^9/L

Serum

Protein electrophoresis gamma globulin spike	Abnormal
Relative serum viscosity	5 cp (Increased)

The diagnosis of Waldenström's macroglobulinemia is suspected. Which of the following antibodies most likely accounts for the abnormal gamma globulin spike on serum protein electrophoresis?

(A) IgA
(B) IgD
(C) IgE
(D) IgG
(E) IgM

(E) is correct. Waldenström's macroglobulinemia is a malignancy of lymphoplasmacytoid cells that secrete excessive IgM. The light chain isotype is kappa in 80 percent of cases. Symptoms are generally complications of the hyperviscosity syndrome. Patients present with weakness, fatigue, and neurologic complaints such as headache and peripheral neuropathy. Choices A, B, C, and D are incorrect. Waldenström's macroglobulinemia is associated with increased levels of IgM.

155. A 63-year-old man with prostate cancer who is undergoing external beam radiation complains of diarrhea, rectal bleeding, and the sensation of incomplete evacuation of stools. Abdominal examination reveals normoactive bowel sounds without peritoneal signs. Anorectal examination reveals hemorrhagic and inflamed mucosa of the distal rectum. Which of the following is the most likely diagnosis?

(A) External hemorrhoids
(B) Fissure-in-ano
(C) Fistula-in-ano
(D) Internal hemorrhoids
(E) Proctitis

(E) is correct. This patient has radiation proctitis. This condition is associated with diarrhea, rectal bleeding, tenesmus, rectal pain, and incontinence. Further complications of this condition include bleeding, stricture, and fistulas. Treatment involves bulking agents, antidiarrheals, and steroid enemas. Choice A is incorrect. External hemorrhoids are abnormally dilated anal veins below the dentate line. They may show a skin tag and occasionally erode through the skin. Choice B is incorrect. Acute onset of perirectal pain associated with straining and blood on the toilet tissue suggests the diagnosis of fissure-in-ano. Risk factors for the development of this condition include straining during bowel movements, constipation, and anal intercourse. Choice C is incorrect. Fistula-in-ano describes perianal pain and a mass in the perianal skin associated with discharge of liquid from the perianal area. Choice D is incorrect. Internal hemorrhoids are veins with mucosa above the dentate line. They are prone to prolapse and bleeding.

156. A 45-year-old white female presents to the emergency department with complaints of headache and blurry vision. Her blood pressure is 200/125 mm Hg with a heart rate of 80 beats per minute. Which of the following is the most appropriate initial treatment?

    (A) Intravenous captopril
    (B) Intravenous nitroglycerin infusion
    (C) Intravenous sodium nitroprusside infusion
    (D) Oral hydralazine
    (E) Oral nifedipine
    (F) Sublingual nifedipine
    (G) Transdermal nitrates

(C) is correct. This patient has accelerated (malignant) hypertension with a diastolic blood pressure greater than 120 mm Hg and neurologic symptoms (headache). Other symptoms of malignant hypertension include acute renal failure and cardiac dysfunction (pulmonary edema or myocardial infarction). The goal is reduction of the mean blood pressure by one-third without rapid overcorrection, which may precipitate cerebral ischemia. Therefore, the best choice for treatment is sodium nitroprusside infusion, which allows for both rapid onset and the best control of blood pressure to avoid overcorrection. Choice A is incorrect. Intravenous captopril in patients with renin-mediated hypertension may precipitate a rapid decline in blood pressure and potentially cause cerebral ischemia. Choice B is incorrect. Intravenous nitroglycerin may precipitate a rapid fall in blood pressure and potentially cause cerebral ischemia. Choice D is incorrect. Hydralazine may precipitate a rapid fall in blood pressure and potentially cause cerebral ischemia. Choice E is incorrect. Oral nifedipine may precipitate a rapid fall in blood pressure and potentially cause cerebral ischemia. Choice F is incorrect. Sublingual nifedipine may precipitate a rapid fall in blood pressure and potentially cause cerebral ischemia. Recently, the Food and Drug Administration issued a warning about the use of sublingual nifedipine in controlling severe hypertension. Choice G is incorrect. Transdermal nitrates may precipitate a rapid fall in blood pressure and potentially cause cerebral ischemia. Their use in the acute setting should be limited to patients with myocardial ischemia.

157. A 16-year-old white male with insulin-dependent diabetes mellitus returns to his primary care physician for a follow-up visit. He had his insulin regimen increased last week for hyperglycemia. This is the fourth such visit in the last several months. A finger stick test reveals a blood glucose of 330 mg/dL. You suspect noncompliance with his insulin regimen. Which of the following is the most appropriate next step?

    (A) Add triglitizone to his medical regimen.
    (B) Confront the patient about your concerns.
    (C) Have his mother give him his insulin.
    (D) Increase his insulin dose further.
    (E) No intervention, 330 mg/dL is adequate glucose control.

(B) is correct. Noncompliance in the adolescent population is a difficult problem. Not discussing your concerns and allowing the patients to express their rationale for their behavior leads to endless cycles of worsening rebellion and noncompliance, which in this case could be deadly (i.e., result in diabetic ketoacidosis). Choice A is incorrect. Triglitizone is a useful adjuvant for many insulin-requiring diabetics. However, adding a second drug does not address the primary suspected problem with this patient's glucose control, noncompliance. Choice C is incorrect. Having his mother give him his insulin, although immediately remedying the suspected problem, does not address the primary concern, which is why the patient is now noncompliant. Choice D is incorrect. Increasing his insulin further does not address the underlying concern and might even be dangerous should the patient begin using the prescribed dosage when, in actuality, he requires far less insulin. Choice E is incorrect. Long-term tight control of glucose levels within the normal range (60–120 mg/dL) has been shown to substantially decrease the long-term sequelae of diabetes. This should be the goal of all diabetic treatment. A blood glucose level of 330 mg/dL is not acceptable.

158. A 5-year-old boy has an 8-month history of passing feces in inappropriate places such as in his clothing and onto the floor. This behavior occurs approximately twice a month and appears to be unintentional. The child was continent of stools for approximately 1 year prior to these events. He is in the 35th percentile for height, weight, and head circumference. Physical examination reveals a well-developed child. Cardiovascular examination reveals a regular rate and rhythm. Pulmonary auscultation reveals no evidence of rales, rhonchi, or wheezes. Gastrointestinal examination reveals normoactive bowel sounds. Anorectal examination reveals good sphincter tone with soft stool in the vault. Which of the following is the most likely associated condition to be seen in this individual?

(A) Anal fissure
(B) Anal fistulas
(C) Functional encopresis
(D) Hemorrhoids
(E) Hirschsprung's disease

(C) is correct. This individual exhibits signs of functional encopresis. This condition is associated with at least 6 months of passage of feces in inappropriate places such as on the floor or into clothing. Fecal passage is involuntary or unintentional. This condition is associated with social embarrassment. Approximately 25 percent of those affected also have functional enuresis. Choice A is incorrect. Anal fissures can occur with functional encopresis secondary to retention of feces and constipation. However, the incidence of this finding is less than 10 percent. Choice B is incorrect. Anal fistulas are rarely seen in association with functional encopresis. Choice D is incorrect. Hemorrhoids are uncommon findings in patients with functional encopresis. Choice E is incorrect. It is important to rule out physical disorders such as aganglionic megacolon in patients with primary encopresis.

159. The probability of a positive test when disease is present defines which of the following terms?

(A) Negative predictive value
(B) Positive predictive value
(C) Relative risk
(D) Sensitivity
(E) Specificity

(D) is correct. Sensitivity is defined as the probability of a positive test when disease is present. Sensitivity involves patients with the disease. It is defined as the number of true positives divided by the number of true positives plus false negatives. It is also known as the true positive rate. Choice A is incorrect. Negative predictive value is the probability of disease being absent when the test result is negative. Choice B is incorrect. Positive predictive value is the probability of disease being present when the test result is positive. Choice C is incorrect. Relative risk is the risk of disease occurrence when a risk factor is present vs. the risk of disease when the risk factor is absent. Choice E is incorrect. Specificity is the probability of a negative test when the disease is absent. Specificity involves patients without the disease.

160. Insulin is infused into a 37-year-old man with diabetes mellitus and hypertension to achieve a steady state plasma concentration of 1 mg/mL. A urine sample after 1 hour has a volume of 60 mL and an insulin concentration of 120 mg/mL. The glomerular filtration rate is

(A) 20 mL/min
(B) 40 mL/min
(C) 80 mL/min
(D) 100 mL/min
(E) 120 mL/min

(E) is correct. Glomerular filtration is determined by the formula urine insulin concentration multiplied by urine volume divided by the plasma concentration of insulin. In the present case, the insulin concentration of 120 mg/mL and the urine volume of 60 mL divided by the plasma concentration of insulin (1 mg/mL) will yield a glomerular filtration rate of 120 mL/min.

161. The probability of a negative test when disease is absent defines which of the following terms?

(A) Negative predictive value
(B) Positive predictive value
(C) Relative risk
(D) Sensitivity
(E) Specificity

(E) is correct. Specificity is the probability of a negative test when the disease is absent. Specificity involves patients without the disease. It is defined as the number of true negatives divided by the number of true negatives plus false positives. Choice A is incorrect. Negative predictive value is the probability of the disease being absent when the test result is negative. Choice B is incorrect. Positive predictive value is the probability of the disease being present when the test result is positive. Choice C is incorrect. Relative risk is the risk of disease occurrence when a risk factor is present vs. the risk of disease occurrence when a risk factor is absent. Choice D is incorrect. Sensitivity is defined as the probability of a positive test when disease is present. Sensitivity involves patients with the disease. It is defined as the number of true positives divided by the number of true positives plus false negatives. It is also known as the true positive rate.

162. A 65-year-old black male presents to his primary care doctor complaining of an exquisitely painful right great toe. The pain began 5 days ago while on a hunting trip. On the trip, he and his friends drank several cases of beer over a two-day period. The patient is unable to bear weight secondary to pain. His right great toe is erythematous and very painful to touch, with a small joint effusion. Joint aspiration is most likely to demonstrate which of the following?

    (A) Crystals resembling "Maltese crosses"
    (B) Negatively birefringent needle-shaped crystals
    (C) Negatively birefringent rhomboid crystals
    (D) Positively birefringent needle-shaped crystals
    (E) Positively birefringent rhomboid crystals

(B) is correct. The crystals of gout are negatively birefringent, needle-shaped crystals when viewed under polarized light. Acute gout may be precipitated by alcohol ingestion. Choice A is incorrect. Maltese crosses are a urinary crystal finding in patients with high cholesterol. Choice C is incorrect. The crystals of gout are negatively birefringent, needle-shaped crystals. Choice D is incorrect. The crystals of gout are negatively birefringent, needle-shaped crystals. Choice E is incorrect. The crystals of calcium pyrophosphate deposition disease, which may occasionally mimic gout in the elderly, are weakly positively birefringent, rhomboid crystals.

163. A 34-year-old white female presents to her primary care physician complaining of fatigue for the last week and easy bruising over the last 2 days. She has prominent pretibial and palatal petechiae. Her white blood count is 62,000/mm³. On her peripheral smear, Auer rods are visualized. Which of the following is the most likely diagnosis?

    (A) Acute lymphocytic leukemia
    (B) Acute myelogenous leukemia
    (C) Chronic lymphocytic leukemia
    (D) Chronic myelogenous leukemia
    (E) Polycythemia vera

(B) is correct. This young patient has presented to her physician with the stigmata of thrombocytopenia and is found to have profound leukocytosis. Auer rods are found specifically in acute myelogenous leukemia. Choice A is incorrect. With the stigmata of thrombocytopenia and profound leukocytosis, acute lymphocytic leukemia is a consideration. However, Auer rods are found specifically in acute myelogenous leukemia. Choice C is incorrect. Chronic lymphocytic leukemia is typically a disease of older patients. The leukocytosis is not as prominent as it is in this patient, and Auer rods are absent. Choice D is incorrect. Chronic myelogenous leukemia, associated with the Philadelphia chromosome, is associated with a more indolent course, and the usual presentation is not with such profound leukocytosis. Auer rods are absent. Choice E is incorrect. Polycythemia vera is a disease of the red blood cell line alone. It is not associated with profound thrombocytopenia or leukocytosis.

164. A 78-year-old male with with a history of anterior wall myocardial infarction several years ago and recurrent episodes of congestive heart failure, atrial fibrillation, chronic renal insufficiency, and hypothyroidism presents to the emergency department with complaints of fatigue, weakness, and a metallic taste in his mouth worsening over the last several days. His current medications include captopril, digoxin, atenolol, nitroglycerin patch, levothyroxine, and one enteric-coated aspirin a day. He has a pericardial friction rub. Laboratory values are as follows:

Serum

Urea nitrogen	100 mg/dL
Creatinine	7.8 mg/dL
Potassium	6.0 mEq/L

Which of the following medications is most likely to have precipitated the patient's renal failure and must be discontinued?

(A) Aspirin
(B) Atenolol
(C) Captopril
(D) Digoxin
(E) Levothyroxine
(F) Nitroglycerin

(C) is correct. Angiotensin-converting enzyme inhibitors interfere with the adaptive responses of the renal microcirculation and may convert compensated renal hypotension to ischemic acute renal failure. For this reason, ACE inhibitors should be avoided in patients with severe chronic renal insufficiency. Choice A is incorrect. Although any inhibitor of cyclooxygenase such as aspirin and other nonsteroidal anti-inflammatory medications may impair renal perfusion and even lead to chronic renal failure when abused, one aspirin a day is unlikely to have precipitated this patient's acute renal failure. Choice B is incorrect. β-blocking medications are not known to precipitate renal failure. Choice D is incorrect. Digoxin is excreted by the kidney, and persons with renal failure are prone to digitalis toxicity. However, digitalis does not precipitate renal failure. Choice E is incorrect. Levothyroxine is not known to precipitate renal failure. Choice F is incorrect. Nitroglycerin, especially when used in conjunction with hydralazine, improves renal blood flow. It is not known to precipitate renal failure.

165. A 39-year-old black female bank executive with a long history of progressive, burning epigastric pain 2 hours after meals that is often nocturnal and relieved by food presents for evaluation. Physical examination reveals a palpable thyroid gland without masses. Cardiac examination reveals no evidence of rubs, murmurs, or gallops. Pulmonary auscultation reveals no evidence or wheezes or rhonchi. Gastrointestinal examination reveals mild tenderness in the mid-epigastric region without focal peritoneal signs. Rectal examination reveals small, internal, nonprolapsing hemorrhoids, and guaiac-negative stool in the vault. Modern views on the etiology of this condition relate to which of the following factors in the pathogenesis?

(A) *Helicobacter pylori*
(B) Impaired gastric blood flow
(C) Impaired gastric epithelial cell turnover
(D) Prostaglandin inhibition
(E) Thinning of the mucous layer

(A) is correct. Modern views of the pathogenesis indicate that there is a major role for *Helicobacter pylori* in the pathophysiology of peptic ulcer disease. This urease-producing organism colonizes the gastric antral mucosa in 100 percent of patients with duodenal ulcer and 70 percent of patients with gastric ulcer. Eradication of this organism is the mainstay of therapy for ulcer disease. Choice B is incorrect. Classical teaching regarding the pathogenesis of peptic ulcer disease considered impaired blood flow to be a key contributor to this condition. Modern views of peptic ulcer disease dispute this finding. Choice C is incorrect. Impaired gastric epithelial cell turnover is not felt to contribute to the pathogenesis of ulcer disease. Choice D is incorrect. Prostaglandin inhibition, while accounting for salicylate and nonsteroidal anti-inflammatory agent ulcer disease, actually contributes to less than 30% of cases of gastric ulcers. Choice E is incorrect. Thinning of the mucous layer may occur as a result of the toxic effects of *H. pylori* on the duodenal mucosa. However, on its own it is a small contributor to the pathophysiology of peptic ulcer disease.

Items 166–167

A 27-year-old man complains of a painless lump in his right groin. He has a prior surgical history of right orchiopexy at age 4. He has no other medical conditions and takes no medications. Cardiac examination reveals a regular rate and rhythm. Pulmonary auscultation reveals no rales, rhonchi, or wheezes. Gastrointestinal examination reveals normoactive bowel sounds. The right testis has a 1.5 cm area of induration on the posterior surface. The right epididymis and vas deferens are palpable. The left testis has no areas of induration. The left epididymis and vas deferens are palpable. Chest x-ray reveals no evidence of effusions, masses, or infiltrates.

166. Which of the following is the most likely diagnosis?

    (A) Embryonal carcinoma
    (B) Endodermal sinus tumor
    (C) Seminoma
    (D) Teratoma
    (E) Teratocarcinoma

(C) is correct. This patient probably has testicular carcinoma. The peak incidence is between the ages of 20 and 40 years. Cryptorchid testes are at increased risk, although early orchiopexy may provide some protection against testicular cancer. Seminoma accounts for 50 percent of cases and is the most common pathology seen. Choice A is incorrect. Embryonal cell carcinoma (20 percent) is a nonseminomatous germ cell tumor of the testis. Choice B is incorrect. Endodermal sinus tumor (5 percent) is a common testicular tumor in newborn males. Choice D is incorrect. Teratoma (15 percent) is a nonseminomatous germ cell tumor of the testis. Choice E is incorrect. Teratocarcinoma (20 percent) is a nonseminomatous germ cell tumor of the testis.

167. Which of the following is the most appropriate initial step in the management of this condition?

    (A) Chemotherapy
    (B) Inguinal orchiectomy
    (C) Radiotherapy
    (D) Radiotherapy and chemotherapy
    (E) Transscrotal orchiectomy

(B) is correct. For all stages of seminoma, treatment first involves inguinal orchiectomy for histopathologic diagnosis and staging. For higher stage disease, retroperitoneal lymph node dissection is undertaken. When positive lymph nodes are found, radiotherapy and chemotherapy are instituted. Choice A is incorrect. Chemotherapy is not the primary therapy for seminoma. Choice C is incorrect. Radiotherapy is not the primary therapy for seminoma. Choice D is incorrect. Chemotherapy and radiotherapy may be required for the treatment of advanced seminoma following orchiectomy. Choice E is incorrect. Transcrotal orchiectomy is not indicated in the treatment of testis cancer. It is possible that during removal of the tumor by this approach, the lymphatic seeding of tumor cells can occur.

168. A 57-year-old man who has worked as a battery manufacturer for 20 years has a long history of osteomalacia. Prior pulmonary function testing suggests emphysema although he is a nonsmoker. Cardiac examination reveals a regular rate and rhythm. Pulmonary auscultation reveals no evidence of wheezing. Gastrointestinal evaluation reveals normoactive bowel sounds without peritoneal signs. Skin examination reveals areas of patchy dermatitis. Urinalysis reveals no evidence of blood or nitrates. However, proteinuria is noted. Which of the following is the most likely etiologic agent?

(A) Arsenic
(B) Cadmium
(C) Manganese
(D) Mercury
(E) Thallium

(B) is correct. Cadmium exposure is often related to occupational risks that occur in the smelting, mining, battery manufacturing, and ceramic industries. Chronic exposure is associated with emphysema, renal tubular damage with proteinuria, renal tubular acidosis, and osteomalacia. Treatment of chronic exposure to cadmium involves large doses of vitamin D. Cadmium inhalation, on the other hand, is treated with glucocorticoids and diuretics. Choice A is incorrect. Arsenic is a heavy metal that can cause various symptoms following chronic exposure. Typical industries that use arsenic include fur and glass. Symptoms include lacrimation, conjunctivitis, anorexia, headache, and vertigo. Physical examination may reveal evidence of dermatitis. Intellectual impairment and drowsiness may also be noted. Choice C is incorrect. Manganese poisoning is associated with headache, hypersomnia, and impotence, as well as uncontrollable laughing and crying spells. Choice D is incorrect. Mercury poisoning is associated with gastritis, bleeding gums, excessive salivation, and coarse tremor with jerky movements. Choice E is incorrect. Thallium poisoning is associated with abdominal pain, vomiting, alopecia, ataxia, retrobulbar neuritis, and impaired consciousness.

169. A 24-year-old man demonstrates evidence of suspiciousness, inappropriate laughter, and impaired judgment. He is cold to the touch and has a dry mouth. He also states that he is hungry. Physical examination reveals a well-developed male with bilateral conjunctival injection. Cardiac examination reveals tachycardia with a regular rhythm. Urine toxicology screen is positive for alcohol and tetrahydrocannabinol. Which of the following is the most appropriate treatment for this patient's symptoms?

(A) Ascorbic acid
(B) Fluphenazine
(C) Haloperidol
(D) Thiothixene
(E) No further treatment is necessary

(E) is correct. Cannabis intoxication produces symptoms of euphoria or dysphoria as well as suspiciousness, intense laughter, time distortion, social withdrawal, and impaired judgment. Signs of intoxication on physical examination include conjunctival injection, increased appetite, dry mouth, and tachycardia. Hypothermia and mild sedation may also be noted. Depersonalization and hallucinations may also occur. Treatment of intoxication is not usually required. Choice A is incorrect. Ascorbic acid is used to alkalinize the urine in patients presenting with an overdose of phencyclidine. Choice B is incorrect. Fluphenazine is a high-potency antipsychotic agent used in the treatment of hallucinogen overdose caused by drugs such as LSD and mescaline. Choice C is incorrect. Haloperidol is a high-potency antipsychotic agent used in the treatment of hallucinogen hallucinosis with psychotic features. Choice D is incorrect. Thiothixene is a high-potency antipsychotic agent that is one of several suggested treatments for hallucinogen hallucinosis with psychosis.

170. A 3-year-old boy presents for evaluation of several days of right otalgia, fever, and generalized discomfort. Right otoscopic examination reveals a hyperemic, opaque tympanic membrane that has poor mobility on pneumatic otoscopy. Left otoscopy reveals no evidence of bulging or retraction, and pneumatic otoscopy reveals good mobility of the left tympanic membrane. Cardiovascular examination reveals tachycardia without murmurs. Pulmonary auscultation reveals scattered wheezes bilaterally without rhonchi or rales. Abdominal examination reveals normoactive bowel sounds. Cultures of middle ear fluid aspirate reveal numerous gram-positive cocci in clusters. Which of the following is the most appropriate treatment for this individual?

    (A) Amoxicillin
    (B) Dicloxacillin
    (C) Erythromycin
    (D) Gentamicin
    (E) Ticarcillin

(A) is correct. This child has evidence of acute otitis media. *Streptococcus pneumoniae* is isolated in 35 percent of middle ear aspirates (the most common). *Haemophilus influenzae* and *Moraxella catarrhalis* were isolated in 25 percent and 15 percent of the cases, respectively. Thus, treatment should be directed against the above pathogens with amoxicillin, trimethoprim-sulfamethoxizole, or cefaclor. Choice B is incorrect. Dicloxacillin is not a first-line agent in the treatment of acute otitis media. Choice C is incorrect. Erythromycin is not a first-line agent in the treatment of acute otitis media. Choice D is incorrect. Gentamicin is an intravenous agent that should be considered in the treatment of sepsis in an acutely ill child. Choice E is incorrect. Ticarcillin is not recommended in the treatment of uncomplicated acute otitis media.

171. A 4-year-old boy is brought to his primary care physician for routine examination. Growth parameters indicate that the child is in the 10th percentile for height, fifth percentile for weight, and fifth percentile for head circumference. The child's mother notes that he does not like to drink milk. Sensory and motor development appear to be age-appropriate. Physical examination reveals normal heart, lungs, and abdomen. Otologic examination reveals no evidence of effusions bilaterally, and both tympanic membranes move well to pneumatic otoscopy. Ophthalmologic examination was not performed.

Laboratory studies are listed below:

Serum

Calcium	7.5 mg/dL
Phosphate	2.2 mg/dL

Typically, this condition occurs due to

    (A) inadequate renal conversion of vitamin D
    (B) lack of sunlight
    (C) malabsorption of vitamin D
    (D) proximal renal tubular acidosis
    (E) saponification

(B) is correct. Rickets is a metabolic disease that affects the growth and development of bone and cartilage. Rickets is unique to childhood and occurs whenever mineral deficiency prevents normal processes of bone mineralization at the epiphyseal plates. Classically, this condition occurs when lack of sunlight interferes with the conversion of vitamin D to its active form. Choice A is incorrect. Inadequate renal conversion of vitamin D to its active form occurs in infancy in vitamin D-dependent rickets. Choice C is incorrect. Malabsorption of vitamin D can be associated with hepatic rickets. Choice D is incorrect. Proximal renal tubular acidosis with alkaline urine can be associated with a rare forms of rickets. Choice E is incorrect. Saponification may be seen in cases of chronic pancreatitis.

172. A 33-year-old woman with a history of depression and chronic fatigue presents for evaluation. She brings her medical records that indicate that she has had an extensive work-up, including blood studies and computed tomography of the head, chest, and pelvis, which were inconclusive. Physical examination reveals a young, well-nourished female in mild distress. Examination of the heart, lungs, and abdomen is within normal limits. You suggest that further testing may be necessary to further elucidate the cause of her symptoms. The patient becomes upset and begins to cry. Which of the following is the best strategy for you to take?

(A) Order follow-up thyroid profile
(B) Call a social worker to further guide this patient
(C) Refer the patient to a psychiatrist
(D) Elicit the patient's perspective and concerns about her condition
(E) Suggest that the patient seek help from another health care professional

(D) is correct. When a physician gets into an emotional discussion with a patient regarding diagnosis, work-up, and therapy, it is best to explore the patient's perspective about the condition. This strategy might make the patient feel more at ease. An effective doctor-patient relationship is essential for patient compliance. Choice A is incorrect. Ordering repeat blood work is not likely to add additional information that will have an impact on the patient's present condition. Choice B is incorrect. Consultation with a social worker is an appropriate selection. However, the physician should explore the patient's concerns before making any further decisions. Choice C is incorrect. Psychiatric evaluation is not appropriate for this patient at this time. Choice E is incorrect. While this patient might ultimately seek care from another physician, it would be advisable for the current physician to determine the patient's perspective about her condition. This may restore the appropriate doctor-patient relationship.

173. A 34-year-old white male presents to the emergency department with complaints of fever and malaise for several days as well as nausea with emesis once. His exam reveals mild right upper quadrant tenderness without guarding or rebound. Laboratory studies are as follows:

Serum

AST	3,350 U/dL
ALT	3,250 U/dL
Bilirubin (total)	6.5 mg/dL
Bilirubin (direct)	6.1 mg/dL

Which of the following is the most appropriate first step in the evaluation of this patient?

(A) Computed tomography of the abdomen
(B) Esophagogastroduodenoscopy
(C) Endoscopic retrograde cholangiopancreatography
(D) Hepatitis serology
(E) Nuclear medicine biliary scan
(F) Ultrasound of the right upper quadrant

(D) is correct. Acute viral hepatitis is the most common cause of markedly elevated liver transaminases in the absence of the ingestion of hepatocellular toxins (like acetaminophen). Choice A is incorrect. Computed tomography is not indicated, as the patient is presenting with the clinical signs and symptoms of viral hepatitis. Choice B is incorrect. Esophagogastroduodenoscopy is very useful for investigating esophageal, stomach, and duodenal pathology, but is not an appropriate initial step in a patient with the clinical picture of hepatitis. Choice C is incorrect. Endoscopic retrograde cholangiopancreatography (ERCP) is a useful tool for investigating pancreatic and biliary pathology, but is not an appropriate first step in the evaluation of a patient with suspected viral hepatitis. Choice E is incorrect. Nuclear medicine biliary scan is a useful test in exploring suspected biliary pathology after an unremarkable right upper quadrant ultrasound, but is not the appropriate initial step in a patient with suspected hepatitis. Choice F is incorrect. Ultrasound of the right upper quadrant is the best initial step in the investigation of biliary pathology, but this patient's hyperbilirubinemia is best explained by hepatitis, not biliary pathology.

174. A 55-year-old male physician is noted by a colleague to be taking diazepam. The colleague has known the physician for many years and knows of no complaints with his medical performance. Which of the following would be the most appropriate first action to take?

(A) Ask the physician who prescribed the medication and for what reason.
(B) Call the physician's family and state that he is taking a controlled substance.
(C) Observe the physician for future occurrences.
(D) Report the physician to the state medical board for taking a controlled substance.
(E) Suggest to the physician that he attend a Narcotics Anonymous meeting.

(A) is correct. Dealing with a substance abuse situation with a colleague is difficult. In this case, it is important to confront the suspicion of substance abuse to remove any doubt that a situation exists. Choice B is incorrect. Important information may go unreported when asking family members about the physician's use of the controlled substance, as his family might not know his medication profile. Choice C is incorrect. By making oneself the investigator in a substance abuse case, one takes on a large responsibility. The self-appointed investigator may not be present during future episodes of substance abuse. Choice D is incorrect. The use of controlled substances is legal in certain situations, for instance if prescribed for a specific medical reason. Choice E is incorrect. To suggest that a person is a substance abuser based on a one-time episode is improper without additional information. If it is discovered that a colleague is abusing the medication, a referral may be appropriate.

175. A 57-year-old white male presents to the emergency department with complaints of bloody diarrhea and dizziness for the last few hours. He has been taking warfarin for the last three months for the treatment of a lower extremity deep venous thrombosis. His blood pressure is 85/50 mm Hg supine with a heart rate of 110 beats per minute. Standing, his blood pressure is 70/40 mm Hg with a heart rate of 140 beats per minute and he is very dizzy. Rectal examination reveals gross bright red blood. Laboratory studies are obtained:

Leukocytes	7,000/mm^3
Hemoglobin	7.5 g/dL
Hematocrit	24%
Platelets	550,000/mm^3
Prothrombin time	>100 seconds
Activated partial thromboplastin time	35 seconds

Which of the following is the most appropriate next step?

(A) Administer fresh frozen plasma
(B) Administer intravenous vitamin K
(C) Administer platelets
(D) Administer protamine sulfate
(E) Administer subcutaneous vitamin K

(A) is correct. This patient has a life-threatening gastrointestinal hemorrhage related to over-anticoagulation with warfarin (as reflected by the extremely elevated prothrombin time). Administration of fresh frozen plasma is most appropriate, as its effects are immediate and last 4 to 6 hours. Support with volume (e.g., fluids) and blood products is also of pressing urgency. Choice B is incorrect. Administration of vitamin K, even the intravenous form, takes 12 to 36 hours to have full effect and reverse the effects of warfarin; too long in this patient with a life-threatening hemorrhage. However, vitamin K is a useful adjuvant to the administration of fresh frozen plasma, as fresh frozen plasma only is effective for 4 to 6 hours after its infusion. Choice C is incorrect. This patient's bleeding disorder is not related to thrombocytopenia or platelet dysfunction. Choice D is incorrect. Protamine sulfate is useful in correcting overanticoagulation with heparin, not warfarin. Choice E is incorrect. Administration of subcutaneous vitamin K takes at least 12 to 36 hours to have full effect and reverse the effects of warfarin; too long in this patient with a life-threatening hemorrhage. However, vitamin K is a useful adjuvant to the administration of fresh frozen plasma, as fresh frozen plasma only is effective for 4 to 6 hours after its infusion.

A 40-year-old male presents to a local health clinic with complaints of shortness of breath worsening over the last several weeks. He has been HIV-positive for several years. He takes no medicines and does not know his last CD4$^+$ count. His temperature is 38.0 C (100.2 F), his heart rate is 100 beats per minute, his respiratory rate is 25 per minute, and his blood pressure is 120/60 mm Hg. His oxygen saturation breathing room air is 88%.

An arterial blood gas is obtained:

PH	7.46
PO$_2$	60 mm Hg
PCO$_2$	24 mm Hg

176. What is the alveolar-arterial oxygen gradient?

(A) 20 mm Hg
(B) 40 mm Hg
(C) 60 mm Hg
(D) 80 mm Hg
(E) 100 mm Hg

(C) is correct. Alveolar-arterial oxygen gradient is calculated by subtracting the arterial oxygen obtained from the alveolar oxygen. When breathing room air, the alveolar oxygen equation simplifies to 150 − (PCO$_2$/0.8). In this case, the alveolar-arterial oxygen gradient is [150 − (24.0/0.8)] − 60 = 60 mm Hg.

177. What is the most likely pathogen that accounts for the symptoms of the patient?

(A) Cytomegalovirus
(B) *Mycobacterium kansasii*
(C) *Mycobacterium tuberculosis*
(D) *Mycoplasma pneumoniae*
(E) *Pneumocystis carinii*
(F) *Streptococcus pneumoniae*

(E) is correct. *Pneumocystis carinii* is a common pathogen in patients with HIV and CD4$^+$ counts less than 200/mm^3. Symptoms are usually progressive dyspnea, cough, and fever, often of several weeks' duration. Often, the alveolar-arterial oxygen gradient is elevated. Choice A is incorrect. In AIDS patients with very low CD4$^+$ counts, cytomegalovirus is a concern. Generally, symptoms are ocular with visual decline, or gastrointestinal with chronic diarrhea. Choice B is incorrect. *Mycobacterium kansasii* is an atypical mycobacterium most commonly isolated as a pathogen in patients who have received bone marrow transplants or are suffering from lymphoma. It is not a common pathogen in patients with HIV. Choice C is incorrect. *Mycobacterium tuberculosis* should always be considered in patients with HIV and pulmonary complaints. However, in this case, hypoxia and an increased alveolar-arterial oxygen gradient argue against this diagnosis. Choice D is incorrect. *Mycoplasma pneumoniae* is a common cause of pneumonia in young adults. It is characterized by a persistent cough, often of several weeks' duration. Lung fields are usually clear, and consolidated pneumonia would be a highly atypical finding. Choice F is incorrect. Patients with HIV infection are at increased risk for developing bacterial pneumonia with any CD4$^+$ count. However, the rapid onset of symptoms and rusty-colored sputum suggestive of *Streptococcus pneumoniae* infection are lacking.

178. A 34-year-old HIV-positive man whose last CD4$^+$ count was 10/mm^3 and who has a viral load of 200,000 copies presents to the emergency department with complaints of fever, chills, a poor appetite, and weight loss worsening over the last several months. His temperature is 38.2 C (102 F), blood pressure is 110/60 mm Hg, and heart rate is 100 beats per minute. He appears cachectic and has marked hepatosplenomegaly. Which of the following is the most likely diagnosis?

 (A) Cytomegalovirus
 (B) *Mycobacterium avium* complex
 (C) *Mycobacterium kansasii*
 (D) *Mycobacterium tuberculosis*
 (E) *Mycoplasma pneumoniae*
 (F) *Pneumocystis carinii*
 (G) *Streptococcus pneumoniae*

(B) is correct. *Mycobacterium avium* complex (MAC) is a group of atypical mycobacteria most commonly isolated as a pathogen in patients with AIDS and very low CD4$^+$ counts (fewer than 50/mm^3). Symptoms include a wasting syndrome with prominent fever, chills, diarrhea, and weight loss. Hepatosplenomegaly is common. The organism often can be cultured from blood or bone marrow aspirate of affected individuals after a 4 to 6 week incubation period. Choice A is incorrect. In AIDS patients with very low CD4$^+$ counts, cytomegalovirus is a concern. Generally, symptoms are ocular with visual decline, or gastrointestinal with chronic diarrhea. Choice C is incorrect. *Mycobacterium kansasii* is an atypical mycobacterium most commonly isolated as a pathogen in patients who have received bone marrow transplants or are suffering from lymphoma. It is not a common pathogen in patients with HIV. Choice D is incorrect. *Mycobacterium tuberculosis* should always be considered in patients with HIV and pulmonary complaints. *Mycobacterium avium* complex (MAC) more commonly produces generalized symptoms in patients with advanced HIV infection. Choice E is incorrect. *Mycoplasma pneumoniae* is a common cause of pneumonia in young adults. It is characterized by a persistent cough, often of several weeks' duration. Choice F is incorrect. *Pneumocystis carinii* is a common pathogen in patients with HIV and CD4$^+$ counts less than 200/mm^3. Symptoms are usually progressive dyspnea, cough, and fever, often of several weeks' duration. Often, the alveolar-arterial oxygen gradient is elevated. Choice G is incorrect. Patients with HIV infection are at increased risk for developing bacterial pneumonia with any CD4$^+$ count. However, the rapid onset of symptoms and rusty-colored sputum suggestive of *Streptococcus pneumoniae* infection are lacking.

179. A 76-year-old white female is brought to the emergency department by ambulance. She has a history of chronic obstructive pulmonary disease and schizophrenia. She is unarousable.

An arterial blood gas is obtained:

pH	7.34
PO$_2$	60 mm Hg
PCO$_2$	100 mm Hg
HCO$_3$ (measured)	40 mEq/dL

Which of the following is the most likely acid-base disorder?

 (A) Acute respiratory acidosis
 (B) Chronic respiratory acidosis
 (C) Increased anion gap metabolic acidosis
 (D) Metabolic and respiratory acidosis
 (E) Normal anion gap metabolic acidosis

(B) is correct. This patient has a profound respiratory acidosis. The large elevation of her bicarbonate indicates renal compensation for a chronic process. In chronic respiratory acidosis there will be an increase in her bicarbonate of greater than 2 mEq/dL for each 10 mm Hg of her 60 mm Hg CO$_2$ increase. Choice A is incorrect. In acute respiratory acidosis, the kidney is unable to compensate by retaining any more than 1 mEq/dL of bicarbonate for each 10 mm Hg increase in the PCO$_2$. Therefore, this patient has a chronic respiratory acidosis with an increase in her bicarbonate of greater than 2 mEq/dL for each 10 mm Hg of her 60 mm Hg CO$_2$ increase. Choice C is incorrect. The patient has an increased PCO$_2$ consistent with a respiratory, not metabolic, acidosis. Choice D is incorrect. This patient has a chronic respiratory acidosis with a compensatory metabolic alkalosis. Choice E is incorrect. The patient has an increased PCO$_2$ consistent with a respiratory, not metabolic, acidosis.

Items 180–181

An 11-year-old boy is a runner on the junior varsity basketball team. During an after-school workout, he collapses while attempting a lay-up shot. According to the coach, he has no prior medical or surgical history. His pre-season physical examination 3 months ago was within normal limits. On the basketball court, he is unresponsive, pulseless, and apneic. Cardiopulmonary resuscitation is begun until the rescue squad arrives. Despite full advanced cardiac life support protocol, he expires on the scene.

180. Which of the following is the most likely cause of death in this individual?

(A) Cardiac mass   10%.
(B) Coronary anomalies   19%.
48% in blacks (C) Hypertrophic cardiomyopathy   36%.
26% in caucos. (D) Myocarditis   3%.
(E) Rupture of the aortic arch   5%.

(C) is correct. Of the cardiovascular causes of sudden death, the most common (accounting for 36 percent of cases) is hypertrophic cardiomyopathy. For reasons that are unclear, this condition is responsible for 48 percent of sudden cardiac deaths in black athletes, but in only 26 percent of sudden cardiac deaths in Caucasian athletes. Choice A is incorrect. Cardiac mass accounts for 10 percent of cases of sudden cardiac death in young, competitive athletes. Choice B is incorrect. Congenital cardiac malformation of the left main coronary artery accounts for 19 percent of cases of sudden cardiac death in young, competitive athletes. Choice D is incorrect. Myocarditis accounts for 3 percent of cases of sudden cardiac death in young, competitive athletes. Choice E is incorrect. Rupture of the aortic arch accounts for 5 percent of cases of sudden cardiac death in young, competitive athletes.

181. The sudden and unexpected death of this athlete has caused the local school board to consider changing the requirements of the pre-athletic physical examination to include more diagnostic testing to prevent such an event from occurring again. Which of the following would be the most useful test to screen athletes prior to their beginning an athletic program in school?

(A) Chest x-ray
(B) Computed tomography
(C) Doppler echocardiography
(D) Electrocardiography with signal averaging
(E) Holter monitoring

(C) is correct. Echocardiography is the test that can diagnose the majority of conditions affecting young, competitive athletes. Hypertrophic cardiomyopathy and idiopathic subaortic stenosis can be diagnosed rather easily with an echocardiogram. In this athlete, likely findings on echocardiography might include abnormal left ventricular outflow tract gradient and systolic anterior motion of the mitral valve. Choice A is incorrect. A chest x-ray can sometimes be useful in the diagnosis of Marfan's syndrome that presents with dilation of the aortic root. Choice B is incorrect. Computed tomography is a low-yield study for the diagnosis of cardiac anomalies in young athletes. Choice D is incorrect. A resting electrocardiograph will not identify the underlying cause of sudden cardiac death in the majority of cases. Choice E is incorrect. Holter monitoring is rarely performed in young, competitive athletes.

182. A 67-year-old white female presents to the emergency department with complaints of nausea, fatigue, and skipped heart beats. She has a history of atrial fibrillation and diverticulitis. Her current medications include digoxin and warfarin. Her blood pressure is 130/70 mm Hg and her heart rate is 70 beats per minute and irregular. An electrocardiogram is obtained and demonstrates normal sinus rhythm with frequent premature ventricular contractions. Which of the following is the most appropriate next step?

(A) Cardiac catheterization
(B) Cardiology consultation
(C) Digoxin level testing
(D) Echocardiogram
(E) Electrical cardioversion
(F) Electrophysiology consultation
(G) Treadmill exercise stress test

(C) is correct. The patient has digoxin toxicity. Early symptoms include anorexia, nausea, and vomiting. The most frequent cardiac disturbance is frequent ventricular premature beats. Choice A is incorrect. Cardiac catheterization is employed to visualize coronary artery anatomy and atherosclerotic disease, as well as to investigate some valvular abnormalities. It has no role in the treatment or diagnosis of digoxin toxicity. Choice B is incorrect. The cause of this patient's premature ventricular contractions is not organic heart disease requiring cardiology consultation, but rather a drug effect. Choice D is incorrect. Echocardiogram is a very useful test to visualize cardiac anatomy and function. However, it has no role in the treatment of digoxin toxicity. Choice E is incorrect. This patient does not have a life-threatening arrhythmia requiring electrical cardioversion. Choice F is incorrect. The cause of this patient's premature ventricular contractions is not a conducting system disease requiring cardiac electrophysiology consultation, but rather a drug effect. Choice G is incorrect. Treadmill exercise stress test is a good screening tool for coronary artery disease, but has no role in the diagnosis and treatment of digoxin toxicity.

Items 183–184

A 12-year-old boy who is not wearing a helmet while batting is struck in the right ear with a baseball thrown by the pitcher during a baseball game. Upon being struck, he falls to the ground and loses consciousness. He is immediately brought to the emergency department for evaluation and treatment. He has no prior medical or surgical history. Physical examination reveals an acutely ill child who is now conscious, alert, and oriented to time, place, and person. He complains that he cannot hear from his right ear. Right otoscopy reveals tearing and perforation of the tympanic membrane. Otoscopy of the left ear reveals a normal tympanic membrane. Facial nerve function paralysis is noted on the right side. The remainder of the physical examination is within normal limits.

183. Which of the following tests should be performed on this patient while in the emergency department?

(A) Computed tomography scan of the temporal bone
(B) Electromyography
(C) Sinus x-ray series
(D) Skull x-rays
(E) Ultrasonography of the neck

(A) is correct. The most appropriate test to order in a patient with a suspected temporal bone fracture is a CT scan. This study should be performed in patients with persistent otorrhea or facial paralysis. This test can be performed in most emergency departments and will likely indicate temporal bone fracture. Choice B is incorrect. Electromyography is not indicated in the management of this patient. Choice C is incorrect. Sinus x-rays are unlikely to be of benefit in the management of this patient. Choice D is incorrect. Skull x-rays are unlikely to be of benefit in the management of this patient. Choice E is incorrect. Ultrasonography of the neck is not likely to provide useful information for the management of this patient.

184. The child's mother arrives at the emergency department and is concerned because her child cannot hear well from his right ear. Which of the following is the most appropriate statement to make to this child's mother?

(A) Hearing loss is due to auditory nerve damage and is permanent.
(B) Hearing loss is due to ossicular disruption and will improve with surgery.
(C) Hearing should return in 4–6 weeks, otherwise specialty consultation will be necessary.
(D) It is likely that hearing loss will also occur in the contralateral ear.
(E) It is likely that the child will develop intermittent seizure activity during the coming weeks.

(C) is correct. Temporal bone fractures do not usually require sophisticated treatment. Patients should be referred to an otolaryngologist if their hearing fails to improve in 4 to 6 weeks. Some patients may be left with residual hearing loss and the cause should be determined. Choice A is incorrect. Auditory nerve damage is unlikely in the majority of cases of temporal bone fracture. Choice B is incorrect. Ossicular disruption is unlikely in the majority of cases of temporal bone fracture. Choice D is incorrect. It is unlikely that hearing loss will occur in the contralateral ear. Choice E is incorrect. Seizure activity is unlikely to occur in this patient.

185. In attempting to counsel a patient about suicide prevention, it is necessary to assess risk of suicide. Which of the following patient profiles would be at highest risk for a suicide attempt?

(A) A 27-year-old man who is of low socioeconomic status, who recently moved from a rural to an urban setting

(B) A 27-year-old woman who is of middle socioeconomic class who lives in the country

(C) A 39-year-old man with schizophrenia who lives in a group home

(D) A 49-year-old woman with a history of major depression who is a recent widow

(E) A 70-year-old man with prostate cancer who works as an office clerk

(D) is correct. Risk for suicide increases starting at age 40, with females attempting suicide more often than males, but males being more successful than females. Minority status is protective against suicide attempts. Concurrent medical, psychiatric, and family problems can escalate one's risk of a suicide attempt. The 49-year-old woman has three risk factors for suicide: She is female, she has a history of depression, and she is a recent widow.

	pH	PCO$_2$	PO$_2$	Sodium	Potassium	Chloride	Bicarbonate
(A)	7.10	78	55	140	4.8	100	28
(B)	7.20	20	98	140	4.8	100	15
(C)	7.25	25	98	140	2.8	110	15
(D)	7.40	35	98	140	4.0	110	20
(E)	7.50	45	98	145	4.0	100	30
(F)	7.50	20	98	145	4.0	110	22
(G)	7.57	40	55	145	2.8	115	25

Match each clinical scenario with the most likely laboratory parameters. Each set of lab values may be used once, more than once, or not at all.

186. A 26-year-old white male with a history of insulin-dependent diabetes is brought to the emergency department by his wife, who notes him to be confused and disoriented. The patient is unable to give any additional history.

(B) is correct. This young diabetic is most likely suffering from diabetic ketoacidosis, which causes an increased anion gap metabolic acidosis. In this case, the anion gap is 25. There is appropriate respiratory compensation with a decrease in the PCO$_2$ of 1.5 times the decrease of the bicarbonate from normal. (As a quick check for metabolic acidosis, the last two numbers of the pH should roughly equal the PCO$_2$.)

187. An 80-year-old white male with a long history of chronic obstructive pulmonary disease is brought to the emergency department by EMS. On arrival of EMS to the scene, he was tachypneic with prominent use of his accessory muscles of respiration. Despite 100% face mask oxygen en route to the hospital, his condition has not improved and now he is cyanotic.

(A) is correct. This patient has a severe acute respiratory acidosis with appropriate renal compensation (for the acute situation, there is an increase of one mEq/L of bicarbonate for each 10 mm Hg increase in the PCO$_2$). Most likely, this patient's drive to breath is via his oxygen pressure, not his carbon dioxide pressure, and the institution of 100% oxygen has precipitated impending respiratory failure.

188. A 72-year-old white female with a history of myocardial infarction and congestive heart failure presents to the emergency room complaining of increasing edema. She takes furosemide and captopril as well as sublingual nitroglycerin for occasional angina. She is in no distress but has prominent dependent edema.

(E) is correct. Use of the loop diuretics often creates a metabolic alkalosis. In this case, the patient has an appropriate compensatory respiratory acidosis, an increase in the PCO_2 of roughly 0.1 to 1 mm Hg for each 1 mEq/dL increase in bicarbonate.

189. A 22-year-old Hispanic female presents to the emergency department with shortness of breath. She notes increasing use of her albuterol inhaler without effect. The patient is tachypneic without use of her accessory muscles of respiration. She has prominent audible wheezes throughout both lung fields.

(F) is correct. This patient has an acute respiratory alkalosis with appropriate renal compensation, a decrease in her bicarbonate by 0 to 2 mEq/dL for each 10 mm Hg decrease in the PCO_2.

190. A 47-year-old white male presents to the emergency department with complaints of profuse, watery diarrhea. He has just returned from a trip to Mexico. His heart rate is 100 beats per minutes and his blood pressure is 120/60 mm Hg. When he stands, he is dizzy and lightheaded.

(C) is correct. This patient with diarrhea has an ungapped metabolic acidosis. There is appropriate respiratory compensation with a decrease in the PCO_2 of 1.5 times the decrease of the bicarbonate from normal. (As a quick check for metabolic acidosis, the last two numbers of the pH should roughly equal the PCO_2.)

(A) Amantadine
(B) Amitriptyline
(C) Buspirone
(D) Diphenhydramine
(E) Fluoxetine
(F) Haloperidol
(G) Levodopa
(H) Levothyroxine
(I) Lithium
(J) Lorazepam
(K) Methadone
(M) Trazodone
(N) Valproate

For each of the patients described below, select the most appropriate pharmacologic agent.

191. A 30-year-old man has evidence of depression. He is usually lethargic with hypersomnia, increased appetite, and a tendency to skip work because he does not want to get out of bed. A few times a year, he feels a surge of energy that makes him feel highly optimistic and powerful. At these times, he is wont to travel to exotic countries, spend excessive amounts of money, and become sexually promiscuous.

(I) is correct. This patient has evidence of bipolar I disorder. Lithium is effective in the short term and prophylactic treatment of bipolar I disorder. Eighty percent of manic episodes respond to therapy. It is also effective in the treatment of depression. Lithium has a narrow therapeutic window, and levels must be monitored. Levels greater than 1.5 mEq/L may lead to gastrointestinal, neurological, and renal complications. Levels greater than 2.5 mEq/L can lead to death.

192. A 25-year-old white male with a history of sickle cell trait has been addicted to heroin for the past 3 years and wishes to quit. He is employed as a stock room manager and would like to keep his job. He drinks 2 to 3 beers per day and smokes 1 pack of cigarettes per day. He uses no other illicit drugs, has no known drug allergies, and takes no medications. Urine toxicology screen is positive for opioids.

(K) is correct. Methadone is a synthetic opioid with a long duration of action used for detoxification and maintenance therapy for patients addicted to opiates. It is a schedule II drug and its administration is restricted by federal laws and regulations.

193. A 28-year-old white female with a history of bipolar I disorder continues to complain of depression and cyclic episodes of mania. She currently takes lithium, and her last level 2 days ago was 1.5 mEq/L. She complains of abdominal pain and dry mouth, and refuses to take any more lithium.

(N) is correct. This patient with bipolar I disorder has failed lithium therapy. Levels greater than 1.5 mEq/L can lead to toxicity. One viable alternative is valproate, shown to be effective in the treatment and prophylaxis of acute mania. It is generally well tolerated and safe.

194. A 50-year-old black male with a history of hypertension has had a long history of alcohol abuse. He usually drinks a bottle of vodka and a fifth of gin every other day. He denies taking any medications. Lately, he has had difficulty with his work as an office manager secondary to conflict with his supervisor. In reaction to these circumstances, he has taken to drinking even more heavily on a daily basis. He arrives in the emergency department after a particularly large binge, agitated and violent.

(J) is correct. This patient with substance-induced agitation should receive lorazepam, a benzodiazepine with rapid intramuscular absorption. Intramuscular lorazepam is the drug of choice to manage substance-induced and psychotic agitation in the emergency room. Benzodiazepines as a class are also used for general anxiety disorder, insomnia, panic disorder, and social phobia.

195. A 75-year-old female nursing home resident with a history of major depression who is currently being treated with amitriptyline is taking haloperidol daily to control a 2-week course of acute psychotic symptoms. Her psychotic agitation is now under control, but she has developed a tremor, festinating gait, and cogwheel rigidity of the bilateral upper extremities. Physical examination is otherwise within normal limits, and the patient is alert and oriented to person, place, and time.

(A) is correct. This patient has neuroleptic-induced parkinsonism. It is especially common in elderly females who take high-potency antipsychotics such as haloperidol. Signs and symptoms include tremor, rigidity, festinating gait, stooped posture, and cogwheel rigidity that develop gradually after 2–3 weeks of therapy. Treatment is decreasing or changing antipsychotics and administering an anticholinergic or amantadine, an antiviral agent serendipitously found to decrease symptoms of Parkinson's disease. Because the patient is already on amitriptyline, a highly anticholinergic drug, amantadine is the drug of choice for this patient.

(A) α-fetoprotein
(B) β₂-microglobulin
(C) Cancer antigen-125
(D) CD 25
(E) Carcinoembryonic antigen (CEA)
(F) Lactate dehydrogenase (LDH)
(G) Prostate-specific antigen (PSA)

Match each of the clinical scenarios with the most likely tumor marker finding.

196. A 45-year-old postmenopausal white female presents to her primary care physician with complaints of abdominal fullness and shortness of breath, both worsening over the last several months. Her abdominal exam reveals both shifting dullness and a fluid wave consistent with ascites. Breath sounds are diminished at the base of the right lung field, with five centimeters of dullness to percussion. She has a palpable right ovarian mass.

(C) is correct. CA-125 is positive in 80 percent of patients with ovarian cancer. It is a useful marker for treatment response and a rise may herald recurrence.

197. A 72-year-old white male presents to his primary care physician with complaints of fatigue worsening over the last several months. He has splenomegaly. His peripheral blood smear demonstrates typical cells of hairy-cell leukemia.

(D) is correct. Hairy cell leukemia is an uncommon, usually indolent hematologic malignancy. It is almost unheard of in patients younger than 55 years old, and is more prevalent in males. Malignant cells are CD 25 positive.

198. A 40-year-old white female presents to her primary care physician with several weeks of fever and night sweats that occasionally soak the bed sheets. She has prominent inguinal and cervical lymph nodes. Her chest roentgenograph demonstrates bulky, hilar lymphadenopathy.

(F) is correct. B-cell lymphomas, in particular, are associated with prominent systemic symptoms such as fever and sweats. Due to the large volume and rapid turnover of malignant cells, LDH is often elevated.

199. A 54-year-old black male presents to his primary care physician with complaints of rib pain that is worse at night and occasionally awakens him from sleep. His serum protein electrophoresis demonstrates an abnormal monoclonal spike.

(B) is correct. Bone pain is the presenting complaint in 70 percent of patients with multiple myeloma, especially pain in the back and ribs. Myeloma cells make osteoclast-activating factor, which prompts osteoclasts to destroy bone. (β₂-microglobulin is the most powerful predictor of survival in multiple myeloma and may substitute for formal staging procedures.)

200. A 25-year-old white male presents to his primary care physician with complaints of a right testicular mass, which has been present for several weeks. Exam confirms a painless, firm mass that is 1 cm in diameter and confined to the right testis. Ultrasound confirms an intratesticular mass.

(A) is correct. Nonseminomatous germ cell tumors are most frequent in the third decade of life (seminomas are most common in the fourth decade). These tumors are comprised of four types of histology, often intermixed in the same tumor: embryonal, teratoma, choriocarcinoma, and endodermal sinus tumor. Most of these mixed tumors secrete both α-fetoprotein and human chorionic gonadotropin.

SECTION 5 BEGINS HERE

Directions (Items 201–250): Each of the numbered items is followed or preceded by a set of options. For each item, select the BEST lettered option to answer the question or complete the statement. Locate the corresponding item number in the appropriate section of your answer sheet and completely fill in the circle containing the lettered option you have selected.

Items 201–204

A 16-year-old girl has been your patient for 10 years. You have been following her for routine preventive care. She has no prior medical or surgical history. She presents for advice regarding contraception. She takes no medications. Physical examination of the heart, lungs, and abdomen is unremarkable. She is a Tanner 5 with regard to sexual development. Her most recent urine pregnancy test is negative.

201. The patient states that she has been involved in a sexual relationship with a male partner for 1 year. She states that neither she nor her partner use contraception. You ask her for reasons for not using contraception during sexual intercourse. Which of the following is the patient's most likely response?

(A) Afraid that my parents would find out
(B) Don't get around to it
(C) My partner objects
(D) Never thought of it
(E) It costs too much

(B) is correct. In a recent survey of 337 female adolescents aged 15 to 19 years regarding why they did not use contraception, several interesting results were noted. Approximately 40 percent of respondents stated that their reason for not using contraception was because they did not "get around to it." This represents the most common reason why teenagers do not use contraception. Choice A is incorrect. Approximately 30 percent of females do not use contraception because they are afraid their family will find out. Choice C is incorrect. Approximately 10 percent of females do not use contraception because their partner objects. Choice D is incorrect. Approximately 15 percent of females do not use contraception because they never thought about it. Choice E is incorrect. Approximately 20 percent of females do not use contraception because they think it costs too much.

202. You begin to discuss information regarding oral contraceptives and consider prescribing a trial for this patient. The patient states that she is concerned about possible side effects of such medications. Which of the following side effects do adolescents fear the most?

(A) Cancer
(B) Heart disease
(C) Nausea
(D) Permanent sterility
(E) Weight gain

(E) is correct. Important barriers to the use of effective contraception in adolescents include their lack of knowledge about services or methods, and perceived side effects. Approximately 82 percent of teenagers perceive the most common side effect of oral contraceptives to be weight gain. This perception may push these individuals away from this method of contraception. Choice A is incorrect. 18 percent of teenagers perceive cancer to be a side effect of oral contraceptives. Choice B is incorrect. 5 percent of teenagers perceive heart disease to be a side effect of oral contraceptives. Choice C is incorrect. 12 percent of teenagers perceive nausea to be a side effect of oral contraceptives. Choice D is incorrect. 11 percent of teenagers perceive sterility to be a side effect of oral contraceptives.

203. Regarding a choice of a contraceptive agent for this individual, which of the following methods has the highest effectiveness for both theoretical and actual use?

   (A) Condom
   (B) Condom with spermicide
   (C) Female condom
   (D) Implantable estrogen-progesterone agents
   (E) Progesterone-only contraceptive

(D) is correct. It is important to consider the theoretical and actual effectiveness of various contraceptive agents prior to selecting one for use in this patient. Implantable estrogen-progesterone agents have the highest effectiveness for both theoretical and actual episodes (99.9 percent). Choice A is incorrect. Condoms, when used perfectly, are 97 percent effective, but experience an 88 percent effectiveness in actual use. Choice B is incorrect. Condom and spermicide, when used perfectly, are 99 percent effective, but experience a 95 percent effectiveness in actual use. Choice C is incorrect. The female condom is 95 percent effective in theory, but is 79 percent effective in practice. Choice E is incorrect. Progesterone-only contraceptives are 98 percent effective in theory, but are 90 percent effective in practice.

204. Over the course of 1 year, this patient tries several different contraceptive methods. You see her 2 years later, and she states that she has been taking oral contraceptives. The agent is triphasic. Which of the following effects is most important for the physician to be concerned about?

   (A) Breakthrough bleeding
   (B) Breast soreness
   (C) Headaches
   (D) Nausea
   (E) Weight gain

(A) is correct. Triphasic oral contraceptives contain varying amounts of estrogen and progesterone. There are several side effects of this formulation. The most common side effect is breakthrough bleeding, which occurs in 66 percent of patients. Choice B is incorrect. Breast soreness occurs in 12 percent of patients on triphasic pills. Choice C is incorrect. Headaches occur in 5 percent of patients on triphasic pills. Choice D is incorrect. Nausea occurs in 10 percent of patients on triphasic pills. Choice E is incorrect. Weight gain occurs in 17 percent of patients on triphasic pills.

205. A 24-year-old woman who is 20 weeks pregnant complains of headache and intermittent right upper quadrant pain. She is a primigravida and weighs 73 kg (160 lb). Her prenatal care has been up to date to the present time. Social history is notable for occasionally drinking wine. She is a former crack-cocaine abuser, but denies usage of substances during the present pregnancy. Blood pressure is 140/90 mm Hg (on 3 separate occasions) with a pulse of 86–92 beats per minute. Cardiovascular examination reveals a mid-systolic click without gallops. Pulmonary examination reveals no evidence of wheezes or rales. Gastrointestinal examination reveals mild tenderness in the lower quadrants bilaterally. Bilateral 1+ pitting edema is also noted. Urinalysis reveals 1+ proteinuria with no evidence of hematuria or glucosuria.

Which of the following is the most appropriate treatment plan for this patient?

   (A) Bed rest
   (B) Hydralazine-intravenous
   (C) Hydralazine-oral
   (D) Prazosin-oral
   (E) Thiazides-oral

(A) is correct. This patient has mild preeclampsia, which is defined as the development of hypertension in pregnancy with proteinuria, edema, or both, usually in the second half of pregnancy. This patient has mild preeclampsia because her blood pressure is less than 160/110 mm Hg, and her proteinuria is less than 2+. Management of mild preeclampsia is bed rest in the lateral decubitus position to maximize uterine blood flow while normalizing maternal blood pressures. Choice B is incorrect. Antihypertensive therapy is indicated if the diastolic blood pressure is repeatedly measured to be above 110 mm Hg. Hydralazine is the agent of choice. Choice C is incorrect. Antihypertensive therapy is indicated if the diastolic blood pressure is repeatedly measured to be above 110 mm Hg. Hydralazine is the agent of choice. This agent can be given intravenously to hospitalized patients. Choice D is incorrect. Prazosin is a direct vasodilator that can be used in the treatment of moderate or severe preeclampsia. Choice E is incorrect. Thiazides cause a decrease in cardiac output and plasma volume, and can be used in the treatment of moderate preeclampsia.

206. A 72-year-old man with chronic obstructive pulmonary disease presents to his primary care physician with complaints of worsening dyspnea on exertion. His current medications include inhaled ipratropium, inhaled albuterol, and an inhaled corticosteriod.

An arterial blood gas is obtained:

pH	7.34
PO_2	62 mm Hg
PCO_2	60 mm Hg

Which of the following is the most appropriate intervention?

(A) Begin 2 liters per minute nasal cannula oxygen
(B) Begin 6 liters per minute nasal cannula oxygen
(C) Begin acetazolamide therapy
(D) Begin corticosteriods
(E) Referral for lung reduction surgery
(F) Referral for transtracheal oxygen therapy

(A) is correct. Patients with severe obstructive pulmonary disease often rely upon their intracranial oxygen content as their central drive to breathe (not their intracranial carbon dioxide concentration, like persons with normal physiology). Instituting high-flow oxygen and normalizing the patient's PO_2 is not desirable, as it might well eliminate his drive to breathe and precipitate respiratory failure. Rather, the goal is to minimize symptoms and prevent cor pulmonale with a minimum of supplemental oxygen. Choice B is incorrect. Instituting high-flow oxygen (6 liters per minute) and normalizing the patient's PO_2 is not desirable, as it might well eliminate the patient's drive to breathe and precipitate respiratory failure. Choice C is incorrect. Acetazolamide, a carbonic anhydrase inhibitor, is used occasionally in efforts to decrease pH to supplement the drive to breathe in patients who retain carbon dioxide and require oxygen supplementation. This is a dangerous intervention and only has a role in refractory patients. Choice D is incorrect. Corticosteriods should be reserved for use in cases of acute decompensation, as the long-term consequences of corticosteriod therapy are severe. Choice E is incorrect. Lung reduction surgery is an experimental procedure reserved for those who fail conventional therapy, and candidates must meet strict guidelines with regard to preoperative pulmonary function. Choice F is incorrect. Transtracheal oxygen is reserved for those patients who refuse nasal cannula oxygen (for aesthetic reasons) or need high-flow oxygen (as it decreases dead space).

A 70-year-old man with a history of myocardial infarction, recurrent ventricular tachycardia, and asthma presents to his primary care physician with complaints of worsening dyspnea on exertion. His current medications include a methylprednisolone inhaler, amiodarone, furosemide, and inhaled albuterol as needed.

Pulmonary function tests are obtained and compared with previous results:

	Today	Two years ago
FEV_1	45% predicted	70% predicted
FVC	48% predicted	72% predicted
DLCO	35% predicted	71% predicted

207. Which of the following best describes his pulmonary function tests?

    (A) New obstructive lung disease
    (B) New restrictive lung disease
    (C) Poor patient effort with pulmonary testing
    (D) Worsening obstructive lung disease
    (E) Worsening restrictive lung disease

(B) is correct. The patient's pulmonary function tests (PFTs) demonstrate a new restrictive pattern. This is evidenced by the reduced FEV_1 and FVC, with a ratio of FEV_1/FVC that is approximately one (which is normal), and severely reduced DLCO. PFTs from two years prior were normal. Choice A is incorrect. Obstructive lung disease is characterized by a reduced FEV_1 with a normal or near normal FVC, giving a reduced FEV_1/FVC ratio. Choice C is incorrect. Poor patient effort may cause spuriously reduced FEV_1 and FVC, but the DLCO measurement does not rely on patient effort. Choices D and E are incorrect. Previous pulmonary function tests from two years ago were normal.

208. Which of the following is most likely to explain the symptoms and pulmonary function tests of the patient?

    (A) Amiodarone toxicity
    (B) Cigarette abuse
    (C) Furosemide toxicity
    (D) Noncompliance with medical therapy
    (E) Methylprednisolone effect
    (F) Worsening asthma

(A) is correct. Amiodarone is a well-known cause of pulmonary fibrosis, which is reflected by the new restrictive pattern of the patient's pulmonary function tests. Choice B is incorrect. When long-standing cigarette abuse causes chronic obstructive pulmonary disease, the pulmonary function tests demonstrate an obstructive pattern. Choice C is incorrect. Furosemide is not known to cause lung disease. Choice D is incorrect. Noncompliance with β-agonist therapy would not cause a new restrictive pattern in the patient's pulmonary function tests. Choice E is incorrect. Use of the long-acting β-agonist methylprednisolone should result in some improvement in the patient's asthmatic symptoms, but not cause new restrictive lung disease. Choice F is incorrect. Worsening asthma would be reflected by a worsening obstructive picture in the patient's pulmonary function tests.

Items 209–211

A 32-year-old white female with a long history of depression and alcoholism is brought to the emergency room by EMS after her husband found her unresponsive and surrounded by several empty prescription pill bottles. The patient had been taking imipramine for her depression, alprazolam for occasional anxiety, omeprazole for a duodenal ulcer, and occasional doses of acetaminophen for headaches. He is unsure of how many of each pill, if any, she had remaining prior to this likely overdose attempt. On exam, the patient is unresponsive with an intact gag reflex, and flushed with warm, dry skin. Her blood pressure half an hour after arrival in the emergency room is 95/50 mm Hg, her heart rate is 125/min, and her respirations are 12/min.

209. Which of the following is the most likely diagnosis?

(A) Acetaminophen intoxication
(B) Alcohol intoxication
(C) Alcohol withdrawal
(D) Alprazolam intoxication
(E) Imipramine intoxication

(E) is correct. The patient is displaying the signs of tricyclic antidepressant overdose, including the hypotension that follows a transient hypertension, tachycardia, and the anticholinergic symptoms of warm, dry skin. Choice A is incorrect. Acetaminophen toxicity does not display anticholinergic symptoms. Choice B is incorrect. Her symptoms and vital signs (the hypotension and tachycardia) as well as her anticholinergic symptoms are inconsistent with alcohol intoxication. Choice C is incorrect. Alcohol withdrawal is associated with hypertension and tachycardia, not hypotension. Choice D is incorrect. Lethargy and coma are common in benzodiazepine overdose, but patients do not display anticholinergic symptoms.

210. Which of the following is the most appropriate initial step in the care of the patient?

(A) Administration of charcoal
(B) Administration of ipecac
(C) Endotracheal intubation
(D) Gastric lavage
(E) Intravenous fluids

(C) is correct. Securing the airway, in this case with endotracheal intubation, is the first step in the resuscitation of any medically unstable patient. Tricyclic antidepressant overdose is a potentially life-threatening emergency. Choices A, B, D, and E are all incorrect. Each of these answer choices is a reasonable intervention in the setting of tricyclic antidepressant overdose. However, securing the airway is paramount.

211. After stabilization in the medical intensive care unit three days after her admission, the patient is transferred to the psychiatric ward. On admission, she is noted by the admitting physician to be tachycardic, hypertensive, and agitated. She has a fine tremor of her hands as well as her tongue. Which of the following is the most appropriate initial step in her care?

(A) Administer lorazepam
(B) Administer nifedipine
(C) Obtain a serum alcohol level
(D) Obtain a urine screen for drugs of abuse
(E) Transfer the patient back to the intensive care unit

(A) is correct. The patient is displaying signs of alcohol withdrawal in the typical pattern (3 days after her admission and last use of alcohol). These symptoms are best managed with administration of benzodiazepines to prevent alcohol withdrawal seizures. Treatment of alcohol withdrawal does not require transfer back to the intensive care unit. Choice B is incorrect. The patient's tachycardia and hypertension are signs of alcohol withdrawal that need to be recognized and treated with benzodiazepines, not symptomatically with an antihypertensive. Choice C is incorrect. The patient is showing signs of alcohol withdrawal, not intoxication. Choice D is incorrect. Although the patient may abuse other drugs, her symptoms and history are consistent with alcohol abuse and withdrawal. Choice E is incorrect. Alcohol withdrawal can be appropriately treated without transfer back to the intensive care unit. Some practitioners now treat alcohol withdrawal on an outpatient basis.

212. A 65-year-old white male with long-standing insulin-dependent diabetes mellitus presents to the emergency department with complaints of chest pain that occurs at rest. His electrocardiogram is unremarkable. Unremarkable cardiac catheterization is performed the following day and is well tolerated. Three days later, he presents to his primary care physician with complaints of nausea and decreased urine output over the last 24 hours. Laboratory studies and a urinalysis are obtained:

Serum

Urea nitrogen	50 mg/dL
Creatinine	3.5 mg/dL
pH	7.0

Urinalysis

Specific gravity	1.010
Protein	1+
Glucose	1+
Blood	1+
Nitrites	Negative
Leukocyte esterase	Negative

Microscopy: Many granular and occasional tubular epithelial casts

Which of the following is the most likely diagnosis?

(A) Acute tubular necrosis
(B) Allergic interstitial nephritis
(C) Cholesterol emboli syndrome
(D) Glomerulonephritis
(E) Renal artery thrombosis
(F) Renal vein thrombosis

(A) is correct. This patient has contrast neuropathy, a form of acute tubular necrosis (ATN). Contrast nephropathy classically presents as an acute (onset within 24 to 28 hours) but reversible (peak 3 to 5 days, resolution within 1 week) rise in BUN and creatinine. It is most common in patients with preexisting chronic renal insufficiency, diabetes mellitus, or congestive heart failure. The urinary sediment contains muddy brown granular or tubular epithelial casts, with little blood or protein on urine dipstick. Choice B is incorrect. Allergic interstitial nephritis follows ingestion of a drug and presents with fever, rash, and arthralgias. The urine sediment often contains white cells (often eosinophils) and occasionally white cell casts. There is usually nephrotic-range proteinuria. Choice C is incorrect. The cholesterol emboli syndrome can follow any manipulation of the aorta, including cardiac catheterization. There are usually other symptoms, such as palpable purpura, hypertension, and livedo reticularis. The urinary sediment is often normal, but may contain eosinophils. Choice D is incorrect. Glomerulonephritis results from glomerular damage generally caused by immune complexes. There is active urine sediment with red blood cell or granular casts, red cells, and white cells. There is often proteinuria as well. Choice E is incorrect. Renal artery thrombosis most commonly occurs in patients with atrial fibrillation or recent myocardial infarction. Patients present with flank or abdominal pain. Choice F is incorrect. Renal vein thrombosis presents with flank pain or occasionally symptoms related to pulmonary embolism. There is proteinuria, often in the nephrotic range, and hematuria.

213. The mother of a 9-year-old girl is concerned that her daughter lags behind in development as compared to other girls in school. Her daughter has not yet begun menses. Developmental history reveals that her speech and language are age-appropriate. She is in the 25th percentile for height and weight. Physical examination reveals a well-developed child with no evidence of sexual hair or breast development. She has limited presence of axillary hair. Cardiovascular examination reveals a regular rate and rhythm. Pulmonary auscultation reveals good breath sounds bilaterally without wheezes. Gastrointestinal examination reveals no guarding, rebound tenderness, or organomegaly. The liver span is 4 cm in the mid-clavicular line. Which of the following is the most appropriate statement to make to the child's mother?

(A) This child's sexual maturation is age-appropriate

(B) This child's axillary hair growth lags behind normal

(C) This child's breast development is delayed

(D) This child's pubic hair development is delayed

(E) This child should already have had a growth spurt

(A) is correct. The first step of sexual maturation in females usually begins between the ages of 10 and 11. However, there is a considerable range in the developmental cycle of young females, and this patient and her mother should be reassured accordingly. Choice B is incorrect. Adult axillary hair growth typically occurs between the ages of 13 and 16. Choice C is incorrect. Breast budding occurs under the influence of estradiol and typically occurs between the ages of 10 and 11. Choice D is incorrect. Pubic hair development occurs under the influence of androgens and typically occurs between the ages of 10.5 and 11.5. Choice E is incorrect. The growth spurt occurs under the influence of growth hormone and typically occurs between the ages of 11 and 12.

214. A 55-year-old black male presents to his primary care physician for a blood pressure check. His blood pressure is 158/93 mm Hg. On two other occasions, his blood pressure readings have been 156/92 mm Hg and 165/96 mm Hg. Over the last month, he has tried to decrease his salt intake and exercise more frequently. Which of the following is the most appropriate initial management of this patient?

(A) Begin an angiotensin-converting enzyme inhibitor

(B) Begin an α-antagonist

(C) Begin a β-blocker

(D) Begin a calcium-antagonist

(E) Blood pressure recheck in one month

(C) is correct. The patient has Stage 2 hypertension by the National Institutes of Health guidelines. His blood pressures have been rechecked to document the elevation. Now the initiation of pharmacologic therapy is appropriate, especially in light of the failure of diet modification and exercise. Two classes of antihypertensive medications are recommended for the initial treatment of hypertension, β-blockers and diuretics. Thus, the initiation of a β-blocker is most appropriate. Choice A is incorrect. Two classes of antihypertensive medications are recommended for the initial treatment of hypertension, β-blockers and diuretics, not ACE inhibitors. Choice B is incorrect. Two classes of antihypertensive medications are recommended for the initial treatment of hypertension, β-blockers and diuretics, not α-antagonists. Choice D is incorrect. Two classes of antihypertensive medications are recommended for the initial treatment of hypertension, β-blockers and diuretics. Some physicians use calcium-antagonists in the initial treatment of hypertension in all African Americans. However, there is little data available to support this, and currently, β-blockers and diuretics are first-line therapy for all races. Choice E is incorrect. The patient's blood pressures have been rechecked to document the elevation. Now the initiation of pharmacologic therapy is appropriate, especially in light of the failure of diet modification and exercise.

Items 215–216

A 23-year-old white male presents to his primary care doctor with complaints of abdominal pain, cramping, nausea and vomiting, and diarrhea. He attended a family picnic several days earlier and ate a "rare" hamburger. He has had no sick contacts. Prior to this episode, he was well and working as an electrical lineman. He has palpable purpura covering his buttocks and lower extremities. His rectal exam is positive for occult blood.

215. Which of the following is the most likely diagnosis?

(A) Eosinophilic fasciitis
(B) Henoch-Schönlein purpura
(C) Hemolytic-uremic syndrome
(D) Idiopathic thrombocytopenia
(E) Thrombotic thrombocytopenia

(B) is correct. Henoch-Schönlein purpura is an immune complex disease with multisystem organ involvement. IgA is the predominant antibody component of the immune complexes, which deposit in a variety of tissues including joints, capillaries of the gastrointestinal tract (accounting for the prominent nausea, vomiting, diarrhea, and guaiac-positive stool), and the skin. The classic lesion of Henoch-Schönlein purpura is most characteristically found on the buttocks and lower extremities and is caused by immune complex deposition. Choice A is incorrect. Eosinophilic fasciitis is a scleroderma-like syndrome of unknown etiology characterized by cobblestoning of the skin. Choice C is incorrect. Hemolytic-uremic syndrome is primarily a disease of children who ingest undercooked hamburger infected with strains of *E. coli* or *Salmonella* sp. The toxins of these bacteria incite an immune reaction that causes the characteristic findings of intravascular hemolysis and renal insufficiency secondary to immune complex deposition in glomeruli. Choice D is incorrect. Idiopathic thrombocytopenia is characterized by petechiae, not purpura. Petechiae appear as platelet counts decrease secondary to antibodies directed against platelets. Choice E is incorrect. Thrombotic thrombocytopenia is classically an idiopathic disease manifested as a pentad of mental status changes, fever, hemolysis, anemia, and thrombocytopenia.

216. Which of the following is likely to be present in the urinalysis of the patient?

(A) High protein levels on dipstick
(B) Many bacteria
(C) Red blood cell casts
(D) Uric acid crystals
(E) White blood cell casts

(C) is correct. Immune complex deposition in the glomeruli incites an inflammatory reaction characterized by red blood cell casts in the urine. Choice A is incorrect. Hemolytic-uremic syndrome may cause mild proteinuria, not heavy proteinuria. Choice B is incorrect. The patient has no urinary symptoms or elucidated risk factors for urinary tract infection or many bacteria in his urinalysis. Choice D is incorrect. There is no mention of prominent symptoms suggesting kidney stones of any variety. Choice E is incorrect. The patient has no urinary symptoms or elucidated risk factors for urinary tract infection, and certainly not for pyelonephritis with white blood cell casts.

217. Electronic fetal heart monitoring is undertaken in a 22-year-old gravida 2 para 1 woman who is at 32 weeks gestation and in early labor. She is HIV-positive and is a crack-cocaine user during the present pregnancy. CD4$^+$ counts are not available. She has not been seen for prenatal care at any time during the present pregnancy. Monitoring reveals an increase in fetal heart rate by 15 beats per minute for greater than 15 seconds on 3 occasions in the last 3 hours. Which of the following is the most appropriate description?

(A) Accelerated fetal heart rate
(B) Early fetal heart deceleration
(C) Late fetal heart deceleration
(D) Variable fetal heart deceleration

(A) is correct. Accelerations of fetal heart rate are defined as an increase in fetal heart rate above baseline of at least 15 beats/minute for 15 seconds. This indicates an intact fetal mechanism that is unstressed by hypoxia and acidemia, and reassures fetal well being. Choice B is incorrect. Early fetal heart deceleration is the slowing of the fetal heart rate, but never below 100 beats/minute. The deceleration begins as the uterine contraction begins, reaches the nadir at the peak of uterine contraction, and returns to baseline at the end of uterine contraction. These early decelerations are due to pressure on the fetal head from the birth canal, causing a reflex vagal response of the fetal sinoatrial node. Choice C is incorrect. Late fetal heart deceleration is a slowing of the fetal heart rate that begins after uterine contraction starts and returns to baseline after the uterine contraction has completed. These decelerations can be associated with uteroplacental insufficiency. Choice D is incorrect. Variable fetal heart deceleration is a slowing of the fetal heart rate that begins before, during, or after the uterine contraction starts, and is characterized by a fall in fetal heart rate to less than 100 beats/minute. These decelerations can be associated with umbilical cord compression and mediated by vagus nerve stimulation with acetylcholine release.

218. A 66-year-old Asian male presents to his primary care physician complaining of increasing abdominal girth over the preceding several weeks, as well as a 14 kg (30 lb) weight loss in the last six months. His past medical history is significant only for a remote history of an intracranial hemorrhage, which was visualized with injection of thorium dioxide, and hypertension controlled with hydrochlorothiazide. Computed tomography reveals a 9 cm in diameter mass adjacent to an area of bright signal intensity suspicious for retained contrast material on the liver. No other suspicious masses are visualized on computed tomography of the chest and abdomen. Which of the following is the most likely pathology of the hepatic mass?

(A) Adenocarcinoma
(B) Angiosarcoma
(C) Carcinoid tumor
(D) Small cell carcinoma
(E) Squamous cell carcinoma

(B) is correct. Angiosarcoma of the liver is associated with exposure to thorium dioxide. Now a well-recognized carcinogen, it was previously used for many vascular contrast studies, including cerebral angiography. By history, the patient has retained thorium dioxide in his liver, and is now presenting with an abutting mass that is highly suspicious for angiosarcoma. Choices A, C, D, and E are incorrect. None of these tumors, although each may be metastatic to the liver, are primary liver neoplasms and have no association with thorium dioxide exposure.

219. Electronic fetal heart monitoring is undertaken in a 22-year-old gravida 3 para 1 woman who is at 32 weeks gestation and in early labor. She has a history of gestational diabetes during the present pregnancy. Cardiovascular examination reveals tachycardia without murmur and pulmonary auscultation reveals clear breath sounds bilaterally. Electronic fetal heart monitoring reveals a fetal heart rate of 150 beats per minute that slows to 100 beats per minute when a uterine contraction starts and returns to 150 beats per minute when the contraction has completed. Which of the following is the most appropriate description?

(A) Accelerated fetal heart rate
(B) Early fetal heart deceleration
(C) Late fetal heart deceleration
(D) Variable fetal heart deceleration

(C) is correct. Late fetal heart decelerations are slowings of the fetal heart rate that begin after uterine contraction starts, and return to baseline after the uterine contraction has completed. These decelerations can be associated with uteroplacental insufficiency. Choice A is incorrect. An acceleration of the fetal heart rate is defined as an increase in fetal heart rate above baseline of at least 15 beats per minute for 15 seconds. Choice B is incorrect. Early fetal heart deceleration is a slowing of the fetal heart rate, but never below 100 beats per minute. The deceleration begins as the uterine contraction begins, reaches the nadir at the peak of uterine contraction, and returns to baseline at the end of uterine contraction. These early decelerations are due to pressure on the fetal head from the birth canal that causes a reflex vagal response of the fetal sinoatrial node. Choice D is incorrect. Variable fetal heart deceleration is a slowing of the fetal heart rate that begins before, during, or after the uterine contraction starts, and is characterized by a fall in fetal heart rate to less than 100 beats per minute. These decelerations can be associated with umbilical cord compression and mediated by vagus nerve stimulation with acetylcholine release.

220. A 15-year-old girl has a persistent fever after receiving penicillin therapy for strep throat 2 weeks ago. She took a 5-day course of penicillin with resolution of throat symptoms. Her oral temperature has been higher than 38.3 C (101 F) every day for the past week with acetaminophen intake. The patient has no localizing signs and symptoms such as headache, cough, abdominal pain, diarrhea, or skin lesions. She has no other medical conditions and currently takes no medications. She has no known drug allergies. Physical examination reveals a temperature of 38.9 C (102 F), a pulse of 120 beats per minute, a blood pressure of 90/60 mm Hg, and respirations of 20/min. The neck is supple. Mucous membranes are moist and without lesions. The oropharynx has swollen adenoid glands. Lungs are clear. Cardiovascular examination reveals tachycardia without murmurs, rubs, or gallops. The abdomen is soft, nontender, and nondistended, with no palpable masses. Extremities are warm and without cyanosis. Laboratatory analyis reveals a white blood cell count of 4,000/mm³, with 5 percent neutrophils, no bands, 80 percent lymphocytes, 8 percent monocytes, 4 percent eosinophils, and 3 percent basophils. Urine culture, blood cultures, and throat cultures are undertaken. The most appropriate next step in management of this patient is

(A) administration of broad-spectrum antibiotics
(B) administration of granulocyte-macrophage colony stimulating factor
(C) administration of a 7-day course of amoxicillin
(D) bone marrow biopsy
(E) repeat 7-day course of penicillin

(A) is correct. This patient with neutropenia (absolute neutrophil count less than 500) and fever should be hospitalized to receive triple-antibiotic coverage and to monitor cultures. The antibiotic regimen usually consists of vancomycin, gentamicin, and a third generation cephalosporin. This patient most likely developed an idiopathic reaction to penicillin, thus causing neutropenia. Choice B is incorrect. The administration of granulocyte-macrophage colony stimulating factor is not the first step. This factor can be given to stimulate the bone marrow in patients whose neutrophil counts do not rise over a given period of time. Choice C is incorrect. The administration of a seven-day course of amoxicillin is not indicated at this time. Choice D is incorrect. Bone marrow biopsy is not the next step. It is indicated if a source of neutropenia is not found. Choice E is incorrect. A repeat seven-day course of penicillin is not indicated at this time.

221. A 45-year-old man with a history of diabetes and hypertension complains of erectile dysfunction for the past 5 years. The patient is managed medically with 10 units of subcutaneous, long-acting insulin in the morning, and 8 subcutaneous units in the evening. His glucose is well controlled during the day, and ranges between 100 and 220 mg/dL. His hypertension is treated with atenolol. The patient expresses some concern about the current care plan for his impotence. During the visit, the patient, visibly upset, begins to raise his voice at the physician. Which of the following is the most appropriate strategy for the physician?

(A) Order repeat blood work
(B) Call a urologist to further evaluate this patient
(C) Refer the patient to a psychiatrist
(D) Ask the patient for his perspective and concerns about erectile dysfunction
(E) Tell the patient to seek care from another health care professional immediately

(D) is correct. When a physician gets into a heated discussion with a patient regarding therapy, it is best to stop the confrontation by displaying empathy toward the patient and asking him to discuss his perspective and concerns about his condition. This strategy might make the patient feel more at ease about his condition. An effective doctor-patient relationship is essential for patient compliance. Choice A is incorrect. Ordering repeat blood work is not likely to reveal additional information that will have an impact on the patient's present condition. Choice B is incorrect. Consultation with a specialist is an appropriate selection. However, the physician should explore the patient's concerns before making any further decisions. Choice C is incorrect. Psychiatric evaluation is not appropriate for this patient at this time. Choice E is incorrect. While this patient might ultimately seek care from another physician, it would be advisable for the current physician to determine the patient's perspective about his condition. This may restore the appropriate doctor-patient relationship.

222. A 40-year-old white woman has difficulty swallowing and constipation. She also complains of thickened, tight skin over her fingertips and on her face. The patient also complains of hypersensitivity to cold in her hands. She has no significant past medical history and takes no medications. She denies tobacco or alcohol use. Physical examination reveals a white female with thickened, mask-like, unsmiling facies. Telangiectases are scattered on the cheeks of her face. There is ulceration and subcutaneous calcification of her fingertips. Lung exam reveals good respiratory effort and clear sounds. Cardiovascular examination reveals normal heart sounds and a normal rate and rhythm. The abdomen is soft and distended, with decreased bowel sounds and negative stool guaiac. There are no focal neurological deficits. Hemoglobin is 10 mg/dL. Electrolytes, liver function tests, and renal function tests are within normal limits. Antinuclear antibody (ANA) is positive. Rh factor is positive. Anticentromere antibody is positive. Anti-Smith antibody is negative. The most likely diagnosis is

(A) CREST syndrome
(B) dermatomyositis
(C) diffuse scleroderma
(D) Sjögren's syndrome
(E) systemic lupus erythematosus

(A) is correct. This patient has calcinosis cutis, Raynaud's phenomenon, esophageal dysmotility, sclerodactyly, and telangiectases—all part of the CREST syndrome. Patients have positive ANA, Rh factor, and anticentromere antibodies. Choice B is incorrect. Dermatomyositis features a heliotrope rash around the eyes, Gottron's papules on the extremities, and elevated creatine kinase levels. Choice C is incorrect. Diffuse scleroderma is CREST with systemic organ (especially renal and pulmonary) involvement. Anticentromere antibody is positive in about 1 percent of patients with diffuse scleroderma, vs. 50 percent of patients with CREST. Choice D is incorrect. Sjögren's syndrome is associated with dry eyes and mouth and rheumatoid arthritis. Choice E is incorrect. Systemic lupus erythematosus features malar rash, immunologic abnormalities, positive anti-Smith antibody, and multisystem involvement, especially renal.

Items 223–224

223. A 5-year-old girl is brought to the emergency department for evaluation of bleeding from the vagina. She has no prior medical or surgical history. Physical examination reveals a tearful child who does not smile at any time during the interview. Cardiovascular examination reveals no evidence of rubs, murmurs, or gallops. Pulmonary auscultation reveals no evidence of wheezes or rales. Gastrointestinal examination reveals mild tenderness to deep palpation in the right and left lower quadrants. Which of the following is the most concerning etiology to be ruled out by the evaluating physician?

(A) Cervical carcinoma
(B) Sexual abuse
(C) Uterine carcinoma
(D) Vaginal carcinoma
(E) Vaginal foreign body

(B) is correct. The most concerning possible etiology of vaginal bleeding in the evaluation of a 5-year-old female is sexual abuse. Up to 11 percent of cases of sexual abuse present with vaginal bleeding, which is more typical than it is in cases of vulvovaginitis or the presence of a vaginal foreign body. Choice A is incorrect. Cervical carcinoma is unlikely in a 5-year-old child. Choice C is incorrect. Uterine carcinoma is highly unlikely in a 5-year-old child. Choice D is incorrect. Vaginal carcinoma is highly unlikely in a 5-year-old child. Choice E is incorrect. Vaginal foreign body is a rare cause of vaginal bleeding in childhood. Suspicion of child abuse is warranted in this case.

224. Which of the following is the most useful tool or diagnostic test to confirm your suspicions in the evaluation of the above patient?

(A) Diagnostic hysteroscopy
(B) Vaginal speculum examination
(C) Diagnostic culdoscopy
(D) Observation of verbal and nonverbal clues when speaking with the patient and family members
(E) Complete blood count and serum electrolytes

(D) is correct. Diagnosis usually depends on the history offered by the child, mother, or friend. Physical examination may be corroborative, but is often not helpful. However, it is also important to be alert to verbal and nonverbal clues to possible abuse when consulting with young patients and their family members. These observations may prove more fruitful than further examination. Choice A is incorrect. There is no role for the use of diagnostic hysteroscopy in the evaluation of a child. Choice B is incorrect. There is no role for the use of vaginal speculum examination. It is often difficult in a prepubertal child, and may be both traumatic and unyielding. Choice C is incorrect. There is no role for the use of diagnostic culdoscopy in the evaluation of a young child. Choice E is incorrect. Complete blood count and serum electrolytes will probably add little to the diagnosis of sexual abuse.

225. A 42-year-old white male presents to the emergency department complaining of weakness and fatigue worsening over the last several days. He has recently recovered from gastroenteritis. Exam reveals poor air entry into both lung fields. Strength in the bilateral lower extremities is 1/5 and in the upper extremities is 2/5. Deep tendon reflexes are absent. Sensation to pinprick and light touch is preserved. Which of the following is the most likely diagnosis?

   (A) Bacterial meningitis
   (B) Left middle cerebral artery stroke
   (C) Guillain-Barré syndrome
   (D) Multiple sclerosis
   (E) Right middle cerebral artery stroke
   (F) Viral encephalitis

(C) is correct. Guillain-Barré syndrome is a rare disease that may follow a *Campylobacter jejuni* gastroenteritis or a viral illness. It is an acute demyelinating polyneuropathy whose features include an areflexic motor paralysis. Management is primarily supportive care. Choice A is incorrect. Bacterial meningitis is accompanied by signs of infection including fever and meningismus with eventual clouding of consciousness, not bilateral flaccid paralysis. Choice B is incorrect. This patient's symptoms and clinical findings are bilateral, and the absence of reflexes reflects a lower motor neuron lesion. Choice D is incorrect. Multiple sclerosis is a slowly progressive disease identified by neurologic findings separated in time and space, not an acute fulminant course. Choice E is incorrect. This patient's symptoms and clinical findings are bilateral, and the absence of reflexes reflects a lower motor neuron lesion. Choice F is incorrect. Viral encephalitis is infection and inflammation of the brain parenchyma. Patients are confused, delirious, and disoriented. Neurologic findings vary greatly and may be localizing.

226. A 67-year-old black male with a long history of alcohol abuse is brought to the emergency department by the police, who found him walking in the middle of the street partially clothed. Physical exam reveals a cooperative but disoriented patient with horizontal gaze nystagmus, a positive Romberg sign, and ataxic gait. Which of the following is the appropriate initial treatment?

   (A) Computed tomography of the head
   (B) Intramuscular B_{12}
   (C) Intravenous folate
   (D) Intravenous glucose
   (E) Intravenous thiamine
   (F) Lumbar puncture
   (G) Magnetic resonance imaging of the head

(E) is correct. This patient has the classic triad of Wernicke's encephalopathy with ophthalmoplegia (evidenced as nystagmus), ataxia, and global confusion caused by thiamine deficiency. Alcoholics are at high risk, and so are other nutritionally deficient patients such as those with starvation, hyperemesis, or cancer. Wernicke's encephalopathy is a medical emergency requiring the immediate administration of thiamine. Choice A is incorrect. Computed tomography of the head is a reasonable study in any patient with confusion without a clear etiology. This alcoholic patient, however, has the classic triad of Wernicke's encephalopathy. Choice B is incorrect. Symptoms of subacute combined degeneration of the spinal cord caused by vitamin B_{12} deficiency include weakness and paresthesia, most commonly in the distal extremities, as well as irritability and mental deterioration. Choice C is incorrect. Folic acid deficiency is a rare cause of subacute combined degeneration of the spinal cord with weakness and paresthesia, as well as irritability and mental deterioration. Choice D is incorrect. Glucose infusion may precipitate or worsen Wernicke's encephalopathy and thiamine must be given prior to glucose in any alcoholic requiring parenteral glucose. Choice F is incorrect. Lumbar puncture is a reasonable intervention in any patient with unexplained mental status changes. However, in this case, the patient has the classic triad of Wernicke's encephalopathy. Choice G is incorrect. Magnetic resonance imaging is an expensive test that should be reserved for patients with mental status changes after normal computed tomography of the head fails to offer evidence of etiology.

227. A 45-year-old white male presents to the emergency department complaining of severe mid-epigastric pain, nausea, and vomiting, which have worsened over the last several days. His abdomen is tender in the epigastrium but without rebound tenderness or guarding. Acute abdominal series demonstrates a nonspecific bowel gas pattern. Laboratories are obtained:

Serum

Alkaline phosphatase	100 U/L
Amylase	445 U/L
Lipase	1000 U/L
Bilirubin (total)	1.0 mg/dL
Sodium	145 mEq/dL
Potassium	4.0 mEq/dL
Chloride	110 mEq/dL
Bicarbonate	25 mEq/dL
Glucose	130 mg/dL
Urea nitrogen	10 mg/dL
Creatinine	1.0 mg/dL
Calcium	9.5 mEq/dL

Which of the following is the most appropriate initial step?

(A) Endoscopic retrograde cholangiopancreatography
(B) Esophagogastroduodenoscopy
(C) Gastroenterology consultation
(D) Nuclear medicine biliary imaging
(E) Place nasogastric tube and set to intermittent suction
(F) Ultrasound of the abdomen

(E) is correct. Based on the history, physical, and laboratory data, this patient has idiopathic pancreatitis. There is no specific treatment for pancreatitis other than bowel rest, pain control, and intravenous hydration. Placement of a nasogastric tube with suction decreases the gastrin release from the stomach and prevents gastric contents from reaching the duodenum. Choice A is incorrect. Endoscopic retrograde cholangiopancreatography is an invasive procedure with risks and complications, especially when performed in the setting of acute pancreatitis. This risk is warranted if specific therapy is likely to be available during the procedure, i.e., sphincterotomy for a common duct gallstone, but not in cases of idiopathic pancreatitis. Choice B is incorrect. There are no clues by history, physical, or laboratory studies to indicate that esophagogastroduodenoscopy would be useful. Choice C is incorrect. It is not necessary to obtain gastroenterology consultation in the initial diagnosis and treatment of pancreatitis, unless there is specific treatment to be offered such as sphincterotomy for a common duct gallstone. Choice D is incorrect. There is no evidence to warrant further evaluation of the biliary tract as an etiology of this patient's pancreatitis. Choice F is incorrect. There is no evidence to warrant further evaluation of the biliary tract as an etiology of this patient's pancreatitis.

228. In 1997, the American Diabetes Association (ADA) made new recommendations for the criteria used to diagnose diabetes mellitus. Previously, anyone with a fasting plasma glucose of 140 mg or higher was classified as having diabetes. Under the new recommendations, the cutoff point for diagnosing diabetes mellitus is a fasting plasma glucose level of 126 mg or higher. What does the change in the cutoff point do to the positive predictive value (PPV) and negative predictive value (NPV) of the fasting plasma glucose test?

	PPV	NPV
(A)	Decreases	Decreases
(B)	Decreases	Increases
(C)	Decreases	Stays the same
(D)	Increases	Decreases
(E)	Increases	Increases
(F)	Increases	Stays the same
(G)	Stays the same	Decreases
(H)	Stays the same	Increases
(I)	Stays the same	Stays the same

(B) is correct. The formula for PPV and NPV is given below.

Gold standard

	Disease Positive	Disease Negative

Diagnostic test

Test Positive	a (TP)	b (FP)
Test Negative	c (FN)	d (TN)

TP = true positive

TN = true negative

FP = false positive

FN = false negative

PPV (the proportion of test positive cases that has disease) = **a/(a + b)**

NPV (the proportion of test negative cases that does not have disease) = **d/(c + d)**

Changing the cutoff point for diagnosing diabetes from a fasting plasma glucose level of 140 mg to a level of 126 mg will decrease the PPV and increase the NPV. The lower cutoff point means that the likelihood of testing positive increases; the PPV therefore decreases because more false positives will be detected. Conversely, the lower cutoff point means that the likelihood of testing negative will decrease; therefore the number of false negatives decreases, causing an increase in the NPV.

229. A 42 year-old white male presents to his primary care doctor with complaints of fever, chills, and a worsening headache over the last several days. He has a several-year history of AIDS with a CD4+ count of $15/mm^3$ and a viral load of 50,000 copies despite a triple-drug regimen including two nucleoside analogs and a protease inhibitor. He is currently taking trimethoprim/sulfamethoxazole as prophylaxis against *Pneumocystis carinii* pneumonia. His temperature is 38.0 C (100.2 F). He has mild photophobia without meningismus. Computed tomography demonstrates several ring-enhancing lesions at the gray/white matter junction. Which of the following is the most likely diagnosis?

(A) Cytomegalovirus
(B) *Haemophilus influenzae*
(C) *Neiserria meningitidis*
(D) *Pneumocystis carinii*
(E) Progressive multifocal leukoencephalopathy
(F) *Streptococcus pneumoniae*
(G) *Toxoplasma gondii*

(G) is correct. This patient has *Toxoplasma gondii* infection based on his history and computed tomography findings. Patients with AIDS and CD4+ counts less than $50/mm^3$ are at greatest risk for *T.gondii*. Ring-enhancing lesions at the gray/white matter junction are highly suggestive. Generally, prophylaxis against *Pneumocystis carinii* with trimethoprim/sulfamethoxazole is also adequate prophylaxis against toxoplasmosis, but there are treatment failures. Choice A is incorrect. In AIDS patients with very low CD4+ counts, cytomegalovirus is always a concern. Generally, symptoms are ocular with visual decline, or gastrointestinal with chronic diarrhea. Cytomegalovirus does not form ring-enhancing lesions. Choice B is incorrect. *Haemophilus influenzae* is a cause of bacterial meningitis. The clinical picture of bacterial meningitis involves photophobia, meningismus, and fever with a rapidly progressive course if untreated. Bacterial meningitis does not produce ring-enhancing lesions. Choice C is incorrect. *Neiserria meningitidis* is a cause of bacterial meningitis. The clinical picture of bacterial meningitis involves photophobia, meningismus, and fever with a rapidly progressive course if untreated. Bacterial meningitis does not produce ring-enhancing lesions. Choice D is incorrect. *Pneumocystis carinii* is a common pathogen in patients with HIV and CD4+ counts less than $200/mm^3$. Symptoms are usually pulmonary, with progressive dyspnea, cough, and fever. Choice E is incorrect. Progressive multifocal leukoencephalopathy is a debilitating, dementing illness of the central nervous system caused by the JC virus. AIDS patients with very low CD4+ counts are at the greatest risk. Ring-enhancing lesions are not a finding. Choice F is incorrect. *Streptococcus pneumoniae* is a cause of bacterial meningitis. The clinical picture of bacterial meningitis involves photophobia, meningismus, and fever with a rapidly progressive course if untreated. Bacterial meningitis does not produce ring-enhancing lesions.

230. A 32-year-old woman, gravida 1 para 0, who has had an unremarkable antenatal course, has painless dilation of the cervix on pelvic examination at 20 weeks. The patient denies fever, abdominal cramping, or backache. Fetal heart tones are detectable by Doppler ultrasound. The uterus is nontender without contractions. Thirty minutes later, the patient's membranes rupture, and an immature infant is delivered and quickly expires. This loss most likely could have been prevented by

(A) antibiotics
(B) cerclage
(C) magnesium sulfate
(D) progesterone
(E) terbutaline

(B) is correct. Incompetent cervix is an important cause of second trimester loss. There is gradual, painless dilation of the cervix with bulging and rupture of the membranes. The fetus is delivered rapidly with little pain and rarely survives. The cause is often obscure, but may be due to connective tissue defects, previous trauma, or in utero diethylstilbestrol exposure. Treatment is with cervical cerclage in the first trimester, with a success rate of 80–90 percent, although it can be done in the second trimester with a lower success rate. The suture can then be removed after 37 weeks of gestation. Choice A is incorrect. Antibiotics can be useful if there is evidence of chorioamnionitis or other signs of infection, which this patient does not have. Choice C is incorrect. There is no evidence that magnesium sulfate is useful in treating an incompetent cervix. Choice D in incorrect. Progesterone has no place in the treatment of incompetent cervix. Choice E is incorrect. This tocolytic agent does not have a place in the management of incompetent cervix if there is no evidence of preterm labor.

231. A 45-year-white male with a long history of alcohol abuse is brought to the emergency department by EMS. He reports a 6-hour history of nausea with several episodes of emesis with bloody vomitus. His worsening dizziness prompted him to summon EMS. His heart rate is 100 beats per minute supine, and 135 beats per minute standing with a supine blood pressure of 120/60 mm Hg and a standing blood pressure of 90/55 mm Hg. He has epigastric tenderness without guarding or rebound tenderness. Bowel sounds are present. Laboratories are obtained:

Serum

Sodium	140 mEq/dL
Potassium	4.0 mEq/dL
Chloride	105 mEq/dL
Bicarbonate	30 mEq/dL
Urea nitrogen	15 mg/dL
Creatinine	1.0 mg/dL
Bilirubin (total)	2.5 mg/dL
Bilirubin (direct)	1.0 mg/dL
AST	160 U/L
ALT	80 U/L
Amylase	80 U/dL
Lipase	150 U/dL

Which of the following is the most appropriate first step?

(A) Computed tomography of the abdomen
(B) Esophagogastroduodenoscopy
(C) Gastroenterology consultation
(D) Insertion of a nasogastric tube
(E) Intravenous fluid resuscitation
(F) Ultrasound of the right upper quadrant

(E) is correct. This chronic alcoholic patient is most likely bleeding from an esophageal varix. However, prior to further diagnostic studies or specific treatment, his hemodynamic instability must be corrected. He is profoundly orthostatic, indicating severe intravascular volume depletion. While awaiting blood products, intravenous fluid resuscitation should be initiated. Choice A is incorrect. No imaging study, including computed tomography of the abdomen, is indicated prior to stabilization of the patient. Choice B is incorrect. Esophagogastroduodenoscopy such as sclerotherapy offers both diagnosis and potential treatment for variceal bleeding, but stabilization of the patient is the first priority. Choice C is incorrect. Gastroenterology consultation for evaluation and treatment is appropriate after stabilization of the patient is achieved. Choice D is incorrect. Insertion of a nasogastric tube might be necessary should the patient continue to vomit, but is generally contraindicated in patients with suspected variceal bleeding. Choice F is incorrect. Right upper quadrant ultrasound is the initial test of choice for suspected biliary pathology, but is not indicated in this acutely ill patient with hematemesis.

232. A 50-year-old man recently suffered the loss of his mother with whom he has always lived. He is distraught because his mother always took care of him, cooking him meals, taking care of bills, fixing an allowance for him, and doing his laundry. He is overwhelmed with his new responsibilities and begs a female coworker to help him at home. She agrees to help him for a brief while, and is amazed at his inability to allocate funds for bills and to perform household chores. After 1 month, she states that she will not be able to assist him further, and the man becomes extremely upset, offering to do anything for her if she will continue to help him. The most likely diagnosis in this man is

(A) histrionic personality disorder
(B) avoidant personality disorder
(C) antisocial personality disorder
(D) dependent personality disorder
(E) borderline personality disorder

(D) is correct. This patient displays a pervasive pattern of dependent and submissive behavior that features the following: difficulty making everyday decisions; a need for others to assume major responsibilities; difficulty doing things without help; helplessness when alone; urgently seeking another relationship as a source of care and support when a close relationship ends. Choice A is incorrect. Histrionic personality disorder features a pattern of behavior that includes being the center of attention, inappropriate sexual seductiveness, insincerity, self-dramatization, and suggestibility. Choice B is incorrect. Avoidant personality disorder features a pattern of behavior caused by low self-esteem and poor self-image. Patients are extremely sensitive to criticism and have few relationships because they are too afraid to risk embarrassment. Choice C is incorrect. Antisocial personality disorder features a pattern of behavior that disregards and violates the rights of others. Patients usually have criminal records and are irritable, hostile, and manipulative. Choice E is incorrect. Borderline personality disorder features frantic efforts to avoid real or imagined abandonment; a pattern of unstable and intense interpersonal relationships; recurrent suicidal behavior, gestures, and threats; affective instability due to a marked reactivity of mood; chronic feelings of emptiness; difficulty controlling anger; and transient, stress-related paranoid ideation.

233. A 60-year-old woman has several tar-colored bowel movements over the period of a week. Past medical history is significant for osteoarthritis and insulin-dependent diabetes mellitus. Medications include insulin and naproxen. She has no known drug allergies. The patient drinks 2 glasses of red wine per day and smokes half a pack of cigarettes per day. The patient denies weight loss, changes in appetite, or abdominal pain. She has never had hematemesis or bright red blood per rectum. Bowel movements were normal before the onset of melena. Physical examination reveals a well-developed, well-nourished woman in no apparent distress. Blood pressure is 130/80 mm Hg. Pulse is 80 beats per minute. Sclera are anicteric. Lung and cardiac exam is normal. The abdomen has mild mid-epigastric tenderness to deep palpation. Bowel sounds are present. There is no hepatosplenomegaly appreciated. Stool guaiac is positive. The extremities are warm and distal pulses are palpable. Hemoglobin is 9 g/dL. Which of the following diagnostic results is most likely to be present in this patient?

(A) Clear bile-stained nasogastric lavage aspirate
(B) Elevated serum ammonia levels
(C) Lower GI series with an apple-core lesion in descending colon
(D) Upper endoscopy with subepithelial hemorrhage, petechiae, and erosions
(E) Upper GI series with gastric ulceration

(D) is correct. This patient most likely has the diagnosis of nonsteroidal anti-inflammatory drug-induced gastritis. The majority of patients with an upper GI bleed present with melena. This patient's major risk factor for bleeding is naproxen use. The diagnostic test of choice is endoscopy, which reveals evidence of erosion and hemorrhage. Choice A is incorrect. Clear bile-stained nasogastric lavage aspirate is unlikely to be found in this patient, as the finding suggests a duodenal source. Choice B is incorrect. Elevated serum ammonia levels would be found if this patient had signs and symptoms of portal hypertension, which she does not. Choice C is incorrect. Lower GI series with an apple-core lesion in the descending colon is unlikely because this patient has no signs or symptoms of colon cancer—bright red blood per rectum, weight loss, and obstruction. Choice E is incorrect. Upper GI series with gastric ulceration is a highly unlikely finding, as these x-rays are unable to detect gastritis.

234. A 23-year-old white woman, gravida 1 para 1, with insulin-dependent diabetes mellitus develops fever and chills. She also complains of back pain, nausea, vomiting, and diarrhea. Urination is more frequent with painful evacuation. She has an insulin pump for her diabetes. Otherwise, the patient takes no other medications and has no known drug allergies. She does not smoke or drink alcohol. She is sexually active with one monogamous male partner. Physical exam reveals a temperature of 38.9 C (102 F), a pulse of 110 beats per minute, respirations of 15/min, and a blood pressure of 100/60 mm Hg. Pupils are reactive to light and equal in size. Sclera are anicteric. Mucous membranes are dry. Lungs are clear. Cardiovascular examination reveals tachycardia with a regular rhythm. There is pronounced costovertebral angle tenderness. The abdomen is soft and flat, with the insulin pump intact and in place. Extremities are warm and without edema. White blood cell count is 15,000/mm^3 with a left shift. Chest x-ray is within normal limits. Abdominal plain film is negative. The finding on urinalysis that is most characteristic of this patient's diagnosis is

(A) bacteria
(B) hyaline casts
(C) red blood cells
(D) white blood cells
(E) white blood cell casts

(E) is correct. This patient has signs and symptoms of acute pyelonephritis: fever, chills, flank pain, and irritative voiding symptoms. This infection of the upper renal tract is most commonly secondary to *Escherichia coli*. White blood cell casts are seen, as they are evacuated from the nephrons and renal tubules. Choice A is incorrect. Bacteria are seen in cystitis. Choice B is incorrect. Hyaline casts are seen in acute tubular necrosis. Choices C and D are incorrect. White blood cells and white blood cells casts are also seen in cystitis and pyelonephritis secondary to adjacent inflamed bowel.

235. A 75-year-old Asian male presents to his primary care physician with complaints of right knee pain and a ringing in his ears. Both of his knees have given him problems for years, but this right knee pain is worse than usual. The pain is worse in the morning, and he takes aspirin during the day with improvement of his symptoms. His right knee is nonerythematous and without significant effusion. There is a large amount of crepitus with passive range of motion. His gait is antalgic. What is the most appropriate next step?

(A) Continue aspirin therapy
(B) Order a salicylic acid level
(C) Order computed tomography of the head
(D) Prescribe enteric-coated aspirin
(E) Prescribe physical therapy

(B) is correct. With new tinnitus and a history of recent use of large amounts of aspirin, this patient may be suffering from salicylate toxicity, which is a medical emergency. The most appropriate first step is a salicylate level. Choice A is incorrect. With new tinnitus and a history of recent use of large amounts of aspirin, this patient may be suffering from salicylate toxicity, which is a medical emergency. Aspirin must be discontinued. Choice C is incorrect. The most likely cause of the patient's new tinnitus is salicylate toxicity. Computed tomography is not warranted. Choice D is incorrect. With new tinnitus and a history of recent use of large amounts of aspirin, this patient may be suffering from salicylate toxicity, which is a medical emergency. Aspirin must be discontinued. Choice E is correct. Although many patients with osteoarthritis benefit from physical therapy, the more immediate issue is the patient's probable salicylate toxicity.

Items 236–238

(A) Asbestos
(B) Beryllium
(C) Coal dust
(D) Silica
(E) Thermophilic *Actinomyces* sp.

Match each clinical scenario with the most likely environmental exposure.

236. A 67-year-old retired factory maintenance worker presents to his primary care physician with complaints of worsening shortness of breath and dyspnea on exertion. Chest roentgenograph demonstrates pleural plaques and pleural thickening. Pulmonary function tests demonstrate a restrictive pattern.

(A) is correct. Asbestos was widely used in construction for its insulating properties. Asbestosis is a diffuse interstitial fibrosing lung disease that causes restrictive lung disease. Chest roentgenography findings are pleural plaques and thickening. Fibrotic changes give a "ground-glass" appearance on chest roentgenography. Asbestos exposure is an important risk factor for both lung cancer and mesothelioma.

237. A 62-year-old former stone cutter presents to his primary care physician with complaints of shortness of breath and dyspnea on exertion. Chest roentgenograph demonstrates eggshell calcification of hilar lymph nodes.

(D) is correct. Silicosis is either an acute or a chronic disease. The acute form is rapidly fatal. Chronic silicosis results from exposure to free silica and is most common in miners and stonecutters. The lung disease may be restrictive or obstructive. Chest roentgenography demonstrates small, rounded opacities in the upper lobes with characteristic eggshell calcification of the hilar lymph nodes. Patients are at increased risk for mycobacterial infections.

238. A 30-year-old white male farmer presents to the emergency department with complaints of the sudden onset of fever, chills, and shortness of breath for the last several hours.

(E) is correct. Farmer's lung results from exposure to moldy hay containing thermophilic actinomycetes. Symptoms begin 4 to 8 hours after exposure with fever, chills, malaise, cough, and dyspnea without wheezing.

Items 239–242

(A) Adrenal cortical neoplasm
(B) AIDS
(C) Cirrhosis of the liver
(D) Cryptorchidism
(E) Iatrogenic gynecomastia
(F) Kallmann's syndrome
(G) Klinefelter's syndrome
(H) Leydig cell tumor of the testis
(I) Lung carcinoma
(J) Nutrition alteration state
(K) Physiologic gynecomastia
(L) Renal failure
(M) Spermatocele
(N) True hermaphroditism

For each patient with gynecomastia, select the most likely etiology.

239. An 18-year-old white male high school student presents for evaluation of bilateral breast enlargement. He reached puberty at age 13. He has no other medical conditions, takes no medications, and has no known drug allergies. He does not smoke or drink alcohol. He denies ever having used illicit drugs. Physical exam reveals a very tall, slim male with long arms. Height is 198 cm (6′6″). Weight is 86 kg (190 lb). Vital signs are stable. Lungs are clear and cardiovascular examination is within normal limits. There is bilateral breast enlargement with no evidence of masses, dimpling, or skin changes. Axillary lymph nodes are not palpable. The abdomen is soft, nontender, and without palpable masses. Testicular examination is notable for firm, small, nontender testes. The patient has scant hair on the chest, arms, legs, and pubic area. Neurological examination is nonfocal. Serum testosterone is 2.0 ng/mL, FSH is 50 mIU/mL, LH is 60 mIU/mL, β-HCG is less than 5 mIU/mL, prolactin is 10 ng/mL, and repeat serum testosterone is 1.0 ng/mL.

(G) is correct. Klinefelter's syndrome is a common cause of primary hypogonadism secondary to the expression of abnormal 47 XXY karyotype. Puberty occurs at the normal time, but virilization is variable. 80 percent have gynecomastia at puberty. Patients also have a tall stature and a crown–pubis length greater than the pubis–floor length. They are at increased risk for breast cancer. 95 percent have azoospermia. Serum testosterone is decreased, FSH/LH ratio is elevated, and prolactin and β-HCG are within normal limits.

240. A 16-year-old white male is seen by his doctor for delayed puberty. As a child, he had no developmental abnormality. He was a full-term infant with an uncomplicated delivery. He takes no medications, alcohol, or cigarettes. Physical examination reveals a tall white male with boyish features. There is no facial, axially, or pubic hair. Limbs are long and thin. Examination is significant for bilateral breast enlargement and a very small penis with palpable testes. Cranial nerves 2 to 12 are intact, but cranial nerve 1 is impaired. Otherwise, there are no other focal neurologic deficits. Serum testosterone is 1.0 ng/mL, LH is 5 mIU/mL, FSH is 10 mIU/mL, and prolactin is 10 ng/mL.

(F) is correct. This patient with hyposmia, hypogonadotropic hypogonadism, and eunuchoidism has Kallmann's syndrome. There is developmental failure of olfactory bulbs as well as a deficiency in luteinizing hormone-releasing hormone secretion. Patients have micropenis and low testosterone, LH, and FSH levels, with normal remaining pituitary function. Treatment is with exogenous luteinizing hormone-releasing hormone.

241. A 13-year-old pubertal boy presents for evaluation of breast enlargement. Developmental history is within normal limits. He does not take any medications or have any known allergies to medications. He does not smoke cigarettes or drink alcohol. He denies any illicit drug use. On physical exam, he is the appropriate height and weight for his age. The right breast is enlarged, while the left breast is normal. There are no palpable breast masses, and axillary lymphadenopathy is not noted. The rest of the physical exam is within normal limits. Serum testosterone, LH, FSH, and prolactin are within normal limits.

(K) is correct. This patient has physiologic gynecomastia. It occurs typically in pubertal males between 12 and 15 years of age. The condition is often unilateral and thought to be due to excess circulating estrogens in relation to circulating serum testosterone.

242. A 24-year-old white male presents for a health examination. Although he is in general good health, he complains of bilateral breast enlargement and decreased libido. He has no other medical conditions, takes no medications, and denies use of cigarettes, alcohol, or illicit drugs. He is sexually active with his wife, but reports a decrease in frequency and in desire. Physical examination reveals normal heart, lungs, and abdomen. The chest has bilateral breast enlargement without associated masses, skin changes, or axillary lymphadenopathy. The patient notes a decrease in hair on chest, axillae, and groin. Testicular examination is significant for a small, firm lump on the right testicle, which does not transilluminate. There is no palpable inguinal lymphadenopathy. Serum estradiol is elevated. Serum testosterone is 9 ng/mL, FSH is 2 mIU/mL, LH is 6 mIU/mL, and β-HCG is undetectable. Chest x-ray is within normal limits. Testicular ultrasound is ordered.

(H) is correct. This patient has signs and symptoms of Leydig cell tumor, a nongerm cell tumor that develops from Leydig cells in the testes. It is usually benign. It is more common in white males, with peak incidence at age 20 to 35 years. This tumor can secrete estrogens and cause feminization. The tumors are usually small and difficult to diagnosis.

Items 243–245

	FEV1	FVC	FEV1/FVC	DLCO
(A)	Decreased	Decreased	Normal	Decreased
(B)	Decreased	Increased	Decreased	Decreased
(C)	Increased	Increased	Normal	Decreased
(D)	Increased	Decreased	Increased	Increased
(E)	Normal	Normal	Normal	Normal

Match each clinical scenario with the most likely pulmonary function tests.

243. A 28-year-old white male with asthma uses a long-acting β-agonist metered-dose inhaler as well as an inhaled corticosteriod. He has never been intubated, but has required three corticosteriod bursts in the last year to control his disease.

(E) is correct. Most asthmatics have normal pulmonary function tests when they are not acutely ill, as the etiology of their disease is reversible bronchospasm.

244. A 67-year-old white female with a 100-pack year history of cigarette abuse uses a ipratropium bromide metered-dose inhaler as well as an inhaled corticosteriod. Additionally, she requires two liters of nasal cannula oxygen to allow her to complete most activities of daily living.

(B) is correct. This patient has chronic obstructive pulmonary disease. She has an increased lung capacity (reflected by an increased FVC, forced vital capacity) but a decreased FEV1. This results in decreased ratio of FEV1/FVC. The DLCO is low, reflecting loss of alveoli for air exchange.

245. A 42-year-old white female with idiopathic pulmonary fibrosis has been symptomatic for the last 2 years, and now requires 3 liters of nasal cannula oxygen to complete activities of daily living. She is awaiting lung transplantation.

(A) is correct. Idiopathic pulmonary fibrosis is the hallmark of restrictive lung diseases. Both the FEV1 and the FVC are decreased, resulting in a normal appearing FEV1/FVC ratio. The DLCO is decreased, reflecting poor air exchange secondary to fibrosis.

Items 246–248

    (A) Mebendazole
    (B) Metronidazole
    (C) Pyrimethamine/Sulfadoxine
    (D) Quinidine
    (E) Tetracycline
    (F) Thiabendazole
    (G) Vancomycin

Match the most appropriate antibiotic choice to each clinical scenario.

246. A 34-year-old plumber presents to his primary care doctor with complaints of severe pruritus. Exam reveals a serpiginous skin eruption on his back and upper arms.

(F) is correct. Cutaneous larva migrans is a serpiginous skin eruption caused by the burrowing larva of animal hookworms, *Ancylostoma braziliense*, in particular. Treatment is thiabendazole.

247. A 23-year-old mother of two toddlers presents to her primary care doctor with complaints of perirectal itching. Microscopic examination of a nocturnal scotch tape test reveals *Enterobius vermicularis*.

(A) is correct. *Enterobius vermicularis* is a common infection of toddlers and school-age children, and occasionally their parents or caregivers. Treatment is mebendazole.

248. A 37-year-old white male with HIV infection presents to his primary care physician with complaints of diarrhea. Evaluation reveals a serum ELISA test that is positive for *Strongyloides stercoralis*.

(F) is correct. *Strongyloides stercoralis*, unlike most other helminths, can replicate in the human body. Patients with HIV are at increased risk for infection, which is best diagnosed by ELISA, as yield from stool is low. Treatment is thiabendazole.

Items 249–250

A 34-year-old white female presents to her primary care physician with complaints of diarrhea for the last 3 months. Over the last several days, she has developed right lower quadrant pain and a fever. Additionally, she notes a 4.5 kg (10 lb) weight loss in the last three months, without any attempts at weight reduction. She is a thin white female. Her temperature is 38.7 C (100 F), heart rate is 100 beats per minute, and blood pressure is 110/60 mm Hg. She has a palpable right lower quadrant mass without any local peritoneal signs. Her stool is positive for occult blood.

249. What is the most appropriate first diagnostic step?

    (A) Air contrast barium enema
    (B) Colonoscopy
    (C) Computed tomography of the abdomen
    (D) Esophagogastroduodenoscopy
    (E) Upper GI series

(A) is correct. This patient's fever, weight loss, and diarrhea are highly suggestive of inflammatory bowel disease. Air contrast barium enema is the test of choice in the initial evaluation of the patient with suspected inflammatory bowel disease. Often, this test will be able to distinguish Crohn's disease from ulcerative colitis, the two inflammatory bowel diseases. Choice B is incorrect. Although many patients undergo eventual colonoscopy for further evaluation or diagnosis of a suspected inflammatory bowel disease, colonoscopy is not appropriate for initial evaluation, as either air contrast barium enema or flexible sigmoidoscopy alone are usually diagnostic. Choice C is incorrect. Computed tomography is useful in the evaluation of intra-abdominal abscesses (a complication of inflammatory bowel disease), but not for initial diagnosis. Choice D is incorrect. This patient's symptoms (diarrhea, weight loss indicating possible malabsorption) and exam findings (a right lower mass) could not be evaluated by esophagogastroduodenoscopy, which can only visualize distally to the duodenum. Choice E is incorrect. This patient's symptoms (diarrhea, weight loss indicating possible malabsorption) and exam findings (a right lower mass) are suggestive of a colonic or perhaps small bowel etiology. Therefore, an upper GI series, especially without small bowel follow-through, would not be the appropriate first test.

250. The patient subsequently undergoes colonoscopy. This study demonstrates rectal sparing with prominent cobblestoning of the ascending colon. Which of the following is the most likely diagnosis?

(A) Celiac sprue
(B) Crohn's disease
(C) Irritable bowel disorder
(D) Ulcerative colitis
(E) Whipple's disease

(B) is correct. By history (diarrhea, weight loss, and stools positive for occult blood), an inflammatory bowel disease is suspected (i.e., Crohn's disease or ulcerative colitis). In this case, the colonoscopy provides the definitive diagnosis. Ulcerative colitis rarely spares the rectum, but rather begins in the rectum and spreads proximally to involve the colon. Fifty percent of instances of Crohn's disease spare the rectum. Cobblestoning is the classic finding in Crohn's disease as well, and is not present in ulcerative colitis. Choice A is incorrect. Celiac sprue is characterized by gluten intolerance. Patients usually present with symptoms of malabsorption. Jejunal biopsy is confirmatory, demonstrating blunting of mucosal villi. Choice C is incorrect. Irritable bowel disorder is characterized by abdominal cramping and alternating diarrhea and constipation. Fever and weight loss are not features. Choice D is incorrect. Ulcerative colitis, an inflammatory bowel disorder, should be considered with this patient's history. However, ulcerative colitis rarely spares the rectum, but rather begins in the rectum and spreads proximally to involve the colon. Cobblestoning is not present, and the affected mucosa appears friable by colonoscopy. Choice E is incorrect. Whipple's disease is a rare systemic disease characterized by arthralgias, abdominal pain, diarrhea, and weight loss. Fever may also be present. The etiologic agent is *Tropheryma whippelii*. Jejunal biopsy is diagnostic, demonstrating macrophages that stain remarkably positive (magenta) with the periodic acid Schiff reagent.

SECTION 6 BEGINS HERE

Directions (Items 251–300): Each of the numbered items is followed or preceded by a set of options. For each item, select the BEST lettered option to answer the question or complete the statement. Locate the corresponding item number in the appropriate section of your answer sheet and completely fill in the circle containing the lettered option you have selected.

Items 251–252

A 65-year-old white woman develops fever, chills, and a headache after complaining of bilateral ear pain for the past week. She is brought to the emergency room disoriented and agitated. Her past medical history is significant for multiple myeloma for which she is being treated with chemotherapy. She has had multiple fractures of the upper and lower extremities. She takes etidronate and a multivitamin. She has no known drug allergies. Physical examination is significant for a thin white female in moderate distress. Temperature is 38.9 C (102 F), pulse is 130 beats per minute, respirations are 20/min, and blood pressure is 90/60 mm Hg. The head is without gross fractures. Both eyes are fixed with pupils at 3 mm that are minimally reactive to light. Neck has nuchal rigidity. Otoscopic examination reveals bulging tympanic membranes bilaterally. Lungs and heart are normal. The abdomen is soft and nontender. Extremities are without edema. Skin is intact. Passive flexion of the neck causes flexion of the hips and knees. White blood cell count is 18,000/mm^3, serum sodium is 140 mEq/L, potassium is 3.5 mEq/L, glucose is 100 mg/dL, calcium is 8.5 mEq/L, and albumin is 5.0 g/dL. Chest x-ray is within normal limits. Lumbar puncture is performed and reveals gram-positive diplococci and many polymorphonuclear leukocytes.

251. Cerebrospinal fluid and lumbar puncture findings are most likely to have

(A) decreased glucose, decreased protein, and elevated pressure
(B) decreased glucose, elevated protein, and elevated pressure
(C) decreased glucose, elevated protein, and decreased pressure
(D) elevated glucose, elevated protein, and elevated pressure
(E) elevated glucose, decreased protein, and decreased pressure

(B) is correct. This patient is presenting with evidence of meningitis, probably secondary to otitis media with extension of pneumococcal infection into the CNS. Patients with multiple myeloma are especially prone to pneumococcal infection. Classic lumbar puncture findings include decreased glucose (less than 70 mg/dL), elevated protein, and elevated opening pressure. Choices (A), (C), (D), and (E) are not typically found in bacterial meningitis.

252. The most appropriate treatment at this time is

(A) ceftriaxone
(B) erythromycin
(C) gentamicin
(D) penicillin
(E) vancomycin

(A) is correct. The gram stain suggests, along with the history, that the causative organism is *Streptococcus pneumoniae*, which is susceptible to ceftriaxone, a third-generation cephalosporin with excellent central nervous system penetration. If this agent does not work, then vancomycin can be used instead. Choices B, C, D, and E are incorrect. These agents are not used to fight *S. pneumoniae* infection.

253. A 37-year-old Zambian male presents to the emergency department with complaints of worsening shortness of breath, nonproductive cough, and fever over the last month. He has a history of HIV infection for which he has refused treatment (last $CD4^+ = 12/mm^3$). His chest roentgenograph demonstrates bilateral interstitial infiltrates.

Arterial blood gas breathing room air:

pH	7.44
PCO_2	24 mm Hg
PO_2	65 mm Hg

What is this patient's alveolar-arterial oxygen gradient?

(A) 12 mm Hg
(B) 25 mm Hg
(C) 55 mm Hg
(D) 65 mm Hg
(E) 72 mm Hg

(C) is correct. For a patient breathing room air at sea level, the alveolar PO_2 is equal to $150 - PCO_2/0.8$ (where 0.8 is the respiratory quotient, a fixed value). The PO_2 is determined by the blood gas. In this case, $150 - 24/0.8 = 120$. The difference between the two is the alveolar-arterial oxygen gradient; in this case, $120 - 65 = 55$. A normal alveolar-arterial gradient is between 3 and 16 mm Hg. An elevated alveolar-arterial gradient is an indication for steroid treatment in patients with *Pneumocystis carinii* pneumonia.

254. A study is designed to evaluate the association between taking one baby aspirin every other day and developing a stroke. Data is extracted from a database of information collected by health care workers between the years 1950 and 1985. One thousand people who reported taken a baby aspirin every other day between 1950 and 1985 are compared to one thousand people who did not take baby aspirin during that time. The incidence of strokes in the group that took baby aspirin was compared to the incidence of strokes in the group that did not take baby aspirin. Which of the following best describes the design of this study?

(A) Case control study
(B) Ecological study
(C) Prospective cohort study
(D) Randomized controlled clinical trial
(E) Retrospective cohort study

(E) is correct. A retrospective cohort study is an observational study in which subjects are chosen based on a particular exposure variable and then evaluated for the presence of a particular outcome or disease. In a retrospective study, both the exposure and outcome (or disease) have occurred prior to the onset of the study. In this case, the exposure is taking a baby aspirin every other day and the outcome is having a stroke. Subjects were chosen based on whether or not they took baby aspirin (the exposure variable). It is retrospective because the data on both variables was collected prior to conducting the study and analyzing the data. Choice A is incorrect. Case control study is an observational study in which subjects are chosen based on a particular disease or outcome variable and then are examined for the presence of the exposure variable of interest. Choice B is incorrect. Ecological study is a comparison of two variables that are analyzed at the level of an entire population, not at the level of individual persons. Choice C is incorrect. Prospective cohort study is an observational study in which subjects are chosen based on a particular exposure variable and then monitored over time for the development of a particular outcome or disease. Choice D is incorrect. Randomized controlled clinical trial is an experimental study in which two or more treatments are being compared. Subjects are assigned by chance to either the study treatment or the control treatment.

255. A 30-year-old black man has the acute onset of fever, chills, and pain in the suprapubic region and low back. He also complains of frequency of urination with marked dysuria. He has no other medical conditions and takes no medications. He reports smoking 2 packs of cigarrettes per day and drinking a 6-pack of beer per week. He denies any intravenous drug abuse. The patient is sexually active with 2 female partners with whom he always uses condoms. Physical examination reveals a black male with malaise and fatigue. Temperature is 40 C (104 F), pulse is 120 beats per minute, blood pressure is 120/80 mm Hg, and respirations are 15/min. The neck is supple. Lungs are clear. Cardiovascular examination reveals a regular tachycardic rhythm. The abdomen has marked suprapubic tenderness with a palpable mass. Bowel sounds are active. There is no rebound tenderness or guarding. Rectal examination reveals a warm, tender, enlarged prostate without fluctuance. The extremities are without cyanosis or edema. White blood cell count is 15,000/mm³ with 90% neutrophils. The most appropriate test to perform in this patient to confirm his diagnosis is

(A) blood culture
(B) intravenous pyelogram
(C) pelvic ultrasound
(D) prostatic fluid culture
(E) urine culture

(E) is correct. This patient has acute bacterial prostatitis—fever, chills, suprapubic pain, and a tender, warm prostate. Diagnosis is with urinalysis and urine culture as patients have bacteriuria, usually gram-negative rods such as *Escherichia coli* and *Pseudomonas* sp. Choice A in incorrect. Blood cultures are not usually positive unless the patient's prostate exam is too rigorous. Choice B is incorrect. Intravenous pyelogram is indicated only if abscess is suspected. Choice C is incorrect. Pelvic ultrasound is indicated if abscess is suspected. Choice D is incorrect. Expression of prostatic fluid is contraindicated as this may cause septicemia or epididymitis.

256. A 54-year-old white male with a history of hypertension and insulin-dependent diabetes mellitus presents to the emergency department with crushing substernal chest pain. Electrocardiogram reveals 3 mm ST segment elevation isolated to leads II, III, and aV_F. What is the most appropriate interpretation of this electrocardiogram?

(A) Anterior wall injury
(B) Anterior wall ischemia
(C) Inferior wall injury
(D) Inferior wall ischemia
(E) Posterior ischemia
(F) Posterior injury
(G) Septal injury
(H) Septal ischemia

(C) is correct. Myocardial injury is typified by ST segment elevation. ST segment depression is a sign of myocardial ischemia. The inferior wall of the heart, with blood supply from the right coronary artery, is represented on the EKG by leads II, III, and aV_F. Choice A is incorrect. The anterior wall of the heart is represented on the EKG by leads V1–V6 and supplied by the left anterior descending artery. Anterior injury would demonstrate ST elevations in these anterior leads. Choice B is incorrect. The anterior wall of the heart is represented on the EKG by leads V1–V6. Anterior ischemia would demonstrate ST depressions in these leads. Choice D is incorrect. Inferior ischemia would demonstrate ST depressions in the inferior leads: II, III, and aV_F. Choice E is incorrect. Posterior ischemia may be difficult to ascertain on an EKG. Choice F is incorrect. Posterior injury is most easily identified by the changes it causes in leads V1 and V2. In particular, a larger wave in V1 is most often a clue to posterior injury. Choice G is incorrect. Isolated septal injury without injury to the anterior wall is seen as ST elevation in leads V1, V2, and occasionally V3. Choice H is incorrect. Isolated septal ischemia without ischemia to the anterior wall is seen as ST depression in leads V1, V2, and occasionally V3.

257. A 66-year-old woman complains of a 1-year history of vaginal itching. She has a prior medical history of hypertension and diet-controlled diabetes. She takes atenolol daily. Physical examination reveals no evidence of murmur or gallops. Pulmonary auscultation reveals clear lungs bilaterally with good inspiratory effort. Gastrointestinal examination reveals guaiac-negative stool in the vault without evidence of hemorrhoids. Vaginal speculum examination reveals no evidence of cervical or vaginal masses and a closed cervical os. There is a 1.5 cm red, ulcerative, exophytic area on the right labia majus. The most likely diagnosis is

    (A) melanoma
    (B) Paget's disease
    (C) squamous cell hyperplasia
    (D) vaginal carcinoma
    (E) vulvar carcinoma

(E) is correct. Vulvar carcinoma accounts for 4 percent of gynecologic malignancies. The typical clinical profile is a female patient over the age of 65 who complains of vulvar pruritus. Physical examination often reveals an ulcerative or exophytic lesion on the labia majus. The etiology of this carcinoma is thought to be prior intraepithelial lesions and human papillomavirus. Choice A is incorrect. Melanoma is a raised pruritic and pigmented lesion of the vulva. Choice B is incorrect. Paget's disease is often associated with underlying disease of the colon and breast and is an intraepithelial disease. Choice C is incorrect. Squamous cell hyperplasia is a hyperplastic lesion associated with skin thickening and excoriation. Choice D is incorrect. Vaginal neoplasia is often multifocal and associated with other lower genital tract intraepithelial or invasive lesions.

258. A 27-year-old woman is brought to the emergency room via ambulance after she slit her wrists. She is stabilized and interviewed for psychiatric evaluation. The patient reports that her boyfriend recently broke up with her after a 6-month long, turbulent relationship. He was her seventh boyfriend in 5 years, and each relationship followed a tumultuous course. This event is her third suicide attempt, the first 2 episodes having involved sleeping pills. The patient is very still and quiet. Affect is blunted. She say she feels nothing but emptiness and wishes to die. Her ex-boyfriend arrives on the scene and answers further questions. He states that their relationship ended because of extreme, unwarranted jealousy on her part. He last spoke to her 2 days prior to her attempt, at which time she had been stable with a positive view of their separation. He notes that she is highly temperamental and prone to temper tantrums and fist fights. Which of the following personality disorders does this patient most likely have?

    (A) Histrionic
    (B) Borderline
    (C) Dependent
    (D) Paranoid
    (E) Narcissistic

(B) is correct. These patients exhibit frantic efforts to avoid real or imagined abandonment; a pattern of unstable and intense interpersonal relationships; recurrent suicidal behavior, gestures, threats; affective instability due to a marked reactivity of mood; chronic feelings of emptiness; difficulty controlling anger; and transient, stress-related paranoid ideation. Choice A is incorrect. Histrionic personality disorder is marked by a pattern of behavior that includes being the center of attention, inappropriate sexual seductiveness, insincerity, self-dramatization, and suggestibility. Choice C is incorrect. Dependent people are unable to make everyday decisions and need others to assume responsibility for most major areas of their lives. They have difficulty initiating projects and go to excessive lengths to obtain nurturance and support. Choice D is incorrect. Paranoid people have a preoccupation with recurrent suspicions, grudges, and reading hidden meanings into benign remarks. Choice E is incorrect. Narcissistic personality disorder features a grandiose sense of self with extreme sensitivity to criticism. Patients have little ability to empathize with others and require excessive admiration.

Items 259–260

A 42-year-old Hispanic male who is HIV-positive presents to the emergency department complaining of a 3-week history of worsening headache and photophobia. He has a stiff neck and his photophobia is confirmed on exam. He has no papilledema or fever. His last CD4⁺ count was 100/mm³. His only medicines include triple-drug therapy for HIV and trimethoprim/sulfamethoxazole.

259. Which of the following is the most appropriate first step?

(A) Computed tomography of the head
(B) Initiation of ceftriaxone
(C) Initiation of amphotericin
(D) Lumbar puncture
(E) Magnetic resonance imaging of the head

(D) is correct. Meningitis should be suspected by the patient's history and physical exam. In the absence of papilledema, it is safe to proceed with lumbar puncture without first obtaining computed tomography of the head. Choice A is incorrect. In the absence of papilledema, it is safe to proceed with lumbar puncture without first obtaining computed tomography of the head. Choice B is incorrect. Lumbar puncture should be obtained prior to the initiation of antibiotics in a stable patient with suspected meningitis. Choice C is incorrect. Lumbar puncture should be obtained prior to the initiation of antibiotics in a stable patient with suspected meningitis. Choice E is incorrect. Magnetic resonance imaging is not indicated as a first step. Should a focal etiology or process involving the posterior fossa be suspected and computed tomography is not diagnostic, then magnetic resonance imaging should be considered.

260. Which of the following pathogens is most likely the etiology of the symptoms of the patient?

(A) *Cryptococcus neoformans*
(B) Cytomegalovirus
(C) *Neisseria meningitidis*
(D) *Streptococcus pneumoniae*
(E) *Toxoplasma gondii*

(A) is correct. This patient with HIV and a CD4⁺ count of 100/mm³ has presented with a subacute course of symptoms consistent with meningitis. With a CD4⁺ count greater than 50/mm³ the most likely pathogen is *Cryptococcus* sp. Choice B is incorrect. Cytomegalovirus is not a common cause of meningitis, even in the immunocompromised. When it causes central nervous disease, it is usually in the form of encephalitis, which presents with confusion. Choice C is incorrect. *Neisseria meningitidis* or meningococcal meningitis, in the absence of treatment, has a rapidly fulminant course, (hours to days, not weeks) and is accompanied by high fever. Choice D is incorrect. Streptococcal meningitis, in the absence of treatment, has a rapidly progressive course, not a subacute presentation. Choice E is incorrect. *Toxoplasma gondii* is an uncommon cause of meningitis in patients with a CD4⁺ count greater than 50/mm³.

A 37-year-old man has the progressive onset of choreiform movements. He has recently had changes in his mood and personality. His prior medical history is notable for amnesia after concussion from a motor vehicle accident as a teenager. His family history reveals hypertension, congestive heart failure, and Huntington's disease in his father that was diagnosed at age 35.

261. Which of the following might explain the cause of the symptoms displayed by this patient?

    (A) Alcohol intoxication
    (B) Atrophy of the basal ganglia and caudate nucleus
    (C) Cerebellar tumor
    (D) Cerebral tumor
    (E) Deficiency of thiamine

(B) is correct. This individual has symptoms of Huntington's disease. This disorder is a genetic autosomal dominant condition characterized by choreiform movements that progressively become more severe. Later, dementia presents, often with psyhotic features. Pathophysiology involves atrophy of the brain with extensive involvement of the caudate nucleus and basal ganglia. Choice A is incorrect. The symptoms and pathophysiology of Huntington's disease are not associated with alcohol intoxication. Choice C is incorrect. The pathophysiology of Huntington's disease does not relate to neoplasia. Choice D is incorrect. The pathophysiology of Huntington's disease does not relate to neoplasia. Choice E is incorrect. Deficiency of thiamine is related to the impairment of short- and long-term memory as seen in the anmestic syndrome.

262. Which of the following associated psychiatric complication is most likely to occur in this individual?

    (A) Dementia
    (B) Depression
    (C) Mood disorder
    (D) Personality changes
    (E) Schizophreniform disorder

(A) is correct. Huntington's disease is associated with several psychiatric complications. Approximately 90 percent of patients will eventually develop dementia, which may first be described by the family as a personality change, and progresses slowly. Choice B is incorrect. Depression is not a typical feature of Huntington's disease. Choice C is incorrect. Approximately 50 percent of patients with Huntington's disease have symptoms of mood disorder. Choice D is incorrect. Approximately 25 percent of patients with Huntington's disease have symptoms of personality change. Choice E is incorrect. Approximately 25 percent of patients with Huntington's disease have symptoms of schizophreniform disorder.

Items 263–265

A 25-year-old Hispanic man with a three-week history of fevers, rigors, and myalgias presents for evaluation. He is a former intravenous drug user and has had sexual relations with both male and female partners during the last year. Physical examination reveals no evidence of cervical or axillary nodes. However, inguinal adenopathy is noted bilaterally. Pharyngeal examination reveals erythema bilaterally. Cardiac examination reveals a regular rate and rhythm. Pulmonary examination is without wheezes, rhonchi, or rales. Gastrointestinal examination reveals no evidence of peritoneal signs. Laboratory studies are as follows

White blood cell count	$6,000/mm^3$
Hemoglobin	15.1g/dL
Hematocrit	46%
Platelet count	$422,000/mm^3$
Serum	
Sodium	138 mEq/L
Potassium	4.0 mEq/L
Chloride	102 mEq/L
Bicarbonate	26 mEq/L
Urea nitrogen	12 mg/dL
Creatinine	0.7 mg/dL
Alanine aminotransferase	44 U/L
Aspartate aminotransferase	47 U/L

263. A standard screening test to be performed in this individual is

   (A) ELISA test
   (B) erythrocyte sedimentation rate
   (C) hepatitis B surface antibody
   (D) polymerase chain reaction
   (E) Western blot test

(A) is correct. The initial diagnostic test for HIV infection is the ELISA (enzyme-linked immunosorbent assay) test. This test is highly sensitive (> 99%) and is quite specific. A positive result of this test must be confirmed with the results of the Western blot test, which is undertaken after the ELISA test is completed. Choice B is incorrect. Erythrocyte sedimentation rate is not a specific test for the HIV virus, but may be elevated due to acute inflammation. Choice C is incorrect. Hepatitis B surface antibody testing in this individual might be positive and indicate a concurrent hepatitis infection. This test is not confirmatory for HIV disease. Choice D is incorrect. Polymerase chain reaction testing can directly culture the HIV virus from tissue, peripheral blood cells, or plasma, but this is most commonly done in a research setting. Choice E is incorrect. Western blot is the most commonly used confirmatory test and detects antibodies to HIV antigens of specific molecular weights.

264. The patient desires information regarding a positive result on the above test. You reply that the seroconversion occurs after transmission within

    (A) 6 to 12 hours
    (B) 6 to 12 days
    (C) 6 to 12 weeks
    (D) 6 to 12 months
    (E) 6 to 12 years

(C) is correct. Seroconversion to HIV positivity in patients exposed to the HIV virus occurs approximately 6 to 12 weeks after transmission. However, the ELISA and Western blot may be negative in a patient who was either recently exposed or is experiencing an acute retroviral syndrome. Therefore, in these individuals, repeat testing at 3 months is suggested.

265. The patient returns 3 years later with persistent abdominal cramps and myalgias. Laboratory testing indicates a CD4$^+$ count of 600/mm^3. Likely findings on physical examination might include which of the following?

    (A) Herpes zoster
    (B) Lymphadenopathy
    (C) Kaposi's sarcoma
    (D) Non-Hodgkin's lymphoma
    (E) Oral candidiasis

(B) is correct. A CD4$^+$ count greater than 500/mm^3 implies early HIV disease for which the most common complication is lymphadenopathy. This finding is considered to be a part of the Group III classification of HIV infection. Group I and II classifications include acute HIV syndrome and asymptomatic infection, respectively. Group IV disease consists of infectious, neoplastic, and neurologic complications of HIV. Choice A is incorrect. Herpes zoster infection typically occurs in patients with CD4$^+$ counts of 200–500/mm^3. Choice C is incorrect. Kaposi's sarcoma occurs in patients with CD4$^+$ counts less that 500/mm^3. Choice D is incorrect. Non-Hodgkin's lymphoma is a neurologic opportunistic infection that occurs with CD4$^+$ counts of 200–400/mm^3. Choice E is incorrect. Oral candidiasis is an infectious (group IV) complication of HIV disease that typically occurs in patients with CD4$^+$ counts of less than 500/mm^3.

266. A 35-year-old woman desires to undergo elective sterilization. A laparoscopic tubal ligation is planned. She has no prior medical or surgical history. Preoperative laboratory studies, including hepatic function tests and coagulation profiles, are normal. Which of the following is the most appropriate method of preventing the development of deep venous thrombosis during the procedure?

    (A) Giving a dose of intravenous heparin prior to pneumoperitoneum
    (B) Giving a dose of warfarin to the patient the night prior to surgery
    (C) Maintaining less than 15 mm Hg pneumoperitoneum
    (D) Use of pneumatic compression devices on the lower extremities
    (E) Use of spinal anesthesia

(C) is correct. By keeping a pneumoperitoneum of lower than the approximate vena cava pressure, one reduces the chance for deep venous thrombosis. Choice A is incorrect. A dose of 50,000 U to 70,000 U of heparin can be toxic, causing immediate hemorrhage. Some studies have advocated the use of low-dose subcutaneous heparin prior to surgery, however doses in this region are dangerous. Choice B is incorrect. Warfarin has a paradoxical effect in the short term of creating a hypercoagulable state. In very rare cases, this has caused skin sloughing. Choice D is incorrect. The use of pneumatic compression devices has been shown to reduce the incidence of deep venous thrombosis. However, in this situation, maintaining a lower vena cava pressure is most important to prevent deep venous thrombosis. Choice E is incorrect. The use of spinal anesthesia for an intraperitoneal operation is generally ill advised because of poor airway control. In this special case, the use of medication to cause an increased peripheral vasodilation will cause increased pooling of blood and possibly increase the risk of deep venous thrombosis.

267. A 52-year-old man has been working as an automobile mechanic for 30 years. He is 5′8″ (172 cm) tall and weighs 200 lb (91 kg). He has smoked one pack of cigarettes per day for the past 35 years. He has no prior medical or surgical history. Physical examination of the heart, lungs, and abdomen is within normal limits. Which of the following single preventive health measures would most significantly impact his future medical care?

    (A) Change to low cholesterol, low fat diet
    (B) Change to high fiber diet
    (C) Increase exercise to 3 times per week
    (D) Lose 20 lb (9.1 kg)
    (E) Stop smoking

(E) is correct. Automobile mechanics, naval shipyard workers, and some construction workers who have worked for many years have been exposed to high levels of asbestos. The risk of lung cancer (mesothelioma) for people who have been exposed to asbestos and cigarette smoke is increased over 100 times. There is also an increased risk of many other health-related disorders from cigarette smoking. Choice A is incorrect. A low cholesterol, low fat diet may help to reduce a person's cholesterol level. However, numerous other interventions, including exercise, reduction in stress, and weight loss are required. Choice B is incorrect. A high fiber diet will reduce the risk of colon cancer. However, in the short term, the reduction in risk is small. Choice C is incorrect. While an increase in the amount of exercise per week will increase the "exercise tolerance" of a person and thus reduce the risk of a myocardial infarction, the cessation of smoking will give the person greater disease prevention than the increase in exercise. Choice D is incorrect. Weight loss without additional interventions has not been shown to greatly influence health in the mildly obese.

268. A 71-year-old man with a history of hypertension has been doing well after aortic aneurysm resection and tube graft 2 years ago. He has been followed by his primary care physician for routine exams and blood tests. His most recent physical examination 1 month ago had the following results: No significant interval change. His blood pressure is 180/90 mm Hg, pulse is 92 beats per minute, and respirations are 16/minute. Cardiac examination reveals a regular rate and rhythm. Pulmomary auscultation reveals clear breath sounds bilaterally. The patient's abdomen is soft, nontender, and nondistended. There is no cyanosis or clubbing of his extremities. Rectal examination revealed no evidence of hemorrhoids, a normal-sized prostate, and guaiac-negative stool in the vault. During the last month, the man has been in good health with no new symptoms. One day after defecation, he noted a streak of bright red blood on the toilet paper. He then phoned his primary care physician to tell him of this finding. Which of the following interventions is most appropriate?

(A) Aortogram
(B) Barium enema
(C) Colonoscopy
(D) Observation
(E) Oral psyllium and docusate

(A) is correct. With a normal physical exam and lack of occult blood one month prior to this event, the index of suspicion in a patient with an aortic graft must be heightened to include aortoenteric fistula. In this case, since the patient is "stable," an emergent aortogram may be obtained. A vascular surgeon should also be immediately contacted in case the patient has an immediate decompensation. Any suspicion of a vascular leak is an emergency until proven otherwise. Choice B is incorrect. The diagnosis of aortoenteric fistula is not made by barium enema. The investigation for neoplastic processes does not preclude the immediate search for an aortoenteric fistula. Choice C is incorrect. Colonoscopy is not a diagnostic method for aortoenteric fistula. In this case, colonoscopy should be delayed until a fistula is ruled out. Choice D is incorrect. A patient with an aortic graft should never be observed, as the risk of a vascular bleed is significant. Choice E is incorrect. Oral medications to loosen the bowels to reduce or prevent hemorrhoids is reasonable first-line treatment in patients without a history of aortic reconstruction. However in this case, one must search for a fistula immediately.

269. A 42-year-old woman complains of nausea after receiving a dose of morphine sulfate for renal colic proven by intravenous pyelogram. Her current medications are haloperidol and acetaminophen with codeine. Physical examination reveals left flank tenderness. Cardiac, pulmonary, and abdominal examinations are unremarkable. Which of the following medications could cause irreversible side effects in this patient when used as an antiemetic?

(A) Cimetidine
(B) Metoclopramide
(C) Ondansetron
(D) Prochlorperazine
(E) Trimethobenzamide

(D) is correct. In a patient taking a neuroleptic antipsychotic, one must be wary of tardive dyskinesia. In this case, giving prochlorperazine, a second neuroleptic, may increase the risk of this serious side effect. ♦Before prescribing any antiemetic, it is important to exclude emergent causes of nausea, i.e., appendicitis. Choice A is incorrect. Cimetidine is a blocker of stomach acid secretion. There is little or no antiemetic effect. Choice B is incorrect. Metoclopramide is a very good medication for the treatment of emesis. Few side effects are noted with the use of metoclopramide. Choice C is incorrect. Ondansetron is a very good antiemetic. It is, however, cost prohibitive to use on a routine basis. Choice E is incorrect. Trimethobenzamide works very well to control nausea. There are few untoward side effects when it is used to treat adults.

Items 270–271

A 55-year-old man who works as a ship builder complains of a 6-month history of progressive dyspnea and dry cough. He also complains of fatigue, anorexia, and a 2.3 kg (5 lb) weight loss over the past 3 months. Physical examination of the heart is within normal limits. Pulmonary auscultation reveals late inspiratory crackles at the posterior lung bases. Abdominal examination is within normal limits. Chest x-ray reveals diffuse reticulonodular markings prominent in the lower lung zones.

270. The physician elects to perform pulmonary function tests in this patient. Which of the following findings would be most likely?

(A) Decreased total lung capacity
(B) Increased forced expiratory volume
(C) Increased residual volume
(D) Increased vital capacity
(E) Unchanged vital capacity

(A) is correct. This patient has evidence of idiopathic pulmonary fibrosis and restrictive lung disease. In restrictive lung disease, pulmonary function testing will indicate alteration in pulmonary functioning. Total lung capacity will decrease, as will residual volume and vital capacity. Detailed work history is important in these patients, who often have occupational exposures to substances such as asbestos, fumes, drugs, or radiation. Choice B is incorrect. Forced expiratory volume will decrease in restrictive lung disease. Choice C is incorrect. Residual volume will decrease in restrictive lung disease. Choice D is incorrect. Vital capacity will decrease in restrictive lung disease. Choice E is incorrect. Vital capacity will decrease in restrictive lung disease.

271. Which of the following is the most important component of the treatment plan for this patient?

(A) Cyclophosphamide
(B) Prednisone
(C) Removal of causative agent
(D) Supplemental oxygen therapy
(E) Tetracycline

(C) is correct. The most important treatment for idiopathic pulmonary fibrosis is removal of the causative agent. In this patient, this involves removing the work exposure to asbestos. Other specific therapy such as glucocorticoids and cyclophosphamide may be considered following removal of the patient from the source of disease. Choice A is incorrect. Cyclophosphamide is often added to the treatment protocol to supplement the anti-inflammatory effects of prednisone. Choice B is incorrect. Prednisone is a first-line therapy for suppression of the inflammatory process following removal of the patient from the source of disease. Choice D is incorrect. Supplemental oxygen is indicated when symptoms of right-sided heart failure and bronchospasm are present. Choice E is incorrect. Tetracycline has no role in the treatment of idiopathic pulmonary fibrosis.

272. A 55-year-old woman who is an administrative assistant at the local community college presents for evaluation of chronic bilateral lower extremity pain. She also complains of intermittent chest pain with exertion. Her weight is 86.4 kg (190 lb) and her height is 157 cm (5'2"). She has hypertension that is controlled with a β-blocking agent. She has a 35-pack year history of smoking and denies alcohol use. Physical examination reveals a woman who appears her stated age. Cardiovascular examination reveals a regular rate and rhythm. There is no evidence of rubs, murmurs, or gallops. Pulmonary auscultation reveals scattered wheezes and rhonchi. Abdominal examination is unremarkable. Rectal examination is guaiac-negative with brown stool in the vault. Which of the following is the single-most preventable risk factor for cardiovascular disease in this patient?

(A) Alcohol abuse
(B) Cigarette smoking
(C) Hypertension
(D) Obesity
(E) Work-related factors

(B) is correct. Cigarette smoking is undoubtedly the single-most preventable risk factor for cardiovascular disease. It is directly responsible for 20 percent of cardiovascular disease in women and 50 percent of acute coronary deaths in women under the age of 55. Choice A is incorrect. Alcohol abuse is not the most preventable risk factor for cardiovascular disease. Choice C is incorrect. Hypertension is a comorbidity that can increase one's risk of developing cardiovascular disease. Choice D is incorrect. Obesity is a comorbidity that can increase one's risk of developing cardiovascular disease. Choice E is incorrect. It is unlikely that work-related factors contribute to this patient's risk of developing cardiovascular disease.

273. A 66-year-old man with biopsy-proven adenocarcinoma of the prostate gland has opted for treatment with a luteinizing hormone-releasing factor agonist-antagonist and an antiandrogen agent. He still suffers from significant bone pain. Which of the following agents might provide him with relief of bone pain?

(A) Estramustine phosphate
(B) Growth factors
(C) Paclitaxel
(D) Retinoids
(E) Strontium-89 chloride

(E) is correct. Strontium-89 chloride is a radiopharmaceutical agent similar to calcium and can provide palliative relief of pain from bony metastasis through calcium metabolic pathways. Approximately 75 percent of patients experience some pain relief and 20 percent are rendered pain-free. Choice A is incorrect. Estramustine is a nitrogen mustard that binds to microtubules and may have promise in the treatment of metastatic prostate cancer. Choice B is incorrect. Growth factors may show promise in the treatment of metastatic prostate cancer. Choice C is incorrect. Paclitaxel binds to cytoplasmic microtubules and inhibits the invasiveness of prostate cancer cells in vitro. Choice D is incorrect. Retinoids bind to nuclear receptors and promote cellular differentiation and may show promise in the treatment of metastatic prostate cancer.

274. A 59-year-old man with a 50-pack year history of smoking has progressive dyspnea with ambulation, orthopnea, and paroxysmal nocturnal dyspnea. He also has a chronic, nonproductive cough. You determine that inhaled bronchodilator therapy would be of benefit for this individual. Which of the following agents has selectivity for both the β-1 and β-2 receptors and has a long duration of action?

(A) Albuterol
(B) Ipratropium
(C) Isoproterenol
(D) Metaproterenol
(E) Metoprolol

(A) is correct. Albuterol is an inhaled bronchodilator that can be used in patients with chronic obstructive pulmonary disease. This agent has selectivity for the β-1 and β-2 receptors and has a duration of action of approximately 4 to 6 hours. Choice B is incorrect. Ipratropium has a long duration of action (4 to 8 hours) but is not selective for the β-receptors. Choice C is incorrect. Isoproterenol is a short-acting agent with selectivity for both β-1 and β-2 receptors. Choice D is incorrect. Metaproterenol is a short-acting agent with selectivity for both β-1 and β-2 receptors. Choice E is incorrect. Metoprolol is not used in the management of chronic obstructive pulmonary disease.

275. A 66-year-old man with an elevated prostate-specific antigen level undergoes a prostate needle biopsy. Pathology reveals a Gleason 3+4 adenocarcinoma on all slides. He does not wish to undergo surgical or medical treatment for his disease. He fully understands the risks and benefits of his decision. Which of the following is the site with the highest frequency of metastasis from prostate cancer?

(A) Femur
(B) Humerus
(C) Pelvis and sacrum
(D) Ribs
(E) Scapula
(F) Skull
(G) Spine

(C) is correct. When prostate cancer metastasizes beyond the organ of origin, the primary tumor initially spreads to bone, with the axial skeleton being the most frequent site of involvement. Sites of metastasis in order of frequency are the pelvis and sacrum, the spine, and the femur. Choice A is incorrect. The femur is the third most common site of metastasis from prostate cancer. Choice B is incorrect. The humerus is an uncommon site of metastasis from prostate cancer. Choice D is incorrect. The ribs are the fourth most common site of metastasis from prostate cancer. Choice E is incorrect. The scapula is the fifth most common site of metastasis from prostate cancer. Choice F is incorrect. The skull is an uncommon site of metastasis from prostate cancer. Choice G is incorrect. The spine is the second most common site of metastasis from prostate cancer.

276. A 33-year-old man with AIDS is hospitalized with *Pneumocystis carinii* pneumonia. He is currently being treated with zidovudine, ganciclovir, trimethoprim-sulfamethoxazole, and delavirdine. Physical examination of the heart is within normal limits. Pulmonary auscultation reveals rhonchi bilaterally with decreased breath sounds at the bases. Laboratory studies have been obtained and are presented below:

Hematocrit	41%
Serum	
Sodium	137 mEq/L
Potassium	4.1 mEq/L
Chloride	104 mEq/L
Bicarbonate	23 mEq/L
Creatinine	1.2 mg/dL

Which of the following adverse reactions is most concerning to the physician who is treating this patient?

(A) Anemia
(B) Headache
(C) Malaise
(D) Nausea
(E) Neutropenia
(F) Peripheral neuropathy
(G) Rash
(H) Stomatitis

(E) is correct. Drug interactions are important to consider in patients who are taking antiretroviral agents. Patients who are taking zidovudine and trimethoprim-sulfamethoxazole are at increased risk of developing neutropenia. It is important to be aware of this interaction when treating such patients. Choice A is incorrect. Anemia is a typical side effect of zidovudine. Choice B is incorrect. Headache is a typical side effect of zidovudine. Choice C is incorrect. Malaise is a typical side effect of zidovudine. Choice D is incorrect. Nausea is a typical side effect of zidovudine. Choice F is incorrect. Peripheral neuropathy is a typical side effect of zalcitabine. Choice G is incorrect. Rash is a typical side effect of didanosine. Choice H is incorrect. Stomatitis is not typically associated with any of the above agents.

277. Investigators are trying to determine the usefulness of a new assay based on the enzyme telomerase to determine the presence of superficial bladder cancer. This assay is based on the presence of telomerase in voided urine specimens. Patients who have indwelling urinary catheters were excluded from the present study. The following data from 200 patients are obtained:

Superficial Bladder Cancer

Telomerase	Cancer present	Cancer absent
Positive	60	40
Negative	20	80

In this study, the specificity is

(A) 10%
(B) 20%
(C) 50%
(D) 67%
(E) 96%

(D) is correct. Specificity is the true negative rate. Specificity is defined as the probability of a negative test when the disease is absent. For the present study, this can be determined by the formula: specificity = true negatives/true negatives + false positives. In this case, specificity is 80/80 + 40 = 67%. Sensitivity, on the other hand, is defined as positivity in disease and can be determined from a collection of data.

Items 278–279

A 38-year-old woman complains of nonprogressive, intermittent dysphagia. She admits to a 9 kg (20 lb) weight loss in the absence of dieting. She also has intermittent tongue pain. Her prior medical history is notable for iron deficiency anemia. Her current medications include iron tablets. Physical examination of the heart, lungs, and abdomen is within normal limits. Upper gastrointestinal endoscopy reveals a distal esophageal ring.

278. Which of the following is the most appropriate treatment for this patient?

(A) Endoscopic esophageal dilation
(B) Intravenous corticosteroids
(C) Monopolar coagulation
(D) Surgical resection
(E) Watchful waiting

(A) is correct. This patient has evidence of an esophageal web. This is a mucosal stricture located anywhere along the esophagus. Intermittent dysphagia is a typical presentation. Plummer-Vinson syndrome is associated with iron deficiency anemia, achlorhydria, glossitis, and stomatitis. Treatment involves endoscopic dilation. Choice B is incorrect. Intravenous corticosteroids may be useful in the treatment of the ingestion of caustic material. Choice C is incorrect. Monopolar coagulation can be useful in the management of bleeding esophageal varices. Choice D is incorrect. Surgical resection is not indicated in this patient. Choice E is incorrect. Watchful waiting is inappropriate in this individual with symptoms and a significant weight loss.

279. The patient is concerned about the risk of future medical problems associated with this condition. Which of the following is the most appropriate statement to make to this patient?

(A) An associated increased risk of esophageal carcinoma is possible.
(B) Avoidance of maneuvers that increase the risk of aspiration is paramount.
(C) Metaplasia occurs in patients with chronic reflux.
(D) Surveillance should begin in 20 years.
(E) Thickening of the hands and feet may occur.

(A) is correct. This patient with a history of iron deficiency anemia, glossitis, and an esophageal web suggests the diagnosis of Plummer-Vinson syndrome. This is a premalignant condition associated with an increased risk of esophageal carcinoma. Choice B is incorrect. Avoidance of maneuvers that increase the risk of aspiration is important in the treatment of acute esophageal obstruction. Choice C is incorrect. Barrett's esophagus is defined as epithelial metaplasia in which specialized columnar epithelium is replaced by stratified squamous epithelium. Choice D is incorrect. Lye ingestion is associated with an increased incidence of squamous cell carcinoma. The risk begins 20 years after exposure. Thus, surveillance should begin at this time. Choice E is incorrect. Tylosis is a rare condition manifested as thickening of the hands and feet and is associated with an increased risk of esophageal carcinoma.

Items 280–281

A 74-year-old man who was released from the hospital 10 days ago after treatment of an acute stroke has a seizure at home. He has been your patient for 5 years and is brought to your office for evaluation. You have treated this patient for hypertension with a calcium-channel blocker. Review of his prior computed tomography scan of the head indicates a large left-sided cortical infarct. Physical examination reveals an elderly man who appears his stated age. He is pleasant and speaks well despite evidence of dysarthria. His heart, lungs, and abdomen are within normal limits. He has a right-sided hemiparesis. You witness no seizure activity during this patient's office visit.

280. Which of the following is the most appropriate treatment for this individual?

(A) Diazepam
(B) Carbamazepine
(C) Phenytoin
(D) Ticlopidine
(E) Watchful waiting

(E) is correct. Approximately 5–10 percent of patients with stroke have seizures, 33 percent of which occur within the first 2 weeks poststroke. Seizures do not affect the overall prognosis, but when status epilepticus occurs, the results can be life threatening. Anticonvulsant prophylaxis is not indicated. Treatment should be initiated only if a seizure actually occurs. Choice A is incorrect. Anticonvulsant therapy is not indicated in this patient. Choice B is incorrect. Carbamazepine therapy is not indicated in this patient. Choice C is incorrect. Therapy with phenytoin is not recommended for this patient. Choice D is incorrect. Ticlopidine is not an anticonvulsant agent.

281. The patient's wife is concerned about the seizure and how it will affect his overall prognosis. Which of the following is an appropriate statement to make to this patient's wife?

(A) Seizures do not affect stroke prognosis.
(B) Seizures suggest the possibility of intracranial neoplasm.
(C) Seizures suggest the possibility of Parkinson's disease.
(D) Seizures suggest the possibility of recurrent stroke.
(E) Seizures suggest underlying intracranial neoplastic disease.

(A) is correct. Overall, seizures do not affect stroke prognosis, but the presence of status epilepticus may be life threatening. As mentioned above, anticonvulsant therapy is not indicated in this patient. Choice B is incorrect. Seizures do not suggest intracranial neoplasm in this patient. Choice C is incorrect. Seizures do not suggest the possibility of Parkinson's disease. Choice D is incorrect. Seizures do not suggest the possibility of recurrent stroke. Choice E is incorrect. It is unlikely that the presence of seizures in this patient is suggestive of a neoplastic process.

A 23-year-old female college student presents to the University Student Health Service complaining of a three-week history of progressive vaginal pain, dyspareunia, and tenderness. She states that she usually uses a vaginal sponge as birth control. Recently, she has switched to using condoms with a new sexual partner. Physical and pelvic examination are performed and reveal an edematous, erythematous, fluctuant mass along the right lateral portion of the labia approximately 1.5 centimeters from the introitus.

282. Which of the following entities is least likely to comprise the differential diagnosis of this condition?

(A) Acrochordon
(B) Bartholin's duct cyst
(C) Epidermoid cyst
(D) Inguinal hernia
(E) Sebaceous cyst

(A) is correct. Acrochordon is a flesh-colored, soft, polypoid tumor that looks like a skin tag. This lesion is usually seen in the vulva, not the labia. Epidermoid cysts, sebaceous cysts, and Bartholin's duct cysts can appear as inflamed, erythematous, fluctuant masses within the vaginal vault. Choice B is incorrect. Bartholin's duct cysts are seen on the vulva. Choice C is incorrect. Epidermoid cysts can appear as inflamed, fluctuant masses. Choice D is incorrect. An inguinal hernia may protrude through the lateral portion of the vaginal walls and give the sensation of a mass lesion. This may also resemble a cystic dilation. Choice E is incorrect. Sebaceous cysts can appear as inflamed, fluctuant masses.

283. Which of the following mechanisms explains the most likely etiology of this condition?

(A) Compression from nearby condyloma lesions
(B) Genitourinary tuberculosis
(C) Retention of secretions and cystic dilation
(D) Subclinical infection
(E) Thinning of cervical mucus

(C) is correct. The symptoms of this patient and physical examination findings suggest a Bartholin's duct cyst. This condition often results from obstruction of the main duct from the Bartholin's gland. This may occur due to clumping of mucus or a narrowing of the duct. The duct may then become secondarily infected. Choice A is incorrect. This condition does not usually coexist with condyloma lesions. Choice B is incorrect. This condition does not usually coexist with genitourinary tuberculosis. Choice D is incorrect. This condition coexists with an acute infection. Choice E is incorrect. Cervical mucus can become pasty and thickened.

284. The patient's 56-year-old mother, who lives in a nearby town, presents to you for evaluation of a similar complaint. Physical examination reveals an edematous, erythematous, fluctuant mass along the left lateral portion of the labia approximately 2 centimeters from the introitus. Which of the following is the most likely cause of this patient's condition?

(A) Bartholin's duct abscess
(B) Bartholin's duct cyst
(C) Female genitourinary carcinoma
(D) Inguinal hernia
(E) Vulvar cyst

(C) is correct. While the findings suggest Bartholin's duct cyst, the patient in this question is older. Therefore, findings of a mass lesion in the lower genital tract must be suspicious for carcinoma. This lesion should be biopsied first before an incision and drainage procedure such as marsupialization is undertaken. Choice A is incorrect. Bartholin's duct abscess would be a rare finding in this patient. Choice B is incorrect. Bartholin's duct cyst would be a rare finding in this patient. Choice D is incorrect. There is no evidence to suggest an inguinal hernia in this patient. Choice E is incorrect. There is no evidence to suggest a vulvar cyst in this patient.

285. A 79-year-old woman with a history of cerebrovascular accident, hypertension, and congestive heart failure is brought to the emergency department for confusion by her daughter. She was found to be walking into walls and repeating the phrase, "I need a dollar." Her current medications include a calcium-channel blocker and digoxin. In the emergency department, she responds to questions by saying, "I don't know." She stares to the left and cannot follow a finger to the right. Cardiac, pulmonary, and abdominal examinations are unremarkable. Computed tomography scan of the head is obtained in the emergency department and reveals cerebral atrophy. Laboratory studies, including serum chemistry, are normal. Which of the following is least likely in the differential diagnosis of this patient?

(A) Meningioma
(B) Myocardial infarction
(C) Pneumonia
(D) Prescription drug interaction
(E) Urinary tract infection

(A) is correct. Prescription drugs are a common cause of a confused state in elderly patients. Confusion can also be the presenting symptom of myocardial infarction, pneumonia, and urinary tract infections. These disorders should be considered when no overt toxin or metabolic disorder is evident. Meningioma is not likely based on the lack of CT findings in this patient. Choice B is incorrect. Myocardial infarction should be considered in the differential diagnosis of this patient. Choice C is incorrect. Pneumonia should be considered in the differential diagnosis of this patient. Choice D is incorrect. Prescription drug interactions should be considered in the differential diagnosis of this patient. Choice E is incorrect. Urinary tract infections can present as an acute confusional state.

Items 286–289

Match each of the following sets of Swan-Ganz catheter readings with the most likely clinical history.

	Cardiac Output	Pulmonary Capillary Pressure Wedge	Systemic Vascular Resistance
(A)	Decreased	Decreased	Decreased
(B)	Decreased	Decreased	Increased
(C)	Decreased	Increased	Increased
(D)	Increased	Normal	Decreased
(E)	Increased	Increased	Increased

286. A 55-year-old nursing home resident presents to the emergency department after the staff notes him to be confused and lethargic. The patient has a history of multiple sclerosis and requires an indwelling Foley catheter. His medical history is significant for hypertension. On exam, his temperature is 39 C (103.5 F), his heart rate is 130 beats per minute, and his blood pressure is 100/50 mm Hg. He is minimally responsive to commands.

(D) is correct. This patient is in septic shock, most likely as a result of gram-negative sepsis due to a urinary tract infection (which he is at great risk for, given his indwelling Foley catheter). His SVR is decreased a result of endotoxins and his cardiac output is high in its attempt to maintain his blood pressure in this profoundly vasodilated state. PCWP remains normal or is sometimes decreased. Choice A is incorrect. In septic shock, cardiac output is expected to be increased. Choices B and C are incorrect. In septic shock, SVR is decreased secondary to the profound vasodilatory effects of endotoxin. Choice E is incorrect. In septic shock, SVR is decreased secondary to the profound vasodilatory effects of endotoxin.

287. A 65-year-old white female presents to the emergency department after two hours of crushing substernal chest pain accompanied by diaphoresis. Her medical history is significant for long-standing hypertension for which she takes atenolol and hypothyroidism for which she takes levothyroxine. She smokes a pack of cigarettes a day. Her blood pressure is 85/45 mm Hg and her heart rate is 120 beats per minute. Her electrocardiogram demonstrates 4 millimeter ST segment elevation in the anterior leads (V1–V4) as well as 2 millimeter ST depression in the inferior leads (II, III, and aVF).

(C) is correct. This patient, in the midst of an anterior wall myocardial infarction, is in cardiogenic shock. As a result of her damaged myocardium, her left ventricular function is severely compromised, reflected by her low cardiac output. In an attempt to maintain her blood pressure, her SVR is increased. Her PCWP is increased, reflecting her profound left ventricular dysfunction. Choice A is incorrect. With profound left ventricular dysfunction, a high PCWP is expected. Additionally, the high SVR is usual, as the patient in cardiogenic shock attempts to maintain the blood pressure. Choice B is incorrect. In cardiogenic shock, a high PCWP is expected, reflecting the profound left ventricular dysfunction. Choices D and E are incorrect. In cardiogenic shock, a high PCWP is expected, reflecting the profound left ventricular dysfunction. Additionally, the high SVR is usual, as the patient in cardiogenic shock attempts to maintain the blood pressure.

288. A 46-year-old white male with a 20-year history of polysubstance abuse presents to the emergency room complaining of worsening shortness of breath and generalized fatigue that have worsened over the last several weeks. He is no longer able to climb a flight of stairs without becoming winded, and on review of systems has new three-pillow orthopnea. He also notes new lower extremity edema that is confirmed by physical exam. He has jugular venous distention and prominent basilar rales bilaterally. He has been drinking heavily (at least a quart of vodka a day) during the last month.

(E) is correct. The patient is suffering alcoholic cardiomyopathy, one of the few causes of high-output heart failure. This is reflected by his high cardiac output, increased PCWP reflecting left ventricular dysfunction, and clinical signs and symptoms of congestive heart failure. Additionally, chronic alcohol consumption results in peripheral vasoconstriction, hence the increased SVR. Choices A, B, and C are incorrect. Alcoholic cardiomyopathy causes high-output heart failure. Thus, the cardiac output would be increased, not decreased. Choice D is correct. Chronic alcohol consumption results in peripheral vasoconstriction, hence an increased SVR.

289. A 26-year-old Asian male presents via emergency medical transport from the scene of his motorcycle accident. Per the EMS team, the patient crashed his motorcycle into a tree and struck his right lower extremity. The patient is awake and complaining of excruciating right thigh pain. His blood pressure is 90/40 mm Hg and heart rate is 120 beats per minute. He has a palpable left dorsal pedis pulse, but no right lower extremity pulses except a femoral pulse.

(B) is correct. The patient is in hypovolemic shock after a right femur fracture with injury to his femoral artery. As a consequence, his has lost a great deal of blood, resulting in hypovolemic shock. His cardiac output is low, as is his PCWP, reflecting his low volume state. His SVR is very high in an effort to maintain his blood pressure in this low volume state. He requires immediate surgical attention. Choice A is incorrect. Although low CO and PCWP are expected, in the profoundly hypovolemic state, a high SVR is predicted. Choice C in incorrect. In a hypovolemic state, a low PCWP is expected, reflecting the profound volume depletion. Choice D and E are incorrect. In the profoundly hypovolemic state, decreased cardiac output is expected, as there is not enough volume to maintain normal cardiac output.

Items 290–294

    (A) Absence seizures
    (B) Benign partial epilepsy
    (C) Complex partial seizures
    (D) Febrile seizures
    (E) Generalized tonic-clonic seizures
    (F) Infantile spasms
    (G) Neonatal seizures
    (H) Night terrors
    (I) Simple partial seizures
    (J) Status epilepticus

For each child with a neurologic symptom, select the most appropriate diagnosis.

290. A 9-year-old boy is brought to the emergency department after an attack of asynchronous clonic movements seen in his face, neck, and extremities that lasted for 20 seconds. Consciousness was maintained during the attack. Physical examination of the heart, lungs, and abdomen is normal. Neurologic examination is unremarkable. Electroencephalogram reveals unilateral spikes and sharp waves.

(I) is correct. This child has evidence of simple partial seizures. Consciousness is maintained during the seizures. Motor activity characterized by asynchronous clonic activity in the face, neck, and extremities is common. A typical seizure lasts for 20 seconds. Electroencephalogram may reveal unilateral spikes and sharp waves during seizure activity.

291. A 6-year-old girl is noted by her teacher to have a blank facial expression with flickering of her eyelids for a 30-second period several times per day. Physical examination of the heart, lungs, and abdomen is unremarkable. Neurologic examination reveals no deficits. Electroencephalogram reveals generalized 3 per second spike-wave discharges.

(A) is correct. This child has evidence of absence seizures. These seizures are characterized by a sudden cessation of motor activity or speech with a blank facial expression and flickering of the eyelids. These seizures are more common in girls who are over the age of 5 years. Electroencephalogram shows characteristic, generalized, 3 per sec. spike-wave discharges during the seizure.

292. A 6-month-old male infant is brought to the physician for evaluation of brief, symmetric contractions of the neck, trunk, and extremities that persist for several minutes. These findings tend to occur during drowsiness or upon awakening. Physical examination of the heart, lungs, and abdomen is unremarkable. Neurologic examination reveals no focal deficits. Electroencephalogram reveals a chaotic pattern of high-amplitude slow waves and spikes.

(F) is correct. This infant has evidence of infantile spasms. These are characterized by brief, symmetric contractions of the neck, trunk, and extremities. Clusters of seizures occur during drowsiness or on awakening. The electroencephalogram typically shows a chaotic pattern of high-amplitude slow waves and spikes, known as hypsarrhythmia.

293. A 2-week-old male infant is brought to the emergency department after being noted to have excessive chewing motions, excessive salivation, and a change in color (to flush red) of the face and skin of the upper extremities. Physical examination reveals a newborn in no acute distress. Cardiac, pulmonary, and abdominal examinations are unremarkable. Neurologic examination fails to demonstrate any abnormality.

(G) is correct. Neonatal seizures are generalized tonic-clonic seizures that occur in the first month of life. Seizures can consist of chewing motions, excessive salivation, blinking, pedaling movements, and change of color. Etiology is typically due to hypoxic-ischemic pathology.

294. An 11-year-old boy is brought to the physician for evaluation of recurrent face and tongue twitching and drooling. He is otherwise healthy. Physical examination of the heart, lungs, and abdomen is unremarkable. Neurologic examination is unremarkable. Electroencephalogram reveals centrotemporal spikes with normal background activity.

(B) is correct. This child has evidence of benign partial epilepsy with centrotemporal spikes. This seizure type has an excellent prognosis. Typically occurring in children ages 10–12 years, attacks feature facial or tongue twitching, speech arrest, or drooling. Seizures often occur during sleep. The electroencephalogram shows a characteristic pattern of centrotemporal spikes with normal background activity.

Items 295–300

    (A) Isoniazid for 6 months
    (B) Isoniazid for 12 months
    (C) Isoniazid/rifampin for 6 months
    (D) Isoniazid/rifampin for 12 months
    (E) Isoniazid/rifampin for 6 months then
        isoniazid for 6 months
    (F) Isoniazid/rifampin/pyrazinamide/
        ethambutol for 2 months then iso-
        niazid/rifampin for 4 months
    (G) Isoniazid/rifampin/ethambutol for 2
        months then isoniazid/rifampin for 7
        months
    (H) No treatment

Match each clinical scenario with the most appropriate treatment regimen.

295. A 32-year-old nurse previously had no reaction to the Mantoux PPD skin test. Now, during her yearly screening, she is found to have a 12 mm reaction to the test.

(A) is correct. Persons at increased risk for tuberculosis such as hospital personnel should be treated with 6 months of isoniazid therapy for any new PPD conversion greater than or equal to 10 mm. A 6-month course of isoniazid reduces the risk of active tuberculosis by 90 percent.

296. A 36-year-old white male presents to the emergency department with complaints of fever, chills, and night sweats accompanied by an 8 kg (20 lb) weight loss in the last 3 months. He was recently released from prison after a 7-year incarceration for armed robbery. Chest radiograph demonstrates upper lobe airspace disease with cavity formation. Sputum stained with Kinyoun stain demonstrates acid-fast bacilli.

(F) is correct. Treatment of pulmonary tuberculosis in almost all patients consists of a 2-month initial phase of isoniazid, rifampin, ethambutol, and pyrazinamide followed by a 4-month continuation phase of isoniazid and rifampin.

297. A 32-year-old Hispanic male presents to his primary care doctor with complaints of fever, chills, night sweats, and a 5 kg (12 lb) weight loss over the last two months. He was diagnosed with HIV infection two years prior and his last CD4+ count was 570/mm^3. Sputum stained by the Ziehl-Neelsen method is positive for acid-fast bacilli.

(F) is correct. Treatment of pulmonary tuberculosis in almost all patients, including those with HIV infection, consists of a 2-month initial phase of isoniazid, rifampin, ethambutol, and pyrazinamide followed by a 4-month continuation phase of isoniazid and rifampin.

298. A 28-year-old white female presents to a local health care clinic with complaints of fever, chills, and night sweats for the last several weeks. She has a cough productive of yellowish sputum. Exam reveals occasional rhoncherous sounds over the bilateral upper lobes. Sputum stained with the Ziehl-Neelsen stain is positive for acid-fast bacilli. Urine pregnancy screen is positive.

(G) is correct. Treatment of pulmonary tuberculosis in pregnant patients consists of a 2-month initial phase of isoniazid, rifampin, and ethambutol followed by a 7-month continuation phase of isoniazid and rifampin.

299. A 30-year-old white female with HIV (last CD4+ count = 400/mm^3) is given a routine Mantoux PPD test by her primary care physician. There is a 7 mm reaction. She previously had no reaction to the Mantoux PPD test.

(B) is correct. Patients who are infected with HIV should be treated for 12 months with isoniazid for a PPD reaction greater than 5 mm.

300. A 35-year-old white male is given the Mantoux PPD test as a routine yearly screen and develops a 15 mm reaction. He previously had no reaction to the test. He is a resident of a chronic care facility secondary to a traumatic brain injury three years prior.

(A) is correct. Patients at high risk for the development of tuberculosis such as residents of chronic care facilities, members of medically underserved populations, or persons born in high-prevalence countries should be treated with 6 months of isoniazid for a tuberculin reaction greater than or equal to 10 mm.

SECTION 7 BEGINS HERE

Directions (Items 301–350): Each of the numbered items is followed or preceded by a set of options. For each item, select the BEST lettered option to answer the question or complete the statement. Locate the corresponding item number in the appropriate section of your answer sheet and completely fill in the circle containing the lettered option you have selected.

301. A 52-year-old man is brought to the emergency department by helicopter. He was found by the side of the road after being ejected from a motor vehicle. He was found unconscious with shallow respirations but a strong pulse. Paramedics intubated the patient prior to placing him in the helicopter. Upon arrival at the hospital, he is evaluated by the trauma service. Which of the following is the first action that should be taken in the emergency department?

(A) Check pulse
(B) Draw complete blood count
(C) Establish intravenous access with large-bore catheter.
(D) Evaluate breath sounds
(E) Obtain chest x-ray

(D) is correct. In all situations, one must make sure that the patient's airway is satisfactory. If the patient was intubated, then transported, one must check to make sure that the endotracheal tube was not dislodged or advanced. The most reliable and rapid method to do this is via auscultation of the chest for equal breath sounds. The rest of the trauma evaluation can continue after this first step is completed. Choice A is incorrect. The first step in resuscitation of any patient is to ensure an adequate airway. Choice B is incorrect. A CBC is a poor method to check for bleeding in a trauma patient. Choice C is incorrect. During many trauma situations, one may be tempted to establish intravenous access. However, one must check the ventilation of the patient first. Choice E is incorrect. Using a chest x-ray to determine endotracheal tube position may take too long to ensure proper oxygenation.

302. A 16-year-old woman comes to the emergency department complaining of right lower quadrant pain for 3 days. The pain has become more severe over the past 4 hours. She also has nausea and vomiting, but no fevers. Her last menstrual period was 2 weeks ago and she states that she has not had any sexual relations for the past month. She has some dysuria. Which of the following laboratory tests would be most important to obtain first?

(A) Complete blood count
(B) Serum electrolytes
(C) Urinalysis
(D) Urine culture
(E) Urine human chorionic gonadotropin

(E) is correct. Even though she denies any recent sexual relations during the last month, it is always important to confirm that she is not pregnant. Choice A is incorrect. The white blood cell count is important to determine if the patient has sepsis. However, the actual number of cells may only allude to a problem. Choice B is incorrect. Serum electrolytes may determine if the patient is dehydrated due to emesis, however the amount and type of hydration may be based upon her pregnancy status. Choice C is incorrect. Urinalysis will tell you if the patient has a urinary tract infection or possible pyelonephritis. However, in general, urinalysis only is another clue that there is a problem, whereas a pregnancy test may give you the reason for her condition. Choice D is incorrect. Urine culture may reveal a cause for her dysuria. However, the result takes too long to return and the treatment may depend upon whether she is pregnant or not.

A 57-year-old previously healthy man is brought to the emergency department after falling from a 7.62 m (25 ft) high scaffold. He was cutting steel beams and lost his balance. He lost consciousness for 2 minutes after the fall. His vital signs are as follows: blood pressure is 128/72 mm Hg, pulse is 92 beats per minute, and respirations are 16 per minute. When he arrives at the emergency department, his cervical spine is immobilized. He is alert and talking, but does not remember anything after hitting the ground.

303. Which of the following pieces of information would be most important to obtain first?

(A) Computed tomography of the head
(B) Complete blood count
(C) Measurement of vital signs
(D) Observation for changes in mental status
(E) Radiograph of the cervical spine

(C) is correct. Vital signs are the most important item in the initial evaluation of the patient. One can evaluate a change in pulse or blood pressure much more rapidly than any laboratory test. Choice A is incorrect. While an evaluation of the brain is important to rule out intracranial bleeds, one must remember to get a baseline set of vital signs prior to continuing on other steps in the evaluation. Choice B is incorrect. Complete blood count is important. However, results take time to return and need to be interpreted based upon the patients clinical status. Choice D is incorrect. It is important to observe the patient for mental status changes. Choice E is incorrect. Radiography of the body can be delayed until an initial evaluation of the patient occurs.

304. Which of the following would be an absolute contraindication to MRI (magnetic resonance imaging) of the head to evaluate this patient's loss of consciousness?

(A) Compound fracture of the right humerus
(B) History of claustrophobia
(C) Intravenous contrast allergy
(D) Multiple artifacts found on cervical spine plain radiograph.
(E) 30-minute delay in obtaining an MRI

(D) is correct. Since this person was working on steel that is metallic, it is important not to expose him to a strong magnetic field. Exposure to metal is not a contraindication to MRI. (However, having a metallic fixture in your body is a contraindication to this procedure.) Choice A is incorrect. Unless the person had a metallic fixator placed, MRI would not be contraindicated. Choice B is incorrect. Claustrophobia is a relative contraindication for MRI. Patients can be placed into new "open" MRI scanners or be sedated if required. Choice C is incorrect. MRI does not involved iodinated contrast, so a history of contrast allergy is not significant in MRI. Choice E is incorrect. An MRI can be performed if the patient is stable. A short delay is a relative contraindication.

305. A patient is unable to provide a urine specimen. Which of the following would be an absolute contraindication to placement of a Foley catheter prior to further evaluation?

    (A) History of transurethral resection of the prostate
    (B) Occult blood found on rectal exam
    (C) Scrotal hematoma
    (D) Severe abdominal pain
    (E) Severe back pain

(C) is correct. Scrotal hematoma, blood at the urethral meatus, or high-riding prostate on digital rectal exam are all absolute contraindications for the placement of a catheter without evaluating the urethra. These are all signs of urethral disruption. A retrograde urethrogram should be performed. Choice A is incorrect. A patient who had a TURP may have had a recurrence of his prostatic hypertrophy that caused him to retain urine. The urethra is still present in patients who had a TURP, and a Foley catheter can be placed. Choice B is incorrect. Occult blood is often found on rectal exam of trauma patients, as a complete rectal exam is often not performed (i.e., not looking for hemorrhoids). If a high-riding prostate is found, a Foley catheter should not be placed. However, occult blood in the stool is not a contraindication. Choice D is incorrect. Abdominal pain in itself is not a contraindication to Foley catheter placement, as the patient may be complaining of urinary retention. It is important to evaluate these patients for the presence of hematuria to exclude bladder perforation or renal injury. Choice E is incorrect. Back pain does not indicate a urethral disruption. However, if additional signs of scrotal or flank hematoma exist, one may consider a retrograde urethrogram to exclude retroperitoneal tracking of urine or blood.

306. A 2-year-old boy with apnea is brought to the emergency department by the paramedics. He was playing with coins and swallowed one. After dislodging the coin and beginning cardiopulmonary resuscitation, intravenous medications are to be given. The best way to obtain immediate intravenous access is via which route?

    (A) Antecubital vein
    (B) Dorsal hand vein
    (C) Femoral venous catheter
    (D) Internal jugular venous catheter
    (E) Intraosseous catheter

(E) is correct. A special intraosseous catheter inserted into the anterior tibia will give prompt and reliable intravenous access in children. Little expertise is required to insert this catheter. Choice A is incorrect. In situations where venous collapse may have occurred, finding a peripheral vein is often very difficult. Choice B is incorrect. In young children, the discovery of a vein on the back of the hand may take significant time and require some expertise due to the small caliber of these veins. Choice C is incorrect. The femoral vein is very close to the femoral artery in children and percutaneous placement of an intravenous catheter is very difficult. Choice D is incorrect. While performing cardiopulmonary resuscitation in children, one should not attempt to insert an internal jugular catheter. Children often have very large necks, making discovery of the vein difficult.

A 29-year-old medical student who has been your patient for 5 years presents to the office for evaluation of a 3-day history of a rash on his right arm. He denies recent exposure to animals. However, he states that he was doing some gardening at his parents' house during the last week. He has no know drug allergies and notes no unusual habits. He states that he has begun to use a new shampoo during the past 6 weeks but has not gotten any of the shampoo on his arms. He has been using hydrocortisone 1% creme without change in the characteristics of the rash. Cardiac, pulmonary, and abdominal examinations are within normal limits. Examination of the right arm reveals scattered erythematous vesicular patches and small vesicles on both hands. The remainder of the skin examination is within normal limits.

307. Which of the following is the most appropriate treatment for this individual?

    (A) Amoxicillin
    (B) Benzoyl peroxide
    (C) Clobetasol propionate
    (D) Metronidazole
    (E) Ticarcillin

(C) is correct. The most likely diagnosis is plant dermatitis. While washing with soap after an exposure may help to prevent sensitization, this will not suffice for an acute eruption. The most appropriate treatment for an acute eruption of plant dermatitis is an ultra-potent topical steroid creme such as clobetasol propionate. Very severe cases may require a course of oral prednisone. Choice A is incorrect. Amoxicillin is an inappropriate treatment for this condition. Choice B is incorrect. Benzoyl peroxide is an inappropriate treatment for this condition. Choice D is incorrect. Metronidazole is an inappropriate treatment for this condition. Choice E is incorrect. Ticarcillin is an inappropriate treatment for this condition.

308. The appropriate medication is prescribed for the patient and he is sent home with a follow-up appointment in 3 weeks. However, he returns to the office in 4 days complaining of intense pruritus and no change in the physical characteristics of the rash. He states that he has diligently taken the medicine you have prescribed. Which of the following is the most appropriate treatment for this patient?

    (A) Amoxicillin
    (B) Benzoyl peroxide
    (C) Clobetasol propionate
    (D) Prednisone
    (E) Tetracycline

(D) is correct. While most cases of plant dermatitis will respond to topical corticosteroid cremes, a few cases will require a course of oral prednisone. An oral corticosteroid is recommended for this patient, who has minimal response to a topical agent. Choice A is incorrect. Amoxicillin is an inappropriate treatment for this condition. Choice B is incorrect. Benzoyl peroxide is an inappropriate treatment for this condition. Choice C is incorrect. Clobetasol propionate is an inappropriate choice for this patient who has shown minimal response to such an agent. Choice E is incorrect. Tetracycline is an inappropriate treatment for this condition.

309. A 24-year-old white female with Turner's syndrome presents to her primary care doctor with complaints of fatigue and dyspnea on exertion worsening over the last several months. Blood pressure is 190/100 mm Hg, and heart rate is 80 beats per minute. Exam reveals a systolic ejection murmur and diminished lower extremity pulses. Chest roentgenograph is notable for rib notching. Which of the following is the patient's most likely cardiac lesion?

(A) Atrial septal defect
(B) Aortic stenosis
(C) Coarctation of the aorta
(D) Mitral regurgitation
(E) Mitral stenosis
(F) Patent ductus arteriosus
(G) Ventricular septal defect

(C) is correct. Coarctation of the aorta results from narrowing of the aortic lumen distal to the origin of the left subclavian artery near the insertion of the ligamenta arteriosum. The lesion is associated with Turner's syndrome. Symptoms vary widely, and include vague fatigue, headache, congestive heart failure, and intracranial hemorrhage secondary to elevated blood pressure. Exam reveals upper extremity hypertension, decreased lower extremity blood pressure and pulses, and a systolic ejection murmur. Chest roentgenograph is often notable for rib notching, cardiomegaly, and a dilated aorta. Choice A is incorrect. Atrial septal defect produces a fixed split second heart sound and a systolic ejection murmur. Choice B is incorrect. Aortic stenosis produces a harsh crescendo-decrescendo murmur, decreased carotid upstrokes, and an absent or diminished second heart sound. Choice D is incorrect. Mitral regurgitation produces a holosystolic murmur heard loudest at the apex with radiation to the axilla. Choice E is incorrect. Mitral stenosis produces a loud first heart sound with a diastolic opening snap and a low-pitched diastolic rumbling murmur. The lesion is strongly associated with previous rheumatic heart disease. Choice F is incorrect. Patent ductus arteriosus is an arterial-venous fistula between the aorta and the left pulmonary artery. The left-to-right shunt produces a continuous machinery murmur. The lesion is usually symptomatic shortly after birth. Choice G is incorrect. Ventricular septal defect produces a left-to-right shunt with a harsh systolic murmur at the left and right upper sternal borders.

310. A 43-year-old white female presents to her primary care physician for a routine physical exam and yearly Pap smear. Her physician notes a hard, solitary thyroid nodule. The nodule is freely mobile and was not present last year. The patient denies any anxiety, fevers, palpitations, diarrhea, or weight loss. Which of the following is the most appropriate next step?

(A) Fine needle aspiration for cytology
(B) Radiolabeled iodine scan with ^{131}I
(C) Reassure the patient that this is normal
(D) Surgical removal of the mass
(E) Ultrasound of the neck

(A) is correct. Fine needle aspiration for cytology is the first procedure in the evaluation of most patients with thyroid nodules. In most cases, it allows for differentiation between benign and malignant lesions while obviating the need for surgical removal. Choice B is incorrect. Radiolabeled iodine scan (or total-body scintiscanning with ^{131}I) should be reserved for evaluation of residual normal or malignant thyroid tissue in the neck or distant metastases after surgical removal of a thyroid nodule. Choice C is incorrect. Although most thyroid nodules are benign, each must be further investigated to ensure that there is no malignancy present. Choice D is incorrect. Efforts to prove the nodule benign with fine needle aspiration should be pursued prior to surgical removal. However, should confirmatory evidence show that a nodule is malignant, resection is indicated. Choice E is incorrect. Ultrasonography of the neck helps to differentiate solid versus cystic neck masses. However, thyroid nodules, whether solid or cystic, require fine needle aspiration.

311. A 27-year-old gravida 4 para 1 woman is now 8 weeks pregnant. She has a history of one spontaneous abortion and one stillborn child. Her mother has diabetes mellitus. Her surviving child weighed 4,500 g (9 lb 14 oz) at birth and is currently 3 years of age and in good health. Physical examination at the present visit reveals a heart rate of 105 beats per minute, a blood pressure of 130/80 mm Hg in the right arm, and 120/80 mm Hg in the left arm. Cardiac examination reveals no murmurs. Pulmonary auscultation reveals no evidence of rhonchi or wheezes. Gastrointestinal evaluation reveals no evidence of peritoneal signs. Laboratory studies obtained are as follows:

Hematocrit	34%
Hemoglobin	11.2 g/dL
Leukocyte count	11,000/mm^3
Platelet count	299,000/mm^3
Serum	
Sodium	135 mEq/L
Chloride	101 mEq/L
Potassium	4.1 mEq/L
Bicarbonate	24 mEq/L
Magnesium	1.6 mEq/L
Urea nitrogen	14 mg/dL

Which of the following interventions is most appropriate?

(A) 1-hour glucose screening at current visit
(B) 1-hour glucose screening at 24 weeks gestation
(C) 1-hour glucose tolerance test at 24 weeks gestation
(D) 3-hour glucose tolerance test at 28 weeks gestation
(E) No further testing is necessary in this patient

(A) is correct. Gestational diabetes is suspected in patients with a prior history of infants weighing more than 4,000 g, repeated spontaneous abortions, unexplained stillbirths, and a strong history of diabetes mellitus, obesity, and glucosuria. This mother has several risk factors for gestational diabetes and should be given a 1-hour glucose screening at the onset of prenatal care. Choice B is incorrect. In patients without risk factors, the 1-hour glucose screening is usually performed between 24 and 28 weeks gestation. Choice C is incorrect. In patients without risk factors, the 1-hour glucose screening is usually performed between 24 and 28 weeks gestation. Choice D is incorrect. The 3-hour glucose tolerance test should be performed for patients whose glucose value on the 1-hour glucose test exceeds 140 mg/100 mL. Choice E is incorrect. The 3-hour glucose tolerance test should be performed for patients whose glucose value on the 1-hour glucose test exceeds 140 mg/100 mL.

312. A 34-year-old woman complains of fever, fatigue, weight loss, arthralgia, and transient patchy alopecia during the last 3 months. Her history is notable for occasional rhinorrhea and cough that responds well to oral decongestant therapy. Her prior surgical history is notable for cesarean section and tubal ligation at age 31. A similar constellation of symptoms occurred 6 months ago during treatment for a cardiovascular disease. Antinuclear antibody testing was positive at her last visit 6 months ago and is still positive at the present time. Presently, her hematocrit is 36% and creatinine is 1.2 mg/dL. The most likely etiology of this constellation of symptoms and findings is related to

(A) ethosuximide
(B) oral contraceptives
(C) hydralazine
(D) phenytoin
(E) procainamide

(E) is correct. Several drugs can cause a syndrome resembling systemic lupus erythematosus (SLE). The syndrome is most commonly caused by procainamide, which induces the presence of antinuclear antibodies in up to 75 percent of individuals within a few months. There is a genetic predisposition to drug-induced lupus determined by drug acetylation rates. Typical symptoms include systemic complaints and arthralgias. The initial therapeutic approach is withdrawal of the offending drug. Choice A is incorrect. Although ethosuximide has been reported to cause drug-induced SLE, case reports have been mainly anecdotal. Choice B is incorrect. Drug-induced lupus is exceedingly rare with the use of oral contraceptives. Choice C is incorrect. Hydralazine is the second-most common cause of drug-induced SLE and induces antinuclear antigen positivity in up to 30 percent of patients taking the medication. Choice D is incorrect. Phenytoin has not been show to cause a lupus-like reaction in clinical studies.

313. Advocates in a large community are concerned about the development of osteoporosis among area residents. Which of the following individuals would be most likely to develop this condition?

(A) A 38-year-old white male marathon runner with a history of diabetes mellitus
(B) A 47-year-old Asian female with a history of hyperthyroidism who weighs 43 kg (95 lb)
(C) A 48-year-old black female with a history of sarcoidosis
(D) A 36-year-old black female who has four children
(E) A 19-year-old white female who binge eats frequently and weighs 68 kg (150 lb)

(B) is correct. Osteoporosis is the progressive reduction and weakening of bone as a result of the aging process. Several important risk factors for osteoporosis have been identified: female, white or Asian race, smoking, early menopause, family history of osteoporosis, and low body weight. Other factors associated with increased risk of osteoporosis may include excessive alcohol intake, low calcium intake, nulliparity, and lack of exercise. The most likely individual to develop osteoporosis is the 47-year-old Asian woman who has a history of thyroid disease and weighs 95 lb. She has three risk factors: female, Asian, and low body weight. Choice A is incorrect. This individual has none of the risk factors for osteoporosis development. Choice C is incorrect. This individual has one risk factor (female) for osteoporosis development. Choice D is incorrect. This individual has one risk factor (female) for osteoporosis development. Choice E is incorrect. This individual has one or two risk factors (female, and possibly overweight and inactive) for osteoporosis development.

314. A 55-year-old woman suffers the loss of her husband in a tragic automobile accident. She is an otherwise healthy woman with no medical problems. She takes no medications. Regarding her grief management and therapy, which of the following strategies would be most successful?

    (A) Encourage internalization of feelings
    (B) Encourage several long visits with her physician
    (C) Encourage open communication with former friends of the deceased
    (D) Routine prescription of antianxiety medications
    (E) Routine prescription of antidepressant medications

(C) is correct. Grief is a normal process following the death of a loved one. Having a small group of people who knew the deceased talk about the person in the presence of the grieving patient may help in the dissipation of grief. Choice A is incorrect. Encourage the ventilation of feelings and allow the person to talk about the loved one. Choice B is incorrect. Frequent, short visits with the physician are better than fewer long ones. Choice D is incorrect. Do not prescribe antianxiety medications on a regular basis. If the person becomes acutely agitated, talk to her before prescribing medication. Choice E is incorrect. Do not prescribe antidepressant medications on a regular basis. If the person becomes acutely depressed, talk to her before prescribing medication.

315. A 34-year-old white female engineering executive presents to her primary care doctor with complaints of fatigue, malaise, and a nonproductive cough. She has recently returned from a long business trip to California and attributes much of her fatigue to her stressful trip. Her temperature is 38.0 C (100.2 F). Her lung fields are clear to auscultation. Chest radiograph reveals a small left pleural effusion. Which of the following is the most likely diagnosis?

    (A) *Cryptococcus neoformans*
    (B) *Coccidioides immitis*
    (C) *Histoplasma capsulatum*
    (D) *Mycobacterium tuberculosis*
    (E) *Mycoplasma pneumoniae*
    (F) *Pneumocystis carinii*
    (G) *Streptococcus pneumoniae*

(B) is correct. This patient has symptoms and chest radiograph findings consistent with a pulmonary process as well as recent travel to California, presumably the San Joaquin Valley, which makes the diagnosis of coccidiomycosis most likely. Chest radiograph may demonstrate infiltrate, hilar adenopathy, or pleural effusion. Diagnosis is confirmed with examination of sputum for the yeast forms or by serologic testing. Choice A is incorrect. *Cryptococcus neoformans* is found in the soil and is concentrated in pigeon droppings. Those most at risk are the immunocompromised, such as patients with HIV infection (CD4+ less than 100/mm^3) and patients receiving immunosuppressive therapy following organ transplantation. Choice C is incorrect. *Histoplasma capsulatum* is endemic to the Ohio and Mississippi River Valleys. It usually produces a self-limited febrile illness. There is no history of such travel in this patient's history. Choice D is incorrect. *Mycobacterium tuberculosis* should always be considered in a patient with pulmonary complaints. However in this case, the lack of usual radiographic findings argues against this diagnosis. Choice E is incorrect. *Mycoplasma pneumoniae* is a common cause of pneumonia in young adults. It is characterized by a persistent cough, often of several weeks duration. Lung fields are usually clear. Choice F is incorrect. *Pneumocystis carinii* is a common pathogen in patients with HIV and CD4+ counts less than 200/mm^3. Symptoms are usually progressive dyspnea, cough, and fever, often of several weeks duration. Choice G is incorrect. In this patient, the rapid onset of symptoms and rusty-colored sputum suggestive of *Streptococcus pneumoniae* infection are lacking.

316. A 15-year-old male is brought to the emergency department by ambulance after collapsing in the park while playing a basketball game with friends. Observers at the scene told the paramedics that the individual was snorting cocaine approximately 1 hour prior to collapsing on the court. Cardiovascular examination reveals no evidence of rubs or gallops. Pulmonary auscultation reveals good breath sounds bilaterally. Gastrointestinal examination fails to reveal peritoneal signs. Which of the following may appear in the patient?

(A) Aortic rupture
(B) Hypotension
(C) Mitral valve prolapse
(D) Pulmonary stenosis
(E) Right ventricular dysfunction

(A) is correct. Cocaine may adversely affect any organ system and is associated with significant morbidity and mortality. Typical cardiovascular effects include left ventricular dysfunction, hypertension, aortic rupture, angina pectoris, cardiac arrhythmia (any type is possible), and coronary artery disease. Choice B is incorrect. The autonomic effects of cocaine use include tachycardia and hypertension. Choice C is incorrect. Mitral valve rupture is a possible cardiac sequelae of cocaine use. Mitral valve prolapse is more common in young females. Choice D is incorrect. Pulmonary valvular dysfunction and pulmonary hypertension can result from cocaine use. Choice E is incorrect. Left ventricular dysfunction is a possible cardiac sequela of cocaine use.

317. A 16-year-old white male presents to his primary care physician with complaints of smoky-colored urine for the last two days. He recently recovered from a streptococcal pharyngitis that was treated with oral penicillin. His blood pressure is 195/100 mm Hg, heart rate is 74 beats per minute, and temperature is 37.2 C (98.9 F). Which of the following is his urinalysis most likely to demonstrate?

pH	Blood	Protein	WBC	RBC	Casts
(A) 7.5	+++	+	20	>50	Erythrocyte
(B) 7.4	+++	+++	0	0	None
(C) 7.3	+	+	>50	5	Leukocyte
(D) 7.4	+	+++	5	30	Renal tubular
(E) 7.4	–	–	2	1	None

(A) is correct. Poststreptococcal glomerulonephritis is the prototypical postinfectious glomerulonephritis and is the leading cause of the nephritic syndrome. Approximately ten days after a pharyngitis infection, the urine often becomes smoky secondary to gross hematuria. There is active urine sediment with red blood cells, red blood cell casts, white blood cells, and mild proteinuria. Only 5 percent of patients develop nephrotic-range proteinuria. Choice B is incorrect. In poststreptococcal glomerulonephritis, there is active urine sediment and usually only mild proteinuria. Choice C is incorrect. This urinalysis represents pyelonephritis, evidenced by the large number of leukocytes (> 50) and leukocyte casts. Choice D is incorrect. This urinalysis presents a picture of acute tubular necrosis (ATN) with prominent proteinuria, hematuria, and renal tubular casts. ATN is often secondary to an ischemic insult. Choice E is incorrect. This urinalysis is normal.

318. A 67-year-old white male presents to his primary care physician with complaints of jaundice, fever, and malaise. He returned from a Caribbean cruise 3 weeks ago. His blood pressure is 130/70 mm Hg, heart rate is 90 beats per minute, and temperature is 38.0 C (100 F). Exam confirms jaundice and a tender 12 cm (4.5 inch) liver span. Which of the following serologic tests is most likely to be positive?

   (A) Hepatitis A IgG
   (B) Hepatitis A IgM
   (C) Hepatitis B antisurface IgM
   (D) Hepatitis B anticore IgM
   (E) Hepatitis B surface antigen
   (F) Hepatitis C IgG

(B) is correct. Hepatitis A is transmitted via the fecal-oral route, usually by contaminated food (especially seafood) and water. The mean incubation period of hepatitis A is four weeks. As an antibody response (first IgM) is generated, there is jaundice, but improvement in the constitutional symptoms. IgG is generated later to confer permanent immunity. Choice A is incorrect. IgG is generated after IgM (the initial antibody response) to confer permanent immunity in hepatitis A infection. Choice C is incorrect. Hepatitis B has a longer incubation period than hepatitis A, often several months, and transmission is blood-borne. Hepatitis B antisurface IgM is the first antibody generated prior to permanent immunity to hepatitis B via antisurface IgG. Choice D is incorrect. Hepatitis B anticore IgM is a marker for early hepatitis B infection. It does not confer immunity. Choice E is incorrect. Hepatitis B surface antigen is a marker for ongoing infection with hepatitis B. Choice F is incorrect. Hepatitis C has a longer incubation period than hepatitis A, often several months, and transmission is believed to be blood-borne. Generation of hepatitis C IgG indicates recovery.

A 65-year-old white female presents her primary care physician complaining of worsening fatigue over the last 4 to 6 months. She denies any change in her sleep cycle and describes her mood as good. She has gained 4 kg (10 lb) since her last office visit 6 months ago. She is also concerned about worsening constipation. Her only other medical problems are gastroesophageal reflux disease, for which she uses over-the-counter ranitidine when symptomatic, and hypercholesterolemia, for which her physician has prescribed simvastatin. The patient has nonpitting pretibial edema, which was not present 6 months ago at her last visit, as well as loss of the lateral half of her eyebrows.

319. Which of the following laboratory tests would be most useful?

(A) Free thyroxine index
(B) Thyroid-stimulating hormone
(C) T3 resin uptake
(D) Total T3
(E) Total T4

(B) is correct. The patient has the classic signs and symptoms of hypothyroidism. The best test to confirm this diagnosis is a thyroid-stimulating hormone level screening. The vast majority of thyroid disease is due to malfunction of the thyroid, not the hypothalamus or pituitary gland. Thus, the level of thyroid-stimulating hormone is the first lab test to become abnormal in the course of thyroid disease. Choice A is incorrect. Prior to the advent of newer and more sensitive assays for thyroid-stimulating hormone, the free thyroxine index was necessary to help differentiate thyroid malfunction from either thyroid-binding protein deficiency or excess. Now the assay is seldom used. Choice C is incorrect. The T3 resin uptake measures the protein-binding capacity for thyroid hormone in plasma. This test was used in conjunction with total T4 to diagnose thyroid conditions. However, the advent of assays for free T4 has eliminated the need to quantify protein binding. Choices D and E are incorrect. The advent of assays for free T4 have eliminated the need to obtain total T3 and T4 levels, along with the T3 resin uptake, because assays for free T3 and T4 are not confounded by protein binding.

320. The patient is placed on a regimen of thyroid replacement therapy. Which of the following laboratory values would be most useful in following her response to treatment?

(A) Free thyroxine index
(B) Thyroid-stimulating hormone
(C) T3 resin uptake
(D) Total T3
(E) Total T4

(B) is correct. The simplest and most cost-effective way to monitor response to thyroid replacement therapy is to follow thyroid-stimulating hormone levels. Choice A is incorrect. Prior to the advent of newer and more sensitive assays for thyroid-stimulating hormone, the free thyroxine index was necessary to help differentiate thyroid malfunction from either thyroid binding protein deficiency or excess. Now the assay is seldom used. Choice C is incorrect. The T3 resin uptake measures the protein-binding capacity of thyroid hormone in plasma. This test was used in conjunction with total T4 to diagnose thyroid conditions. However, the advent of assays for free T4 has eliminated the need to quantify protein binding. Choices D and E are incorrect. The advent of assays for free T4 have eliminated the need to obtain total T3 and T4 levels, along with the T3 resin uptake, because assays for free T3 and T4 are not confounded by protein binding.

321. A 24-year-old restrained driver in a head-on collision is brought to the emergency department. He has signs of significant head and facial trauma, but no other obvious injuries. His past medical history is noncontributory. Vital signs include a blood pressure of 68/48 mm Hg and a pulse of 105 beats/minute that is thready. Respirations are 8 per minute and shallow. Cardiac and pulmonary examinations are unremarkable. Abdominal examination reveals mild tenderness in the left upper quadrant and no peritoneal signs. Digital rectal examination is normal. His Glasgow Coma Scale is 8. Which of the following is the most appropriate test to assess for intraperitoneal bleeding?

(A) Abdominal x-ray
(B) Aortogram
(C) Computed tomography scan
(D) Diagnostic peritoneal lavage
(E) Ultrasonography

(D) is correct. This patient has no indications for an immediate laparotomy, but is hemodynamically unstable. Diagnostic peritoneal lavage is sensitive, rapid, and does not require moving the patient from the emergency department to be performed. Therefore, it is the procedure of choice to evaluate for intraperitoneal bleeding in the unstable patient. Choice A is incorrect. This procedure is unlikely to provide useful information about intra-abdominal bleeding. Choice B is incorrect. This procedure is unlikely to provide useful information about intra-abdominal bleeding. Choice C is incorrect. CT scanning will require moving this unstable patient from the emergency department to complete the procedure. Choice E is incorrect. Ultrasonography will require moving this unstable patient from the emergency department to complete the procedure.

322. A 24-year-old Asian female presents to her primary care physician complaining of a nontender lump in her right breast. She noticed the lump a few days ago. She is in the middle of her menstrual cycle. Exam confirms a 1 cm, smooth, rubbery, and freely mobile mass in the right lower quadrant of her right breast. There is no axillary adenopathy. The left breast is normal. Which of the following is the most appropriate first step?

(A) Excisional biopsy
(B) Fine needle aspiration
(C) Follow-up appointment after her menses
(D) Referral to a breast surgeon
(E) Ultrasound exam

(C) is correct. This patient has a fibroadenoma by history and physical examination. There is no need for further evaluation, other than a recheck to assure the patient that it is benign after her next menstrual period. Choice A is incorrect. This patient has a fibroadenoma by history and physical examination. There is no need for further evaluation, other than a recheck to assure the patient that it is benign. Choice B is incorrect. This patient has a fibroadenoma by history and physical examination. There is no need for further evaluation, other than a recheck to assure the patient that it is benign. Fine needle aspiration is a good starting point when there is any concern about malignancy. Choice D is incorrect. This patient has a fibroadenoma by history and physical examination. There is no need for further evaluation, other than a recheck to assure the patient that it is benign. Choice E is incorrect. This patient has a fibroadenoma by history and physical examination. There is no need for further evaluation, other than a recheck to assure the patient that it is benign. Ultrasound is a good starting point when there is any concern about malignancy, especially in a patient with fibrocystic breast disease.

323. A 52-year-old Hispanic male presents to his primary care physician with complaints of "turning yellow." He denies any abdominal pain, nausea, or vomiting. He admits to a 4 kg (10 lb) weight loss in the last two months. He is jaundiced but well-appearing. His abdomen is without masses but his gallbladder is palpable. Which of the following is the best first step?

(A) Computed tomography of the abdomen
(B) Endoscopic retrograde cholangiopancreatography
(C) Liver biopsy
(D) Magnetic resonance imaging of the abdomen
(E) Nuclear medicine biliary scan
(F) Ultrasound of the abdomen

(F) is correct. This patient has jaundice, weight loss, and a palpable gallbladder. These symptoms are suspicious for pancreatic cancer. The best first step in the evaluation of his jaundice is ultrasound of the abdomen, which will image the hepatobiliary system as well as the pancreas. Choice A is incorrect. Computed tomography is a useful tool in the evaluation of pancreatic masses. However, ultrasound is the best first step, especially in the patient with jaundice. Choice B is incorrect. Endoscopic retrograde cholangiopancreatography (ERCP) is an important tool in the evaluation of pancreatic masses and other biliary pathology, but it is not an appropriate first step. Choice C is incorrect. Liver biopsy is an invasive procedure with inherent risks. It is not the appropriate first step in the evaluation of any patient with jaundice. Choice D is incorrect. Magnetic resonance imaging has a role in evaluating pancreatic masses, especially insulinomas, but is not the best first step. Choice E is incorrect. A nuclear medicine biliary scan is an excellent test for confirming cholelithiasis prior to proceeding with cholecystectomy. However, ultrasound is the best first step in the evaluation of a patient with jaundice.

324. A 29-year-old man with no prior medical history presents to the emergency room complaining of a 12-hour history of tearing pain with defecation and bright red bleeding per rectum noted on the toilet tissue. Vital signs are as follows: blood pressure is 138/90 mm Hg, pulse is 90 beats per minute, respirations are 14 per minute, and temperature is normal. Urinanalysis reveals no evidence of microhematuria, glucosuria, or proteinuria. Cardiovascular examination reveals a regular rate and rhythm. Pulmonary auscultation reveals no evidence of rales, rhonchi, or wheezes. Good air exchange is noted bilaterally. Gastrointestinal examination reveals tenderness to deep palpation in the lower left quadrant with no localizing peritoneal signs. Anoscopy reveals a split in the anoderm at the posterior midline with fresh blood oozing from the site. Which of the following is the most appropriate treatment?

(A) Ampicillin-intravenous
(B) Metronidazole-oral
(C) Rubber band ligation
(D) Stool softeners, sitz baths, and bulking agents
(E) Surgical excision and sphincterotomy

(D) is correct. Anal fissure is a split in the midline of the posterior anoderm 90 percent of the time. Symptoms of acute fissures include tearing pain on defecation and blood in the stool or on the toilet paper. Treatment of choice for acute fissures includes stool softeners, sitz baths, and dietary bulking agents. Choice A is incorrect. There is no role for intravenous antibiotic therapy in the management of acute anal fissures. Choice B is incorrect. There is no role for oral antibiotic therapy in the management of acute anal fissures. Choice C is incorrect. Rubber band ligation is an appropriate treatment for hemorrhoids. Choice E is incorrect. Surgical therapy is reserved for chronic, nonhealing fissures, and the procedure of choice is lateral sphincterotomy.

325. A 31-year-old man with a history of depression has recently begun a sexual relationship with a new female partner. Since the beginning of this relationship, he has had a pattern of ejaculation that occurs with minimal sexual stimulation, often immediately after vaginal penetration. Physical examination reveals an uncircumcised penis with a patent urethral meatus. The testicles are descended bilaterally without evidence of palpable masses. Cremasteric reflexes are present bilaterally. Which of the following is the most appropriate treatment for this condition?

(A) Behavioral techniques
(B) Directive marital therapy
(C) Pharmacologic therapy
(D) Psychodynamic approaches
(E) Surgical resection

(A) is correct. It is estimated that 30 percent of the male population suffers from premature ejaculation. This condition is more prevalent in the young and those with a new sexual partner. This dysfunction is most amenable to cure when behavioral techniques are used in the treatment protocol. Choice B is incorrect. Directive marital therapy is effective in the treatment of dyspareunia. Choice C is incorrect. Pharmacologic therapy is not considered to be a primary treatment for premature ejaculation. Choice D is incorrect. Psychodynamic approaches are considered to be effective therapy for dyspareunia. Choice E is incorrect. Surgical resection is not considered to be an effective therapy for premature ejaculation.

326. A 36-year-old white male in brought to the emergency department by EMS. He has a history of schizoaffective disorder for which he takes lithium and haloperidol. He summoned EMS after feeling dizzy and confused. His laboratory values are as follows:

Serum

Sodium	122 mEq/L
Potassium	4.0 mEq/L
Chloride	88 mEq/L
Bicarbonate	22 mEq/L
Creatinine	0.9 mg/dL
Urea nitrogen	8.2 mg/dL
Osmolality	270 mOsmol/kg

Urine

Sodium	40 mEq/L

Which of the following is the most likely etiology of his electrolyte disturbance?

(A) Dehydration
(B) Haloperidol therapy
(C) Lithium therapy
(D) Primary hyperaldosteronism
(E) Psychogenic water intoxication

(C) is correct. Chronic use of lithium commonly results in a nephrogenic diabetes insipidus, in which the distal tubule is unresponsive to antidiuretic hormone and thus is unable to maximally concentrate urine. Therefore, the urine sodium would be increased. Choice A is incorrect. Dehydration commonly results in hypernatremia. Choice B is incorrect. Haloperidol is not known to cause hyponatremia. Choice D is incorrect. Primary hyperaldosteronism results in excessive sodium, and therefore water resorption (secondary to increased aldosterone) and hypernatremia. Choice E is incorrect. In psychogenic water intoxication, urinary sodium is decreased.

327. A 19-year-old white male presents to the student health center at his university with complaints of a painless ulcer on his penis. The lesion appeared several weeks ago. Since beginning college last fall, he has had unprotected sex with multiple partners. His last unprotected intercourse was about a month ago after a fraternity party. He denies any medical problems and has never had a sexually transmitted disease in the past. He notes difficulty breathing and a rash when given penicillin that required treatment with epinephrine some time in high school. Which of the following is the most appropriate treatment?

(A) Azithromycin 1 gram by mouth
(B) Benzanthine penicillin 2.4 million units by intramuscular injection
(C) Cephalexin 500 mg by mouth four times a day for 28 days
(D) Ciprofloxacin 500 mg by mouth twice a day for 28 days
(E) Desensitization and treatment with penicillin
(F) Doxycycline 100 mg by mouth twice per day for 28 days

(F) is correct. This patient has primary syphilis. Usual treatment involves 2.4 million units of benzanthine penicillin by intramuscular injection. However, this patient describes an anaphylactic reaction to penicillin. The alternative regimen for the penicillin allergic is either doxycycline or tetracycline for 28 days. Choice A is incorrect. Although azithromycin has excellent activity against *Chlamydia trachomatis*, it is not appropriate treatment for syphilis. Choice B is incorrect. This patient describes an anaphylactic reaction to penicillin. The alternative regimen for the penicillin allergic is either doxycycline or tetracycline for 28 days. Choice C is incorrect. First-generation cephalosporins lack activity against *Treponema pallidum*. Also, the patient's apparent anaphylactic reaction to penicillin is a contraindication for the use of a cephalosporin. Choice D is incorrect. Fluoroquinolones lack activity against *Treponema pallidum*. Choice E is incorrect. Desensitization, which poses a risk to the patient and requires a lengthy process, is warranted only in cases without alternative appropriate therapy, such as pregnant women requiring treatment for syphilis and for patients with neurosyphilis (a case in which penicillin is the only efficacious therapy).

328. A 37-year-old white male presents to the emergency department with complaints of crushing substernal chest pain that began 30 minutes ago. An electrocardiogram demonstrates 2 mm of ST segment elevation in leads II, III, and aV_F. The patient is a nonsmoker, has no family history of myocardial infarction, and no personal history of diabetes mellitus or hypertension. His total cholesterol was 120 mg/dL last year. Cardiac catheterization is performed and demonstrates transient coronary artery spasm with the injection of intracoronary acetylcholine. Which of the following is the most appropriate first step in the long-term management of this patient?

(A) Oral hydralazine
(B) Oral metoprolol
(C) Oral narcotics as needed for pain
(D) Oral short-acting nifedipine
(E) Oral sustained-release verapamil
(F) Transdermal clonidine

(E) is correct. This patient has Prinzmetal's angina. This an uncommon form of angina that usually occurs in patients at rest in their 30s and 40s. It may produce ST segment elevations. Diagnosis is confirmed by witnessing coronary vasospasm during cardiac catheterization after provocation with intracoronary acetylcholine or intravenous ergonovine. Treatment is long-acting calcium channel-blockers. Choice A is incorrect. Hydralazine has a role in the management of refractory hypertension, not Prinzmetal's angina. Choice B is incorrect. There is no role for the use of β-blockers in the treatment of Prinzmetal's angina. Choice C is incorrect. The use of narcotics may relieve symptoms of Prinzmetal's angina, but would not treat the etiology of the pain, coronary vasospasm. Choice D is incorrect. There is a role for short-acting calcium channel-blockers in the treatment of acute Printzmetal's angina, but not its long-term management. Choice F is incorrect. Transdermal clonidine is useful in the management of refractory hypertension, not Prinzmetal's angina.

An 81-year-old white male presents to the emergency room after being found unconscious by his neighbor. The patient lives alone and had not been seen in several days. The patient is resuscitated with several liters of normal saline. His mental status improves significantly and he is able to relate falling about twenty hours prior to admission after tripping on the rug. He denies any musculoskeletal complaints. No ecchymoses are noted on physical exam. His prostate is normal size without nodules. Over the next several hours, he is noted to be oliguric.

329. Which of the following is the most appropriate next step in the evaluation and treatment of his oliguria?

    (A) Computed tomography of the pelvis
    (B) Intravenous pyelogram
    (C) Pelvis roentgenographs
    (D) Renal ultrasound
    (E) Urinalysis with microscopy

(E) is correct. The patient's history is suggestive of rhabdomyolysis secondary to a long period of time prior to his neighbor's intervention. The most effective test to confirm this diagnosis is to obtain a urinalysis that demonstrates large amounts of hemoglobin by dipstick without red blood cells by microscopy. These findings suggest the presence of myoglobin in the urine, a product of the patient's rhabdomyolysis. With this diagnosis confirmed, the need for more extensive testing to exclude other causes of acute renal failure is obviated. Choice A is incorrect. Computed tomography of the pelvis would be useful to explore pelvic anatomy contributing to possible urinary obstruction, e.g., a large retroperitoneal mass. But patient's history is suggestive of rhabdomyolysis, and the most effective test to confirm this diagnosis is a urinalysis. Choice B is incorrect. An intravenous pyelogram (IVP) is a useful test to evaluate ureteral patency, e.g., in the evaluation of a possible kidney stone. This patient's history does not suggest a stone or other ureteral obstruction, and therefore an IVP is not indicated. Choice C is incorrect. There is no history or physical exam finding indicating pelvic fracture, thus pelvic roentgenographs would not be of benefit. Choice D is incorrect. Renal ultrasound is useful in evaluating kidney size and excluding hydronephrosis. However, the history suggests rhabdomyolysis, not obstruction.

330. Several weeks after discharge from the hospital, the patient is again brought to the emergency room by his neighbor. Now, the neighbor is concerned because the patient is increasingly confused and forgetful since discharge from the hospital 21 days ago. Additionally, he is now walking with a new stagger. Other than a new headache, he denies any additional symptoms. The patient denies any use of alcohol and is taking no medicines, including over-the-counter remedies. What is the most appropriate diagnostic intervention?

    (A) Carotid duplex ultrasonography
    (B) Computed tomography of the head
    (C) Electroencephalogram
    (D) Lumbar puncture
    (E) Urinalysis

(B) is correct. With the patient's history of a recent fall, the suspicion of a subdural hematoma is high. The best test to confirm this diagnosis is computed tomography of the head. Choice A is incorrect. Although the patient's symptoms initially could have been consistent with a transient ischemic attack and thereby justify a search for an embolic source, the time course (several weeks, not less than 24 hours) makes this diagnosis unlikely. Choice C is incorrect. There is no suggestion of seizure in this patient that would require an EEG. Choice D is incorrect. Lumbar puncture is not recommended when the diagnosis of subdural hematoma is considered, as such intervention may worsen any tissue shifts. Choice E is incorrect. Although urinary tract infections can be a source a mental status changes, especially in the elderly, this patient's history gives no clues to support this diagnosis, but rather favors subdural hematoma.

331. A 40-year-old white male presents to the emergency department with complaints of crushing substernal chest pain that began while playing basketball one hour ago. The pain radiates to his left arm and jaw and is accompanied by diaphoresis and nausea. Electrocardiogram demonstrates 3 mm of ST segment elevation in leads II, III, and aV_F. Which of the following the most likely location of this patient's coronary artery lesion?

(A) Circumflex artery
(B) Left anterior descending artery
(C) Left coronary artery
(D) Marginal branch of the left anterior descending artery
(E) Obtuse marginal branch of the circumflex artery
(F) Right coronary artery

(F) is correct. The right coronary artery supplies blood to the inferior wall of the heart, which is represented on the electrocardiogram as leads II, III, and aV_F. ST segment elevation represents myocardial injury. Choice A is incorrect. The circumflex artery is most closely represented on an electrocardiogram by leads V_5 and V_6. Choice B is incorrect. The left anterior descending artery is most closely represented on electrocardiogram by leads V_1, V_2, V_3, and V_4. Choice C is incorrect. The left coronary artery or "left main" supplies the entire anterior and lateral wall of the heart through its two branches, the left anterior descending artery and the circumflex. Therefore, an occlusive lesion of the left coronary artery would result is electrocardiogram changes in V_1, V_2, V_3, V_4, V_5, and V_6. Choice D is incorrect. The left anterior descending artery has multiple marginal branches. Occlusion of these branches results in changes on electrocardiogram in leads V_1, V_2, V_3, and V_4. Choice E is incorrect. The circumflex artery usually has several obtuse branches. These branches are most closely represented on electrocardiogram by leads V_5 and V_6.

332. A 60-year-old woman, gravida 2 para 2, has been hospitalized for 1 week for the management of neutropenic fever. Blood, urine, and throat cultures have been negative. On the eighth hospital day, the patient develops acute right lower quadrant pain with distention, nausea, and vomiting. She has no change in bowel habits and is passing flatus. She is currently taking vancomycin, ampicillin, and gentamicin intravenously. She has a history of breast cancer for which she recently underwent autologous bone marrow transplant. Physical examination reveals a thin white woman in distress. Temperature is 39 C (102.2 F), pulse is 120 beats per minute, respirations are 25 per minute, and blood pressure is 80/60 mm Hg. Examination of the head, eyes, ears, nose, and throat reveals no lesions or abnormalities. Peripheral intravenous sites are clean and intact without swelling or erythema. Lungs are clear. Cardiovascular examination reveals tachycardia. The abdomen is distended with diffuse tenderness to light palpation, especially in the right lower quadrant. Extremities are without skin lesions, cyanosis, or edema. Abdominal plain film reveals massive dilated loops of bowel with thumbprinting of the bowel walls. The most likely diagnosis is

(A) appendicitis
(B) diverticulitis
(C) pseudomembranous colitis
(D) toxic megacolon
(E) typhlitis

(E) is correct. In patients with neutropenic fever and acute abdominal pain, the diagnosis of typhlitis should always be considered. This entity is an infection of the bowel by enteric organisms, seen especially in neutropenic patients. Treatment requires anaerobic antibiotic coverage and possible surgical intervention. Choice A is incorrect. Appendicitis has a presentation similar to the one described above. However, the abdominal plain film points to the diagnosis of typhlitis. Choice B is incorrect. Diverticulitis is not likely to present as acutely and is more likely to produce pain in the left lower quadrant. Choice C is incorrect. Pseudomembranous colitis presents with diarrhea, which this patient does not have. Choice D is incorrect. Toxic megacolon is not the most likely diagnosis in this neutropenic patient with no change in bowel habits and no predisposing condition, such as inflammatory bowel disease.

333. A fine needle aspiration test is often used to determine if a breast mass is malignant. At one laboratory, the results of the fine needle aspiration test are categorized as: (1) insufficient material to adequately assess the tissue sample; (2) benign; (3) suspicious but not definitely malignant; and (4) malignant. How would the sensitivity and specificity of the fine needle aspiration test differ if the lab chose to call suspicious tissue samples negative as opposed to positive?

	Sensitivity	Specificity
(A)	Higher	Higher
(B)	Higher	Lower
(C)	Higher	The same
(D)	Lower	Higher
(E)	Lower	Lower
(F)	Lower	The same
(G)	The same	Higher
(H)	The same	Lower
(I)	The same	The same

(D) is correct. The formula for sensitivity and specificity is given below.

Gold standard

	Disease Positive	Disease Negative
Diagnostic test		
Test Positive	**a** (TP)	**b** (FP)
Test Negative	**c** (FN)	**d** (TN)

TP = true positive
TN = true negative
FP = false positive
FN = false negative

Sensitivity (ability to include people with disease) = a/(a + c)

Specificity (ability to exclude people without disease) = d/(d + b)

In this problem, different "cut-off points" for the fine needle aspiration test are being compared. If suspicious tissue samples are considered negative, the likelihood of getting a positive result will be less than if suspicious tissue samples are considered positive; thus there will be fewer false positives and the specificity will be higher. At the same time, the likelihood of getting a negative result will be higher. There will be more false negatives and the sensitivity of the test will be lower.

334. A husband-wife couple turns to a marriage counselor for guidance. The wife complains that her husband of 10 years is arrogant, manipulative, and unloving. He is a partner in a large law firm and often works long hours. He expects his wife to wake up when he does to make him a hot meal each morning. He expects the same when he arrives home, usually past 8 PM, and frequently gets angry at his wife for cooking "inedible" meals. In the meantime, he does not help at all with household chores. He recently had an affair with another lawyer in his firm and did not apologize to his wife when she found out. He states that all women want to sleep with him, so it was a natural course of events. The husband becomes visibly upset during this discourse and claims that his wife does not understand him because she is not as "special" or "unique" as he is. He claims it is difficult for him to continue to be successful, as she keeps "dragging him down" with her foolish complaints. The most likely diagnosis of the husband is

(A) borderline personality disorder
(B) histrionic personality disorder
(C) narcissistic personality disorder
(D) antisocial personality disorder
(E) dependent personality disorder

(C) is correct. This patient displays the following: a grandiose sense of self-importance; belief that he is special and unique; requirement for excessive admiration; a sense of entitlement; interpersonal exploitation; lack of empathy; and arrogant and haughty behavior and attitude. These qualify him for narcissistic personality disorder. Choice A is incorrect. Borderline personality disorder features frantic efforts to avoid real or imagined abandonment; a pattern of unstable and intense interpersonal relationships; recurrent suicidal behavior, gestures, and threats; affective instability due to a marked reactivity of mood; chronic feelings of emptiness; difficulty controlling anger; and transient, stress-related paranoid ideation. Choice B is incorrect. Histrionic personality disorder features a pattern of behavior that includes the need to be the center of attention, inappropriate sexual seductiveness, insincerity, self-dramatization, and suggestibility. Choice D is incorrect. Antisocial personality disorder features a pattern of behavior that disregards and violates the rights of others. Patients usually have criminal records and are irritable, hostile, and manipulative. Choice E is incorrect. Dependent personality disorder features an inability to make everyday decisions and a need for others to assume responsibility for most major areas of life. Patients have difficulty initiating projects and go to excessive lengths to obtain nurturance and support.

335. A 28-year-old white woman has bright red hematemesis. She recently binged on a large pizza and a 6-pack of beer and then vomited several times. After purging herself, she vomited one more time, this time with bright red clots. Physical examination is unremarkable except for poor dentition and dental caries. Nasogastric lavage yields blood clots. Upper gastrointestinal tract endoscopy reveals longitudinal mucosal tears at the gastroesophageal junction and arterial bleeding. With nonoperative management, the patient's condition will most likely

    (A) lead to increased mortality
    (B) progress to full esophageal perforation
    (C) recur
    (D) stabilize until emergent surgery can be
         performed
    (E) stop spontaneously

(E) is correct. This patient has Mallory-Weiss syndrome, an acute upper GI bleed from longitudinal esophageal tears after repeated vomiting. A severe bleed can occur. Nonoperative management such as decompression and antiemetics are usually sufficient to stabilize the patient until the bleeding stops spontaneously. Choice A is incorrect. Mallory-Weiss tears rarely lead to death. Choice B is incorrect. Mallory-Weiss tears do not lead to full esophageal perforation. Choice C is incorrect. Mallory-Weiss tears rarely recur. Choice D is incorrect. Mallory-Weiss tears rarely require emergent surgery.

Items 336–338

    (A) Absent A waves
    (B) Cannon A waves
    (C) Prominent V wave
    (D) Sharp y descent

Match each venous wave form finding with the most likely clinical scenario.

336. A 45-year-old white female presents to her primary care doctor with complaints of nervousness, weight loss, and palpitations. She appears anxious, with prominent bilateral proptosis. Her cardiac rhythm is irregular with a rate of 135 beats per minute.

(A) is correct. This patient has atrial fibrillation that was likely precipitated by hyperthyroidism. The A wave is produced by venous distention during atrial contraction. The A wave is absent in atrial fibrillation.

337. A 72-year-old white male presents to the emergency department with complaints of dizziness. An electrocardiogram demonstrates a junctional rhythm with a rate of 50 beats per minute and no other abnormalities.

(B) is correct. Cannon A waves occur when the right atrium contracts against a closed tricuspid valve such as in a junctional rhythm or complete heart block.

338. A 68-year-old white male presents to his new primary care doctor to establish medical care. His past medical history includes a bout of tuberculosis that he notes caused his heart to "stiffen up," and has left him chronically short of breath and intolerant of exercise.

(D) is correct. The negative descending limb of the jugular venous pulse is the y descent. It is produced by the opening of the tricuspid valve and the rapid inflow of blood into the right ventricle. A sharp y descent is characteristic of constrictive pericarditis such as might follow tuberculosis.

Items 339–342

    (A) Hypovolemic
    (B) Cardiogenic
    (C) Obstructive
    (D) Distributive
    (E) Associative
    (F) Commutative

For each of the following critically ill patients, select the most appropriate form of clinical shock.

339. A 28-year-old man who sustained several gun shot wounds to the abdomen and lower extremities is left in the field for 2 hours before being brought to the emergency department.

(A) is correct. In hypovolemic shock, there can be a decline in cardiac output and systemic vascular resistance due to fluid loss. This condition can result from loss of blood (hemorrhage), loss of plasma fluids (burn patients), and loss of fluid and electrolytes (third-spacing seen in pancreatitis).

340. A 51-year-old man who had a myocardial infarction 4 weeks ago suddenly falls to the ground while walking in front of his home. As emergency personnel arrive on the scene, he is apneic and pulseless. Electrocardiogram reveals asystole. Autopsy studies later reveal rupture of the intraventricular septum.

(B) is correct. Cardiogenic shock can result from cardiac pump failure or valvular failure. As described by the scenario in this question, rupture of the intraventricular septum can also occur with immediate decline in cardiac output and systemic vascular resistance.

341. A 39-year-old woman with a history of diabetes mellitus and hypertension presents with left-sided chest pain that improves when she sits up. A presumed diagnosis of pericarditis is made.

(C) is correct. Etiologies of obstructive shock include tension pneumothorax, pericardial diseases, disease of the pulmonary blood vessels, cardiac tumor (left atrial myxoma), mural thrombus, and valvular obstructive diseases. In this condition, there is a decrease in cardiac output and an increase in systemic vascular resistance.

342. A 41-year-old man with a history of chronic pancreatitis is readmitted to the hospital with recurrent abdominal pain and persistent vomiting. His mucous membranes appear dry.

(A) is correct. This patient has hypovolemic shock. Loss of electrolytes and fluid, known as third-spacing, is a major contributor to shock in patients with acute pancreatitis. There can be a decline in cardiac output and systemic vascular resistance due to fluid loss.

Items 343–346

Match each type of chest exam findings with the most appropriate clinical scenario.

	Tactile Fremitus	Egophony	Percussion Note
(A)	Absent	Absent	Hyperresonant
(B)	Decreased	Absent	Hyperresonant
(C)	Decreased	Absent	Dull
(D)	Increased	Present	Dull
(E)	Increased	Present	Hyperresonant
(F)	Increased	Absent	Hyperresonant

343. A 22-year-old white male arrives to the emergency department with complaints of the acute onset of shortness of breath and sharp, right-sided chest pain that is most severe upon inspiration. By exam, the patient is tall and thin and in mild distress.

(A) is correct. This patient has a pneumothorax. With pneumothorax, breath sounds are absent in the affected lung, the percussion note is hyperresonant, and tactile fremitus is absent. Spontaneous pneumothoraces in tall, thin young men are not uncommon and may require chest tube placement, depending upon the degree of the pneumothorax.

344. A 72-year-old white female with metastatic breast cancer presents to the emergency room complaining of worsening dyspnea on exertion and new shortness of breath at rest. By exam, the patient is a cachectic-appearing elderly female in mild respiratory distress.

(C) is correct. This patient has a large pleural effusion. Malignant pleural effusions are common in end-stage breast cancer and occasionally respond to pleuridesis. With large pleural effusions, breath sounds are absent and without egophony, the percussion note is dull, and fremitus is decreased (unlike the increased fremitus over an area of consolidation).

345. A 36-year-old Asian male presents to the emergency department complaining of the acute onset of fever of 38.8 C (103 F), shaking chills, and cough productive of rusty-colored sputum. In the emergency department, the patient's temperature is 39.0 C (103.5 F). On exam, the patient is ill-appearing, but in no respiratory distress.

(D) is correct. This patient has classic features of pneumococcal pneumonia (acute onset of high fever, rigors, and rusty-colored sputum). The findings consistent with lobar pneumonia (the typical pattern for pneumococcal pneumonia) include increased tactile fremitus (not the decreased tactile fremitus as with an effusion), egophony, and dullness to percussion (over the affected lobe).

346. A 28-year-old female with a long history of difficult to control asthma presents to the emergency department complaining of increasing shortness of breath and wheezing without improvement with multiple uses of her albuterol metered-dose inhaler.

(B) is correct. This patient has known asthma and now presents with an asthma exacerbation. Typical chest exam findings include hyperinflation of the lungs with hyperresonance to percussion, a prolonged expiratory phase with wheezing but no egophony (as with consolidations), and decreased tactile fremitus.

Items 347–348

(A) congenital cytomegalovirus (CMV) infection
(B) congenital toxoplasmosis
(C) herpes zoster
(D) intrauterine parvovirus B19 infection
(E) maternal mumps infection
(F) maternal rubella infection
(G) maternal rubeola infection
(H) varicella

For each of the following patient descriptions, select the most likely infectious etiology.

347. A 6-month-old male infant was born at 35 weeks gestation in a pregnancy complicated by intrauterine growth retardation and premature labor. At birth, he was found to have chorioretinitis, anemia, jaundice, seizures, and intracranial calcifications. In addition to these findings, he is now noted to have psychomotor retardation. He is currently being treated with pyrimethamine and sulfadiazine.

(B) is correct. Congenital toxoplasmosis is caused by transplacental transmission of *Toxoplasma gondii*, with the most severe results of congenital infection occurring in the first trimester. Babies are often asymptomatic, but may show the above signs and symptoms. Late sequelae include auditory impairment, psychomotor retardation, and microcephaly. Treatment is long-term pyrimethamine and sulfadiazine.

348. A 23-year-old primigravida at 20 weeks gestation develops fever, headache, and conjunctivitis. Three days later, she has a rash on her face that spreads to the trunk, arms, and legs. The patient also has pain in her joints and enlarged lymph nodes on the back of her head. The rash is gone in 3 days.

(F) is correct. Maternal rubella infection occurs with the characteristic prodrome of fever, headache, and conjunctivitis. 1–5 days later, a macular rash develops with arthralgia and lymphadenopathy that can be posterior auricular, suboccipital, or posterior cervical in location. The rash is gone in 3–5 days. When infection occurs before 20 weeks gestation, the infant is at risk for congenital rubella syndrome—cardiac, ocular, neurologic, hepatic, and dermatologic abnormalities.

349. A 7-month-old male infant who is breast-fed develops a skin rash consisting of the eruption of multiple 1 to 2 mm in diameter vesicles on an erythematous base. These lesions are on the right abdomen and do not cross the midline. The infant is irritable and inconsolable.

(C) is correct. Vertical transmission of V2V can occur if a pregnant woman contracts chickenpox. For the first 6 months, the mother's protective antibodies ward off infection. After this time, the infant can get herpes zoster. The transplacental infection risk is 25 percent, but most infants don't develop sequelae.

350. A 2-year-old male child who was normal at birth now develops sensorineural hearing loss. He is found to have mental retardation and psychomotor developmental delay. The boy occasionally has seizures. The child's mother had an uncomplicated prenatal course except for a mononucleosis-like illness in the first trimester. The mother had no exposure to cats and did not eat raw meat during the pregnancy. CMV-specific IgM antibody and *Toxoplasma gondii* serologies were negative during antenatal testing.

(A) is correct. Primary maternal infection that is usually asymptomatic but can present as mononucleosis-like illness can result in congenital CMV infection. CMV IgM antibody is only present in 80 percent of patients with primary infection. Most infants are asymptomatic at birth, but get late sequelae including hearing, motor, and psychomotor abnormalities. The mortality rate if symptomatic at birth is 20–30 percent.

Directions (Items 351–400): Each of the numbered items is followed or preceded by a set of options. For each item, select the BEST lettered option to answer the question or complete the statement. Locate the corresponding item number in the appropriate section of your answer sheet and completely fill in the circle containing the lettered option you have selected.

351. A 27-year-old primigravid patient has insulin-dependent diabetes mellitus, White's class B. She is in her first trimester and has thus far been without complaints except for some nausea and vomiting during the morning hours. She is on a fixed regimen of insulin 3 times a day, and checks her capillary blood glucose 4 times a day. At this time, this patient is most at risk for development of

(A) hydramnios
(B) hyperglycemia
(C) hypertension
(D) hypoglycemia
(E) urinary tract infection

(D) is correct. This first trimester patient with IDDM on a fixed insulin injection regimen is at risk for hypoglycemia. During the first half of pregnancy, patients on fixed injection regimens who have nausea and vomiting, which decreases oral intake, can develop hypoglycemia. Choice A is incorrect. Hydramnios is a common problem in patients with poorly controlled glucose levels. This phenomenon occurs secondary to increased levels of amniotic fluid glucose, which acts as an osmotic agent and brings in excess water. Choice B is incorrect. Hyperglycemia commonly occurs during the second half of gestation in IDDM patient. It occurs secondary to insulin resistance, requiring patients to increase their insulin dosages. Choice C is incorrect. Hypertension occurs commonly in IDDM patients later in gestation. Choice E is incorrect. If glucosuria is severe, there is an increased risk of urinary tract infection, especially if blood glucose levels have been high. Increased plasma levels lead to increased glomerular filtration, with the resultant creation of a urinary medium perfect for bacterial proliferation.

352. A 45-year-old man is in a stable marriage and works as an accountant. He is known to be a scrupulous citizen of outstanding moral beliefs by his church, which he attends regularly. Outside of church, he has no social contacts. He prefers to work and spends long hours at the office. He and his wife have never gone on vacation because it is a waste of money. They live in a modest home, although they could afford a much larger one. His relationship with his children is constricted. They often argue with their father because he is overly strict with them. Because he is "captain" of the house, he personally takes charge of all financial matters, delegating regimented funds for bills and for spending money, which the rest of the family members claim is too parsimonious. However, he believes in "saving for a rainy day" and even keeps all of his old clothes and shoes from 20 years ago, "just in case" of a catastrophe. The most likely defense mechanism employed regularly by this man is

(A) dissociation
(B) isolation
(C) splitting
(D) projection
(E) passive aggression

(B) is correct. This patient remembers the truth in fine detail but without affect. The man shows self-restraint, overly formal social behavior, and obstinacy. These are the characteristics of obsessive-compulsive personality disorder, in which patients most often use the defense of isolation. Choice A is incorrect. Dissociation is the "forgetting" of unpleasant feelings and associations. Choice C is incorrect. Splitting is the division of individuals into all good and all bad. Choice D is incorrect. Projection involves attributing to another person the thoughts or feelings of one's own that are unacceptable. Choice E is incorrect. Passive aggression occurs when resistance is indirect and often turned against self.

353. A 35-year-old primigravida presents at 16 weeks gestation for maternal serum α-fetoprotein (MSAFP) screening. She has had an uneventful prenatal course with regular care. She has no pre-existing medical conditions. She does not smoke cigarettes or drink alcohol. The physical examination is within normal limits. Fetal heart tones are reassuring. The MSAFP level returns as 0.4 MOM. Repeat ultrasound verifies the gestational age. Based on these findings, this fetus may be at increased risk for

(A) cystic hygroma
(B) Down syndrome
(C) gastroschisis
(D) hydrocephalus
(E) neural tube defect

(B) is correct. MSAFP levels are used as a screening tool for neural tube defects and for chromosome abnormalities at 15–19 weeks gestation. Low levels are associated with chromosomal disorders, especially trisomy 21. Further studies are indicated in this high-risk patient and fetus. Choices A, C, and E are incorrect. Cystic hygroma, gastroschisis, and neural tube defects are associated with increased MSAFP levels. Choice D is incorrect. Hydrocephalus is a closed defect and is not associated with changes in MSAFP levels.

354. A 25-year-old white man has bloody diarrhea. This patient has about 6 bloody bowel movements per day, accompanied by a sense of an urgent need to defecate and abdominal cramps. This pattern has been occurring for the past week. He also complains of weakness, fever, and a 5 kg (11 lb) weight loss over this time period. He has no past medical or surgical history. He does not take any medications. He drinks about 2 beers per week but denies cigarette or illicit drug use. Family history is significant for a father who died of colon cancer at age 48. Physical examination reveals a pale white male in mild distress. Temperature is 38.3 C (101 F), pulse is 100 beats per minute, blood pressure is 100/70 mm Hg, respirations are 14 per minute. The skin is intact and without rashes. Sclera are anicteric and pale. Mucous membranes are moist and without lesions. Lungs are clear. Cardiovascular examination reveals tachycardia with a regular rhythm. The abdomen has bilateral lower quadrant tenderness to palpation without rebound tenderness or guarding. Bowel sounds are present and no masses are palpable. Stool guaiac is positive. Hemoglobin is 8 g/dL, white blood cell count is 10,000/mm^3, erythrocyte sedimentation rate is 30 mm/hr, serum albumin is 3.0 g/dL. Sigmoidoscopy reveals friable, edematous mucosa with erosions. Lower GI series reveals a homogeneous sigmoid colon with loss of haustral markings. The most likely diagnosis is

(A) colon carcinoma
(B) Crohn's disease
(C) ischemic colitis
(D) toxic megacolon
(E) ulcerative colitis

(E) is correct. This patient with bloody diarrhea, lower abdominal cramps, anemia, family history of colon cancer, and a classic sigmoidoscopy and lower GI series has ulcerative colitis. This disease usually involves the rectum and the left colon. Patients have an increased risk of colon cancer, especially after 10 years of the disease. Choice A is incorrect. Colon carcinoma is not likely given the lower GI series findings. Choice B is incorrect. Crohn's disease is more likely to reveal a lower GI series with bowel strictures and fistulae. This disease can occur anywhere along the GI tract, and rectal bleeding is uncommon. Choice C is incorrect. Ischemic colitis occurs in older patients with abdominal pain and a relatively unremarkable abdominal exam. Choice D is incorrect. Toxic megacolon is seen in ulcerative colitis when severe disease results in massive colonic dilatation. It occurs in fewer than 2 percent of patients.

355. A study is designed to determine if there is an association between the rate of HIV infection and the rate of tuberculosis (TB) infection. Data on the incidence rates of HIV infection and the incidence rates of tuberculosis infection for all 50 states are obtained from the Centers for Disease Control. The data is plotted on a graph with incidence of TB infection on the y-axis and incidence of HIV infection on the x-axis. Linear regression analysis is used to determine if a relationship exists between these two diseases. Which of the following best describes the design of this study?

    (A) Case control study
    (B) Ecological study
    (C) Prospective cohort study
    (D) Randomized controlled clinical trial
    (E) Retrospective cohort study

(B) is correct. An ecological study is a comparison of two variables that are analyzed at the level of an entire population, not individual people. In this case, the rates of HIV infection and tuberculosis infection for each state are compared. Data is collected at the population level, with each state representing a different population. This is in contrast to studies that collect and compare data on individuals. Choice A is incorrect. A case control study is an observational study in which subjects are chosen based on a particular disease or outcome variable, and then are examined for the presence of the exposure variable of interest. Choice C is incorrect. A prospective cohort study is an observational study in which subjects are chosen based on a particular exposure variable, and then monitored over time for the development of a particular outcome or disease. Choice D is incorrect. A randomized controlled clinical trial is an experimental study in which two or more treatments are being compared. Subjects are assigned by chance to either the study treatment or the control treatment. Choice E is incorrect. A retrospective cohort study is an observational study in which subjects are chosen based on a particular exposure variable and then evaluated for the presence of a particular outcome or disease. In a retrospective study, both the exposure and outcome (or disease) have occurred prior to the onset of the study.

Items 356–357

A 35-year-old white male is brought to the emergency department by EMS. He struck his head earlier in the day falling out of a tree that he was trimming. Afterwards, he had a severe headache but no other complaints. He went to take a nap, and two hours later his wife could not arouse him. In the emergency room, he is minimally responsive to deep pain. His pupils are asymmetric, with the left 5 mm and the right 3 mm. Both pupils react to light.

356. Which of the following is the most appropriate first step?

    (A) Carotid duplex Doppler study
    (B) Computed tomography of the head
    (C) Lumbar puncture
    (D) Magnetic resonance imaging of the head
    (E) Transcranial duplex Doppler study

(B) is correct. In light of the patient's fall and rapidly progressive signs and symptoms, an emergent computed tomography of the head is indicated. Computed tomography is the best test to visualize intracranial bleeding, as well as to assess impending herniation quickly. Choice A is incorrect. With the patient's rapidly declining status but nonfocal exam (except for anisocoria, a sign of increased intracranial pressure), computed tomography should be the first test performed. If he had a focal neurologic exam and normal computed tomography, the next test should be a carotid Doppler study. Choice C is incorrect. Lumbar puncture must not be performed when increased intracranial pressure is suspected by exam. Choice D is incorrect. Bleeding is the suspected etiology of this patient's rapidly deteriorating mental status. Computed tomography is the best imaging study to visualize blood in the brain. Also, it has the advantage of begin far less time-intensive. Choice E is incorrect. Transcranial Dopplers are useful in assessing intracranial blood flow and for following the status of vascular lesions over time, not in the setting of evolving neurologic compromise.

357. What is the most likely explanation for the symptoms in this patient?

- (A) Brainstem stroke
- (B) Carotid dissection
- (C) Epidural hematoma
- (D) Subarachnoid hemorrhage
- (E) Subacute subdural hematoma

(C) is correct. This patient fell out of a tree and struck his head, with likely rupture of his middle meningeal artery, causing an epidural hematoma. A brief lucid period is common after this injury. His anisocoria is due to increasing intracranial pressure. The oculomotor nerve, with its long intracranial course, is commonly affected early in the face of rising intracerebral pressure. Choice A is incorrect. Although a brainstem stroke might cause unequally sized pupils, strokes are not generally associated with trauma, but with other risk factors such as hypertension and cerebrovascular disease. Choice B is incorrect. Carotid dissection, which can be secondary to trauma, usually presents with focal neurologic deficits, e.g., dense contralateral hemiplegia and language difficulty if the dissection is on the left side. Additionally, patients have local neck pain over the carotid, Horner's syndrome, and ipsilateral headache. Choice D is incorrect. Rupture of an intracerebral aneurysm leading to a subarachnoid hemorrhage would have a similar presentation, severe headache and a brief lucid period. However, rupture is spontaneous and not related to trauma. Choice E is incorrect. Subacute subdural hematomas caused by tearing of the bridging veins are usually secondary to trauma in the elderly and alcoholics. The lucid period is often days to weeks prior to the onset of symptoms, as veins are a low-flow system and a longer time is needed for the accumulation of blood. However, acute subdural hematomas are trauma-related and progress much as epidural hematomas do.

358. A 35-year-old woman delivered a healthy, full-term infant 2 months ago. Since then, she has been breast-feeding without difficulty. In the past 24 hours the patient has developed redness, tenderness, and warmth in her right breast. On physical examination, the patient has a temperature of 37 C (98.6 F) with an obvious cellulitis of her right breast tissue. There is no expressible pus, and the nipple appears fissured. There is no palpable area of fluctuation. The physical examination is otherwise within normal limits. The next most appropriate step in management is

- (A) blood culture
- (B) incision and drainage of breast abscess
- (C) discontinuation of breast-feeding
- (D) administration of antibiotics against *Staphylococcus aureus* for mother
- (E) administration of antibiotics against *Staphylococcus aureus* for child

(D) is correct. This mother has puerperal mastitis. It is usually caused by *S. aureus*, and leads to a red, tender, warm breast. The patient may have a fever and develop a breast abscess. The most appropriate management is to continue breast-feeding to decrease breast milk stasis, and to give antibiotics to the mother. The child usually thrives without any intervention. If there is no improvement, then there is a need to reassess for abscess. Choice A is incorrect. Blood cultures are not required because it is a local infection. Choice B is incorrect. Incision and drainage of the breast abscess is not necessary at this time. This patient can undergo less invasive intervention, with observation to check for improvement. Choice C is incorrect. Breast-feeding should continue to discourage milk stasis. Choice E is incorrect. The administration of antibiotics against *Staphylococcus aureus* for the child is not necessary.

359. A 39-year-old white male presents to his primary care doctor with complaints of fever, chills, and cough productive of rusty-colored sputum over the last 12 hours. He has a history of HIV infection with a CD4$^+$ count of 450/mm^3 and a viral load of 20,000 copies three months ago. He takes no medications. His temperature is 38.8 C (103.2 F). He has egobronchophony throughout the left lower lobe lung field with increased fremitus and tubular breath sounds. Which of the following is the most likely pathogen?

(A) Cytomegalovirus
(B) *Mycobacterium kansasii*
(C) *Mycobacterium tuberculosis*
(D) *Mycoplasma pneumoniae*
(E) *Pneumocystis carinii*
(F) *Streptococcus pneumoniae*

(F) is correct. Patients with HIV infection are at increased risk for developing bacterial pneumonia with any CD4$^+$ count. Recurrent bacterial pneumonia is an AIDS-defining illness. This patient's physical exam findings indicate a left lower lobe consolidation consistent with a bacterial pneumonia. Additionally, the rapid onset of symptoms and rusty-colored sputum are suggestive of *Streptococcus pneumoniae*. Choice A is incorrect. In AIDS patients with very low CD4$^+$ counts, cytomegalovirus is a concern. Generally, symptoms are ocular with visual decline, or gastrointestinal with chronic diarrhea. Choice B is incorrect. *Mycobacterium kansasii* is an atypical mycobacterium most commonly isolated as a pathogen in patients who have received bone marrow transplants or are suffering from lymphoma. It is not a common pathogen in patients with HIV. Choice C is incorrect. *Mycobacterium tuberculosis* should always be considered in patients with HIV and pulmonary complaints. However in this case, the consolidated pneumonia and acute onset of symptoms argue against this diagnosis. Choice D is incorrect. *Mycoplasma pneumoniae* is a common cause of pneumonia in young adults. It is characterized by a persistent cough, often of several weeks duration. Lung fields are usually clear to auscultation, and consolidated pneumonia would be a highly atypical finding. Choice E is incorrect. *Pneumocystis carinii* is a common pathogen in patients with HIV and CD4$^+$ counts less than 200/mm^3. Symptoms are usually progressive dyspnea, cough, and fever often of several weeks duration, not twelve hours.

360. A 65-year-old white male presents to his primary care physician complaining of shortness of breath worsening over the last several weeks. Exam reveals diminished breath sounds in the lower half of the right lung field with dullness to percussion. Chest radiograph demonstrates a right-sided pleural effusion. Thoracentesis is performed and malignant cells are visualized on cytologic analysis. Which of the following is the most consistent with the fluid analysis of this pleural effusion?

Appearance	pH	Protein (gm/dL)	WBC/mm^3	RBC/mm^3
(A) Clear	7.4	1.0	50	5,000
(B) Clear	7.4	1.0	500	7,000
(C) Milky	7.25	4.0	2,000	5,000
(D) Reddish	7.35	4.0	2,000	20,000
(E) Reddish	7.2	2.0	500	10,000
(F) Turbid	7.2	4.0	2,000	5,000

(D) is correct. Malignant pleural effusions are exudative, with a protein count greater than 3.0 gm/dL. Additionally, malignant effusions are often bloody, with elevated red blood cell counts. Choices A, B, and E are incorrect. Pleural effusions with protein counts less than 3.0 gm/dL are transudative. The most common causes of transudative pleural effusions are congestive heart failure, nephrotic syndrome, and liver disease. Choice C is incorrect. Milky-appearing pleural effusions are suggestive of a chylothorax and are exudative. Choice F is incorrect. Exudative pleural effusions with low pH and white blood cell counts greater than 1,000/mm^3 are usually a result of infection.

361. A 25-year-old woman complains of vulvar itching, burning, and vaginal discharge with rancid odor for 2 weeks. She has a prior medical history of gestational diabetes mellitus and asthma for which she takes no medications. She is gravida 1 para 1 with a healthy 1-year-old male child at home. Currently, she lives alone and has had unprotected sexual intercourse with multiple male partners during the past several weeks. The vaginal discharge is yellow-green in color, frothy, and has a pH of 7.0. Vulvovaginal examination reveals vulvar edema, erythema, and petechiae on the cervix. The vaginal vault has no evidence of mass lesions. Wet smear reveals large numbers of mature epithelial cells, white blood cells, and a fusiform protozoan organism. The most appropriate treatment includes

(A) amoxicillin
(B) ampicillin
(C) metronidazole
(D) miconazole
(E) terconazole

(C) is correct. *Trichomonas vaginalis* is a protozoan organism that may colonize the urethra and vagina. This organism can be freely transmitted during sexual intercourse. Symptoms of infection include vulvar itching, burning, copious discharge with rancid odor, dysuria, and dyspareunia. Examination may reveal edema and erythema of the vulva and petechiae of the upper vagina and cervix. The secretions are often yellow-green with a pH higher than 6.5. Wet smear will reveal the *Trichomonas* organism. Treatment is by oral metronidazole and one-day therapy regimens results in a 90 percent cure rate. Choice A is incorrect. Amoxicillin is not an appropriate treatment choice for *Trichomonas vaginalis*. Choice B is incorrect. Ampicillin is not an appropriate treatment choice for *Trichomonas vaginalis*. Choice D is incorrect. Miconazole is a topical synthetic imidazole used for the treatment of vaginal candidiasis. Choice E is incorrect. Terconazole is a topical synthetic imidazole used for the treatment of vaginal candidiasis.

362. A 25-year-old black woman dies suddenly. She had a prior medical history of mitral valve prolapse, hypothyroidism, and gestational diabetes. She was gravida 2 para 2 and worked as an administrative assistant. Both of her children are well except for lactose intolerance and sickle-cell trait in one of the children. Given only the demographic information provided above, the most likely cause of death in this individual was

(A) acquired immunodeficiency syndrome
(B) acute leukemia
(C) chronic lymphoma
(D) domestic violence
(E) myocardial infarction

(A) is correct. Acquired immune deficiency syndrome is the third-leading cause of death among women in the 25- to 44-year-old age group. The disease is the leading cause of death among black women in this age group. Women have become the fastest-growing group of AIDS patients in the United States. Choice B is incorrect. Hematologic malignancies typically cause death in young and old patients. Choice C is incorrect. As mentioned above, hematologic malignancies typically cause death in young and old patients. Choice D is incorrect. Domestic violence is also a common cause of death of women in this age group. Choice E is incorrect. Myocardial infarction is a common cause of death in men older than age 44.

363. A 42-year-old status post renal transplant several years prior presents to his primary care physician with complaints of a cough productive of scant yellowish sputum. The cough has worsened over the last four weeks and now he is having fevers. His current medications include cyclosporine, azathioprine, and prednisone. Chest roentgenograph demonstrates diffuse bilateral interstitial infiltrates. A bronchoalveolar lavage is performed. Silver stain of the lavage specimen demonstrates multiple cysts. Which of the following is the most appropriate treatment?

(A) Acyclovir
(B) Amphotericin
(C) Ampicillin
(D) Ceftriaxone
(E) Erythromycin
(F) Trimethoprim/Sulfamethoxazole
(G) Tetracycline

(F) is correct. Pulmonary infection with *Pneumocystis carinii* is common in transplant patients, especially those on the combination of azathioprine, cyclosporine, and prednisone who do not take trimethoprim/sulfamethoxazole prophylaxis. Bronchoalveolar lavage frequent yields silver-staining cysts, which confirm the diagnosis of *Pneumocystis carinii*. Choices A, B, C, D, E, and G are incorrect. None of these antibiotics has action against *Pneumocystis carinii*. Treatment alternatives to trimethoprim/sulfamethoxazole in the allergic patient include dapsone and pentamidine.

364. Malpractice can be defined as a professional's lack of skill or care that results in injury to the patient. Which of the following clinical outcomes is most likely to result in a malpractice suit against a physician?

(A) A 29-year-old man under psychiatric care for schizophrenia commits suicide.
(B) A 37-year-old woman with panic disorder states that her physician did not obtain informed consent for a procedure.
(C) A 39-year-old woman with depression claims that her physician became sexually active with her.
(D) A 59-year-old man with depression undergoes electroconvulsive therapy and fractures his femur 1 week later.

(A) is correct. Malpractice can be defined as occurrences in a professional practice that result in injury to the patient that is a consequence of the professional's lack of skill or care. Suicide of a psychiatric patient nearly always raises the question of malpractice and is the most common basis of lawsuits in psychiatry. Therefore, careful documentation of all patient encounters and treatment is essential. Choice B is incorrect. The alleged failure of a physician to obtain informed consent can infrequently be the basis of a malpractice suit. Choice C is incorrect. Sexual activity with patients is considered to be criminal in a number of states, and is deemed unethical by several physician organizations. Choice D is incorrect. Negligent administration of medications in electroconvulsive therapy is the second-largest source of malpractice lawsuits in psychiatry.

365. A 64-year-old white female presents to her new primary care physician after noticing a lump in her left breast about a week prior to her visit. Exam confirms a hard, 2 cm by 2 cm mass in the outer lower quadrant of her left breast that is fixed to the underlying tissue. Which of the following is the most appropriate first step?

(A) Excisional biopsy
(B) Fine needle aspiration
(C) Mammography
(D) Referral to a breast surgeon
(E) Ultrasound exam

(C) is correct. This mass is very suspicious for malignancy. The first step in the evaluation of any concerning breast mass is mammography. Choice A is incorrect. This mass is very suspicious for malignancy and will likely require referral to a surgeon for an excisional biopsy. However, the first step in the evaluation of any concerning breast mass is mammography. Choice B is incorrect. Fine needle aspiration is an appropriate step after mammography, especially in masses that are likely cystic, e.g., in patients with fibrocystic breast disease. Choice D is incorrect. This mass is very suspicious for malignancy and will likely require referral to a surgeon for an excisional biopsy. However, the first step in the evaluation of any concerning breast mass is mammography. Choice E is incorrect. Ultrasound is an appropriate next step after mammography, especially in masses that are likely cystic, e.g., in patients with fibrocystic breast disease.

366. In the town of Smallville, there are 7,500 women between the ages of 14 and 44 years old. In 1997, 1,500 women became pregnant. 100 women had an abortion before the 20th week of gestation. Intrauterine fetal deaths occurred in 50 women after the 20th week of gestation. 75 babies died within the first 28 days of life. What was the neonatal mortality rate in Smallville in 1997?

(A) $(250/1,500) \times 1,000$
(B) $(125/1,500) \times 1,000$
(C) $(125/1,350) \times 1,000$
(D) $(75/1,500) \times 1,000$
(E) $(75/1,350) \times 1,000$

(E) is correct. The neonatal mortality rate is defined as the number of infants dying during the period beginning after birth and continuing up to the first 28 days of life per 1,000 live births. In this case there were 75 babies that died in the neonatal period. There were $1,500 - (100 + 50) = 1,350$ live births. In order to express the neonatal mortality rate as number of deaths per 1,000 live births, you must multiply the number of neonatal deaths divided by the number of live births by 1,000. This is not to be confused with the perinatal morality rate, which is defined as the number of fetal deaths occurring from the 20th week of gestation until the 28th day of life per 1,000 live births. Choice A is incorrect. Choice A includes intrauterine fetal deaths in the numerator and denominator. Choice B is incorrect. Choice B includes intrauterine fetal deaths after 20 weeks gestation in the numerator and all intrauterine fetal deaths in the denominator. Choice C is incorrect. Choice C is a calculation of the perinatal mortality rate. Choice D is incorrect. Choice D includes all intrauterine fetal deaths in the denominator.

367. A 40-year-old white man develops fever, chills, and muscle aches 1 week after returning from a camping trip. He also has had a rash during this time on his thigh that has been getting larger. The patient has no significant past medical history and takes no medications. He smokes about 1 pack of cigarettes per day and drinks 6 beers per week. The patient reports no change in bowel movements or urination, and no chest pain or syncope. The patient complains of a headache. Physical examination reveals a well-developed, well-nourished white male in mild distress. Temperature is 38.3 C (101 F), pulse is 90 beats per minute, blood pressure is 120/80 mm Hg, and respirations are 15 per min. The neck is supple and lungs are clear. Cardiovascular examination is within normal limits. The abdomen is soft, nontender, and nondistended with normal bowel sounds. There is a 10 cm raised red lesion on the right thigh with central clearing. Extensive lab studies including HIV, VDRL, and blood cultures are negative. Serum antibodies to *Borrelia burgdorferi* are positive. If untreated, in the near future this patient can expect to develop

   (A) acrodermatitis chronica atrophicans within 1 month
   (B) Bell's palsy within weeks
   (C) second-degree heart block after years
   (D) leukoencephalitis within days
   (E) subacute encephalopathy within weeks

(B) is correct. This patient has Lyme disease—early localized infection with erythema migrans, flu-like symptoms, and positive antibody titers. Bell's palsy (unilateral demyelination of cranial nerve VII with facial paralysis and inability to close the eyelid) occurs in Stage 2 (days to weeks) after seeding of the central nervous system by this treponemal bacterial species. Choice A is incorrect. Acrodermatitis chronica atrophicanis a late manifestation of this disease, occurring months to years later. Choice C is incorrect. Second-degree heart block occurs days to weeks later. Choice D is incorrect. Leukoencephalitis occurs months to years later. Choice E is incorrect. Subacute encephalopathy is another late manifestation that occurs months to years later.

Items 368–369

A 37-year-old white female presents to her primary care physician complaining of worsening fatigue over the last several months. She is able to do her usual activities in the morning, but by the afternoon she is profoundly fatigued and some days even has difficulty working at her computer. Her symptoms improve dramatically if she takes a nap after work. She has bilateral ptosis.

368. Which of the following is the most likely diagnosis?

   (A) Chronic fatigue syndrome
   (B) Major depression
   (C) Mononucleosis
   (D) Myasthenia gravis
   (E) Still's disease

(D) is correct. Myasthenia gravis is an autoimmune disease that commonly presents in the third and fourth decades. Autoantibodies are produced against the acetylcholine binding site of the neuromuscular junction, blocking the binding of acetylcholine. Ptosis is common, as is profound fatigue ameliorated by sleep. Choice A is incorrect. Chronic fatigue syndrome, a diagnosis surrounded by much controversy as to its etiology and even its existence, is a diagnosis of exclusion. Choice B is incorrect. There is no mention of other symptoms of depression to warrant this diagnosis (crying, overwhelming sadness, constitutional symptoms). Choice C is incorrect. Mononucleosis is a disease of children and adolescents. Most people are infected and immune to it by their adult years. It may cause profound fatigue, but not ptosis. Choice E is incorrect. Still's disease is an uncommon disease characterized by high fevers (intermittent) and a salmon-colored rash in addition to profound fatigue.

369. Which of the following is most likely to confirm the clinical diagnosis of the patient?

    (A) Computed tomography of the head
    (B) Edrophonium test
    (C) Erythrocyte sedimentation rate
    (D) Magnetic resonance imaging of the head
    (E) Monospot test

(B) is correct. The edrophonium test is able to confirm the diagnosis of myasthenia gravis is most cases. Significant symptomatic improvement occurs after the administration of edrophonium, an acetylcholinesterase inhibitor, which may be scored by a trained observer. However, the improvement is only momentary. Choice A is incorrect. There is no history of trauma or focal neurologic findings to suggest a central nervous system etiology of the patient's fatigue, weakness, and ptosis to warrant computed tomography of the head. Choice C is incorrect. The erythrocyte sedimentation test is a nonspecific indicator of inflammation and does not help to confirm the diagnosis of myasthenia gravis. Choice D is incorrect. There is no history of trauma or focal neurologic findings to suggest a central nervous system etiology of the patient's fatigue, weakness, and ptosis to warrant magnetic resonance imaging of the head. Choice E is incorrect. Mononucleosis is a disease of children and adolescents. Most people are infected and immune to it by their adult years and, as it does not cause ptosis, would be an unlikely cause of this patient's symptoms.

370. A 28-year-old HIV-positive man who acquired the disease through intravenous drug use presents to his physician for evaluation of progressive visual disturbance presenting as a decrease in visual acuity. Funduscopic examination reveals bilateral large white areas with perivascular exudates and hemorrhages. The patient does not remember his last CD4$^+$ count and has been noncompliant with his medications. The presence of the above clinical findings suggests that the patient's current CD4$^+$ count is approximately which of the following?

    (A) 50/mm^3
    (B) 100/mm^3
    (C) 200/mm^3
    (D) 300/mm^3
    (E) 450/mm^3

(A) is correct. This patient with HIV disease complains of decline in visual acuity, and physical examination reveals large white areas with perivascular exudates and hemorrhages ("cottage cheese and ketchup"), which is suggestive of cytomegalovirus (CMV) retinitis. CMV retinitis often occurs when the CD4$^+$ count is less than 50/mm^3. Thus, patients with low CD4$^+$ counts should see their eye doctors regularly for examination.

371. A 10-year-old boy has a one-year history of recurrent eyeblinking, head jerking, and facial grimacing. Recently, he has progressed to multiple coughing attacks as well as grunting and sniffling. During the last week he has begun to repeat his own words and the words of his family members. Teachers in school have noted that the child has a short attention span and occasionally hits himself and jumps up and down. Which of the following is the most likely diagnosis of this individual?

(A) Elective mutism
(B) Mood disorder of childhood
(C) Schizophrenia of childhood
(D) Tourette's disorder
(E) Undifferentiated attention deficit disorder

(D) is correct. This patient exhibits signs and symptoms of Tourette's disorder. Multiple motor and vocal tics occur several times daily. Simple motor tics can include eye blinking and facial grimacing. Simple vocal tics include coughing and grunting. Complex motor tics include hitting self and jumping, while complex vocal tics include repeating one's own words and the repeating of other's words. Excessive swearing can also be noted. 85 percent of patients improve with haloperidol and its associated sedative properties. Choice A is incorrect. Elective mutism is the persistent refusal to talk in a child who both speaks and comprehends. Choice B is incorrect. This rare disorder of childhood relies on the adult criteria for depression for diagnosis. Choice C is incorrect. Schizophrenia of childhood requires the presence of delusions and hallucinations. This condition is diagnosed using the adult criteria. Choice E is incorrect. Undifferentiated attention deficit disorder describes very inattentive children who are not hyperactive.

372. A 41-year-old man has a long history of heartburn and is resistant to lifestyle modifications and over-the-counter antacids. He has weekly episodes of nocturnal regurgitation. Cardiac examination reveals a regular rate and rhythm. Pulmonary auscultation reveals clear lungs bilaterally without wheezes or rhonchi. Abdominal examination reveals some mild tenderness in the mid-epigastric region. Rectal examination is guaiac-negative with stool in the vault. What would be the most appropriate next step in the management of this patient?

(A) Addition of cimetidine to the treatment regimen
(B) Addition of famotidine to the treatment regimen
(C) Referral to a gastroenterologist for endoscopy
(D) Referral for ambulatory 24-hour pH monitoring
(E) Watchful waiting

(C) is correct. Endoscopy provides a wealth of information to the examining physician. First, it rules out markers of more severe disease such as esophageal ulceration, Barrett's esophagus, or an early stricture. It also allows for the early discovery of esophagitis. Thus, it is an important adjunctive test for this patient to undergo. Choice A is incorrect. In a patient with a long history of heartburn, endoscopy is an important and informative test. Choice B is incorrect. In a patient with a long history of heartburn, endoscopy is an important and informative test. Choice D is incorrect. 24-hour pH testing is useful to exclude the diagnosis of acid reflux, but is costly and somewhat invasive. Choice E is incorrect. Watchful waiting does not allow the physician to evaluate more serious disease as mentioned above.

373. A 27-year-old woman complains of 3 months of fatigue and shortness of breath during her daily jog. She denies abdominal pain, nausea, vomiting, constipation, or the passage of black or bloody stools. She denies excessive bleeding during or between her menstrual periods or nose bleeds. Cardiac, pulmonary, and abdominal examinations are within normal limits. Stool is guaiac-negative. Laboratory studies reveal a hemoglobin level of 9.7 g/dL and a platelet count of 637,000 cells/mm^3. The mean corpuscular volume is 68 fL. Peripheral smear suggests hypochromasia and microcytosis. What would be the most appropriate next step in the management of this patient?

    (A) Administration of oral iron therapy
    (B) Barium enema
    (C) Colonoscopy
    (D) Upper gastrointestinal barium series
    (E) Watchful waiting

(C) is correct. This patient has evidence of iron deficiency anemia. Although her stool guaiac test is negative, she still might have intermittent bleeding. Sources to consider include cancers of the large bowel or large polyps. Colonoscopy is a good test to consider in this patient. Choice A is incorrect. The cause of iron deficiency anemia needs to be pursued before treatment is instituted. Choice B is incorrect. Colonoscopy is the preferred management strategy for this patient. Choice D is incorrect. Upper gastrointestinal endoscopy would be preferred over a barium study. Choice E is incorrect. The cause of iron deficiency should be pursued vigorously.

374. A 55-year-old businessman developed acute diarrhea 7 days after returning from a business trip. He spent 3 days in Mexico City, ate no food outside the hotel, and took no prophylactic antibiotics. He was well while in Mexico and for the first week after his return. His diarrhea consisted of 7 to 10 watery stools per day that were devoid of blood or mucus, but were preceded by abdominal cramps that were temporarily relieved following each bowel movement. Cardiac and pulmonary examinations are unremarkable. Abdominal examination reveals tenderness to deep palpation in the right and left lower quadrants. Peritoneal signs are absent. Stool is guaiac-negative. What is the next most appropriate step in the management of this patient?

    (A) Administration of a 4-day course of ciprofloxacin
    (B) Administration of doxycycline capsules
    (C) Administration of metronidazole
    (D) Examination of stool for ova, parasites, and stool cultures
    (E) Treatment with corticosteroid enemas

(D) is correct. This patient has evidence of acute diarrhea. One must consider causes such as *Escherichia coli*, *Campylobacter* sp., *Salmonella* sp., and *Shigella* sp. Thus, a good first step in the evaluation of the patient with acute diarrhea is examination of the stool for ova, parasites, and stool cultures. Choice A is incorrect. Quinolones are an effective treatment for *Campylobacter* sp. infections. Choice B is incorrect. Doxycycline is an effective treatment for *Escherichia coli* infections. Choice C is incorrect. Metronidazole is an effective treatment for amebiasis. Choice E is incorrect. Corticosteroids can have devastating consequences in patients with severe amebic colitis.

375. A 23-year-old primigravid woman is 24 weeks pregnant. She complains of dizziness and fatigue. Both of her parents have insulin-dependent diabetes mellitus. Her mother has diabetic retinopathy. Physical examination of the heart, lungs, and abdomen is within normal limits. Urinalysis reveals glucosuria. Serum glucose is 180 mg/dL. Which of the following is the appropriate time for an initial ocular examination in this patient?

(A) At the time of diagnosis of diabetes
(B) Within 1 year of the diagnosis of diabetes
(C) Within 5 years of the diagnosis of diabetes
(D) Within 10 years of the diagnosis of diabetes
(E) Within 15 years of the diagnosis of diabetes

(A) is correct. Young patients with insulin-dependent diabetes mellitus should undergo an initial ocular examination within 5 years of diagnosis. However, this patient with gestational diabetes should be examined as soon as the diagnosis of diabetes is established. Choices B, C, D, and E are incorrect. Young, nonpregnant patients with diabetes mellitus should have an ocular examination within 5 years of the diagnosis.

376. A 36-year-old woman has a positive home pregnancy test. She presents to her physician for a confirmatory examination. She has a history of recurrent urinary tract infections, seizure disorder, headaches, and deep venous thrombosis. Her current medications include acetaminophen, ciprofloxacin, warfarin, valproic acid, and methotrexate. She drinks 2 beers per day. Physical examination of the heart, lungs, and abdomen is within normal limits. Urine and serum β-HCG testing are positive. Which of the following medications taken by this patient does not require adjustment during pregnancy?

(A) Acetaminophen
(B) Ciprofloxacin
(C) Methotrexate
(D) Valproic acid
(E) Warfarin

(A) is correct. Women often ask about the safety of medications during pregnancy. Analgesics such as acetaminophen, codeine, lidocaine, and morphine are considered safe during pregnancy. Antibiotics such as penicillin, erythromycin, and cephalosporins are also considered safe for use during pregnancy. Choice B is incorrect. Ciprofloxacin is contraindicated in pregnancy. Choice C is incorrect. Methotrexate is contraindicated in pregnancy. Choice D is incorrect. Valproic acid is contraindicated in pregnancy. Choice E is incorrect. Warfarin is contraindicated in pregnancy.

377. A 66-year-old man with a 1-year history of benign prostatic hyperplasia (BPH) complains of ejaculatory dysfunction for the last 5 months. He is able to attain a weak erection and sense ejaculation, but is not able to ejaculate. He has a history of hypertension controlled with a calcium channel-blocker and an angiotensin-converting enzyme inhibitor. He also has peptic ulcer disease treated with an H2-blocker. His BPH is treated with terazosin. Physical examination reveals an uncircumsized phallus with small testes bilaterally. The prostate is approximately 40 g and nontender. Which drug is most likely to be responsible for this patient's complaint?

    (A) Diltiazem
    (B) Enalapril
    (C) Monopril
    (D) Ranitidine
    (E) Terazosin

(E) is correct. This patient has multiple medical problems and is taking terazosin, which is a sympatholytic antihypertensive agent. This medication is rarely associated with impotence, but can cause retrograde ejaculation. This phenomenon is the result of relaxation of the smooth muscles of the prostatic urethra and bladder neck. Choice A is incorrect. Calcium channel-blockers are a rare cause of impotence. Choice B is incorrect. Angiotensin-converting enzyme inhibitors are a rare cause of impotence. Choice C is incorrect. Angiotensin-converting enzyme inhibitors are a rare cause of impotence. Choice D is incorrect. H2 receptor blockers are often associated with impotence, but are less likely to cause retrograde ejaculation, which is what this patient is describing.

378. A 71-year-old man complains of ejaculatory dysfunction for the last 10 months. He is able to attain a weak erection and sense ejaculation, but is not able to ejaculate. The patient's serum testosterone level is 220 mg/mL. He is concerned that his low testosterone level is contributing to his erectile dysfunction and urges his physician to consider testosterone supplementation. Which of the following tests should be carried out prior to beginning this therapy?

    (A) Complete blood count
    (B) Serum electrolytes
    (C) Serum prostate-specific antigen level
    (D) Serum thyroid-stimulating hormone level
    (E) No further testing is necessary at this time

(C) is correct. When a decreased serum testosterone level is detected and before supplementation is considered, a serum prostate-specific antigen level should be drawn. This test is essential to rule out an androgen-sensitive tumor (prostate cancer) prior to initiating testosterone therapy that would further stimulating such a tumor, if present. Choice A is incorrect. This test is not specific for androgen-sensitive tumors. Choice B is incorrect. This test is not specific for androgen-sensitive tumors. Choice D is incorrect. This test is not specific for androgen-sensitive tumors. Choice E is incorrect. The presence of an androgen-sensitive tumor must be excluded before hormone supplementation can begin.

379. A 59-year-old man with diabetes mellitus and hypertension complains of erectile dysfunction for 2 years. He is able to attain a weak erection but is not able to ejaculate. The patient's serum testosterone level is 240 mg/mL. He is concerned that his low testosterone level is contributing to his erectile dysfunction and urges his physician to consider testosterone supplementation. The patient is begun on methyltestosterone daily and is scheduled to return for follow-up visit in 2 months. Which of the following important effects of this agent should the treating physician be aware of?

    (A) Acalculous cholecystitis
    (B) Hepatic carcinoma
    (C) Hepatocellular cystic degeneration
    (D) Splenic infarction
    (E) Testicular torsion

(B) is correct. Oral androgen preparations have erratic gastrointestinal absorption and can cause cholestatic jaundice, as well as hepatic carcinoma. Thus, these agents should be used for only a short time. Parenteral androgens are preferred. These agents should be avoided in patients with liver disease. Choice A is incorrect. Oral androgens can cause cholestatic jaundice. Choice C is incorrect. Oral androgens are associated with the development of hepatocellular carcinoma. Choice D is incorrect. Oral androgens are not associated with splenic infarction. Choice E is incorrect. Oral androgens are not associated with testicular torsion.

380. Tomorrowland, a large city of 1 million people, has a university cancer care center. Of 200 patients in the center, 50 have lung cancer. Of these 50 patients, 45 are smokers. Of the remaining 150 hospitalized patients who do not have lung cancer, 60 are smokers. What is the odds ratio for smoking and the risk of lung cancer?

    (A) 5
    (B) 13.5
    (C) 18.5
    (D) 45
    (E) 60

(B) is correct. Odds ratio is determined by the ratio of people who are smokers with lung cancer multiplied by the number of people without lung cancer who are nonsmokers. This number is divided by the number of people who are nonsmokers with lung cancer multiplied by the number of smokers without lung cancer. Thus, (45) (90)/(5) (60) = 13.5. The risk of lung cancer is 13.5 times higher in people who smoke that in those who do not smoke.

31. The systolic blood pressure in a community is normally distributed with a mean of 120 mm Hg and a standard deviation of 10. What percentage of people have a systolic blood pressure at or above 140 mm Hg?

    (A) 1.9%
    (B) 2.5%
    (C) 13.5%
    (D) 34%
    (E) 64.2%

(B) is correct. The systolic blood pressure of 140 mm Hg in this community is 2 standard deviations above the mean of 120 mm Hg. The area under the curve between 2 and 3 standard deviations is about 2.35 percent plus about 0.15 percent (everything above 3 standard deviations). Thus, a total of 2.50 percent of the people will have blood pressures at or above 140 mm Hg.

$$z = (\bar{x} - x)/s$$

$$\frac{120-140}{10} = \frac{-20}{10} = -2 \text{ (meann)}$$

382. A 14-year-old girl consults her family physician because she believes that she has contracted a sexually transmitted disease. Physical examination of the heart, lungs, and abdomen is normal. Gram stain of urethral discharge reveals the presence of gram-negative diplococci. What is the most appropriate course of action for the physician to take?

    (A) Counsel the patient about safe sex practices

    (B) Get verbal permission from her parents before treatment

    (C) Get written permission from her parents before treatment

    (D) Report the case to the local health authorities

    (E) Telephone her sexual partner regarding this condition

(A) is correct. Prior to the treatment of this patient, the physician should counsel her on safe sexual practices. Parental consent is not required for treatment of minors in cases of sexually transmitted disease, pregnancy, and substance abuse. Choice B is incorrect. Parental consent is not required for treating minors in cases of sexually transmitted disease. Choice C is incorrect. Parental consent is not required for treating minors in cases of sexually transmitted disease. Choice D is incorrect. This case can be reported to local health authorities after treatment has begun. Choice E is incorrect. This patient should notify her partner if she is found to have a sexually transmitted disease.

383. A 51-year-old man presents to the emergency department complaining of a 6-hour history of left-sided chest pain. Which statement will elicit the most information from this patient?

    (A) "Is there a history of heart disease in your family?"

    (B) "Point to the area in your chest that hurts."

    (C) "Tell me about the pain."

    (D) "Tell me about the pain in your left chest."

    (E) "When did the pain begin?"

(C) is correct. Although direct questioning can elicit information, the open-ended type of question and interview is most likely to produce a good clinical relationship, aid in obtaining information about the patient, and not close off potential areas of pertinent information. Choices A, B, D, and E are incorrect. They are examples of direct questions.

384. A 55-year-old woman comes to the emergency department complaining of a 10-hour history of progressive, dull abdominal pain in the mid-epigastric region. She seems agitated and says that she is afraid that she has cirrhosis of the liver and then suddenly stops speaking to the physician. What will best encourage her to continue speaking?

    (A) "Do you drink?"
    (B) "How much beer do you drink?"
    (C) "I can see that you are very upset."
    (D) "Please go on."
    (E) "Why did you wait so long to come in for evaluation?"

(D) is correct. This question illustrates the concept of facilitation. This is a basic interviewing technique used by the physician to encourage the patient to elaborate on an answer. Choice A is incorrect. This response does not encourage facilitation. Choice B is incorrect. This response does not encourage facilitation. Choice C is incorrect. This response illustrates the concept of empathy, but might not encourage the patient to elaborate further about her situation. Choice E is incorrect. This response illustrates the concept of confrontation.

385. A 9-year-old boy is brought to the emergency department after a 22.7 kg (50 lb) box fell on his knees while he was asleep. He has no prior medical or surgical history. Physical examination reveals erythema and edema of both knees. Joint motion testing was not undertaken. Radiographic examination of the knees reveal focal narrowing of the epiphyseal plate and effusions bilaterally. What is the most likely outcome for this child?

    (A) Fat embolism
    (B) Focal bone-growth arrest
    (C) Nemaline myopathy
    (D) Osteoporosis
    (E) Pulmonary edema
    (F) Pulmonary embolism

(B) is correct. This child has suffered a type V physeal fracture. The physis is crushed by severe compressive forces. X-ray studies often indicate focal narrowing of the epiphyseal plate with an associated joint effusion. Focal bone-growth arrest is a likely complication. Choice A is incorrect. Fat embolism is not the most likely outcome for this child. Choice C is incorrect. Nemaline myopathy can be associated with severe muscular weakness and is characterized by rod-shaped granules in the type I muscle fibers. Choice D is incorrect. Osteoporosis is characterized by a decrease in bone mass caused by impaired synthesis of bone matrix protein. Choice E is incorrect. Pulmonary edema would be an unlikely complication in this child. Choice F is incorrect. Pulmonary embolism would be an unlikely complication in this child.

(A) Balanced electrolyte solution (Ringer's lactate)
(B) Dextrose 5% solution
(C) Isotonic saline (0.9% solution)
(D) Hydroxyethyl starch
(E) Human serum albumin
(F) Normal saline

For each clinical scenario, select the most likely resuscitation solution that the patient received.

386. A 49-year-old man with end-stage renal disease on hemodialysis is admitted to the hospital with chest pain. Electrocardiograms are unchanged from prior studies. He is started on intravenous fluids and is later found unresponsive by nurses. Computed tomography of the head suggests an infarct in the distribution of the right middle cerebral artery. His serum lactate level is now 9 mg/dL and serum osmolarity is 600 mOsm/L.

(B) is correct. Dextrose is available as a 5 percent solution in saline or water. This intravenous fluid provides 170 kcal/L and contributes approximately 280 mOsm to a solution. Infusion of dextrose can fuel the production of lactic acid in ischemic organs, such as in this individual who has renal insufficiency and stroke. Thus, serum lactate levels will rise. Serum osmolarity will also rise since this fluid is hyperosmolar.

387. A 44-year-old man with chronic renal insufficiency presents to the emergency room with chest pain. Electrocardiography reveals T-wave inversion in the precordial leads. He is placed on intravenous fluids. Twelve hours later, his serum potassium is 5.4 mEq/L and serum calcium is 12.5 mg/dL.

(A) is correct. Ringer's lactate is a balanced electrolyte solution that substitutes potassium and calcium for some of the sodium in isotonic saline. Lactate is added as a buffer. The added potassium can be detrimental to patients with renal insufficiency. Serum calcium levels may also rise due to the added calcium.

388. A 56-year-old man with dehydration and diverticulitis has a blood pressure of 90/50 mm Hg, a pulse of 110 beats per minute, and a urine output of 0.8 cc/kg/hr despite intravenous fluids running at a rate of 120 cc/hr. Three days later, his serum amylase is 300 U/L and his creatinine rises to 1.6 mg/dL.

(D) is correct. Hydroxyethyl starch is a synthetic starch that was introduced as an inexpensive alternative to albumin. This solution is cleared by the kidneys and the largest particles can take several weeks to clear. Thus, elevations in serum creatinine are possible. The serum amylase level can rise to three times normal and is a normal response to degradation of hydroxyethyl starch and does not indicate pancreatitis. Serum lipase must be used to diagnose and follow pancreatitis when it is used.

389. A 31-year-old woman with a thyroid nodule is scheduled to undergo a right hemithyroidectomy. She has a prior medical history of mitral valve prolapse. She currently takes no medications. She is placed on intravenous fluids prior to the induction of anesthesia. The solution she is placed on is slightly acidic and is hypertonic to plasma. Upon completion of surgery, serum chloride is 116 mEq/L.

(C) is correct. Isotonic saline is the standard crystalloid fluid and contains 9 grams of sodium chloride per liter (a 0.9 percent solution). This fluid is slightly hypertonic to plasma and has an acidic pH. This solution may produce a hyperchloremic metabolic acidosis.

Items 390–397

    (A) Dietary modification of carbohydrate intake
    (B) Discontinuation of iatrogenic drug
    (C) Intravenous fluid resuscitation
    (D) Intravenous gentamicin and clindamycin
    (E) Intravenous metronidzaole
    (F) Intravenous vancomycin
    (G) Loperamide
    (H) Methotrexate
    (I) Omeprazole
    (J) Oral metronidazole
    (K) Oral vancomycin
    (L) Prednisone
    (M) Sulfasalazine
    (N) Tap water enema

For each patient with diarrhea, select the most appropriate treatment.

390. A 29-year-old white woman, gravida 1 para 0, has a history of intermittent bloody diarrhea for the past 10 years. She now has about 1 bowel movement per day that is loose with occasional blood and mucus. She has no other significant past medical history. Physical examination is notable for a temperature of 37 C (98.6 F), a pulse of 80 beats per minute, and a blood pressure of 110/70 mm Hg. Skin is without rashes. Lungs are clear. Cardiovascular examination is unremarkable. The abdomen is gravid and stool guaiac is positive. Bowel sounds are active. There is mild lower quadrant abdominal tenderness. Stool cultures are negative. Urinary HCG is positive. Hemoglobin is 10 mg/dL. Erythrocyte sedimentation rate is 10 mm/hr. Sigmoidoscopy reveals a friable edematous mucosal appearance.

(M) is correct. This patient with ulcerative colitis has mild disease, as evidenced by normal stool frequency, normal temperature, and a normal erythrocyte sedimentation rate. She needs a maintenance program to control her disease. Since this patient is pregnant, the best choice is sulfasalazine, which has no adverse effects on the fetus.

391. A 58-year-old white man has the recent onset of left lower quadrant abdominal pain radiating to the back and diarrhea. He also complains of fever and chills. The patient denies urgency or frequency of urination, or blood in stools. He has a history of hypertension and takes enalapril with good control. Physical examination reveals a well-developed, well-nourished white male in mild distress. Temperature is 38.3 C (101 F), pulse is 100 beats per minute, and blood pressure is 130/90 mm Hg. Lungs are clear. The heart is without murmurs, rubs, or gallops. The abdomen is soft and nondistended, with left lower quadrant tenderness to light palpation. Bowel sounds are present. Stool guaiac is negative. There is no costovertebral angle tenderness. White blood cell count is 11,000/mm³. Urinalysis is negative for nitrites, blood, and bacteria. Abdominal plain film is unremarkable.

(D) is correct. This patient has acute diverticulitis—left lower quadrant abdominal pain, fever, chills, and diarrhea. Treatment consists of hospitalization for intravenous antibiotics and bowel rest. Intravenous gentamicin and clindamycin provide good coverage for enteric organisms.

392. An 80-year-old female nursing home resident, gravida 6 para 6, develops rectal bleeding and diarrhea. She complains of a feeling of rectal fullness. The patient denies any abdominal pain, nausea, vomiting, fever, or chills. Her last bowel movement was 2 weeks ago, and she is usually continent of stool and urine. Past medical history is significant for left hemispheric infarct 5 years ago, with gradual improvement of right hemiparesis and aphasia. On physical examination, the patient is afebrile, alert, and oriented to person, place, and time. The lungs and heart are within normal limits. The abdomen is soft and nontender with a mass palpable in the left lower quadrant. On rectal examination, hard stool is present in the vault and stool guaiac is negative. Plain film of the abdomen reveals a large amount of feces in the large bowel, no obstructive pattern, and air in the rectum.

(N) is correct. This patient has overflow stool incontinence from fecal impaction. The patient needs a good bowel regimen, including regular bowel movements with enemas, stool softeners, and a high-fiber diet.

393. A 25-year-old white man has severe, gnawing, mid-epigastric pain, and voluminous diarrhea. The pain is worse with eating. The patient denies bright red blood in his stool or tar-colored stools. He has no fever, chills, nausea, or vomiting. He has no significant past medical history except for ulcers, for which he uses over-the-counter famotidine. Physical examination reveals a nondistended, nontender abdomen that is flat with normal bowel sounds. Stool guaiac is positive. Stool cultures are negative. Serum gastrin is 2,000 pg/mL. An upper gastrointestinal series reveals multiple duodenal ulcers.

(I) is correct. This patient has Zollinger-Ellison syndrome (ZES), caused by a gastrinoma in the pancreas or duodenum. These patients have severe refractory peptic ulcer disease and diarrhea secondary to fat malabsorption. Serum gastrin levels exceed 500 pg/mL and an upper GI series reveals multiple ulcers. Medical therapy aims to control acid hypersecretion, the drug of choice being omeprazole.

394. A 42-year-old man has crampy abdominal pain and diarrhea with palpitations and sweating, noted to occur about 30 minutes after eating his mother's spaghetti and garlic bread meals. He has no bright red blood per rectum and abdominal pain always precedes the diarrhea. Three months ago, the patient had surgery for refractory peptic ulcer disease. He has recovered uneventfully except for this diarrhea. Physical examination is unremarkable.

(A) is correct. This patient has dumping syndrome, cramping abdominal pain and diarrhea with diaphoresis and palpitations secondary to rapid movement of gastric contents through the GI tract. It is related to the high-carbohydrate meal. The patient most likely had pyloroplasty or pyloric bypass surgery. Treatment includes dietary modification limiting carbohydrate content of meals, and having 6 small meals throughout the day.

395. A 30-year-old black man with a history of peptic ulcer disease develops fever, nausea, one episode of vomiting, bloody diarrhea, and abdominal cramps 12 hours after attending a family reunion and barbecue. He takes ranitidine for his duodenal ulcer. He has no known drug allergies. On physical examination, temperature is 38.3 C (101 F), respirations are 20 per minute, supine blood pressure and pulse are 120/80 mm Hg and 90 beats per minute, and upright blood pressure and pulse are 100/60 mm Hg and 120 beats per minute, respectively. The skin is intact and without rashes and mucous membranes are dry. Lungs are clear. Radial pulses are thready and symmetrical. The abdomen is soft with mild tenderness to deep palpation of the left lower quadrant. No masses are felt and stool guaiac is negative. Neurological exam is without focal deficits. Labs show evidence of hypokalemic metabolic acidosis. Stool cultures are positive for *Salmonella* sp. Stool ova and parasite exam is negative. Fecal leukocytes are present. Blood cultures are negative after 2 days of incubation.

(C) is correct. This patient has acute *Salmonella* gastroenteritis, the most common form of *Salmonella* infection. The patient has no extra-intestinal manifestations of infection, such as Rose spots (small, pale red, blanching macules on chest and abdomen), abdominal distention, or cough that would be suggestive of typhoid fever. Therefore, antibiotic therapy is not indicated and may in fact prolong the course of disease. Instead, the most appropriate treatment is intravenous fluid resuscitation, as the patient is orthostatic from vomiting and diarrhea.

396. A 50-year-old Hispanic woman, gravida 2 para 2, has the acute onset of voluminous, watery diarrhea with lower abdominal cramps for 1 day. She denies seeing any blood or mucus in the stools and has had about 5 bowel movements since the onset of symptoms. She denies any dietary changes or ingestion of raw or undercooked food. Past medical history is significant for recent strep throat, treated with a 7-day course of ampicillin 1 month ago. Otherwise, the patient is taking no medications and has no known drug allergies. The patient does not drink alcohol or use tobacco products. Physical examination is significant for a temperature of 38 C (100.4 F), mild left lower quadrant abdominal tenderness to deep palpation, and a positive stool guaiac test. Flexible sigmoidoscopy reveals yellow plaques scattered over the colonic mucosa, with intervening areas of hyperemic mucosa. Biopsies and cultures are pending.

(J) is correct. This patient has antibiotic-induced pseudomembranous colitis secondary to ampicillin use 1 month ago. The flexible sigmoidoscopy findings are classic and stool cultures are not useful. The demonstration of *Clostridium difficile* toxin is diagnostic in most cases. The treatment of choice is oral metronidazole. An alternative, equally effective regimen is oral vancomycin, which is poorly absorbed in the gastrointestinal tract. However, because metronidazole is considerably less costly and because vancomycin-resistant organisms seem to be proliferating of late, oral metronidazole is the first choice.

397. A 45-year-old black woman, gravida 1 para 1, with a history of asthma develops diarrhea and shortness of breath. Bowel movements are formed, soft, and frequent, about 3 times a day. The patient has difficulty breathing but no chest pain. She has had no changes in her diet. She was recently diagnosed with hypertension and begun on propanolol. Her asthma has been quiescent for years. The patient takes no other medications and has no known drug allergies. She does not smoke and reports drinking about 2 beers per day. She denies illicit drug use. She has no headache, bright red blood per rectum, melena, syncope, abdominal pain, or cough. On physical examination, the patient is afebrile with respirations of 30 per minute, a pulse of 110 beats per minute, and a blood pressure of 100/70 mm Hg. Pulmonary auscultation reveals scattered wheezes. Cardiovascular exam reveals tachycardia. The abdomen is soft, nontender, and nondistended with guaiac-negative stool. Extremities show no evidence of clubbing or edema. Chest x-ray is within normal limits. Ventilation perfusion scan of the lungs is low probability. Stool cultures are negative.

(B) is correct. This patient has diarrhea and shortness of breath secondary to propanolol use. This β-adrenergic blocker causes constriction of lung air passages and increases bowel motility. The most appropriate therapy is to discontinue the drug and to switch to another agent for hypertension.

Items 398–400

    (A) Alprazolam
    (B) Clonazepam
    (C) Ethosuximide
    (D) Phenytoin
    (E) Valproic acid

Match each clinical scenario with the most appropriate pharmacologic treatment.

398. An 18-year-old presents to his new primary care physician with complaints of poor school performance since entry into college. His professors have noted that he often has periods of "blanking out" with lapses in his concentration. He had similar episodes throughout high school, but was still able to keep up in school. He denies ever hurting himself during these episodes or any urinary or fecal incontinence.

(C) is correct. This patient is describing typical absence seizures, which usually begin in childhood and present as poor school performance. Ethosuximide is the drug of choice for the treatment of uncomplicated absence seizures.

399. A 26-year-old white male presents to his primary care doctor after his fiancée noted several episodes of lip-smacking and disjointed movements of his right arm. During these episodes that last 10 to 15 minutes, his fiancée is unable to arouse him.

(D) is correct. This patient is having complex partial seizures with automatisms. Phenytoin and carbamazepine are the initial drugs of choice for the treatment of partial seizures. Phenytoin has the benefit of once-a-day dosing, but carbamazepine has a side effect profile that is often better tolerated.

400. A 23-year-old white male presents to his primary care doctor with complaints of recurrent seizures. He suffered several seizures as a child, but stopped taking his seizure medication as a teenager. He has now had several episodes for which he has no memory that were accompanied by loss of bladder control. His muscles are sore afterward, and on one occasion he bit his tongue.

(E) is correct. This patient is having generalized tonic-clonic seizures. Valproic acid is the best initial choice for the treatment of generalized and tonic-clonic seizures.

ABOUT THE AUTHOR

John J. Mariani, M.D., a graduate of the New York University School of Medicine, is the Director of Research and Development for Medical Licensing Programs at The Princeton Review. He has worked closely with USMLE students while teaching Princeton Review USMLE courses and is responsible for guiding the work of dozens of M.D.'s and Ph.D.'s who contribute to the Princeton Review's course material.

ART/ PHOTO CREDITS

p. 64 Reproduced with permission from *Practical Electrocardiography*, Fig. 26.1 by Henry, Marriot 8th ed. Published by Williams and Wilkins.

p. 74 Reproduced with permission from *Harrison's Principles of Internal Medicine*, by Anthony Fauci, 14th ed., page 2369. Published by the McGraw-Hill Health Professions Division.

p. 101 Reproduced with permission from *Harrison's Principles of Internal Medicine*, by Anthony Fauci, 14th ed., page 2354. Published by the McGraw-Hill Health Professions Division.

p. 103 Reproduced with permission from *Harrison's Principles of Internal Medicine*, by Anthony Fauci, 14th ed., page 2414. Published by the McGraw-Hill Health Professions Division.

p. 118 Reproduced with permission from *Exercises in Fetal Monitoring*, by Barry Schifrin, page 57. Published by W. B. Saunders Co.

p. 120 Reproduced with permission from *Exercises in Fetal Monitoring*, by Barry Schifrin, page 119. Published by W. B. Saunders Co.

p. 122 Reproduced with permission from *Exercises in Fetal Monitoring*, by Barry Schifrin, page 25. Published by W. B. Saunders Co.

p. 124 Reproduced with permission from *Exercises in Fetal Monitoring*, by Barry Schifrin, page 31. Published by W. B. Saunders Co.

p. 173 Reproduced with permission from *Nelson's Textbook of Pediatrics*, by Richard Behrman, 15th ed, page 1202. Published by W. B. Saunders Co.

p. 262 Reproduced with permission from *Harrison's Principles of Internal Medicine*, by Anthony Fauci, 14th ed., page 1657. Published by the McGraw-Hill Health Professions Division.

p. 275 Reproduced with permission from *Principles of Surgery*, by Seymour Schwartz, 7th ed. page 713. Published by the McGraw-Hill Health Professions Division.

NOTES

NOTES

NOTES

NOTES

NOTES

NOTES

NOTES

NOTES

NOTES

NOTES

NOTES

FIND US...

International

Hong Kong
4/F Sun Hung Kai Centre
30 Harbour Road, Wan Chai,
Hong Kong
Tel: (011)85-2-517-3016

Japan
Fuji Building 40, 15-14
Sakuragaokacho, Shibuya Ku,
Tokyo 150, Japan
Tel: (011)81-3-3463-1343

Korea
Tae Young Bldg, 944-24,
Daechi- Dong, Kangnam-Ku
The Princeton Review- ANC
Seoul, Korea 135-280,
South Korea
Tel: (011)82-2-554-7763

Mexico City
PR Mex S De RL De Cv
Guanajuato 228 Col. Roma
06700 Mexico D.F., Mexico
Tel: 525-564-9468

Montreal
666 Sherbrooke St.
West, Suite 202
Montreal, QC H3A 1E7 Canada
Tel: (514) 499-0870

Pakistan
1 Bawa Park - 90 Upper Mall
Lahore, Pakistan
Tel: (011)92-42-571-2315

Spain
Pza. Castilla, 3 - 5º A, 28046
Madrid, Spain
Tel: (011)341-323-4212

Taiwan
155 Chung Hsiao East Road
Section 4 - 4th Floor,
Taipei R.O.C., Taiwan
Tel: (011)886-2-751-1243

Thailand
Building One, 99 Wireless Road
Bangkok, Thailand 10330
Tel: (662) 256-7080

Toronto
1240 Bay Street, Suite 300
Toronto M5R 2A7 Canada
Tel: (800) 495-7737
Tel: (716) 839-4391

Vancouver
4212 University Way NE,
Suite 204
Seattle, WA 98105
Tel: (206) 548-1100

locations

National (U.S.)
We have over 60 offices around the U.S. and
run courses in over 400 sites. For courses and locations
within the U.S. call 1 (800) 2/Review and you will be
routed to the nearest office.

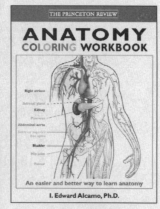